PSYCHOLOGY

Realizing Human Potential

Eighth Edition

RENE V. DAWIS, PH.D.
ROSEMARY T. FRUEHLING, PH.D.

PARADIGM

Developmental Editor: Cynthia Miller
Copyeditor: Carol Kennedy
Production Manager: Joan Silver
Text Design and Composition: Jung-Ah Suh
Art Direction: Queue Publishing Services

Acknowledgements

We wish to thank the following instructors and technical experts who contributed to this book:

Mr. David E. Spence, Instructor
Monterey Peninsula College
Pebble Beach, California

Dr. Brian Engdahl
University of Minnesota
Minneapolis, Minnesota

Ms. Paula Brown-Weinstock
Bryant & Stratton Business Institute
Buffalo, New York

Dr. Nambury S. Raju
Georgia Institute of Technology
Atlanta, Georgia

Library of Congress Cataloging-in-Publication Data

Dawis, Rene V.
    Psychology : realizing human potential. -- 8th ed. / Rene
V. Dawis. Rosemary T. Fruehling.
      p. cm.
    Includes bibliographical references and index
    ISBN 1-56118-341-5
    1. Psychology, Industrial.   I. Fruehling, Rosemary T.,
II. Title.
    [DNLM: 1. Psychology, Industrial.]
    HF5548.8L23 1996
    158.7--dc20   94-20886
                                            CIP

© 1996 by Paradigm Publishing Inc.
           Published by **EMC**Paradigm
           875 Montreal Way
           St. Paul, MN 55102
           (800) 535-6865
           E-mail publish@emcp.com

Printed in the United States of America

10 9 8 7 6 5 4 3

UNIT I HUMAN POTENTIAL

UNIT II THE BIOLOGICAL BASIS OF BEHAVIOR

CONTENTS

IV

CONTENTS

UNIT III HUMAN DEVELOPMENT

CONTENTS

UNIT V   WORK ADJUSTMENT

CONTENTS

AUTHORS

Dr. Rene V. Dawis is currently professor of psychology and adjunct professor of industrial relations at the University of Minnesota. An Internationally known teacher, Dr. Dawis has taught at the University of the Philippines and the University of Minnesota, where he received the H. G. Heneman Award for Teaching Excellence.

Dr. Dawis is also widely known as a researcher. He received research awards from the American Rehabilitation Counseling Association in 1965 and 1974 and from the American Personnel and Guidance Association in 1960 and 1967.

Dr. Dawis has published more than 100 works, including journal articles and monographs since 1958. He is coauthor of three books, *Psychology: Realizing Human Potential, Adjustment to Work* and *A Psychological Theory of Work Adjustment.*

Dr. Rosemary T. Fruehling is an internationally known educator and lecturer in the field of business education, president of Paradigm Publishing Inc., and has taught office education at both the high school and postsecondary levels. She has also conducted business education teacher-training seminars for the United States Department of Defense and for the McGraw-Hill International Division.

Dr. Fruehling has served as a consultant to such business firms as Honeywell, General Mills, International Milling, Crocker Banks, and Warner-Lambert Pharmaceutical Company. In addition Dr. Fruehling served as director of the Office of Software Technology Development for the State of Minnesota. Before that appointment, she was postsecondary vocational education section manager in the Division of Vocational-Technical Education of the Minnesota State Department of Education.

Dr. Fruehling is coauthor of a number of textbooks, including, *Psychology: Realizing Human Potential; Working at Human Relations; Business Correspondence: Essentials of Communication; Business Communication: A Case-Method Approach; Office Systems: People, Procedures, Technology; and Your Attitude Counts.*

Psychology as a science got its start in the university and, seeking respectability, modeled itself after physics, the paramount science. Thus, for half a century, until the 1950s, basic, experimental, or theoretical psychology reigned supreme in departments of psychology. "Applied" psychology was kept out of most leading departments, finding its home in colleges of education as educational and school psychology; in schools of business administration or management as industrial-organizational psychology; and in medical schools as clinical psychology. Not even the spectacular success of applied psychology in World Wars I and II nor the popularity of Freud among the intellectuals and the educated of the 1930s and 1940s could loosen the dominance of basic psychology in departments of psychology. This dominance over applied psychology extended to the American Psychological Association (APA), founded in the 1890s by academic psychologists. Finally, in the late 1940s, the applied psychologists left APA to form their own organization, but a rapprochement was achieved, and APA officially became more hospitable to applied psychology.

The situation in departments of psychology also started to change, due in large part to a pattern of research funding that developed after World War II. A dramatic increase in federal funding, especially in the fields of defense, education, health, and labor served to fuel an explosion of research in applied psychology, effectively ending the "second-class" status to which it had been relegated in the past. Today, it is the academic psychologist who has a difficult time finding support for research, because the overwhelming proportion of available research funds is allocated for "applied" programs.

Along with this shift has come a change in the way science is viewed as a human and as a societal institution. This shift rides the wave of social revolutions occurring after World War II that have radically changed our ways of thinking and our values. Today we demand that science be accountable to society and that it make a positive contribution. Psychology, too, has this responsibility.

▼ OVERVIEW OF THE EIGHTH EDITION OF
PSYCHOLOGY: REALIZING HUMAN POTENTIAL

The eighth edition of *Psychology: Realizing Human Potential* has been updated to reflect the changes that are occurring in the field of psychology. It is intended to introduce students to the theories, research, and applications that constitute the science, and also to demonstrate how the material is applied to everyday life. The text not only includes coverage of the traditional topics of psychology, such as the biological basis of behavior, human development, cognition, and perception, but also emphasizes social and work psychology, making it particularly unique among psychology textbooks: it draws from theoretical and applied approaches.

Furthermore, this text has been updated to enhance instruction. The chapters have been reorganized into five units that relate to a particular subtype of psychology, such as developmental psychology (Unit III) and social psychology (Unit IV). These self-contained units allow instructors to choose and omit topics to fit their course syllabi. Two new chapters (one on the brain, the other on abilities) enhance the scope of coverage of the text, and the latest research and material on stress, critical thinking, gender differences, and the changing workforce is also included.

PREFACE

The following features are common to every chapter and unit:

Chapter Quotation. Each chapter opens with a quotation that relates to the topic of the chapter and gives students a reference point from which to begin their study.

Chapter Introduction. Following the quotation, the introduction expands on the reference point and helps bridge the gap between what students already know and the subsequent chapter content.

Marginal Definitions. Definitions appear beside all important terms discussed in the chapter to help students better understand the topics being discussed. There is also an end-of-book glossary.

To The Point. Within each chapter, two or three To the Point boxes describe contemporary research, pivotal studies, interesting applications, and psychology at work.

Chapter Summary. At the end of each chapter, a summary provides a concise synopsis of all major points covered within the chapter.

Questions for Review and Discussion. Questions that apply the chapter concepts to real world topics appear at the end of each chapter to provide students the opportunity to actively review the material presented within the chapter.

Activities. For further research, out-of-classroom activities are suggested to enhance what students learned within the chapter.

Key Terms. A list of key terms for the student to define is also provided at the end of each chapter.

Cases. One or two Case studies appear at the end of each chapter and present situations that students must analyze. These exercises enhance critical thinking skills.

Research Studies. New end-of-unit studies require students to read and analyze research that relates to what was learned in the unit. The student is required to "think like a psychologist."

For Further Research. A bibliography appears at the end of the text.

▼ ANCILLARY MATERIALS

Student Study Guide. Reviewed by instructors and developed in consultation with a learning theory expert, this valuable study guide by Rene Dawis and Rosemary Fruehling reinforces concepts presented in the text and integrates them with activities to facilitate learning.

- An introductory section explains how to study and how to use the study guide effectively with the text.

- A Chapter Outline provides a brief synopsis of the main points covered in the chapter.

- Questions are presented in a variety of formats and reflect the actual tests students will face in the classroom.

- Vocabulary review exercises increase students' knowledge of terminology.

Instructor's Guide. Designed to enhance classroom instruction, this valuable resource provides general teaching suggestions, objectives, enrichment suggestions, and transparency masters. A test bank and answer keys for both the text and study guide are also provided.

In sum, *Psychology: Realizing Human Potential* is an enlightening textbook that focuses on showing students how to reach their highest potential in their personal lives and in their environment. By citing the most up-to-date research in academic and applied psychology, this text incorporates the theme of human behavior as it unfolds in the individual's interaction with the environment, especially the work environment.

▼ REALIZING YOUR HIGHEST POTENTIAL

Note that we said "realizing your <u>highest</u> potential, not " realizing your potential <u>fully</u>" or "<u>completely</u>." No one can do that because we have not one but many potentialities, and we cannot realize them all. It is something like having cable TV. You may have 50 channels, say, or 100, but when you are tuned in on one channel, you cannot see what is happening on the other 49 or 99. Likewise, just think how many careers or occupations there are that you could have entered with a reasonable chance at being successful. You could not become all of them. For most of us, one occupation is enough because preparing for more than one occupation would take up a lot of time and expense. Besides, to do justice to two occupations at the same time may be too demanding and stressful for most of us. So, we have had to choose, and when you choose to realize one of your potentialities, you deny yourself the opportunity to realize your other potentialities. Self-actualization is about realizing not all of your potentialities, but your highest potential.

▼ THE USES OF PSYCHOLOGY

This brings us to the purpose of this textbook, which is to teach you about psychology. <u>Psychology is the science that studies human potential and how human potential is realized in human behavior.</u> As a result, psychology as a science can serve humanity when it <u>helps people know more about their potential and appreciate better how their potential can be realized through their behavior.</u> When it does that, psychology avoids being a "science without humanity." To bring it to a personal level, learning psychology should help you understand your potential better, which in turn should help you realize your highest potential.

What will psychology tell you in this textbook that might help you learn more about your potential? We won't repeat the detail given in the different chapters. Rather, in this introduction, we shall discuss some of the "big picture" lessons taught by the science of psychology that may help you better understand your potential and its role in your behavior–for it is in your behavior that your potential is realized.

Mind and Behavior

You will learn that psychology is about two things: <u>mind</u> and <u>behavior.</u> You cannot understand mind without looking at behavior, and you cannot account for behavior without bringing in mind. You cannot study psychology without studying both. The two intersect and interact: mind influences behavior and behavior influences mind. Is this another instance of the chicken-egg problem? Actually, this old dilemma is easily resolved if you know which <u>particular</u> chicken and which <u>particular</u> egg are involved, because then you can tell whether it is a chicken laying or an egg hatching. Similarly, there are instances when it is mind that influences behavior and other instances when behavior influences mind. Much of psychological research is directed at finding out which instances are which. You will learn some of these instances. For example, your attitudes (mind) can lead you to work harder (behavior). On the other hand, physical exercise (behavior) can ease your feelings of anxiety (mind). By knowing when and how each can influence the other, you can better appreciate why you behave the way you do and why you think and feel the way you do.

INTRODUCTION

Internal and External

Because psychology is about both mind and behavior, it is no surprise that one of the major dimensions in psychology is the inside-outside or internal-external dimension. You will read that introversion-extraversion is one of the major traits of personality. People differ in their tendency to attend more to the inside (matters of mind) or more to the outside (matters of behavior). You will also read about how internal (self) reinforcers are contrasted with external (environmental) reinforcers, and how your motivation, your self-esteem, your satisfaction, and your behavior can depend on what you believe to be the more effective reinforcers for you, the internal or the external. To become an autonomous person, one who is self-initiated and self-sufficient, you have to learn how to use internal reinforcers more because, in general, you can exercise more control over internal than external reinforcers.

Whole and Part

Psychology also studies the functioning of the whole human being, in contrast to physiology and other biological sciences, which study the functioning of the human being's parts. Psychology stresses the difference between the whole and the sum of its parts, because the two are NOT equal. The functioning of the whole human being is more than just the sum of the functioning of its parts: it is functioning of a different kind! For example, what is it that you see? You can study the functioning of the parts of the visual system, from the eye all the way to the brain areas that monitor vision; you can study the physics, physiology, and biochemistry of vision, and yet such knowledge alone cannot answer the question, what do you see? Because what you see is affected by your memories, your emotional state, your expectations, the visual cues you have learned in the past, what you are thinking of at the present moment–in other words, by the functioning of the whole of you. Realizing that you function as a whole can give you better insight into your behavior and your thoughts and feelings.

Biology and Psychology

You must not forget that you are a biological being. Your mind and behavior occur because of the functioning of biological mechanisms. The most important of these from the standpoint of psychology are your brain mechanisms, which come into play when you gather information about the outside world, when you process that information, when you react to it, when you use your abilities to act on the information you have gathered–in short, whenever you do something, anything. These brain mechanisms are incredibly complex, and an introductory text can provide little more than an introduction to that complexity. This complexity underscores one point: that we cannot (yet) easily trace the causal pathways between biology and behavior. Sometimes what you think and feel is caused by biochemical events in your brain; at other times your thoughts and feelings can cause biochemical changes in your body. What is important is to realize that any explanation of your behavior has to take into account your biology. What you are–your potential, your predispositions, your preferences, and even your prejudices–all will show the stamp of your biology–your genetic inheritance and your physical, psychological, and social development. You might say that your biology sets limits on your psychology, although not to the extent (as some people believe) that "biology is destiny."

Psychology can transcend biology. Altruism is a case in point: sacrificing one's life (even if only one's day-to-day life) for the sake of others overturns the biological law of self-preservation. Then there are the stories of incredible feats of heroism, like the one about the 100-pound grandmother whose 18-year-old grandson was trapped under and slowly being crushed by the car he was working on that had slipped from its blocks. Without a moment's hesitation, the grandmother lifted the car all by herself, just long enough for her grandson to slip out from under the car. You must know many similar stories of extraordinary heroism. Motivation can produce miracles, and psychology can indeed override biology.

Motivation and Cognition

Another important lesson psychology teaches is that your perceptions and cognitions, not just your behavior, are influenced by your motivation. True, environment limits what it is possible for you to perceive physically, but there is a sense in which you see what you want to see and hear what you want to hear. You even "reason out" toward conclusions that your motivation has already led you to select beforehand. People rarely reason by starting with premises and using logic to lead them to "logical conclusions." Rather, they start with the conclusion they want to reach and reason logically back to premises, and then they adopt these premises as their own–thus appearing (even to themselves!) to be very rational in their reasoning. To know yourself is to know what your beginning premises (or "first principles") are. It is to be aware that many of your conclusions are preconceived. It is to be honest with yourself about which came first, which premises and which conclusions. Furthermore, psychology teaches that your premises and conclusions–in other words, your biases–enter into your perception by screening out what is against your bias and allowing in what is in favor of your bias, thereby leading you to "see what you want to see and hear what you want to hear." (Panel discussions on TV or your newspaper's opinion pages provide ample instances of this phenomenon.)

Individual and Environment

Another important lesson psychology teaches is that you cannot understand behavior by studying "person" alone. Neither can you do it by studying "environment" alone. Only by studying person-in-environment–or more precisely, this-person-in-this-environment–can you expect to understand behavior. It is said that "personality does not exist in a vacuum." Learning about your personality is a giant step toward knowing yourself, but it is not enough. The environment or the situation–the context–also has something to say about your behavior. On the other hand, knowing only about environments and situations is also not enough. You cannot tell what effect a given environment or situation will have on different people unless you also know their personalities. Different personalities react differently to the same situation, not to mention different situations and environments. (That is precisely the reason we can say that the personalities are "different.") But we must also point out that personalities and environments tend to go together. To put it another way, "personality seeks its own environment." Like personalities tend to seek like environments, and conversely, similar environments tend to get to be peopled by similar personalities. "Like attracts like" is scientific fact as well as folk wisdom. We tend to prefer and favor those who are like us. Conversely, we tend to respond negatively to those who are unlike us, a tendency that–unchecked–can lead to social fractionation or worse.

How do we go about counteracting this tendency? In a culturally diverse world, how do we establish community with those who are unlike us? Psychology suggests that we can begin by acting on the very tendency itself–by finding areas in which we are alike, by focusing attention on these areas, and by using them to build community. By emphasizing similarities and downplaying (though not denying) differences, we might be able at least to tolerate one another and perhaps eventually to learn to respect one another as well.

Development and Learning

Personalities and environments change and develop. Development is change, change in an ordinarily ordered sequence of steps or stages. Learning is also change in a sequence of steps, but "learning" is change in the short term, whereas "development" is change over the long term. Much of your development can be explained by the mechanisms of learning.

Habits

Learning contributes to development through what you learn–habits. Habits are the products of learning, and much of your behavior is habitual behavior. Even your skills are habits. Therefore, knowing how to develop the right habits–such as the right skills–is very important to developing your potential. By teaching you how to develop the right habits, psychology can contribute to helping you realize your highest potential.

Development and Choice

But we sometimes overlook the fact that your development also depends on your <u>choices</u>. What you choose sets the direction and the potential outcomes of your later development. If you choose to drop out of school, your development takes a different turn than if you choose to stay in school. If you stay in school, in college, say, the major you choose can make quite a difference in your later development. So, one might say, "choice is development."

If development depends on choice, choice is ironically the product of development. Arriving at a choice point often takes some doing. You do not get to choose a college unless you completed high school with grades good enough to get you into college. You do not get to choose a college major unless you completed your first two years of college successfully. And so on. You do not get to the choice point unless you develop.

Development and Opportunity

At each choice point, you could choose NOT to choose, which effectively stops your development at that point. But sometimes, you arrive at a choice point and there are no alternatives to choose from. People with no alternatives do not choose—they have nothing to choose from. Their development is effectively arrested at that point. Having alternatives is what is meant by "opportunity." Opportunity equals having alternatives equals being able to choose equals the chance to develop. Opportunity is the precondition for development, and conversely, lack of opportunity leads to lack of development.

There is an opportunity-development spiral that can move up or down. Having opportunity can lead to development, and more development leads to more opportunity, which leads to more development, and so on, in an upward spiral. The downward spiral can also happen: lack of opportunity leads to lack of development, which in turn leads to less opportunity, which leads to less development, and so on. Which spiral are you on? What if you find yourself on a downward spiral, how do you break out of it? You break out by "creating" your own opportunity; by being alert and taking advantage of any passing opportunity; by embarking on a program of self-development, which in turn prepares you for more kinds of opportunity. Any of these can "jump start" you on the way up the upward spiral.

Practice and Learning

Psychology teaches that, besides its role in your development, learning also plays an important role in your everyday behavior. Of all the "laws of learning," the one most involved in everyday behavior is the "law of practice." Do you always procrastinate? Are you often easily upset by actually inconsequential matters? Do you frequently "fly off the handle" too quickly? Why do these or other "bad" habits persist as habits with you? One answer, simple-minded though it may seem, is: because you practice them. Each time you repeat a habit, you are practicing the habit—and practice makes the habit grow stronger. Therefore, to break a habit, you must start first by NOT practicing it. The less you practice it, the weaker the habit gets. The weaker the habit gets, the better your chance of substituting a new ("good") habit for the old ("bad") one. You do not "get rid" of a habit; rather, you "trade it in" for another. And the more incompatible the new habit is with the old one, the better the chance of the new supplanting the old. ("Incompatible" means that if you do one thing, you cannot physically do the other. For example, standing up and sitting down are incompatible.)

Emotional Habits

Our emotional habits are especially worth examining. Emotions may have complex origins and complex mechanisms, but they too are subject to the law of practice. This applies to common everyday "negative" emotions such as anger and anxiety. You can begin to "manage" or gain some control over these emotions either by avoiding situations that trigger them (therefore you avoid practicing them) or by practicing an incompatible habit when the offending emotion is aroused. For example, when you are anxious, get angry; when you are angry, laugh—"practice" finding humor in the situation. (Incidentally, laughter—we now know—has very real healing properties.)

In fact, with regard to emotions, we cannot do better than follow the old belief: "accentuate the positive, eliminate the negative." There is no better prescription for mental health than to practice "positive" emotions and avoid practicing "negative" emotions. The old saying that it is "healthy" to "let off steam" or "release your (pent-up) anger" turns out not to be completely wise. Practice leads inevitably to habit–the more you practice, the stronger your habit–so that "practicing" letting off steam can eventually turn you into a habitually short-tempered person.

"Practicing" anger is responsible for much of the stress of everyday life. For example: when you make a mistake, knowing that you made a mistake makes you feel bad; in a real sense, that knowledge is already a punishment. So, when you are scolded or when someone gets mad at you for making a mistake, your punishment is doubled. To get angry at someone for making a mistake is effectively to double that person's punishment. If the person is not aware of making the mistake, the thing to do is to let the person know about it factually–you do not have to get angry. If you can keep from getting angry, not only are you NOT practicing the emotion (thereby weakening the "bad" habit), you are also helping to diminish the unbelievable amount of emotional punishment that we unnecessarily inflict upon one another in everyday life and experience as "stress."

Please note that in trying to "apply psychology," such as applying the suggestions in this introduction and elsewhere in this book, you may succeed–and then again you may not. Human behavior, human thought and feeling, and human situations are usually much more complicated than can be depicted in a textbook. As a general rule, when applying anything as a beginner, it is best to do it under the supervision of an expert or a practiced (professional) person. "Applying psychology" by beginners should be supervised by a psychologist or someone trained and experienced in the particular application.

Individual Differences

Before leaving the subject of learning, why–you may have often wondered–can't our educators get it right, why is there a never-ending argument about the "right" method for teaching reading or math or anything else for that matter? The answer psychology gives is: because there are large differences among learners, and what works for one learner may not work for another. No method winds up being "right" for everyone, not even, oftentimes, for the majority. People differ in many ways, on just about any conceivable human attribute (psychology calls this "individual differences"). It is a wonder we can find any method at all that works for more than just a few individuals. The situation is partially helped by the fact that most people are flexible (psychology also calls this the "plasticity" of human behavior), and most people are willing to accommodate (you will read of the personality trait of agreeableness). The best method for a few may be good enough for many, and so the problem becomes one of searching for the method that is good enough for the most people at the least cost. The important lesson here is that the fact of individual differences must always be taken into account when designing anything–things or procedures–for human beings. Part of learning about self is finding out how you are individually different from others, because, while you are "like many in some respects and like some in many respects," you are "like none in all respects."

Choosing and Deciding

The "good enough" principle is useful in other human domains as well. It is especially useful in choosing or deciding. Rational choice or decision requires the consideration of all alternatives, otherwise the decision calculations will be incomplete and thus open to error. (How many times have we chosen or decided on something, only to find a better alternative afterwards, much to our regret?) Yet, consideration of all alternatives is impossible or impractical in most real-life situations. The practical, workable thing to do is to use the "good enough" standard. But when you choose or decide on the basis of " good enough," you should not expect complete satisfaction, according to Herbert Simon, the Nobel laureate, who is the world's top expert on decision making. Rather than full satisfaction, you should aim at "satisficing" (a word coined by Prof. Simon to denote satisfaction with a choice or decision based on the "good enough" standard.)

For it to work, you cannot second-guess yourself. Once you have decided on the basis of all the information available to you (provided you had not "jumped the gun" and decided too early) you should make up your mind to be satisfied with your decision or choice. The ability to do this is one of the keys to maturity and inner peace. And the more you practice it, the more of a habit it will become.

"Satisficing" does not mean that you shouldn't change when you realize you made a bad mistake. Neither does it mean that you should be easily content and aim low in life. As in other aspects of life, there is a trade-off involved here, one between aspiration and satisfaction. The higher your aspiration is, the higher the potential prize, but also the greater the chance of being disappointed and becoming dissatisfied. Conversely, the lower your aspiration is, the lower your potential achievement or accomplishment, but also the less your chance of the disappointment and dissatisfaction that come with failure. You have to make up your own mind as to what you value more: a chance at achievement with a higher risk of disappointment and dissatisfaction, or a guarantee of success but with lower accomplishment. What you value will determine what you regard as "good enough."

Setting Goals

Psychology has confirmed that setting high—and therefore difficult—goals and achieving them is not only very rewarding but also very satisfying. (One should differentiate between setting difficult goals and setting impossible goals which only ensure failure.) But setting high and difficult goals can also set you up for failure. This can happen when your progress toward the goal is slow and you fail to persevere. When progress toward the goal is slow, you can help yourself by setting up intermediate goals that are more readily attainable. Each intermediate goal you attain will reinforce you and boost your motivation. The marathon is a good example to illustrate this technique, which psychology calls "successive approximation." If you think about the final goal some 26 miles away, it seems so distant and unattainable. But if you take it one mile at a time, each mile being your immediate goal, you can take satisfaction at achieving your immediate goal and maintain your motivation for the longer run. The successive approximation technique is one of the most useful techniques to help you realize your highest potential.

INTRODUCTION

Choosing Environments

It is obvious from the previous paragraphs that, to realize your highest potential, you must choose your "environments" carefully. This applies especially to your "work environment" (your job and your career), because, as the pioneering work psychologist Anne Roe observed, in our modern world, work is the best place to realize our highest potential. How should you go about choosing your "environments"? There is an old and simple formula for doing this, still very much in use. It has three parts. First, know yourself. (Socrates's wisdom reaches across 2,500 years.) Know your requirements and your capabilities. Second, know your environments. Know about their requirements and their capabilities. Third, choose the environment most correspondent with you and with which you are most correspondent. "Correspondence," as you will read in Chapter 17, means that the environment fulfills your requirements and you fulfill the environment's requirements. If you don't have confidence in your ability to know yourself or to know your environments or to choose well, seek the help of a counseling psychologist or other professionally trained advice-giver.

Having chosen your environments carefully, you must next work at maintaining and even increasing the correspondence between you and your environment. This means (as you will read in Chapter 17) "acting on" the environment and yourself to fulfill requirements on both sides to a higher degree. For you, it can mean learning to be more flexible and more persevering–more willing to tolerate discorrespondence. It means practicing adjustment habits.

What if work doesn't realize your highest potential? This is the case for many workers, and for others who do not work for pay. The answer, of course, is to be found in non-work or off-work activities–avocations, hobbies, leisure-time activities, and non-work careers (homemaking, volunteer work.) Here again, the three-part formula applies: know yourself, know your "environments," and choose correspondence. Realizing your highest potential outside of work presumes, however, that your everyday life needs are taken care of, either by someone else or by your job, the work that may not realize your highest potential. Unfortunately, this presumption does not apply to those at the bottom rungs of our society, whose life needs are not met, and who may never get the chance to realize their highest potential.

But for the rest of us, it all comes down to this: You need first to know yourself well if you are to figure out what you can become–to realize your highest potential. And this is where psychology comes in.

Human Potential

Psychology is the science that studies what human beings are capable of doing; their behavior potential and how and when this potential is actualized or realized as human activity. Psychology has learned a great deal about human potential and human behavior by using the methods of science. By studying psychology, you will begin to learn more about your potential; and by learning about yourself, your potential and your behavior, you can learn a lot about other people as well, about their potential and their behavior.

In this unit, you will learn about the need to be aware of your self, your talents, and your values and about the many factors that affect your development. You will also learn about the development of psychology as a science and how early psychologists explained behavior. This knowledge will give you a basis for study of your self through-out the rest of this book.

CHAPTER 1

▶ PSYCHOLOGY:
The Drive to Know
Ourselves

Know then thyself.
Alexander Pope

Alexander Pope wrote the line "Know then thyself" in 1733, more than 100 years before psychology became a formal science. Yet it and a subsequent line, "The proper study of mankind is man," could be considered a summation of the relatively young science, conveying not only psychology's aim but also its value.

Pope wrote long before people had become aware of the prejudicial effects of sexist language, and in writing "mankind" and "man," he was referring to all people—men and women. And that is what the "proper study"—psychology—is all about: the study of all people, how they behave, and why they behave as they do.

Our raised consciousness about sexist words and their potentially injurious effect on both men and women is itself an example of psychology in action. Language evolved to suggest a superior-inferior relationship between men and women. The work of psychologists, among others, has shown that this description of the relationship is inaccurate. Sexist language does not reflect a fact; it perpetuates a myth.

▼ SELF-AWARENESS

What kind of person am I? What is my personality like? What are my talents? What are my values? How can I realize my potential? These are typical questions people ask themselves, often in vague, wondering ways.

Being **self-centered** is not productive or healthy. Being **self-aware** is productive and healthy. Learning about yourself and others is a key to a successful life.

The kind of person you are determines how you select your goals and go about achieving them. People who are unaware of themselves can make unwise choices. Being unaware of your strengths is likely to have a negative effect because it may cause you to interact poorly with others. Those who are most successful and satisfied in life are often those who understand themselves. Self-awareness is the first step toward a successful career and a fulfilling life.

Later in this book you will learn how you grow and develop. For now, be aware that you are as you are and behave as you do because of a number of factors. These factors can be divided into two general categories: biological and environmental.

Biological factors include the physical characteristics that you inherit from your parents and ancestors. Among them are such apparent ones as your hair, eyes, nose, mouth, height, and weight, and less apparent ones, such as your nervous system, brain, and spinal cord. Your inherited

self-centered
excessively preoccupied with yourself

self-aware
sensibly aware of your worth and potential

biological
referring to physical characteristics inherited from ancestors

physical characteristics came through your **chromosomes**, which are those parts of a human cell that transmit physical characteristics. Chromosomes themselves in turn contain **genes** that are responsible for specific characteristics. For example, there are genes for brown eyes and genes for blue or other colors.

Environmental factors include your surroundings, factors outside of you that affect your development and behavior. Your environment begins influencing you from the moment of conception. As you grow, the environment that influences you changes.

Both biological and environmental factors are important and very much intertwined. Some biological factors—a person's sex or a physical handicap—might appear to be strongly dominant, that is, exercising the most influence. But experience teaches that this is not necessarily so.

Your Changing Self

Being aware of what you are is important so you can deal with the pluses and minuses realistically. The set of complex interrelating physical and mental characteristics that constitute you is not static. What you are today is not what you were yesterday or will be tomorrow. You are constantly changing, even if you are not aware of it.

Sometimes something forceful or dramatic will happen to you— graduation, successful completion of a project, or conquering of a long-held fear. Then you are aware of the change. Most often you are not aware of the changes taking place. You might become aware of them when you look at a photograph taken of you years earlier. You might laugh at that strange person you were. These changes are both **voluntary** and **involuntary**.

Your Right to Develop Your Potential

To a large extent you can direct your change, your growth and development. The degree to which you possess this capability sets you and all human beings apart from all other living things. Lower animals realize their potential on one level. A racehorse, for example, will grow strong and fast. It can be trained by humans to realize its potential to race.

▼ TALENT

Potential, talent, and ability are words you will encounter often throughout this text. People frequently use them interchangeably, and to some extent they are similar. Unused talent or ability remain potential. "Actualization" or "realization" means using talent or ability. Talent is the broader term; you

---

chromosomes
parts of a human cell that transmit physical characteristics

genes
parts of a chromosome that determine specific characteristics, such as eye or hair color

environmental
factors outside the individual that affect the individual's development and behavior

voluntary
resulting from one's own choices

involuntary
outside or beyond the individual's conscious control

TO THE POINT

Nothing more dramatically illustrates the point that the relative influence of biological and environmental factors is not fully understood than the changed and changing views about women. It was once believed that their gender prevented women from doing many things that women do today. For example, women, conventional wisdom had it, could not run a 26-mile, 385-yard race (the standard length of a marathon). Even after women competed in other athletic events, this "wisdom" continued to prevail. It was not until 1984 that a women's marathon was allowed in the Olympics.

Women can indeed run marathons. In 1994 a woman won the New York City Marathon (a 26.5 mile trek). Her time was faster than that of any man in all the Olympic marathons run from 1896 to 1964.

A Closing Gap

Today the difference between the time of men and that of women is only about 5 minutes and is closing fast—a remarkable feat considering that women have been running marathons for only three decades. Some people have begun to think that if a person's gender does affect long-range running, it favors women. That is ironic, since their gender and its perceived limitations have kept women out of marathons in the past.

Handicap No Bar

For one further example of why you cannot assume biological factors are always dominant, consider a physically handicapped person. Certainly a disability will dominate a person's life.

But will it really?

Many people with disabilities participate and succeed in sports that require tremendous physical training.

Think about it.

You, however, can decide what physical attributes to develop. Even more important, you can develop your mind—your mental attributes. You can recognize your potential and deliberately work to develop it. All humans have this capability. You exercise it when you attend school and study and when you investigate careers, select one, and prepare for it.

To shape your growth and development effectively, you must be aware of your potential and your values, what is important to you. Consider that your potential is your raw material and your values determine how you shape that raw material. You will read more about values later in this chapter and in Chapter 10.

could consider ability as narrowly focused talent. In Chapter 6 you will read of ability defined in technical terms.

What Is Talent?

Psychologists have learned that **talent** is not easily defined. As in all sciences, knowledge in psychology continues to accumulate. As new facts are discovered and new ways of looking at things are invented, concepts such as talent are refined and redefined. However, a good working definition of talent is that it is the potential for learning to perform an activity considered important in a society.[1] In principle, everyone has a unique pattern and combination of abilities that produces one's unique talent.

talent
potential for learning to perform activities important in a culture

The fact that people with apparently similar potential and from similar backgrounds do develop in different ways is a frequent theme in novels and movies. A classic film of the 1930s, Angels With Dirty Faces, starring James Cagney and Pat O'Brien, used this as a plot device. Cagney became a gangster, while his boyhood chum became a priest. The film suggests that their differences in development stemmed from the fact that Cagney was caught and sent to reform school for a minor crime in which both were involved. O'Brien escaped. In real life the influential factors are often less clear.

TO THE POINT

Talents Used/Talents Wasted

Few, if any, of us realize the full potential of our talents. Also, the degree to which people realize their potential differs. Some develop and use many of their talents, while others do not. There are many reasons why this is so, some of them known but many unknown. In one sense psychology is a search for these reasons. By learning what causes some people to develop their talents and others to fail to do so, scientists hope to increase everyone's capacity for development.

Psychologists have determined that to realize your potential, you must have the desire to develop your talent. The greater your desire, other things being equal, the greater your development and use of talent. This relationship between realization of potential, talent, and desire has been popularized in this simple formula:

Performance (realization) = Ability (talent) x Motivation (desire)

Motivation is a condition or conditions that cause you to act. You will read more about motivation, what it is and where it comes from, later in this text. For now, we will just say that without motivation, you do not realize or use your talent. Your values play a big role in determining your motivation.

▼ VALUES

values
in everyday usage, standards for evaluating things and events; a sense of what is important

As you go through life you acquire **values**. In Chapter 10, you will learn a more technical definition of values. At any one time, you can have many values, and sometimes they conflict. But essentially you are motivated to achieve what you value. In some situations, your circumstances help determine your values: A person deprived of water for a long time will value a drink of water above all else. Put another way, you value your life and health. So if circumstances, such as lack of water, appear to threaten either, you react accordingly. But in normal everyday life, values are not so clearly influenced by immediate circumstances.

Often it is difficult to understand why people value some things and not others. Everyone values a secure, decent life and will work to earn the money needed for it. Some people, however, value money and power above all else; and in a single-minded drive to acquire these assets, they may sacrifice friends and family.

One person may value work for its own sake and derive great satisfaction from doing it apart from pay or other rewards. Another may dislike work but will do it to achieve other things that are valued, such as lifestyle or recognition or power.

Values Help Focus Talents

You could live your life without ever identifying your values. It has been said, however, that the unexamined life is not worth living. Those without a clear idea of their values will find themselves in the wasteland described by the poet T. S. Eliot, asking repeatedly the mournful questions:

> *What shall I do now?*
> *What shall I do?*
> *What shall we do tomorrow?*
> *What shall we ever do?*

Knowing what your values are will help you focus your talents, plan ahead, and choose to act rather than react. When the time comes to select a career, you will more likely select one that you can do well and enjoy. Knowing what you value will make it easier for you to make decisions when faced with conflicting choices. For example, your answers to the following questions will have a bearing on the kind of job you will enjoy and do well:

- Do you value working with people or things?
- Do you value independence or security?
- Do you value certainty or challenge?

How You Acquire Values

You will learn later in this text of the needs everyone has that govern behavior. These needs range from obvious biological ones, such as a need to eat, to psychological ones, such as a need for affection. You experience many needs and many ways to satisfy them. Out of this experience, you distill your values. You learn to value some needs above others and learn preferred ways to meet them. You develop these distinctions and acquire values from two sources: experience and other people.

Experience

Experience begins molding your values from the moment of your birth. Many social scientists believe that by age five you have formed your basic values. Experiences in these early years strongly shape the values you hold for life.

Persons deprived of love and affection as children may value them so greatly as to spend most of their adult life seeking them, never feeling fully satisfied. A person given much love and affection as a child will value them in later life because the experience was rewarding. But in this situation

Peanuts

Fig. 1-1

Others may influence our values,
though not often this quickly.

the individual, having experienced love and affection, would not value acquiring them so highly; rather, this person would value giving them to others.

Experience is a powerful shaper of values and can be more powerful than schooling or even the home. That is because what actually happens to you can have a stronger effect on you than what people tell you or show you by example.

Other People

Experience may be a most powerful shaper of values. Some independent people may rely solely on personal experience, ignoring all advice and examples of other people. But it is impossible for you to shape your values without being influenced by other people.

Parents exert the first and strongest influence on your values. Parents decide for a child what is right and what is wrong, and for the child, that is all there is to it. A mother might stress sharing: "Be nice to other children. Let them play with your toys." As a result the child might learn to value sharing and kindness. Or a mother might continually say, "Be careful with your toys. They're expensive. The other children might break them." This child might learn to value possessions over people.

When you leave home, other people exert an influence on you. At first it will be mostly people in authority, such as teachers and religious leaders. Between the ages of 12 and 18, people often reject their parents, others in authority, or most older people as a source of values. At this age you are most influenced by your peers.

Many parents make the mistake of attempting to force a set of values on their children. This may backfire, as each person is a unique individual, who must develop in his or her own way. Without pressure, most children will develop values similar to those of their parents, however. With pressure, children may deliberately cultivate different values. People may develop a particular set of values simply to avoid another set.

How You Clarify Values

Acquiring and clarifying values is a lifelong process. Carl Jung, an early psychoanalyst, called this process individuation. Many people become confused about their values because they live in a time of constant change and also because they live in a society made up of many differing groups. It is difficult to establish a consistent set of values. Often you will find it necessary to compromise some of your values. The problem is in deciding when to compromise your values without becoming a hypocrite or when to hold to your values without becoming a fanatic.

Compromising

When many people must live, study, or work together, it is not possible for all of them to satisfy their values completely. Upholding the value of total individual freedom, for example, is not always practical and can be self-defeating. You may often need to consider compromise. For example, you may value good grades and want to spend an evening studying but find yourself in a social situation in which you feel it necessary to go out for a pizza because you also value being accepted socially.

If you habitually compromise, however, you are in danger of failing to reach some of your goals. If you always give in to pressure and go get a pizza instead of studying, your grades will suffer. You are also becoming a hypocrite because you are acting against your stated values (achieving good grades). Acting against your values can give you negative feelings, unhappiness, and guilt. Mature people try to live by their values. For example, taking a token drink may be an acceptable compromise once in a while as a way to be accepted, but giving in to peer pressure and drinking heavily is not a compromise but an immature reaction.

This story of the wealthy man and his child illustrates that experience can be a more powerful force than other people in shaping values. Although he had become extremely wealthy, the father continued all his life to be frugal and to save, acting on values he had learned as a youngster. He tried to teach his child to value saving as he did. But the child never acquired this value. The child was a spendthrift, valuing the pleasure of spending money above that of saving it.

When a friend asked the father why the child did not follow his example of saving money, the father replied, "My father was poor, but my child's father is rich."

The child and the father each developed values about the use of money. The father learned when young that it was hard to get, so valued saving it. The child learned when young that it was plentiful, so valued spending it.

TO THE POINT

Inflexibility

Because compromise often is necessary, it helps to know which values you hold as most important. Not all values are equal. Some values you will defend with your life. Others are less important. Mature people are those who can maintain their important values and be willing to compromise less important ones. Another way of saying this is that mature people value getting along with others and recognize the need to do so above some other values.

People who hold strongly to unrealistic values become fanatics. A sage once said, "Fanatics are people who, having lost sight of their goals, have redoubled their efforts."

An example of a fanatic is the terrorist. Terrorists value their group's cause above human life. No matter how righteous their cause, by destroying life, including their own, they destroy the possibility of reaching any goals, including their own most cherished cause.

Mature people fall between the two extremes of the hypocrite with meaningless values that are compromised from day to day and the fanatic who rigidly maintains a value no matter how unrealistic it is or how destructive it has become.

▼ THE NEED FOR CONTINUAL SELF-AWARENESS

Occasionally examine and reevaluate your values. Ask yourself such questions as:

- Are my values appropriate, fitting, or proper in terms of what I am doing now?

- Do my values fit in with the changes that have occurred in my life?

- Are my values meaningful in the current environment?

If the answer to any of these questions is no, then you must consider examining your values. You will not always change them, of course, because your values may not be at fault. You might decide to keep your values and change your circumstances insofar as that is possible.

The point is to be open to the possibility of changing. In an entry-level job, respect for authority is a value that may be functional because you have little experience. Lacking that experience, you should value the experience of mentors or supervisors. But as you gain experience and move to more demanding jobs, you should begin to value more independence and the ability to make your own decisions. Otherwise, you will not continue to grow in the job and will eventually become dissatisfied.

Continual self-awareness is necessary for at least three basic reasons:

1. You grow physically and mentally.
2. Your personality changes as you grow and mature.
3. Your environment, especially in today's technological society, continually changes.

Self-Awareness Through Psychology

You have read about the importance of talents and values and the need for you to know yours—to be self-aware. Where does psychology fit in? Psychology comprises the scientific study of people's behavior. The more you know about psychology, the more you can know about yourself.

▼ DEFINITION OF PSYCHOLOGY

Psychology is the scientific study of human behavior—physical and mental. The roots of the word psychology suggest its meaning. It is made from two Greek words: psyche ("breath, soul"; later, "mind") and logos ("reason, word"; later, "study"). They were combined in psychology to mean "the study of the human soul."

The development of human **consciousness** occurred far back in the history of human beings. But as long as humans have been conscious of themselves, they have wondered and asked questions about why they behave as they do. So even though psychology dates back only to the nineteenth century, its roots go back much farther.

Modern psychology grew out of **philosophy**. Earlier philosophers attempted to explain human behavior by **subjective** reasoning. The distinguishing characteristic of psychology today is that it is a scientific study of human behavior.

consciousness
the state of having knowledge, being aware of one's own existence

philosophy
the study of first principles or ultimate questions

subjective
based on a mental idea or feeling; not observable; not verifiable

Tools and Concepts

Scientific study implies the use of **objective** procedures and tools. In their effort to understand and explain human behavior, psychologists use many different tools. They methodically observe humans and animals. Yes, much of what has been learned about humans came from the study of animals. They record their observations so others can check and verify them.

Psychologists pose specific questions and then attempt to answer them through observation and experimentation. The questions can be general ones, such as:

objective
actually observable as opposed to being a mental idea or feeling; verifiable

Fig. 1-2

In Greek myth, Psyche was represented by a beautiful maiden with the wings of a butterfly; she symbolized the soul. Originally psychology—the study of the soul—was a branch of philosophy.

- What are talents?
- Where do values come from?
- What motivates us?
- What is the relationship between our biology and our behavior?

More often the questions are specific, or narrowly stated:

- What effect does background noise have on people's ability to study?

- To what extent is an individual's behavior influenced by the group the individual is in?

Long-standing questions psychologists seek answers for include:

- How can thinking (which is nonphysical) affect the body (which is physical)?

- Do we run away because we are afraid, or are we afraid because we run away?

In seeking answers, psychologists not only observe people and animals in natural surroundings, but also often conduct experiments with rigid controls. Psychologists also use many different kinds of tests to identify attitudes, aptitudes, and intelligence. Through their studies, psychologists hope to learn how to predict human behavior as well as how to control some aspects of it. The goal is to make it possible for all people to develop their potential to the fullest.

Human behavior is obviously a very broad subject for study. Because of this, psychology has evolved into several different specialties, each focusing on certain aspects of human behavior. Not surprisingly, psychologists in different areas and even in the same area occasionally come to different conclusions. For example, psychologists continue to disagree about the relative influence of biological and environmental factors.

Subfields of Psychology

One person could not possibly be an expert in all of psychology. Thus, depending on their focus, psychologists specialize in subfields that exist within the broad science of psychology. Within these subfields the work that psychologists do can generally be divided into four broad categories:

1. Teaching
2. Practical application, such as counseling and treating people
3. Research and experimentation
4. Operation of clinics, consultant agencies, and the like

Table 1-1

MAJOR SUBFIELDS OF PSYCHOLOGY	
SUBFIELD	NO. IN FIELD*
Experimental	1,118
Clinical	6,470
Evaluation and Measurement	1,407
Social/Personality	2,687
Developmental	1,209
Educational	1,948
School	2,104
Industrial/Organizational	2,519
Counseling	5,318

* Based on 1993 APA Division Memberships

There are many thousands of psychologists in the United States. The 1993 American Psychological Association (APA) directory lists 115,129 members. The directory shows that its members belong to 49 different divisions, reflecting the many specialties or subfields within psychology.

Here is a brief description of 9 of the 49 major subfields in which psychologists work. Keep in mind, however, that while the different subfields focus on different aspects of human behavior, they are all interrelated and often overlap. Also, the subfields themselves are often divided into narrower specialties. See Table 1-1.

Experimental

The name of this subfield is slightly misleading. **Experimental psychologists** do not limit their research to experiments. At the same time, psychologists in all other subfields do experiments.

Experimental psychologists do carry out experiments, however. These experiments, with animals and people, explore our basic behavioral processes (Figure 1-3):

experimental psychologists psychologists who use the experimental method in attempting to understand and explain basic behavioral processes

- **Sensation and perception:** How do we respond to light, sound?

- **Learning and memory:** How do we learn? How do we remember?

- **Cognition:** How do we think?

- **Motor skills:** How do we acquire skills? Maintain them?

- **Motivation:** What makes us do what we do? What are our values?

- **Emotion:** What is love? anger? fear?

Clinical

clinical psychologists
psychologists with specialized training in the treatment of emotional and behavioral problems

In essence, **clinical psychologists** use their knowledge and skill to help people. This is the largest and best known grouping of psychologists. You have probably heard jokes about being an "armchair psychologist." This expression is applied to people who are always attempting to explain or influence the behavior of others.

On a serious level, clinical psychologists examine and treat people for emotional and behavioral problems. They are similar to psychiatrists and psychoanalysts. This is a good place to clarify the differences among these three types of professionals. Clinical psychologists, psychiatrists, and psychoanalysts often do similar work; the difference among them is their training. **Psychiatrists** have degrees in medicine as well as training in treatment of mental disorders. **Psychoanalysts** in the United States also usually have medical degrees. They are psychiatrists who have studied and who practice Sigmund Freud's treatment methods. They have also undergone psychoanalysis themselves.

Psychiatrists
individuals with degrees in medicine and specialized training in the treatment of mental disorders

Psychoanalysts
psychiatrists who study and practice Sigmund Freud's personality theories and treatment methods and have undergone psychoanalysis

Clinical psychologists generally have doctor of philosophy degrees (Ph.D.'s) in psychology. Clinical psychologists have training in the treatment of emotional and behavioral problems from a psychological (rather than a medical) perspective. See Figure 1-4.

Psychometrics

Have you ever taken a test? How about the Scholastic Aptitude Tests (SATs)? Perhaps you have heard of the initials IQ, which stand for "Intelligence Quotient." If so, you are acquainted with the work of psychometric psychologists. Psychometric psychologists construct tests designed to measure many different things: intelligence, interests, aptitudes, personality.

To prepare these tests, these psychologists must identify the characteristics they wish to measure, construct the test, and determine how to interpret the test results based on tryouts and statistical analysis. Test interpretation, to be acceptable, has to be based on experience and observation, not just on theoretical (speculative) expectations.

This is one of the more controversial areas of psychology. Experts continue to debate what "intelligence" really is, as well as how to measure it correctly. There is also debate over the extent to which tests are culturally biased, that is, favoring only those people raised in particular environments.

Social

In large part, this book deals with **social psychology**, which is the study of how people interact. One focus of this text is preparation for entering, and effective interaction in, the workplace.

How do people influence each other? Why will individuals go along with the group even at times when they do not agree with it? How do people react to aggressive behavior in others? Social psychologists seek answers to questions such as these. Their studies can have practical consequences because they deal with how people act when they are with others, such as at work.

Developmental

Developmental psychologists study how behavior develops from birth (and even before) to death. They try not only to describe that development but also to predict and modify it. Within this field psychologists specialize even further. Some concentrate on child development; others on old age; and still others on continuing developmental processes, such as learning as a lifelong process.

Questions that developmental psychologists ask include these: What skills are present at birth? When do we begin to perceive shapes or color? In the last decade, as the average age of our population rose, interest in the effects of aging grew. Continuing studies began to suggest that, contrary to popular belief, mental abilities did not necessarily decline with age.

Educational

Educational psychologists attempt to determine what environment fosters learning and what hinders it. They want to find out how schools can best educate both gifted and learning-disabled students and how schools can help overcome social, emotional, and physical handicaps. They construct materials and develop techniques and procedures to be used in the classroom.

School

School psychologists study people in relation to educational environments. In some respects, they represent a specialized form of educational psychology (see above) or counseling psychology (see next page).

They are similar to educational psychologists in that they develop programs to help students learn. But they also train teachers who work with students who have special learning problems. It is estimated that between 20 and 30 percent of children in the United States experience school-adjustment problems. School psychologists work in schools, and they also work for children and youth service agencies and in criminal justice departments.

Fig. 1-3

Much of what we know about human behavior has come from scientific study and experimentation with animals in the laboratory.

social psychology
the study of how people interact

developmental psychologists
psychologists who study how behavior develops from (and even before) birth to death

Educational psychologists
psychologists who study factors that influence learning

School psychologists
psychologists who study people in relation to educational environments

Fig. 1-4

Clinical psychologists work in a clinic or office, using their knowledge of human behavior to help people with behavioral problems.

industrial/organizational psychologists
psychologists who study how people behave in their workplace environment

Industrial/Organizational

This subfield is similar in some aspects to educational psychology. The difference, of course, is that **industrial/organizational psychologists** operate in work organizations.

Fig. 1-5

Psychometric psychologists use tests to acquire knowledge of human behavior.

Industrial/organizational psychologists focus on how people behave in the workplace. Businesses of all kinds increasingly recognize the importance of this subfield of psychology. Anything that can be done to help workers realize their potential and increase their satisfaction on the job will increase their productivity and their value to the organization.

Industrial/organizational psychologists have been particularly important in helping work organizations and workers adjust to the introduction of new technologies into the workplace. For example, they help workers handle cyberphobia (fear and dislike of computers). These psychologists might study anything from the effects of glare from a computer screen to the effects of stress caused by fear the computer will eliminate jobs. Based on their studies, industrial/organizational psychologists help businesses set up adequate training programs.

Counseling

Counseling psychologists usually work one-on-one helping individuals understand themselves, make choices or decisions, and solve personal problems. They interview, observe, and test individuals to help with self-understanding, decision making, and identification of problems, and suggest ways to correct them. You will find counseling psychologists in businesses, in private practice, and in educational institutions (perhaps your school has one who helps you with setting career goals or finding solutions to problems with your studies).

counseling psychologists
psychologists who help individuals understand themselves, make choices and decisions, and solve personal problems

TO THE POINT

To give you an idea of how specialized psychology has become, here is a breakdown of the field of social psychology into the specialties recognized by the APA.

Social Psychology
- Interpersonal processes
    - Influence and communications
    - Interpersonal relations
    - Social perception and motivation
    - Aggression
- Intra- and intergroup processes
    - Group conflict and attitudes
    - Group decision making and performance
    - Group structure
    - Leadership
    - Sensitivity and encounter groups
- Communication
    - Mass media communication
    - Language
    - Nonverbal communication
- Attitudes and opinions
- Values and moral behavior
- Alcohol use
- Drug use
- Smoking
- Sexual Behavior
    - Birth control
    - Sexual life styles
    - Sex roles and sex differences
- Psychology and the arts
- Culture and social processes
    - Ethnology
    - Socioeconomic structure and roles
    - Religion
    - Cross-cultural comparison
    - Family
    - Social change and programs
    - Crime reduction
- Deviant behavior

SUMMARY

1. _____ Psychology is the study of people's behavior, not only how but why they behave as they do.

2. _____ Those who best know themselves have the best chance of being successful and satisfied in life.

3. _____ Factors influencing your behavior fall into two general categories: biological and environmental.

4. _____ The set of complex interrelating physical and mental characteristics that constitute you is not static. It changes as you encounter new experiences and grow. These changes are both voluntary and involuntary.

5. _____ Your ability to direct your change, your growth and development, sets you as a human being apart from all other living things.

6. _____ A good, working definition of talent is that it is potential for learning to perform activities important to society. Each individual has a unique combination of abilities that produces unique talent.

7. _____ Few if any of us realize the full potential of our talent. Some reasons for this are known; many are not.

8. _____ Psychologists have determined that you must desire to develop your talent. The greater your desire, the greater your development of talent. Performance = Talent X Motivation

9. _____ You are motivated to achieve what you value. Often it is difficult to understand why people have certain values and others do not.

10. _____ Knowing what your values are helps you focus on your talent, plan ahead, and choose rather than just react.

11. _____ Acquiring and clarifying values is a lifelong process. You acquire values mainly from two sources: experience and other people.

12. _____ Many people become confused about their values in this time of continuing change in a complex society. They have difficulty establishing a consistent set of values without becoming hypocrites or fanatics.

13. _____ Psychologists strive to understand human behavior, to learn how to predict it, as well as how to modify some aspects of it.

14. _____ Psychology has evolved into several different specialties, each focusing on certain aspects of human behavior.

KEY TERMS
Define the following:

Biological
Chromosomes
Clinical psychologists
Consciousness
Counseling psychologists
Developmental
    psychologists
Educational
    psychologists
Environmental
Experimental psychologists
Genes
Individuation
Industrial/organizational
    psychologists
Involuntary
Motivation
Objective
Philosophy
Psychiatrists
Psychoanalysts
Psychology
Psychometric psychologists
School psychologists
Self-aware
Self-centered
Social psychology
Subjective
Talent
Values
Voluntary

QUESTIONS FOR REVIEW AND DISCUSSION

1. Briefly explain the difference between being self-centered and being self-aware. Which do you prefer and why?
2. What are the two general categories of factors that determine how we look and behave, and how do they influence us?
3. To shape our growth and development successfully, what two things must we know about ourselves?
4. Why do few of us realize the full potential of our talent?
5. Of the two sources of your values, experience and other people, which is the more influential of the two? Why?
6. What is philosophy? How does it relate to psychology?
7. How does social psychology relate to experimental psychology?
8. What do psychometric psychologists do? Why is their work sometimes controversial?

ACTIVITIES

1. Look in the *APA Membership Directories* published by the American Psychological Association for the names of several psychologists, and see what kinds of work they have been doing. Also look at the back of the directory for Divisional Memberships (of the association), and notice where psychologists live by state and city and where they are employed. Your school or local library might have a copy of this directory.
2. Choose an article in *Psychology Today* that might interest you, and read the article. Did you feel that this article could be understood by a person not trained in psychology? What did you gain from reading the article?
3. Look around your community for examples of people with handicaps who have led successful lives, or think of any famous people who overcame handicaps. Make a list of these people and what they accomplished.
4. In recent years, an issue of concern has been smoking in public places. The U.S. Surgeon General, relying on extensive studies, determined that smoking is dangerous not only to the smoker's health but also to nonsmokers inhaling the contaminated air. One result has been to pit those who value health against those who value total individual freedom (expressed, in this case, as the right to smoke anywhere). The question essentially is whether one person in pursuit of individual freedom should be allowed to endanger another's health, or whether one person's health should be allowed to severely restrict another's freedom. What do your values make you think about this? How would you resolve the problem?

5.   Our values are shaped by other people and by our experiences. Which of the two would you consider the more powerful influence? Why do you suppose this is true? Think of examples in your own life in which experience helped shape one of your values. Think of examples in which other people shaped one of your values. Make a two-column list of the examples you can think of.

CASE 1

What Is Self?

It is not just psychologists and modern late-20th-century people who have been puzzled about the nature of "self." Avicenna, a 10th century Arab philosopher, argued that self had to be different and separate from the body and its parts:

> For I am myself, even if I am unaware that I possess a hand, a foot, or any other member (of the body). . . Or rather, I think that these members depend on myself, and I believe that they are instruments which belong to me, which I employ for my needs; if these needs did not exist, I would have no need to possess them, but would still be myself, though they would not exist.

1.   Do you agree with Avicenna? Why or why not?
2.   How do you view "self"?

From *The Roots of Psychology*, edited by Solomon Diamond, Basic Books, 1974.

CASE 2

Why Study Psychology?

A famous psychologist, Henry Murray, left a promising career as a biochemistry researcher to become a psychologist because, in his own words, he. . .want(ed) to know why man, "like an angry ape, plays such fantastic tricks before high heaven"; why he laughs, blasphemes and frets, cheers at a spangled cloth and bleeds for a king; why he blushes over four-letter words and hides his genitals, and falls in love with so and so and later strangles her, why he mourns in isolation, lacerates himself with guilt, invents a purgatory and a paradise.

1.   What are <u>your</u> reasons for studying psychology--besides, of course, to fulfill program requirements?

2.   Although you haven't read this textbook yet, do you think (from your present knowledge) that Murray can find what he is looking for in the science of psychology?

From *The Life of Henry A. Murray: 1893-1988,* by James Anderson.

THE METHODS AND MODELS OF PSYCHOLOGY: How We Study Human Potential

Oh Wad th power the giftie gie us To see oursels as others see us! It would frae monie a blunder free us,...
Robert Burns

You can never see yourself as others see you, but the poet was right in suggesting that the more you know about yourself, the fewer blunders you are likely to make. How do you learn about yourself? Primarily in two ways:

1. From your observations of your own behavior—how you act and react, how you think and feel, what is important and not important to you, what you do well and don't do well, your likes and dislikes, your hopes and fears

2. From your observations of how others behave in relation to you, including what they communicate to you about yourself, whether spoken or unspoken

There is a third way that you can learn about yourself. It is through the science that studies human behavior—the science of psychology.

Psychology will not really tell you about yourself. Rather, psychology will tell you how and why people behave as they do. You still have to figure out if what psychology tells you about human behavior applies to you and, if it does apply, what you can learn from it about yourself.

What can psychology tell you about yourself that you don't already know? Plenty—because psychology is expert knowledge. A mechanic can tell you much more about your car than you'll ever learn by yourself, even if you bought the car new and no one else has been driving it for the last ten years. A physician can tell you more about your body than you may want to know.

This is the age of experts, of specialized knowledge, and the field that specializes in human behavior is psychology. The psychology that you are studying in this book is scientific psychology. It is the psychology—the knowledge of human behavior—that has been produced by the scientific community of scholars and research workers, which means that:

- This "knowledge" is the product of a particular group of humans.

- The fund of knowledge continues to grow.

- Other scientists besides psychologists contribute to psychological knowledge, although psychologists contribute the most.

▼ THE SCIENCE OF PSYCHOLOGY

Psychology has been defined as the science of human behavior. You will examine first what is meant by science. Later in this chapter you will examine what is meant by *human behavior*.

Science

The term *science* used to mean "ordered and orderly knowledge." Disorderly knowledge leads to mental confusion. Orderly knowledge gives you a mental "grasp" on things, or what is called comprehension. With ordered knowledge, you can see the larger picture more clearly, enabling you to say, "I understand."

Modern science, like older science, is aimed at improved or increased understanding. Modern science differs somewhat from older science in that its focus is less on ordering knowledge (although that is still very much a concern) and more on discovery and invention. Modern science's goal, simply put, is to learn more and more about the universe, the world, and all life. To explore the unknown, scientists invent tools to help in their observations, instruments—at times exotic—that have become the hallmark of modern science.

Invention in modern science is not confined to instruments, however, important though these may be in achieving the breakthroughs of which all scientists dream. Even more important are the scientists' invention of new ways of thinking about their observations. Scientists would say they invent new theories about their data.

Data and Theory

Data and theory are the essence of modern science. Scientists observe to gather data. On the basis of their data they construct **theories**, which are simply ways of looking at the larger reality beyond the data. A theory is an attempt to describe and explain some aspect of reality.

theories
attempts to describe and explain reality

Each theory provides new directions for more observations that, in turn, lead to new or modified theories and sometimes the dropping of a theory altogether. The goal of all scientific enterprise, *as science*, is theory.

How you interpret reality has profound implications for your behavior. That is why science has become such an important part of your life. The point to be stressed, however, is that scientific activity leads to theory.

Technology

What people do with scientific theory is another, separate matter. People will inevitably use theory. When scientific theory is used to address and solve

Fig. 2-1

Theoretical science and applied science (technology) are two different things. When the two are confused, theoretical science is both blamed for the ills and credited for the good caused by technology.

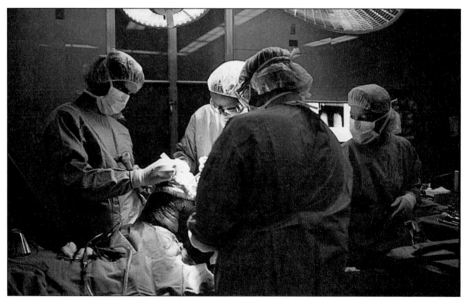

applied science
scientific study of the use of science to address and solve human problems

technology
the use of scientific theory and knowledge to address and solve human problems

human problems, it is called **applied science** or **technology**. It is technology (the use of science) that affects ordinary people most. As a result, they see technology and science as being the same. Seeing them as the same thing, people often blame science for the ills that technology creates or credit science for the good that technology does.

In recent times, for example, scientists studying heredity (genetics) have made incredible advances using new tools of observation provided by the sciences of physics and chemistry. These advances have given rise to a new technology known as bioengineering, or genetic engineering, some aspects of which have become controversial. Using the new knowledge, for example, technicians have created new life forms for commercial use, such as plants resistant to cold, microorganisms beneficial to plants, and one species of livestock with implanted genes of another species. Critics worry about unforeseen long-term effects of such bioengineering.

▼ THE METHODS OF SCIENCE

How do scientists "know" about things? Scientists' methods have, in recent times, reached such levels of complexity and sophistication that only another expert or specialist can competently discuss scientific methodology in a given field. No longer can we talk about *the* scientific method, because there are many methods. Nonetheless, four basic methods can be described: the comparative method, the grouping method, the analytic method, and the deductive (experimental) method.

The Comparative Method

The **comparative method** is probably the most basic scientific method. It consists of comparing two observations (events, objects, persons, groups, situations, conditions, etc.) and attempting to identify similarities and differences. As you will read in a following section, psychologists have used differences among individuals to develop an elaborate methodology for research.

A variant of the comparative method, much used in clinical psychology, might be called the **method of limits**. Scientists learn about a phenomenon by studying the extremes, or limits, of the phenomenon. For example, if you want to learn about temperature, you study the extremes of temperature, hot and cold. If you want to learn about human behavior, you study the extremes of human behavior, such as genius and mental retardation.

The Grouping Method

The **grouping method** basically consists of categorizing or classifying observations (most frequently things rather than events). This could be the oldest scientific method, one associated with the older idea of science as ordered knowledge. By grouping objects, scientists discover an underlying rule or principle that explains the grouping. For example, Carolus Linnaeus (1707–1778, a Swedish botanist who originated the Linnean system of classifying plants and animals) found a hierarchy of complexity that was explained later by the theory of evolution.

comparative method
the method of comparing and contrasting observations, attempting to identify similarities and differences

method of limits
a variant of the comparative method. The study of the extremes, or limits, of a phenomenon

grouping method
the method of categorizing or classifying observations in order to identify underlying rules or principles about the things observed

The Analytic Method

analytic method
the method of breaking the object of study into component parts in order to see how the whole functions as a result of the functioning of the parts

To analyze means "to break down" or "to reduce to simpler parts." The **analytic method** is a favorite among scientists. It consists of breaking down the object of study into its component parts in order to see how the whole functions as a result of the functioning of the parts.

The study of the human body is a good example of this approach. By breaking down the object of study—from whole body to systems to parts to cells—scientists develop a clearer picture of how the body works. The power of this method can be seen in the incredible advances in physics, chemistry, and biology. By studying a small atom, for example, physicists have developed theories on the behavior of large objects, even solar systems, galaxies, and universes.

The Deductive (Experimental) Method

deductive method
the method of studying current theory to deduce (arrive at) a suggested explanation of an existing condition, then devising experiments to disprove the explanation or find evidence for it

hypothesis
an explanation deduced (arrived at) from theories about an object, event, or condition

The **deductive method** consists of studying current theories to deduce (to determine by inferring from a general principle) a suggested explanation of an existing condition and then devising experiments to disprove the explanation. Scientists call the explanation or tentative assumption they deduce from theories a **hypothesis**.

Scientists also sometimes refer to the deductive method as the **experimental method**. To experiment means "to try out." By trial and learning from error, scientists eventually piece together the "truth"—that is, they gain more understanding.

The goal in experimentation is to devise a procedure that disproves all guesses except the experimenter's. Typically, there will be two explanations of a phenomenon. The ideal experiment has two mutually exclusive outcomes, one outcome favoring one explanation and the other outcome favoring the other explanation.

An example of a simple experiment designed to test two possible explanations of a phenomenon is Galileo's famous experiment in the Leaning Tower of Pisa. Galileo (1564–1642) wanted to test whether two objects of different masses actually will fall at the same rate. It seemed common sense in his day to assume that a larger, heavier stone would fall faster and land sooner than a light, small stone.

The experiment could have only one of two possible outcomes: Either the stones would land at the same time, or one would land before the other. Galileo took two stones of different sizes to the top of the tower and let them fall, while an observer stood at the bottom. When in fact both stones landed at the same time, he was able to demonstrate that the speed of a falling object is not affected by its size or weight. Objects of different sizes and weights fall at the same speed. This is not true of things like feathers or

Fig. 2-2

Trial and error—the experimental methods of science.

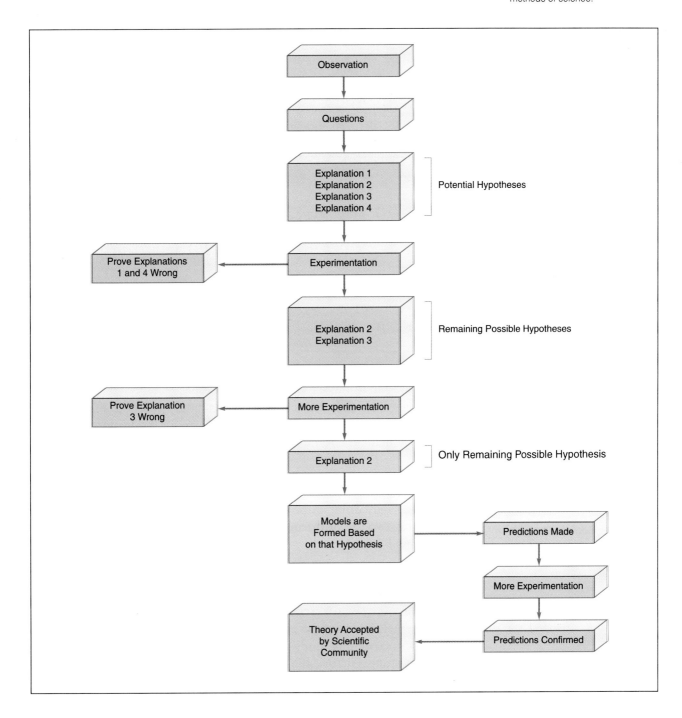

TO THE POINT

In the deductive (experimental) method, proving is not as important as disproving because all psychological experiments must begin with a "no effect" or "null" hypothesis. To illustrate, suppose psychologists wanted to find out whether a sales force would increase sales if the force were offered a bonus for all sales over $100,000 a month. They would set up an experiment to prove or disprove the null hypothesis that:

Even if salespeople are offered a bonus for all sales over $100,000, this will not affect their sales records.

The null hypothesis is the opposite of the hypothesis deduced from theory, which is that the chance to earn more money will cause people to work harder.

dandelion seeds, but that is because of wind resistance. On an airless planet, they too would fall at the same speed as the stone.

Mastery of the deductive (experimental) method enabled the sciences of physics and chemistry to make the incredible advances in knowledge that have made them the models for other sciences.

Common Characteristics

Although they may differ in procedure, all scientific methods share certain characteristics. Two are of the utmost importance: replicability and what we will call accessibility.

Replicability

replicability
the ability to be repeated

Science deals only with repeating, repeated, repeatable phenomena. **Replicability** means having the ability to be repeated. If something happens only once, science cannot study it. The study of things that happened once belongs to history. Historical phenomena that repeat themselves can be studied by science if they are likely to repeat themselves in the future.

Confirmation in science is achieved by replication; that is, by repeating the experiment or study. Thus, the first requirement for a scientific study is that it be replicable. This allows doubters to check independently on the original study.

Accessibility

The second shared characteristic for a scientific method goes hand-in-hand with the first. **Accessibility** means that all scientific study should be available to the public. Anyone interested should have access to the procedures and results of a study. A study cannot be kept secret and be part of science. The superiority of the scientific approach lies in its self-correcting mechanism. This mechanism depends on the accessibility of all scientific study without exception.

accessibility
the idea that all scientific study should be available to the public

▼ HUMAN BEHAVIOR

As the term is generally used by psychologists, **human behavior** refers to more than just the observable actions ordinarily thought of as "behavior" (as in "Junior's behavior today was very bad."). Some psychologists do prefer to limit the term to mean only observable behavior. Most psychologists, however, use the term to mean functions that are not directly observable, such as thoughts and feelings, as well. You can see the result of thinking and feelings, but not the processes.

You can never see other people's thoughts, although you can, of course, observe your own. For many psychologists, it is the unobservable behavior—like thoughts and feelings—that is the more interesting and that makes the observed behavior of interest to them.

Another term used in psychology to refer to behavior is response. **Response** originally meant "behavior in reaction to a **stimulus**." Stimulus, in turn, was defined in a circular fashion as a condition that elicits a response. Then, psychologists found out that the relationship between stimulus and response was not so simple and actually could be extremely complex.

Soon, psychologists began to use response without meaning "elicited by a stimulus." In fact, what happened after a response and its effects on future responses became more interesting than the immediate cause and result. The term *response* began to be used as synonymous with *behavior*.

As a simple illustration of this shift in the meaning, consider what you do when handed a hot potato. You drop it. Initially, your "response" is limited to the immediate reaction: dropping the hot potato. But, unless you are very slow, you have also learned something and will change your subsequent behavior: you will avoid handling hot things. Thus, according to

human behavior
human acts or activities, both mental and physical

response
originally, a term that referred to a reaction to a stimulus. Later expanded to mean behavior generally, especially learned behavior

stimulus
a condition that elicits a response

the broader meaning given it, your "response" was not merely the reaction of dropping one hot potato, but the learning response as well that affects your future actions. Like *behavior*, the term *response* was enlarged to include human functioning that is not directly observable.

Human behavior does not occur in a vacuum. It occurs in an environment. The "environment" for a given behavior can be narrow or broad, immediate or distant, temporary or (relatively) permanent, stable or unstable, structured or unstructured.

The environment may be physical or it may be psychological. The same physical environment may be different psychological environments for the infant, the child, the adolescent, the young adult, the old adult. Any definition of behavior is incomplete unless it includes specification of the environment in which the behavior takes place.

The work environment, for example, is obviously different from the home environment. You act differently in one than in the other. At work you are more formal and you carry out tasks that may not immediately please you. At home you are less formal and more often tend to do what immediately pleases you.

TO THE POINT

Some areas of scientific research and development are not readily accessible today. In two particular areas—industrial and business research and military research—secrecy is more the rule than the exception.

Scientists of all nations deplore this need for secrecy. Fortunately for the advancement of science, such secrecy, when it occurs, is mostly at the level of applied science. At a more basic level of scientific endeavor, pure research for which there is not apparent practical application of the results, accessibility rules.

Despite differences among nations on political matters, scientists throughout the world do share their work in most subjects. Russian and American scientists, for example, share research on disease or the discovery of new information about the solar system.

In areas where secrecy prevails, no matter how necessary, scientific research is probably handicapped.

A Complex Chain of Events

Scientists today appreciate the fact that all human behavior (or response) is a complex chain of events that loops back and forth between the individual and the environment. You could use the environment as an arbitrary starting point and trace the chain of events through the human's sensing apparatus (eyes and ears, for example) to the brain, out of the brain, to the individual's movement apparatus as expressed by actions taken, and back to the environment.

Or you could arbitrarily start in the human brain, go out to the movement apparatus, into the environment, from the environment into the sensing apparatus, and back to the brain. Either way, the loop keeps going round and round.

Three Divisions of Behavior

Looking at human behavior in the manner just described leads to categorizing it in three divisions:

1. **Sensory and perceptual behavior:** Starting from the environment and ending in the brain

2. **Central processes:** What goes on in the brain

3. **Motor behavior:** Starting from the brain and ending in the environment

The central processes can be divided into two subcategories:

1. **Cognitive behavior:** Based primarily on the functioning of the cortex (the higher brain).

2. **Affective behavior:** Based primarily on the functioning of the lower brain, especially the hypothalamus (small section of brain that controls body temperature and influences hunger, thirst, and sexual behavior).

You can continue subdividing the central processes. For example, cognitive behavior includes information processing (including reasoning), memory (information storage and retrieval), and language functions, among others.

Affective behavior refers to behavior involving your emotions—love, hate, fear, and so on. In psychology, *affect* as a noun is another word for *emotion.* Affective behavior includes positive affect (pleasurable emotion) and negative affect (disagreeable emotion), which are considered two different kinds of behavior. As you can see, the term human behavior used in this comprehensive way includes a wide variety of human functioning, both observable and unobservable.

▼ THE METHODS OF PSYCHOLOGY

Describing human behavior and explaining it are the tasks of the science of psychology. To describe human behavior is in a sense to explain it. As description becomes more and more elaborate, it is organized into theories, as you have read. Theories can be after-the-fact explanations (Monday-morning quarterbacking). Such theories are a dime a dozen. More important theories are those that predict what will happen. To rise beyond the merely speculative, theories must be tested. To test a theory requires that its predictions be observed and checked out. Experimentation is essentially checking out predictions made from theory.

The great psychologist Kurt Lewin said, "There is nothing so practical as a good theory." A good theory is one whose predictions are confirmed (or, more correctly, not disproved). The more the theory's predictions check out, the more confidence you have in the theory. Some theories gain such widespread acceptance that they become "laws." **Laws of science** are theories that are so universally accepted and unchallenged as to be taken for granted. You have heard of the "law of gravity" and can use it to predict that when a heavy object is thrown up in the air, it will fall back down.

When you have such a good theory, you can use that theory to your advantage. A good theory of human behavior enables you to do something about human behavior, to alter it, to change destructive behavior, in other words, to control it. Control of human behavior is possible when you are able to make predictions about it with great confidence. Being able to predict is the first step to, and the necessary condition for, control. Description, prediction, and control, however, all begin with observation.

Observation in Psychology

Scientific observation in psychology is done in a variety of ways. It can be done in laboratories where environments are controlled, in clinics where there is a mixture of controlled and uncontrolled conditions, and in the field, where there is little control of conditions and the environment is in its "natural state."

Observation varies according to where it is taking place. A scientist observing animal behavior in the laboratory might stand in sight of the

laws of science
theories that are so universally accepted and unchallenged as to be taken for granted (such as, "the law of gravity")

animal and use many sensitive instruments to gather and record data. But a scientist in the field might need to hide and use nothing more than binoculars and paper and pencil for notes. The manner of observation can also vary in other ways.

Observation Varies in Duration

Observation can be done for a short time (a few minutes, a few hours) or a long time (days, months, even years). Scientists studying how animals, such as gorillas or baboons, live in the wild spend years in the field making observations. A scientist studying how people react in a certain situation makes observations for only as long as the situation exists. But observations that are carried on only briefly at any given time may themselves be repeated over an extended period of time as conditions permit.

Observation Varies in Objectivity

Observation can be objective or subjective. Objective observation deals with objects independent of the observer. The observer tries to put aside emotions or personal thoughts while recording what is being observed. Subjective observation involves the observer's thoughts and feelings. In objective observation, agreement about what is observed is very high. In subjective observation, opinions may differ about what is observed.

Observation Varies in Standardization

Observation is most often done in a standardized way—a set procedure is followed. It can also be done, however, in an unstandardized, open-ended way, in which the observer knows what to observe, but does not wish to influence when the observed phenomenon appears.

There are times when psychologists do not want their subjects to be aware that they are being observed. We call this unobtrusive observation. However, this is done only with the prior consent of the subjects or of their parents if the subjects are children.

Observation Varies in Instruments Used

Observation varies according to the instruments used. In the laboratory, psychologists use apparatuses, such as mechanical or electronic equipment, to make and record the observations. In the field, they use tests and questionnaires. One result of inventing, developing, and using instruments for observation is that scientists can agree about their data.

Tests

Psychologists invented the psychological test to measure human mental ability. Measurement is simply observation in a way that produces readings that can be expressed by numbers. By recording the subjects' responses in solving problems presented in the test, psychologists are able to get a reading or measurement (test score) on the subjects' abilities.

There are many human abilities, so that psychologists must be sure that:

- The various test items measure the same ability.

- The test measures an adequate range of the ability.

- The test scores are reliable (the same subject gets the same reading on separate occasions).

- The test really measures what it is supposed to measure.

Questionnaires

The questionnaire is a standardized way of asking questions in such a way that the subject's responses can be translated into numbers or scores. The questionnaire borrows much from the psychological test. The same basic principles are used to construct questionnaires and tests. Tests and questionnaires are used to make observation more objective.

Experimental and Correlational Methods

Psychology's development as a science has followed two major methods. The first was in the laboratory, in academic settings, where theory was the foremost concern. The other was in the field and clinic, in school and work settings, where application was the foremost concern. These two pathways have been called the experimental and correlational methodologies, respectively.

Experimental Method

variable
a factor that can take on different values in an experiment

constant
a factor that always has the same value in an experiment

The experimental method starts with two variables. A **variable** is some changing aspect of the person or thing being studied. Height, weight, and age are variables. The opposite of a variable is a **constant**. For example pi is a constant, because the circumference of any circle divided by its diameter gives the *same value*, no matter what the size of the circle. Size, circumference, and diameter, however, are variables.

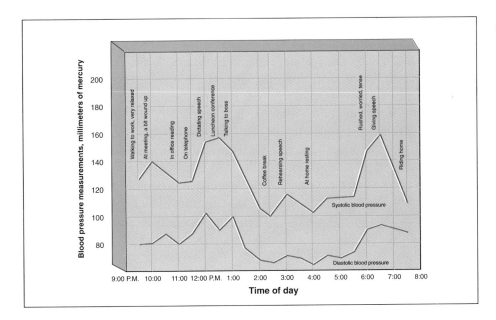

Fig. 2-3

By using instruments, psychologists can "observe" a subject's reactions when they are not with the subject. For example, a male patient with difficulty handling stress wore a portable blood pressure measuring device that recorded his blood pressure throughout the day. The patient kept a diary of his activities. Psychologists could compare his reactions, as indicated by blood pressure, with his activities to learn what was stressful to him. This chart resulted from the use of such a device.

One of the two variables is called the **dependent variable** (the condition or activity which the experiment is designed to measure), and the other is the **independent variable** (the factor or condition which the experimenter controls). The dependent variable is not directly controlled by the experimenter, because the point is to see how changes in the independent variable will affect it.

dependent variable
the condition or activity which the experiment is designed to measure

independent variable
in a scientific experiment, the factor or condition controlled by the experimenter

Basic Purpose

The basic purpose of an experiment is to see how the dependent variable changes as a result of changes in the independent variable. The experiment explores the basic *If-Then* relationship. Here are some simple examples: *If* students study longer hours (independent variable), *Then* they will get better grades (dependent variable). *If* auto dealers reduce prices (independent variable), *Then* they will sell more cars (dependent variable).

The experimenter tries to find if there really is an If-Then relationship and, if so, what kind (positive or negative) and how strong. Perhaps the relationship between studying longer and good grades is negative! Or perhaps there is a point beyond which the number of hours studying will not result in improved grades. Or too much studying might even result in lower grades. Or perhaps there is no relationship.

The more precise the experiment, the more accurately the experimenter can say how much change occurs in the dependent variable with each change in the independent variable. The use of more sensitive instruments makes experiments more precise.

Repeating the experiment many times and using many different subjects make it more reliable. If the same results occur with many repetitions and many subjects, you have great confidence in the findings.

Usually, more than one independent variable affects the dependent variable. Experiments have to be devised to identify the effects of each factor by itself and in combination with other factors.

Experimenting often requires repeating the experiment with the same dependent variable but with different independent variables or conditions.

In the simplest experiments, subjects are randomly assigned to two groups, called the experimental and control groups. The experimental group experiences the changing values of the independent variable such as the varying noise level in an experiment to determine what are the best conditions for studying. The control group does not experience any change in the independent variable; for them it's "business as usual."

Interpreting Results

After an experiment, the experimental group and the control group are measured. If the changes in the independent variable have any effect on the dependent variable, the two groups should differ in their scores on the dependent variable. For example, in an experiment to determine the effect of a bonus on sales performance, the experimental group receiving the bonus should show a higher rate of sales than the control group if bonuses do influence a person's rate of sales.

In the case of the experiment to determine what makes a good environment for studying, the subjects would be tested to see how much information they retained under different conditions. The results of the tests would be compared with each other as well as with the results for a control group to see what effect the changing conditions had on studying.

Knowing there is a difference, however, is not yet enough to allow drawing conclusions. Psychologists must know whether the difference in the dependent variable (for example, selling) between the two groups was really the result of the changes in the independent variable (bonuses). It could have been a fluke. The salespeople in the experimental group might just have been having a good day or those in the control group, a bad day. Or there may be other, not yet identified, independent variables, such as the competition's going out of business or an increase in prices.

Psychologists use statistical tests to determine whether differences between two groups are the result of changes in the independent variable or simply a random, chance result.

If the statistical test shows that the odds are 1 in 20 (5 percent) or less that the changes could have occurred by chance, the conclusion is that the results did not occur by chance and are therefore the result of the independent variable—bonuses do improve sales performance. If the probability is higher than 5 percent, doubt exists about bonuses being effective in improving sales performance.

The experimental method is used not just by experimental psychologists but also by applied psychologists. It is a favored way of evaluating new methods for teaching or for treating a behavior disorder.

Well-thought-out procedure and logic have made the experiment the most acceptable way of producing evidence about a **causal** relationship. Some psychologists accept no other evidence. But there are too many situations in the study of human behavior in which conducting an experiment is too costly, or just not possible. For such situations, psychologists have recourse to the other major approach to research, the correlational method.

causal
referring to a cause-and-effect relationship

Correlational Method

Like the experimental method, the **correlational method** measures two variables, but unlike the experimental method, the relationship between the variables is not considered causal. That is, neither one can be considered the cause or the effect. Sometimes there may be a causal relationship, but the correlations by themselves do not prove it exists.

correlational method
a major method in psychology based on the study of correlations between variables

What has become known as the Hawthorne Studies is a classic example that illustrates the experimental method. The study was conducted in the late 1920s at the Hawthorne Works of the Western Electric Company in Chicago. The hypothesis to be tested was that better lighting (independent variable) would improve productivity (dependent variable).

Several women workers were selected to be the experimental group and the rest of the workers were used as the control group. The lighting levels (constant condition) were kept the same for the control group. In the room for the experimental group, the lighting levels were changed (changing experimental condition). The intent was to find the "right" lighting level for the most productivity.

The observers were surprised by what happened. Productivity increased in the experimental group regardless of what lighting level was used.

Clearly another independent variable was influencing the dependent variable of production. Harvard psychologists under Dr. Elton Mayo eventually determined that the women in the experimental groups were motivated to work harder by having special attention paid to them. You will read more about motivation later in this text.

TO THE POINT

Correlation attempts to express the extent to which one variable changes in relation to the values in another variable. Here are some examples: Is there a correlation between leg length and ability to jump? Is there a correlation between scores on Scholastic Aptitude Tests (SATs) and college grades? Is there a correlation between hair color and temperament?

Types of Correlation

Correlation can be either positive or negative. In *positive* correlation, the values of both variables go up or down more or less together. For example, the more time spent practicing the guitar, the more songs you could play. Values of both variables increase in this positive correlation.

In *negative* correlation, as the values of one variable go up, the associated values in the other variable generally go down. The correlation of the price of an object and number of objects sold could be negative: as the price is increased, the number sold could decrease.

If the values of both variables move in unison, either up or down, you have *perfect* correlation. Perfect correlation rarely occurs in real life.

Uses of Correlation

Correlation has found many uses in the psychologist's study of human behavior. One of the most important is the role it has played in the evolution of the psychological test. Intercorrelation among test items or the correlation of each item with total test score is used to refine the test. Correlation between two halves of the test, between two forms of the test, or between two administrations of the test is used to demonstrate the reliability of the test.

Correlations with other tests and with other variables known as *criterion variables* are used to demonstrate the validity of the test. Criterion variables help demonstrate that the test measures what it is supposed to measure. A test of scholastic aptitude should correlate with school grades. That is, persons with high scores on a scholastic aptitude test should also tend to have high grades in school; those with low scores should on average have low grades.

Another major use of correlation is in making predictions. When there is correlation between two variables, one variable can be used to predict the other variable and vice versa. Thus, for example, if there is a correlation between a test and school grades, you can use test scores to predict school grades, and school grades to predict test scores.

Being able to predict allows you to do other things. For instance, taking the previous example, you can predict who would do well in school and give them scholarships, or you can predict who won't do well in school and give them additional help, such as tutoring.

It is this ability to predict using correlation that applied psychologists use in much of their work serving the needs of individuals and organizations. Correlation is so effective that studies have shown that correlational formulas alone are practically as reliable as the predictions made by trained clinicians.

▼ MODELS OF HUMAN BEHAVIOR

Since psychology became a modern science in the late nineteenth century, several schools of thought or ways of thinking about human behavior have been advanced and developed. These schools of thought emphasize different aspects of human behavior and organize the data in different ways. They constitute different models of human behavior.

Structural Model

The earliest school of thought in scientific psychology was the one that Wilhelm Wundt (1832–1920) set up in Germany. A student of Wundt's, Edward Bradford Titchener (1867–1927) of Cornell University, who brought the work to America, named it **structuralism**. Those who used the structural model saw psychology as the study of conscious experience. They focused on the elements of consciousness and the attributes of these elements: sensations, images, emotions.

structuralism
the first school of thought in scientific psychology, which emphasized the structure of consciousness and its elements: sensations, images, and emotions

Modern psychologists continue to study the subject matter but not with the methods structuralists used. The early structuralists used introspection exclusively. Also, they refused to consider how their findings could be applied to benefit humans. They wanted a "pure" science. These positions led to their loss of a following among practical-minded American psychologists.

Later structuralists moved beyond merely studying elements and their attributes to the study of wholes or systems. The whole (the system) is greater than the sum of its parts, its elements. Knowing what each element can do won't tell you what the whole can do; you have to know how the elements are put together. The idea of a system involves the idea of unique relationships among the elements in the system. What the whole can do only comes about when the elements are related in a particular way. This unique set of relationships is what psychologists call "structure." Modern psychologists continue to search for the "structures" that explain behavior.

Functional Model

The **functional model** developed in part in protest against structuralism but more so because it captured the spirit of American practicality. This model

functional model
a school of psychology that emphasized the functions of consciousness rather than its structure and the importance of psychology for practical purposes

Wilhelm Wundt (1832–1920), who founded the Structural Model school of psychological thought in Germany, has been called the father of psychology.

proposed the study of mental processes (or functions) in addition to mental content (or structures).

Influenced by evolutionary theory, it proposed that mental processes have functions in the adjustment and adaptation of human beings to their environment. Influenced by pragmatic (practical) philosophy, it also proposed that the study of psychology should help in solving human problems. Thus "functional" in functionalism had several meanings.

The early functionalists also believed that mental processes combine with physical processes in a unified whole. Unlike the early structuralists, they were willing to study behavior as well as consciousness, thus paving the way for the behaviorists. The functionalists' model disappeared not because it was an inferior model of human behavior but because it gave rise to—and eventually had to give way to—other developments in psychology, particularly behaviorism.

Behavioral Model

The earliest behaviorists took functionalism to one extreme and proclaimed that only behavior (and not consciousness) could be the subject matter of a science of psychology. Because behavior (or response) cannot be defined without referring to the environment in which the behavior or response occurs, the behavioral model quickly took on a stimulus-response cast and became known as the S-R model.

The goal of behaviorists was to describe the relationships between stimuli and responses. The discoveries of conditioning and reinforcement gave them the conceptual tools with which to develop a psychology of learning and to describe how behavior is acquired, maintained, modified, suppressed, and extinguished.

Conditioning is the process of making a neutral stimulus effective in causing response as a result of association with an effective stimulus. This process was discovered by the Russian scientist Ivan Pavlov. If you consistently show a hungry dog food after ringing a bell, the sound of the bell (neutral stimulus) becomes an effective stimulus in making the dog salivate by associating the tone with food (effective stimulus). See Figure 9-3 on page 235.

Reinforcement is the shaping and modification of behavior by the positive or negative consequences of responding. If a child throws a temper tantrum and you pay attention to the child, your attention "reinforces" the child's behavior and makes the tantrums more likely in the future. If you ignore the child, this behavior is not reinforced and will become less likely. Thus behavior can be explained, predicted, and controlled by knowing the individual's behavioral history and its consequences and the stimuli currently affecting the individual.

The behaviorists made psychology into a natural science and, some felt, into a subfield of biology. Introspection was banished and experimentation with animals became the accepted procedure for discovering the laws of learning. To the behaviorists, all behavior is subject to the basic laws of learning. To the critic of behaviorism, the leap from a few types of animal experiments, even if conducted in a thousand variations, to the complex level of human behavior, is unsupportable.

Gestalt Model

To the **Gestalt** psychologists the real world is not the same as the world as we perceive it, and the perceived world is all we really ever know. Furthermore, perceptions come as wholes, and it is a mistake to break perceived wholes into their component parts, because the whole is not just the sum of its parts.

Gestalt
a school of psychology asserting that perception and cognition could not be broken into constituent parts: "The whole is greater than the sum of its parts"

Wholes must be understood independently of their parts, for wholes have qualities of their own independent of the qualities of their parts. The "insights" you get in problem solving and productive thinking are examples of this. When you have an insight you have reorganized perceived parts into a whole that is more than, or different from, the parts.

If you are familiar with jigsaw puzzles, you have an idea of how a whole is different from its parts. When you first dump the pieces out of the box, you just have a jumble of pieces with interesting shapes and colors. Only after you have put them together in the proper way, do you see the full picture.

Like the early structuralists, the Gestaltists studied consciousness along with behavior. Unlike the early structuralists—and the behaviorists—the Gestaltists viewed psychology as being more than merely studying responses to stimuli. The key to understanding behavior, according to the Gestalt method, is to study the whole that contains the ego and the behavioral environment. The ego is your personal identity that maintains itself separate from the perceived, behavioral environment.

Essentially, the Gestaltists believed that you cannot understand a person by studying functions or responses individually any more than you could understand a musical composition by studying the notes individually. You have to look at the whole person and the whole situation, just as you have to consider the whole musical score to appreciate it.

Although the Gestaltists managed to attract a loyal following, much of their early evidence was "soft" (unquantified and subjective), and for years their following, even if influential, has been and remains small.

TO THE POINT

The most widely used test to assess personality and mental health is the Minnesota Multiphasic Personality Inventory (MMPI). It was developed in the 1940s by S. R. Hathaway, a psychologist, and J. R. McKinley, a psychiatrist. Since its development, the MMPI has been taken by millions of people both in this country and in other countries. The test has been updated recently to reflect changes in our society. About 14 percent of the test items are being revised to eliminate outdated or sexist language.

The test is considered an objective personality assessment as opposed to a subjective assessment, such as would result from an interview. It has validation scales, such as a "lie scale" to evaluate how honestly people respond to the questions. The lie scale includes such questions as "I do not always tell the truth" and "I get angry sometimes." If a person consistently answers false to such questions, the assumption is the person may be lying. Another validation scale rates a person's tendency to be overly critical of herself or himself.

The new MMPI2 has 567 true-false items and takes about one to two hours to complete.

As part of the process of evaluating and standardizing the test, it has been given to some 20,000 people around the country, including a standardization sample of 2,600 adults chosen to be representative of the U.S. population. Working on the revision are psychologists James Butcher and Auke Tellegen, University of Minnesota; Grant Dahlstrom, University of North Carolina; and John Graham, Kent State University in Ohio.

Psychoanalytic Model

psychoanalytic model
school of psychology originated by Sigmund Freud, stressing unconscious motivations and defining the mind as made up of three regions: id, ego, and superego

More than any other model, the **psychoanalytic model** of human behavior left a lasting mark on the intellectual and cultural landscape of our times. Literature, art, drama, and cinema as well as the human sciences (psychology, anthropology, and sociology) felt its influence. The psychoanalytic model is also referred to as the Freudian model in honor of Sigmund Freud (1856–1939), its originator.

The central tenet of the psychoanalytic model is that human behavior is determined largely by unconscious motives. How this happens is described by invoking a complex "mental apparatus" that Freud constructed to account for his theories. There are, Freud said, three "mind regions." He called them id, superego, and ego.

The Id

id
used in the psychoanalytic model to refer to unconscious, unlearned, inborn instincts

The **id** is completely unconscious and the repository of your inherited, unlearned, inborn instincts that must be satisfied for the sake of self-preservation or species preservation. These instincts, therefore, become your *primary* motives for behavior.

The Superego

The **superego** is conscious and preconscious, insofar as it is under our control to bring thoughts to awareness or consciousness. But parts of it are unconscious to the extent that we cannot bring thoughts voluntarily into awareness. The superego represents our making our own the culture's traditional moral values and ideals, the standards of society that we learned from our parents and that are enforced by a system of rewards and punishments. These standards provide secondary (learned, social) motives for our behavior.

The Ego

The **ego**, also conscious, preconscious, and partly unconscious, is the executive of your mind, the seat of your free will and perception, thought, and memory. You behave because of the ego's attempts to satisfy the demands of both the id and the superego while coping with reality. Satisfying the id produces pleasure; satisfying the superego produces pride.

Failure to satisfy the id produces **neurotic anxiety**. Neurotic anxiety is a functional disorder of the mind, emotions for which there is no apparent physical cause but which can cause people to think there is something physically wrong with them.

Failure to satisfy the superego leads to **moral anxiety**, or guilt. Moral anxiety is a disorder arising from the belief that you have failed to meet standards you have been taught.

Your motives, both primary and secondary, are powered by the **libido**, psychic or mental energy that originates in the id. Consequently, your primary (or unconscious) motives are the more powerful. To handle this power and still satisfy the superego, your ego resorts to **displacement**— redirecting the libido to more acceptable objects or activities.

There are several other well-known ego-defense mechanisms: repression, regression, substitution, rationalization, identification, and disassociation. The activation of such defense mechanisms in reaction to stress is discussed in Chapter 18.

Freud believed that behavior is motivated by a few basic motives, mostly the sexual instinct, but that because of displacement most behavior does not appear to be sexually motivated. Only with psychoanalysis is the true motivation revealed.

The psychoanalytic model is criticized on the grounds that it provides an explanation for every contingency, thus making it impossible to

superego
used in the psychoanalytic model to refer to a portion of the mind in which are stored cultural and traditional morals, ideals, and values, learned primarily from parents

ego
used in the psychoanalytic model to refer to an area of the mind thought to be the seat of free will and perceiving, thinking, and remembering

neurotic anxiety
a functional disorder of the mind, or emotions for which there is no apparent physical cause, arising out of a failure to satisfy the demands of the id

moral anxiety
a disorder of the mind, or emotions for which there is no apparent physical cause, arising out of a failure to satisfy the demands of the superego

libido
psychic or mental energy that originates in the id

displacement
redirection of the libido to objects or activities that are acceptable to the superego

Fig. 2-5

Sigmund Freud developed the psychoanalytic model of human behavior. This model describes behavior as being determined by unconscious motives

humanistic model
a school of psychology known as the "Third Force," after behaviorism and psychoanalysis, rejecting the determinism of the latter two and emphasizing free will, action as opposed to reaction, creativity, and the "whole person" in the Gestalt sense

determinism
the doctrine that behavior is determined, completely produced by, and resulting from stimuli or unconscious motive

disprove, which, therefore, renders it unscientific. Nonetheless, Freudian theory has been the stimulus for many inquiries into the human mind, and remains one of the most influential theories in psychology's history.

Humanistic Model

The **humanistic model** arose as a "third force" in opposition to the determinism of both behaviorism and psychoanalysis. **Determinism** is the doctrine that behavior is determined, that is, completely produced by and resulting from stimuli (behaviorism) or unconscious motives (psychoanalysis). Humanistic psychologists argue that you are active, or striving, not just reactive. They maintain you are free-willed, or free to choose, rather than confined to determined paths. In their view you are creative, or productive, instead of being just a product. Finally, they maintain that you are a unique whole person in the Gestalt sense and not simply a collection of parts.

They feel psychology should study the "experiencing person," and only personally or socially significant problems. Science and psychology exist only for the betterment of humankind, they argue. The objective of psychology should be understanding, not explaining, and the application of psychology should result in increased self-understanding as well as increased understanding of others.

The humanistic model shares tenets with the existential and phenomenological models. All three have some roots in the Gestalt model. All three share a philosophy of science that differs considerably from the prevailing one. The existential and phenomenological models are hard to distinguish from each other and from the humanistic model. Followers of one model are often also followers of either or both of the other two. The difference may be one of emphasis.

Cognitive Model

The scientific challenge to the behavioral model came not from the psychoanalysts or humanists but from students of cognition. In rapid succession, they discovered that:

- Your capacity to take in information at any one time is limited.

- The process by which you take in information and store it could be charted in step-by-step fashion.

- The "strategies" you use over several acts could explain problem-solving behavior better than the examination of separate acts (S-R combinations).

It became clear to this new generation of psychologists that what went on between stimuli and responses is supremely important, not only in understanding behavior but in its own right as subject matter for study.

Behavior is more than mere combinations of reactions. It involves action as well as reaction, feedback, and adjustment on the basis of feedback. It involves the mind. Once again, psychologists found it fashionable to study sensation and perception, reasoning and remembering, how you mentally solve problems, how you think to arrive at a choice.

Once again human subjects rather than animals began to populate experimental laboratories. A wide variety of problems involving cognition were studied. People spoke of the cognitive revolution as overturning the behavioral model.

Newer Models

You may indeed be witnessing the beginnings of new sciences that may transform psychology. That something occurs in the mind (or the brain) between stimulus and response is not a new idea. What is new are the specifics of the models that psychologists are inventing to describe what goes on. The computer has provided a machine comparison, and many scientists are studying artificial intelligence, that is, getting the machine to behave like a human. But even if a machine behaves like a human, a human rarely behaves like a machine.

We have discussed several models of human behavior in psychology's attempt to understand human nature. All of them are right in some ways, wrong in other ways. The new, succeeding model typically improves on and is better than the old, or at least so we believe. Each new model adds new touches to the emerging portrait. Each new model advances your knowledge of yourself.

SUMMARY

1. Psychology tells you how and why people behave as they do. You still have to figure out if what psychology tells you about human behavior applies to you, and, if it does apply, what you can learn about yourself from it.

2. Modern science, like older science, is aimed at improved or increased understanding. Modern science differs somewhat from older science in that its focus is less on ordering knowledge (although that is still very much a concern) and more on discovery and invention.

3. Data and theory are the essence of modern science. Scientists observe to gather data. On the basis of their data, they construct theories, which are simply attempts to describe and explain reality, ways of looking at the larger reality beyond the data.

4. The right of the scientists to unfettered study probably lies beyond the law and ultimately in the nature of human beings. It is human nature to want to know.

5. There are four basic methods of science: the comparative method, the grouping method, the analytic method, and the deductive or experimental method.

6. All scientific methods share two basic characteristics: replicability, that is, they can be repeated in different places and with different subjects; and accessibility, that is, their methods and results are public knowledge.

7. Human behavior refers to both obvious behavior and unseen behavior, or thoughts and feelings. Some psychologists consider the terms response and behavior to mean the same thing. All human behavior is a complex chain of events looping back and forth between the individual and the environment.

8. There are three divisions of behavior: sensory and perceptual, central or mental processes, and motor.

9. Scientific observation in psychology is done in a variety of ways and places. It can vary in duration, objectivity, standardization, and the instruments used, among which tests and questionnaires are prominent.

10. Psychology developed as a science following two major methods: experimental and correlational. The experimental method begins with two variables and attempts to determine how the independent variable affects the dependent variable. The correlational method seeks only to determine whether two variables will change in concert. There may or may not be a causal relationship between them.

11. Various schools of psychologists have emphasized different ways of viewing human behavior. Psychological models that have been developed include: structural, functional, behavioral, Gestalt, psychoanalytic, humanistic (existential and phenomenological), and cognitive models.

QUESTIONS FOR REVIEW AND DISCUSSION

1. Briefly define the term *science*. Explain the different emphasis between older science and modern science.
2. Explain the difference between science and technology.
3. What are the two common characteristics all scientific methods share? Why are they important?
4. What two prominent instruments do psychologists use in the field to obtain information about human behavior? Describe each one.
5. Briefly describe the experimental method as used in psychology.
6. In what significant way does the correlational method differ from the experimental method?
7. Tell how the behavioral model of psychology differs from the structural and functional models.
8. What sets the humanistic model apart from the other models, especially behaviorism and psychoanalysis?

ACTIVITIES

1. Go to your school library or local library. Look for scientific publications such as the *Journal of Applied Psychology, Journal of Experimental Psychology, Psychological Science*, or the popular magazine *Psychology Today*. Browse through them for reports on psychological experiments. When you find such an article, read it, and write a brief report. Note particularly how the experiment was conducted. Identify the dependent and independent variable.
2. Be a psychologist. Think of some theory that you would like to prove or disprove. Let your imagination go. Do you have a theory that you do your homework better watching MTV? Perhaps you have a theory about how having their own cars improves students' grades, or a theory about how students do more homework on rainy days. Construct a hypothesis to test your theory. Identify the

KEY TERMS
Define the following:

Accessibility
Affective behavior
Analytic method
Applied science
Causal
Central processes
Cognitive behavior
Comparative method
Conditioning
Constant
Correlational method
Deductive method
Dependent variable
Determinism
Displacement
Ego
Experimental method
Functional model
Gestalt
Grouping method
Human behavior
Humanistic model
Hypothesis
Id
If-Then
Independent variable
Laws of science
Libido
Method of limits
Moral anxiety
Motor behavior
Neurotic anxiety
Psychoanalytic model
Reinforcement

Replicability
Response
Sensory and perceptual
* behavior*
Stimulus
Structuralism
Superego
Technology
Theories
Variable

dependent and independent variables. Determine how many subjects you will need and how you will divide them.

3. The difference between the experimental and correlational methods is that the first seeks a cause-and-effect relationship between the variables, whereas the second seeks only to see if the two variables change in unison, either going up or down together (positive correlation) or one going up while the other goes down (negative correlation). The fact that two variables correlate does not mean that they are causally related. People often see cause-and-effect in correlation where in fact none exists. Think of and make a list of at least three pairs of variables that might be highly correlated but are not related as cause and effect. For example, the size of the big toe is correlated with intelligence (but only for growing children). There is a correlation (across the states) between pig production and the production of pig iron. In European cities, the size of the stork population is correlated with the number of childbirths.

4. Review the various psychological models of human behavior that psychologists have presented over the years. Which one appeals most to you? Write a brief description of the model you prefer with your reasons.

CASE 1

What Is in an Experiment?

Stephen Williams, a psychologist at the University of Ulster at Coleraine, Northern Ireland, had this theory: The initial letter of your last name helps determine how fast you think and follow instructions.

Do you agree? Consider this. Williams set up an experiment to test his theory. His null hypothesis was that the initial letter of your last name does not affect how fast you think or follow instructions.

He tested 26 people by reading them 16 sentences and a list of numbers to remember. His directions on how to respond were deliberately confusing. He tested each person separately to make the results comparable.

He found that there was indeed a correlation between the first initial of last names and faster thinking and remembering. Those with initials near the beginning of the alphabet performed better than those whose initials appear toward the end.

1. What kind of psychologist would Williams likely be?
2. How would you describe the subjects' responses?
3. What explanation can you think of for this behavior?

CASE 2

The Roles of Science and Technology

In trying to solve the terrifying problems that face us in the world today, we naturally turn to the things we do best. We play from strength, and our strength is science and technology. Threatened by a nuclear holocaust, we build bigger deterrent forces and antiballistic-missile systems. We try to stave off world famine with new foods and better ways of growing them. Improved sanitation and medicine will, we hope, control disease, better housing and transportation will solve the problems of the ghettos, and new ways of reducing or disposing of waste will stop the pollution of the environment. We can point to remarkable achievements in all these fields, and it is not surprising that we should try to extend them. But things grow steadily worse, and it is disheartening to find that technology itself is increasingly at fault. Sanitation and medicine have made the problems of population more acute, war has acquired a new horror with the invention of nuclear weapons, and the affluent pursuit of happiness is largely responsible for pollution.

We need to make vast changes in human behavior, and we cannot make them with the help of nothing more than physics or biology, no matter how hard we try. It is not enough to "use technology with a deeper understanding of human issues," or to "dedicate technology to man's spiritual needs," or to "encourage technologists to look at human problems." Such expressions imply that where human behavior begins, technology stops, and that we must carry on, as we have in the past, with what we have learned from personal experience or from those collections of personal experiences called history, or with the distillations of experience to be found in folk wisdom and practical rules of thumb. These have been available for centuries, and all we have to show for them is the state of the world today.

What we need is a technology of behavior.

1. Based on what you have read in this chapter, what would you say this quoted passage says about science and technology? Do you think the writer's views have validity?

2. Think of the various models of human behavior that psychologists have constructed (structural, functional, behavioral, Gestalt, psychoanalytic, humanistic, and cognitive). In which one of these schools of thought would you say the writer of this passage belongs? Explain why you think so.

Excerpt from B. F. Skinner, *Beyond Freedom and Dignity* (New York: Alfred A. Knopf, 1971): 3–5.

Unit I

RESEARCH STUDY

A Case of IQ

An article reports on a study of the average IQs for different groups. Data in the study show the following: (a) When persons are classified according to socioeconomic status, the group at the highest socioeconomic status (or SES) level also has the highest average IQ, the next highest SES group has the next highest average IQ, and so on in order, with the lowest SES group having the lowest average IQ. (b) When persons are classified according to educational level, the group with the highest level of education also has the highest average IQ, the next highest educated group has the next highest average IQ, and so on in order, with the least educated having the lowest average IQ. (c) When persons are classified according to geographical location, the groups in the northern states have the higher average IQs, and those in the southern states have the lower average IQs.

1. What implications or conclusions can you draw that are consistent with the data? Write them down so you can examine them critically. The critical test to apply is that the implication cannot be ruled out by the data. List as many implications as you can regardless of your opinion (whether you agree with them or not), examine them according to the critical test, revise them as needed and remove those that don't pass the critical test.

2. Take one of the implications you have listed that you do NOT believe is the case, that you think is wrong. How would you explain why the data seem to support the implication?

3. Can you think of a study that would disprove the implication in 2 above? That is, what data are needed to disprove the implication?

This is the way scientists generally work. One scientist reports findings and draws implications consistent with the findings. Another scientist who does not believe an implication and thinks there is another explanation for the findings goes and designs a study or studies to (a) check out the finding (make sure it is dependable), (b) disprove the implication, and (c) support the alternative explanation.

The Biological Basis of Behavior

Because behavior is best viewed as the functioning of the whole human body, you begin your study of psychology with a look at the part of the human body most responsible for the control of behavior: the nervous system—in particular, the brain. To understand human behavior better, you have to understand how the brain functions: how it takes in information, stores it, and retrieves it for use; how it goes about its functions, and how its functions are affected by different internal and external conditions.

In this unit, you will not only learn how behavior is affected by biology, you will also study how human behavior capabilities are organized around what are called abilities, and how these abilities underlie the rich diversity of human skills. Finally you will look at where human potential originates – in genes – and how potential is shaped into actuality by the interaction of genes with the environment.

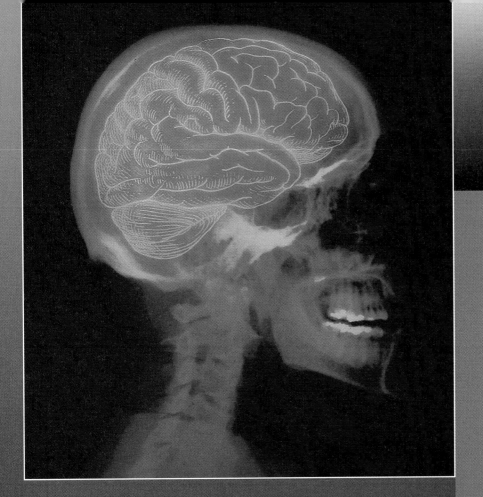

CHAPTER 3

▷ BIOLOGY, BRAIN, AND BEHAVIOR:
Why We Are Individuals

Suppose that the eye were an animal; then seeing would be its soul.
Aristotle

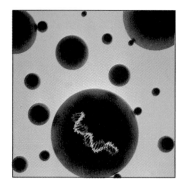

Recall that in Aristotle's time, psychology was the "study of the soul," but that over the years, psychology has come to mean the study of behavior. If we understand Aristotle correctly, "soul" would be to the body (the "animal") what seeing is to the eye—that is, Aristotle's "soul" is actually not too different from contemporary psychology's term, behavior. "Behavior" is, after all, what the body does.

No one today expects to understand seeing, or vision, without some knowledge of the eye. Similarly, following on Aristotle, neither should anyone expect to understand human behavior without some knowledge of the human body.

In this chapter, you begin your study of behavior with some facts from biology about the one part of the human body that is most important to understanding how you behave—your nervous system, especially your brain. Because psychology depends so much on biology, we oftentimes refer to psychology as a biological science.

Do you know the origin of the word "individual"? It comes from the same root as the word "indivisible." "Individual" literally means "cannot (or even should not) be divided further." In that way, "individual" is like the word "atom," which originally meant "cannot be cut up or split further."

We often use "individual" to refer to a single human being. This is because when you are "behaving," you act as a single undivided entity, as an integrated whole (compare with your use of the term "personal integrity"). Of course there are exceptions, but when these happen, we speak of "abnormal" behavior. "Normal" human behavior is integrated behavior.

▼ THE NERVOUS SYSTEM

nervous system
body system made up of the brain and spinal cord, nerves, ganglia, and parts of the sensory organs

What enables you to behave as a whole? As a single integrated entity? Biology tells us that it is largely because of your body's **nervous system**, especially your brain. Your nervous system is the main control system of your body. It has four functions:

1. It coordinates and regulates all of the body processes that keep you alive as a biological organism (such as respiration, digestion, blood pressure, and heart rate).

2. It gathers information about the outside world, as well as information about your own body.

3. It interprets and stores this information for immediate or future use.

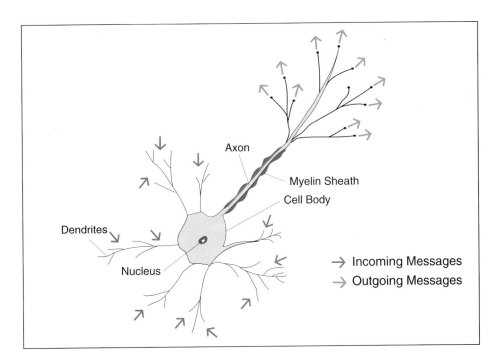

Fig. 3-1

The neuron.

4. It directs your behavior (walking, talking, etc.)—your response to newly received information combined with old remembered information.

In your body, these four functions are happening simultaneously all the time, and all the while your nervous system coordinates these functions into one seemingly smooth flow. (In some ways, your nervous system functions like a computer system that takes in information and uses the information to control and direct some machines, like in your car. But even the most advanced computer system in the world is very primitive and very simple when compared with your nervous system.)

Because your behavior depends so much on the functioning of your nervous system, you need to learn about the nervous system before we can begin our study of human potential.

We start with the basic unit of your nervous system, which, as it is for other parts of your body, is the **cell**. The nervous system has over a trillion cells that are of two kinds: **neurons** and **glia** (or glial cells). The neurons are specialized information-transmitting cells that do the nervous system's work. The glia are the cells that surround the neurons to provide them with their "work environment." The glia maintain this environment and do "housekeeping" (bringing in nutrients from the bloodstream, getting rid of wastes). To understand how the nervous system works, you need to know something about how the neurons work.

cell
basic unit of the body

neuron
individual nerve cell that forms the basic structure of the nervous system

glia
cells that surround the neurons

neural networks
interconnected groups of neurons

cell body
the central part of the cell

axon
a long fiber that conducts information away from the cell body of a neuron

dendrite
short fibers that conduct information from other neurons to the cell body

myelin sheath
a layer of myelin surrounding some nerve fibers

nerve
a bundle of neuron fibers supported by connective tissue located outside the brain

nerve tract
a bundle of neuron fibers located inside the brain

neural impulse
an electrical signal transmitted from receptor cells or from neurons to other neurons, muscles, or glands

synapse
the space between two neurons over which neurotransmitters travel

neurotransmitters
chemical "messengers" that convey neural impulses between neurons

receptor sites
areas on the surface of neurons at which neurotransmitters "dock"

The Neuron

The neuron is the "building block" of your nervous system (Fig. 3-1). Neurons are organized into groups called **neural networks**. As the word suggests, neurons within a network are interconnected, and networks are interconnected with other networks, forming larger networks. The whole is, of course, your nervous system.

A neuron is made up of a **cell body** and fiberlike extensions that look like roots. One of these fibers, the **axon**, is much longer than the rest. The other, shorter fibers are called **dendrites**. Dendrites are the "receiving" fibers of the neuron, whereas the axon is the "sending" fiber. Axons are like the telephone cables of your body, with many axons being bound together in one cable by a sheath (the **myelin sheath**). It is these "cables" that we refer to as **nerves** when located outside the brain or as **nerve tracts** when in the brain.

Neurons provide your body with a communication system through their unique ability to transmit electrical signals called **neural impulses** (Fig. 3-2). These neural impulses are the "messages" of your body's communication system. A neuron may receive neural impulses from receptor cells or other neurons, and may transmit neural impulses to other neurons or to the muscles or glands.

A neural impulse is transmitted in a complex procedure that involves an electrical change in the axon. When a neural impulse shoots down the axon (we say that the neuron "fires"), the neural impulse is transmitted without loss of signal strength along the whole length of the axon. Once started, the neural impulse goes all the way or it does not start at all. (This is known as the "all or none" law.)

After a neuron fires, it rests a bit before it fires again. This rest period is so brief, however, that a typical neuron can fire as many as a hundred times per second.

The place where one neuron makes contact with another neuron, or with a receptor or a muscle, is called a **synapse** (from a Greek word meaning "to clasp"). Upon reaching the far end of the axon, the neural impulse is transmitted across the synapse, typically from the axon of one neuron to the dendrite of another neuron (there are some variations, such as axon to another axon, axon directly to cell body) (Fig. 3-3). Transmission is either electrical or chemical. In electrical transmission, the neural impulse is conducted directly (like electric current) from one neuron to the other. In chemical transmission (which is more common), the neural impulse is conveyed through the use of chemical "messengers" called **neurotransmitters**. The axon terminals produce many kinds of neurotransmitters, each kind with its own specific **receptor sites** in the receiving dendrites. To transmit a neural impulse across the synapse, a neurotransmitter is "sent" across

Fig. 3-2

A neural impulse is like a tiny biological battery ready to be discharged. These impulses send messages throughout your body.

the divide to "dock" at its specific receptor site in the receiving dendrite. When it "docks," the neurotransmitter causes an electrical change in the dendrite that spreads to the receiving neuron's cell body. Because a neuron has many dendrites (dozens, even hundreds), it can receive many neural impulses at the same time. The received neural impulses accumulate as a "sum," and this "sum" can "tell" the receiving neuron to fire or not to fire. The "summing up" process is technically called **synaptic integration**, the result of which is either **excitatory** (to fire) or **inhibitory** (not to fire). Synaptic integration is the basis for all of the activity of the brain—and the

synaptic integration
the accumulation of neural impulses

Fig. 3-3

A magnified view of a synapse. Transmitters cross the synaptic gap to affect the next neuron.

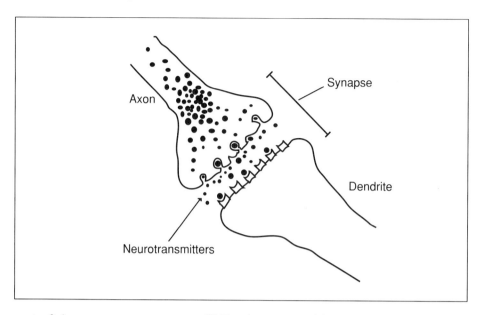

Axon

Synapse

Dendrite

Neurotransmitters

rest of the nervous system as well! To give you an idea of how much activity is going on in your brain, consider this: The average adult human brain has about 10 billion neurons, and each neuron has about 10,000 synapses with other neurons. That means that there are about 100 thousand billion possible synapses, which in numbers is 20,000 times the earth's current population of 5 billion!

Why is synaptic integration so important? Because it determines the degree of control you have over your behavior. Excitation and inhibition are opposing forces that are used to tilt behavior one way or the other or to maintain a balance, like the accelerator and the brake, with the steering wheel, of your car. To the degree that you can excite and/or inhibit the transmission of neural impulses, to that degree do you have control over your behavior. And much of this control depends on the functioning of neurotransmitters.

Neurotransmitters

Because neurotransmitters play such critical roles in synaptic integration, they are important players in your body's communication and control system. Among the best known of the 50-plus neurotransmitters that have been identified so far are the following:

- **Acetylcholine:** Functions in the areas of the brain responsible for sensory perception, movement, speech language, learning, and memory (in Alzheimer's disease, the brain has abnormally low levels of acetylcholine)

- **Dopamine:** Is involved in our experience of reward or pleasure and is also involved in movement (dopamine deficiency is thought to underlie Parkinson's disease, a movement disorder)

- **Norenpinephrine:** Contributes to arousal and is involved in learning, in sleep and wakefulness, and in the regulation of mood (it has been linked to depression)

- **Serotonin:** Affects mood and sleep, but also appetite (eating a lot of carbohydrates can produce more serotonin; in turn, increasing serotonin will decrease the appetite)

- **Glutamate:** Speeds up transmission across the synapses in the brain, and is thought by some to be at the very foundation of learning (the theory is that learning depends on repeated use of particular synapses; on the other hand, too much glutamate can cause neurons to fire themselves to death!)

- **GABA (gamma amino butyric acid):** Is the major inhibitory neurotransmitter in the nervous system (it is also involved in sleep), so that when it malfunctions, the excitatory neurotransmitters are "out of control" and a variety of behavioral disorders result, such as severe anxiety and uncontrollable movement of the limbs

- **Endorphins (endogenous morphines):** Behave like opiates (morphines) in relieving pain, producing euphoria, and inducing sleep

There are many other neurotransmitters, including the neuropeptides, whose role is only beginning to be understood. The new field of **psychopharmacology** is the study of how drugs affect behavior, and an important area in this field is the study of how neurotransmitters are affected by drugs. For example, addiction is best explained as the result of a drug's interfering with the normal functioning of the neurotransmitters.

Now that you have viewed your nervous system from the bottom up, let us examine it from the top down.

Parts of the Nervous System

Your nervous system has two main divisions: the central nervous system and the peripheral nervous system (Fig. 3-4). The **central nervous system** (or **CNS**), as its name suggests, is at the center of the action. It is the part that exercises control, the part to which information is sent, processed, and stored; it is the "chief executive" of the system. The **peripheral nervous**

psychopharmacology
the study of the effect of drugs on the mind and behavior

central nervous system
the brain and spinal cord as a combined system

peripheral nervous system
all portions of the nervous system lying outside the brain and spinal cord

system ("periphery" means "edge") is the rest of the nervous system that is not part of the central nervous system.

The central nervous system has two main components: the brain and the spinal cord. Both of these are encased in bone (the skull and the spinal column), and are protected by coverings and fluid—testimony to their importance in human evolution. It is through the fluid that the brain is fed with nutrients, especially oxygen and glucose. Did you know that, although your brain is only about 2 percent of your body weight, it consumes about 20 percent of your oxygen as well as 20 percent of your glucose intake? And that one-fifth of the blood your heart pumps is required for your brain? Yet, because the brain is packed with neurons and glial cells so very tightly, it is hard for substances in the blood (including toxic substances) to enter the brain—constituting what scientists call the **blood-brain barrier** that protects the brain.

blood-brain barrier
a barrier that makes it hard for substances in the blood to enter the brain

The peripheral nervous system also has two main components: the somatic nervous system (which carries information from the sense organs to the CNS and relays "orders" from the CNS to the muscles), and the autonomic nervous system (which carries messages back and forth between the CNS and the visceral organs, the heart, the lungs, and the glands, and is responsible for the "emergency response" of the body). We shall examine all four components of the nervous system in some detail, but we shall concentrate on the brain, the most important organ in your body.

Fig. 3-4

Divisions of the nervous system.

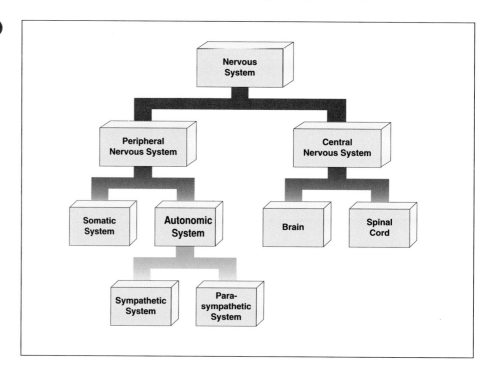

▼ THE CENTRAL NERVOUS SYSTEM

The Brain

The **brain** is the most complex organ of the most complex living being on planet Earth, so complex that few scientists can claim to be experts on the whole brain; most brain scientists can only specialize on some specific brain structure or function. Our study will barely skim the surface.

The brain is made up of many, many parts (Fig. 3-5). One way to sort out the parts is to follow the brain's development in the human being. The human brain develops from a tube of cells in the human embryo called the neural tube. As the neural tube grows, it forms three enlargements at one end that become the **forebrain**, the **midbrain**, and the **hindbrain** (named, as you can guess, according to their location). The rest of the neural tube eventually becomes the spinal cord.

The forebrain becomes the largest and most recognizable part of the fully developed brain, the cerebrum. This is the part that you immediately see when the brain is exposed. Other major brain structures that develop from the forebrain are the thalamus and the limbic system.

The midbrain and hindbrain become what is called the brain stem. The midbrain develops into several structures that we won't list. The hindbrain develops into the cerebellum (or "little brain"), the medulla (medulla oblongata) and the pons. Let us examine these major brain structures and the roles they play in behavior.

forebrain
the front part of the brain, including the cerebrum, hypothalamus, thalamus, and corpus callosum.

midbrain
the middle part of the brain consisting of structures linking the forebrain and the brainstem

hindbrain
the back part of the brain including the cerebellum, pons, and medulla oblongata

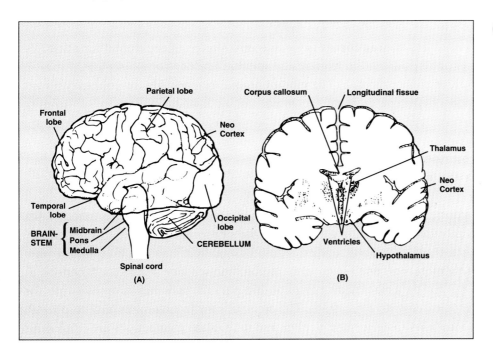

Fig. 3-5

Sections of the Brain

cerebrum
the enlarged upper part of the brain that is the seat of conscious mental processes

cerebral hemisphere
the right or left half of the cerebrum

corpus callosum
the large bundle of fibers connecting the right and left cerebral hemispheres

frontal lobe
the front of the cerebrum that includes sites associated with the control of movement, the processing of smell, and higher mental functions

occipital lobe
the back of the cerebrum that includes areas where vision registers in the brain

parietal lobe
the top of the cerebrum that includes sites where bodily sensations register in the brain

temporal lobe
the side of the cerebrum where hearing registers in the brain

neocortex
the cerebrum's surface covering of neuron cell bodies

sensory cortex
area of the neocortex that receives sensory or motor information

motor cortex
area of the neocortex associated with control of voluntary movements

association cortex
all areas of the neocortex that are not specifically sensory or motor in function

The Cerebrum

The **cerebrum**, the largest structure of the brain, is wrinkled and grayish-looking on the outside (hence, "gray matter") but whitish in the inside ("white matter," which is made up of lots of axons). It is divided into two halves, the left and right **cerebral hemispheres**. The two cerebral hemispheres are connected by a bridge of compact white matter called the **corpus callosum**, which contains upward of 200 million axons.

Each cerebral hemisphere is divided by grooves into sections called lobes. The front section is the **frontal lobe**, the back section is the **occipital lobe**, the section between the frontal and occipital lobes on the top of the head is the **parietal lobe,** and the section below the parietal lobe on the ear side of the head is the **temporal lobe.**

The cerebrum's surface is covered by a 3- to 4-millimeter-thick layer of neuron cell bodies called the **neocortex** (Latin for "new bark"). Your neocortex (also called the cerebral cortex) is responsible for your conscious experience—your thought and reasoning and imagination and memory and feeling—and for your conscious, voluntary movements.

The neocortex consists of three types of areas: sensory cortex, motor cortex, and association cortex (Fig. 3-6). The **sensory cortex** areas are located in the occipital, temporal, and parietal lobes and have to do with your sensing abilities. The occipital section (called the *visual cortex*) receives neural impulses from the eyes; the temporal section (the auditory cortex), from the ears; and the parietal section (the somatic sensory cortex), from the skin (touch, temperature, and pain).

The **motor cortex** is located on a stretch of the frontal lobe that lies right alongside and in front of the somatic sensory cortex, separated from it by a prominent groove. The motor cortex is responsible for voluntary movement. Different areas of the motor cortex initiate movement in different parts of your body (an area for the hand, an area for the mouth, etc.). These areas are arranged so that they pair up (in a kind of mirror image) with a corresponding area of the somatic sensory cortex to "cover" the same part of the body.

The **association cortex** areas are the largest and perhaps most important areas of the neocortex. They are located in all the lobes of the cerebrum and include all areas of the neocortex not part of the sensory cortex and the motor cortex. These association areas receive information from more than one sense organ or combine sensory and motor functioning.

The association cortex is the part of your brain responsible for complex cognitive functions. The areas in your frontal lobes have to do with your ability to deliberate, to plan, and to regulate your actions and with your

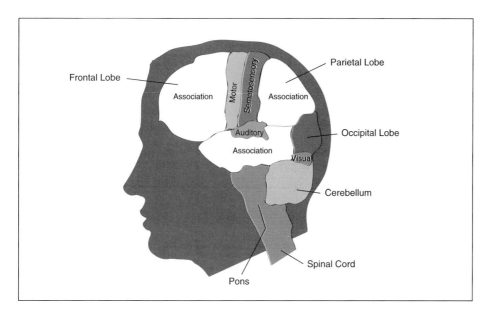

Fig. 3-6

The three areas of the neocortex.

your ability to anticipate the future, especially to estimate the effects of future actions. It is the frontal lobes that are involved when you excitedly await for, or are worried and anxious about, an upcoming event. The association areas in your occipital lobes have to do with your visual perception; they help out the visual cortex. (More about this in the next chapter). Your ability to connect visual with auditory information, to recognize spoken words, to recognize faces, to remember language, are all located in your temporal lobes. Your ability to orient yourself in space (in three dimensions), to use symbols, to recognize printed words, to read and make maps, all reside in your parietal lobes.

As you might expect, damage to the neocortex causes a deficit in all kinds of ability, depending on where the damage occurs. For example, if your frontal lobes are damaged, you may lose caution as well as initiative (and anxiety too, hence the use of prefrontal lobotomy—cutting away parts of the frontal lobe—in an attempt to control abnormal anxiety). Damage to your occipital lobes will affect your vision and your visual perception. And so on.

Why do we have two cerebral hemispheres? For one thing, each hemisphere receives sensory information from, and sends movement messages to, one half (one side) of your body—the opposite side! That is, the left hemisphere is responsible for the right side of your body and the right hemisphere for the left. As a rule, the hemispheres operate in symmetrical or mirror-image fashion, but there are important exceptions. One of these involves speech: the speech centers of the brain are found, in adults, only in the dominant hemisphere—which, for the majority of people, is the left hemisphere. Hemisphere dominance is related to handedness, but not completely. Thus, only one-third of left-handed persons have their speech centers located in their right hemispheres (or sometimes in both), and about 5 percent of right-handed persons have their speech centers in their right hemispheres.

Research by Roger Sperry (for which he won the Nobel Prize in 1981) and others has shown that the left (or dominant) hemisphere controls not only speaking and writing, but also logical and analytical thought, and mathematical calculation. On the other hand, the right (or nondominant) hemisphere controls creative and artistic thinking, visualizing of space, and the comprehension and interpretation of music.

Enclosed by the cerebral hemispheres, situated right in the middle of the brain, are two lobes of gray matter. This is the thalamus. The thalamus relays information from the sense organs to the sensory cortex (except for smell). Your thalamus can recognize in a crude way whether the sensation you are about to experience is pleasant or unpleasant. (Some speculate that this might form a basis for what we often call "intuition.")

Groups of neuron cell bodies, called the **basal ganglia**, are found in front of and partly surrounding the thalamus. These are important in motor functions, in producing and controlling muscle movement.

Perhaps more important than the thalamus because of its role in emotion and memory is the brain structure that surrounds it— the limbic system.

The Limbic System

The **limbic system** is the primitive core of the brain and is strongly associated with emotion. The limbic system is not a single structure but rather a group of structures that form a border around the thalamus (Fig. 3-7). ("Limbus" is Latin for "border"; "system" means a group of interconnected parts that function as a whole.) The limbic system is made up of the **hypothalamus**, the **hippocampus** (Latin for "sea horse", which it is supposed to look like), and the **amygdala** (Latin for "almond", which it resembles in shape), plus clusters of neuron cell bodies known as nuclei.

The hypothalamus is located under the thalamus ("hypo" means under). It is one of the major communications crossroads of the brain, with tracts (axon bundles) leading down to the spinal cord. It helps regulate your body's life support systems dealing with appetite, thirst, body temperature, cardiovascular functioning, and water and salt metabolism. It is involved in fighting behavior, sexual behavior, sleep and wakefulness, and the experi-

basal ganglia
groups of neuron cell bodies found in front of and partly surrounding the thalamus

limbic system
a system of interconnected structures in the forebrain that are closely associated with emotional response

hypothalamus
the small section of the brain that controls body temperature and influences hunger, thirst, and sexual behavior

hippocampus
brain structure in the limbic system involved in memory

amygdala
almond-shaped brain structure in the limbic system involved in aggression and fear

ences of pleasure and pain. Although it is part of the limbic system, the hypothalamus is also linked up with the autonomic nervous system and the endocrine system of the body, all of which are involved in the experience we call *emotion* (and whose primary biological function is emergency response).

The hippocampus plays a major role in your ability to remember and recall, especially your short-term memory. If your hippocampus is damaged, you may not be able to remember things that happened only a few hours ago. The hippocampus is connected with the hypothalamus, the thalamus, and the brain stem by a massive bundle of axons called the *fornix* (the largest nerve tract in the brain, containing over 2 million axons).

The amygdala, a cluster of neuron cell bodies, is connected with the hypothalamus and shares in its life-support functions. More important, it is involved in aggression and fear. Removing the amygdala will make a ferocious animal tame as a lamb. Stimulating it can arouse a peaceful animal into a frenzy. Sometimes, tumors in the limbic system can cause a personality change from normal to violent, even murderous, behavior.

The limbic system also includes the **olfactory cortex**, which has to do with smell. Recall that all information from the sensory organs, except for smell, is relayed to the neocortex through the thalamus. Smell is relayed directly to the limbic system. Smell, of course, is one of the senses we use when we eat, and smells help (or hinder!) our appetite. It is also worth noting that, in animals, smell is important in sexual (mating) behavior; for insects, it is an absolute necessity. For humans, however, because our sense of smell is poorly developed, we rely more on the other senses (sight, sound, and touch) in our sexual behavior, but smell can still play a rudimentary role!

olfactory cortex
site on the frontal lobes where information on smell registers

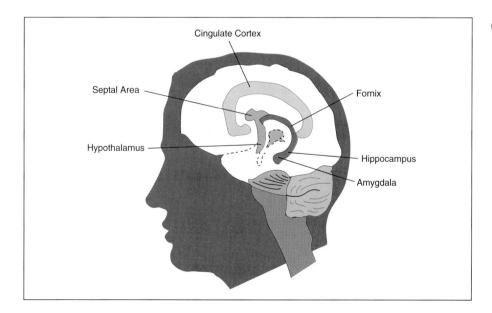

Fig. 3-7

Parts of the limbic system.

The Brain Stem

brain stem
the lower portions of the brain, including the cerebellum, medulla, and reticular formation

midbrain
part of the brain consisting of structures linking the forebrain and the brainstem

cerebellum
a projection at the base of the brain associated with motor response

reticular formation
network of neurons within the medulla associated with attention, alertness, and activation of higher brain areas

medulla
enlarged stalk at the base of the brain that connects to the spinal cord and controls vital life functions

pons
mass of nerve fibers that connect the cerebellum and medulla

As you have read, your **brain stem** comprises the midbrain and the hindbrain (cerebellum, reticular formation, medulla, and pons). Among its most important functions is to maintain your body posture and balance.

The **midbrain** is not prominent in humans (unlike in birds and fish, where it is a very important brain structure). Your midbrain structures help relay information from your sense organs (eyes, ears, skin) to the neocortex. They also help in starting movement smoothly and in controlling certain automatic behaviors (such as when your eyes automatically compensate when you move your head).

The **cerebellum** (in adults, about the size of a baseball or a fist, and even more wrinkled than the cerebrum) is located under the occipital lobes. Your cerebellum, together with the basal ganglia, have major roles in your motor response system. The cerebellum receives neural impulses from the neocortex (sensory and motor areas) and is involved in the control of the limbs and of body movements, posture, and equilibrium. Among its main functions is controlling finely coordinated movements (such as when you thread a needle). It holds the memory for such well rehearsed motor skills as playing the piano or typing.

The **reticular formation**, also called the **reticular activating system**, is a network of neurons ("reticular" means netlike) that spreads through the brain stem up to the thalamus and into the forebrain (neocortex). Your reticular formation governs arousal-waking and attention as well as sleep. When stimulated, your reticular formation makes you more attentive. If you are "put under"—given general anesthesia in surgery—it is your reticular formation that is "disabled," put out of commission.

The **medulla** contains nuclei (neuron cell bodies) from the cranial nerves. It helps control your "vital functions" (life maintaining functions) such as blood pressure, heart rate, breathing, and swallowing.

The **pons** is an arched structure, looking like a humped bridge ("pons" is Latin for "bridge"), that sticks out below the midbrain structures. It contains tracts (axon bundles) that connect the cerebellum with the medulla. It also has nuclei (neuron cell bodies) from the cranial nerves that have to do with several behaviors such as eyeball movement, chewing, taste sensation, facial movement, sound sensation, equilibrium, and the control of breathing. (The 12 *cranial nerve* pairs, so named because they are located in the cranium or skull, are part of the peripheral nervous system.)

We know that certain abilities are located ("localized") in specific areas of the brain, and that if one of these areas is destroyed the area will not grow back again. Is the ability, then, lost permanently? Usually, yes. However, for some people we find that, with time, the person can regain some of the lost ability and relearn lost skills. This happens not because the brain regrows to replace the lost area, but rather because other areas of the brain take over the lost function. For example, we find some stroke victims who have lost their speech are able, with time, to regain some or even most of their speaking ability. This shows the ability of the brain to take over functions lost when an area is damaged or destroyed—an amazing ability!

What about the other side of the coin? Can you "improve" your brain? Research with animals has shown that when the environment is "enriched" with more stimulating sights and sounds, more challenging playthings, more "playmates" or companions, the result is changes in the structure and chemistry of the brain. The neocortex becomes thicker, the neuron cell bodies larger, the dendrites longer; there are more synapses, and even more glial cells. These changes happened regardless of the age of the animals! Although we can't do this kind of research with humans, it is not unreasonable to think that a stimulating environment can also have a good effect on your brain.

The Spinal Cord

The **spinal cord** is the extension of the brain stem downward out of the skull and into the spinal column. It links the brain with the peripheral nervous system. This is where what is "central" and what is "peripheral" gets pretty confusing. For example, take the motor neurons that "tell" the muscles to move on orders of the brain. Their axons (that extend to the muscles) are part of the peripheral nervous system, but their cell bodies are in the spinal cord and therefore are part of the central nervous system. On the other hand, the sensory neurons (that send information from the skin and joints) belong to the peripheral nervous system, except the ends of their axons, which are in the spinal cord and therefore are part of the central nervous system.

Thirty-one pairs of nerves (bundles of axons), called **spinal nerves**, issue out of the spinal cord. Each nerve has two "roots" connecting it to the spinal cord. The root closer to the back is for sensory axons (incoming signals) and the root closer to the front is for motor axons (outgoing signals). The two roots join up a short distance from the spinal cord where they become one nerve. The roots are part of the central nervous system, but the nerves, as you have read, are part of the peripheral nervous system.

The spinal cord serves as the communications pathway between the brain and the rest of the body. Besides this function, the spinal cord has another important function: it is responsible for **reflex behavior.**

Have you ever had a physician tap your kneecap with a rubber hatchetlike instrument while you were seated with your legs dangling, and did your lower leg jerk upward involuntarily? That is known as the "knee-

spinal nerve
one of 62 major nerves that channel sensory and motor information in and out of the spinal cord

reflex behavior
actions monitored by the spinal cord

jerk reflex," a good example of reflex behavior. A *reflex* is so named because a sensory signal comes to the spinal cord and a motor signal is immediately "reflected out" to the muscles by the spinal cord without waiting for "orders" from the brain. (The brain, of course, eventually receives the sensory signal, but by then the reflex has occurred.) Pulling your hand away automatically when you touch something hot is another example of a reflex. A reflex happens very fast because only a few synapses are involved. The **reflex arc** involves only the sensory neuron, a few special connecting neurons in the spinal cord called **interneurons**, and the motor neuron. Reflexes are a holdover from an earlier evolutionary stage and have to do with the most basic and primitive of biological needs: survival and reproduction.

reflex arc
the pathway that leads from a stimulus to the spinal cord to an automatic response, such as a knee jerk

interneuron
a neuron that links other neurons

▼ THE PERIPHERAL NERVOUS SYSTEM

The Somatic Nervous System

As you have read, the **somatic nervous sytem** is the part of the peripheral nervous system that carries signals from the sense organs to the brain and from the brain to the muscles. It also carries signals from the muscles to the brain, to let the brain know how the muscles are doing, and from the brain to the sense organs, telling the sense organs what to do.

somatic nervous system
the system of nerves that carries signals from the sense organs to the brain and from the brain to the muscles

The somatic nervous system consists of the cranial nerves and the spinal nerves that you have read about. Some of these nerves are shared with the autonomic nervous system. At this point, you do not need more detail about the somatic nervous system. You will learn more about the sense organs of the body in the next chapter. You will learn more about complex human abilities in Chapters 5 and 6, abilities that depend on the smooth functioning of the somatic nervous system.

The Autonomic Nervous System

The autonomic nervous system, or ANS, is the name given to a special group of cranial and spinal nerves, plus supporting CNS neurons, that regulate your blood pressure, heart rate, body temperature, bodily processes such as digestion, and emotional responses such as blushing. Most of your body's internal organs (heart, stomach, intestines, bladder, and sex organs) are served by nerves from the ANS. The name was originally given the ANS because it was thought to act independently of conscious control, that it was under its own control (autonomous). We now know this is not strictly true, and that with training (with the use of what is called *biofeedback*) we can gain some measure of control over our blood pressure, heart rate, and even body temperature. The ANS is very much involved in our experience of emotion, and so we will look at it in a little more detail.

The ANS is divided into two parts: the **sympathetic division** and the **parasympathetic division**. The two divisions typically work in opposite ways. Generally, the sympathetic division excites or stimulates, whereas the parasympathetic division inhibits. For example, the sympathetic division will make your heart beat faster, the parasympathetic division will make it beat slower. But there are exceptions: for example, the parasympathetic—not the sympathetic—is responsible for penile erection and vaginal dilation during sexual behavior, and the sympathetic is responsible for the opposite calming effect.

The sympathetic division basically is responsible for the emergency response of your body—named the *"fight or flight"* response by the noted physiologist W. B. Cannon. Your body prepares for emergency action by such measures as increasing the pumping action of your heart and mobilizing your blood sugar reserves. In prehistoric times, humans needed the emergency response either to kill some prey they needed for food or to fight or flee from some deadly enemy. Today you rarely need to kill prey for food, nor do you often need to fight or escape from deadly enemies. But many other everyday events have taken the place of these prehistoric situations to arouse your emergency response—injury or pain or the threat of it, events that try your patience like traffic jams and long waiting lines, encounters with extremely sexually attractive persons, quarrels and heated arguments, and even strenuous exercise. When you are euphoric and elated or fearful and anxious or angry, it is your sympathetic nervous system that is responsible.

The sympathetic division is distributed widely over your whole body, but the parasympathetic division has a more limited distribution. Because of this, it does not have a full counterpart to the emergency response of the sympathetic division. The parasympathetic division's basic function has to do with protecting and conserving your body's energy resources and reserves. It slows down your heart rate and lowers your blood pressure; it stimulates your saliva secretion and your digestion; it helps store up energy resources in the form of blood sugar.

One other difference between the two ANS divisions is in the type of neurotransmitters they use. The parasympathetic division uses acetylcholine, whereas the sympathetic division uses norepinephrine (also called noradrenaline), both of which you have read about. An interesting thing about noradrenaline is that chemically it is very similar to the hormone produced by the adrenal gland, called adrenalin. In fact, before neurotransmitters were discovered, scientists had observed that the action of adrenalin was similar to the action of the sympathetic nervous system, practically mimicking it.

Which brings up the matter of hormones. At the beginning of this chapter, you were told that the nervous system was the main communica-

sympathetic division
a branch of the autonomic system responsible for activating the body at times of stress

parasympathetic division
a branch of the autonomic system responsible for quieting the body and conserving energy

tions system of your body, but it is not the only one. Your body does have another communications system—a chemical one—called the endocrine system.

The Endocrine System

The endocrine system consists of a number of glands within your body that don't have ducts (they are also called "ductless glands"). They secrete right into the blood or the lymph of your body. Their secretions are called **hormones**. Like neurotransmitters, hormones are chemical "messengers." Their role is to regulate various body functions: metabolism, growth, development, sex, and the secretion of other hormones. The following are

hormones
body chemicals carried by body fluids that have an effect on bodily functions and behavior

TO THE POINT

One Brain Or Three?

Did you know that you may actually have three brains rather than one? This is what Paul MacLean, a top government scientist, thinks. According to Dr. MacLean, what may have happened during evolution was that instead of an old brain evolving into a new one, the old was just kept on and the new added onto it—and in the process humans acquired three different brains. This would explain why we have the brain structures that we do.

According to Dr. MacLean, the spinal cord, the hindbrain, and the midbrain together form some kind of "neural chassis" (like the chassis of a car), the basic nervous system structure responsible for the basic biological functions of self-preservation and reproduction. But the neural chassis cannot operate without a "driver," without a "brain." Enter the three brains, in very slow succession.

The first brain, which evolved several hundred million years ago during the age of the reptiles and dinosaurs, is what Dr. MacLean calls the R-complex (R for reptilian). The second brain is the limbic system, evolving about 150 million years ago. The third brain is the neocortex, the newest development, appearing only tens of millions of years ago.

The R-complex, which surrounds the midbrain, governs behavior that has to do with establishing dominance, hence giving rise to the traits of aggressiveness and competitiveness. This explains why the first, the most common, and the most lasting basis on which we judge others is in terms of superiority-inferiority. Even when we were very young, we always thought in terms of winning or losing, leading or following. The R-complex also has to do with ritualistic behavior, the

the major glands of your endocrine system:

- **Pineal body:** Located between the two lobes of the thalamus. Its hormone acts on the hypothalamus and influences the activity of the gonads (ovaries and testes).

- **Pituitary gland:** Located in the middle of the brain behind the optic nerve crossing. Its hormones regulate the secretion of other glands such as the thyroid and adrenals, and are involved in growth, especially development during puberty.

- **Thyroid gland:** Located in the neck around the larynx. Its hormone regulates your body's heat and energy production.

compulsion to follow the same routine when doing something—a form of persistence that must have been useful because so many animals exhibit it.

The limbic system, which in turn surrounds the R-complex, has to do with emotion and mood. In this, it contrasts sharply with the "cold-blooded" quality and lack of (emotional) color of the R-complex. The appearance of the limbic system on the evolutionary scene may have been responsible for the development of altruistic behavior (or "love," if you will), which probably happened when emotion came to be associated with sexual or mating behavior and its consequences.

The neocortex, which in final turn surrounds the limbic system, contributes an explosion of human capabilities: planning, deliberation, reasoning, initiative, invention, abstraction, anticipation, communication, memory. It is to the neocortex that we attribute the characteristic that most distinguishes humans from other animals: intelligence.

What does it mean to have three brains rather than one? For one thing, it explains why humans are such bundles of contradiction. Can you imagine three drivers attempting, all at the same time, to drive your car? But doesn't this happen when, for instance, your head tells you to go one way but your heart tells you to go another? For another thing, this means that when we learn, we do not and cannot learn fully unless we engage all three brains at once and have them all participate in the learning. We need to attend not just to the subject matter (neocortex), but also to the emotions and motivations of the learners (limbic system) and to their social-group dynamics as well as their preferred ways of doing things (R-complex). Think back to the teachers whom you considered to be good teachers, and chances are that they would have engaged all three of your brains.

What do YOU think it means to have three brains in one?

- **Parathyroids**: Four small bodies behind the thyroid. Their hormone regulates calcium levels in the blood.

- **Thymus:** Located above the heart, in front of the heart's main artery, the aorta. Its hormone promotes the growth of lymphatic tissue. It also produces the lymphatic T-cells that are used by your immune system (the system that guards your body against "foreign invaders" such as disease germs).

- **Adrenal glands:** Located above each kidney. The adrenals' insides (also called a medulla) produce the hormones that are used to prepare the body for emergency response and exertion. The adrenals' outside rind (also called a cortex) produces hormones that regulate kidney function, maintain the body's blood sugar reserves, and govern the secondary sexual characteristics of the person.

- **Pancreas:** Located near the stomach and liver. It produces insulin, the hormone essential to glucose metabolism.

- **Gonads:** Ovaries (for females) and testes (for males). They produce hormones that regulate sexual development and the functioning of the reproductive organs, including for women menstruation and pregnancy. These hormones also help determine the person's secondary sexual characteristics.

As you can see, the hormones have quite a bit to do with your behavior. Sometimes you behave in ways that you do not expect (such as becoming very irritable), or you are not able to behave as you expected (such as losing your usual level of energy). One of the possibilities to check out would be the functioning of your hormones. Of course, you should ask a physician to do the checking. As a general rule, when abnormal behavior takes place, it is useful to have a physician check the person in order to rule out any malfunctioning of the body's organs and systems.

In this chapter, we have concentrated on the nervous system, especially the brain. But of course there are other parts to your body, all of which contribute to the way you are and the way you behave. As complex as the brain, the nervous system, and the human body are, knowing about the parts and the functions of the brain, the nervous system, or the body will not really tell you how people will behave. It will not tell you what people will think, what they will say, or what they will do. You still have to study behavior itself and what brings it about. In the chapters that follow, you will learn more about the many behaviors of which humans are capable, which collectively we call human potential.

1. Your body's nervous system enables you to behave as a whole by coordinating and regulating all of the body processes; by gathering information about the outside world; by interpreting and storing information for immediate or future use; and by directing your behavior--your response to newly received information combined with old remembered information.

2. The nervous system is made up of billions of cells that are of two kinds: neurons and glia. Neurons provide your body with a communication system by transmitting electrical signals called neural impulses. These signals are passed from neuron to neuron through synapses. Glia surround the neurons and provide them with their "work environment."

3. Neurons release chemicals called neurotransmitters at the synapse. Over 50 kinds of neurotransmitters have been identified, and each carries different messages to your body to react in specific ways.

4. The nervous system can be divided into the central nervous system (the brain and spinal cord), and the peripheral nervous system (the somatic and the autonomic nervous system).

5. The brain can be divided into three parts: the forebrain, the midbrain, and the hindbrain.

6. Major brain structures that develop from the forebrain are the cerebrum, which is responsible for cognitive activity; the thalamus, which relays information from the senses to the brain; and the limbic system, which consists of a group of structures that have to do with eating, drinking, sleeping, and emotion.

7. The hindbrain develops into the cerebellum, which maintains coordination, posture and muscle tone; the medulla, which controls vital functions; and the pons, which regulates eyeball and facial movement, chewing, taste, sound sensation, and breathing.

8. The spinal cord links the brain with the peripheral nervous system. It serves as the communications pathway between the brain and the rest of the body.

9. The endocrine system provides chemical communication in the body through the release of hormones into the blood stream.

10. Hormones are released directly into the lymph or the blood stream by the endocrine glands. Each gland secretes a special hormone that affects your body in different ways.

KEY TERMS
Define the following:

Acetylcholine
Adrenal glands
Amygdala
Association cortex
Auditory cortex
Autonomic nervous system
Axon
Biofeedback
Blood-brain barrier
Brain stem
Cell
Cell body
Central nervous system
Cerebral hemispheres
Cerebrum
Corpus callosum
Dendrite
Dopamine
Endorphins
Excitatory
Fornix
Frontal lobe
Forebrain
GABA
Glia
Glutamate
Gonads
Hindbrain
Hippocampus
Hormones
Hypothalamus
Inhibitory
Limbic system
Medulla
Midbrain
Motor cortex
Myelin sheath
Neocortex
Nervous system
Neuron
Neural network
Nerve
Nerve tract
Neural impulse
Neurotransmitter

QUESTIONS FOR REVIEW AND DISCUSSION

1. What is the basic unit of the nervous system?
2. How does the nervous system carry electrical and chemical messages from one part to another?
3. How are the central nervous system and the peripheral nervous system related?
4. How can an understanding of the nervous system help clinicians to relieve disease and pain?
5. How is the spinal cord related to behavior?
6. How do the two halves of the brain operate independently of each other?
7. What would happen if the cerebellum were injured?
8. How do hormones affect behavior?

ACTIVITIES

1. Consult an encyclopedia or science yearbook--material written for laypersons. Look up "allergy" or "psychosomatic illness or disease." Is there some basis for believing that "it's all in your mind" when you suffer from these ailments?
2. Interview a physiological psychologist or a neuropsychologist (your local university, medical school, or VA medical center should have one). Ask about their research interests. Make sure you understand what part of the research is "body," what part is "mind" or "behavior," and what links the two together.
3. Look for a newspaper article about the brain (most papers have sections or parts of the paper devoted to science reporting).What information did the article give you beyond what you read in Chapter 3?
4. See if your psychology department laboratory has a reaction time apparatus. If you can use it, check the difference between your fastest simple reaction time, your choice reaction time, and your judgment reaction time. (You may need an Introductory Laboratory Psychology workbook to guide you in setting up the different reaction time procedures.) Can you visualize what goes on in your brain to account for the difference between choice RT, judgment RT, and simple RT?
5. Do some extra reading (encyclopedia, science yearbook, etc.) about one (or more) of the neurotransmitters. Note especially how their action (or inaction) can affect behavior. What would happen if you increased (or decreased) your body's supply of the neuro-transmitter?
6. Do some library research and write a short (5-10 page) paper on the topic, "Head size and IQ" (or "Head size and intelligence"). Reference the studies that report actual data on the topic.

CASE 1

The Preeminence of the Brain

Eddie and Bobby were having another of their many "academic" arguments. "I think the brain is more important," declared Eddie. "All you really need is a brain that can remember well and think fast, and the rest will follow." "No," countered Bobby, "no matter how good your brain is, what really counts is what's in it--its contents. I read where the thing that is different between experts and beginners is not the amount of brain power but the knowledge the experts have that the beginners don't have. And the brain's contents can come only through your senses. So, it is even more important to have good sense organs." "Oh, yeah?" says Eddie. "There's this one guy in my school who is called a genius by all the teachers, but he is legally blind and has hearing problems as well; he even needs a tape recorder for class. How do you explain that?" And on it goes.

1. If you had to choose, with whom would you side? Why?

2. Pretend you are Eddie's "lawyer." Is there anything in Chapter 3 that you can use to defend Eddie's position?

CASE 2

The James-Lange Theory of Emotion

One of the most controversial theories about emotion was advanced by William James, America's foremost psychologist, and independently at the same time by Carl Lange, a Danish scientist. The crux of the theory is captured in James's declaration: "We are afraid because we run." Ordinarily, we would say, "We run because we are afraid." Yet, James and Lange have a point: if we do not run and stand our ground, we may lose our fear and even feel brave. Much of military training and discipline is intended to do just that--by training soldiers to stand their ground, they foster bravery and absence of fear in the troops. Similarly, by kneeling in church, we foster in ourselves a sense of reverence. What would happen if in church we laughed and kidded around like we do on the playground?

1. From what you read in Chapter 3, can you figure out an explanation for the James-Lange theory?

Norepinephrine
Occipital lobe
Olfactory cortex
Pancreas
Parasympathetic division
Parietal lobe
Parathyroids
Peripheral nervous system
Pineal body
Pituitary gland
Pons
Psychopharmacology
Receptor site
Reticular formation
Reflex behavior
Serotonin
Sensory cortex
Somatic nervous system
Sympathetic division
Synapse
Synaptic integration
Temporal lobe
Thymus
Thyroid gland
Visual cortex
Vous system

2. Do you think James-Lange explains our "rituals" like saluting the flag, singing the national anthem, standing when an important person enters the room? If you don't "buy" James-Lange, what other explanation or theory better accounts for these behaviors?

CHAPTER 4

▷ PERCEPTION:
How We Obtain Data
About Our Environment

*The senses are the beginning and the end of human
knowledge....The uncertainty of our senses makes
everything they produce uncertain....*
Montaigne

The Chapter Quotations from an essay Montaigne wrote four hundred years ago, state the simple, yet perplexing, truth about our senses. Everything we know about ourselves and the world about us we gather with the use of our senses. At the same time, experience teaches us that our senses often mislead us.

We hear, smell, taste, touch, and see to gather the information that forms our knowledge. As Montaigne wrote, "We would know no more than a stone, if we did not know that there is sound, smell, light, taste, measure, weight, softness, hardness, roughness, color, smoothness, breadth, depth."

That your senses can mislead you is easily shown. You have no doubt had many experiences of this happening. Simple "facts" such as what is hot and cold can become confused by the senses.

- If you have been out skiing or skating and come in quite cold, tap water that would ordinarily feel cold to you will feel warm (sense of touch).

- If you have just eaten a very sweet cookie, a cup of tea that had seemed sweet will seem less so, almost sour (sense of taste).

- A candlelit room that at first seems very dark to you, becomes brighter the longer you remain (sense of sight).

- An echo gives you the impression that a sound comes from in front of you or all around you (sense of hearing).

- A common initiation practice is to put cold spaghetti strands on a blindfolded person's hand and say they are worms. To the blindfolded person, they feel like worms (sense of touch).

This last example reveals another aspect of your senses, which is that what goes on in your brain can affect your senses. Thus, as with so much else affecting you, there is a two-way interaction when you use your senses. Senses affect the brain and, in turn, are affected by it.

Because the senses can be demonstrably unreliable, should you mistrust them altogether? Certainly not. In the first place, they are all you have; more to the point, they do a more than adequate job of helping you understand the world around you.

▼ SENSING AND PERCEIVING

In none of the situations listed above did the external "facts" change. Furthermore, the senses transmitted essentially the same data. Yet the brain interpreted it differently. Water that would ordinarily seem cold, in the example, seemed warm. The examples illustrate that when you gather information from your surroundings you carry out two broad functions: sensing and perceiving.

Sensing is the act of receiving data through your sense organs or receptors. It is largely a physical and chemical process. As you will read, it is a complex process carried out by intricate sense organs, such as your eyes, ears, nose, tongue, and sensitive cells in the surface of your skin.

Perceiving is the act of interpreting and organizing the data you receive through your senses. This interpretation is carried on in the brain. As you will read, your memories, motivation, and emotions affect your perception.

perceiving
the act of interpreting and organizing the data received through the senses

Our External Senses

The familiar five senses are sight, hearing, smell, taste, and touch. In addition to these familiar senses, several others have been identified that can be classified as internal senses. Let's look at each of these and learn how they work, what happens when there are problems, and how the data these senses gather are perceived.

▼ SIGHT

Most of your knowledge of your environment comes to you through your sense of sight. What you see can even influence your other senses. An example of how sight influences other senses can be found in your everyday experience with television or movies. When you are looking at the screen and seeing the moving lips of a person talking, your sight convinces you that the sound is coming from the person's mouth. Actually, it is coming from speakers elsewhere in the television console or, in a movie theater, from some place completely removed from the location of the screen.

The next time you are at the movies try shutting your eyes for a few seconds to see if your ears detect where the sound is actually coming from. With open eyes, your sight will convince you that, regardless of its actual source, the sound comes from the pictures on the screen.

What Sight Is

Sight comes to you in the form of light energy. Light moves in waves. But light waves are described differently from waves created when you throw a rock into a pond. Those water waves are *mechanical* in nature: displacement of the water by the rock is being passed on. Light waves are *electromagnetic* in nature; they behave differently from mechanically produced waves. For instance, whereas water waves travel at speeds measured in miles per hour, light waves travel at 186,000 miles per *second.*

Like all waves, light waves have peaks and troughs. The height of the peaks and the distance between them determine the quality of the light we see. The distance between peaks of light waves is known as the **wavelength**. The shorter the distance between peaks, the more wavelengths there are for the same distances. Wavelengths determine what you perceive as color.

The height of the light waves is known as the **amplitude**. Amplitude determines the brightness of a color, ranging from light to dark.

Another characteristic of color that you see is known as saturation, which refers to the purity of the color. If you are receiving only one wavelength, the color is purest or most saturated. If all of the color wavelengths are present, the color is fully unsaturated and you see what is called white.

Humans cannot see all of the light waves that exist. In fact, they cannot see most of them. Scientists measure wavelengths of light in **nanometers**. The word *nano* comes from a Greek word meaning dwarf. A nanometer is one billionth of a meter. That means that it takes 1,000,000,000 nanometers to equal 1 meter, and a meter is only a hand's width longer than a yard!

Human vision ranges from about 375 to about 775 nanometers, which is a very small portion of the electromagnetic energy range. The colors you see in this range run from violet to red.

The Eye

Your organ of sight is, of course, the eye. The *American Heritage Dictionary* describes the eye as a "hollow structure . . . having a lens capable of focusing incident light on an internal photosensitive retina." Notice the similarity between the definition of the eye and the dictionary's definition of "camera": "a light-proof enclosure having an aperture and a shuttered lens through which the image of an object is focused and recorded on a photosensitive film or plate."

Your eyes take pictures continually when your eyelids are open. Eyelids are like the shutter in a camera. When open, they allow light to pass through. Light waves entering your eyes first strike the **cornea**, which is a transparent tissue covering the front of your eyeballs.

---

wavelength
the measurement of the distance between the peaks of two consecutive waves

amplitude
the measurement of the height of a wave

nanometers
a unit of measure for light wavelengths, consisting of 1 one-billionth of a meter

cornea
a transparent tissue covering the front of the eyeball

The light next passes through the **anterior chamber**, which is filled with a watery fluid. It then strikes the pupil, which is the opening in the **iris**, the colored part of your eyes. The iris controls the opening of the pupil. In bright light the pupil closes to reduce the amount of light entering. In darkness it opens to increase the amount of light.

The light next passes through the lens, where it is focused onto the **retina**. The retina is the photosensitive part of your eyes. The retina can be compared to the film in a camera. The comparison of an eye to a camera can be carried too far, however, because the eye is an active organ and is much more complex.

Many light waves strike the retina at any given moment of seeing. The light waves stimulate the cells of the retina, which then send signals (neural impulses) along the optic nerve to the brain. Sight, like all your other senses, requires two actions: the sensing and the perceiving. When your brain receives the signals from the retina, you then perceive or interpret them as pictures and color.

Sight Filters

Your sense of sight can be affected by physical defects, illness, fatigue, and drugs. It is important to have your eyes tested periodically. Doctors who specialize in eye care recommend a yearly checkup. Eye defects, even slight ones, can reduce your efficiency in school or on the job.

iris
the colored part of the eye that controls the opening of the pupil

retina
the photosensitive part of the eye onto which light is focused through the lens

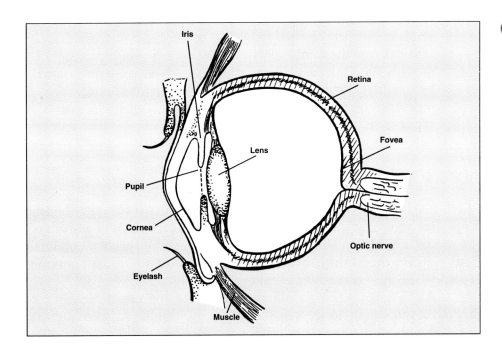

Fig. 4-1

This diagram shows the major parts of the human eye in cross section.

Visual Defects

Some of the more common defects people have with their eyes are:

- **Myopia:** Known as nearsightedness. People with this defect can see near objects clearly, but they cannot see objects far away clearly. This condition can be corrected with glasses or contact lenses.

- **Hyperopia**: Known as farsightedness. This is the opposite of near sightedness. Persons with hyperopia can see objects far away more clearly than they can see objects that are nearby. Glasses or contact lenses also help people overcome this defect.

- **Astigmatism:** The condition in which the eye's lenses are defective. They are not spherical or symmetrical and, as a result, distort the image. A person with astigmatism looking at the spokes of a wheel will see some of the spokes clearly, while others will appear blurred. Glasses or contact lenses can help correct this defect.

- **Color blindness:** The inability to distinguish colors. Color blindness can make it difficult if not impossible for a person to perform certain jobs. Such a person could hardly be an artist or interior decorator, for example. Color-coded wires are often used in electronics, which can make it impossible for some color-blind persons to do such work.

- **Dyslexia:** A reading impairment whereby the dyslexic perceives words or numbers reversed from their proper order, and might, for example, read the word *may* as *yam.* Words may also appear to move on the page. Recent research suggests dyslexia may be caused by abnormal development of the brain's hemispheres during pregnancy. Dyslexics can, especially with professional help, overcome or compensate for their disability. Thomas Edison and Albert Einstein are both thought to have been dyslexic.

Illness, Fatigue, Drugs

Illness, fatigue, and drugs affect your ability to see and to perceive or under-stand what you see. If you are ill, tired, or under the influence of any drugs, you should avoid activities that require good eyesight. Virtually all occupa-tions require the ability to see well. And one of the most common activities—driving—demands excellent eyesight.

Alcohol and other drugs are particularly dangerous because, while they affect your ability to see well, they often give you the mistaken impres-sion that you not only see as well but are seeing better. Activities, such as driving, that demand good eyesight should be completely avoided when taking alcohol or other drugs.

Drugs known as **hallucinogens**, such as LSD and mescaline, cause the users to have vivid pictorial experiences. The effects are in the brain, not the eye. Users "see" unreal images with exaggerated colors. The following excerpts from an article on hallucinogenic drugs discuss this mental phenomenon.

hallucinogens
drugs that cause the user to have vivid sensory experiences that do not correspond to reality (hallucinations)

> One subjective experience that is frequently reported is a change in visual perception. When the eyes are open, the perception of light and space is affected; colors become more vivid and seem to glow; the space between objects becomes more apparent, as though space itself had become "real," and surface details appear to be more sharply defined. Many people feel a new awareness of the physical beauty of the world, particularly of visual harmonies, colors, the play of light and the exquisiteness of detail.

The article goes on to describe vivid images appearing in the mind when the eyes are closed. It refers to hallucinations ranging from abstract forms to exotic creatures in imaginary times and places.

> The "hellish" experiences include an impression of blackness accompanied by feelings of gloom and isolation, a garish modification of the flowing colors observed in the "heavenly" phase, a sense of sickly greens and ugly dark reds. The subject's perception of his own body may become unpleasant; his limbs may seem to be distorted or his flesh to be decaying; in a mirror his face may appear to be a mask, his smile a meaningless grimace. Sometimes all human movements appear to be mere puppetry, or everyone seems to be dead. These experiences can be so disturbing that a residue of fear and depression persists long after the effects of the drug have worn off.[3]

Visual Perception—External Clues

As mentioned above, sight comes to you in light waves that strike your eyes and are transmitted along the optic nerves to your brain as neural impulses. What your brain makes of them—perceiving these impulses as meaningful "pictures"—depends on several factors. Some of these factors are external. That is, they are clues in the environment that your brain uses to make sense out of the visual data.

Your brain always tries to see the "whole" picture. It is always taking all the various visual stimuli coming in and trying to organize them into pictures that are more than the sum of their parts. (Recall reading of Gestalt psychologists in Chapter 2. "Gestalt" means whole.)

Gestalt Perception Rules

Gestalt psychologists identified several "rules" your brain follows in organizing data into whole, understandable patterns. These are:

continuity rule
tendency to extend perception of part to perception of whole

- **The rule of continuity:** Your brain continues to extend the picture based on what familiar stimuli are shown. If you see part of a car sticking out from behind a garage, your brain can complete the image of a car.

closure rule
perceptual tendency to complete figures by "closing" or ignoring small gaps

- **The rule of closure:** You see several separate parts of an incomplete object or pattern, and your brain tends to "complete" them to make a familiar whole.

similarity rule
tendency to group items on the basis of similarity

- **The rule of similarity:** You tend to group similar items. A simple illustration might be found in sports: You instantly group players together who are wearing the same uniforms

proximity rule
tendency to group items on the basis of closeness to each other

- **The rule of proximity:** You tend to group things according to how close they are to each other. You see one team as a whole because the players are usually grouped together.

Related to these rules is another way your brain organizes visual stimuli. You tend to divide stimuli into *figure*, which is what you focus on, and *ground*, which is the background. How this figure-ground separation works is illustrated in the familiar faces-vase picture shown in Figure 4-3.

Constancy

constancy
the brain's ability to recognize that an object retains its size, shape, and color under varying conditions of perspective and lighting

Another principle that helps your brain make sense out of visual stimuli is known as **constancy**. As a person moves away from you, that person's image naturally becomes smaller on your retina. Your brain, however, does not interpret that as a shrinking person. It maintains a constant impression of

Fig. 4-2

Moviegoers can alter their perception of some movies by wearing specially designed glasses.

Fig. 4-3

This classic picture illustrates how we separate images into figure and ground. Depending on which we see as the figure, we are looking at either a white vase or two silhouetted faces.

the person as the same size. The same is true of shapes and colors. A round or rectangular object will continue to appear round or rectangular, even when viewed from an angle that makes it appear stretched out or flattened. A white shirt will still seem white even if in the dark it appears to be gray.

It is this constancy that allows you to perceive depth. By knowing the size of an object, you can estimate its distance from you by how small or large it appears to be. This perceptual process is known as the **unconscious inference theory**. This theory states that we make subconscious explanations about our surroundings when an object seems different. That is, when a person seems smaller than you know him or her to be, your brain decides the person is far away. Your brain interprets sound in the same way. If you hear faintly a noise your experience has taught you is loud, you "know" it is far away.

Another theory offered to explain constancy is the **ecological theory**. According to this theory, it is the relationship of one object to another that clues the brain as to distance. As you look at a person in the distance, the relationship of that person's size to objects nearby remains constant. You thus know they are all at the same distance.

unconscious inference theory
a theory that explains constancy as the result of unconscious "inferences" or explanations of the difference between the perceived object and what it is known from prior experience to be

ecological theory
a theory that explains constancy in terms of the perceived relationships of objects to one another

Optical Illusions

What you perceive is not necessarily what you see. Your brain is very good at interpreting what your eye sees, but sometimes the very clues that it uses to make sense of a visual image cause it to make a mistake. When that happens, you experience optical illusions. A common optical illusion is the

Fig. 4-4

The Ames room creates an optical illusion by destroying visual clues. The person who appears smaller is farther away, although the size of the windows on the back wall suggests they are the same distance from the viewer.

appearance that two parallel lines, such as railroad tracks, converge as they move into the distance. You know from experience that the tracks remain parallel. Such illusions are common, and everyone has experienced them. In a normal eye, the light waves may be accurately received, but the brain does not always interpret them correctly.

How surrounding clues can trick the mind is demonstrated by the Ames room, designed by the American psychologist Adelbert Ames. The back wall slants away from the viewer, but windows are painted on it to appear the same size so that those clues to depth perception are distorted. Looking into the room, you would see a person standing in the far corner as smaller than a person standing in the near corner because the clues are telling you the two people are the same distance from you.

Visual Perception—Internal Influences

How your brain perceives or interprets the light waves that reach it as neural impulses along the optic nerve depends on *internal* factors as well as external ones. Your perception is affected by your attitudes, habits, and values. Your culture and training will influence how you perceive, as will what you think is important.

Experience Filters

As a simple example of how your conditioning affects your perception, read the following sentence only once counting the Fs you see in it.

> Finished files are the result of years of scientific study
> combined with the experience of years.

How many Fs did you see with just the one reading? Dr. Paul D. Leedy, who gave this test in his book *Improving Your Reading, Understanding, and Enjoyment,* reported that most readers see only three of the six Fs. Finding three Fs is poor, four is fair, five is good, and all six is excellent.

Your perception is often influenced by what you think is important. The *ofs* in Dr. Leedy's sentence are not important to most people and so they miss the Fs in them, even though their eyes see these words. What you think is important results from your experience. Newborn children see things mechanically in the same way that older people do, but the children perceive very little because at that age they do not have the experience to give meaning to what they see. As children grow older, experience will allow them to find meaning in the things they see, and they will begin to perceive more.

Your learning will affect your perception. For example, when a clothing designer walks into a room, she or he will immediately notice what the people are wearing and not notice much about the room's furnishings. On the other hand, an antique dealer will immediately notice the room's furniture and not what the people are wearing.

Perceptual Set

This tendency to perceive what you have been trained to perceive or have experienced is known as **perceptual set**. It is very helpful, but at times it can be a filter that prevents us from seeing all we should. Your other senses are influenced by perceptual set as well. For example, when your experience with a particular person makes you think you know what that person is going to say, you often do not listen fully and thus miss hearing what the person does say.

perceptual set
the tendency of an individual to perceive what she or he expects to perceive

▼ HEARING

Your sense of hearing is a vital part of your ability to communicate. (Chapter 12 discusses the communication process.) If humans could not hear, speech might never have developed. Your sense of hearing rounds out your ability to talk. Your sense of hearing also helps you gather information from your environment that is important to your survival. If a car roars down on you from behind, your hearing warns you of the danger. Your sense of hearing also brings you enjoyment when some sounds, such as musical notes arranged in a certain order, please you.

Your sense of hearing is working all the time. But you are not always aware of the sounds reaching you. For one reason or another your brain "tunes them out." You are not listening. There are many reasons why you filter the sounds reaching you, some of which you will read about later. The point now is that the process of hearing involves the acts of sensing (the physical act) and perception (the mental act of filtering, interpreting, or organizing).

hearing
the act of sensing sound; specifically: the special sense by which noises and tones are received as stimuli

A simple way of stating this is that **hearing** is the physical act of sensing, and **listening** is the mental act of perception. As you will read, there can be physical disabilities that prevent hearing and mental blocks that prevent listening. (Listening as a part of the communication process is discussed further in Chapter 12.)

listening
the act of perceiving sound

What Sound Is

What your brain interprets as "sound" are vibrations of air. The motion of air vibrations comes in the form of waves, and thus we speak of sound waves. An action, such as someone blowing out breath, creates some sound waves. When these sound waves reach your eardrum, a thin tissue inside your ear, it vibrates. Your brain eventually interprets that vibration as words or other identifiable sounds.

cycle
the passage of a single wave from peak to trough to peak

Like light waves, sound waves have peaks and troughs. Peaks represent loud points of the sound waves and troughs represent soft points of the sound wave. A peak followed by a trough is called a **cycle**. Scientists determine the frequency of sound by counting the number of cycles that occur in 1 second. One cycle per second is called a hertz (Hz).

pitch
highness or lowness of a sound, determined by frequency of cycles

Frequency determines **pitch**, which is highness or lowness. This is not volume, which refers to **loudness**. You have heard people with low voices or high voices. That is pitch. The more cycles per second the higher the pitch. You can hear frequencies between 20 and 20,000 Hz and are most sensitive to frequencies from 2,000 to 4,000 Hz.

decibels
units of measurement of the loudness of a sound

Volume, or what we call loudness, is affected by increasing or decreasing the height of individual sound waves. Loudness is measured in units called **decibels**. A whisper from 5 feet away measures around 20 decibels. A rock music group with amplifiers turned up to full volume will measure over 100 decibels. Potential ear damage can occur at 85 decibels and could be caused by something as common as a lawnmower or a food blender.

The Ear

Your organs for hearing are, of course, your ears. The familiar, visible portions of them are only a small part of the overall hearing organ. But these outer ears serve an important function beyond that of supporting your eyeglasses or earrings. They serve as traps for sound. Scientists divide the ear into three separate sections for study: the outer ear, middle ear, and inner ear.

The Outer Ear

The outer ear, most of which can be seen (the auricle), serves as the trap to catch the sound waves and direct them inward. In addition to the auricle, there is the **auditory canal**, which is the opening through which the sound waves pass to the middle ear.

The Middle Ear

The middle ear begins at the **eardrum**, which vibrates when struck by incoming air waves. The eardrum, in turn, activates three tiny bones in the middle ear: the anvil, the hammer, and the stirrup, so named because of their appearance. The last of these bones, the stirrup, transmits the sound vibrations to a thin membrane, called the **oval window**, that sends them on to the liquid of the inner ear.

A passage called the **Eustachian tube** runs between the middle ear and the throat area. One of its functions is to help balance the air pressure in the ear. You may have noticed when going up in an airplane or in an elevator in a high building that your ears hurt. This discomfort can be eased by opening your mouth and yawning. This act helps equalize the pressure in the middle ear cavity.

The Inner Ear

Through the oval window, sound waves enter the inner ear, which is known as the cochlea. The **cochlea** looks like a snail shell and is filled with fluid. Within the cochlea is the **basilar membrane**, which supports the primary receptors of sound. These primary receptors of sound are minute hair cells known collectively as the **organ of Corti.** The vibrations of the fluid in the cochlea move the hairs that activate **auditory nerve** cells under them. These cells transmit signals triggered by sound to the brain in the form of neural impulses.

Hearing Filters

Age, noise, drugs, disease, and physical injury can all cause hearing problems. Individual hearing ability can extend from being able to hear all sounds within the range for human beings through varying degrees of hearing loss to being totally deaf and unable to hear anything.

---

auditory canal
the opening through which sound waves pass from the outer ear to the middle ear

eardrum
a thin tissue in the middle ear that vibrates when struck by sound waves, activating the anvil, hammer, and stirrup, which in turn activates the inner ear

oval window
the oval fenestra (opening) of the inner ear

Eustachian tube
a passage that runs between the middle ear and the throat area

cochlea
the inner ear

basilar membrane
a membrane in the cochlea supporting the organ of Corti

organ of Corti
minute hair cells in the cochlea that rest on the inside surface of the basilar membrane

auditory nerve
either of the eighth pair of cranial nerves connecting the inner ear with the brain and transmitting impulses concerned with hearing and balance

Age

Age is the most common cause of hearing loss. As people grow older, their ability to hear drops steadily. Scientists have found that people in their forties experience a drop of some 80 Hz about every six months in their reception of high-frequency sounds. This happens because with age the membranes and hair cells of the inner ear become less pliable and thus less able to vibrate.

Noise

Next to age, noise is the great destroyer of hearing. As you probably are aware, a sudden, loud noise, such as an explosion, can cause momentary deafness. Repeated exposure to loud noise will cause permanent hearing loss.

Studies have shown that both loudness and high frequencies can cause hearing loss. The ability to hear frequencies up to 3,000 Hz (cycles per second) is important for understanding speech. Higher frequencies are considered noise. The ability to hear frequencies above 3,000 Hz, however, is needed to enjoy music. Because high frequencies will cause hearing loss, especially as you age, you should minimize your exposure to high frequencies and loudness.

Because loudness and high frequency do hasten the decline of hearing, federal and state laws require companies to provide workers with ear plugs when they must work in very noisy conditions. One such law is the federal Occupational Health and Safety Act. If you have ever flown, you

Fig. 4-5

This diagram shows the major parts of the ear. Scientists consider the ear to be composed of three different sections: the outer, middle, and inner ear.

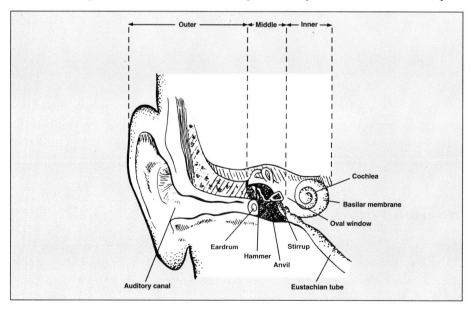

probably noticed that persons working on the ground around jet airplanes wear noise protectors over their ears. Noise generated by loud music in closed spaces often exceeds levels at which the law requires industry to provide protection for workers.

Drugs

Hallucinogens or drugs that cause changes in perception also can cause both temporary and permanent hearing loss. A person under the influence of drugs may "hear" music or conversations that do not exist. Such hearing deceptions are called *auditory hallucinations.*

Although in some instances the hearing sensations caused by drugs may seem pleasant, like beautiful symphonies, the real danger lies in sensations that are destructive to the auditory nerves, for these can result in permanent deafness.

Disease

Once a major cause of hearing loss, disease today causes less damage than noise or drugs. Antibiotics have greatly reduced problems of ear infections, most of which can now be treated and cured before surgery is necessary or there is any hearing loss.

Physical Injury

Physical damage to your ear could also result in loss of hearing. A blow on the ear could rupture an eardrum or cause other damage, for example. Nonpermanent hearing loss can also be caused by wax buildup in the ear. Sometimes, people need to have excess wax removed by doctors.

How We Listen

Listening, as noted, is the perception part of the hearing process. It is organizing and interpreting the information that the hearing sense receives. Effective listening is essential for a successful social and work life. Because listening depends on the ability to hear, the first step toward effective listening is to be aware of your hearing acuteness. A person aware of having a slight hearing loss, for example, can make an effort to be near the person speaking.

Today, specialists have sophisticated instruments that can measure degrees of hearing loss. There are also sophisticated hearing aids that fit almost invisibly in the ear and that can selectively amplify ranges of sound. If a person has lost hearing in the upper range, such a device is necessary in

Fig. 4-6

Repeated exposure to loud music can cause permanent hearing loss. Pete Townshend, formerly of the Who, today has hearing loss due to more than 20 years of exposure to amplified music.

order to avoid amplifying sounds in the lower range, which the person can hear well.

Listening Filters

The fact that there is nothing wrong with your hearing ability does not mean that you will mentally receive, organize, and interpret all the sounds reaching you. Many other filters, some useful, some not so useful, work to prevent or impede listening.

Some of these filters—background noise, for example—are obvious. If you are at a crowded, noisy party, you must raise your voice to be heard. But raising your voice, of course, increases the noise level and thus also adds to the problem.

Repetition also serves as a filter. If the same noise continues at the same level, you eventually tune it out mentally. Your ears still receive the same stimuli, but your brain does not act on it. Examples range from such things as a constantly ticking clock to heavy traffic roaring nearby. People who live constantly with such noise soon stop "hearing" it. You will read more about this filter later in this chapter in the section on adaptation.

Tuning out repetitive noise probably has survival value. To listen constantly, always registering such noise, would be at best irritating and at worst actually damaging to your mental well-being.

You also develop your own mental filters that obstruct listening. One major filter is *inattention*. As you listen to a person speak, your mind might wander. This happens because your mind works faster than people speak. People speak at an average rate of 100 to 150 words a minute, but the brain processes words several times as fast.

This becomes a particular problem if the subject being discussed does not interest you. In such a situation, you are apt to begin using the idle time your faster brain gives you to think about subjects that do interest you. You begin to daydream instead of concentrating on what is being said. Nichols and Stevens give an example of how this happens in their article "Listening to People":

> *A,* the boss, is talking to *B,* the subordinate, about a new program that the firm is planning to launch. B is a poor listener. In this instance, he tries to listen well, but he has difficulty concentrating on what *A* has to say.
>
> *A* starts talking and *B* launches into the listening process, grasping every word and phrase that comes into his ears. But right away *B* finds that because of *A's* slow rate of speech, he has time to think of things other than the spoken line of thought.
>
> Subconsciously, *B* decides to sandwich a few thoughts of his own into the aural ones that are arriving so slowly. So *B* quickly dashes out onto a mental sidetrack and thinks something like this: "Oh, yes, before I leave I want to tell *A* about the big success of the meeting I called yesterday." Then *B* comes back to *A's* spoken line of thought and listens for a few more words.
>
> There is plenty of time for *B* to do just what he has done, dash away from what he hears and then return quickly, and he continues taking sidetracks to his own private thoughts. Indeed, he can hardly avoid doing this because over the years the process has become a strong aural habit of his.
>
> But, sooner or later, on one of the mental sidetracks, *B* is almost sure to stay away too long. When he returns, *A* is moving along ahead of him. At this point it becomes harder for *B* to understand *A,* simply because *B* has missed part of the oral message. The private mental sidetracks become more inviting than ever, and *B* slides off onto several of them. Slowly he misses more and more of what *A* has to say. When *A* is through talking, it is safe to say that *B* will have received and understood less than half of what was spoken to him.[3]

Effective listening requires that you do not let unwanted filters block out wanted or needed messages. Because so much of your learning and ability to interact successfully depends on your listening skill, you should work to make it strong.

Effective Listening

Even with ears that hear well, most people do not know how to listen. Tests administered to business and professional people at the University of Minnesota showed that immediately after hearing a talk, those involved remembered only about half of what they had heard. Other research has indicated that after 2 months, the average listener actually retains only 25 percent of what was heard.

In the 1950s, people—especially those in business—began to realize that good listening was essential and that listening was something that could be improved with practice and learning. Nichols and Steven's article, quoted on pages 101 and 103, describes the growing awareness of listening as an important and necessary skill.

TO THE POINT

Even noises you are not aware of hearing can affect you. Although not listening to them and not conscious of them, on another level you are aware of them.

All sensory data that reach you below your active conscious level affect you on what is called the **subliminal** level. These could include noise below your normal threshold of hearing. Although this level is below your active consciousness, so you are not aware of receiving the sensory stimuli, you can still be affected by it.

The knowledge that subliminal noise can affect behavior is sometimes put to use. For example, in large shopping malls where shoplifting is a serious problem, especially around Christmas, the sound of jail doors closing is played at a subliminal level along with the Christmas carols.

The theory is that people prone to shoplifting will decide not to do so in reaction to the subliminal reminder of what could be in store for them. They are not aware of why they make this decision or even of hearing jail doors closing. But on a subliminal level, their brain has heard it and delivered the message, disguised though it is.

The realization that people—such as advertisers—could use subliminal messages to persuade people to do something, such as buy a product, has aroused concern. Subliminal messages can be visual as well as sound. Responsible advertisers shun such practices, however.

Recently the top executives of a major manufacturing plant in the Chicago area were asked to survey the role that listening plays in their work. Later an executive seminar on listening was held. Here are three typical comments made by participants:

"Frankly, I had never thought of listening as an important subject by itself. But now that I am aware of it, I think that perhaps 90 percent of my work depends on my listening to someone, or on someone else listening to me."

"I've been thinking back about things that have gone wrong over the past couple of years, and I suddenly realized that many of the troubles have resulted from someone not hearing something, or getting it in a distorted way."

"It's interesting to me that we have considered so many facets of communication in the company, but have inadvertently overlooked listening. I've about decided that it's the most important link in the company's communications, and it's obviously also the weakest one."[4]

Here are some suggestions for effective listening:

- Think along with the speaker.

- Give the speaker complete attention (through eye contact if it is a face-to-face exchange).

- Don't interrupt the speaker except to ask for clarification.

- Have your hearing checked at least once a year.

- Do not doodle or read when listening.

- Take notes if necessary, but make them brief; do not let note taking replace listening.

- Block out distracting sights and sounds.

- Occasionally mentally review and sum up the speaker's points.

- Look for nonverbal signs (facial expression; body language) to help you understand what is being said.

- Mentally rephrase what you consider the main ideas.

- Occasionally respond to the speaker by nodding or, if in a one-on-one situation, by repeating back points to be sure you understood.

TO THE POINT

Be a positive, active listener. Become and stay involved mentally in what you are hearing. Use idle brain time to organize and sum up points heard. Concentrate and try to absorb as much as you can of what is being said to you. The ability to listen well is a must for any working person. When people fail to hear and understand each other accurately, costly errors occur. Misinterpreting a spoken order, transposing a customer's telephone number, failing to recognize a customer's irate tone, and failing to remember an important client's name—all because of ineffective listening—have resulted in lost business and lost jobs.

▼ SMELL AND TASTE

These two senses work closely together. Your sense of smell affects your sense of taste. As you probably know from experience, when a cold blocks your nasal passages and dulls your sense of smell, you also lose your sense of taste to a large degree. Although these senses may not be as important to your survival as your senses of sight and sound, they nevertheless play a considerable part in your enjoyment and safety.

Both of these senses are considered chemical senses. Whereas your senses of hearing and sight respond to sound and light waves, your senses of smell and taste respond to chemical substances in the environment.

Smell

olfactory sense
the scientific term for the sense of smell

The scientific term for your sense of smell is **olfactory sense**. Your nose, your primary olfactory organ, is lined with *olfactory mucosa* that contain the olfactory receptors. When air (entering either through your nose or mouth) passes over them, signals are transmitted to your brain, which then interprets the odor. If air cannot pass over these olfactory receptors, your ability to detect odors is reduced. This explains why you lose your sense of smell when you have a cold.

Just as three primary colors have been identified, researchers have identified seven "primary" odors. As with the colors, these seven primary odors can be blended into many different ones. Most of us can detect more odors than we think we can. We do not identify them all because we do not know their names.

The seven primary odors are camphoraceous (like a moth ball), ethereal (as in dry-cleaning fluid), floral, minty, musky, pungent (as vinegar), and putrid (like a rotten egg).

Your sense of smell adds pleasure to your life by making it possible for you to enjoy pleasant odors and by enhancing your taste. Although your sense of smell is not nearly as sensitive as that of many animals that depend on it for survival, it still serves a useful survival function for you. With it you can detect life-threatening chemicals in the air, such as smoke or gas. Scientists today believe that the olfactory sense was the first one developed in the evolution of animals.

Taste

The scientific term for your sense of taste is **gustatory sense**. This sense plays an even lesser role than smell in your survival today, although in the evolution of humans and other animals, it has been important. That is because most poisonous substances have a bitter or unpleasant taste.

Your tongue is your taste organ. It holds thousands of taste receptors, that are called **taste buds**. Scientists are still not completely certain why things taste exactly as they do. Research has indicated that the taste buds in the tip of your tongue are most sensitive to sweet tastes, those along the side to sour and salty tastes, and those at the back to bitter tastes. But all areas can detect all tastes.

The four basic tastes—sweet, sour, salty, and bitter—are the only ones that your taste receptors recognize. But again, as with colors and odors, these four basic tastes mix in many combinations that your brain perceives as different kinds of taste sensations.

You have to learn to like some tastes. The culture you live in will influence what you like. But you are also probably born with taste buds that will incline you toward some tastes and against others. Experiments, for example, have shown that some people lack taste buds for particular bitter tastes.

Your tastes change as you age. One reason for this is that your taste bud cells die and are replaced about every two weeks, but as you grow older, fewer new taste buds are generated.

▼ TOUCH

Touch is the sensation you have when something physical comes into contact with your body. Your whole skin covering contains the sensory receptors for touch. Actually, what you think of as a sense of touch is really one of four basic sensations that you experience through the sensory receptors near the surface of your skin. These include pressure (the sense of touch itself), pain, heat, and cold.

These sensations have apparent survival value, particularly pain. Pain alerts you when something is wrong, because of either an accident or illness, in any part of your body. The importance of pain as a survival mechanism was illustrated in a study of lepers in India by Paul Brand.

Fig. 4-7

Most people can distinguish seven primary odors.

gustatory sense
the scientific term for the sense of taste

taste buds
structures on the tongue that contain the receptor cells for taste

Taste influences what foods people eat.

One of the symptoms of this dreaded disease had been the crippling of hands. In his work, Dr. Brand showed that people afflicted with leprosy lost sensation in their extremities. They were unable to feel pain. As a result they frequently unknowingly injured themselves. It was these injuries and not, as had long been believed, the disease itself that caused the crippling.[4]

On the face of it, pain seems to be the most objective of our senses. That is, it would seem that with pain, unlike with hearing and seeing, there could be little difference between the sensation and the perception. After all, if we hurt, we hurt. But even this sense can be affected by our experience, our culture, and our training.

You have no doubt heard an old story that shows a culture's effect on a person's reaction to pain. It happened in Sparta, an ancient Greek state, where honor and the ability to ignore pain were prized. In the story, a Spartan boy who hid a wolf in his jacket endured fatal bites without crying out or acknowledging that he had hidden the wolf.

Our own present-day society is a pain-conscious one. While your other senses are appealed to constantly by merchandisers hoping to sell their wares, your sense of pain has the distinction of being itself a major target of these appeals. In TV commercials, on the radio, in the newspapers and magazines, countless advertisements appear for aspirin and other pain killers. One such product was marketed with the claim that it was for those "who had no time for pain" in their lives.

This emphasis on pain and relieving it may not be in your best interests. As mentioned earlier, pain is a warning that something is wrong somewhere in your body. Finding out what is wrong and treating it is the wisest course. Pain itself is just a symptom.

▼ OUR INTERNAL SENSES

In addition to the five familiar senses you have just read about, scientists identify other senses that can be grouped broadly in the category of internal senses. These are not new or mysterious senses. People have always had them even if they have not thought of them as regular senses. The difference between these internal senses and the other five is that the former react to stimuli from within the body instead of to stimuli from the environment outside of the body.

The scientific name for these senses is **proprioceptive senses**. The proprioceptive senses include three different kinds of sensing receptors: vestibular, kinesthetic, and internal.

proprioceptive senses
internal senses that react to stimuli from within the body instead of stimuli from the environment outside of the body

Vestibular Sensors

If you have ever suffered from motion sickness or seasickness, you have miserably experienced this sense reacting to stimuli. Your **vestibular sensors** help you keep your sense of balance. They tell you when you are moving and in what direction. They work closely with your sense of vision, and it is when the close working relationship of these two senses goes awry that you experience motion sickness.

The vestibular sensors are located in your inner ear. They consist of receptor cells arranged throughout a series of canals that are filled with a fluid. Movement of the fluid stimulates the receptor cells that then send signals to the brain.

A person subject to seasickness is less likely to experience it if she or he is actually steering the boat, because this allows the person to see and anticipate movement and compensate for it. This illustrates the close relationship of vision and vestibular sensors. Riding in the front rather than the back seat of a car has a similar effect.

Kinesthetic Sensors

Your **kinesthetic sensors** are located throughout your body in blood vessel walls just under your skin. They allow you to sense the movement of parts of your body in relation to each other. In other words, you know, even with your eyes closed, whether your left arm is hanging by your side or raised above your head.

Internal Sensors

Internal senses include a third kind of sensor, known loosely as **internal sensors**. These sensors receive data from your internal organs, such as your heart. Through them you sense fast heartbeats or the pain of a kidney stone.

Relatively recently, scientists have developed instruments that increase our awareness of or sensitivity to the workings of our inner organs. The use of these instruments has produced interesting findings, not the least of which is that people can control organs and muscles that had been considered completely involuntary. That is, the muscles operate without conscious effort, and it was thought that they could not be consciously controlled.

But with use of an instrument that allows a person to see on a screen or graph the result of changes in heartbeat, that person can be trained to change his or her heartbeat rate at will by concentrating on it. Somehow, being able to see the results makes the person able to do this. This process is called biofeedback, which you read of in Chapter 3.

vestibular sensors
proprioceptive sense receptors, located in the inner ear, involved in the sense of balance and in determining when the body is moving and in what direction

kinesthetic sensors
proprioceptive sense receptors, located throughout the body in blood vessel walls just under the skin, that allow the individual to sense the movement of parts of the body in relation to each other

internal sensors
proprioceptive sense receptors that receive data from internal organs such as the heart

▼ PERCEPTION FILTERS

You have been reading about the senses individually, first sight, then hearing, and so on, as if each were independent and not connected with the others. Obviously, however, all of your senses work together, and what you know or perceive of the world and your place in it is a result of absorbing the information from all your senses and organizing it into an understandable whole.

Your brain does a remarkable job in converting all the sensory stimuli into a meaningful whole. There is so much coming in that a most important step in understanding it all is to filter or block out some of it. Filtering is an essential part of perceiving, but it is also a danger. If you filter out the wrong sensory information, you could misunderstand what is happening or even endanger yourself.

You read of filters that affect individual sensory organs. These filters generally affect all senses; they can be grouped into three categories: sensory thresholds, adaptation, and what we will call predisposition, which includes your values, interests, motives, emotions, and expectations.

Sensory Thresholds

There is a limit—threshold—below which your brain will not perceive sensory stimuli. Thresholds differ among senses and, to a degree, among people. To a large extent sensory thresholds are determined by your physiological makeup, but they are also affected by your psychological makeup. Consequently, they will also differ for you from time to time, depending on your motives or interests and the surrounding conditions.

For example, if you are sitting in the back of a lecture hall near an open window on a spring day listening to a dull speaker talk about a subject that does not interest you while you can see people outside having fun, your threshold for hearing the speaker will be high, which is to say you will not hear much.

Because so many factors can affect a sensory threshold, scientists are careful about defining its level exactly. For example, they might say that under ideal conditions the average person should be able to hear the sound of an ordinary watch ticking at a distance of 20 feet.

Scientists have defined two types of thresholds for our perception of physical stimuli: absolute threshold and difference threshold.

Absolute Threshold

absolute threshold
the smallest amount of a physical stimulus that the brain will notice 50 percent of the time

Absolute threshold refers to the smallest amount of a physical stimulus that the brain will notice 50 percent of the time. Hearing the ticking of a watch from 20 feet away is an example of an absolute threshold for hearing. Other thresholds established under perfect conditions are perceiving the equivalent of one candlepower of light at 17 miles or detecting a teaspoon of sugar in two gallons of water.

Your absolute threshold will change according to surrounding conditions and your own condition. If you are sleepy, your absolute thresholds will be higher than when you are fully awake.

Difference Threshold

Difference threshold refers to the smallest amount of change in a physical stimulus that will be noticed 50 percent of the time. Difference threshold is also known as **just noticeable difference (jnd)**.

Your difference threshold is, if anything, more variable than your absolute threshold. That is because it is affected by the amount of the existing stimulus. For example, if you were to add a lump of sugar to an already sweet drink, such as cola, you would not notice it much, if at all. But if you add the sugar to a bitter drink, such as lemon juice, you would notice it immediately.

difference threshold
the smallest amount of change in a physical stimulus that will be noticed 50 percent of the time

Adaptation

Adaptation refers to the fact that if any sensory organ is subjected constantly to the same stimulus, it will eventually stop responding to or noticing it. You experience this phenomenon daily. You lose your sense of background noises in your own house, for example. If you have an air conditioner that hums or central heating that rumbles, you do not hear them, although a visitor probably will. Adaptation affects your thresholds.

You experience adaptation in another way whenever you enter a movie theater. In the bright outside, your sight sensors have increased your threshold for sight so that harmful brightness beyond what you need to see is shut out. Consequently, when first entering the dark movie theater, you cannot see. You must wait until your threshold for sight is lower so that your sensors become aware of more light.

Because of adaptation, you become unaware of odors. If you entered a photographer's darkroom, you would be very much aware of the smell of the chemicals. However, if you were a photographer working in there, you would quickly reach the point (adapt) at which you would not smell the chemicals at all. If you left the darkroom for a long time and then returned, you would at first notice the chemicals' smell again.

Predisposition

Several psychological factors and your past experiences can affect your sensory thresholds. Your values, interests, motives, emotions, and expectations all play a part, either depressing or heightening what can be called your sense of awareness. These factors will either increase your attention or decrease it in regard to general or specific sensory stimuli.

Motivation is a strong influencer of your sensory thresholds. In the lecture hall situation described earlier, if you were strongly motivated to learn about the speaker's topic, you would probably block out distracting sounds and sights to listen carefully. You will read about motivation in Chapter 10.

If you are feeling depressed, you probably have a higher threshold for many of your sensory receptors than you have when feeling good or optimistic. If you are walking around in a fog of gloom, you very likely will not notice pleasant odors or attractive, colorful scenes. On the other hand, if you are feeling great, all your senses might be fully awake and everything will look bright and lovely.

If your emotions can influence your senses, what you sense can also affect your emotions. A pleasant odor, such as the smell of freshly baked bread or a delightful perfume, may be enough to jolt you out of a down mood and propel you into a good mood.

Your expectations will also affect your senses. For example, if you believe that the *probability* is high that a certain sound or sight will materialize, you are more likely to hear or see it than if you believe that the probability is low. Safety experts apply this principle when they educate people to drive defensively. They want drivers to believe that a high probability of an accident exists so their awareness of factors that can cause accidents will be increased.

In this chapter you have read of sensing and perceiving: how sensory stimuli reach you and how your brain organizes these stimuli so you can make sense of the physical world. In the next chapter you will read about how you think about and apply these data.

SUMMARY

1. Your senses may sometimes mislead you, but overall, you must trust them because they do a wondrous job in helping you understand the world around you. They are affected by many factors, including the brain, which they, in turn, can affect.

2. When you gather information from your surroundings you carry out two broad functions: sensing, which is the act of receiving data, and perceiving, which is the act of interpreting and organizing the data.

3. In addition to the five familiar senses—sight, hearing, smell, taste, and touch—you have several others known as internal senses.

4. Most knowledge of the environment comes through the sense of sight.

5. Sight comes to you in the form of *electromagnetic energy,* known as light waves. Like all waves, light waves have highs and lows. The height of the peaks and the distance between them determine the quality of the light you see. You see only a very small portion of the electromagnetic energy range. Your sense of sight can be affected by physical defects, illness, fatigue, and drugs.

6. Your brain uses clues in the environment as well as your experience and training to make sense out of (or perceive) the visual data received through your eyes.

7. "Rules" describing how your brain organizes clues from the environment include *continuity,* which means your mind continues to build a picture based on what familiar stimuli suggest; *closure*, which means that if you see an incomplete object or pattern, you tend to fill in the missing parts to make a familiar whole; *similarity,* which means you tend to group similar items; *proximity*, which means you tend to group things according to how close they are to each other.

8. Figure-ground and constancy are two other ways by which your brain makes sense out of visual stimuli it receives. It separates the stimuli into *figure,* which is the point of focus, and *ground*, which is the background. *Constancy* refers to the brain's ability to retain a constant impression of an object. That is, a distant object is not perceived as smaller than it actually is.

9. Your perception is affected by your attitudes, habits, and values. Your culture and environment influence how you perceive, as does what you think is important.

_____ 10. The tendency to perceive what you have experienced or what you have been trained to perceive is known as perceptual set. It usually is very helpful, but at times it can be a filter that prevents you from perceiving all you should.

_____ 11. What your brain interprets as "sound" are vibrations of air known as sound waves. Your sense organ—the ear—is activated by these sound waves, and your brain eventually interprets the stimuli as words or other identifiable sounds.

_____ 12. Like light waves, sound waves have highs and lows. The height of the waves and the distance between them determine the quality of the sound you hear.

_____ 13. Age, noise, drugs, disease, and physical injury can all cause hearing problems. Age is the most common cause of hearing loss. Disease is not the major cause of hearing loss that it once was.

_____ 14. In addition to physical filters that prevent you from hearing, you have many mental filters that prevent you from listening. One major filter is *inattention*, which occurs because brains work faster than people talk. Effective listening requires that you not let unwanted filters block out wanted or needed messages.

_____ 15. In addition to the five external senses—hearing, sight, smell, taste, and touch—you have *proprioceptive*, or internal, senses that include a sense of balance (vestibular sensors), a sense of your body's position (kinesthetic sensors), and a sense of conditions in your internal organs.

_____ 16. Sensory thresholds, adaptation, and predisposition (motivation, interest, background) are factors that affect your overall perception.

KEY TERMS
Define the following terms:

Absolute threshold
Adaptation
Amplitude
Anterior chamber
Astigmatism
Auditory canal
Auditory nerve
Basilar membrane
Closure
Cochlea

QUESTIONS FOR REVIEW AND DISCUSSION

_____ 1. When you gather information from your surroundings you carry out two broad functions. What are they? Briefly define them.

_____ 2. Describe briefly how your eyes work.

_____ 3. How your brain perceives the neural impulses reaching it as the result of light waves striking your eyes depends on external and internal factors. Explain what this means. Describe some of these factors.

_____ 4. Why do we speak of sound "waves"? Briefly explain the characteristics of sound waves that determine the quality of the sound.

5. What you think of as a sense of touch is really one of four basic sensations that you experience through the sensory receptors near the surface of your skin. What is meant by this statement?
6. What are the proprioceptive senses?
7. What is meant by the phrase "sensory thresholds"?
8. Give an example of adaptation as it refers to sensory perception.

ACTIVITIES

1. To get an idea of how important your senses are to you, try doing without them for a 15-minute period. Join with a partner and take turns being blindfolded and wearing earplugs to reduce your hearing while the other leads you carefully for a short walk. Afterward, describe how you felt. What senses could you still use? Did they help you keep your orientation? For example, did you know directions, where parts of your body were?
2. Identify the general physical or psychological sensory filters affecting the individuals described below. More than one filter might apply in any one situation. The filters to consider are adaptation (A), absolute threshold (AT), difference threshold (DT), and predisposition (P).
    *   Jerry was studying in his room, just barely aware of others talking in the hall. He could hear only a word now and then in the general murmur.
    *   When Bill began to complain once again about the work, Jan heard only the first few words and then her mind wandered and she stopped listening.
    *   Janice pulled a large sled with two youngsters on it. A cat jumped into the lap of one of the youngsters. Janice did not notice it, but when another youngster got on the sled, Janice looked around.
    *   John, a fisherman, noticed the pictures of boats when he visited his friend's house for the first time.
3. Which "laws" or principles of perception—closure (C), figure-ground (FG), continuity (CT), proximity (P), constancy (CS), or similarity (S) explain the following:
    *   The sun and moon appear the same size, although the sun is thousands of times bigger.
    *   From a hill, you see a river disappear behind a smaller hill. When it appears on the other side, you know it is the same river.
    *   You are looking at a crowd of people hurrying by when a familiar face suddenly jumps out at you.
    *   You are looking at a group of people passing by. You

Color blindness
Constancy
Continuity
Cornea
Cycle
Decibels
Difference threshold
Dyslexia
Eardrum
Ecological theory
Eustachian tube
Gustatory sense
Hallucinogens
Hearing
Hertz
Hyperopia
Internal sensors
Iris
Kinesthetic sensors
Listening
Myopia
Nanometers
Olfactory sense
Organ of Corti
Oval window
Perceiving
Perceptual set
Pitch
Proprioceptive senses
Proximity
Retina
Saturation
Sensing
Similarity
Subliminal
Unconscious inference
  theory
Vestibular sensors
Wavelength

notice many are wearing yellow jackets and realize they are members of a team or work force.

- When you look at a TV screen and see full-length images of people only ten inches high and then images of just their faces filling the same ten-inch area, it all looks normal to you.

4. Practice determining what your own thresholds are and learn how they can be changed by your motivation and interests. Try reading and listening to a record. Read different things, ranging from what interests you very much to something you are not interested in but must read. Try to notice now and then when you are more aware of the sound of the record than of what you are reading.

5. Several of you look at the same picture for about 15 seconds. Then each writes down what she or he noticed. Compare notes. Ordinarily, people notice first those things that relate to their occupations or to what interests them.

CASE 1

Dangerous Perception Filters

"Sal, come into my office just as soon as you have parked your truck," Viv, the warehouse supervisor, called as Sal drove into the yard. Sal backed the truck into one of the empty loading bays and walked into the office.

"Martha Nelson just called," Viv said.

"Oh?" Sal replied. "I was just there delivering the furniture she bought."

"It was the second time she called. She was furious," Viv said sternly.

"What's the matter with her?" Sal asked. "I told you, I just delivered the stuff."

"Yes, you did just deliver the stuff. After three in the afternoon. I told you this morning that Mrs. Nelson had to have the furniture delivered before one o'clock. She had an appointment this afternoon and is giving a party tonight. So she wanted the furniture before she had to go out."

"Oh, I guess I didn't hear you say she wanted it by one o'clock today. I thought you just said she wanted it delivered today," Sal explained. "Sorry about that."

"Even with another delivery, Sal, I don't see how you could have gotten there so late. Did anything else happen?" Viv wanted to know.

"No," Sal said. "Oh, I did have a little trouble finding her house."

"Why?" Viv asked. "The address was clearly written down."

"Oh, I just read it wrong, I guess. I didn't look too closely and thought she lived on West 80th Street instead of East 80th. Seems most of our customers live on the west side, you know. So, I thought she did," Sal explained.

"Well, she lives on the east side. You must have lost about an hour's time because of that."

"I'm sorry, but at least she has her furniture now," Sal said.

"Sal, you have been working for us for several months now, and this is not the first time that you either have been late, have gone to the wrong address, or have gotten the order wrong. You have a problem. You make things very difficult for us. The company cannot afford to lose customers like Mrs. Nelson. I'm afraid, Sal, that I am going to have to put you on probation. You must simply learn to pay attention. If you cannot, the company cannot afford to keep you employed. You are our last contact with the customer, and if they begin to feel they cannot depend on you, they will decide they cannot depend on the company."

1. Describe briefly what you think Sal's problems are.

2. Specifically identify sensory perception problems, the various filters or the perception clues that Sal may be misusing.

3. What can Sal do to avoid his problems?

CASE 2

How Perceptions Are Shaped

Even the simple act which we describe as "seeing someone we know" is to some extent an intellectual process. We pack the physical outline of the person we see with all the notions we have already formed about him, and in the total picture of him which we compose in our minds those notions have certainly the principal place. In the end they come to fill out so completely the curve of his cheeks, to follow so exactly the line of his nose, they blend so harmoniously in the sound of his voice as if it were no more than a transparent envelope, that each time we see the face or hear the voice it is these notions which we recognize and to which we listen. And so, no doubt, from the Swann they had constructed for themselves my family had left out, in their ignorance, a whole host of details of his life in the world of fashion . . . details which caused other people, when they met him to see all the graces enthroned in his face.

In this excerpt from *Remembrance of Things Past* by Marcel Proust, the author vividly describes how our brains work to create the images we see.

- Discuss this passage in terms of what you have just read about perception.

- Identify the various senses, principles, and filters that seem to be at work in this passage.

COGNITION:
How We Process and Use Information

O, What a world of unseen visions and heard silences, this insubstantial country of the mind!...an invisible mansion of all moods, musings, and mysteries...A whole kingdom where each of us reigns reclusively alone...
Julian Jaynes

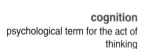

In Chapter 4, you read of how your senses absorb and your brain perceives data. All of this activity has to do with acquiring, storing, and retrieving data. This chapter deals with how you use or manipulate—that is, *think* about—data.

The act of thinking, of being aware of ourselves, of being able mentally to relive the past or envision the future, is what makes humans different from all other animals. Well, humans *think* it makes them different. No one can be really sure. No one has yet precisely described or defined just what it is that humans do when they think. The terms used to talk about this process—*think, dream, plan, create, reason,* and so on—are imprecise and open to broad interpretation. Scientists even wrestle with such questions as, Do people use language because they think, or do they think because they use language?

The act of thinking is connected to *consciousness* and to *intelligence*, which two terms are themselves difficult to define. Freeman Dyson, an outstanding British astrophysicist, has advanced the idea that even subatomic particles are in a way conscious. The American psychologist Julian Jaynes, on the other hand, has argued that people themselves only very recently developed consciousness. And Sir Fred Hoyle, a leading astronomer, has suggested that the universe itself is intelligent. These are exciting thoughts, examples themselves of the power of the human intellect as well as of the scope of the problem of defining "thinking."

Despite the perplexing questions about the exact nature of the thinking process, consciousness, and intelligence, much is understood. If they cannot be completely explained, their existence can certainly be demonstrated, as you are doing right now. Your reading these words involves thinking, consciousness, and intelligence.

▼ THE ACT OF THINKING

cognition
psychological term for the act of thinking

The act of thinking involves changing, combining, and otherwise manipulating information received through your senses and stored in your memory. Psychologists refer to the act of thinking as **cognition**, which comes from a Latin word meaning to get to know.

Because the thinking process cannot be observed, scientists, such as cognitive psychologists, who study it must develop ingenious experiments that make it possible to draw conclusions about what happens when you think. Some of these experiments look very simple. For example, in one experiment on the thinking process, subjects were shown pairs of letters and instructed to push a "same" button if both letters were vowels or both were

Fig. 5-1

Thinking, consciousness, and intelligence are all terms that are difficult to define precisely or identify exactly. Scientists have different theories to explain them. One has suggested that the universe itself has intelligence, and another, that even subatomic particles have a form of consciousness.

consonants. They pushed a "different" key if one of the pair was a vowel and the other a consonant.[4]

This experiment was designed to measure the time it takes for a thought process to occur. Time is important in the study of thinking because it provides scientists with one way to measure a process that is unobservable. Based upon the time it takes subjects to carry out different mental tasks, scientists can draw some conclusions about the process. The time intervals involved are fractions of seconds.

In the simple task of identifying and matching vowels and consonants, it was found that reaction time was fastest when the paired letters were identical (AA), somewhat slower when the letters were the same but in different shapes (Aa), and slowest when the letters were different (AE). In other words, subjects were able to process the information fastest when it was in the form of identical symbols, less fast when the appearance differed even if the two letters had the same name, and slowest when the two letters were only in the same class, that is, vowels or consonants.

Thinking and Images

That it takes longer for a person to respond when the two letters are different and less time when they are obviously the same may appear self-evident. But scientists must still ask why. Answering that question can lead to several conclusions about how you think. In simple terms, the experiment suggests you think first in terms of physical identity, second in terms of the "name" of the object, and third in terms of its broader classification.

Much of your thinking relies on your memory. Even if you are thinking about or responding to newly received stimuli, you call up information already in your memory to help you use it. As you will read in Chapter 9, you have short-term and long-term memory as well as effortless and effortful retrieval. All of this is part of the overall thinking process.

Mental Shortcuts

abstraction
general words or images that stand for all the common characteristics of a group of similar objects or images

The simple tests of recognizing similar letters also indicate another characteristic of your thinking process. You use abstractions. An **abstraction** is a general word or image that stands for all the characteristics of a group of similar things or images. Your ability to abstract is a key part of your thinking.

Abstractions

Using abstractions speeds up your thought processes. You do not need to think of every little detail, just the general word. As a simple example, consider the word cat. When you hear or read that word, your mind may immediately invoke an image of a cat, probably one with which you are familiar, or one you own. You do not consciously go through a step-by-step mental process of creating the image of a cat. And the image of a cat you invoke will depend on your previous experiences with cats.

There can be several levels of abstraction. The word *cat* is an abstraction for all those small, furry, four-legged creatures people keep as pets. *Pets* is a higher-level abstraction that includes cats and many other different animals. *Animals* is an even higher-level abstraction that includes pets and all other animals, even people.

Using abstractions has its dangers. If your abstraction of cat includes the characterization of *friendly*, you may receive an unpleasant surprise trying to pick up an unfriendly cat. In Chapter 12 you will read how abstractions can sometimes hinder communication.

In the experiment to identify letters, the levels of abstractions range from the physical appearance of a letter to its name to its class—vowel or consonant. The indications are that the higher the level of abstraction, the slower you think.

Schemata

To handle all the sensory data coming to it, the brain has developed another useful shortcut of organization and manipulation. It quickly puts together different bits and pieces of information, including abstractions, to create a meaningful whole. Your brain creates mental structures almost automatically and very rapidly, often after having received only a few clues from the environment.

An example is the mental structure you develop for a job. After being on the job for a while you stop thinking of each step or task that must be done. If you are a secretary, you have a mental structure of what to do when the mail arrives, when you receive dictation, when a visitor arrives. In essence you have several structures within the overall job structure. All these mental structures make it possible for you to carry out the responsibilities of your job quickly and efficiently.

These mental structures are known as **schemata** (singular: **schema**). As you can tell, this word is close to the word *scheme*, which means a systematic plan of action. Both come from the same Greek root word meaning form or plan. A mental schema is a summary or outline in the sense that it is based on many different bits of information.

schemata
mental structures, summaries, or outlines that are based on many different bits of information, used to handle all the sensory data to which an individual is exposed

Though necessary for organized, fast thinking, these schemata can create problems. Relying too heavily on them could cause you to miss important new clues in the environment that would, if you saw them, alter your thinking on how to respond in a particular situation.

Say that you are a secretary in a busy office that is rarely visited by clients without appointments but is often visited by salespeople without appointments. Your schema for handling visitors without appointments would be to give them as little time as possible and move them out quickly. If one day a client, perhaps one with a complaint, came into the office without an appointment, you would create problems for your company if, failing to notice the new clues, you let your usual schema for handling unexpected visitors prevail:

Fig. 5-2

We mentally organize the many demands of our job into a usable whole, known as a schema, so we can do it efficiently by reacting to a few clues without thinking of all the details. If we miss important clues about changes, then our schema causes us to err.

"Do you have an appointment?"
        "No, but..."
"I'm sorry, we do not see people without appointments."
        "Look, I'm..."
"I'm very sorry, but we are too busy to talk with you now.
Please call for an appointment. Here's our card. Goodbye!"

And then acting on your schema, you would turn to an incoming call or go back to typing, leaving one very irate client. Schemata can stop you from listening, a particularly dangerous habit in occupations in which you must work with people. "Do you have ginger beer?" the customer asks. "Oh sure," the waitress replies, and brings a bottle of ginger ale.

Thinking and Concepts

Although you think often in images, not all of your thoughts occur as images. At a high level of abstraction you think in terms of general ideas, which are known as **concepts**. Honor, friendship, charity, and bravery are examples of concepts. You often use a combination of imagery and concepts.

concepts
general ideas on a very high level of abstraction, which, together with images, are the primary form that thoughts take

Concepts are similar to schemata in that they are based on several different bits of information. If someone ignores danger to her own life and jumps into a freezing river to rescue another person, your mind puts together these events and comes up with the concept of bravery. Factors in your environment obviously color your concepts. If the woman risking her life lived in a culture that believed people should only look out for themselves, witnesses to her act would develop a concept of foolishness.

You use a combination of images and words in your thought processes. When thinking about concepts, words play a larger part because it is difficult to have images for such things as trust, honor, or bravery. You can and do imagine specific acts that embody these concepts, but words are your primary way of thinking about concepts.

Thinking and Language

Although all animals communicate, humans alone use language. Some birds, such as parrots, can be taught to mimic spoken words. Some higher-level animals, such as chimpanzees, have been taught to use a rudimentary sign language indicating recognition of some words. But no animals other than humans have exhibited the ability to *use* language.

Scientists are working to develop computers that can use language, but as of this writing, they have had little success. They have created machines that can recognize words, that can put words together into meaningful sentences, and that can actually speak words. But they have so far failed to develop a machine with automatic language recognition that has even a fraction of a human's capability to understand and use language.

One of the first tasks that scientists thought computers would be able to do easily was to translate one language into another. Such a task seems rather straightforward, well within a computer's capability: It must simply convert one series of sounds and symbols into another series of sounds and symbols that have the same meaning. So far, no computer capable of making valid translations has been created. The task of translation has proved much more complex than it at first appeared to be. Despite their marvelous capabilities, computers are not (at least, not yet) thinking machines.

It is not the fact that there are more than 3000 languages in the world that makes translation difficult for a machine. Actually, despite this great diversity, all languages have surprising similarities in the way they are structured. Difficulties arise because language is very complex, and it is shaped to some extent by the environment while at the same time influencing how the environment is perceived.

Inuits (native to Alaska and northern Canada), for example, have many names for snow. They have a word for packed snow, one for icy snow, one for falling snow. This does not mean that non-Inuits cannot recognize different kinds of snow. If you have ever skied, you learned very quickly the difference among a dry, soft snow; a hard, crusty snow; and a wet, soggy snow. You can and are able to describe the different kinds of snow even if you do not have one word for each. You, however, are not as aware of the different kinds of snow as an Inuit is.

You are capable of perceiving many different shades of color, although you may not identify them because you do not know the names for them. A Stone Age tribe was discovered that had only two words for color—essentially "dark" and "bright." People from that tribe could nonetheless identify and remember different colors.

But language does reflect thought patterns, and influences them as well. Scientists who study language and its effect on behavior are known as **psycholinguists**.

You rely on many clues when you use language. These include sound, meaning, and structure (which is the way words are put together.) Many animals make sounds. Many use sounds to communicate. Only humans have created words from sounds, and sentences and meanings from words. People then use these words to think; they even use words to talk or think about words.

An animal sound, such as the caw of a crow, will send a message of alarm to other crows. But these crows cannot think of a concept such as danger and then discuss it later. In a moment you will read of some theories on how humans learn language. But first let's look at the sounds themselves, because that is how language begins, and at meaning and structure.

Sounds

Words are made up of a series of separate sounds. Each word has its own sound, and this is one way to identify the word when it is spoken. Even small words are made up of separate sounds. The word *day*, for example, is made up of the sounds of *d* and *a*. The basic units of sound you make when speaking are known as **phonemes**. A phoneme is the smallest elemental sound that can be distinctly recognized. The *a* sound, *b* sound, and *d* sound are examples of phonemes, as is the *ch* sound in *church* (it cannot be broken down into any smaller, recognizable sound). By themselves, phonemes have no meaning. You put phonemes together to make words that have meaning. The smallest units of sound, small words actually, that have meaning are known as **morphemes**. The words *day* and *man* are morphemes, so are prefixes and suffixes, such as *pre-* and *-ly*, which have meaning when attached to other words.

There are about 46 phonemes in English. Other languages may have as few as 15 and as many as 85. People find it difficult often to pronounce phonemes that are not in their native language. For example, French does not have the English phoneme represented by the *th* sound in thin. Consequently, a French speaker might say instead "sin."

psycholinguists
scientists who study language and its relation to behavior

phonemes
the smallest sounds in a language that can be distinctly recognized, such as "b" or "ch"

morphemes
the smallest units of sound that have meaning in a language, such as "by" or "-ly"

Meaning and Structure

Words have meanings. If you heard the one word *look*, it would have meaning for you and you would probably take some action, such as looking around. All words have their own meanings that they carry around with them. You can look in a dictionary to find the meaning or definition of any word.

A dictionary is limited though, because though it can give you the meanings of all words and even the many different meanings of one word, it

The way you think can affect your health and success, research has increasingly indicated. That is, studies have shown that persons who think optimistically tend to be healthier, enjoy longer life, score higher on achievement tests, and succeed more at work. According to Edward E. Jones, a Princeton University psychologist, "Our expectancies not only affect how we see reality, but also affect the reality itself."

Scientists are studying how people react to failures. In one study they found that when people are disappointed, such as after being turned down for a job, optimists respond by coming up with a plan of action and seeking help and advice from others. Pessimists, on the other hand, decide there was nothing they could have done and try to forget the rejection.

We tend to explain our failures in a set way, according to Martin Seligman, a University of Pennsylvania psychologist. Pessimists blame themselves and, when they flunk an exam, decide it was the result of a personal deficit that cannot be remedied. Optimists see such failures as the result of mistakes they can correct.

The extremes of optimism and pessimism are illustrated in the old story of the man with two sons, one an optimist and the other a pessimist. Because their attitudes were so extreme, the father felt he had to teach them a lesson. So, one Christmas he gave the pessimistic son many beautiful and elaborate presents. For the optimistic son, he had a load of manure dumped in the yard.

When he came downstairs that morning, he found the pessimist seated among all the beautiful presents nearly in tears. Irritated, the father asked what was wrong, and the pessimist said, "I figure that with all these presents there has to be a catch here somewhere."

The father sighed and went out in the yard to find his optimistic son jumping around with joy. "Why are you so happy?" the father asked, "You didn't get any nice presents." "Gee, Dad," the optimist said, "I figure that with all this manure, there has to be a pony somewhere!"

Most of us are a mixture of the two extremes.

TO THE POINT

cannot give you all the possible meanings a word can take on from its surroundings; the surroundings can be either other words or the nonverbal environment. That is because the number of combinations is limitless, and that is what makes language, especially English, so useful and sometimes confusing. *Look* is a simple word, but even it can take on quite different meanings:

- "Look!" A command to look and see something interesting.

- "That person looks good." A reference to a person's appearance.

- "Look, I haven't the time to do this work." The speaker is not asking the hearer to use eyes to see something. "Look" is an exclamation here, possibly directed at the "mind's eye."

- "Look out!" Hearing this, you might duck or fall to the ground, not wasting any time to look around because you would know that was not the prime meaning.

So, words have meanings of their own as well as meanings determined by their place in a sentence, by other words used with them, by the manner in which they are said, and by the environment or situation in which they are used. Sometimes they can take on meanings that are different from any given in the dictionary.

Our marvelous language is so flexible, in fact, you can make words mean the exact opposite of what they really mean by your tone of voice. You no doubt have experienced this and have done it yourself. "Oh, yeah, sure." An exclamation and two positive words of *agreement*, which, given the right tone, can be made to mean *disagreement*.

Learning Language

Scientists have been able to identify various stages in a child's development of language, but they still disagree about exactly how humans acquire the ability to use language. In one sense it just seems to happen. When children learn to talk, no one is telling them about nouns and verbs and objects and how to put them together to make sentences. Children just do it.

Observations show a rather consistent progression from meaningless sounds to words at about one year of age. Then children begin putting the words together to make meaningful sentences at about two years. The development appears to go from one word utterances to combining two words into simple sentences. After that, children begin combining more words to make sentences. There is no three-word stage.

Three major theories have been put forward to explain what is happening as a child learns a language: the imitation theory, the reinforcement theory, and the innate ability theory.

Imitation Theory

As its name implies, the **imitation theory** of learning language holds that you simply imitate what you hear and continue to do so until you get it right. Because you have to have other people to imitate, imitation theory is also known as social learning theory. (You will read more about this in Chapter 9.)

imitation theory
a theory of language learning that holds that individuals imitate what they hear and continue to do so until they get it right

Reinforcement Theory

Behaviorist psychologists put forth the **reinforcement theory** of learning language, which holds that children learn or are conditioned to use language correctly by being reinforced for correct usage and punished when they make errors. Reinforcement theory is also known as operant conditioning theory. (You will also read more about this in Chapter 9.)

reinforcement theory
a theory of language learning that holds that children learn or are conditioned to use language correctly by being reinforced for correct usage and punished when they make errors

Innate Ability Theory

Some scientists believe humans are born with an ability to acquire and use language. That no one has to teach people the "rules" about understanding and using the different meanings of a word appears to support this belief. Humans have a natural ability to form or learn the rules of language.
Noam Chomsky, a linguist at the Massachusetts Institute of Technology, calls this **innate ability theory** the language acquisition device. His argument, simply put, is that our brains are naturally programmed to recognize the "rules" that govern language and that all we need to activate this ability is the experience.

innate ability theory
a theory of language learning that holds that humans are born with the ability to learn the "rules" that govern language

Language and Writing

You learn to speak before you can write, and your personal development in this reflects the development of humankind. Humans learned to speak before they could write, and it was only fairly recently in the history of humans that writing developed. Even today, some languages exist that have only an oral tradition. That means they are spoken, not written.

It is not surprising that people speak before they write. Considering the complexity of language, it is a miracle that humans developed the ability to write, that they invented symbols to represent the various sounds of human speech that could be written down.

word writing
a system of writing in which symbols stand for entire words or concepts

The first written language was made up of pictures, or images. A picture of a horse meant a horse; one of a house, a house. This is **word writing** in the sense that the image represents a whole word. These images eventually became uniform and lost detail. They became symbols and began to stand for the sound of saying the thing they stood for, as well as for the thing itself. Egyptian hieroglyphics are one example of this kind of early writing.

syllable writing
a system of writing in which symbols represent sounds and stand for parts of words, or syllables

A more abstract and flexible form of written language that appeared was **syllable writing**, which involved putting two or more symbols together to make up syllables of another word. With this kind of writing, people were able to express even more things by writing. For example, Japanese *kana* evolved from Chinese characters, but, unlike the characters, *kana* represent sounds and syllables, not concepts or whole words.

alphabet writing
a system of writing in which each symbol (letter) stands for a distinct sound or phoneme

Another development of written language was **alphabet writing**, which is what we use when writing English. Having an alphabet in which each letter more or less stands for a distinct sound (phoneme) results in a written language of tremendous flexibility. Using these letter symbols, you can write down anything you can utter. To understand how flexible this system is, consider that a good unabridged dictionary lists more than 450,000 words that are made with the 26 letters of our alphabet.

Thinking and Logic

You do not need to take a formal course in logic to use logic in your thinking. You and everyone else use logic when thinking all the time. You use it when you *reason*. Using logic involves putting together or organizing two or more pieces of information to arrive at or develop a new piece of knowledge. Or it involves seeing relationships between two different bits of information that lead to a new bit of knowledge.

There are two basic kinds of reasoning, or logic, that you normally carry out, often without much conscious thought:

1. **Inductive logic:** Beginning with specific facts that you have observed or know and drawing a general conclusion from these specific facts.

2. **Deductive logic:** You begin with a general observation or principle and make a specific conclusion about a specific situation.

Here is an example of inductive reasoning:

> On cold days you notice that your cat always curls up in a spot in the sun.

Using inductive reasoning, you conclude from seeing your cat doing this many times that all cats will seek warm spots on cold days.

Here is an example of deductive reasoning:

The company always fires people who are more than an hour late on three occasions.

Bill has been more than an hour late three times.

Bill will be fired.

If you studied formal logic you would know that the three statements about Bill and the company are in the form of a **syllogism**. A syllogism is a form of deductive logic consisting of a *major premise* (the company rules on being late), a *minor premise* (Bill's record of tardiness), and a *conclusion* (Bill will be fired).

You will recall reading in Chapter 2 that scientists often use deductive reasoning and that a particular method of studying general theories to arrive at specific hypotheses is known as the deductive experimental method.

You use the deductive and inductive methods of reasoning even if you are not always aware of creating a syllogism or going through the various steps of the process. It is by this kind of reasoning that you increase your awareness and understanding of your world.

The fact that you use the logical process, however, does not mean that you will always come to the right conclusion. If either one of your premises is wrong, for example, your conclusion will be wrong. Consider this example of deductive reasoning:

All birds fly.
Ostriches are birds.
Ostriches fly.

There is nothing wrong with the logic in this syllogism; the problem is that the major premise "all birds fly" is wrong, so the conclusion "ostriches fly" can be wrong. Many people make mental errors not because they cannot reason adequately, but because their basic information is incomplete or wrong.

syllogism
a form of deductive logic consisting of a major premise, a minor premise, and a conclusion

Thinking and Intelligence

As you read in Chapter 1, no other area of psychology arouses such debate as the study of intelligence. We all learn to think that some people are "smart" and some are "stupid." We even put such labels on ourselves. Although we think we know exactly what we mean by such labels, they are really very imprecise descriptions of reality.

As a simple example of the difficulty in determining intelligence, how would you describe people who followed the logical steps you read earlier that led to the conclusion ostriches could fly? Are such people "stupid" or not intelligent? Not so. There was nothing at all "stupid" about their reasoning. It was intelligent. They had just never heard about birds that could not fly. Does that make them "stupid," or does it just mean they need more information?

Kinds of Intelligence

Howard Gardner, a research psychologist, has suggested that people have different, often unrelated, kinds of intelligences. In his book *Frames of Mind: Multiple Intelligences* (New York: Basic Books, 1983), Gardner distinguishes seven different kinds of intelligences, or ways of understanding the environment:

- **Linguistic:** The ability to use language, which is one of the three varieties of intelligence that intelligence tests measure

- **Logical-mathematical:** The ability to reason deductively and inductively and to use numbers, which is the second variety most intelligence tests measure

- **Spatial:** The ability to visualize space and to manipulate it mentally, the third variety measured by intelligence tests

- **Musical:** The ability to recognize and make pitch and rhythmic patterns

- **Motor:** The ability to use your hands or body, such as a fine craftsman or a dancer

- **Interpersonal:** The ability to understand and react with other individuals

- **Intrapersonal:** The ability to be aware of self and have a sense of identity

▼ SOLVING PROBLEMS

Your thinking occurs in one of two broad patterns: organized and deliberate to achieve a desired goal or unorganized and free-flowing, as when you

As an example of the difficulty of defining intelligence, consider this old story:

A motorist had a flat tire just as he was driving by a mental institution. He pulled over to the curb and began to change tires. He took off the flat tire and carefully put the four lugs (bolts) that held the tire to the wheel in the hub cap.

Unfortunately for him, as he was rolling the spare tire up to the wheel, it hit the hub cap and all four lugs fell out and down a nearby storm sewer. The man could not get them back out, and he stood there not knowing what he was going to do because he saw no way to attach the spare tire to the wheel.

A patient at the institution had been leaning on a fence watching the man, and when she saw he did not know what to do, she told him to take one lug off each of the other three wheels and use them on the fourth wheel. Then each wheel would be held on by three lugs—enough to get safely to a garage and buy other lugs.

The man was very thankful but somewhat astonished, "Gee, thanks a lot, but how come you're in there?"

"I may be crazy," the woman said, "but I'm not stupid."

Although crudely stated, the point the woman made was a very good one. The driver had a narrow view of what intelligence is and was surprised when a person whose situation caused him to assume she could not reason showed that she could do it very well.

TO THE POINT

are daydreaming. This section will look at systematic, organized thinking.

Organized thinking occurs in reaction to internal or external situations. Something happens, and you are motivated to think along a certain line. Usually, especially when the motivation comes from an external situation, you in essence solve a problem. The "problem" could be nothing more complex than deciding when it is safe to cross the street, or it could be as complex as deciding what career you want to follow.

Problem solving and decision making are closely related. Solving a problem involves making a decision. In this section you will read of problem solving in a broad sense, in terms of meeting and dealing with day-to-day situations. In Chapter 16, you will learn a step-by-step approach to making a specific decision, such as when faced with several alternatives in a career. To solve a problem, you go through four mental steps:

1. Interpreting or identifying the problem
2. Thinking of solutions
3. Picking the best solution
4. Reviewing and adjusting

Identifying the Problem

This first step is the most crucial. If you do not interpret the problem correctly, you will not be able to solve it easily, if at all. Consider your interpretation of the problem as the major premise from which you will work to a conclusive solution. Recall what happens when the major premise in a syllogism is wrong: the conclusion can be wrong.

The importance of the first step is easily illustrated. You have experienced examples of it often. Riddles are deliberately designed to obscure what the real problem is so that you will have difficulty thinking of the answer. Consider this classic:[6]

> Two trains, 50 miles apart, begin moving toward each other simultaneously traveling 25 mph. At the same time, a bird springs into the air in front of one train and flies to the front of the other. The bird continues to fly back and forth between the two approaching trains until they meet. The bird flies at a speed of 100 mph. How many miles does the bird fly?

If you are like most people, you will probably accept the interpretation of the problem as stated and struggle to determine the number of miles the shuttling bird flew, using algebra if you can. If, instead of interpreting the problem originally as how far the bird flies, you interpret it as how much time the bird flies, the problem becomes very simple.

The two trains began 50 miles apart and traveled toward each other at 25 miles per hour. Thus, they will each cover half the distance between

Fig. 5-3

How you interpret a problem will determine how you go about solving it. This puzzle concerning how far the bird flew between two approaching trains before they met can be solved easily if you interpret it in terms of how long the bird flies.

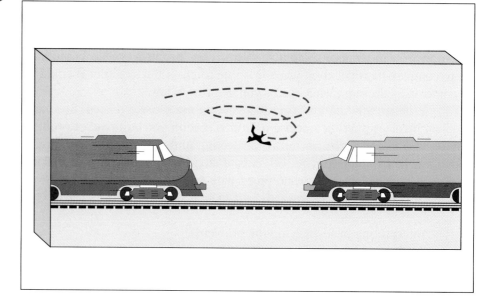

them and meet in one hour. Given its flight speed of 100 mph, the bird obviously has flown 100 miles when the trains meet.

How you interpret a problem determines how you go about solving it. Even simple situations require care in identifying the problem. For example, your problem on a given evening might be whether to watch a favorite TV program or to prepare for the next day's examination. Whether you interpret this problem in terms of immediate satisfaction or in terms of delayed satisfaction will obviously influence your conclusion.

Thinking of Solutions

Most problems have more than one possible solution, and you should think of as many as you can before coming to any conclusion. In everyday life, you frequently go through possible alternatives automatically, and quickly select the solution you want. Two approaches to generating solutions are:

1. Mentally go through all the possible solutions, one by one, until the right one appears.
2. Take a shortcut by using prior knowledge to eliminate obviously wrong solutions.

Dressing for the day requires you to solve several problems. In the first approach, you would try on everything you have until you had on what appears to be the right combination. In the second approach, you would consider the weather, your destination today, and other factors to arrive at a solution faster.

Picking the Best Solution

After generating as many solutions as possible, you pick the best one to the extent of your knowledge. If your problem is how to get across a stream, you reject trying to jump over, stepping across on slippery rocks, or wading, and decide to use a plank you see lying across it.

Often, you know immediately if you have chosen the best solution. In this instance, you either cross safely or fall in if the plank breaks. In any event, you know after the fact. But you cannot know before the fact. All you can do, and should do, is generate as many solutions as possible and select what appears to be the best one.

Reviewing and Adjusting

If you fall into the creek, all you can do is climb out and walk home wet. Frequently, if your solution turns out to be unfavorable, you have the opportunity to review and adjust it. Rarely can anyone come up with a perfect solution that will do for all situations. A change in conditions can ruin the best-laid plans. This is particularly true in regard to decisions.

As an example of how conditions can change, suppose that your problem is to find exactly the right house to buy, in which you plan to raise your family and live the rest of your life. Imagine that you spend a lot of time looking for this house, gather information, look at many different houses, compare each with what you know about yourself and your needs, and, finally, make a choice and purchase a house. The house is near your work, close to good schools, and in a countrylike setting, which particularly suited you because you want your children to have places to run and play in. Two years after you move in, the state announces that a new superhigh-

TO THE POINT

Reviewing and adjusting or changing decisions may be more difficult than you might imagine. Studies have suggested that once we have made a decision our inclination to support it as the "right" decision increases. In 1957 Leon Festinger suggested this in his theory of **cognitive dissonance reduction**.

A study reported in the *Journal of Social Psychology* supported this theory. The researchers, Paul Rosenfeld, John G. Kennedy, and Robert Giacalone, took advantage of a "Great Gumball Guess" contest at a large shopping mall in northwest Pennsylvania.

They asked a random sampling of people to estimate their chances of winning on a scale from 1 to 100. The sampling included 24 people prior to their making a guess, 17 who had already guessed, and 21 who were not guessing. This last group made up the control group.

The researchers found that the people who had already guessed had more confidence in their decisions than did those in either of the other groups, whose expressed level of confidence was about equal.

The desire to save face may be one reason why people express greater confidence in their decision after the fact. Cognitive dissonance holds that people attempt to reduce mental inconsistency or dissonance because it is an unpleasant state. Inconsistency occurs when a person, having decided on one of several possible alternatives, subsequently thinks of the potential negative benefits of the chosen alternative compared with the potential positive benefits of those not chosen.

Guessing the number of gumballs in a machine is not a terribly important decision to make. Decisions affecting your career and life always are.

way will be constructed right next to your house. In order to deal with the situation, you review and adjust.

▼ CREATIVE THINKING

In one sense all problem solving is creative thinking. You mentally relate pertinent facts to create a solution that did not exist for you before. Activities that are creative in the conventional sense—composing a song or poem, writing a book, designing a building—are themselves exercises in problem solving. The problem for the composer is to arrange the notes or words so as to provide new pleasure and insights. The problem for the writer is to select the right words and arrange them in an apt way to convey an exact meaning. The problem for the architect is to create a design that is sturdy, functional, and aesthetically pleasing.

Yet creative problem solving is different from ordinary problem solving. Ordinary problem solvers, no matter how intelligent, deal with the data rather as they find them and work toward one acceptable conclusion or answer. Creative problem solvers reinterpret the data in different ways to arrive at different conclusions or solutions. They look at things in many ways; for them there is no one correct way or one correct solution.

Just as there is disagreement among psychologists in defining what intelligence is, there is disagreement about what creativity is and how to measure it. They agree that intelligence and creativity are not the same thing. Very intelligent people are not necessarily creative. And very creative people are not necessarily highly intelligent, although studies do indicate that creative people are of above-average intelligence.

Convergent and Divergent Thinking

Psychologists have characterized two ways of thinking to distinguish creative thinking from conventional thinking. According to this theory, conventional thinkers are convergent thinkers, whereas creative thinkers are divergent thinkers.

Conventional or **convergent** thinkers, when solving a problem, follow established paths to arrive at one correct solution. **Divergent** thinkers do not follow established paths but think of new ones to arrive at different solutions. Creative thinkers seem to have fewer constraints or blocks on how they look at or identify a problem.

James Adams, in his book *Conceptual Blockbusting: A Guide to Better Ideas*, reported several creative solutions that he received to the classic nine-dot problem shown in Figure 5-4. Most people fail to solve the problem because of a perceptual block. They do not think of drawing lines

convergent thinking
designates "conventional" thinking, characterized by the use of established thought paths to arrive at one "correct" solution

divergent thinking
a term to designate "creative" thinking, characterized by the use of new thought paths to arrive at unconventional solutions

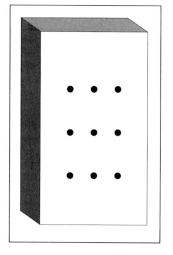

Fig. 5-4

The problem in the nine-dot puzzle is to draw no more than four straight lines that go through all nine dots without lifting your pencil from the paper. Solutions to the problem indicate to some extent the difference between convergent and divergent thinking.

incubation period
as used here, a period of inactive or unconscious thought following intense concentration on a problem, often followed by the sudden appearance of a solution

outside the boundaries of the box created by the arrangement of dots, although there is nothing in the statement of the problem to prevent this. They are convergent thinkers.

People who think about extending the lines beyond the apparent boundaries of the box solve the problem as shown in Figure 5-5.

Other creative or divergent thinkers not only ignored the apparent boundaries created by the arrangement of dots, they rearranged the dots. Nothing in the statement of the puzzle prevents this. Adams reported receiving solutions in which the solver simply cut up the paper, rearranged the dots in one row, and connected them with one straight line! Others rolled the paper into a cylinder, making it possible to draw one line as a spiral through all the dots. And one young girl drew one very fat line that went through all the dots.[8]

Incubation

Another characteristic of creative thinking is that it often involves a period during which the individual has stopped thinking about the problem. What happens is that the thinker will wrestle with a problem, thinking hard about it for some time. Then, perhaps weary of it, the thinker will stop. At some time later, without the person's consciously thinking of the problem again, perhaps even while he or she is sleeping or daydreaming, a solution or an answer comes.

Psychologists refer to this period of inactive or unconscious thought as an **incubation period**. You probably have experienced flashes of insight or intuition when an answer to a problem that has been perplexing you suddenly jumps into your mind. This happens when you have stopped thinking of the problem and have gone on to other things. The process seems to follow roughly these stages:

- A period of intense thought on the problem
- A decision to stop working on the problem
- A period of rest, even sleep or daydreaming
- The sudden appearance of the solution

We can all work to increase our creativity. As you read earlier, the most important step in problem solving or decision making is the first step, when you identify the problem. To reach a sound solution, you must first correctly interpret the problem. When you are at that first step, you can try to interpret the problem in different ways that may help you arrive at creative solutions.

You can also try to use the incubation process. If you have failed to come up with a satisfying answer or solution after a period of intense concentration, decide to put the problem away for a while. The answer might come to you even while you sleep or are just daydreaming about other things.

In everyday life, problems happen all the time, and so you have to learn how to think creatively. Another kind of situation that happens all the time in everyday life also requires you to think, but in a different way: situations where you are called on to evaluate or judge. For example, a company claims that their product is the "best" on the market. Or, you read an article claiming that the author's method is the "best" method for handling stress. Or your friend insists that leasing a new car is "better" than buying a new car. How do you evaluate such claims?

▼ CRITICAL THINKING

Critical thinking is the thinking that you do when you have to evaluate a claim. As the examples above show, a claim is an assertion that something is a fact or is the case. Where problem solving requires creative thinking, evaluating claims requires critical thinking.

Over the years, people like philosophers, teachers, legal thinkers, and scientists have had to evaluate claims in the course of their work. Over the years, these "claim-evaluators" have put together procedures for thinking critically. These procedures can be condensed into the following questions:

1. What is the claim being made?
2. What evidence has been offered to support the claim?
3. How good is the evidence?
4. Can the evidence support a different claim?
5. Is there evidence that disproves the claim?
6. Which evidence is stronger, the evidence for the claim or the evidence against the claim?

Let us look at each of these questions.

What is the claim being made?

The claims people make range from the simple to the complex, from the straightforward to the subtle or disguised, from the unimportant to the important. The simple and straightforward offer little problem, especially if they also are unimportant. However, the other extremes may offer problems to the beginner. You need the proper background of knowledge and information before you become adept at identifying and understanding

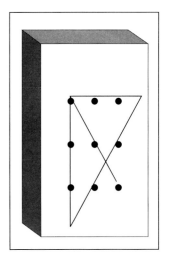

Fig. 5-5

This is a divergent-thinking solution to the nine-dot problem, in which the solver overcame the perceptual block most people have and drew the lines outside the boundaries.

Fig. 5-6

This advertisement makes a claim that many people would like to believe. In fact, people without training in the field of dentistry don't have the expertise to evaluate this claim effectively.

complex claims. You need experience and practice before you become adept at identifying disguised or hidden claims. You need a clear set of values that you are able to apply to situations before you can tell what is important and what is not. (More about values appears later in the chapter.)

Complex claims require specialized information. For example, not many of us who are untrained can understand the claims (or counterclaims) made in science and medicine, or in health and diet (Fig. 5-6). Even "experts" may be incompetent if the matter is outside their expertise. This is one reason people go (back) to school: to increase their fund of knowledge so that they will be able to evaluate complex claims.

Hidden claims usually give the beginner some trouble. We may illustrate hidden claims by the case of false or misleading advertising. For example, a vegetable food product is advertised as having NO CHOLES-TEROL. At first glance, the claim is straightforward: that the product has no cholesterol. But advertising it as having NO CHOLESTEROL is being used to make a hidden claim: that the product is good for you—because cutting your intake of cholesterol is good for you. Which claim, then, should you evaluate: that the product has no cholesterol or that the product is good for you? The evidence you need to evaluate each claim will be different. If you had the appropriate science background, you would know that, being vegetable, the product could not possibly have cholesterol because cholesterol only comes with animal fat, and therefore the first claim is absolutely correct. However, is the product, then, good for you? That would require more information about the nutritional content of the product (not to mention taste, cost, etc.). It may turn out that the only thing good about the product is that it has no cholesterol, but on other grounds the product is no good at all.

If you have problems identifying the claim being made, you might wish to list all the possible claims that you think are being made. Then you can focus on the most important one(s). After some experience, you will find that identifying claims becomes easier for you. (A good practice is to write down the claims to allow you to examine all the possible claims all at once. You can look at the claims two at a time and pick the more important one. By a process of elimination, you can settle on the one or the few most important claims.)

Because life is so short, you have to pick and choose the claims that you think are important enough to evaluate. Often, because of lack of time, you have to defer to the opinion of those who know more and have more experience than you. But it doesn't hurt to try your hand at identifying the claim and evaluating it yourself.

What evidence has been offered to support the claim?

People often make claims without offering any evidence to support them. If you analyze what they say, you find that they just repeat the claim in so many other words, in several different ways. If you are sympathetic to the claimant, you tend to accept the claim; if you are antagonistic, you tend to reject the claim—without examining the evidence. This is why it is best to suspend judgment, not to allow yourself to feel sympathetic or antagonistic to the claimant. To think critically, you should neither accept nor reject a claim without first examining the evidence, and certainly not judge a claim on the basis of feelings for the claimant. If no evidence has been offered, you should ask for it or—sometimes—look for it. (Some people may not be articulate enough to present their evidence, but their claim might be honest. And correct!)

Looking at the evidence offered, you should ask yourself, What exactly is the evidence? Is it factual (can you see or check it out for yourself) or is it opinion? Oftentimes, the opinion of others is used as "evidence" (this is what we call "testimonials") (Fig. 5-7). To think critically, you should prefer facts, rather than opinion, as evidence.

Even when facts are presented as evidence, they may be "dressed up" in nice-sounding words. You have to strip away the propaganda. "The absolutely fantastic price of $199" should be read simply as "the price of $199." Beware of adjectives and adverbs. One reason scientists have over the years come to prefer numerical description to verbal description is that numbers, unlike words, rarely carry along any extra meanings. Words, on the other hand, are loaded with them, so that many times their meaning lies, like beauty, "in the eye of the beholder."

How good is the evidence?

There are three grounds on which you can judge how good the evidence is that is being offered to support the claim: relevance, reliability, and consistency. Relevance takes precedence. No matter how reliable and consistent the offered evidence is, if it is irrelevant, it does not count. Judging relevance is usually straightforward, but there are times when you may find it a problem. When in doubt, you could either allow the evidence or disallow it. Either course runs some risks: If you allow it and the evidence turns out eventually to be irrelevant, you have wasted your time. If you disallow it, and unbeknown to you, the evidence turns out to be relevant and even critical to the claim, you might reach an incorrect conclusion about the claim. If the claim is very important to you, you would be better off allowing the doubtful evidence than disallowing it. If it is not all that important, you might just as well disallow the doubtful evidence.

Advertisers often use testimonials of celebrities to try to sell their products.

"Reliability" means you can trust the evidence because it comes from a reliable source and is factual and accurate. If the evidence comes from an unreliable source, you are in the same position as having evidence of doubtful relevance, so you can proceed in much the same manner.

How do you check on the accuracy of the facts? You could use the old rule of "independent confirmation." This rule is used by journalists when they require verification from an independent source, by lawyers and judges when they require corroboration by another witness, and by scientists when they require independent confirmation of experimental results by a different laboratory. If the facts are taken from one textbook, you might check them against another textbook; if given by management, you might check them against labor's facts; if given by government, you might check them against facts compiled by public interest groups; and so on. A desirable situation is when you can check the facts with an opponent or antagonistic source, or a source that has nothing to gain from confirming the facts.

Finally, evidence does not often come whole; it frequently comes in fragments. The evidence for a claim may require several different facts. When it does, you can use the third yardstick for appraising the worth of the evidence: consistency—the requirement that the different parts or the different facts of the evidence jibe or fit in with one another. Consistency is embodied in some old rules, for example, that "the whole must equal the sum of its parts," otherwise something is inconsistent. Or the "transitivity" rule, which says if A is greater than B and B is greater than C, then A should be greater than C, otherwise something is inconsistent. Or the "double negation" rule in logic, which says if not-A is not the case, then A is the case, otherwise, something is inconsistent. As you can see, applying the yardstick of consistency to the evidence may require some logic, and perhaps some mathematics.

If the "evidence" is not factual and is nothing more than the opinion of others (that is, testimonials), then the reliability and competence of the source is of paramount concern. We add "competence" to the requirements because the opinion is only as good as the source's competence as a critical thinker, no matter how reliable the source.

Up to this point, critical thinking as applying the three questions might be considered to be basic critical thinking. You can apply the three questions to just about any claim in everyday life. If you answer the three questions adequately, you usually can reach a satisfactory decision about the claim. However, specialists (scientists, etc.) in critical thinking have added three more questions that, so to speak, raise the quality of critical thinking to a higher level.

Can the evidence support a different claim?

If you have pinned down the claim being made, established what evidence is offered to back it up, and ascertained that the evidence is good, you probably would think, "That's good enough for me," and accept the claim. But scientists (and philosophers before them) have learned from hard experience that that may not be the end of the story. In science, sometimes the same set of facts supports opposite claims. This was the case when Copernicus first proposed that it was the earth that revolved around the sun and not vice versa. The facts known at the time supported either theory. So scientists have learned to ask if the facts advanced to support a particular theory may not also support another, perhaps opposite, theory. If they do, then the scientists have to design the "crucial experiment" that can support only one theory, not the other.

You may not yet have the knowledge and experience of scientists, but you can apply the fourth question in your critical thinking just as the scientists do. The arena of political claims is a good place to practice applying the fourth question (remember, you have to suspend judgement first). Write down the claims of one party (perhaps start with one claim), then the evidence advanced to support the claim. Then check to see if the evidence is acceptable. Now look at the claim of the other party (if the two parties disagree). Does the first party's evidence support the second party's claim? (See Fig. 5-8.) If it does, you will have to go to the fifth question. (You can expand your practice in critical thinking to include opposing claims in current social issues, besides the political.)

Is there evidence that disproves the claim?

If the evidence can support a different claim, you are in the same position as the scientists who have to design a "crucial experiment" or as a police detective who has unearthed clues that point equally to two suspects. You have to figure out what evidence can disprove the original claim.

This part of critical thinking is very much like creative problem solving. It requires creative thinking, about which you have already read. Aside from "persevere," there are really no good rules to offer on how to think creatively, because each person's creativity is unique to that person.

Looking for evidence that might disprove the original claim is like letting the defense have its day in court. It is said that there are always two sides to a question. Looking at both sides will bring you closer to the truth. Looking for disproving evidence will enable you to think more critically about the claim—which leads to the final question.

Fig. 5-8

Candidates for President often make opposing political claims. Practice applying the fourth question in critical thinking using current political claims.

Which Evidence is Stronger, the Evidence for the Claim or the Evidence against the Claim?

This is the last step before you decide for or against the claim. In science, the decision is usually tentative, and the search goes on for new evidence. Eventually, the weight of the evidence is overwhelmingly for one theory or another, and the losing theory is abandoned for good. In real life, decisions on some claims may be final (for example, critical thinking about claims concerning a particular car model will end when you buy the car—or buy a different one). However, decisions about other claims may have to be tentative, and, like the scientists, you may have to keep looking for more evidence, or at least leave yourself open to receiving other evidence.

To sum up: critical thinking is a particular way of thinking about claims. It can be described by six questions:

1. What is the claim being made? If you can answer this question, then you go on to

2. What evidence has been offered to support the claim? If there is no evidence, disregard the claim. If there is evidence, then you go on to

3. How good is the evidence? If the evidence is no good, disregard the claim. If the evidence is good, then you go on to

4. Can the evidence support a different claim? If it does not, then accept the claim. If the evidence supports a different claim, then you go on to

5. Is there evidence that disproves the claim? If there is, then you can disregard the claim. If not, then you can ask the same question about the other claim. If there is evidence that disproves the other claim, you can accept the original claim. If there is no evidence that disproves either claim, you need a tie-breaker, which is the final question

6. Which is stronger, the evidence for the claim or the evidence against the claim, the evidence favoring the claim or the evidence not favoring it?

Critical Thinking and Values

Critical thinking is simply learning to "think for yourself." During childhood, you learned to accept your parents' word. If they said something was "good," you usually took their word for it. In school, as you were growing up, you usually took the word of your teachers or others whom you respected (those we call "role models"). In effect, you trusted your role models to do your thinking for you. But as you grew older, you did not always have your role models around to ask or listen to. Sometimes, you were no longer fully satisfied with their judgments or their reasoning. More and more, you needed to—and you began to want to—"think on your own."

As you began to think on your own, you probably started by consciously or unconsciously imitating your role models. Without your intending to, you had learned the grounds on which you could evaluate claims and assertions (more accurately, you learned your role models' grounds). These grounds are called **criteria** (singular, **criterion**). Criteria are the standards on which you base your evaluation of claims and assertions.

criteria
standards on which a judgment or decision may be based

Usually, different criteria are used for different situations. Regardless of the situation, the criteria reflect what you consider to be important to you, what we call your **values**. Your criteria reflect your values and your values show up in the criteria you choose. We will discuss values in more detail in Chapter 10.

values
a sense of what is important.

SUMMARY

1. No one has yet adequately described or defined just exactly what it is that people do when they "think." The terms used to talk about this process—think, dream, plan, create, reason, and so on—are imprecise and open to broad interpretation.

2. The act of thinking involves changing, combining, and otherwise manipulating information received through your senses and stored in your memory. Psychologists refer to the act of thinking as cognition, which comes from a Latin word meaning to get to know.

3. Experiments suggest you think first in terms of physical identity, second in terms of the "name" of the object, and third in terms of its broader classification. Your ability to abstract is a key part of your thinking.

4. To handle all the sensory data coming to it, your brain has developed some useful shortcuts of organization and manipulation. In addition to abstractions, your brain puts together many different pieces of information to create mental structures that are known as schemata.

5. People think in concepts, which are high-level abstractions for thoughts that have no physical existence, such as honor, charity, friendship. Concepts are similar to schemata in that they are based on several different bits of information.

6. Language reflects the thought process and influences it as well.

7. The basic units of sound made when speaking are known as phonemes, which are the smallest elemental sounds that can be distinctly recognized. The a, b, and d sounds are examples of phonemes. By themselves, phonemes have no meaning. The smallest units of sound that have meaning are known as morphemes.

8. Words have not only meanings of their own but meanings determined by their place in a sentence, by other words used with them, by the manner in which they are said, and by the environment or situation in which they are used.

9. Scientists have been able to identify various stages in a child's development of language, but they still disagree about exactly how we acquire the ability to use language. Observations show a rather consistent progression from meaningless sounds to words at about one year of age, then to putting two

words together to make meaningful sentences at about two years. After that, children begin combining more words to make sentences.

10. Three theories about how people learn language are the imitation (social learning) theory, the reinforcement theory, and the innate ability theory.

11. Writing began first as word writing. Pictures were drawn, then the pictures were used to represent the sounds of the item, and eventually an alphabet evolved with the letters representing various sounds of speech.

12. There are two basic kinds of reasoning or logic that people normally carry out, often without much conscious thought: inductive and deductive.

13. There is considerable discussion over exactly what intelligence is. In addition to the kinds of intelligence measured by most tests—linguistic and logical-mathematical—Howard Gardner, a research psychologist, has identified five other kinds: spatial, musical, motor, interpersonal, and intrapersonal.

14. Your thinking occurs in one of two broad patterns: organized and deliberate to achieve a desired goal, or unorganized and free-flowing, as when you are daydreaming. Organized thinking occurs in reaction to internal or external situations. Something happens and you are motivated to think along a certain line to solve a problem or make a decision.

15. To solve a problem you go through three steps: interpreting, generating solutions, and picking the best solution. The first step is most important because if you do not identify the problem correctly, you cannot come up with good solutions.

16. Creative thinking involves divergent thinking. That is, the creative thinker uses new ways of looking at data (a problem) and coming up with different solutions. Most people, even very intelligent ones, use convergent thinking, which means they accept the data (statement of problem) as is and move toward one "correct" solution.

17. Creative conclusions or solutions often come after a period of incubation. This is a period of rest, perhaps even sleep or day dreaming, when the answer to a problem you have been struggling with will suddenly come into your mind.

18. Critical thinking is thinking about and evaluating claims. Critical thinking requires answers to these questions: What is the claim being made? What evidence has been offered to support this claim? How good is the evidence? Can the evidence support a different claim? Is there evidence that

disproves the claim? Which evidence is stronger, the evidence for the claim or the evidence against the claim?

19. _____ Your critical thinking shows the standards, or criteria, on which you base your evaluations. These criteria, in turn, reflect your values.

KEY TERMS
Define the following terms:

Abstraction
Alphabet writing
Cognition
Cognitive dissonance
  reduction
Concepts
Convergent thinking
Criteria
Deductive logic
Divergent thinking
Imitation theory
Incubation period
Inductive logic
Innate ability theory
Language acquisition
  device
Morphemes
Phonemes
Psycholinguists
Reinforcement theory
Schemata
Syllable writing
Syllogism
Values
Word writing

QUESTIONS FOR REVIEW AND DISCUSSION

1. _____ Explain why time is important to scientists who study the thinking process.
2. _____ Identify two mental shortcuts people use. Describe their advantages and dangers.
3. _____ What three clues do people rely on when using language? Explain them.
4. _____ Define and give an example of inductive and deductive logic.
5. _____ What are the seven areas of intelligence according to the research psychologist Howard Gardner?
6. _____ In what ways do creative and normal thinkers differ?
7. _____ What is meant by "incubation" in creative thinking?

ACTIVITIES

1. _____ The way language is used and developed indicates a lot about the thinking process. For an idea of the complexity and richness of this thought, consider how many different meanings some simple words can take through use and analogy. Take the word tap, for example. How many different meanings can you think of for it? Make a list of them and of some other simple words with many meanings. Try to trace the development and relationship of the different meanings.
2. _____ Consider some forthcoming decision that you must make, such as what to do on your next vacation or this coming summer, or on a major purchase, and so on. Following the steps in the problem-solving process, write out your interpretation or definition of the problem, including all the facts. Then see how many different alternatives you can generate. Evaluate the alternatives, pick the one you think is best, and write why you think so.
3. _____ Construct five syllogisms illustrating deductive reasoning or logic from facts in your own life. These should consist of a major premise, a minor premise, and a conclusion. Be careful of faulty major premises, such as in this syllogism: People who get up early

are wise. I get up early. I am wise. Or: Teams that win the first game of the month end as winners. Our team won the first game of the month. Our team will end as a winner.

4. Many exciting experiments are being conducted on cognition, the way people think, how their thinking patterns affect them. Visit your school library or public library, and look for magazines, such as Science or *Psychology Today*, that carry reports of such experiments. Find one that interests you, and summarize the findings in a report of no more than two pages.

5. Will incubation work for you? Try it. Consider some problem (look in a puzzle book of logic from the library if necessary). Follow the stages of creative thinking as far as you can: Think very hard for a time about the problem and try to solve it. After a reasonable time, put it away and out of your mind. Go on to other activities. Note whether, at some time during the next few days, a solution occurs to you.

6. Think about some mental structures or schemata that you have that help you perform tasks without much conscious effort. (Riding a bike is one example.) Try describing the details of them. Consider whether you could perform more effectively if you consciously thought of the details involved all the time. Identify potential dangers of relying completely on schemata.

7. Take an issue on which you haven't yet formed an opinion. Use it to practice your critical thinking skills. Go through each of the steps (the 6 questions) as systematically as you can. But don't spend too much time on any one question or on the whole process. Set reasonable time limits for each question and for the process. After you are done, evaluate the exercise and see if it has helped you improve your critical thinking ability.

CASE 1

Logic, Intelligence, Creativity

In a faraway land long ago there was once a wise and good village chief who had a most exciting announcement. "Of utmost importance," he reminded his villagers, "is the ability to travel to the port to trade our jewelry for food. Until recently those traveling to the port simply left our village and wandered aimlessly until they either found the port or died. I am happy to announce that thanks to the efforts of our most wise and scientific medicine man we have captured the essence of travel. We have discovered that all travel is based upon footprints. Follow footprints precisely and you will never get lost going to or from the port again.

"But what about trees?" asked one villager.

"Trees are not footprints, and thus should be ignored," replied the chief.

"May we consider the stars?" questioned another.

"Don't be foolish," commanded the chief "What could be farther from footprints than stars? Have I not told you already? There is no travel without footprints. Footprints are the essence of all travel. Understand footprints and the concept of travel is yours forever. You will never be lost again."

That was many years ago. And since that time many villagers have come and gone from the port never taking their eyes off the footprints. Some of the more scholarly villagers over the years have studied and refined footprintology, writing long, scholarly discourses on the many things footprints show and of the many truths to be found through careful scrutiny of footprints.

Over the years the methods of observing footprints have been refined to such an exact science that many years of studying with rigorous examinations are required to truly practice and teach footprintology. In fact, before each young man is able to leave the village he must be thoroughly educated in footprintology as the essence of travel, lest someday he look up at the trees or stars and lose sight of that essence that the wisest of wise know as travel.

1. Discuss this story in terms of what it shows about intelligence, logic, and creativity.

From Dan S. Bagley III, "Footprints: A Parable About Knowledge," *Journal of Creative Behavior* 13, no. 4 (1979).

CASE 2

Solving a Problem

"I'm going to flip a coin!" Maxine said impatiently. "I just can't decide which career I want."

"That's no way to decide on your career," her friend Lorraine said. "Especially now, after all the exploring we have done to find out what our interests and aptitudes are."

"That's part of the trouble," Maxine said. "I spent all that time doing that, and now I'm confused. All my life I was sure of what I wanted to do. I love the outdoors, so I have planned to be a forester, or a conservationist, something like that."

"So what changed?" Lorraine prodded.

"Well, I found that my interests and abilities suited me for being a forester and working outdoors, but the program also indicated that I would be good working with people, maybe teaching. So I worked as a tutor for primary grade kids, and I loved it!" Maxine almost wailed. "And I was good at it."

"Lucky you found out in time," Lorraine said. "Now you can be a teacher."

"No," Maxine snapped. "You don't understand. Now I want to do both things. So I'm going to toss a coin and let that decide."

"Well, I think you had better talk to our counselor first. It seems to me that there is a better way to resolve this," Lorraine said.

"I don't know," Maxine said. "The best I can think of is to be a teacher and then get a job working outside during the summer vacation."

"That sounds like one possible solution to your problem," Lorraine said. "There may be other things, too, that you could do to combine your interests better."

Maxine said, "I wish life were simpler. Maybe it was better back when people just did what their parents did."

"I doubt it," Lorraine laughed. "It's more complicated for us because we have more choices today. But if we get it all together, I bet we will have more satisfying and rewarding lives. We just have to know how to make the right decisions."

1. What step or steps in the problem-solving process is Maxine skipping over?

2. What other alternatives can you think of for her?

6

ABILITIES:
How Our Human
Potential Is Organized

"Like all in some respects; like some in many respects; like none in all respects."

Psychology is the science that studies what humans are capable of doing. This is probably the most important contribution of psychology to society. The first psychology-scientists (like Wilhelm Wundt, Hermann Ebbinghaus, and Francis Galton) studied such human capabilities as speed of reacting (reaction time), discriminating, judging, estimating, remembering, imagining, and learning. They studied visual, auditory, and tactile perception, visual and auditory memory, concept formation, forgetting, even susceptibility to illusions. They studied human capabilities by using instruments and procedures that eventually became what today we call ability tests. We will learn more about ability tests later.

▼ INDIVIDUAL DIFFERENCES

The early psychologists concentrated on learning as much as they could about human capability (ability, for short). They discovered three important facts about human abilities:

✳ 1. **Interindividual differences:** When a large number of persons are tested for the same ability, there is quite a difference between the best and the worst (which difference they called a "range"). For most abilities, the largest number of persons score in the middle of the range and successively fewer persons score higher or lower than midrange. If we diagram the numbers of persons at each ability

Fig. 6-1

Diagram of frequency distribution.

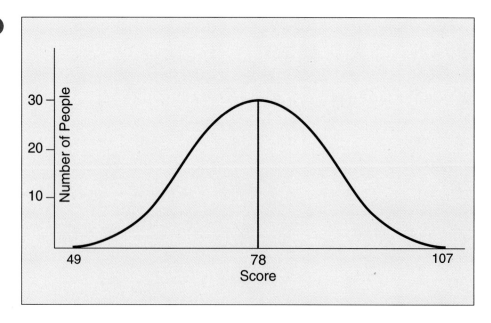

level, we get a picture that (for most abilities) looks like a symmetrical mountain or, as it is most often described, like a bell, as in Fig. 6-1. This figure is a diagram of a **frequency distribution** (how many people scoring each score).

frequency distribution
a graph that shows how many people have the same score

✳ 2. **Intraindividual differences:** When we take one person and look at that person's standing or rank in the frequency distributions for different abilities, we find that one does not always have the same standing on all abilities and may rank high on some abilities, average on others, or low on still others. We can show how one person differs in ability level over many different abilities by means of a graph known as a **test profile** (or ability profile), as illustrated in Fig. 6-2.

test profile
a graph that shows a person's relative standing on different abilities

✳ 3. **Correlation:** When we take a group of people and order them according to their standing (rank) on one ability, their "rank order" may or may not be similar to their rank order on a second ability. When rank orders are similar, psychologists call the two abilities **correlated**, and when they are not, the two abilities are said to be **uncorrelated**. Mathematicians describe the amount of correlation more exactly with what is called a **correlation coefficient**. The coefficient, symbolized by r, is given in decimal form and goes from +1.00, for perfect positive correlation, down to 0.00, which is no correlation, and through negative decimals to -1.00, which is perfect negative correlation. Positive correlation (positive decimals) occur

correlated
ranking people (or observations) in a similar way

correlation coefficient
a number that indicates the degree of correlation between two variables

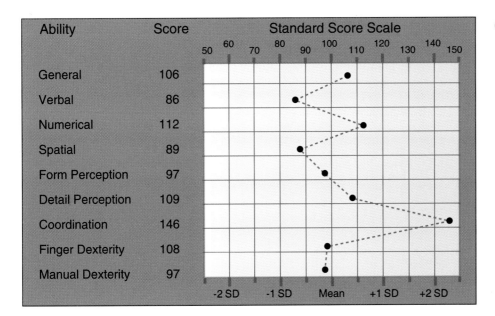

Ability	Score
General	106
Verbal	86
Numerical	112
Spatial	89
Form Perception	97
Detail Perception	109
Coordination	146
Finger Dexterity	108
Manual Dexterity	97

Fig. 6-2

Ability profile showing a person's relative standing on different abilities. The average (mean) score for the gneral population is 100 and the standard deviation (see Figure 6-1) is 20.

when the rank orders are similar in direction, and negative correlation (negative decimals) occurs when they are opposite. The decimals give the degree or amount of correlation regardless of whether it is positive or negative; the closer to +1.00 or -1.00, the higher the correlation, and the closer to .00, the lower the correlation.

These three findings stem from a basic reality that underlies all of human ability, the phenomenon psychologists call individual differences.

Fig. 6-3

Although identical twins have similar looks, they are not identical in all of their abilities

People are bound to differ on any given ability, and the same person is bound to be different in ability level for different kinds of ability. Individual differences show that, although you are "like all" in having human abilities, and "like some" in how good or poor you are in certain abilities, you are "like none" in the profile of all your abilities. Even identical twins are never 100 percent alike in all of their abilities (Fig. 6-3).

Descriptive Statistics

Not only did psychologists discover that individual differences were often distributed in a bell shape, they discovered that the bell shape could be described mathematically. The shape was what mathematicians called a **normal curve**. To draw the curve requires two bits of information: the average or midpoint value, called the **mean**, and a measure of how wide the range is, called the **standard deviation**. Interestingly, the means and standard deviations of two abilities are used to calculate the coefficient, *r*, of the correlation between them. With these discoveries, psychologists started to use mathematics—especially statistics—to describe and analyze their data. Today, you have to know some statistics in order to understand the reports that psychologists write of their research.

normal curve
a bell-shaped curve having known mathematical properties

mean
occupying a position about midway between extremes

standard deviation
a measure of the dispersion of a frequency distribution

▼ ABILITY TESTS

To study abilities more intensively, psychologists "invented" the **ability test**. Actually, the invention of the ability test did not happen all at once, but rather it developed gradually to its present form. It started with instruments used in the laboratory, such as the reaction time chronometer (timing instrument). For many abilities, all that was needed to construct a test were instructions on what to do (such as: add or subtract numbers, solve arithmetic problems, give the meaning of words), paper and pencil, and a stop watch with which to time the person being tested. This made it possible for psychologists to go out of the laboratory and into the "field" (classroom, workplace, etc.) to measure many human abilities. They learned that they had to use standard operating procedures so that they could compare results for different testings. You can see how this eventually led to the modern-day ability test.

As you read in Chapter 1, people have complained about ability tests, especially intelligence tests. One reason for this might be that ability tests, like medical tests, can be "bearers of bad news." With medical tests, the bad news refers to your physical health. With ability tests, the bad news refers, among other things, to your self-image—how capable you see yourself as being—so that it can have unwanted repercussions on your self-esteem,

ability test
an instrument and a set of standard procedures designed to measure a particular ability

your self-confidence, your aspirations and ambitions. Critics have called ability tests biased, favoring one gender over another, one ethnic group over another, one social class over another. More severe critics have called ability tests useless, incapable of doing the job of measuring abilities. Other critics have questioned not so much what ability tests are as how they are used, that they are used to discriminate against certain groups. Let us explore those two questions more carefully: what an ability test is, and how it is used.

Basic Structure of an Ability Test

An ability test is an instrument and a set of standard procedures designed to measure a particular ability. The instrument itself is typically printed material ("paper-and-pencil tests") or apparatus ("performance tests," such as a pegboard). In the past few years, more and more test instruments have been "computerized," programmed for the computer to administer. The set of standard procedures includes instructions to the test administrator on how precisely to give the test, how much time to give, whether the test taker should be seated or standing, etc., and instructions to the test taker on how to take the test (what exactly is one being asked to do).

test items
problems that measure particular abilities

The instrument is basically a set of problems (called **test items**) for the test taker to solve. The type of problem identifies what particular ability is being measured. For example, verbal ability might be measured with items that ask you to pick out words with the same meaning (synonyms) or words that fit the given definitions. Or the items might ask you to locate typographical errors, and these would measure clerical ability. Some tests (such as intelligence or general mental ability tests) have a mix of items because the idea is to sample a wide variety of problems for the test taker to solve. More and more, however, the practice has been to limit one test to one type of item (hence, one ability), and if you want to measure "intelligence" or "general mental ability," to give several tests together (called a **test battery**) so as to get the variety of problems desired (Fig. 6-4).

test battery
a group of tests given to the same individual

The test instrument is useless, of course, without the set of instructions that tell you what to do. The "test" (instrument plus instructions) is designed to get you to perform in a particular way. Your performance is then evaluated in a way that produces a **test score**.

Tests are scored in a number of ways. The most common way is by counting the total number of items you get right. A variation of this is to count the number of problems solved in a set time period; for example, how many addition or subtraction problems can you solve in two minutes? Yet another method is to find out how long it takes you to do a particular task, such as reassembling a disassembled piece of apparatus. With computerized

Fig. 6-4

SAT tests measure general mental ability.

tests, it is possible to get two or more scores at the same time, such as how many problems you solve and how much time you take to solve each problem. Whatever scoring method is used, the important thing is that the score produced is objective; that is, the score does not depend on the subjective judgment of some human scorer. Most ability tests are scored objectively and even automatically, but some abilities (such as creative abilities) are so complex that tests for them cannot be scored objectively with the available methods. For such tests, psychologists have developed judgment or estimation methods of scoring that come close to being as objective as the usual scoring methods.

objective
verifiable

How can you tell how good a test is? Psychologists use two yardsticks: reliability and validity.

Test Reliability

"Reliability" means you can rely on something, and a test is reliable when you can depend on the score you get as being correct. Speaking technically, a test is reliable when its error in measuring is small; the smaller the error, the more reliable the test. Test reliability is about the amount of error that is always present during any kind of measurement. The amount of error can be expressed as a plus-or-minus factor attached to the score (for example, your score is 89 plus-or-minus 3). This is similar to the error factor we attach to other measurements (for example, your weight on your bathroom scale, plus-or-minus 1 pound). The idea is that you really do not know what the "true score" is; you only have an "observed score," which may be off a wee bit in either direction.

reliability coefficient
index of the ability of a test to yield the same score each time it is given to the same person

Although a plus-or-minus error factor is easy enough to understand, test reliability is not typically given in terms of such a factor because the practice among psychologists has been to use a **reliability coefficient**. A reliability coefficient is a two-place decimal between .00 and 1.00; .00 means the test is completely unreliable and 1.00 means the test is perfectly reliable (which no test is). Typical reliability coefficients are in the .80s for good tests, in the .90s for the best tests, and in the .70s for the minimally adequate tests. Persons trained in psychometrics (see Chapter 1) can easily convert a reliability coefficient to a plus-or-minus factor.

How do you find out how much error there is in a test? There are three common methods for evaluating test reliability:

1. **Retest method:** You give the test to a (preferably large) group of people and then, after a wait of usually two weeks, you give the test again to the same people;

2. **Alternate-forms method:** You give the test to the group along with another test (called an alternate form) that was designed to be equivalent to the first test; and

3. **Split-half method:** You give the test to the group, but before scoring it, you first divide the test into two halves (usually odd-numbered items versus even-numbered items) and compute scores for each half. For all three methods, you compute the correlation between the two sets of scores obtained by the same group of people, and the correlation coefficient that results is the reliability coefficient. There are several other, more technically advanced, methods of evaluating test reliability, but these three basic methods are still much in use.

Test Validity

valid
when a test measures what it is supposed to measure

content validity
when the content of a test appears to measure what it is supposed to measure

convergent validity
when a test correlates with other tests that measure the same thing

A test is **valid** when it measures what the test is supposed to measure. Evaluating test validity is more difficult than evaluating test reliability. More evidence is needed for validity because much of validity evidence is indirect. To evaluate a test's validity, you can begin by examining the test items to see if they appear to be tapping the ability that the test is supposed to measure. This is called **content validity**. Some jokingly call it "face validity" because, like a face, it can be deceiving. Content validity may not be convincing evidence of validity, but it is necessary because otherwise, people—especially those taking the test—may lose confidence in the test.

Next you might look at how the test correlates with other tests that are supposed to measure the same ability. This is known as **convergent validity**. If the correlation is not high, then one of the tests, or both, is not measuring the ability.

Then you might look at how the test correlates with other tests that are supposed to measure other abilities. This is known as **discriminant validity**. This time, the correlation should not be high because if it is, the two tests are measuring the same thing and not two separate abilities. Again, this means that one or both tests may not be valid.

discriminant validity
when a test does <u>not</u> correlate with other tests that measure different things

Convergent and discriminant validity are parts of a more general type of validity known as **construct validity**. Evaluating construct validity requires some theory about the ability being measured (which is technically called a **construct**). The theory is supposed to tell the test developer what the test should be correlated with and what it should not be correlated with. Then it becomes a simple matter of checking things out: the test should correlate when theory says it should correlate, and should not correlate when theory says it should not correlate. The more you find this, the more the evidence of construct validity. As you can see, evaluating construct validity can go on and on, and you stop only when you finally are confident that the test is valid.

construct validity
when a test's pattern of correlations with other tests and other variables is consistent with theory

To be valid, a test must first be reliable, but a test can be reliable and not valid at the same time. This is why both criteria have to be used when examining how good an ability test is.

▼ USES OF ABILITY TESTS

Like all other instruments for measurement in science, the ability test's first use is for description. As you will read later, ability tests are used to describe human potential. Beyond description, ability tests are used for two basic purposes: **selection** and **placement**.

In selection, you give one or more ability tests to a group of people (applicants) and then use the test scores to select whom you want among the group. Examples include selecting for admission to a college, for scholarships, for employment positions, for members of a team. Usually, the highest scoring persons are the ones selected, but not always. For example, we know that high scorers on a test of spatial ability make poor salespersons, so that in this case, high scores can be used to select out and not in.

selection
a process that results in the choice of some individuals but not of others

In placement, you give one or more (usually more) ability tests to a person (client) and then use the test scores to find out what "place" is best for the person. Examples of "places" would be college majors, career fields, occupations, jobs, retirement activities. This, of course, is what counseling is all about. High school counselors, college academic counselors, vocational counselors, career counselors, employee counselors in industry, employment service counselors, retirement counselors—all of them have the same goal of "placing" the person in the most suitable place or "environment".

placement
the assignment of a person to a suitable place (as a job or a class in school)

Misuse of tests

Ability tests are, by intention, designed to discriminate among people. What good is a test where everyone gets the same score? No better than a thermometer that gives the same reading regardless of time of day, weather conditions, or season of the year. But because ability tests are designed to discriminate, they are open to abuse and exploitation by unethical individuals. Tests can be constructed to be biased against certain groups. One protection against this possibility is to demand full disclosure of the details of test construction in the test manuals. This is now required by the ethical standards set for psychologists.

validate
to test for effectiveness for a particular use

Even with properly constructed ability tests, there is room for misuse. Proper use requires that tests should be **validated** for any particular use, in much the same way that the government requires medical drugs to be tested for effectiveness before they are placed on the market. Even well-constructed ability tests are misused when they are used in situations or for purposes for which the tests have not been validated.

criterion-related validity
the validity of tests for particular uses

The validity of ability tests for particular uses is known technically as **criterion-related validity**. The criterion is something that represents the use for which the test is valid. For example, one criterion for college scholarships is grades; another might be performance on tests, such as the board exams for physicians or the bar exams for lawyers. If an ability test is to be used in selecting persons for scholarships, then the test must be shown to correlate with a criterion, such as grades in college. Only when the test has been shown to correlate with college grades (or another criterion) can it be valid for use in selection for scholarships. (When a test correlates with a criterion, we say that the test "predicts" the criterion.) Another example: one criterion for job performance is supervisors' ratings. To be valid for use in selection for a job, the test must predict supervisors' ratings of workers on that type of job. In both examples, as in all criterion-related validation, the higher the correlation the more valid the test. Also, you can see that a test may be valid for one criterion but not for another, and one test may be more valid than another test for the same criterion. The psychologists' ethical standards require that any use that is claimed for a test should be backed by evidence of criterion-related validity for that use, and that tests should not be used for unvalidated purposes.

▼ DESCRIBING HUMAN POTENTIAL

skill
capability to perform a given task or tasks

Before we can describe potential, we have first to establish the actual. What is your actual capability? A straightforward answer would be to list everything you can do—all of your **skills**. Skills are the basic units of human capability, because any behavior, or behavioral performance, can be described as the collective and coordinated functioning of skills.

A skill may be defined as an identifiable, repeatable response sequence in response to some task demand. "Identifiable" means you can tell one skill from another. And if you can't repeat it, it isn't a skill. "Response sequence" means a skill is more than just a twitch of the muscle, but more like a coordinated series of movements. By this definition, an eye blink is not a skill, but if you can blink in Morse code, then you have a skill. A "task" is something to be done—produce a product, produce a result, perform a service, or perform in a prescribed manner. Who demands the task? Others, of course (home, school, work, etc.), but also yourself. In fact, many tasks are self-imposed. When you do a task, you show a skill. If you can't do the task, you show lack of skill, or if you do the task poorly, you show a low level of skill. There is a bit of circularity in definition here—you need a task to define a skill and you need a skill to do a task.

Humans have a variety of skills. *Motor* skills are most familiar. We usually associate the word *skill* with motor behaviors like riding a bike or shooting a basketball or playing a piano. But we also have *perceptual* skills, such as seeing detail, recognizing faces, identifying forms and shapes. Furthermore, we have *cognitive* skills, such as imagining and remembering and reasoning. And finally, we have *emotional* skills, such as being able to control our feelings of anger or fear or even love, or being able to express them on call like actresses and actors do. But skills are not just motor *or* perceptual *or* cognitive *or* emotional. In fact, *all* skills have motor, perceptual, cognitive, and emotional components. We just name them according to the component that is most responsible for differences among people (that produces the most individual differences).

There are thousands of human skills. If a task defines a skill, every time a task is invented, a new skill is also in the making. When computers were invented, one of the tasks was to program the computer, thus creating the new skill of computer programming. This possibility—that new skills are being "invented" all the time—can make listing all the skills of one person, not to mention listing all existing human skills, an endless task. Another problem with the idea of listing skills (besides their huge and growing number) is that skills can be combined to form more complex skills, and vice versa, skills can be broken down into simpler skills. For example, typing skill can be combined with proofreading skill, filing skill, skill in running various office machines, among others, to make up secretarial skill or office-work skill. In turn, typing skill can be broken down into finger dexterity, eye-hand coordination, word knowledge, detail perception, and other more elemental skills. If you try to list skills without some system for classifying them that takes the skill-combining possibilities into account,

you will wind up with much duplication and overlap. You can see why listing skills may not be practical as a way to describe actual human capability.

Using Ability Tests to Describe Skills

Many psychologists, especially those in counseling and industrial/organizational psychology, have preferred to use a different method of describing human capability. This method makes use of ability tests. Ability tests can be used to estimate (using correlation) your *standing* (or *level*) on a skill (how skillful you are compared with others), in much the same way that ability tests are used to predict a criterion in criterion-related validity. Most of the time, one's skill level on a particular skill can be estimated by using three to five different ability tests. For example, University of Minnesota researchers found that mechanical skill level can be estimated by using four ability tests: a spatial relations test, a manual dexterity test, a form perception test, and a mechanical information knowledge test. Each of these ability tests could be used with other tests to estimate standing on other skills. For example, the spatial relations test can be used to help estimate carpentry skill level.

In this way, standing on any skill can, in principle, be described by a small number of ability tests. This was what the U.S. Employment Service (USES) found out: with 12 tests measuring nine abilities, they found they could estimate the job proficiency of workers in each of about 500 different occupations. For each occupation, they found one to four ability tests, as well as the minimum score for each ability, required to estimate satisfactory job proficiency. (In our terms, an "occupation" could be considered to be one large complex skill composed of many less complex skills, so that we can speak of engineering skill, carpentry skill, secretarial skill, managing skill, janitoring skill, or lawyering skill.)

Using Ability Tests to Assess Potential

How, then, do we describe human potential? The USES's work shows us how we might be able to do it with ability tests. We know that if you are proficient in a given occupation, you have the skills required to do the job, and you also have the minimum levels of ability or abilities measured by the USES tests for that occupation. The question is, is the opposite true? If you have the minimum levels of ability on the USES tests used to estimate job proficiency in an occupation, would that mean you also have the required skills? No, not necessarily; not unless you had been trained for the occupation. In other words, if you have the skills, we know you have the abilities (as measured by the tests), but if you have the abilities, we do not know if you have the skills.

TABLE 6-1

GATB ABILITY TESTS AND SCORES

Occupational Group	Required Minimum GATB Test[1] Scores			
Artistic Occupations				
1. Literary Arts	G100	V100	Q100	
2. Visual Arts	G100	S100	P85	
3. Performing Arts: Drama	G100	V100		
4. Performing Arts: Music	G110	V100	Q100	
5. Performing Arts: Dance	G100	S95		
6. Craft Arts	S90	P85	M85	
Scientific Occupations				
7. Physical Sciences	G115	V105	N110	S110
8. Life Sciences	G115	V105	N110	S110
9. Medical Sciences	G115	V105	N110	S110
10. Laboratory Technology	G105	N100		
Plant and Animal Occupations				
11. Managerial Work: Plants and Animals	G100	N90		
12. Animal Training and Service I	G95	M85		
13. Animal Training and Service II	K85	M85		
14. Elemental Work: Plants and Animals	K85	M80		
Protective Occupations				
15. Safety and Law Enforcement	G100	Q95		
16. Security Services	G95			
Mechanical Occupations				
17. Engineering	G115	N105	S110	
18. Mangerial Work: Mechanical	G105	V100	N100	S95
19. Engineering Technology	G105	N100	S100	
20. Air and Water Vehicle Operation	G105	N100	S100	
21. Craft Technology	S90	P85	M85	
22. Quality Control I	N90	S90	P85	
23. Land and Motor Vehicle Operation	S85	P80	M85	
24. Materials Control I	G95	N85	Q90	
25. Materials Control II	Q85	K85		
26. Crafts I	S85	P80	M85	
27. Crafts II	P80	K85	M85	
28. Equipment Operation	S85	P80	M85	
29. Elemental Work: Mechanical	K85	M80		

GATB ABILITY TESTS AND SCORES

Occupational Group	Required Minimum GATB Test[1] Score			
Industrial Occupations				
30. Production Technology I	N85	S90	P85	
31. Production Technology II	S85	P85	M85	
32. Production Work	P80	K85	M85	
33. Quality Control II	P80	K85	M85	
34. Elemental Work: Industrial	K85	F80	M80	
Business Detail Occupations				
35. Administrative Detail	G100	N95	Q100	
36. Mathematical Detail	G95	N90	Q100	
37. Financial Detail	G95	N90	Q100	
38. Oral Communications	G95	Q95		
39. Records Processing	G95	Q95		
40. Clerical Machine Operation	G95	Q100	K95	
41. Clerical Handling	Q90	K85		
Selling Occupations				
42. Sales Technology	G100	V100	N95	Q100
43. General Sales	G95	N90	Q90	
44. Vending	K85	M80		
Personal Service Occupations				
45. Hospital Services	G95			
46. Barber and Beauty Services	S85	P85	K90	M85
47. Passenger Services	S85	M85		
48. Attendant Services	K85	M80		
Humanitarian Occupations				
49. Social Services	G105	V100	N110	Q95
50. Nursing, Therapy, Specialized Teaching Services	G105	V100		
51. Child and Adult Care	G95			
Specialized Professional Occupations				
52. Mathematics and Statistics	G115	V100	N110	S100
53. Educational and Library Services I	G100	V100	N95	Q100
54. Educational and Library Services II	G95	Q95		
55. Social Research I	G110	V100	N105	
56. Social Research II	G100	V100	N105	
57. Law I	G110	V100	N105	

TABLE 6-1, continued

GATB ABILITY TESTS AND SCORES

Occupational Group	Required Minimum GATB Test[1] Score			
58. Law II	G100	V100	N95	Q100
59. Business Administration	G105	V95	N100	Q100
60. Finance	G110	V95	N105	Q100
61. Services Administration	G105	V95	N100	Q100
62. Communications	G100	V100	N95	Q100
63. Promotion	G105	V95	N100	Q100
64. Regulations Enforcement	G105	N95	Q95	
65. Business Management	G100	V95	N95	Q100
66. Contracts and Claims	G100	V95	N95	Q100

[1] G = General Cognitive Ability, V = Verbal Ability, N = Numerical Ability, S = Spatial Ability, P = Form Perception Ability, Q = Detail Perception Ability, K = Eye-Hand Coordination, F = Finger Dexterity, M = Manual Dexterity. Scale has a mean of 100 and a standard deviation of 20. Adapted from Table 1, Manual of the USES General Aptitude Test Battery, Section II: Occupational Aptitude Pattern Structure. Washington, DC: U.S. Department of Labor, 1979.

But—and this is the important thing the USES (and other researchers) have found—if you had the required abilities (the required minimum levels on the required ability tests) and you were given the required training, you would be able to learn the skills required for the occupation. In other words, the scores on the ability tests could be used to predict whether or not you could be trained for an occupation. More than that, the ability test scores could be used to predict how well you would learn the occupation and how well you would do in the occupation. And this can be done for each of the 500 occupations studied by the USES without your having to try out each occupation. In other words, by using nine ability scores on the USES tests, we can estimate your potential for each of 500 occupations. This is how we can assess human potential. This is why the USES tests are called the **General Aptitude Test Battery** (or **GATB**). "Aptitude" is another word for "potential."

Aptitude

"Aptitude" means how likely it is that, given training and that you are motivated to learn, you will learn a given skill. This is your aptitude for that skill. How likely it is that you will learn a set of skills for a job or occupation is your job or occupational aptitude. How likely it is that, given training, you will learn the skills taught in school is your scholastic aptitude. How likely it is that, given training, you will learn the skill to play the piano (or other musical instrument) is your musical aptitude or, in this case, your aptitude for the piano. If your aptitude for the piano is high, you will likely learn to play the piano easily and quickly, or learn to play the piano very well. Conversely, if your aptitude is low, it likely will take you a longer time than usual to learn to play, or you will not learn to play the piano well at all.

Of course, until you have undergone the experience, nobody knows for sure whether with training you can learn quickly or slowly, whether you can learn well or poorly. But who has the means or the time to try out learning every skill to find out which ones can be learned quickly and learned well? We need some good way (which does not take so long or cost so much) to find out where our best chances are. And that is where ability tests can be used to good advantage. With the backing of research, ability tests can be used to identify your best aptitudes, or to check out how much aptitude you might have for a particular skill or set of skills (e.g., job, occupation) that you might be interested in.

As you read earlier, only a few ability tests are usually needed to estimate aptitude for occupations. Researchers have found that adding more tests (beyond four or five) does not improve estimation enough to warrant the extra tests. The USES, for example, uses from one to four abilities to estimate aptitude for each of about 500 occupations it has studied. Table 6-1 lists the minimum scores for GATB ability tests required to estimate aptitude for groups or occupations. This will give you an idea of what the "aptitude profile" for each occupational group looks like.

▼ THE VARIETY OF HUMAN ABILITIES

In the early days of ability testing, psychologists developed tests for every ability they wanted to measure. Soon there were so many ability tests that, among other problems, they began to duplicate and overlap one another. Some psychologists realized that test duplication, though a problem, was actually no different in principle from alternate-forms reliability (which you have read about). Studying the problem further, they discovered that what each item in a test measured could be divided into two parts: a part that the item measured in common with the other items, and a part that the item measured only by itself. They also discovered that the total score on a test reflected the common part measured by the items, and further, that the correlation between two tests represented an overlap in the common parts measured by the two tests' items. What's more, they found out that what applied to items also applied to tests, that is, that an ability test measured something in common with other ability tests (reflected in their correlations), and something unique that only the test measured by itself.

In time, the **psychometricians** developed a technique called **factor analysis** that allowed them to tease out the parts (which they called **factors**) and to understand what abilities the tests were actually measuring. We can summarize their research findings—borrowing in large part from John Carroll's comprehensive 1993 survey, entitled *Human Cognitive Abilities*—as follows:

Types of factors

Ability tests measure three kinds of "common factors" (the part measured in common with other tests):

1. **General ability factor:** Measured by all ability tests to some extent;

2. **Broad ability factors:** Measured by a combination of several tests; and

3. **Narrow ability factors:** Measured by a few tests of a particular type. As you recall, each test also measures a part that no other test measures, called a **specific** factor (specific to the test).

The General Ability Factor

The general ability factor, called **g**, consists of an overall ability to "apprehend experience" (be aware of what is happening) and to "deduce relations" (make connections, see and understand relationships of various kinds). This is the factor measured by most conventional intelligence tests. You recall that one characteristic of intelligence tests is that they are made up of tests of several different kinds of ability, most prominent of which are verbal ability, numerical ability, spatial ability, and reasoning ability.

Broad Ability Factors

Eight broad ability factors have been well identified. These are:

1. **Fluid intelligence:** A broad ability that involves basic cognitive processes and is thought to depend heavily on biological inheritance and biological development. You measure it by a combination of tests of inductive reasoning, visualization (or spatial visualization), deductive reasoning, numerical (or quantitative) reasoning, idea fluency, and spatial relations.

psychometric psychologist
a psychologist who studies testing

factor analysis
a statistical technique to find out the parts (factors) that tests measure in common

factor
what a test measures in common with other tests with which it is correlated

2. **Crystallized intelligence:** A broad ability that depends heavily on experience, learning or training, and cultural influences. You measure it by a combination of tests of verbal ability, language development, reading comprehension, general information, spelling, and numerical (or arithmetic) computation.

3. **Hybrid (or mixed):** A broad ability that is a mix of fluid and crystallized intelligence. You measure it by a combination of verbal, spatial, numerical, and reasoning ability tests. This is the factor measured by most tests of scholastic aptitude. It looks like g, but is not a general factor in that it is not measured by all ability tests.

4. **Visual perception:** A broad ability that you measure by a combination of tests of visualization, spatial relations, and perceptual speed.

5. **General memory**: A broad ability measured by a combination of associative memory, memory span, meaningful memory, and other memory tests.

6. **Memory retrieval:** A broad ability to readily recall concepts, ideas, names, etc. from long-term memory. You measure this broad ability by a combination of idea fluency, originality or creativity, expressive fluency (fluency of expression), associational fluency, figural fluency, and other fluency tests.

7. **Speediness:** A broad speed ability that you measure by a combination of speed tests such as tests of perceptual speed, numerical computation, reaction time, writing speed, and speed of test performance.

8. **Auditory perception:** A broad ability measured by combinations of tests that measure both perception of speech and perception of music.

Narrow Ability Factors

Each of the abilities mentioned above as tests contributing to the measurement of broad abilities are themselves narrow abilities. These include: verbal ability, spatial visualization, numerical reasoning, deductive reasoning, numerical computation, inductive reasoning, spatial relations, language development, reading comprehension, knowledge of general information, associative memory, memory span, idea fluency, associative fluency, expressive fluency, figural fluency, perceptual speed, reaction time, writing speed, speech perception, and music perception. Each of these narrow abilities can be measured by a number of published tests. Ability test batteries are designed to measure several of these abilities, usually verbal, numerical, spatial, and reasoning abilities.

There are a number of **sensory** abilities of even narrower focus than the narrow abilities mentioned above. These abilities refer to thresholds of sensation (how low or how high is the stimulus you can sense) and sensory acuities (sharpness of your sensitivity to stimuli) for the different senses you read about in Chapter 4.

sensory
of or relating to sensation or to the senses

Also, a number of **physical** and **psychomotor** (or motor) abilities have been identified, largely through the work of Edwin Fleishman and his research team. These include the following abilities: reaction time (mentioned above), choice reaction time, speed of limb movement, wrist-finger speed, finger dexterity, manual dexterity, control precision, rate control, arm-hand steadiness, multilimb coordination, gross body coordination, gross body equilibrium, static strength, dynamic strength, explosive strength, extent flexibility, dynamic flexibility, and stamina.

physical
of or relating to the body

psychomotor
of or relating to motor action directly proceeding from mental activity

This, then, is the variety or range of human abilities—at least the human abilities identified and measured with reliable and valid tests developed by psychometrician/psychologists. They represent sensory-perceptual or "input" abilities, cognitive or "central processing" abilities, and physical-motor or "output" abilities. Only emotional abilities are not represented. This is because ability tests are designed and intended to explore the limits of human performance (or **maximum performance**, as the psychometricians term it). It is, of course, unethical—and operationally very difficult as well—to probe for the limits of your emotions. For this reason, emotional abilities are not measured; rather, they are estimated by judgments on rating scales.

maximum performance
the limits of human performance

A Radex Structure of Abilities

The variety of human abilities we just surveyed can be represented by a diagram, technically called a **radex**, that resembles a target, as shown in Fig. 6-5. At the bulls-eye of the target lies g or general ability. The first ring around the bull's-eye represents the broad ability factors. The next ring around the bull's-eye represents the narrow ability factors. The ring farthest from the bull's-eye represents the specific factors that are unique to each ability test. Different regions of the circumference represent the different types of test content, mainly three types for paper-and-pencil tests: linguistic, numerical, and figural. (A fourth type might be apparatus tests.) As you move toward the bull's-eye, the content of the ability test becomes more complex (has more kinds of factors). It is at its most complex at the bull's-eye. As you move away from the bull's-eye, the content of the ability test becomes more simple—it measures fewer and fewer kinds of factors until, at the last ring, it measures only one specific factor.

radex
a diagram that surveys the variety of human abilities

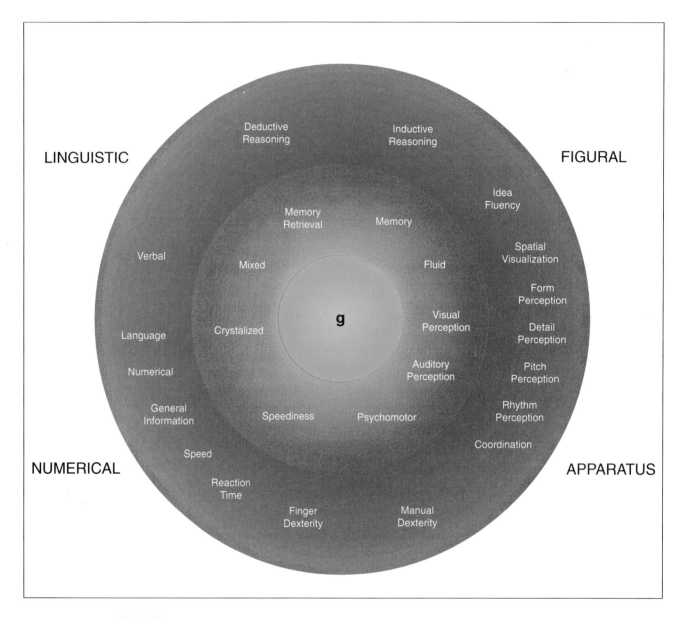

Fig. 6-5

A Radex representation of the organization of human abilities

SUMMARY

1. When tested for the same ability, people obtain different scores. The largest number of people score in the midrange; with fewer people scoring above or below the midrange. If this **frequency distribution** were to be diagrammed, it would look like a bell.

2. A **test profile** demonstrates how one person differs in ability level over many different abilities. If the levels for two abilities are similar across many persons, psychologists call the two abilities **correlated**.

3. **Individual differences** show that although all people have human abilities, people differ on any ability, and although many people have the same level on some abilities, no two persons have the exact same level on all abilities.

4. An **ability test** is an instrument and a set of standard procedures designed to measure a particular ability. Ability tests are useful to psychologists for (1) description of people's abilities, (2) selection of people according to their ability level, and (3) placement of people according to their pattern of abilities.

5. There is an amount of error that is always present during testing. A test is **reliable** when its error in measuring is small. A test is **valid** when it measures what the test is supposed to measure.

6. Because ability tests are designed to discriminate among people, they are open to abuse and exploitation by unethical individuals. They can be constructed to be biased against certain groups. For this reason, they should always be validated. The validity of ability tests for particular uses is known as **criterion-related validity**.

7. Counseling and industrial psychologists use ability tests to describe human capability. They believe that one's standing on any skill can be described through a very small number of ability tests. The U.S. Employment Service (USES) uses 12 tests measuring 9 abilities to estimate job proficiency of workers in about 500 occupations.

8. **Aptitude** is how likely it is that, given training, you will learn a given skill or that you will learn a set of skills for a job or occupation.

9. Ability tests measure three kinds of common factors: general ability, broad ability, and narrow ability. General ability is the overall ability to comprehend relationships; broad ability demonstrates basic cognitive, perceptive, or associative processes; narrow ability focuses more on specific abilities, such as spatial visualization, idea fluency, perceptual speed.

KEY TERMS
Define the following:

Ability test
Alternate-forms method
Auditory perception
Broad ability
Construct validity
Content validity
Convergent validity
Correlated
Correlation coefficient
Criterion-related validity
Crystallized intelligence
Discriminant validity
Factor analysis
Factors
Fluid intelligence
Frequency distribution
General ability
*General Aptitude Test
  Battery*
Hybrid broad ability
Maximum performance
Mean
Memory
Memory retrieval
Narrow ability
Normal curve
Placement
Physical
Psychomotor
Radex
Reliability coefficient
Retest method
Selection
Sensory
Skills
Specific factor
Speediness
Split-half method
Standard deviation
Test battery
Test profile
Uncorrelated
Validate
Visual perception

QUESTIONS FOR REVIEW AND DISCUSSION

1. Think about five different people you know well. Select people who are different in age, background, and occupation. List at least five different narrow abilities of each. Discuss similarities and differences.

2. Make a list of your own narrow abilities. Compare your list with that of the people you selected for activity 1. How do the lists differ? If you have the same ability as someone else, are you both at the same level of ability?

3. Find a magazine or newspaper article that deals with human ability. Discuss in class.

ACTIVITIES

1. Compile all your records of ability tests you have taken. (You might have to ask your parents or your former schools if they have any records they can give you.) Organize your scores according to Carroll's ability factors. Then make an ability profile of your scores, following the lead of Figure 6-2. Try to put all the scores on the same measure or metric, such as percentiles (your best bet). Of course the norm groups will differ, but disregard them for the moment.

2. Look up the Guinness Book of Records (or some similar resource) for instances of exceptional special ability, such as feats of memory or strength or various kinds of skill. Make a list of these (to remind you of what humans can do).

3. Borrow from your school or public library and read an old book by David Wechsler entitled, The Range of Human Capacities (1935, Baltimore: Williams & Wilkins). (This is the Wechsler of WAIS and WAIS R fame.) Wechsler had this idea that if, for every 1,000 people you left out the top and bottom persons in a ranking on any human ability, the difference between the second highest person and the person second from the bottom (or 2nd vs. 999th) is usually in the range of 2 to 1, the second highest person having twice the ability of the 999th person. (The top, or 1st person and the bottom, or 1000th person, Wechsler thought were unusual, extraordinary, bordering on the abnormal.) See how plausible Wechsler's idea is for different kinds of ability (perceptual, cognitive, psychomotor).

4. Find out if the science museum in your community has apparatus to evaluate different kinds of ability (hearing acuity, manual dexterity, spatial visualization, problem solving ability, and the like). Test yourself several times until you're satisfied you have reached your "personal best." Check to see how you compare

against the museum's norms for abilities, or figure out some way to determine how well you do on each task. Keep some record of your performance and add it to your records for Activity 1 (if you did that activity).

5. Discuss with a good friend or your brother/sister what each of you is good at and what you're not good at. Focus on past performances, not interests or beliefs about your abilities. Compare your patterns for similarities and differences. How are you "alike in some or many respects but like none in all respects"?

6. Write a 5-10 page paper--and feel free to speculate--about the conditions that should be present in order for you to develop your talent(s) to its (their) fullest and still be realistic about everyday living. Do you roller-blade well? How much practice time each day would you think would be ideal (but also practical)? Do you write poetry or short stories? Would you need a mountain (or seashore or other) hideaway? for how many months a year? Do you play the piano? Would you need to take lessons from the university music department or from some well-known music school? Are you a mountain climber? Which mountain should you climb next, and which after that? Do you tinker with car engines? What model engine would you love to get your hands on? Etc. Do this for every one of the talents you think you have.

CASE 1

Who Is Better Than Whom?

The two children were playing the ancient game of "I'm better than you are." "I'm better than you in school," said the first child. "No, you're not," said the second. "You may be better than me in reading, but I'm better than you in arithmetic." "Well, I'm also better in spelling," said the first. "But not in geography," said the second. "I'm better in social studies," bragged the first. "I'm better in music," countered the second. "I can run faster than you." "I can walk farther than you." "I can skip rope better than you." "I can stay under water longer than you." "My bowling scores are higher than yours." Pause. "I can think up more ways that I'm better than you than you can. So there."

1. What does this exchange tell you about human abilities?

2. Can you describe the two children in terms of Carroll's ability factors?

CASE 2

The Case for General Intelligence

The psychologist William Cooley makes the following case for the concept of general intelligence—the g factor:

- If you give a set of cognitive tasks—any set—to a large group of unselected adults, the tasks will correlate positively with one another, and its principal component (the general factor, g) will account for about one-fourth of the variance (individual differences) in the group.

- If you administer two different sets of cognitive tasks, their principal components will correlate .80 or higher. It doesn't matter what the tasks are; the g factor is always there.

- The best predictor of academic performance at any educational level is g measured at the previous educational level.

- The best predictor of what happens to youth vocationally upon leaving school is g.

1. Is the argument persuasive?
2. If you do not agree with Cooley, what are your counter-arguments?

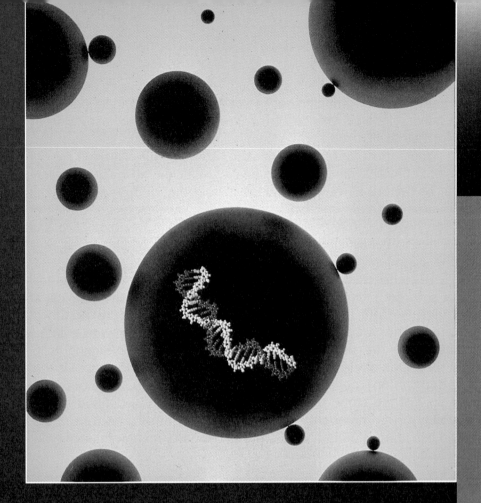

7

▶ HEREDITY AND
ENVIRONMENT:
How Our Human
Potential Is Shaped

*{We have} emerged from two quite different processes of
evolution: the biological evolution responsible for the human
species and the cultural evolution carried out by that species.*
B.F. Skinner

Do you look like a relative of yours—perhaps an aunt or uncle, a grandfather or grandmother? People in a family tend to look alike. "Like father, like son" goes an old expression that could just as easily be "like mother, like son," or "like father, like daughter."

You expect to see similarities in facial appearance, in height or build, or in physical characteristics among relatives. How about similarities in behavior? Have you ever been told that you laugh like your great-uncle or great-aunt, that you walk like your mother or father, or that you have the mannerism of a cousin? Again, we expect to see similarities in behavior and in behavior tendencies among those born into the same family.

Because children frequently resemble their parents, people talk of the children "inheriting" their "characteristics"—be these physical or behavioral—from their parents. You can observe other kinds of "parental inheritance." A seed from an apple tree grows up to be another apple tree, not a pear tree. A tulip bulb grows into another tulip, not a rose. One of the most basic forces of "parental inheritance" is that a life form in one species can give rise to—reproduce—another life form only of the same species. In fact, a species is defined by the capability of its members to mate with each other and reproduce. Individuals from different species cannot ordinarily mate with each other and reproduce.

▼ BIOLOGICAL HEREDITY

One mechanism that underlies these phenomena is biological heredity. Until the turn of the century, much of what was known about biological heredity could be summed up in the phrase "like begets like." Only members of the same species are born within the species, and traits run in families. So farmers learned to keep the "good seed" to sow for the next year's crop and to prize the offspring of the best-performing animals, those that were the fattest or that produced the most milk.

The principles of good breeding were known hundreds of years ago. It was not until relatively recently, however, that people learned how to classify living things. In the eighteenth century the scientist Linnaeus (as you read in Chapter 2) developed the classification system by which every living being is now classified. Classification of the species in turn led to one of the most intriguing of questions in science: How did species originate?

Theory of Evolution

The answer was not long in coming. In 1859, Charles Darwin's (1809-1882) *Origin of Species* was published, containing his theory of evolution that showed how species can originate and how changes in species can occur.

The theory's most startling implication was that the human species was not a unique creation but rather only the last of an evolutionary line

TO THE POINT

Here is a brief summary of the start of the famous voyage of Charles Darwin (1809-1882) a British naturalist who developed the theory of natural selection, explaining how species can originate and change. His observations led to a profound change in our knowledge about how the various species originated. It also reveals something of how a scientist works.

When H.M.S. Beagle, "of 234 tons, rigged as a barque, and carrying six guns," slipped from her moorings in Devonport harbour on 27 December, 1831, the events which were to end in the writing of *On the Origin of Species* were being set in motion. She had on board Charles Darwin, a young Cambridge graduate, son of a wealthy physician of Shrewsbury, in the role of naturalist. On the last day of February 1832 the Beagle reached South America and Darwin, just entered on his twenty-fourth year, stepped ashore on a continent which was destined to raise serious but secret doubts in his mind concerning the origin of living things. He was not a naturalist who was content merely to collect specimens, to note habits, to chart distributions, or to write accurate descriptions of what he found; he never could restrain his mind from searching into the reason of things.

Questions were ever rising in his mind: Why should those giant fossil animals he dug from recent geological strata be so near akin to the little armor-plated armadillos that he found still alive in the same place? Why was it that, as he passed from district to district, he found that one species was replaced by another near akin to it? Did every species of animal and plant remain just as it was created, as was believed by every respectable person known to him? Or did each and all of them change, as some great daring skeptic had alleged?

In due course, after surveying many uncharted coasts, the Beagle reached the Galapagos Islands, five hundred miles to the west of South America. Here his doubts became strengthened and his belief in orthodoxy shaken. Why was it that in those islands living things should be not exactly the same as in South America but yet so closely alike? And why should each of the islands have its own peculiar creations? Special creation could not explain such things. South America thus proved to be a second university to Charles Darwin; after three and a half years spent in its laboratories he graduated as the greatest naturalist of the nineteenth century.[9]

Charles Darwin

that presumably can evolve even further. This went against some people's religious beliefs, and Darwin's theory has been controversial ever since.

The Discovery of Genes

Revolutionary as it was, Darwin's theory did not answer the question of how biological inheritance is transmitted. It was an obscure Austrian monk, Gregor Mendel (1822–1884), who discovered the mechanism of heredity. By crossbreeding pea plants that had different characteristics, and by keeping careful records of the results, Mendel produced evidence that parents carried certain "elements" (later to be called **genes**, which you read about in Chapter 1) that were transmitted to their offspring.

genes
the part of a chromosome through which genetic information is transmitted

Mendel found that the combination of characteristics from both parents determined the characteristics that showed up in the offspring. The offspring, in turn, passed on these characteristics to their own offspring. What was remarkable about Mendel's work was that he discovered the *rules* that govern the transmission of these characteristics, and understood them well enough so that he could predict what characteristics would show up in the offspring.

In essence he discovered that offspring inherit two genes—one from each parent—for a given characteristic. These genes are either **dominant** or **recessive**. If both a dominant and a recessive gene are present, the offspring will have the characteristic of the dominant gene.

dominant
Mendelian characteristic that is always shown

recessive
Mendelian characteristic that is not shown if paired with a dominant one

These first-generation offspring could pass on either a dominant or a recessive gene to the second generation. About every fourth offspring in the second generation would have a pair of recessive genes and so would exhibit that characteristic. All other offspring would have the characteristic of the dominant gene.

At the time no one paid much attention to Mendel's findings. Fortunately, they were "rediscovered" 35 years later in 1900. This rediscovery triggered a period of vigorous research and the launching of a field now known as **genetics**, which concentrates on the study of how and which traits are passed on from one generation to another.

genetics
the study of how traits are passed on through the genes from one generation to another

Step by step, the complicated machinery of biological inheritance was uncovered, culminating in 1953 in the discovery of the chemical structure of the gene, the so-called **genetic code.** This makes it possible to change genes in the laboratory. The field of genetics has continued to rocket forward at a dizzying pace. Even so, there are still a lot of mysteries to be solved. Also, new discoveries are being made all the time that force us to revise our thinking about genes and about biological inheritance.

genetic code
the chemical structure of genes

One Gene or Many?

We now know that the rules about biological heredity that Mendel discovered apply only to certain traits whose "expression" (manifestation in the offspring) depends on only one gene. (Mendel was lucky that the characteristics he worked on turned out to depend on only one gene. Such characteristics are now known as **Mendelian traits**.) The expression of other traits—and many behavioral characteristics belong to this group—do not behave according to the Mendelian rules. When the expression of a characteristic in a population (large group of individuals) takes the form of a *normal distribution* (see Chapter 6), scientists figure out that the characteristic has to depend on many genes. Such characteristics are therefore called **polygenic traits** ("poly" means many).

Mendelian traits
characteristics that depend on only one gene

polygenetic traits
characteristics that depend on many genes

Inheritance and Behavior

What exactly do you inherit, and how does this inheritance influence your behavior? Answers to these questions are exceedingly complex. The following, however, provides some simplified, nontechnical answers.

To begin with, you inherit genes from your parents—*not* traits, characteristics, or mannerisms. Half of your genes come from each of your parents. Genes carry the biochemical "instructions" for making proteins, and **proteins** are the "stuff of life."

In particular, **enzymes** (an important kind of protein) are produced on the basis of the genes' instructions. Enzymes, in turn, are necessary for the development of the organ systems of your body: your nervous system including your brain, your musculoskeletal system, your visceral systems (digestive, excretory, and respiratory), your glandular system, and your cardiovascular system.

proteins
chemical compounds that are essential to the growth and development of the body

enzymes
proteins produced by genes involved in the development of the body's organ systems

These organ systems account for your functioning, all of which are involved in your behavior. The pathway from genes to behavior is long and often not clear, and the direct influence of the genes diminishes at each step. Even so, the influence of genes on individual differences remains.

Genes do not operate in a vacuum but in a biochemical environment. The technical details of how they operate are complex, but even laypersons are aware of the powerful effects of environment. We have learned, for instance, that taking drugs can adversely affect the sex cells, the sperm and ova. A pregnant woman's exposure to certain chemicals can drastically alter the normal course of the fetus's development and result in birth defects. The exposure of a growing child to chemicals will influence the behavioral development of the child.

Fig. 7-2

If a mother and father each have both dominant and recessive genes for their hair color, for example dark (B) and blond (b), their own hair will be dark. If they have children, statistically three would have dark hair and one would be blond.

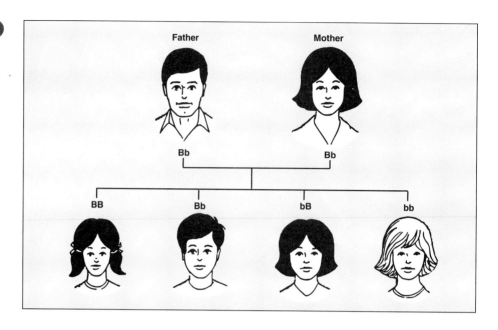

In other words, as you trace the pathway from genes to behavior, you find the environment exerting its influence at each step of the way. Biological heredity does not operate except in the context of particular environments.

You Inherit Potential

potential
an inherent range of capacity for growth

What you inherit can be called potential. **Potential** means an inherent range of capacity for growth and development. You inherit a variety of potentials. Their ranges, which may be large or small, depend on your biological heredity—the genes you inherit from your parents.

When the ranges of potential exhibited by parent and offspring are small, scientists commonly ascribe the characteristic (or trait) to biological heredity. Many physical characteristics such as eye color, hair color and texture, skin color, head shape, height, and build are commonly thought of as being "inherited" because the range of potential passed on by parent to offspring is typically small.

By contrast, many behavior characteristics, such as types of skills acquired, amount and kind of information stored, and preferences for food, hobbies, and so on, have larger ranges (between parent and offspring) and therefore are said to be "not inherited." Countless arguments have occurred on whether an attribute is "inherited" or not.

Scientists work hard and go to considerable trouble to increase our knowledge of human behavior. Because twins, both identical and non-identical, are excellent subjects for studying the relative effects of heredity and environment, scientists are always searching for them. In their search, they are innovative and resourceful. Here is a letter that appeared in the September 1986 issue of the *AARP News Bulletin* (a monthly newsletter of the American Association of Retired Persons) that illustrates the type of research scientists conduct with twins and a resourceful way of finding possible subjects.

Search for Twins

My colleagues and I at the Medical College of Virginia are working to establish a nationwide register of twins aged 50-95. Twin research can make an important contribution to our understanding of the genetic and social influences on aging and aging-related health problems. We want to hear from both identical and fraternal twins, even if one twin is now dead. We also would like to hear from anyone who is a child or spouse of a twin. Contact us by calling, toll free, (800) URA-TWIN.

[signed] Lindon Eaves
Professor of Human Genetics
Medical College of Virginia
Richmond, VA

TO THE POINT

▼ HEREDITY OR ENVIRONMENT

How do scientists know whether heredity or environment affects the range of capacity for growth and development? Scientists use several methods to find this out, but we will describe only the simplest ones. These methods are "simplest" only in the sense that they rest on two simple premises:

1. If environment can be held constant, whatever range you see must be due to biological heredity.

2. Conversely, if heredity can be held constant, the range you observe must be due to environment.

Scientists cannot really observe a range for any one individual, but only the actual appearance of the trait. They can only deduce what the range might be by studying many individuals under the same conditions. The differences among individuals would be due to heredity if environments are similar, and due to environment if heredities are similar.

Holding environment constant or equal is a very difficult task. There are some excellent "constant" environments to study (such as the service academies at West Point, Annapolis, and Colorado Springs), but the individuals entering these environments have already been exposed to different environments.

Nature, however, has provided instances in which biological heredity is equal: identical twins, who came from a single fertilized egg. By comparing the differences between twins from identical pairs with the differences between twins from fraternal, or nonidentical, pairs (who came from two fertilized eggs), scientists have been able to assess the relative influences of biological heredity and environment on behavior. By comparing the differences between twins from identical pairs who were separated at birth (or shortly thereafter) and who were reared apart, scientists have been able to study the effects of environment on behavior.

Scientists have studied differences between the partners in twin sets by measuring their performances on ability tests and their responses to preference questionnaires.

Heritability Index

heritability index
measure of the relative influence of heredity on a plant or animal characteristic

Scientists express their assessment of the relative influence of biological heredity on plants and animals (including humans) with a **heritability index** (symbolized by h^2). The higher the h^2 (it ranges between 0 and 1.00), the more the characteristic being studied is influenced by biological heredity.

Typical h^2 values are: 0.5 to 0.6 for height, weight, and IQ; 0.3 to 0.4 for personality and preference (interests, values) variables measured by self-report inventory; 0.1 to 0.2 for reproductive traits such as litter size and egg production.

High heritability is desirable for those characteristics that plant and animal breeders want to "breed in" their populations, but paradoxically, it is the characteristics with low heritabilities that matter more in evolution. In human populations, high heritability for a behavior characteristic could mean that the environments influencing the expression of the characteristic are limited in range; that is, they are more alike than different.

The Gene's Influence

The extent to which genes shape behavior is affected by a variety of environments. The environments in the cell nucleus, in the cell, in the organ system, in the body—all affect the influence of the genes. The surprise is that, in spite of this, the influence of genes in adult behavior can still be detected, to a greater extent for some characteristics than for others.

Nature or Nurture: The Case of IQ

IQ is one of the best known of psychological terms; it is also one of the most controversial. This is because of the nature-nurture argument, with both camps completely convinced that their factor—nature or nurture, heredity or environment—is the main reason for IQ.

As you read, the IQ test is actually a test of many abilities, so that the IQ score is, on analysis, a measure of the general ability factor (see Chapter 6). On the IQ scale, 100 is the average score and 15 is the standard

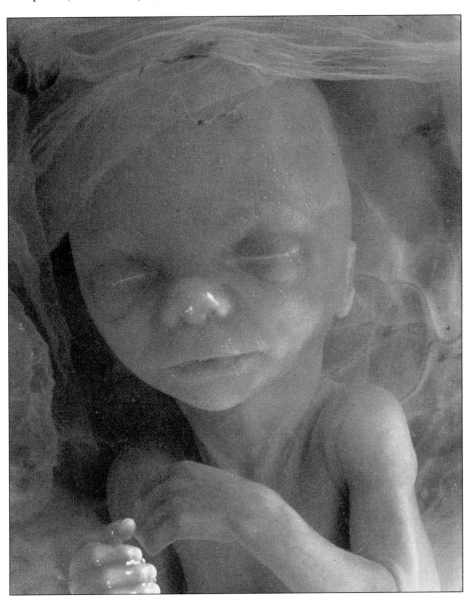

Fig. 7-3

Genes shape behavior. Once born, this child has the *potential* to behave in very specific ways.

deviation, which means that about 68 percent of the population have IQs between 85 and 115, and only about 2 1/2 percent have IQs higher than 130 or less than 70.

Because IQ in the general population is in the form of the normal distribution, you might think that it is a polygenic trait. It is, but some cases of mental retardation (IQ below 70) are known to be due to a single gene or an extra chromosome (the carriers of the genes in the cell). Also, a normal distribution can be produced by having many different environments just as well as having many different genes.

When we divide people into degrees of relationship (how closely related they are biologically), we find that the closer the biological relationship, the more similar the IQs. But then, the closer the biological relationship, the more similar their environments also tend to be. And for those of the same degree of relationship, those who are raised together have more similar IQs than those raised apart.

In one much cited study, children of parents whose IQs were low (85 and below) were adopted and raised by parents with high IQs (115 and up). The average IQ of the children later on was found to be 105, which was generally taken as showing the dominant influence of environment. But when the children were rank-ordered according to IQ, their rank order was similar to the rank order in IQ of the *biological* parents, but not to the IQ rank of their adoptive parents—which showed the strong influence of heredity.

As you can see, the nature-nurture or heredity-environment controversy is a noncontroversy. Both are influential in determining IQ, and both are influential in determining other behavioral characteristics as well.

▼ OUR DIFFERENT ENVIRONMENTS

Many environments influence your behavior. For many kinds of behavior, genes have less influence than these environments. Whereas the genes stand for potential, these environments signify *opportunity* or its opposite—handicap. It is as if the genes spread out the possibilities and the environments choose which possibility to realize. Different kinds of environments and their influence can be identified. Let's look at some of them.

The Internal Environment

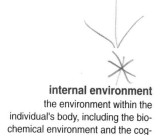

internal environment
the environment within the individual's body, including the biochemical environment and the cognitive environment

The first environment that is important in shaping your behavior is your **internal environment**. It is the environment within your skin. This environment has possibly two parts:

1. The biological and biochemical environment that appears to underlie your moods, temperaments, and emotional states
2. The cognitive or conscious environment that "surrounds" your "self," the "I" or your psychological center

The two parts appear to interact so that one can affect the other and vice versa. Since the biological and biochemical discoveries of the 1950s, especially the discovery of mood-altering drugs such as tranquilizers, the treatment of mental illness has changed radically. Scientists now accept the fact that people can change their mental states by changing their internal environment. In the late 1960s, the reverse discovery was made. That is, it was shown that mental states could change physiological responses previously considered to be "involuntary," such as heart rate, blood pressure, skin temperature, and the like.

To change these involuntary physiological responses, a feedback apparatus is required that tells the person how well he or she is succeeding at the attempt (see Chapter 3). Feedback is a necessary condition for any learning. A whole new field of **biofeedback** has emerged. Professionals in this field have developed ways and instruments to help people monitor and mentally control these involuntary functions.

What the work in biofeedback has shown is that it is possible to change internal environments by changing mental states. This is not a new idea by any means. What is new is that now the mechanism that underlies the phenomenon is understood better. Before these scientific discoveries,

biofeedback
a field of study or the process involved in monitoring and mentally controlling functions previously considered involuntary, such as heartbeat, blood pressure, skin temperature, and so on

Fig. 7-4

Environment shapes behavior by providing the opportunity or handicap for specific behaviors.

Fig. 7-5

Our physical environment takes many forms, and all of them can have a bearing on our behavior. Climate, for example, has a big effect on how we dress, build our houses, and participate in sports or hobbies. For example, those living in the cold climates might become skiers. Those living in the tropics will probably turn to surfing, swimming, or other hot-weather activities.

people had to accept on faith the idea of conscious mental control of involuntary functions.

The Physical Environment

The **physical environment** refers to your surroundings described in physical or material terms. One such environment that has an effect on behavior is climate.

The difficulty of determining whether environment or genetic makeup has the most influence on personality was demonstrated again by a study conducted by Denise Daniels, a researcher, and Robert Plomin, a psychologist, at the University of Colorado at Boulder's Institute for Behavioral Genetics.[10]

Shyness, a tendency to keep to oneself and to move away from the center of attention, would seem to be mostly influenced by environment. Studies have shown, however, that a disposition toward shyness may be genetically inherited.

In their study, Daniels and Plomin compared 152 families with adopted children to 120 families bringing up children born to them. They used many personality and temperament questionnaires to determine degrees of shyness exhibited by babies at 12 months and 24 months. They also rated the home environments as well as the personalities of the adoptive and biological parents.

They found, among other things, that adopted babies taken from their birth mothers within three months of birth tended toward shyness if their birth mothers were shy, regardless of what their adoptive parents were like. This was interpreted as strongly indicating a genetic connection between the personalities of parent and child.

TO THE POINT

The Effects of Climate

Cultures—that is, ways of living—have been shaped by climate. Ways of dressing and housing, types of leisure activities, pace of working, schedules of cyclical (regularly repeated) activities, child-rearing practices, superstitious behavior, eating practices, sleeping practices—to name but a few—are all influenced by climate.

Other Physical Aspects

Other physical aspects of the environment that have an impact on behavior include:

- Crowding and isolation
- Sensory overstimulation and understimulation
- Noise and silence
- Varying versus uniform physical background
- Monotony versus variety of physical stimuli
- Artificial (human-made) versus natural surroundings
- Chemical substances

physical environment
natural settings, such as forests or beaches, as well as environments built by humans, such as buildings, ships, cities

Fig. 7-6

During the school years, peers, friends, and classmates exert a very strong influence on behavior.

Psychologists have studied in minute detail the impact that various physical aspects of the environment have on behavior. One finding that they observed over and over again was that people differed in their response to the same physical aspect. One person hates crowds, another is afraid of them, and a third just loves them. Young people may like their music deafeningly loud, but many older people can't stand the "noise." Different people react differently to monotony—or to variety. When findings are reported about the impact of the physical environment on people, they are of necessity reported as averages. What we tend to overlook is the range of variability around the average, which may be small for some aspects of the environment but large for other aspects.

The Social Environment

The social environment refers to the other human beings with whom you are in contact and your interactions with them. Because humans are social beings, the social environment exercises a great influence. The long period of your dependence on your parents guarantees the strength of the social environment as an influence on your behavior. You learn your emotional responses while interacting with your parents.

A Powerful Influence

Although hereditary factors are involved, your parents' treatment of you has much to do with your emotional behavior. You imitate your parents and model much of your behavior—cognitive, emotional, and even motor—on them.

As you interact with other persons besides your parents, you learn other behavior by watching and imitating these other persons or through the effects or consequences of their responses to you. During your school years, your peers—your friends, classmates, age group—exert a very strong influence on you. You can remember back in grade or high school how you "would not be caught dead" wearing something or doing something because "nobody does it." You learn to model your behavior on some person or "personality" (TV, movie, sports, etc.). Even now, you catch yourself making a particular gesture or using a particular expression, and you suddenly realize that you have been unthinkingly imitating some other person.

Because much of your life you are interacting with other humans, the social environment, although not the only force shaping your behavior, is one of the most powerful forces at work.

Self-Concept

The social environment plays the pivotal role in shaping one particular aspect of your psychological life. This is your **self-concept**, the view that you have of yourself. To some psychologists, the self-concept is the key to understanding much of a person's psychology—the person's motives, values, interests, needs, wants, desires, aspirations.

Feedback from the social environment is the key to the formation of the self-concept. When you think of yourself as good in one thing, average in another, poor in a third, it is in large measure due to the reactions and evaluations of others. Indeed, the self-concept can be said to begin with self-consciousness caused by the attention paid to us by other people.

The Cultural Environment

The **cultural environment** is the system of ways of behaving expected within a community of human beings. We are all born into a community, and we are all born into a cultural environment. Like the physical environment, the cultural environment can be described in terms of its various aspects. As noted above, climate, an aspect of the physical environment, can influence the cultural environment. How you dress, the kind of house you have, and what you do for recreation are part of the cultural environment.

Customs

Customs are accepted habitual ways of behaving that everyone observes. They have the force of unwritten law. Standing when the national anthem is played is an example of a custom. Customs can change. At one time in this country, it was the custom for stores to close on Sundays and for virtually all commerce to stop. Today, many stores open for business on Sundays.

Taboos

Taboos, which forbid specific kinds of behavior, are among the most powerful customs. Some practices, like walking around without clothes, are taboos in our culture. Especially strong taboos forbid murder, incest, and cannibalism.

Etiquette

Social and business **etiquette** are examples of customs that influence behavior in a society. Being polite and courteous is an example of social etiquette. Using utensils to eat with instead of fingers is another example. Business etiquette also includes being polite and courteous, for practical as well as

self-concept
an individual's view of himself or herself

cultural environment
the system of ways of behaving expected within a community of human beings

customs
accepted, habitual ways of behaving observed by all members of a community

taboos
powerful customs that forbid specific kinds of behavior, such as murder or incest

etiquette
the conduct or procedure required by good breeding or prescribed by authority to be observed in social or official life

social reasons. An example of business etiquette is a sales representative's buying lunch for a potential customer.

Cultural Values

cultural values
the values attached to various objects and activities by the majority of people in a given culture

Cultural values are the prevailing set of standards and beliefs held by a community that define what is and what is not important to it. Our society values people who succeed, particularly those who worked their way up from a poor background. Our culture values independence and owning one's own home.

Social Roles

social roles
community expectations about social position and function, which define the power relationships in the community

Social roles are patterns of behavior determined by community expectations about an individual's social position and function. Social roles define the power relationships in the community. Their object is to maintain the stability of these power relationships. People who take an active part in running the community develop this power and help maintain stability.

All of these aspects of the cultural environment shape the behavior of a culture's members. Certain ways of doing things become the "natural" way of behaving. Certain ways of thinking and certain attitudes are taken for granted, and other ways of thinking and other attitudes are considered strange, weird, incomprehensible, even harmful. The cultural environment will determine whether it is "normal" or "abnormal" to show affection or other emotions. You need only cross over into another culture to realize how much of your behavior is shaped by your cultural environment.

One environment is of particular interest to us in this text, and that is the work environment. The way our lives are organized (at this time in history and in this society), the work environment plays a huge role in how we realize our potential, in how human potential is shaped by the environment. To understand how this comes about, we need to look at the work environment in more detail.

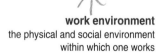

The Work Environment

work environment
the physical and social environment within which one works

Your **work environment** is more than just the physical place in which you work and the machines or tools with which you work. It includes the people with whom you work: your work group, your immediate boss, and the higher-ups or top management. It also includes other people with whom you come in contact in your work: clients and customers, workers in other groups or organizations, and the general public.

Because work is a social enterprise, the social aspect is the most important part of your work environment. Your work environment, therefore, is not passive; on the contrary, it is active, reactive, and interactive (Fig. 7-7).

Work Requirements

Your work environment makes demands on you all the time. Thus it is said that the work environment has **requirements** of the workers. Many of these requirements are *formal*. They are stated in a formal manner and usually written down. The job description and especially the job specifications are formal, written listings of these requirements. They typically describe your functions in the organization, your specific duties, and the tasks you are expected to perform.

requirements
the demands made upon workers by the work environment

Sometimes they do not describe precisely how you are to perform your tasks; instead, some job specifications state what you are expected to accomplish—for example, sell *X* dollars worth of goods during the year. Sometimes the tasks are minutely described, as in the musical notation for a particular piano composition that a concert pianist is to perform.

Many of the work environment's requirements are *informal*, that is, not set down in writing. For example, you may not be told what clothes to wear, but if your work group dresses up, you will feel compelled to dress up also. If everyone treats the boss in a formal, "Mr. or Ms. X" manner, you would not address the boss informally by his or her first name. Each work group and each work organization develops a *culture* of its own that is most in evidence in the informal requirements it makes of its members. This culture, while it may not be formally acknowledged by the organization, can often have far-reaching effects on the habits, attitudes, and even values of its members. Working with a group of people on a daily basis and for years at a time, often in close proximity, sharing experiences, goals, and expectations, can have a profound impact on the way you see and react to the world.

Work Reinforcers

The work environment is not all requirements. It has a "flip side" that consists of what it offers to meet *your* requirements. In psychology, these are called **work reinforcers**, although they are more familiarly known as rewards. They are called reinforcers because they *maintain* work behavior. That is, their presence encourages you or motivates you to perform the necessary work. Work reinforcers, like work requirements, are also formal and informal.

work reinforcers
the rewards given to workers by the work environment

Formal work reinforcers consist of your pay, benefits, and other parts of the organization's reward system for its employees. They are frequently written down, sometimes in a contract between the workers

Fig. 7-7

The work environment is more than a place to work; it is a social environment.

(often represented by a union) and the organization, often times in a company policy booklet, which represents the company's promise to provide certain things.

Informal work reinforcers may be many, depending on your requirements, that is, your needs. If you require a challenging job that demands both physical and mental effort and the company provides you with such a job, that is a work reinforcer. If you need to work with persons congenial to you and your coworkers are congenial, they are work reinforcers. Other reinforcers, which are mostly informal, are:

- Ability utilization
- Achievement
- Activity
- Advancement
- Authority
- Creativity
- Independence
- Moral values
- Recognition
- Responsibility and autonomy
- Social service
- Social status
- Variety

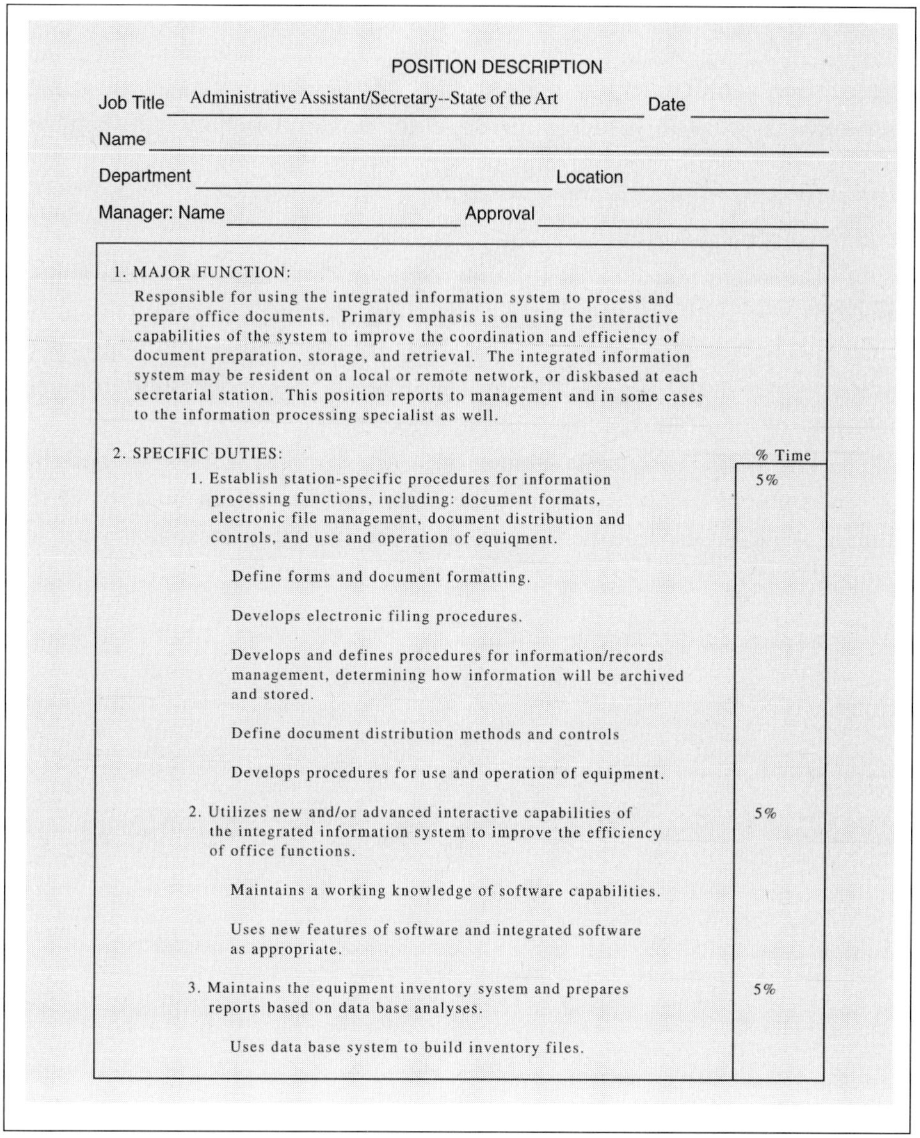

POSITION DESCRIPTION

Job Title Administrative Assistant/Secretary--State of the Art   Date _____

Name _____

Department _____ Location _____

Manager: Name _____ Approval _____

1. MAJOR FUNCTION:

Responsible for using the integrated information system to process and prepare office documents. Primary emphasis is on using the interactive capabilities of the system to improve the coordination and efficiency of document preparation, storage, and retrieval. The integrated information system may be resident on a local or remote network, or diskbased at each secretarial station. This position reports to management and in some cases to the information processing specialist as well.

2. SPECIFIC DUTIES: % Time

1. Establish station-specific procedures for information   5%
   processing functions, including: document formats,
   electronic file management, document distribution and
   controls, and use and operation of equiqment.

   Define forms and document formatting.

   Develops electronic filing procedures.

   Develops and defines procedures for information/records
   management, determining how information will be archived
   and stored.

   Define document distribution methods and controls

   Develops procedures for use and operation of equipment.

2. Utilizes new and/or advanced interactive capabilities of   5%
   the integrated information system to improve the efficiency
   of office functions.

   Maintains a working knowledge of software capabilities.

   Uses new features of software and integrated software
   as appropriate.

3. Maintains the equipment inventory system and prepares   5%
   reports based on data base analyses.

   Uses data base system to build inventory files.

Fig. 7-8

The work environment requirements of workers are both formal and informal. Formal requirements are often written down. A job description outlines the duties and tasks a worker must perform, which are examples of formal work environment requirements.

To summarize, the work environment is that part of the world of work that immediately concerns you. It has two aspects: requirements and reinforcers. The responsibilities, duties or functions, tasks of the job, and the other expectations of superiors, coworkers, and other people with whom you have contact on your job are the requirements of the work environment. The monetary rewards and other conditions that meet your requirements constitute the reinforcers of the work environment.

▼ HEREDITY-ENVIRONMENT PARTNERSHIP

These, then—internal, physical, social, cultural, work—are the major environments that influence your development and behavior. When you consider them and their strong influence, it makes you wonder if your biological inheritance—your genes—plays any substantive role at all in shaping your behavior.

But when you look at the data on twins and studies of heritability, especially the findings showing an amazing similarity in adult identical twins who were separated at birth or early infancy and reared apart, your thinking takes a 180-degree turn. You now begin to wonder if environment plays any role at all in shaping your behavior.

The truth, of course, is that both are important. Neither heredity nor environment functions without the other. The important question at the moment is, What environment can realize the most potential that your (or anyone else's) hereditary brings?

SUMMARY

1. One of the most basic forces of biological heredity is that a life form in one species can reproduce another life form only of the same species. Although the principles of breeding were known thousands of years ago, scientists only relatively recently learned how to classify living things.

2. In 1859, Charles Darwin's Origin of Species was published, containing his theory of evolution on how species can originate and how changes in species can occur. The theory's most startling implication was that the human species was not a unique creation but rather only the most recent of an evolutionary line that presumably will continue to evolve.

3. Gregor Mendel (1822-1884) discovered how the mechanism by which biological inheritance is transmitted works. Using pea plants, he produced evidence that each parent passes on genes to offspring that transmit potential for particular traits. Mendel discovered some genes are dominant and others recessive. If both genes are present in an offspring, the off-spring shows the characteristic of the dominant gene.

4. In 1953, scientists discovered the chemical structure of the gene, the so-called genetic code. This makes it possible to modify genes in the laboratories.

5. Some traits depend on one gene (Mendelian traits), whereas others depend on many genes (polygenic traits).

6. Genes themselves are affected by an environment—a bio-chemical environment. Taking drugs can adversely affect the sperm and ova. A pregnant woman's exposure to certain chemicals can drastically alter the normal course of the fetus's development and result in birth defects.

7. What you inherit with genes is a potential that reflects an inherent range of capacity for your growth. If the range of potential is small, genes probably play an influential role in determining your characteristics; if the range is great, environment probably plays the influential role. Scientists express their assessment of the relative influences of biological heredity and environment with an heritability index (symbolized by h^2).

8. The nature-nurture controversy shows how both are important and necessary contributors to individual differences in IQ.

9. The major environments that influence your development are internal, physical, social, cultural, and work.

10. _____ Neither heredity nor environment operates without the other. The important question is, What environment can realize your potential best?

KEY TERMS
Define the following:

Biofeedback
Cultural environment
Cultural values
Customs
Dimensions
Dominant
Enzymes
Etiquette
Genetic code
Genetics
Heritability index
Internal environment
Mendelian traits
Physical environment
Polygenic traits
Potential
Predispose
Proteins
Recessive
Reinforcers
Requirements
Self-concept
Social roles
Taboos
Work environment

QUESTIONS FOR REVIEW AND DISCUSSION

1. _____ Briefly explain what is meant by *parental inheritance*. What is one of the most basic forces of parental inheritance?
2. _____ Why is Charles Darwin's book *Origin of Species* important?
3. _____ Who was Gregor Mendel, and why was his work important?
4. _____ What is the implication of the statement "Genes do not operate in a vacuum"?
5. _____ Explain why scientists look for identical twins as subjects in their study of the influence of heredity or environment.
6. _____ What are the major environments that influence our behavior? Give an example of each.
7. _____ Which is more important in determining our behavior—heredity or environment? Explain your answer.

ACTIVITIES

1. _____ Consider your own immediate family (parents, siblings, grand parents) and all close relations (cousins, your parents' brothers and sisters, who are your aunts and uncles). Make a list of some of the traits and characteristics—both behavioral and physical—that the family and relatives share. Make a list of the differences. Identify those that seem to be mostly the result of heredity. Identify those that seem to be mostly the result of environment. In what ways do you think environment created some of the differences? Were you surprised at the number of similar traits and characteristics? Do some of the differences surprise you?
2. _____ Construct a rough family tree for four generations of a family, showing how two physical characteristics—one dominant and one recessive—would show up in each succeeding generation.
3. _____ We are all influenced by the environment, which has four broad categories: physical, cultural, social, and internal. Try to identify some of the various environments that you must operate in and that may influence your behavior. Two obvious physical-cultural ones are your home and school. Identify others and how they influence you. For example, what is the climate like where you live, and how has that influenced some of the things you do or like?

CASE 1

Heredity and Environment

George reached his full size when he was still a teenager. He was large, standing 6 feet 2 inches and weighing 195 pounds. For a large person, he was very quick and also had excellent eye-hand coordination. In high school he starred on the football team and also played on the basketball and baseball teams. That made his father, also a large man and a former college football player, proud. It also made George popular.

George was not altogether happy about playing all these sports, however. He liked them well enough, but they took up too much time, which he would have preferred to use doing something else.

Ever since he was a very young boy, he had been interested in drawing and had displayed considerable talent for it. His mother was an interior decorator, and like her he seemed to have a sense for color and design. While he was in high school, he got a job in the local art supply store working weekends and summers. He met many artists because the area where he lived had a famous artist's colony. He also joined the high school art club, but sports took up most of his time.

In college, to please his father and many of his peers, who felt that given his size and talent he should play for the school, George went out for the football team and other sports his freshman year. But the sports took up even more time, and he became more dissatisfied. He decided to major in art and to devote all his extracurricular time developing his skill and interest in art.

Although he knew it would distress his father as well as sports fans of the college, he withdrew from the major competitive sports. He continued to play sports, which he liked and was good at, but only for recreation and pleasure. He concentrated most of his energy on his art.

1. Of the traits and characteristics that George has, which were most likely to have been influenced by heredity and which by environment?

2. Name and describe some of the environments George lived in.

3. What reinforcers would you say George valued most highly in college? Explain.

Unit II

RESEARCH STUDY

A School Behavior Problem

A young elementary-school age child is referred to you. According to the teachers, the child is not performing well at school in practically all subjects and has become a "behavior problem." Based on your experience, you figure that the "behavior problem" is largely the consequence of poor school performance. Your first task, therefore, is to find out why the child is not performing well.

1. Develop a list of hypotheses (technical name for "hunches") about what underlies the child's poor performance. Use the chapters in this unit to generate the hypotheses (plural for "hypothesis"). Start with Chapter 3 and go chapter by chapter as you develop your hypotheses. Develop at least two hypotheses per chapter.

2. What kind of data do you need to test each hypothesis? Which data (plural for "datum") are readily available to you—if this were a real-life situation—and which would require you to send the child out for further and more extensive evaluation than you do?

3. If the data confirm the hypothesis, what can be done about it to help the child perform better? (You are, of course, limited to what you know, including your knowledge acquired outside of this course. Use all your knowledge to best advantage.) Do this for each hypothesis for which data are readily available.

UNIT III

Human Development

There are two basic aspects to development: maturation and learning. Biological maturation follows the same course for humans as for all other life: growth, stability, decline. It is in learning, especially in cognitive learning, that humans differ from and far outstrip other species. Furthermore, humans learn not only skills and abilities, not just information and knowledge, but also preferences and values, interests and attitudes, and motivations.

In this unit you will study the development of your personality – how you express yourself in behavior. You will see how your personality is shaped in the growing years, how it becomes stable when you reach adulthood, and how it changes during your life.

CHAPTER 9

▶ STAGES OF DEVELOPMENT:
How We Grow

The Child is Father of the Man
William Wordsworth

The child is father of the man (or mother of the woman) neatly sums up the psychological truth that life is an unbroken continuum and that your early years shape your later years. While it is true that life proceeds in an unbroken line extending from conception to death, it is also true that as you age, you go through several distinctly different stages. You are not ordinarily aware of the stages as they occur. Normally you sense the wholeness of your life, the continuum. It is only after you have experienced them and can look back to them over a few years that you recognize different stages in your life.

Psychologists focus on different stages of life to learn what happens in each of them and how the stages interact to form the whole. In their studies of human development, psychologists identify these stages generally on the basis of age, but specifically on physical, mental, social, and moral development.

The stages of development can be based only loosely upon age because development varies among individuals. These age divisions reflect an abstract average. Averages are very useful quantitative concepts, but they must be kept in perspective. It has been said, with more truth than humor, that the "average" person does not exist. Real people develop on their own individual schedules.

Overly anxious parents sometimes forget this and make the mistake of pushing a child when they feel the child has not begun to crawl, or walk, or talk at the "right" age. The "right" age for normal development is a broad interval, which for some is an earlier and for others a later age. Only a marked variation from the normal interval should cause concern.

The *order* in which the stages occur seems to be more significant than the precise age at which they occur. Psychologists have found that development proceeds in a set order. Everyone moves through similar patterns of development in the same general sequence, if not at the same age. This appears to be true of physical and mental development, and social and moral development.

▼ AN AGE-IRRELEVANT SOCIETY

As some have noted, this society is becoming an age-irrelevant society—one that makes age increasingly meaningless, especially in the adult years, for categorizing people. This is worth noting as the population is growing older. People live longer. There are more people over 45 and over 65 than ever before. In the last decade, the over-65 segment of the population increased faster than any other segment.

While the population is growing older in the sense that it contains more older people, in another sense it is getting younger. That is to say that people are healthier and more active than ever before. The stereotype of the white-haired, somewhat fragile, grandmother and grandfather rocking on the porch does not reflect today's reality. Grandmother and grandfather are living the lives of healthy, vigorous, active people. Grandmother's hair is probably blonde, and she is either out jogging or knocking a ball across a tennis net. Grandfather might be fishing, but he also might be taking a 10-mile sprint on his bicycle. Or they may have decided not to retire and have started new careers.

The increasing number and vigor of older people have resulted in a change in society's perceptions—among them, ideas about when workers should retire. For many years, businesses required people to retire at age 65. Laws today prohibit such forced retirement before age 70. For a further discussion of the changing nature of work and the work force see Chapter 16.

▼ FOUR AREAS OF DEVELOPMENT

Psychologists have studied four broad areas of development:

1. Physical and motor
2. Cognitive and mental
3. Social and moral
4. Emotional

Fig. 8-1

Anxious parents may sometimes push an infant to develop faster if they think the child is not developing at the right age. Although on average all people develop on similar schedules, some develop sooner and others later. There is no "right" age.

TO THE POINT

Shakespeare, in one of his most quoted passages (*As You Like It*, act II, scene vii), referred to seven stages in the development of humans:

And one man in his time plays many parts,
His acts being seven ages. At first the infant,
Mewling and puking in the nurse's arms.
And then the whining school-boy,
...creeping like snail
Unwillingly to school. And then the lover,
Sighing like furnace, with a woeful ballad
Made to his mistress' eyebrow. Then a soldier,
Full of strange oaths, and bearded like the pard,
Jealous in honor, sudden and quick in quarrel,
Seeking the bubble reputation
Even in the cannon's mouth. And then the justice,
In fair round belly with good capon lined,
With eyes severe and beard of formal cut,

...The sixth age shifts
Into the lean and slipper'd pantaloon,
With spectacles on nose....
...Last scene of all,...
Is second childishness, and mere oblivion,...

Shakespeare wrote these lines in 1599. Although his descriptions are rather unflattering, his age-based stages are not so far from those recognized by psychologists today as significant:

Infancy, first stage, birth to 18 months
Infancy, second stage, 18 months to 3 years
Preschool, 3 to 5 years
Preadolescence, 6 to 11 years
Adolescence, 12 to 18 years
Young adulthood, 19 to 45 years
Middle age, 46 to 65 years
Old age, 65 years to death

These areas are interrelated, and development in all of them is influenced by both heredity and environment, as you read in Chapter 7. In their studies, psychologists try to determine not only how people develop, but why they develop as they do. They seek to answer the how and why not only in a general way to determine basic rules governing everyone's development but also in specific terms to explain a particular individual's development.

▼ PHYSICAL AND MOTOR DEVELOPMENT

Physical development refers to bodily changes. Individuals grow most quickly during their first three years and again in adolescence. Children increase in height and weight so quickly that persons seeing them only occasionally, such as on holidays or special occasions, invariably say, "My, how you've grown." Adolescents, self-conscious about their bodies during this period of great outward development, often come to dislike hearing this expression.

Early Motor Skills

Accompanying this physical growth is an increasing ability to use muscles purposefully, to make them do what is wanted. This is **motor development**. People are born with some motor ability. But newborn infants must develop many motor skills. They do so rapidly. These learned motor skills include turning over in a crib, crawling, standing, and, eventually, walking. Newborn babies react to stimuli, such as light, pain, and touch. If a newborn feels a touch on the side of the cheek, the baby turns toward it. All of these motor skills have survival value. Turning toward a touch on the cheek facilitates nursing. Within a week, a baby can recognize his or her mother's voice and smell.

Holdover Reflexes

Interestingly, babies are born with some **reflexes** (see Chapter 3) that they later lose, some of which must be relearned. A newborn baby will instinctively clutch something that touches its palm. Later it loses this ability to grasp and must relearn it. Psychologists call this the *Darwinian reflex*. They speculate that this holdover reflex once helped human babies hold on to their mothers, much as newborn monkeys and other furbearing animals do.

Another holdover reflex has been called the *Moro reflex*. Newborn babies exhibit this reflex when they are startled. They arch their backs, fling out their arms, and then pull them in as if to hug something. One theory is that this reaction made it easier for a mother to pick up the infant in a crisis.

Although these holdover reflexes appear to serve no direct survival need today, they do still serve a useful function. If newborn babies do not exhibit these reflexes, physicians are alerted to possible muscular or nervous system problems.

How Motor Skills Develop

Psychologists have discovered that babies develop motor skills in a head-to-toe sequence. That is, a baby first controls the muscles that move the head.

Fig. 8-2

Thanks in part to an increased knowledge of living that has come from the work of psychologists, we have the apparent paradox of our society becoming younger as it becomes older. The paradox is more apparent than real: While the number of older people in our society has been increasing, their health and mental outlook remain more like what was once considered typical of middle, rather than old, age.

physical development
development of the body

motor development
development of the ability to use muscles purposefully, to make them do what is wanted

reflexes
automatic physical responses to stimuli

Can the development of motor skills be sped up or slowed down by environments? This, of course, is part of the question of which is more important in development, heredity or environment. Motor skills seem to be more influenced by heredity.

Training can speed up motor development only marginally, if at all. An environment with little stimulus or human contact can slow down the development of motor skills. But the effect of environment, even in such cases, is not lasting, except in extremely severe cases.

A classic study of the effects of deprivation on motor development involved 174 children in three institutions in Iran.[1] In two of the institutions, the infants received minimal attention from attendants. They were not picked up, turned in their cribs, given toys, or held while being fed.

These deprived infants did not develop motor skills at the ages of normal children. They did not sit up or crawl until later, but they did catch up by school age.

[1]W. Dennis, "Causes of Retardation among Institutional Children," *Journal of Genetic Psychology* 96, pages 47-59 (1960).

The baby lifts and turns it from side to side. Then comes the ability to lift the chest, and next the ability to control arms, and finally legs.

▼ COGNITIVE AND MENTAL DEVELOPMENT

cognitive development
development of the ability to think, remember, learn, and use language

introspective method
the examination of one's own thoughts in order to understand cognitive processes

Thinking, remembering, learning, and using language are all part of **cognitive development**, which may also be called intellectual development. As long ago as the time of ancient Greek civilization, humans thought about "thought." And until recently, people had only the Greeks' **introspective method** to explore this activity.

Aristotle

Using the introspective method, those ancient Greeks developed theories of thinking that form the basis of many theories held today. Among other things, they recognized the importance of memory and realized that in order to think, we must have memory.

Fig. 8-3

Cognitive development is stimulated by an environment that values learning.

Aristotle (384-322 B.C.) developed the theory of **association,** which maintains that our thinking tends to run from one idea to another related idea. He said ideas were associated by *contiguity* (meaning that they occurred together), *similarity*, or *contrast*. He also recognized that memory alone was not enough to explain thinking and that another process, the use of logic, was necessary. Aristotle's "laws of association" remain part of the basis for the study of thinking today.

association
a theory, developed by Aristotle, that our thought tends to run from one idea to another related idea

Jean Piaget

The man recognized as the most prominent modern researcher of cognitive development is Jean Piaget (1896-1980). Piaget and his coworkers are credited with having produced more valuable research and theories than any other group in the first half of this century.

In the second half of this century, researchers using increasingly sophisticated techniques and often building on the work of Piaget are generating new evidence and understanding that show that some of Piaget's conclusions must be altered. This would probably not bother Piaget, who viewed his work, especially in his earlier years, as a beginning and a way to stimulate further research.

Piaget's contributions to the study of cognitive development began when he was a young man, helping to create standardized tests to measure intelligence. In such testing, the focus is on the child's ability to give the correct answer. Piaget, however, became interested in the incorrect answers they gave.

He discovered that children of the same age often gave the same wrong answers. He found that common wrong answers were given at different ages. He became interested in finding out why these similar wrong answers were given. Eventually he concluded that the difference between younger and older children was not that the latter were brighter. There was, he said, a qualitative difference in the way children thought at different ages.

Fig. 8-4

Born on August 9, 1896, in Switzerland, Jean Piaget did much to advance the study of cognitive development. His first interest was in nature and the biological sciences. When he was 11, an article he wrote was published in a natural history magazine. He later became interested in the development of intelligence.

Factors in Cognitive Development

As in all development, heredity and environment play roles in cognitive development. Heredity is particularly influential at and shortly after birth. Thereafter environmental factors play an increasing role. Heredity influences cognitive development in two ways:

1. It sets broad limits on cognitive functions.

2. It transmits automatic behavioral reaction.

Piaget echoed the Greeks in suggesting that we inherit two basic tendencies: accommodation and assimilation.

The way an experiment is set up can influence the outcome. Psychologists are aware of this and are becoming increasingly sophisticated in designing experiments to test development. Cases in point are the experiment Piaget conducted and one conducted in the 1980s by psychologist Renee Baillargeon and colleagues at the University of Illinois. Both experiments were designed to determine at what age babies realize that two objects cannot occupy the same space.

Piaget simply moved an object from a child's view by hiding it under a blanket. If the child lifted the blanket to look for it, Piaget theorized the child had exhibited a degree of the object permanence ability and had realized that two objects could not occupy the same space at the same time. His research led him to believe this occurs at about 9 months.

The recent researchers used a mirror and a trap door. When the trap door was opened, it hid the object but rested against it. Using the mirror, the researchers sometimes made it appear that the trap door passed through the object—an impossibility. Babies did not appear to be fooled. When the object was there but hidden by the door, they looked behind the door for it.

They looked for the hidden object as early as 5 months, indicating they had already reached a stage Piaget thought was not reached until about 9 months. Those conducting the new experiment theorized that lifting a blanket required muscular control beyond the abilities of younger babies, hence the apparently mistaken assumption by Piaget.

This indicates that how an experiment is structured is very important. It also suggests that all research is a search for truth, and no one experiment is likely to produce the final truth.

TO THE POINT

- **Accommodation:** The tendency to adjust ourselves to the environment.

- **Assimilation:** The tendency to organize new experience according to our way of thinking.

Piaget's Stages of Cognitive Development

Piaget theorized that normal humans go through the same stages of cognitive development in the same order and at approximately the same age. Here are Piaget's stages of cognitive development: sensorimotor, preoperational, concrete operational, and formal operational.

Sensorimotor

This is the stage of reflex and learning through action, roughly from birth to 2 years. Reflexive reactions change to organized reaction to stimuli. Babies touch and move things, learning about them through their senses. During this period they learn that objects continue to exist even when out of their sight. Piaget called this ability to realize an object has a reality of its own **object permanence**.

object permanence
the ability to realize that an object has a reality of its own

Piaget demonstrated object permanence by hiding an object while the infants watched. Even though they saw what was happening, the babies continued to look for the object in its original place until, at about 12 months of age, they began to look for it in the new hiding place. Note that subsequent experimenters, using different techniques, have apparently demonstrated that babies develop object permanence at an earlier age, which Piaget did not realize because of the nature of his experiment.

Preoperational

This stage is marked by a growing ability to use language and numbers. Children begin to talk about things they cannot see. But their logical thinking is still limited. At this stage the child tends to be **egocentric**. The child is unable to see more than one aspect of a situation at a time. This stage very loosely covers the ages of 2 to 7 years.

egocentric
believing that one is the center and cause of all that happens

Concrete Operational

This stage marks a move from egocentricity to a realization that others exist and have different points of view. This stage is roughly from 7 to 11 years. Children now develop what Piaget called **conservation**. That is, they realize that equal quantities of matter remain equal regardless of their shape. The

conservation
as used here, the ability to understand that equal quantities of matter remain equal regardless of their shape

same amount of clay rolled in a ball or rolled out like a worm remains the same amount of clay. The ability to recognize conservation indicates that the child understands:

- **Reversibility:** Realizing the image of the worm can be reversed to the ball.

- **Identity:** Realizing the clay is the *same* in either shape, that nothing has been taken away or added.

- **Compensation:** Realizing that a ball is shorter and thicker, but a worm is longer and narrower.

At this stage, children can apply these abilities only to objects they know from concrete experience. Hence the name of this stage. They can not yet deal with abstract symbols.

Formal Operational

Starting about age 12, when children are entering adolescence, they begin thinking in abstract terms. At this stage they can play "what if" games with reality. "What if I become a writer?" "If I were a parent, I would..." This level of abstract thinking does not rely on concrete experience. They can handle conflicting ideas, set goals for themselves, and hold ideals based on such concepts as love and service to others.

reversibility
the ability to understand that a quantity of matter converted to a different shape can be reversed to its original shape

identity
as used here, the ability to understand that a single quantity of matter formed into two different shapes remains the same amount of matter

compensation
the ability to understand that when a quantity of matter changes shape, its dimensions also change

Fig. 8-5

When children realize that equal quantities of matter remain equal regardless of their shape, they have developed what Piaget called conservation.

▼ SOCIAL AND MORAL DEVELOPMENT

You are more than the sum of your physical and mental abilities. You learn to speak, but to what end? You learn to coordinate your eyes and hands, but for what purpose? To survive, yes; yet humans have developed a complex society to ensure survival. And to live successfully in that society, you must also develop both socially and morally, which is known as psychosocial development.

The social and moral uses toward which you put your mental and physical skills define you as an individual. Your social and moral development shapes your personality. Heredity and environment help shape your social and moral development, with environment perhaps having the greater influence on the outcome.

Social Development

social development
the process of learning that one is not the center of the universe and that it is necessary to interact with others and the environment

As you read earlier, people begin life as egocentric. The infant believes that he or she is the center and the cause of all action. **Social development** is the process of learning that one is not the center of the universe, and that it is necessary to interact with others and the environment. Experts disagree about whether infants are totally egocentric and when they become aware of and interact with others. Scientists keep discovering that children realize at earlier ages than previously thought that they must adapt their behavior to others.

Some activities that children indulge in, once thought to be egocentric, are today being looked at in another light. Piaget noticed that young children talked to themselves a lot. He called this "unsuccessful communication" and a sign of egocentricity. Later research found that this private speech is not antisocial but a learning tool. Young children need to think about tasks they are performing. Those who talk to themselves perform better. Also those who talk to themselves a lot when doing a task tend to be more sociable and interested in talking to others than those who do not use private speech. People come equipped, so to speak, with the desire and the ability to be sociable. Such an ability has obvious survival value in humans, who must depend heavily on one another.

Erik Erikson, a noted psychoanalyst and psychologist who was born in 1902, was one of the first to put forth a theory of social development to cover our entire life span. He suggested people pass through eight stages, at each of which they encounter a "crisis." Their successful social development depends on how they react at each stage or turning point.

Erikson's theory has been faulted because the stages are not defined well enough to permit objective verification. His theory also has been criticized as biased against women. Despite its possible weaknesses, Erikson's theory is valued for the insights it offers on human behavior. Here briefly are the eight stages.

Trust Versus Mistrust

This stage covers the first 18 months. Infants learn to what extent they can trust the world by the care and nourishment given them, primarily by their mothers. If care and nourishment is adequate, they develop a sense of trust. They feel safe in the world. If care is cold and inadequate, they do not learn to interact well with others.

Autonomy Versus Shame and Doubt

Autonomy is the state of being independent. During this stage, which lasts to age 3 years, babies move out to explore the world and to assert their independence. Their abilities are still very limited, and they doubt themselves. They begin to sense right and wrong. They cannot be permitted unlimited independence at this stage because they might hurt themselves or others. At the same time, too much control will suppress their willingness to be independent later.

Initiative Versus Guilt

At this stage, which lasts to age 6, children begin initiating actions as well as imitating others. They compete for approval and to impress their parents. They try things, fail, and realize a sense of failure for the first time. Feelings of guilt arise that cause them to govern their own behavior rather than being solely governed by punishment from outside. They need to experience enough success to continue growing and experimenting, tempered with enough sense of guilt to control themselves.

Industry Versus Inferiority

This is the stage, lasting until age 12, during which children begin learning that society and people other than parents set rules. They must learn to adapt at school and in many new situations. Learning the many new rules requires hard work. Children do not always succeed and sometimes feel inferior. Too many failures cause them to retreat instead of moving ahead to other stages.

Fig. 8-6

Erik Erikson, a psychoanalyst and psychologist who was born in 1902, theorized that a pattern of social development covered the entire human life span. He suggested that we pass through eight different stages, at each of which we face a particular "crisis." Our successful social development depends on how we respond to the crisis.

autonomy
state of being independent

Identity Versus Role Confusion

This is a time of many changes as individuals move from childhood through adolescence to beginning adulthood at age 19. Peer pressure conflicts with their desire to be individuals. Tremendous physical changes occur. Sexuality begins to assert itself. Individuals begin wondering who they are and particularly what they will be. At this stage they begin the first serious thinking about future careers.

Graduating from high school, going to college, getting your first job, thinking about how you want to spend the rest of your life are among the major events you encounter at this stage. This stage is important because it is when you begin serious preparation for a career. Your choices and preparation are important because much of the remainder of your adult life will be taken up with work.

Despite its importance to them, many high school seniors do not seriously think about and prepare for their future careers, according to some recent studies. At the same time, more high-school-aged students are now in the workforce than there have been in more than 20 years. Whatever their reasons for working, teenagers holding jobs are not necessarily gaining experience useful to them in making good career choices. For one reason, the kinds of jobs they have do not train them in skills that will be useful in career advancement. Working teenagers may learn to handle money and interact with others in a work situation, but in general, work experience may not be as useful as good academic preparation for future career success.

In this stage, teenagers face many choices and demands, including whether to work or not, or how to balance a need to work with a desire for further education. How individuals handle all these confusing demands shapes their adult life.

Psychologists once thought that personality was fixed for life at this stage. Erikson, however, identified the three additional stages described below, at which he said further development occurred.

Intimacy Versus Isolation

At this stage, in early or young adulthood, individuals form attachments with others, marry, and give up some part of themselves for the sake of maintaining a relationship. They also form bonds with coworkers and other acquaintances. At the same time, they maintain a strong sense of themselves. If individuals have not successfully resolved role confusion at the Identify versus Role Confusion stage, they may have difficulty forming bonds and, as a result, feel lonely and isolated.

Generativity Versus Stagnation

Through work or children, individuals attempt to make a contribution to life. Because they cannot be constantly active and creative, they have periods of stagnation during which they build up strength. Those who have not developed successfully through earlier stages may become more stagnant than generative at this point, middle age, and focus on their own comfort and needs.

Integrity Versus Despair

Those who have gone through all the previous stages successfully will have a good feeling about their life—a sense of integrity—at this stage, which is old age. Those with more failures than successes will feel more despair at this time. Everyone has experienced some successes, and even the most successful people have had some failures. The balance is what is important, Erikson feels.

You read Shakespeare's description of the different stages of life, which included a rather negative view of old age, in the To The Point box on page 206. Another poet had a different view of old age. These lines from the poem "Rabbi Ben Ezra" by Robert Browning (1812–1889) project a more optimistic, positive view of life's later stages:

> Grow old along with me!
> The best is yet to be,
> The last of life, for which the first was made.

Moral Development

As you read, social development involves learning that you are not the center of the universe and that you must interact with other people. **Moral development** involves the growing recognition of the concept of right and wrong. At the egocentric stage, infants know only what pleases or displeases them. They eventually learn that the universe does not revolve around them and that there are other people with desires that they must consider. Children learn that doing certain things will result in punishment, so they avoid doing them.

Eventually, children **internalize** certain ideas, which means that they make the ideas a part of their way of thinking. As a result, they avoid some actions not because of a fear of outside punishment or reward but because of internal feelings of guilt and shame or pleasure and contentment.

Piaget believed that the essence of moral behavior is a willingness to follow rules that regulate interpersonal activities. To study the development

moral development
the development of the concepts of right and wrong

internalize
make an idea, value, or attitude a part of one's way of thinking

of morality in young children, Piaget observed how they played games of marbles. He selected marbles because it was a game for children and in playing it and following rules, the players were most likely following their own thought patterns and not imitating adults.

Piaget's observations led him to suggest three stages of moral development, any two of which could be overlapping: egocentrism, incipient cooperation, and genuine cooperation. Let's look briefly at each of these stages. You will note similarities to the stages of cognitive development that you read about earlier.

Egocentrism

In this stage (about 4 to 7 years of age) children do not follow or understand rules but say that they do. This stage is illustrated by two youngsters Piaget observed playing a game of marbles in which each followed his own set of rules. They were, in effect, playing two independent games, but acted as if they were playing together.

Incipient Cooperation

This stage (about 7 to 11) marks the beginning of real social awareness. Understanding of the rules is not complete, but children do cooperate as they compete with each other. They cooperate by agreeing to follow the basic rules as they compete to win. Because understanding is incomplete, there are many arguments and discussions about what the rules are.

Genuine Cooperation

At about 11, children begin to master the rules. In fact, at this stage, the rules can become as important as the game itself. Children settle differences of opinion by referring to the rules. They also like to invent rules to cover all imagined possibilities.

Developing Concept of Rules

After studying how children apply rules, Piaget then sought to determine how they thought about them. Again he observed stages in the developing sense of what rules were. These stages coincided with those of applying or practicing the rules. He identified two stages of this moral development, further dividing the first stage into two parts. Essentially, children move from a blind, unknowing acceptance of rules to a mature subjective attitude about the formulation and application of rules.

Fig. 8-7

According to Piaget, at about age 11, children begin to master the rules of a game.

Stage One (4 to 10 Years)

This stage is divided into two parts. In both, children believe some authority has created the rules and that the rules are unchangeable. In the first part of stage one, called *absolutistic*, children believe rules come from an authority who invented the game and they cannot be changed, but *do* allow rule changes to be made. Piaget believed the contradiction existed because the children's understanding of rules is so limited. They do not recognize the changes as such, but see them as other versions of the rules.

With a greater understanding of the rules in the second part of stage one, children begin to reject alterations. At the same time, however, they still fail to understand the purpose of rules and continually break them. Remember that this stage coincides with the egocentric period of development, during which children see themselves as the center of everything.

It is during this period that children exhibit what Piaget called **moral realism**. He meant by this that they judge an action solely by results and not by intent. Piaget used the clinical method to develop his theory of moral realism. In one experiment, he told children a story about two boys. One boy wanted to help his father by filling an inkwell. In doing so, he

moral realism
a tendency exhibited by younger children to judge an action solely by results and not by intent

made a large ink stain on the table cloth. The other boy was just playing with the inkwell and he made a small blot on the cloth.

By questioning them, Piaget determined that the children judged by the result. They judged the boy who made the larger stain more guilty, even though he wanted to be helpful, than the one who made a smaller stain, even though he was just fooling around. Intentions, Piaget theorized, were not relevant to the children's concept of responsibility and guilt.

Stage Two (About 10 Years)

At about age 10, children begin to realize that rules can be changed, that people make them up, and that they can as well. They start to understand that rules work only when everyone agrees to them. They move from an absolutist morality to a more flexible one and eventually no longer simply accept rules to follow but select the rules they and others agree to.

Children eventually develop a subjective responsibility. This comes about as they move further out in the world and away from the influence of only their family. They see there are different points of view and different rules. They begin to judge an act by intent as well as result. As they move away from egocentricity, they become aware that rules serve purposes for all. They develop the realization that cooperation is necessary and rules are needed to govern the interaction of humans.

Kohlberg's Theory

Whereas Piaget considered the use and understanding of rules to be indicative of moral development, the psychologist Lawrence Kohlberg interpreted moral development in terms of what people think about moral issues. He attempted to create a structure that would show the development of a sense of justice.

Kohlberg posed moral dilemmas for people to solve. A typical dilemma was whether it is right to steal medicine for a dying person. He created a system of scoring the answers people gave. As a result of his research, he divided the development of morality into three stages. As you read them, note the similarities between Kohlberg's and Piaget's theories of moral development.

Stage One: Preconventional Level (4 to 10 Years)

The child is under extreme control. Others impose rules, which children follow because of fear of punishment or desire for rewards.

Stage Two: Conventional Level (10 to 13 Years)

A desire to please develops. Children learn rules that others have made and follow them so that people important to them will praise them and consider them good. They are able to identify with authority figures enough to determine what will be considered good or bad. They become interested in doing what is right and keeping the social order.

Stage Three: Postconventional Level (13 Years or Older)

Cognitive abilities have developed to the point at which individuals can mentally put themselves in other people's places. Children before adolescence are not capable of this kind of thinking. Some people never do reach this stage of development. At this stage individuals have made the rules their own—they have internalized them. They behave according to what they believe is the right thing to do. Actions are not influenced solely by external rewards and punishment. How individuals feel about themselves and their actions is more important.

At this level, people recognize that two accepted standards of behavior can conflict and that they must often make hard choices between the two. Choices are based on a sense of what is right and wrong. Generally, when faced with conflicts, people tend to follow the law, but in some cases they may ignore the general law and the opinion of society. In the latter situation, they are governed by strongly held beliefs and their knowledge that if they do not act in accordance with their beliefs, they will not like themselves.

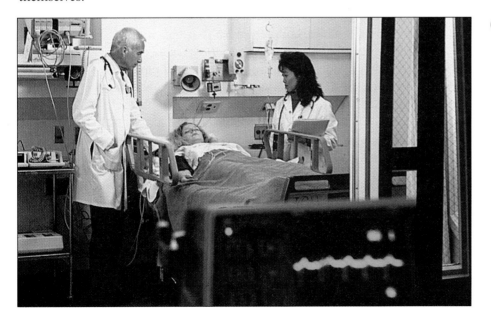

Fig. 8-8

To study moral development, Kohlberg asked people to solve moral dilemmas. He evaluated the answers and scored them on a scale to indicate stages of development. A typical problem he posed was whether or when to turn off the life-support systems of a terminally ill person.

▼ EMOTIONAL DEVELOPMENT

Infants interact with few people and things. At preschool age, they have more interaction, but it is still mostly within the family. At school age, they move out of the home environment and into a new environment, where they encounter many new people and experiences. All these changes require new responses, which shape **emotional development**. Basic emotional traits become established at an early age, but these traits change and modify as new conditions are encountered. In terms of emotional development, psychologists have identified the following stages. Again, note how emotional development reflects development in other ways.

emotional development
development of emotional traits; feelings

Attachment and Dependency

During a child's first 18 months, emotional development can be characterized by the terms *attachment* and *dependency*. At this age, children learn that a certain person—usually a mother—is the source of warmth, food, and comfort. Children become *attached* to and *dependent* on that person. If the object of attachment and dependency is removed, children suffer anxiety.

Attachment is not love, although love may grow out of attachment. As children mature, explore more, and are allowed more freedom by their mothers or caretakers, the next stage in emotional development begins.

Autonomy and Independence

Between 18 months and 3 years, children develop autonomy and independence. In this stage great changes occur. From the crib and the environment of only parents and siblings, children move to a big world and discover that not all of it is there to please, amuse, or comfort them.

This period of adjustment strongly influences emotional development. Overly protective parents may cause their children to become timid. A child constantly hearing, "don't touch," "be careful," "come back," "stop," may become reluctant to experiment and have difficulty facing new experiences as an adult. Parents, of course, must teach children that they cannot do whatever they want. Actions have consequences. Striking a match could cause a fire. The ideal is for the child to learn that exploring is good, but that sometimes it is necessary to be careful. Through the interplay of the need to explore and the need for care, children develop autonomy and independence.

Identification and Imitation

Identification and imitation play a part in emotional development, and at this stage, beginning about age 3, when young children unconsciously

Fig. 8-9

In our first months we develop an attachment to a person, usually our mother. Attachment and dependency are our main characteristics. If the object of our attachment is removed, we suffer anxiety. If we receive adequate care and love during this period, we develop a sense of security in the world and are ready to move to the next stage of development.

imitate selected models, identification and imitation dominate. As children begin to notice physical differences between the sexes, they start to identify their own sex roles. Children tend to identify and imitate parents of the same sex. Some theorists believe that moral values emerge at this stage.

Conscience and Moral Development

Initially, children's decisions to do what is right and avoid what is wrong stem from a desire to be rewarded or to avoid punishment. Later, they do what is right to please people they like. At a still later age, older children and young adults do what they feel is best for society. At this stage individuals have developed adult emotions. This corresponds to the final level of moral development in Kohlberg's stages. Not everyone fully achieves this level of development.

▼ WORK AND DEVELOPMENT

This chapter has discussed how you develop psychologically to become the person you are and have the personality you do. This final section briefly reviews the importance of work and development. Most of your waking hours as an adult will be devoted to work, which to a large degree will define you. How you have developed helps determine the work you do, and the work in turn influences your development. Not only the specific work you do but society's perception of work in general helps shape you.

TO THE POINT

Recent research shows that parents influence their children's cognitive and moral development in many subtle ways of which the parents are often unaware.

Gerald Patterson, a psychologist at the Oregon Social Learning Center, conducting a study of more than 500 families, reported that most parents do not know the real messages that their children get from them. Frequently it is the opposite of what is intended.

For example, in disciplining children, parents frequently teach them to be disobedient. Once a child has been asked to do something, such as clean up her room, Dr. Patterson said, the parents must follow through. Many don't, and the child learns disobedience pays off.

On the other hand, insisting on absolute obedience to authority seems to impair cognitive growth, according to a study by Earl Schaefer and Marianna Edgerton at the University of North Carolina. In a related study, Elaine Blechman, a clinical psychologist at Albert Einstein Medical College in New York, said there is a relationship between performance in social and academic life and how well family members work together to resolve conflicts. Children from families in which conflicts are resolved by everyone participating and discussing problems adjust better socially than those from families in which one person dictates the solution.

Findings quoted in the July 29, 1986, issue of *The New York Times.*

The meaning of work has changed through time depending on conditions, retaining throughout, to different degrees and with different emphasis, three basic meanings:

1. Work is a hard necessity, painful and burdensome.
2. Work is a means toward ends.
3. Work is a creative act that is good for its own sake.[2]

The meaning of work to an individual also differs within the person's lifetime, depending on that person's age and condition. A worker facing mandatory retirement gives work a different meaning than does a worker just beginning a career. An unemployed person needing a job gives work a different meaning than does a gainfully employed person.

Studies have shown changing and contrasting feelings about work between generations of workers. Workers in the 1950s, coming out of a Great Depression and a world war, valued their work highly and identified with their jobs. Workers today are less likely to identify themselves with their jobs; they stress the importance of leisure activities and put their family role above their work role. You will read more about the changing work force in Chapter 16.

As Lloyd Lofquist and Rene Dawis state in their book *Adjustment to Work*, we have inherited a cultural view that "work is central to [personal] development and total life adjustment; and . . . work provides a situation for satisfying needs." Whatever views you have of work, it is a large part of your life.

SUMMARY

1. Psychologists focus on the different stages of life to learn what happens in each of them and how the stages interact to form the whole. The various stages occur only roughly at the same age for everyone. They do occur in the same sequence.

2. The significant basic stages people go through are infancy (birth to 3 years), preschool (3 to 5 years), preadolescence (6 to 11 years), adolescence (12 to 18 years), young adult (19 to 45 years), middle age (46 to 65 years), and old age (65 years to death). The ages serve only as a rough guide.

3. Psychologists study four broad aspects of development: physical and motor, mental and cognitive, social and moral, and emotional.

4. Babies are born with some motor ability but must develop many motor skills. They do so rapidly. Learned motor skills include moving the head, turning over in a crib, crawling, standing, and, eventually, walking. Newborn babies react to stimuli (any agent, action, or condition that causes a response), such as light, pain, and touch.

5. Babies are born with some "holdover reflexes" that serve no obvious direct need but are useful indicators of normal development. They lose these reflexes quickly.

6. Thinking, remembering, learning, and using language are all part of cognitive development. The psychologist recognized as the most prominent modern researcher of cognitive development is Jean Piaget.

7. Piaget determined that the difference between younger and older children was not that the latter were brighter but that there was a qualitative difference in the way children thought at different ages.

8. Heredity influences cognitive development in two ways:
   a. It sets broad limits on cognitive functions.
   b. It transmits automatic behavioral reactions.

9. Social and moral (psychosocial) development is necessary to survive in a complex society in which people are dependent on each other.

10. Social and moral development are also shaped by heredity and environment. Environment may be the greater force of the two, but that is still not definitely known.

11. Erik Erikson put forth a much discussed theory of social development to cover the entire human life span.

12.   In the final stage of moral development, individuals internalize ideas. They avoid doing some things not because of outside punishment or reward but because of internal feelings of guilt and shame or pleasure and contentment.

13.   Piaget interpreted moral development as the way people learn, understand, and use rules. Lawrence Kohlberg interpreted moral development in terms of what people think about moral issues.

14.   Whatever views you have of work, it is a large part of your life. It is central to your development and total life adjustment, and it provides you with a way of satisfying your needs.

QUESTIONS FOR REVIEW AND DISCUSSION

1.   Explain briefly the relationship of age to stages of development. What is more significant than age in the development stages?

2.   What are the broad age-based stages psychologists group people in? What stage are you in now? What can you recall of previous stages?

3.   Explain briefly what physical development is. What does motor development refer to?

4.   What did Piaget's study of the wrong answers children gave on tests reveal to him?

5.   In what two ways does heredity influence cognitive development?

6.   What is our psychosocial development?

7.   Briefly sum up Erik Erikson's theory of social development.

8.   What are the characteristics of Kohlberg's Postconventional Level (Stage 3)? At what age do we reach it?

ACTIVITIES

1.   The psychologist Erik Erikson said we all pass through eight stages of social development, each characterized by a crisis. Think back on your life. Can you recall being in any one of the stages? What can you remember about it? What crisis did you encounter? Can you recall trying to impress your parents or an older sibling? What was the result? Write a one-page description of some episode that reflects one of the stages.

2.   At your school or public library try to find a biography (either a book or an article in a publication) of Jean Piaget or another psychologist mentioned in this chapter. Read it. Make a one-page outline of the major events in the individual's life.

KEY TERMS
Define the following:

Accommodation
Adaptation
Assimilation
Association
Autonomy
Cognitive development
Compensation
Conservation
Egocentric
Emotional development
Identity
Internalize
Introspective method
Moral development
Moral realism
Motor development
Object permanence
Organization
Physical development
Reflexes
Reversibility
Social development

3. To get an idea of the patience and concentration that psychologists must have when conducting experiments or observing people, spend an hour observing some activity and making notes of all you see. You can watch children playing in a playground, people playing ball or other games at a park, or people in bleachers watching others. Or you can observe the activities of a young relative or a pet. Your observing must be unnoticed and not interfere with the natural behavior. Your notes should be thorough, because the observer never knows what is important and what is not.

4. Lawrence Kohlberg described three stages, or levels, of moral development. He called the highest or last one the Postconventional Level. People begin reaching this level at 13. Some, he said, never fully reach it. At this level a person's moral behavior is essentially based on what that person believes is right or wrong. Rules have been internalized. Rewards and punishment do play a major part in influencing behavior. Think about people you know or have read about (they can be real or fictional). Think of someone you know whose behavior indicates she or he has reached this level. Describe the person's actions that demonstrate your belief.

5. Look for periodicals or newspapers in which there are articles about how people develop. Try to find articles about recent experiments or theories that relate to what you have been reading in this chapter. (Psychology Today is one example of a publication; the science section in the Tuesday editions of The New York Times is another possible source.) Write a one-page report on the major points of an article. Note any different results from those of previous researchers.

CASE 1

Why Children Behave as They Do

Some second graders were each asked to perform a small task. As a reward each was given a bag of M&M candies. They were then asked to share the candies with other second graders who were coming in and who had not received any. The youngsters were asked to share in three different environments:

1. When only they and the other children were present
2. When they could see themselves in a mirror
3. When an adult was present looking at them

Based on research by William Froming, psychologist at the University of Florida at Gainesville.

1. Describe how you believe the children behaved when asked to share their candies in each of the three different situations.

2. Can you relate their behavior to any of the stages of social or moral development you have read about in this chapter?

3. Is it possible to anticipate further development?

CASE 2

Stages of Moral or Social Development

Leo and Nadine carried their lunch trays around the aisles of the company cafeteria, looking for a place to sit. All the tables were taken.

"Looks like everyone is eating in today," Nadine said. "I don't see a single place."

"Well, let's walk around again," Leo said. "I hope we get a table soon, my soup is getting cold."

They continued to walk slowly. "Look over there," Nadine said as she stopped and pointed to a table for four. "Those people have finished eating and are playing cards. Boy, that's not very thoughtful with so many of us waiting to sit down to eat."

"Yeah," Leo agreed. "They know they're not supposed to do that. The company puts little notices on the tables asking people not to keep tables when they finish eating if the place is crowded."

Leo and Nadine stared at the four card players for a few seconds. The players ignored them, and Leo and Nadine continued looking for a table.

"Hey," Leo said. "Over there is a guy just reading at a table for two. Let's ask him to let us have the table. He can go read anyplace."

"Okay," Nadine replied, and they went over to the table.

"Hi," Leo said. "I see you're finished with lunch. I wonder if we could have this table."

The reader barely looked up. "I haven't finished my coffee," he snapped, and pointed to a cup that had about a swallow left in it.

"But—" Nadine began to sputter in protest. "You. . ."

"We're just about done," a woman at a nearby table said. "You can sit here." Her lunch companion nodded in agreement.

"Oh, but you haven't finished your dessert," Nadine said.

"Don't worry," the other woman assured her. "I've really eaten all I should. Here, sit down."

The two women took two final hasty swallows of their coffee and got up. Leo and Nadine sat down, telling the two women how grateful they were. The man at the nearby table who had refused to get up kept on reading.

"Boy, people certainly are different," Leo said in a voice he hoped the reader could hear. "Those two women weren't even really finished with their lunch and they gave us their table—while that guy. . ." He left the sentence unfinished.

1. What stages of moral or social development do the people in this vignette exhibit?

MECHANISMS OF DEVELOPMENT: How We Learn

There is no desire more natural than the desire for knowledge. We try all the ways that can lead us to it. When reason fails, we use experience.
Montaigne

Learning is something you do all your life. Sometimes you learn as the result of conscious effort, such as when you memorize facts or a passage as part of school work. Sometimes learning just "happens" to you. Learning is an exciting topic of research and investigation among psychologists and other scientists today. How do people learn? What do they learn? What is learning? With facts gathered in experiments and observations using new instruments and technologies, scientists are developing new theories to answer these old questions.

▼ WHAT IS LEARNING?

Simply defined, learning is behavior modification. Or, stated another way, learning is development. Both statements are accurate to some extent, but neither is completely accurate or sufficiently broad. Not all behavior modification or development results from learning. As you read in Chapters 7 and 8, physical development is largely a result of your inherited genes, and it occurs in similar stages for all humans. Your cognitive and emotional development results from a combination of heredity and learning. Your social and moral development is largely a result of learning.

You could also say that learning is an attempt to acquire knowledge of the environment so as to operate in it successfully. As you read in Chapter 7, you are always interacting with your environment, changing it and being changed by it, and this is part of the learning experience. Your learning now is focused on modifying your behavior so you will be successful in future social and career environments when you leave school. At the same time, you are constantly learning in an informal, almost unconscious, way how to behave in your current environment.

Because learning results in behavior modification, it follows that observing a change in behavior is the best way to determine if learning has taken place. The most common example of this technique is one with which you are very familiar: testing. You study a topic in school and then are tested to determine how much of it you have retained. Although observation of behavior modification is the only way to determine if learning has taken place, it is not a perfect way because there is a difference between learning and performance—a fact you no doubt have experienced first hand.

For example, if you have ever had to take a test on a well-known subject when you have been emotionally upset or physically ill, your performance almost certainly did not reflect your learning. Also, some people suffer from test anxiety and as a consequence their efforts on tests do not really reflect their learning. If shy persons must perform or speak before a large number of people, their behavior will probably not accurately reflect their learning.

Fig. 9-1

Children are constantly learning, sometimes in an informal, almost unconscious way, how to behave in their environments.

Learned and Unlearned Behavior

As used in this text, **learning** means changing behavior more or less permanently by acquiring knowledge, understanding, or skill through experience. In this sense it differs from **maturation**, which means behavioral change resulting from biologically predetermined processes. Overall development results from both learning and maturation.

Many abilities and skills result from maturation and not from learning. Flinching or ducking to avoid being hit, for example, is not a learned skill but a reflex performed automatically. You are born with these reflexes. You do not need to learn the biological act of eating. You do, however, need to learn the social act of eating—that is, using a knife and fork.

Different Kinds of Learning

Psychologists have identified several different ways in which you learn. The simplest kind of learning is called **habituation learning**. It is through habituation that you learn how to behave or cope in your current environment. It means getting used to something.

When you enter a new environment—say a new school or a new job—you at first feel uncomfortable and uneasy. This is true even if you have the necessary skills to do the required work. In a very short time, you begin to feel comfortable in the new environment. This is an example of habituation. You have become used to the new environment.

A higher level of learning is called **associative learning**. This kind of learning results from the interaction between you and your environment. As

learning
changing behavior more or less permanently by acquiring knowledge, understanding, or skill through experience

maturation
behavioral development or change resulting from biologically predetermined patterns

habituation learning
learning by becoming used to something

associative learning
learning that results from things going together

the name implies, learned behavior (a response) results from or is associated with a particular stimulus. Two kinds of associative learning have been identified: *classical conditioning* and *operant conditioning*. These have been long studied by behavioral psychologists, and you will read more about them later in this chapter.

A third kind of learning, which is attracting more and more attention today, is **cognitive learning**. This kind of learning stresses the process that occurs in the mind or brain between the time a stimulus occurs and the time a response is made. Cognitive psychologists are trying to determine just what the mind—a nonphysical entity—is and how it relates to the brain—a physical entity. Unlike the behaviorists, they do not believe that all learning is the result of associating a response to a stimulus. They believe another step occurs—thinking. You will look at each of these learning viewpoints in more detail below.

cognitive learning
higher-level learning involving thinking, knowing, understanding, and anticipation

▼ CLASSICAL CONDITIONING

You were introduced to the concept of conditioning in Chapter 2. Conditioning is another word for a certain type of learning. Ivan Pavlov, a Russian scientist (1849–1936), was one of the first to conduct experiments that demonstrated **classical conditioning** in animals. He gave food to dogs while a tone sounded. The dogs became conditioned to expect food at the sound of the tone, and as a result, they reacted to the sound of the tone as to a piece of meat.

classical conditioning
the process whereby a neutral stimulus becomes an effective stimulus in causing a specific response

Classical conditioning occurs when what is originally a **neutral stimulus**, one that does not produce any particular response (in this experiment, a tone), becomes a **conditioned stimulus**, one that does, or is made to, elicit a particular response. The tone became a conditioned stimulus and caused the same reaction (salivating) in the dogs that a piece of meat did. The dogs associated the tone with food.

neutral stimulus
a stimulus that does not produce any particular response

conditioned stimulus
a previously neutral stimulus that acquires the capacity to evoke a response

Subsequent studies and observations have proved that humans can and do learn behavior modification in the same way. Most people will exhibit the same kind of conditioning as Pavlov's dogs. Have you ever felt your mouth water when someone was describing a great meal they had? The *conditioned stimulus* was the spoken description, which caused your conditioned response. The description, of course, was a *neutral stimulus* until associated by you with food.

Conditioning Emotions

Pavlov's experiments showed how classical conditioning can affect physical reactions. An American psychologist, John Watson, showed that emotional reactions can also be conditioned. Watson believed that people are born with three basic emotions: fear, rage, and love—and that they can be conditioned to express them in response to a given stimulus. In an experiment that would not be allowed today, Watson and his associates used an 11-month-old boy to demonstrate how a fear response can be conditioned.

The boy initially had no fear of a white rat, which was thus a neutral stimulus. The experimenters then made a loud sound directly behind the baby's head whenever the white rat appeared. The sound frightened the boy. Eventually, the boy reacted with fear when the white rat appeared even if no noise was made. The neutral stimulus had become a conditioned one eliciting the emotion of fear.

Everyone has experienced similarly conditioned responses. Have you ever had to give a speech in front of a group of people and were frightened by the situation? Subsequently, just the thought alone will cause you to experience symptoms of anxiety and fear. Of course, if you frequently make speeches and they go well and you are applauded, your emotional response may change. You may learn to like the experience. Consequently, the thought of making a speech may cause you to experience emotions of pleasure.

Fig. 9-2

The famous early experiments on classical conditioning were carried out by a Russian scientist, Ivan Pavlov. He showed how dogs could be "conditioned" to begin salivating at the sound of a tone.

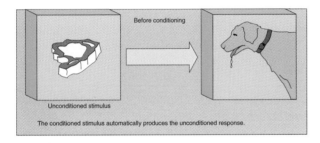

Before conditioning

Unconditioned stimulus

The conditioned stimulus automatically produces the unconditioned response.

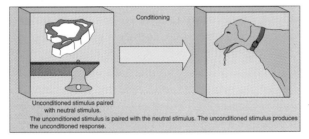

Conditioning

Unconditioned stimulus paired with neutral stimulus.
The unconditioned stimulus is paired with the neutral stimulus. The unconditioned stimulus produces the unconditioned response.

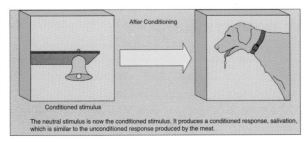

After Conditioning

Conditioned stimulus

The neutral stimulus is now the conditioned stimulus. It produces a conditioned response, salivation, which is similar to the unconditioned response produced by the meat.

Fig. 9-3

Conditioning occurs in three stages as illustrated here.

If you have ever played the game Simon Says, you have experienced classical conditioning. In the game, one person is the leader. The leader performs simple actions, such as raising an arm, clapping, waving, bending. The group is to imitate the leader's action only when the leader uses the full expression, "Simon says 'do this!'" If the leader does not say "Simon says 'do this!'" but only "Do this!" the followers are not supposed to imitate the action. If the leader uses the full command several times as she or he moves and then suddenly says only "Do this!" many followers conditioned to follow the leader's action will do so now although it means losing the game.

Counterconditioning

counterconditioning
conditioning to replace a conditioned response with a different response

If a young boy can be conditioned to fear a white rat, it would seem logical that the boy could be reconditioned, so to speak, not to fear the rat. Experiments have proven that such **counterconditioning** is possible. If a stimulus elicits a conditioned response of fear, for example, one way to change the response is to associate the stimulus with one that elicits a pleasant or secure feeling. When the white rat appeared, the young boy could be given a treat, such as candy or ice cream. Eventually, he would associate the white rat with a feeling of pleasure and stop reacting with fear when the rat appears.

 ## ▼ OPERANT CONDITIONING

operant conditioning
the process whereby behavior is influenced by its consequences

Classical conditioning focuses on the way in which stimuli influence behavior: a tone sounds, a dog salivates. **Operant conditioning** focuses on how behavior is influenced by its consequences.

You see examples of operant conditioning daily in your own and in others' lives. For example, people generally arrive on time for work or class.

They try to arrive on time because they have learned that arriving late has bad or negative consequences for them: their pay is cut, they are fired, they miss some important information, or they must stay after school. If they arrive on time, they keep their job, receive full pay, get the important information, or do not need to stay after school. The stimuli, called *consequences* in these situations, come *after* the action.

Consequences of behavior are also called *reinforcers*. They are so called because they *reinforce* a certain behavior. There can be *negative* reinforcers (not being fired) and *positive* reinforcers (obtaining the important information). You read about reinforcers and the role they play in your development in Chapter 7. Reinforcers are consequences of your actions that make you want to take the same action over again.

The behavior that you exhibit to obtain a desired result or avoid an undesired one *operates* on your environment accordingly. Hence the name *operant conditioning*. B. F. Skinner, the famous American psychologist, was the proponent of operant conditioning. He developed what has become known as a Skinner box for experimenting with animals. The box is designed to allow the animal to behave in a certain way, such as pressing a bar or pecking at a key, and as a consequence of that behavior, to receive food. Food reinforces food-getting behavior (bar-pressing, key-pecking).

Reinforcement Levels

In addition to the two *kinds* of reinforcers—positive and negative—there are two *levels* of reinforcers: primary reinforcers and secondary reinforcers.

Primary reinforcers are important because they meet biological needs. Primary reinforcers include water, food, sex, and safety.

primary reinforcers
reinforcers that meet biological needs

Secondary reinforcers are learned. When eating out, for example, good food presentation (design, trimmings, color) can reinforce your going to a certain restaurant. This is an example of a secondary reinforcer. These secondary reinforcers are important only as they relate to the primary reinforcers. If food meant nothing to you, good food presentation would be meaningless. Money is a prime example of a secondary reinforcer. The money itself is valuable only for how it is associated with primary reinforcers. Nonetheless, as money proves, a secondary reinforcer can be very powerful.

secondary reinforcers
learned reinforcers that derive their effectiveness from their association with primary reinforcers

Incidental Reinforcers

For a consequence to be considered a reinforcer, it must increase the frequency or likelihood of the behavior. If it doesn't, it is not a reinforcer. At the same time, it is not always easy to identify a reinforcer. A parent may

B. F. Skinner, the American psychologist who popularized operant conditioning, developed this box, in which an animal could push a bar (operant behavior), which released a pellet of food into the cage (consequence and reinforcer).

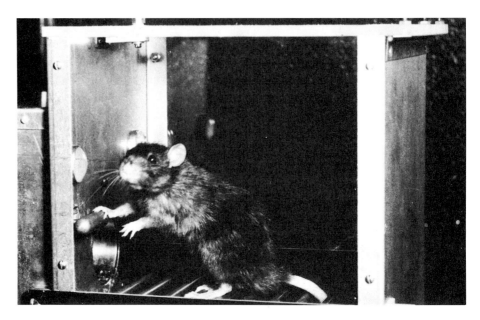

scold a child for its bad behavior. But if the child wants attention and gets it in no other way, then scolding becomes a reinforcer of bad behavior! Such a parent is achieving the exact opposite reaction from what is desired. Similar examples can be found in the workplace, where managers might unwittingly reinforce unwanted behavior by paying special attention to those who create problems.

Reinforcement Schedules

For a reinforcement to be effective, it must quickly follow the behavior. If the consequence of our behavior comes later, it will be a weak reinforcer. This can best be illustrated by operant behavior that has two possible consequences. The consequence that occurs first will be the stronger. A person will drink alcohol (operant behavior) because the immediate consequence is a feeling of pleasure. The other consequence—sickness and possibly an early death—is delayed and thus weaker.

To be effective, a reinforcer does not need to follow every occurrence of the behavior that brings it about. Psychologists have discovered that reinforcement occurs on a specific pattern or schedule. The two major schedules are continuous reinforcement and intermittent reinforcement.

Continuous Reinforcement

continuous reinforcement
reinforcement that occurs each time the operant behavior occurs

Continuous reinforcement means that every time the operant behavior occurs, it is reinforced. Every time the rat pushes the bar, it receives food.

Every time you eat, you satisfy your hunger. Many simple types of operant behavior result in continuous reinforcement. If you are cold, you put on more clothes or turn up the heat. If the light hurts your eyes, you move it or turn it off. In each case, your behavior is reinforced by the consequences: warmth or less light. With more complex behavior, however, intermittent reinforcement is more common.

Psychology has many useful and practical applications. A relatively new practice is one aimed at helping pets. Pet psychology is a growing field. To some this might seem frivolous, but pet psychology grew out of many laboratory experiences, and it can have beneficial side effects for humans.

Knowing about operant conditioning and reinforcers can be useful. An owner was unable to stop his dog from making a mess on the carpet while he was away at work. Every evening he returned home to find a mess, and every evening he scolded the dog.

According to a veterinarian psychologist, the dog was seeking attention. If the animal could be said to verbalize its thoughts, it seemed to be saying, "All I need do is mess on the floor, and I get all kinds of attention."

The dog's operant behavior was making a mess, and the scolding was a reinforcer to the dog's need for attention. The owner changed the dog's behavior by ignoring it when it made a mess and paying attention to it when it did not.

TO THE POINT

Intermittent Reinforcement

intermittent reinforcement
reinforcement that occurs only sometimes when the operant behavior occurs

ratio schedule
in conditioning, a situation in which reinforcement depends on repeating operant behavior a certain number of times

interval schedule
in conditioning, a situation in which reinforcement depends on the passage of time, regardless of how many times the behavior is repeated

As you are aware, your behavior is not always reinforced by a rewarding consequence. Nonetheless, you will continue a particular behavior if it is sometimes reinforced by the desired consequence. This is **intermittent reinforcement**. For example, if a rat receives food only every sixth time it hits the bar, it will continue to hit the bar.

In this case the reinforcement depends on repeating the operant behavior a number of times. This is known as a **ratio schedule**. Intermittent reinforcement can also occur as the result of the passage of time, in which case it is known as an **interval schedule**. That is, reinforcement occurs hourly, daily, or weekly regardless of how many times the behavior is or is not carried out.

Generally speaking, ratio schedules generate a higher rate of operant behavior than interval schedules. The reason for this is that in an interval schedule, you cannot control the passage of time, so you can do nothing to speed up your reinforcement. In a ratio schedule, you can control the rate at which you behave and thus exercise some control over when you receive the reinforcement.

These two schedules—interval and ratio—can be further defined as either *fixed* or *variable*. So altogether you have four different schedules of intermittent reinforcement:

1. Fixed interval schedule
2. Variable interval schedule
3. Fixed ratio schedule
4. Variable ratio schedule

Each has its own effect on our operant behavior. Let's examine them individually.

Fixed Interval Schedule

The weekly paycheck is a good example of a reinforcer that comes at a fixed interval. You work five days, and every five days you receive the reinforcement. Even though you are not being reinforced constantly—or even hourly or daily—you are still motivated to work (your operant behavior) because you know that after the agreed amount of time, you will receive your reinforcement in the form of a paycheck. In addition to the paycheck, workers on a five-day week enjoy another reinforcer at the end of each work period: two free days. This reinforcer is particularly important to those workers who are paid only every other week or only once a month.

Animals show a drop in their response or operant behavior immediately after receiving the reinforcement because they have learned that it will be some time before they are reinforced again no matter what they do. They tend to increase their behavior as the time for the reinforcement approaches. This might be reflected by humans in the workplace and explain the "Monday blues." Workers know that it will be several days before payday, and in addition to feeling "down," they may not work as energetically on the first day as they do later in the week.

You probably experience a similar change in your operant behavior. You study hard just before the scheduled midterm and not quite so hard immediately after it. The fixed interval schedule generally results in an uneven behavior pattern.

Variable Interval Schedule

In this schedule, the reinforcements occur after a passage of time, but at different intervals. Promotions at work are one example of reinforcers on a variable interval schedule. Promotions definitely come, but they usually come as the result of retirements, resignations, or increased business, none of which occur at regular or fixed intervals. People continue working (operant behavior) in the hope of a promotion (reinforcement) even if they do not know exactly when it is likely to come.

The variable interval schedule has no distinctive effect on the rate at which the operant behavior is exhibited. While you might speed up just before and slow down just after payday or a test, the possibility of a future promotion does not have that effect on our behavior. The possibility does, of course, keep you coming to work each day and not slowing down too much on those blue Mondays—at least not if you really want a chance at a promotion.

Fixed Ratio Schedule

Under this schedule, reinforcement occurs every time a specific number of responses has been performed by the subject. For the rat, food always appears after it has pushed the bar for the fifth time in a row. A common example of fixed ratio schedule reinforcement in the workplace is piecework. With piecework, pay depends on the number of units a worker completes. For example, a worker is paid X dollars for every ten microchips he or she installs.

Those on a fixed ratio schedule of reinforcement tend to display a response pattern similar to that of those on a fixed interval schedule. That is, they show higher interest and productivity as they near completion of the required number of responses and lower interest and productivity right after reinforcement.

Variable Ratio Schedule

This schedule refers to a pattern in which the subject must perform a certain number of times before being reinforced, but the number of times varies. For instance, the rat might be reinforced with food after striking the bar 5 times, then after 3 times, then after 13 times, then after 1 time, and so on.

All the subject can know is that there will be a reinforcement if a particular behavior is carried out, but the subject never knows when the behavior will result in a reinforcement.

This schedule would seem to be the weakest conditioner, and the subject would be most likely to stop performing the operant behavior. Given the irregular pattern of rewards, one might expect that the operant behavior (pushing the bar) would quickly become *extinguished*. The opposite, actually, is true. Variable ratio schedules are *strong* conditioners of behavior. The rat, for example, not knowing at which bar press food will appear, presses the bar all the more often and rapidly.

Gamblers exhibit the kind of operant behavior conditioned by variable ratio schedules of reinforcement. They never know when they will win, only that if they keep playing they will sometimes win. That occasional win, even if the amount doesn't cover their losses, strongly reinforces their gambling behavior. The variable ratio reinforcment schedule could lead to gambling addiction, which is a growing problem in this country.

Random Reinforcement

If reinforcement follows no apparent schedule, the result can be odd behavior. Much superstitious behavior (behavior for which there appears to be no logical explanation) results from random reinforcement. If the rat is given food at irregular intervals, regardless of what it is doing, it might develop "superstitious" behavior. If the food happened to appear just as it scratched its right ear, it might subsequently continue to scratch its right ear when it wanted to obtain food. Sometimes food would come. Sometimes it would not.

You have seen examples of this behavior many times. The tennis pro who decides to wear a hat to shade his eyes and then wins the tournament might decide the hat is "lucky" and wear it thereafter whenever he plays. Sometimes he wins, and that reinforces his superstitious behavior.

Random reinforcement has been used to control and confuse people. Dictators exercise control by not letting people know when or what behavior will be reinforced (by either rewards or punishments). The same behavior at one time results in reward and at another time punishment. The result is people are confused and always uncertain about what they should do.

Fig. 9-5

A variable ratio schedule of reinforcement is one of the strongest. The subject, knowing that a certain behavior will be rewarded but not knowing when, feels compelled to repeat the behavior as frequently as possible. Gamblers are responding to a variable ratio schedule of reinforcement and the expectation that they will eventually be rewarded can make gambling addictive.

This is a favorite device of incompetent managers in large organizations. Because reinforcement is random, workers do not know what is expected of them and thus are never sure of their survival. Consequently, they feel powerless and unable to protect themselves from authority.

Punishment

Everyone has been punished for unwanted behavior: a smack on the rear, a harsh word, loss of allowance or some privilege. Although punishment is a form of conditioning that results in learning, punishment itself is *not* a reinforcer, but avoiding or escaping punishment *is*.

Negative reinforcement occurs when the operant behavior is intended to avoid or escape from unpleasant stimuli. If you are sitting in a cold draft, you can move or put on a sweater. The unpleasant situation existed before your behavior that was intended to change it. If you succeeded in changing it, your behavior is reinforced. Behavior that results in escaping or avoiding punishment is reinforced—negative reinforcement.

Punishment is often used in trying to change behavior. But many experiments and observations have shown that it is not an effective way to modify human behavior. Punishment may cause a change in behavior, but often not the desired one. It may result in the unwanted behavior being hidden or exhibited in other ways.

To Sum Up

Operant conditioning refers to behavior learned because of the reinforcement that follows it. Behavioral psychologists feel that most behavior—human or nonhuman—can be explained on the basis of reinforcement principles. As a rat learns to push a bar to get food, humans learn behavior that will result in reinforcement. A certain behavior becomes associated with a certain reinforcement, and thus the subject—human or lower order animal—learns to use that behavior for that result. The behavior patterns you learn are the ones associated with the results you want. These behavior patterns are thus reinforced, and you repeat them whenever you want the associated results.

▼ COGNITIVE LEARNING

While acknowledging that classical and operant conditioning play a large part in the behavior people learn, cognitive psychologists say that people also learn in other ways. Learning, they believe, often involves more than simply associating stimulus and response. Other paths are followed.

In a famous experiment involving three groups of rats and a maze, cognitive psychologists demonstrated the difference between operant conditioning and cognitive learning. One group was always fed upon successfully completing the maze. After some trial-and-error runs, this group learned the maze—a typical example of operant conditioning.

A second group was not given food for completing the maze until the third day. For the first two days, these rats wandered around the maze. They took as long to finish the maze and made as many errors at the end of the second day as they did the first day in the maze. They showed no signs of learning the maze. After receiving food, however, they went through the maze quickly.

The third group was not given food for completing the maze until seven days into the experiment. Their feeding had no connection to running the maze. For those first seven days, they wandered haphazardly through the maze, making many wrong turns each time and seemingly not learning how to get through it quickly. After receiving food for getting through the maze on the seventh day, they thereafter immediately ran the maze quickly.

So far all this sounds like typical operant conditioning. But there is a difference—a very significant one. The rats receiving food after three and those after seven days *immediately* thereafter began to run the maze well. Even though they had not shown it, these rats had in fact been learning the maze all along. Only after they were given a goal—food—did they put the learning to use to run through the maze without error. This interesting experiment also reflects on the difficulty of determining if learning has taken place. About the only way is through observing changed behavior.

Goal-Oriented Learning

All the groups of rats had to learn the maze. Even those given food from day one made errors on several runs before they learned it. The rats not at first given food demonstrated when finally given food that they had indeed also learned the maze. They had not used that learning until given a reason or goal in the form of food.

Edward Tolman, one of the American psychologists conducting such experiments, concluded that animals can be *goal-oriented* as well as *response-oriented*. Although a stimulus does lead to a response, he said, there is a brain process—cognition—that takes place between the two. He argued that by using this brain process, animals are selective as to which stimuli they will respond to.

Observational Learning

One kind of cognitive learning is **observational learning**. As the name implies, this is learning by observing others. This is also known as *imitation*, *vicarious learning*, or *modeling*. The collective theory under which psychologists group these explanations of learning is called *social learning theory*.

observational learning
learning by observation of others; imitation, vicarious learning, or modeling

Social Learning Theory

According to social learning theory, you imitate what you see. A well-known demonstration of this was filmed by Albert Bandura, a Stanford psychologist. Nursery school children watched a movie in which an adult struck a doll with a hammer and took other aggressive action. When the children played with the doll, many of them displayed similar behavior.

Experiments such as this have caused psychologists to worry about the effect of TV and movie violence on children. The general belief, however, holds that imitation is *not* automatic or without other influences. Developing or learning through imitation is a continuous and complex thing. All observations, not just a single one, such as viewing a violent scene on television, influence which behavioral patterns are learned.

Observational Learning Steps

According to Bandura, observational learning is a four-step process:

1. Paying attention and seeing the relevant behavior
2. Remembering the behavior in either words or mental images

Fig. 9-6

Cognitive psychologists have demonstrated that rats can learn to run a maze without reinforcement.

3. Converting the memory into action
4. Adopting the behavior

If you think about things you have learned in your lifetime, you quickly understand how influential and necessary observational learning is. Every game you learned was probably learned by watching others play it or demonstrate to you how to play. If you did not observe someone else doing it, you would have a difficult time learning how to jump rope, shoot marbles, play tennis, drive a car, or sail a boat.

▼ MEMORY

Without memory you would need to learn the same things over and over. What is memory? Where is memory? Psychologists, particularly over the last decade, have begun making significant gains in finding answers to these questions. Memory is associated with our mind, but what is the mind and how does it relate to the brain? Stephen Kosslyn, a Harvard psychologist and leading researcher into the workings of the brain, has answered the question this way: "The mind is what the brain does."

Associations, Not Facts

Scientists continually gain new insights into how you remember and how memory is related to learning. Recent experiments, for example, have indicated that memory is not so much a copy of facts or experience as it is the storage of the connections or associations between aspects of experience.

In this view of memory, learning requires mastering the proper strengths of the connections between different experiences or facts. These relationships appear to be encoded (stored) in groupings or patterns of cells.

Kinds of Memory

Psychologists speak of **memory systems**, which are the sets of common mechanisms for storing information. They also refer to **memory codes**, which are the different forms in which items are stored in the memory system.

Memory systems are divided into two subsystems: *active memory* and *long-term memory*. Keep in mind that these categories are based upon observations and experiments on how you use memory. Though they are useful distinctions in helping you to understand how memory works, the line between them is not definite or precise.

Active Memory

Active memory is much the smaller of the two kinds of memory systems. As its name implies, active memory is what you use when carrying out tasks. Psychologist Donald Broadbent has used the analogy of a desktop to describe active memory. In this analogy, active memory is like a desktop on which you place all related materials you need to perform a particular task.

Some of this related material comes from long-term memory, which can be compared to file cabinets or desk drawers. Psychologists refer to this related material as **operational memory**. It is memory you have stored away in long-term memory and have now activated for use.

Other related material enters into your active memory (onto your desk top) from outside experiences. Someone says something or hands you a report. This is called **short-term memory**. When you receive new information into active memory, you are likely to forget it quickly unless it is reinforced.

Active memory, whether short-term or operational, has limitations. If you have ever been interrupted while doing a math problem or just copying down a list of numbers, you probably lost your place. Psychologists believe that if you are told a list of random digits (they enter your short-term, active memory), the most you can repeat after a single trial is about eight. The same limit also applies to information you bring up out of long-term memory into operational memory. This limit on what you can hold in active memory curtails your ability to solve problems.

Psychologists have proposed that the basic mechanism of active memory is a continuing electrical process in the brain. Long-term memory, they theorize, involves more permanent structural changes in brain cells.

memory systems
cognitive mechanisms for storing information

memory codes
the different forms in which items are stored in the memory system

active memory
used in tasks currently being performed, consisting of short-term memory and operational memory

operational memory
material stored in long-term memory that has been activated for use in active memory

short-term memory
material that enters active memory directly from the environment and is unlikely to be retained unless reinforced

Long-Term Memory

long-term memory
all remembered material (associations) that is not in active memory

contiguity
the state of being close together

Long-term memory is all memory that is not in active memory. What is stored is *associations*. An example of the simplest kind of association was that made by the dog between a tone and food in Pavlov's experiment. This also illustrates one of the essential requirements of association: **contiguity**. Contiguity is the state of being close together. If the appearance of the food had not been contiguous with the sounding of the tone, the dog would never have associated the two. In all memory, contiguity is essential.

Insofar as the process is understood, scientists theorize that long-term memory stores associated material together in "memory cells." Old associations can give meaning to new input, which is then stored in its own "memory cell." The concept of a "memory cell" is theoretical. Their existence has not yet been proved. (Compare this concept with Piaget's concept of assimilation, Chapter 8.)

The way in which information is first stored is very important because this will determine how it will be used in the future. Say, for example, you are an avid skier and you are introduced to a person who is described as a skier. Your memory of that person will be filed in a memory cell associated with skiing, and you would most readily remember that person as someone to talk about skiing with or to plan a ski trip with. The person may also be a computer expert, but at the one time you hear this, it is of little interest to you.

Later, however, say you have developed an interest in computers and want advice from someone who knows about them. You probably would not think of your skiing friend as a source, at least not without effort or having your memory jogged by something else. So you can have a lot of information in your long-term memory, but its use depends to a large extent upon how you have filed it away in your memory cells.

Retrieval

effortless retrieval
recall of information occurring in a familiar context; recall without effort

effortful retrieval
recall of information occurring in an unfamiliar context; recall with effort

Retrieval is the process by which you recall information stored in long-term memory. Psychologists recognize two types of retrieval: effortless and effortful.

Effortless retrieval occurs when input comes to you in a familiar context. Your ability to recall the meaning of the common words in this book is an example of effortless retrieval.

Effortful retrieval occurs when input comes to you in an unfamiliar context. If you have ever encountered a person you know in one setting (say a teacher at school) in completely different surroundings (say at a disco), you may struggle a few minutes before you recall who the person really is.

Most psychologists also believe that *recall* and *recognition* are two different processes, although both are aspects of memory. Recall is the act of bringing something up from your memory. Recognition is the act of identifying something or someone on sight. For example, multiple-choice tests require a form of recognition, whereas essay tests require recall. Which do you think is easier? If you like multiple-choice tests better, you are in a majority because it does seem easier to recognize something than to recall it from memory. Some studies, however, suggest that this is not always true.

Memory Codes

The brain stores information in certain forms known as memory codes. Three such codes have been identified: imagery, motor, and symbolic.

You can conduct simple experiments to illustrate how important associations are in memory. Everyone easily remembers the sequence of numbers from zero to nine. They represent an organized sequence in long-term memory.

If you asked someone to say a number immediately after you say one, they most often would say the next one in the sequence. If you said "four," they would most often say "five."

Also ask someone to answer as quickly as possible whether a number you give them belongs in a given sequence, say one to four. If you then said "nine" at one time and "five" at another, their response would be faster with the nine because it is farther away from the sequence. The difference in the response time may be too small for you to register without instruments, but it is there. In active memory, you can temporarily rearrange associations. You can have someone remember numbers in different sequences, for example. Instead of four, five, six, have them remember five, six, four. They will be able to repeat the sequence immediately after you and probably for a short time thereafter. But, still later, after they have been distracted with other activities, they will forget this new temporary sequence. It will leave their active memory, and the normal sequence held in long-term memory will be the only one they remember.

Of course, you do store numbers in many different sequences in long-term memory: telephone numbers, social security numbers, ZIP Codes. But the less often you use special sequences of numbers, the harder it can be to bring them up into active memory.

TO THE POINT

Imagery

Einstein is quoted as having said that his most original ideas came to him in mental pictures, not in words or numbers. Aristotle believed that thought is impossible without images. **Imagery**, the internal representation of an outside reality, is probably the most common way in which you store information.

Psychologists have studied imagery since the early 1900s, but recently have been giving it much more attention. In the 1980s, they discovered some interesting information. They discovered that some people constantly have images in their mind, shifting and changing. Others have very few. But only about 3 percent of all people do not seem to have any mental pictures at all.

The most common use of imagery is to make a decision or solve a problem. You can no doubt easily remember doing this yourself. For example, when trying to decide what to wear, have you ever pictured yourself in the different choices available? Also, if you have to make a choice between two activities—playing tennis or going swimming—you may have pictured yourself in each to test which you felt most strongly about.

Many people even use mental images to solve purely logical problems. Experiments by Janellen Huttenlocher, a psychologist at the University of Chicago, showed that people used images to solve such logical puzzles as the following: John is smarter than Bill, and Susan is smarter than John. Is Susan smarter than Bill? Huttenlocher's research showed people solved this by picturing a line and putting dots on it to represent the individuals in the premise. Dots to the right represented the smarter person.

Motor Codes

The philosopher Gilbert Ryle in 1949 distinguished between remembering *that* and remembering *how*. Remembering "that" refers to remembering information. Remembering "how" refers to motor skills that you have acquired and that you can perform without conscious thought.

Riding a bike, typing, tying a knot are all examples of motor skills that you store as motor codes. Once they are learned, you perform these activities without thinking about them. Indeed, if you do try to think about them—that is, visualize how you do them—you are likely to be unable to do them well.

Have you ever been asked to give directions on how to get to a certain place and were unable to do so even though you know perfectly well how to get there and travel the route often? This is an example of having stored something in motor codes, which you now have difficulty transferring to another code.

Computers, used so extensively today in all areas of business, are mechanical and electronic brains that work in many ways as human brains do. Computers can store, process, and retrieve memory. They have long-term memory on diskettes or tape. They have short-term memory or active memory that exists only when the power is on and disappears unless stored into long-term memory when power is shut off.

Computers store information in codes or symbols, usually an arrangement of 1s and 0s. They have memory that can be altered (random-access memory, or RAM) and memory that can be used but not changed (read-only memory, or ROM).

Despite the many similarities between computers and the human brain, there is one striking difference: these "thinking" machines cannot, in fact, think. They cannot yet make the associations that constitute thinking in humans. Increasingly successful efforts are being made to give these machines what is called "artificial intelligence," or AI. But experts consider it unlikely that computers will ever be made that can "think" as humans can. Computers have a mechanical brain, but they lack a mind, that vaguely understood entity which is "what the brain does."

Because of their huge and growing capacity to store information ("memory") and call it up quickly in different forms, computers, created by thinking humans, enhance the power of the human mind.

TO THE POINT

Fig. 9-7

We remember motor skills in a different way than we remember other information. Once we learn to ride a bike, we remember the technique and can do it without conscious thought. Psychologists say this type of memory is stored as motor codes, one way our brain stores information. Other types of storage codes are imagery and symbols.

symbol
something that stands for another thing

interference
as used here, the occurrence of new information that drives out or makes recovery of old information more difficult

Selecting the right numbers on a push-button phone is another example of motor skills. Some people can remember the pattern of the numbers and push them automatically. When asked to say what the numbers are, they must actually go through the motions to remember them. Typists have the same experience when asked to name the keys on a blank typewriter keyboard.

Symbolic Codes

A **symbol** is something that stands for another thing. You use symbols all the time. They are quite common on traffic signs along highways, and they are used to help people find their way around such places as large airports.

Language, of course, is our universal symbol. You use words all the time to stand for something else. Words themselves can become images—you can see words in your mind—but their basic function is as symbols. Words are powerful symbols, as many tests have shown. In one test the word *yellow* was written in blue ink. People could easily read the word and were not bothered by the actual color. When asked to name the color, however, they hesitated because of the power of the word.

Forgetting

Have you ever gone into a room or into a store and then couldn't remember what you were there for? A little frightening? A blow to the ego? Actually, this is a very common occurrence and not a cause for concern. We all forget. You will probably not be surprised to learn that one of the most common incidents of forgetting is to forget the name of a person you have just met at a social gathering. Other common types of forgetting are to forget to bring up a point you wanted to make in a conversation and, upon waking up, to forget immediately what you had just been dreaming.

These common occurrences are good examples of the major cause of our forgetting: **interference**. Essentially, the interference theory of forgetting suggests that new information drives out old information or makes its recovery more difficult. When you are introduced to someone, especially in the midst of a social gathering, a lot is happening, and new information is coming at you rather quickly. Thus, it is difficult for you to retain the new acquaintance's name.

Once something has been stored in long-term memory, you never completely lose it, although you may have difficulty bringing it up into active memory. Information held only in active memory is completely erased once it has been forgotten.

Experiments suggest that you retain and can use information that is unique. This might explain why, once learned, you can remember odd facts. Such information has its own memory cell and nothing else *interferes* with it or changes it. People with good memories apparently have the ability to treat many data as unique.

Research indicates that people tend to remember more than they believe they do. Also, contrary to popular belief, memory does not become worse with age, although people may remember different things in different ways. Older people tend to order their lives so as to aid their memories, and they also rely more on help, such as lists. Younger people believe they are able to remember more easily than they really can. They are a little "cocky" about their memory but at the same time tend to complain more about forgetting.

▼ MASTERY: THE ULTIMATE LEARNING

All of us are experts in many of the daily activities that we must carry out. We have mastered these tasks completely. But how do experts achieve that high level of performance? Cognitive psychologists have studied and compared the performances of novices and experts to come up with some answers. One thing they have found is that expertise does not necessarily rest on a superior memory.

In a pioneering study of chess players, it was found that first of all, the expert did not look ahead any greater number of moves than the less

Fig. 9-8

We use symbols—things that stand for other things—all the time, as these familiar signs attest. They are almost universally understood and are thus very useful when people of different languages mingle. Words are, of course, the ultimate symbols in our everyday life.

TO THE POINT

There are simple measures you can take to aid and improve your memory. Here are a few:

GENERAL
Think positively. Believe you can remember what you want to. Be confident about it. Experiments have shown you remember more when you feel confident you can remember.

REMEMBERING NAMES AND FACES
Concentrate on hearing the name the first time.
Repeat it immediately.
Use it as often as possible at first (or repeat it in your mind).
Associate the name with a physical characteristic of the person or a feeling you have of the person.
Look for outstanding or different characteristics of the person (red hair, blue eyes, loud voice, very tall, honest face).

IMPROVING YOUR MEMORY
Concentrate or pay attention. Much memory loss occurs because you were not paying attention in the first place.
Take notes or write notes to yourself. Taking notes is especially important when studying a new subject. Writing notes to remind yourself of something is a good practice to avoid forgetting an appointment or a task.
Reduce the interference. Try to concentrate on one thing at a time. Do not study for two different subjects, one right after the other. Study one, then go do something else. Give your memory time to integrate the new material before attempting more.
Use mnemonics. Mnemonics are devices—usually words in an easily remembered pattern, such as a rhyme to help you recall items. Many people use the jingle

> Thirty days has September,
> April, June, and November.
> All the rest have 31
> Excepting February alone,
> Which has but 28 in fine,
> Till leap year gives it 29.

Use rote exercises. You can fix things in your memory by hearing them over and over or by repeating them to yourself often. This is how you memorize poetry and actors memorize lines.

Fig.9-9

Chess players have mastered the game by recognizing patterns that appear on the board.

capable player. The difference between expert and beginner was the former's ability to recognize a few patterns in the positions of the pieces after a five-second glance at the board. This ability was related to superior knowledge of the game, not superior memory.

Note that the expert recognized patterns, not necessarily all the positions of the individual pieces. This seems to give further evidence that you remember associations rather than specific facts.

Two general principles of expertise are that skill depends on the knowledge base and that the more practice, the better the performance.

Paderewski, the great pianist, made the point about practice when he said, "If I miss one day's practice, I notice it. If I miss two days, the critics notice it. If I miss three days, the public notices it."

In their book *Mind Over Machines*, Hubert and Stuart Greyfus of the University of California, Berkeley, list five stages through which a novice in any activity must pass before becoming an expert:

1. **Novice:** Follows rules.

2. **Advanced Beginner:** Uses experience as well as rules. (If you are learning to drive a car with a standard shift, you might always shift gears at a specified speed at first. When you are more experienced, you may be guided by the sound of the motor.)

3. **Competence:** Uses more experience and organizes information; makes plans and concentrates only on most important elements.

4. **Proficiency:** Moves with rapid, fluid motions; acts sometimes without conscious thought.

5. **Expertise:** Moves, makes decisions, and solves problems without applying rules; in effect does what has now become second nature.

1. Learning may be defined as behavior modification. Or, stated another way, learning is development. Both statements are accurate to some extent, but neither is completely accurate or sufficiently broad. Not all behavior modification or development results from learning. Cognitive and emotional development results from a combination of heredity and learning.

2. Because learning results in behavior modification, observing a change in behavior is the best way to determine if learning has taken place, but it is not a perfect way because there is a difference between learning and performance.

3. Overall development is the result of learning and maturation (behavioral change resulting from biologically predetermined processes).

4. Two broad categories of learning are habituation learning, which results from becoming used to the environment, and associative learning, which results from interaction with the environment. A third category of learning is cognitive learning, the process that occurs in the mind or brain between the time a stimulus occurs and the time a response is made.

5. Associative learning is further divided into two subcategories: classical and operant conditioning. Classical conditioning, discovered by Pavlov, happens when a neutral stimulus becomes a conditioned stimulus, as when dogs salivate at the sound of a tone. The stimulus occurs, and the behavior follows. In operant conditioning, the behavior comes first and the consequences reinforce the behavior, making it more likely to be repeated the next time the stimulus occurs.

6. There are two kinds of reinforcers: positive and negative. Positive reinforcers are desired results or consequences, whereas negative reinforcers enable you to avoid or end undesired results or consequences. And there are two levels of reinforcers: primary and secondary. Primary reinforcers meet your biological needs, such as water, food, sex, and safety. Secondary reinforcers are learned. You need food (a primary reinforcer), but you learn to prefer certain restaurants (secondary reinforcers).

7. Reinforcement occurs on a specific pattern or schedule. The two major schedules are continuous reinforcement and intermittent reinforcement.

8. Intermittent reinforcement occurs as the result of the passage

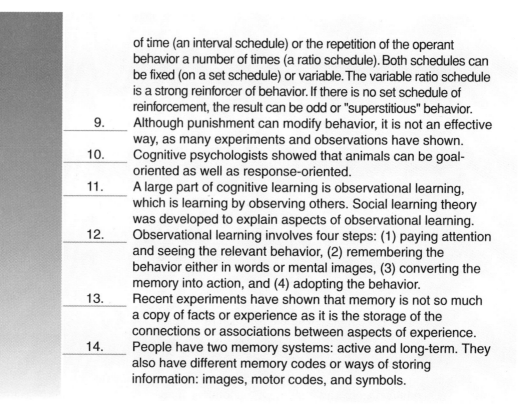

of time (an interval schedule) or the repetition of the operant behavior a number of times (a ratio schedule). Both schedules can be fixed (on a set schedule) or variable. The variable ratio schedule is a strong reinforcer of behavior. If there is no set schedule of reinforcement, the result can be odd or "superstitious" behavior.

9. Although punishment can modify behavior, it is not an effective way, as many experiments and observations have shown.

10. Cognitive psychologists showed that animals can be goal-oriented as well as response-oriented.

11. A large part of cognitive learning is observational learning, which is learning by observing others. Social learning theory was developed to explain aspects of observational learning.

12. Observational learning involves four steps: (1) paying attention and seeing the relevant behavior, (2) remembering the behavior either in words or mental images, (3) converting the memory into action, and (4) adopting the behavior.

13. Recent experiments have shown that memory is not so much a copy of facts or experience as it is the storage of the connections or associations between aspects of experience.

14. People have two memory systems: active and long-term. They also have different memory codes or ways of storing information: images, motor codes, and symbols.

KEY TERMS
Define the following:

Active memory
Associative learning
Classical conditioning
Cognitive learning
Conditioned stimulus
Contiguity
Continuous reinforcement
Counterconditioning
Effortful retrieval
Effortless retrieval
Habituation learning
Imagery
Interference
Intermittent reinforcement
Interval schedule
Learning
Long-term memory

QUESTIONS FOR REVIEW AND DISCUSSION

1. What is the best way to determine if learning has taken place? Explain why it is not a perfect way to measure learning.

2. Explain the sentence "Our overall development is the result of learning and maturation."

3. Briefly explain the difference between classical conditioning and operant conditioning.

4. Identify the two levels of reinforcers and give an example of each.

5. Which schedule of reinforcement is the stronger one? Why?

6. A classical experiment with three groups of rats running a maze was said to demonstrate cognitive learning. One group was reinforced as soon as they learned the maze; the second group, only on the third day; and the third group, not for several days thereafter. How did the rats behave, and what did it show to support the idea of cognitive learning?

7. Describe the four steps of observational learning.

8. Briefly describe the two memory systems.

9. In what three forms do we store information? Briefly describe each.

ACTIVITIES

Maturation
Memory codes
Memory systems
Neutral stimulus
Observational learning
Operant conditioning
Operational memory
Primary reinforcers
Ratio schedule
Secondary reinforcers
Short-term memory
Symbol

1. You can experience how your active or short-term memory works by playing the card game "Concentration." You will also appreciate how people remember by association. This is a two-person game. Cut the deck to see who plays first (high card). The game is simple. Lay out the cards face down in rows and columns (with the jokers you can have six rows and nine columns). The first player turns over two cards at random. If they match in value (both nines, for example, or queens), the player takes both. If they do not match, the player turns them face down again and the second player goes. The goal is to acquire the most cards by matching them. The trick is to remember which cards have been turned up and where they are located.

2. There are three basic types of learning: classical conditioning, in which a stimulus causes a response; operant conditioning, in which we behave on account of the consequences; and cognitive learning. Think back over your life for the past few years. Try to remember at least one example for each of the basic types of learning that you have experienced. Briefly describe it so as to show which type of learning occurred.

3. Psychologists and others continue to carry on exciting research into how we learn and how we remember. New information is being discovered and reported frequently. Check at your school or local library for publications that carry such news. These would be large newspapers that have science sections and many magazines such as *Psychology Today*, *Omni*, or *Scientific American*. Try to find an article on some recent research in these areas. Read it and write a one-page summary of it.

4. Psychologists believe that using your memory to recall something or to recognize something are two different activities. Recognition is believed to be easier than recall, but some experiments suggest that this is not always so. Try this experiment on yourself or friends. It is one that Michael Watkins, a Yale University psychologist, used to show that conventional belief about recall and recognition is not always so. Go to step 1.

Step 1 Supply the missing two letters to make each of the following a word:
SPANI_____EXPLO_____CODI_____SUPP_____
After completing the words, put the paper where you or the subject cannot see it. Wait about 15 minutes, then do the next step.

Step 2 Select the two-letter pair you have seen before from this list: LY; EL; SH; DE; FY; UR; RE; ES. Which steps did you find easier? Which step was using recall? Which step required recognition?

CASE 1

Types of Learning

Marie was up an hour early again this morning because she wanted to continue training her new puppy, a golden retriever. Her first goal was to have it learn its name and to come when called. She put the dog on a long line. Then she repeatedly called its name, Goldie, and gently pulled on the rope. She would say, "Here, Goldie," and pull the dog toward her. When the dog was next to her, she petted and praised it.

Next she walked with the dog. When it moved ahead, she would pull on the rope and say "heel" to make it walk beside her. After it learned to come and to heel, she took off the rope and walked the dog along a fence around the edge of the property. She wanted to train it never to leave the property. Whenever it started to go through one of the open gates, she shouted "No!" and made a loud noise. After that happened several times, the dog kept away from the gates.

She also taught it to sit and shake hands, giving it a piece of dog biscuit whenever it performed the trick.

One day she was surprised when the dog came to her with an empty water bowl in its mouth. She remembered that she had forgotten to fill it earlier. She laughed and filled it. Thereafter, if she did not fill either the food or water bowl, the dog would bring them to her.

When the morning lessons were finished, Marie took the dog inside, praised and petted it, and gave it a bowl of food.

1. Identify the various types of learning or conditioning strategies that Marie used to train her golden retriever.

2. Match the different kinds of conditioning with the specific things Marie was teaching the dog.

3. Were any other kinds of learning exhibited?

CASE 2

Remembering Under Pressure

"Welcome aboard, Len. I'm certainly glad to see you. We really need help. As you know, I'm Carol Johnson, the store manager. Call me Carol. Now today, I want you to work here in the photo department while you get acquainted. It is very simple. Top drawer on the right is where the returned slides are; middle drawer for standard black and white; bottom drawer for overflow. All right? Everything is filed alphabetically by the last initial of the customer. Right?"

"Uh, right," Len answered.

It was Len's first day at work. He had been hired as a clerk in a large drugstore that sold just about everything. He was very pleased to have the job, but today he was feeling more confused and frightened than pleased. He was wondering how he was going to remember everything that Carol was telling him. He was thinking he would ask her a few questions, when she continued.

"Got to hurry," Carol said. "Store opens in a few minutes, and we'll be mobbed. We're having a sale today. Most items are half price, but not all of them. Cosmetics, cough syrups, other nonprescription medicines. If people ask, tell them that. Otherwise check with me. But your main concern is photos, and there is no sale on here."

Len tried to make a mental note of the items Carol said were on sale, but she was continuing with more information.

"Of course, we do have sale prices on enlargements. Price list is on the left side of the cash register if anyone asks. Let's see now. Oh, the envelopes for film to be developed are in the drawer in the middle. Envelopes for pictures to be enlarged are on the end. Put all that material in the mail bag in the corner. It is picked up just before noon and again just before 5 P.M. when you leave. Don't forget to put the right information on the envelopes when people bring in film. Mark whether it is slides or prints and get the name, first initial, and phone number.

"I guess that's it. Must run. The store is opening. Oh, don't accept credit cards for purchases below $10. Got it? Good. Call if you need me. I'll check back later. Good luck."

Carol hurried away as the doors opened for the first customers. Len stood there with his head spinning. "I'll never make it," he thought, but the first customer was already at the counter.

1. Which memory system was Len most likely using as he listened to Carol and prepared to wait on the first customer?

2. What mental codes did Len most likely use?

3. What could Len do to help himself through the first tough day?

► NEEDS, VALUES,
INTERESTS, AND
ATTITUDES:
How We Get Motivated

Where there's a will, there's a way.
Old Saying

Essentially, the old saying "where there's a will, there's a way" means that if you want—really want—to do something, you will find a way to do it. In other words, you must be motivated to act. The stronger your motivation, the more likely you are to accomplish your purpose. The weaker your motivation, the less likely you are to reach your goal.

▼ THE KEYS TO REALIZING TALENT

In the last chapter you learned about how learning takes place, what the process or mechanism of learning is. But a well-equipped learning environment by itself will not make a person learn. One more ingredient is needed—something we believe is in the learner. That is the desire or motivation to learn.

Another old saying, "You can lead a horse to water, but you cannot make it drink," illustrates this point. Unless the horse is motivated to drink, you cannot make it do so. You can, of course, induce thirst in the horse by denying it water for a long time. But first you must know that a horse can get thirsty. Does a rock get thirsty? If it does, then perhaps you can make it thirsty, and you can lead it to water, and it can drink! Absurd, because you know that a rock does not get thirsty. But do you know what motivates human beings? If you do not, you will not know how to motivate the learner to learn.

Motivation is important not only in the process of learning. It is also important in the application of what you have learned. Learning a skill is one thing; using it is another. Learning facts and figures is one thing; using them is another. Using your skills and your knowledge involves motivation, among other things. When you are motivated to use the skills and knowledge you have learned, then you are on your way to realizing your talent, your potential.

Motivation is a necessary condition if you are to learn, and it is a necessary condition if you are to use what you learn.

▼ WHAT IS MOTIVATION?

Sometimes the answer seems quite clear. Being thirsty, for example, motivates you to drink. But often what motivates you is not so clear. Consequently, there are many answers to the question "What is motivation?" You have read about theories. The formal answers to the question about motivation are called theories of motivation. Because it is a complex question, many theories of motivation exist.

Some theories focus on outcomes—*why* people are motivated. Others focus on process—*how* people are motivated. This chapter presents a view of motivation distilled from several theories of motivation.

Most theories agree that motivation involves these basic processes:

- First, the individual is energized. That is, there is a change of energy level in the individual to a perceptibly higher level.

- Second, this increased energy is directed at a specific target (goal, objective, or outcome) through a channel, mechanism, or process.

To describe motivation requires knowing its "triggering mechanism" or what starts it, its intensity or strength, and its direction or the goals toward which it is aimed.

People Are Motivated Organisms

The concept of motivation applies only to self-propelled organisms. If all movement could be explained as being caused by outside forces, the concept of motivation would be unnecessary. Trees or rivers or clouds are not thought of as being motivated. They are not self-propelled, but move only as the direct result of outside forces.

Humans are self-propelled, and therefore are called motivated organisms. Not all human movements are self-propelled, however. If a car hits you, you might "fly" for a few hundred yards but not of your own accord. However, even if human behavior is brought about by the environment, because you are self-propelled, you can behave in different ways. For example, if it is dark, you may turn on a light or you may not; if it is cold, you may put on more clothes, or you may not if it is the fashionable thing to do. Scientists believe that much behavior is the result of something going on in a person, rather than simply an automatic response to the environment.

Care must be exercised in making flat assertions that behavior results from something within a person as opposed to something in the environment. Knowledge in this area, although great, is still incomplete. As scientists learn more, they may discover that behavior now thought of as being self-propelled or motivated is really the result of the environment. As of now, however, the concept of internal motivation is a leading explanation of much human behavior.

For motivated behavior to occur, according to most theories, three conditions must be met:

Fig. 10-1

Activities that children do well or spend a lot of time on may give clues to their capabilities.

1. The individual must be *capable* of behavior.

2. The individual must have the *opportunity*, and in some cases be encouraged by the environment, to behave.

3. The individual must either *require* something of the environment or *be required* by the environment to behave.

Capability

Your capabilities not only set the limits on what you can do but also help determine what you want to do. There are obvious examples: A blind person who wants some recreation would not think of going to a movie or playing basketball. Such a person might think instead of listening to records or swimming. A deaf person, on the other hand, would choose going to the movies over listening to records, and might consider playing basketball. Your capabilities shape the things you are motivated to do.

Capabilities and motivation act on each other. The more capable you are, the more motivated you become, and, on the flip side, the more motivated you are, the more capable you become. This is true with interests that require special abilities, such as the performing arts (music, dancing), the creative arts (painting, sculpting, composing, writing), mathematics, science, and the skilled crafts (carpentry, mechanics, woodworking). But this relationship between interests and abilities is not high in general because many interests are served by the same abilities, and several abilities may serve the same interests.

Parents with growing children should watch for the things the children do well and encourage them along those lines. Parents should also watch for those activities on which the children spend a lot of time. These activities may give clues as to the children's capabilities.

In any event, young adults *should* have a good idea of what their capabilities are—their strengths and weaknesses in the matter of ability. This will provide them with clues to what their motivations might be. Using capabilities to the fullest is highly motivating. Why this is so will become clearer as you read along.

Opportunity

Like capability, opportunity sets limits on what you can do. Examples again are obvious. Few people in the tropics ski or are motivated to ski for the simple reason that they do not have snow. Someone who lives by the seashore or near an available swimming pool might be more likely to go swimming than someone who does not. If a home has many books or a piano, a child is more likely to read or to learn to play the piano.

Opportunity depends on the environment. Environments can be hostile, friendly, or neutral with respect to given behaviors. A budding musician or mechanic might find the home environment discouraging, neutral, or encouraging .

Opportunity interacts with capability. If the environment is neutral, capability has a chance to develop. If the environment is benign or friendly, capability can develop at a faster rate. If the environment is hostile, capability development will be retarded or even suppressed.

Capability plus opportunity, however, still does not mean that behavior will occur. Consider a car parked on a road. The car is *capable* of traveling. The road provides the *opportunity*. But gas is needed to provide the *motive* power and a spark to set things in motion. This is what motivation is—it converts capability in the presence of opportunity into a reality. The "spark" that energizes the system is "requirement."

Requirement

One characteristic of the living organism is that it has *requirements*: requirements for survival and maintenance, requirements for well-being. You know that you need food, water, and air in order to live. You need rest and exercise. You need the companionship of other humans. When you have what you need to live, when your rest and exercise cycle flows in a smooth rhythm, when you have the companionship of other humans, you feel at your best.

Physiological (or biological) and psychological *needs* are requirements the individual has of the environment. The physiological needs are requirements that stem from your biological nature. The satisfaction of these needs is essential to sustaining the life of the individual. Psychological needs derive from physiological needs, depend a lot on learning, and differ from individual to individual and from culture to culture.

The environment, in its turn, has requirements of the individual. The family has requirements of the family member, the work group of the work group member, the society or culture of the member of society or the culture. Even the physical environment can be thought of as having

TO THE POINT

If you need to be motivated in order to act, it follows that the greater your motivation, the more effective you can be. That seems logical, and you often see coaches, for example, giving pep talks to their teams to fire up their motivation as high as possible.

Studies, however, have shown that there can be such a thing as being too highly motivated. There is such a thing as trying too hard. Remember that motivation means you are energized to do something; you are aroused. If you get too energized or aroused, you may not perform as well as you would otherwise.

This has been verified by many studies. The first famous one was conducted in 1906 by R. M. Yerkes and J. D. Dodson. They found if a person was doing something complicated, being too motivated actually hurt performance. You have probably witnessed or experienced this situation: the great athlete fails at a crucial moment, or you are unable to perform a simple task under pressure. What has become known as the Yerkes-Dodson law states that the best level of motivation varies depending on what you are doing. If you are doing something easy, the more motivation, the better. If you are doing something complicated, a moderate level of motivation seems best.

"requirements" of the human inasmuch as the human is part of a total physical system. For example, whereas humans require oxygen, which plants provide, plants require carbon dioxide, which humans (among others) provide. From a motivational point of view, then, human behavior occurs to *satisfy* the individual's requirements and also the requirements of the environment. *You behave in order to fulfill or meet these requirements.*

▼ NEEDS SHAPE MOTIVATION

The individual's requirements of the environment are called **needs**. As mentioned earlier, you have two kinds of needs, physiological (also called biological) and psychological.

Physiological Needs

Physiological needs have to be satisfied for the individual to survive. As such, physiological needs are basic and for that reason are called **primary needs**.

The term *need* implies a lack, a deficiency, a deprivation. Such a definition clearly applies to physiological needs, which can be induced by depriving the individual of whatever is required to satisfy the need—air, food, water, sex, exercise, and sensory stimulation.

In studies of animal behavior, scientists have found that these satisfiers of physiological needs can be used to mold the animal's behavior. The animal will behave (it is *motivated* to behave) in order to obtain what satisfies the need—called the **need-satisfier**. Because receiving these need-satisfiers causes the animal to maintain the behavior that resulted in obtaining them, they are called *reinforcers* as you read in Chapter 9. Whatever satisfies a physiological need is a potential reinforcer.

As you read, there are positive and negative reinforcers. Positive reinforcers include such things as food, water, and air that provide something the animal needs. Animals also have physiological needs to avoid or escape life-threatening or distressing stimuli. Such stimuli are called **aversive stimuli.** Thus, any behavior that enables an animal to avoid aversive stimuli is reinforced. Such reinforcers are negative reinforcers.

Psychological Needs

Another group of needs are derived from the physiological needs. Because these derived needs have to do with the psychological or mental well-being of the individual, they are called **psychological needs**. Because they are derived, presumably according to the laws of conditioning, they are also called **secondary needs**.

needs
the individual's requirements of the environment

physiological needs
needs that must be satisfied for survival

primary needs
needs that must be satisfied for the individual to survive (also known as biological or physiological needs)

need-satisfier
behavior, object, or event that satisfies a need

aversive stimuli
life-threatening or distressing stimuli

psychological needs
needs having to do with the psychological or mental well-being of the individual

secondary needs
another term for psychological needs

Much is still to be learned about how psychological needs are derived from physiological needs. Derivation appears to occur in different ways. For example, your need for food (a primary reinforcer) leads you to develop a need for being with people (who become a secondary reinforcer).

Infants depend on other humans, primarily parents, to provide food. Because infants require other humans to satisfy their primary need for food, other humans as satisfiers of this requirement become reinforcers. Inasmuch as other humans are reinforcers, infants develop a psychological requirement for them, just as they have a physiological requirement for food. What has happened is that they have acquired a need for **affiliation**, which is a need to be associated with others.

affiliation
as used here, the need to be associated with others

To take a different example, you have a primary need for exercise. As you exercise, you find that you have an effect on your environment. Other humans such as parents give you feedback about what you have accomplished. This makes you feel good. You do more things to obtain this feeling. The feedback, which leads to the feeling of accomplishment, becomes a reinforcer. You like the feeling of accomplishment, which becomes a need.

Some Unknowns

How much psychological needs come about by learning and how much they are influenced by your inherited genetic makeup has not been determined yet. Part of the reason scientists are not sure about this is that they do not have an agreed-upon list and definition of psychological needs. They do know that the more frequently a reinforcer functions as a reinforcer, the more an individual will develop a "requirement" for that reinforcer. The requirement for reinforcer X can be called a need for X or an X need.

Secondary needs are derived from primary needs, but not all secondary needs are psychological *needs*. This text will limit the term psychological needs to those needs that have to do with mental (cognitive-emotional) well-being. Physiological needs can have a psychological component, but they have to do primarily with physical well-being.

Learned Versus Genetic

You might say that physiological needs have more of a genetic component in that they are more inherited and less learned, whereas psychological needs are more learned. Therefore, peoples of all cultures will have the same set of physiological needs, but they may have different, if overlapping, sets of psychological needs.

Fig. 10-2

We have a primary need for exercise, but satisfying this primary need can sometimes turn into a way of satisfying higher needs. If we get positive feedback—praise—for exercising, that leads to a feeling of accomplishment, and this feeling is a reinforcer. We like it. Therefore we develop a need for achievement. Marathon runners, for example, exercise far beyond the level necessary to satisfy their primary need. They endure the pain to satisfy a higher need.

What are some of your psychological needs? Henry A. Murray, who was the foremost advocate of needs as determiners of motivation, listed the following:[1]

Abasement. The need to submit, to accept defeat, to surrender.

Achievement. The need to accomplish something difficult or challenging.

Affiliation. The need to be close to and be loyal to a friend.

Aggression. The need to fight, attack, injure, or overcome the opposition of another.

Dependence. The need to yield eagerly to an acknowledged superior.

Dominance. The need to master, control, and direct others.

Exhibition. The need to be seen and heard by others, to make an impression.

Harmavoidance. The need to avoid pain, injury, death; to escape from danger.

Infavoidance. The need to avoid humiliation or embarrassment.

Nurturance. The need to help, support, comfort, and protect others.

Order. The need to keep things in order, neat, tidy, and precise.

Play. The need to do things for fun and pleasure, and for no other reason.

Autonomy. The need to be independent, unattached, free.

Counteraction. The need to make up for a failure by trying harder.

Rejection. The need to distance oneself from another considered inferior.

Sentience. The need for sensuous experiences.

Sex. The need for sexual experience.

Succorance. The need to be helped, supported, comforted, and protected.

Understanding. The need to know, to get answers to questions, to speculate and theorize.

Vocational Needs

The above 19 needs are general needs that cut across a variety of sit-

Levels of Needs

Needs are motivating and behavior occurs in order to satisfy needs when the opportunity arises and the person has the necessary capabilities. Abraham Maslow (1903–1970), a well-known American psychologist, advanced the idea that needs are organized in a hierarchy such that lower-level needs have to be satisfied before higher-level needs become motivating.

uations. The following list of specific needs, taken from the Minnesota Importance Questionnaire, are called *vocational* or *work needs* because they refer to the work situation.

Ability utilization. The need to use one's abilities.

Achievement. The need to get a feeling of accomplishment.

Activity. The need to be busy all the time.

Advancement. The need for opportunities to advance.

Authority. The need to be able to tell others what to do.

Company policies and practices. The need for fair administration of company policies.

Compensation. The need to be paid well in comparison with others.

Coworkers. The need for coworkers who are easy to make friends with.

Creativity. The need to try out some of one's own ideas.

Independence. The need to be able to work alone on the job.

Moral values. The need to be able to work without feeling it is wrong.

Recognition. The need for approval and acknowledgment for the work one does.

Responsibility. The need to make decisions on one's own.

Security. The need for steady employment.

Social service. The need to be able to do things for other people.

Social status. The need to be "somebody" in the community.

Supervision—human relations. The need for a boss who backs up the workers.

Supervision—technical. The need for a boss who trains the workers well.

Variety. The need to do something different every day.

Working conditions. The need for good working conditions.

These 20 vocational needs were found by research to be those most frequently required by most workers. Of course, not all may be required by any one worker, who may also have other needs not on this list.

According to Maslow, the hierarchy of needs is as follows (listed from highest level to lowest):

- Self-actualization need
- Self-esteem need
- Love and belonging needs

- Safety needs
- Physiological needs

Your higher-level needs generally are your psychological needs, which, you remember, are also called secondary needs. This is another way of remembering that they come second; your physiological (primary) needs usually must be satisfied first. It is not always clear why some needs are more important than others. Research has shown, however, that needs do tend to organize in an hierarchical order, with some needs being more important than others. The ordering of the needs seems to be different for different persons, although some patterns are found more frequently than others.

For example, for most people physiological needs are at a lower level than psychological needs and, therefore, are *prepotent* (they have to be satisfied ahead of psychological needs).

For many people, safety needs are at a lower level than the other psychological needs and, therefore, are more prepotent. This, however, is not true for many other people. For some, love and belonging are more prepotent than self-esteem and even self-actualization, and the reverse is true for others.

Maslow believed that self-actualization is the highest level need of all and that once it is satisfied, no other need will matter. However, self-actualization can only happen if:

- Your important needs are regularly satisfied (needs never remain satisfied).

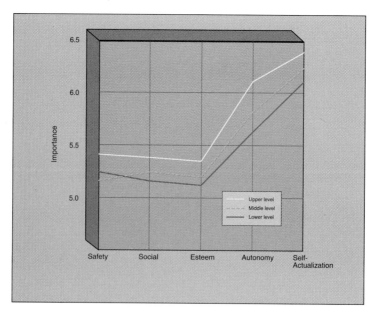

Fig. 10-3

How important are the different levels of needs in a work organization? This chart shows how three different levels of managers ranked five needs in importance. Not surprisingly, perhaps, the higher-level needs were more important to them.

- Your capabilities are realized to the fullest extent. (This would mean that you must have had the opportunity to actualize self, a condition that is denied to many.)

Compensation

One of the characteristics of human adaptability is the ability to **compensate**. To compensate means that you learn to substitute one important need for another. Because several needs often require satisfaction simultaneously, this is important. You compensate for not satisfying one need by satisfying another. You are thus able to achieve the same level of overall satisfaction by satisfying different needs at different times.

The substitution of one important need for another tends to occur within clusters. For example, a person may be satisfied with the use of all of her or his abilities at one time and have the feeling of accomplishment at another time, even if both needs (to use all abilities and to have feeling of accomplishment) are never fully satisfied at the same time.

Discovering what needs you can satisfy to compensate for other needs you cannot satisfy is an important step in self-understanding. Compensation is particularly important when you wish to maintain your level of motivation. It is not always possible to have the preferred reinforcers available. Compensating one with another is one way to maintain motivation.

compensate
to substitute satisfaction of one important need for another

▼ VALUES

You have seen that what are called psychological needs are, upon analysis, actually the individual's *requirements for reinforcers*. Studies of reinforcer requirements have shown that they cluster into groups that appear to have dominant requirement themes.

Because such a group theme is basic and describes what is important to people who have the related cluster of needs, the theme is identified as a **value**. A value can be defined as the theme underlying a cluster of related psychological needs that describes what is of basic importance to the person. Six values have been identified as underlying the 20 vocational needs listed on page 273. These are:

value
theme underlying a cluster of related psychological needs

1. **Achievement:** The importance of reinforcers that accompany accomplishment

2. **Autonomy:** The importance of reinforcers that accompany self-sufficiency and self-initiated activity

3. **Status:** The importance of reinforcers that provide recognition and enable dominance

4. **Altruism:** The importance of reinforcers accompanying service to others and harmony with them

5. **Comfort:** The importance of reinforcers associated with the absence of stress and the presence of pleasant feelings

6. **Safety:** The importance of reinforcers associated with order, predictability, and freedom from harm

Values can be classified further by the types of reinforcers they involve. For example, the six vocational values can be associated with certain types of reinforcers as shown in Table 10-1.

Of course, social reinforcers are also external and environmental. They are classified as a separate group to emphasize the fact that social reinforcers constitute one of the most powerful of the motivational forces that influence human behavior.

Conflicting Values

Research has found that certain values appear to oppose each other in the sense that satisfying the requirements of one seems automatically to rule out being able to satisfy the other. These "opponent" values are:

- Safety versus Autonomy
- Comfort versus Achievement
- Status versus Altruism

Take, for example, status versus altruism. Satisfying your needs for status requires you to put self ahead of others, whereas to satisfy your altruism needs requires you to put others ahead of self. Likewise, achievement is not satisfied without some sacrifice, but comfort is not satisfied if one makes sacrifices. Safety is best upheld by structured situations, but structured situations deny the exercise of initiative required by autonomy.

A person can have opposing values, but such a person will seesaw from satisfying one value to satisfying the other value and will appear to others to be inconsistent and unpredictable.

Table 10-1

SIX VALUES UNDERLIE THE 20 VOCATIONAL NEEDS		
Values	Corresponding Vocational Need Clusters	Reinforcers
1. Achievement (importance of accomplishment)	1. Ability utilization 2. Achievement	Internal
2. Autonomy (importance of initiative)	3. Creativity 4. Responsibility	Internal
3. Status (importance of recognition and prestige)	5. Advancement 6. Recognition 7. Authority 8. Social status	Social
4. Altruism (importance of harmony with and service to others)	9. Coworkers 10. Social service 11. Moral values	Social
5. Comfort (importance of comfort, absence of stress)	12. Activity 13. Independence 14. Variety 15. Compensation 16. Security 17. Working conditions	External environmental
6. Safety (importance of predictability, stability)	18. Company policies 19. Supervision— human relations 20. Supervision— technical	External environmental

▼ INTERESTS

interests

preferences for activities; likes or dislikes as opposed to needs or values

Interests are motives that differ somewhat from needs and values. Needs and values are preferences about what is important—important reinforcers (for needs) and important basic themes in requirements (for values). Interests are preferences about what you like and dislike. Your interests may coincide with, but are not the same as, your needs and values.

Interests are your liking or disliking for activities. Activities involve both capabilities and reinforcers. The combination of the right set of abilities with the right set of reinforcers is what makes for interest. *Right* means that the activity requires the set of abilities that the individual has. *Right* means that the activity provides the set of reinforcers that the individual requires. In other words, interest depends on the individual's capabilities and requirements.

Interests that are based on internal or self-reinforcers are stable. For example, an interest resulting from your being able to use your best abilities and having a feeling of accomplishment will be stable.

Interests based on external, including social, reinforcers tend to be less stable. In this sense, interests are influenced by the individual's reinforcer requirements (needs and values). One clue, therefore, to an individual's needs and values lies in that individual's interests.

Although different from needs and values, interests may influence needs and values. If because of an interest you persist in an activity, that persistence not only may improve your capabilities, but also enable you to acquire a preference for reinforcers present in the activity. In this way, interests feed into needs and values as well as capabilities, and, in turn, needs and values as well as capabilities feed into interests.

Interest Themes

Research by the vocational psychologist John Holland and others, has shown that six major themes underlie the work-related interests expressed by people through the medium of questionnaires such as the *Strong Interest Inventory*. These six interest themes are:

- **Realistic:** A liking for hands-on activities like working on cars or gardening or building things with tools; for physically strenuous activities; for concrete rather than abstract problems; for activity requiring physical or motor skills; for the outdoors; and a dislike for or unease with social situations that require much interpersonal interaction and conversation

- **Investigative:** A liking for thinking rather than acting; for acquiring knowledge and information; for science and other scholarly activity;

Fig. 10-4

An interest will be stable if it results from our being able to use our best abilities and to have a feeling of accomplishment. Because of this we will be highly motivated to achieve.

for dealing with abstract problems; and a dislike for selling and commercial activity

- **Artistic:** A liking for activities emphasizing the aesthetic; for creative and self-expressive opportunities; for form rather than content; for "fine arts" activities like music and museums; and a dislike for routine, rules, and the predictable

- **Social:** A liking for being with people; for interacting (especially verbally) with people; for working and playing in groups; for activities that benefit people; for social occasions; and a dislike for being alone and out of touch with people

- **Enterprising:** A liking for activities involving selling, leading, or dominating; for risk-taking ventures (especially of the money-making variety); for activities that bring power, status, and wealth; and a dislike for scientific and abstract activities

- **Conventional:** A liking for well-ordered environments; for systematic and well-structured activities; for rules, norms, and standard operating procedures; and a dislike for the ambiguous and unpredictable

These six interest themes were found, by repeated research, to be related in such a way that you could depict them as points on a hexagon (six-sided figure), as shown in Figure 10-5. This order (R-I-A-S-E-C) remained the same regardless of the group answering the questionnaires. This order reflects similarity of interests—the closer together, the more similar the interests, and the farther apart, the less similar the interests. People with interests on opposite sides of the hexagon would have the least similar interests; these are the Realistic and the Social, the Investigative and the Enterprising, the Artistic and the Conventional.

These six interest themes do not, of course, exhaust the possible interests that people have, not even the work-related. But most people's work interests can be classified into one, or some combination, of these six themes. Actually, the six themes can be organized along two dimensions, as depicted in Figure 10-5. The horizontal dimension represents interest in *people* at right end and interest in *things* at the left end. The vertical dimension represents interest in *ideas* at the upper end and interest in *data* at the lower end. Most interests can be plotted in terms of coordinates on these two dimensions, much as we do on a map.

▼ WORK ATTITUDES

attitudes
learned tendencies to respond to people, objects, or institutions in a positive or negative way

Interests are a special case of a more general class of motives known as attitudes. An **attitude** is a predisposition or tendency to accept or reject an *attitude-object*. The attitude-object (target of the attitude) may be a person, thing, idea, or event, that is, you have an attitude toward or about a person, thing, idea, event. This is the cognitive component of the attitude, which also has an emotional component. The emotional component gives the attitude its intensity—you are strongly (or mildly) for (or against) this person (or thing, idea, event).

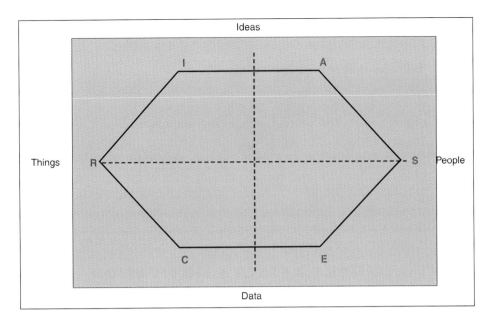

Fig. 10-5

Holland's Hexagon Arrangement of Six Interest Themes

Attitudes are learned, and like other things learned, they can be reinforced. The most powerful reinforcers of attitudes are social—your family, your friends, your peer group, your work group, your community. Many attitudes are acquired by imitation or "osmosis"—from parents, friends, or peers, from your readings, TV, or other social media. This explains why many attitudes are uninformed, why, for example, we may have strong attitudes about members of a minority group without knowing much about the group.

Attitudes may be weak (easily changed) or strong (resistant to change). Strong attitudes have strong emotional components, mostly of fear or hate; these are the attitudes that are hardest to change. Even education or convincing information may not be enough to change some attitudes with strong emotional components.

Of most interest to us in this text are the attitudes associated with work. We have already discussed work-related interests. Other work-related attitudes might be grouped into three:

- **Attitudes toward self:** Examples include self-esteem and self-confidence. These attitudes toward self color all your dealings with the environment and therefore they affect how well you realize your potential.

- **Attitudes toward work:** Known variously as "work ethic," "job involvement," or "work commitment." These include attitudes that (a) work is central, (b) the work must go on, regardless, (c) hard work is good for the soul, (d) doing a good job is its own reward, (e) leisure is to be taken only after all the work is done.

- **Attitudes toward work institutions:** These include attitudes toward the work organization ("organizational commitment"), toward one's profession or trade (including one's professional/trade association or organization), toward one's union and unionism in general, and toward various other work institutions (federal and state law, federal and state agencies, etc.). *Organizational commitment* is your identification with, and involvement in, your work organization. The behavior that results from organizational commitment may look very much like the behavior that results from *work commitment*, but the two attitudes are separate, even if related.

▼ ENVIRONMENT AFFECTS MOTIVATION

Ordinarily motivation is thought of as something that originates within, causing certain behavior. Behavior, in turn, is expected to affect the environment. Thus, if at work you are motivated, you work hard and you do your job well. This, in turn, affects your coworkers, your supervisor, your customers, your organization, all presumably in a positive, beneficial way— "presumably" because effects are never certain. Negative effects or reactions can occur through no fault of your own. For example, your working hard may be viewed by some as "rate busting," that is, pushing up the work requirements for all the other workers.

In any event, ordinarily, motivation is thought of as affecting the environment. The opposite is also true: the environment affects motivation. The environment affects motivation in a number of ways.

Environment Defines Opportunity

The environment provides or limits opportunity for the development of capability as well as opportunity for the practice of particular behaviors, such as work skills. Opportunity comes in either *passive* (permissive) form or *active* (encouraging) form. "Affirmative action plans" designed to help minorities obtain jobs from which they had previously been barred are examples of active opportunity. The difference between active and passive lies in the number and type of reinforcers that come into play. The more active, the greater the reinforcement.

Development of capability differs from use of capability. The use of capability requires development of capability. But the fact that capability has been developed does not mean that the opportunity to use it will exist. It is only in fairly recent times that society has become aware of this situation. Minority group members, women, and people with disabilities have often been denied the opportunity to use developed capabilities. Denial of opportunity affects motivation, usually negatively.

Environment Shapes Preferences

The environment influences motivation by the kind and quantity of reinforcers that are present in it. Recall that motivation is powered by needs, and needs are your reinforcer requirements. The environment helps shape your reinforcer preferences and, therefore, your reinforcer requirements, by making some reinforcers but not others available to you.

For example, the environment helps shape your food preferences and, therefore, your food requirements. If you are brought up near the ocean, you will probably develop a liking for seafood. If you are brought up in one culture, you may develop a liking for spicy food; in another, a liking for bland food.

It is possible that you inherit some of your preferences for reinforcers. Research so far has resulted in mixed findings. Regardless of the size of the genetic component, however, environment plays a decisive role in that it determines *exposure* to reinforcers. You cannot develop a need for social reinforcers if you are not exposed to other people. Environment affects your motives only to the extent that needs—reinforcer requirements— are shaped by environment.

Environment Requirements

Yet another way in which environment affects motivation is to be found in the requirements environment has of people. Success or failure in any endeavor can result from the extent and nature of these requirements. In our complex society, there are many environment requirements in the form of laws, social requirements, and demands of other people. One requirement, for example, is the ability to read.

The environment can require you to behave in a manner that is not within your capability, or that runs counter to your capability. When this happens, the result is failure, which usually is a powerful *de*motivator. Continuous failure can drive motivation down to zero.

Sometimes people identified as lazy and good-for-nothing are people who have had a history of nothing but failure. The environment— home, school, work—required these people to behave in ways beyond their capability. Or there are people considered rebellious, antisocial, weird, or delinquent. Such people have kept their motivation to behave in spite of their continuing failure to meet the requirements of their social environment, but they behave in ways not socially valued or approved.

Fig. 10-6

Jim Abbott, major league pitcher for the New York Yankees, has capitalized motivationally on success. Although physically handicapped, he did not become discouraged by failure, which helped him to succeed.

TO THE POINT

Although, as extensive research has shown, Maslow's hierarchy of needs reflects a general order in which different needs become motivating, care must be taken to avoid assuming that this hierarchy is exactly the same for everyone or always the same for the same person. It is not, in either case. Different individuals can have different orders of needs. And the hierarchy can change according to circumstances for individuals. History and literature are filled with examples of this.

Obvious examples are the individuals who risk their own lives to save others in dangerous situations: diving into the freezing water, running into the burning building, putting their own body between another individual and a life-threatening situation. These people are ignoring their lower needs for safety and comfort to satisfy needs of a higher order.

Less dramatic examples can be found in your daily life. How often have you ignored a physiological need for sleep to prepare yourself thoroughly for an important examination. Of course, some physiological needs can be ignored only so long and then they will assert themselves—they must be met or the individual will suffer.

Sometimes, individuals with very strong higher motivation reject their physiological needs to the point of ill health or even death. One sad example of this is the hunger strike frequently used by individuals seeking to achieve a goal that means much to them. They are motivated by one of the higher needs: love, self-esteem, or self-actualization.

We have always recognized the implied hierarchy of needs by commonly characterizing the actions of individuals who ignore lower needs as sacrifices. Several famous examples of individuals whose motivation did not follow the usual hierarchy were once recorded by William Herbert Carruth in these famous lines from his poem "Each in His Own Tongue":

> *A picket frozen on duty,*
> *A mother starved for her brood,*
> *Socrates drinking the hemlock*
> *And Jesus on the rood.*

The environment can require you to behave in ways well within your capability, or, even better, in concordance with your capability. In such instances, the environment affects motivation in a positive way. The old adage "nothing succeeds like success" recognizes that nothing is as motivating as success. Continuous success drives motivation up. The success-motivated individual appears self-confident, sure of himself or herself, optimistic, enthusiastic, and energetic.

Of course, few people experience either continuous failure or continuous success. For most, the behavior that the environment requires may lie within their capabilities at some times and not at other times. You learn to capitalize motivationally on your success and not to become too demotivated by your failures.

The environment's behavior requirements also help shape preferences for reinforcers. Achievement values and preference for achievement reinforcers may be acquired through success experiences, whereas safety values and preference for safety reinforcers may be acquired from failure experiences. Changes in the strengths of your motives—your values and preferences for reinforcers—may occur with changes in your success and failure experiences. It is a continuous developmental process.

▼ MOTIVES INFLUENCE DEVELOPMENT

It is apparent that life is an interactive system and that cause and effect flow both ways. Just as your previous developmental history exerts great influence on what your present motives (need, values, interests, attitudes) are, so do your present motives exert great influence on your future development.

Motives Screen Reality

Your motives influence your perception. You are more likely to be aware of reinforcing stimuli for which you have strong preference than of stimuli that have not been reinforcing in the past or for which you do not have strong preference.

You are more likely to be sensitive to information related to your motives. For example, if you are motivated strongly by a need for physical comfort, you will most likely be more aware of the discomfort of doing demanding physical exercise than of the good feelings and other benefits derived from it.

Motives Distort Reality

At times you even distort your perception of reality to conform to your needs, values, interests, and attitudes. Distortion of reality occurs mostly in your fantasies and your dreams. Psychologists have found that fantasies and dreams can reveal a person's motives, even those the person would like to hide and keep secret. This was one of Freud's basic discoveries.

People, of course, differ in this regard as in any other. There are those at one extreme, who rarely fantasize or dream, and those at the other extreme, whose prolific fantasies and dreams clearly reveal their motives.

Distortion of reality can be very subtle. You may believe you perceive reality objectively when you have actually distorted your perception. It always comes as a great surprise and even shock when you realize the degree to which you have distorted reality in your perception.

attitude
a learned tendency to respond to people, objects, or institutions in a positive or negative way

Attitude refers to your "leaning" toward or away from some object (person, idea, institution, event). Your attitude toward something can be positive or negative, favorable or unfavorable, and that attitude will influence how you perceive that object. Your motives function, in a manner of speaking, as a screen that filters your perceptions of the outside world.

Motives Shape Learning

Your motives also shape your learning. You learn skills and acquire information more readily when the learning activity is of interest to you and is coupled with your preferred reinforcers. On the other hand, you learn skills and acquire information with difficulty if the learning activity is not interesting and is coupled with stimuli that do not reinforce you. You have no doubt had the experience of learning very quickly a subject that interested you and struggling to learn a subject that did not interest you at all.

Just as your motives can distort your perception, so can your motives "distort" your learning. You learn some things and some ways to reason and solve problems in order to justify holding on to your motives. The abused child or spouse learns to tolerate pain and solve conflict problems by submission in order to justify the high value in which they hold the abusive parent or spouse.

You might learn to lie, cheat, and even commit murder in the service of a motive such as patriotism. Fortunately, such extreme distortions in learning brought about by your motives are not every day occurrences for most people.

Motives Influence Lifestyles

Finally, your motives influence your lifestyle. Most normal development—during which your development shapes your motives and your motives shape your development—eventually settles down to what has been called a lifestyle. This occurs when your motives (needs, values, interests, attitudes) become relatively stable and your environment, too, becomes relatively stable. Then your behavior also becomes relatively stable and predictable. You become a creature of habit. Your motives are satisfied with regularity, and your behavior is characterized by regularity.

SUMMARY

1. A well-equipped learning environment by itself will not make a person learn. One more ingredient is needed—the desire or motivation to learn. Motivation is important in the process of learning and also in the application of what is learned.

2. Motivation involves an increase in the individual's energy level, which is directed at a target. The concept of motivation applies only to self-propelled organisms.

3. Motivated behavior rests on three conditions: capability, opportunity, and requirement.

4. The individual's requirements of the environment are called needs, of which there are two kinds: physiological (biological) and psychological. Physiological needs have to be satisfied for the individual to survive; for that reason they are called primary needs. Psychological needs grow out of physiological needs, are largely learned, and so are termed secondary.

5. Needs are satisfied by reinforcers. There are positive and negative reinforcers. Positive reinforcers include food, water, and air. The removal or avoidance of aversive stimuli is a negative reinforcer.

6. Needs tend to be organized in a hierarchy in which lower-level needs have to be satisfied before higher-level needs.

7. Because several needs require satisfaction simultaneously, you learn to compensate for not satisfying one need by satisfying another, by substituting one important need for another. The substitution of one important need for another tends to occur within clusters.

8. A value can be defined as the theme underlying a cluster of related psychological needs that describes what is of basic importance to the person.

9. Certain values appear to oppose each other: satisfying the requirements of one seems automatically to rule out being able to satisfy the other.

10. Needs and values are preferences about what is important. Interests are preferences about what the individual likes and dislikes. Interests that are stable are based on internal reinforcers or self-reinforcers.

11. An attitude is a tendency to accept or reject something. Examples include your attitudes toward yourself, work, and work institutions. Attitudes have a strong emotional component that may make them difficult to change.

12.   Motivation affects the environment. The opposite is also true: the environment affects motivation in many ways.

13.   Your motives influence your future development. They screen reality, distort reality, shape learning, and influence lifestyles.

KEY TERMS
Define the following:

Achievement
Affiliation
Altruism
Attitudes
Autonomy
Aversive stimuli
Comfort
Compensate
Interests
Need-satisfier
Needs
Physiological needs
Prepotent
Primary needs
Psychological needs
Safety
Secondary needs
Status
Value

QUESTIONS FOR REVIEW AND DISCUSSION

1.   Describe the fundamental processes that, according to most theories, are involved in motivation.

2.   Identify the three conditions that must be met for there to be motivated behavior.

3.   Give some examples of positive and negative reinforcers.

4.   Briefly explain the difference between physiological needs and psychological needs.

5.   Identify in their correct order (either from highest to lowest or lowest to highest) the needs in Maslow's hierarchy of needs.

6.   Explain the statement "Interests are motives that differ somewhat from needs and values."

7.   List and briefly describe some of the ways in which the environment affects motivation.

8.   In what ways do motives influence your development? Explain.

ACTIVITIES

1.   Think a little about what motivates you. Try to identify two or three of your strongest motivations. Write them down. Consider whether and how your motivations may have changed during your life. Try to think of some motivation you once had, but no longer do. Of your current, strong motivations, try to describe how you developed them.

2.   Imagine you had to motivate a friend or family member to do something. If possible, have a real person in mind. Perhaps some one you know still smokes and you want to motivate them to stop. Or perhaps you have a friend in class who has decided the work is too hard and is discouraged from studying and trying. You want to motivate the person to work and study. Describe how you would go about motivating someone.

3.   Pick one or two of your favorite characters from a TV program. Write down their actions and decisions during one segment. Then

try to identify in general what needs they were satisfying in terms of Maslow's five levels of needs.

4. As you read in this chapter, it is not always possible to satisfy all your needs. Sometimes they conflict. Sometimes circumstances just will not permit it. Think of a time when you had conflicting values or when you could not satisfy a need. Try to remember what you did, how you compensated.

5. Go to your local library and look through several recent issues of major daily newspapers. Try to find news stories that contain: (1) an example of someone whose actions indicated she or he did not have Maslow's hierarchy of needs, (2) an example of efforts to change the environment to provide people with opportunity they might otherwise have lacked, (3) an example of an individual or individuals with capability and opportunity, (4) an example of an individual or individuals with capability but no opportunity.

CASE 1

How Motivation Differs with People and Time

"I'm very upset!" Pamela declared. "I really don't think it's fair."

"Pamela, you have been with us a year, and we do think highly of your work," Eileen, the office manager, said.

"Well, if that's the case, why am I the one being let go?"

"As you know, we're putting in new equipment and reducing our staff as a result," Eileen explained. "We do not need as much clerical help now. Earlier this year, we notified the staff that we would be installing a word processing system. We invited those interested in learning how to operate a word processor to attend several evening courses at our expense. You decided not to."

"Well, I just graduated from school last year," Pamela explained. "I didn't feel like taking classes again. I figured that was behind me now. Besides, I'm a very good typist and file clerk."

"Yes, you are," Eileen agreed. "But now we need people who have other skills or who are willing to learn them."

"It still doesn't seem fair," Pamela repeated. "I studied hard in school and learned my skills well. School is over for me now. I don't see why I should be expected to go back and take more courses."

"We live in a fast-changing society, Pamela," Eileen explained. "Some jobs change constantly with new technology. To keep our jobs and get ahead, all of us must be learning all the time."

"Do you mean to tell me that you still take courses, go to school?" Pamela asked.

"You bet I do. Even after ten years with the company and four years as office manager," Eileen said, "I'm still learning. I took the word processing course even though I'm not going to work as a word processor operator. But I felt I should know about them in order to supervise others. Next month I begin a course on managing people. I take at least one formal course or seminar each year."

Pamela's eyes opened wide. "Gee, I thought once you graduated you were done with all that. I figured from now on I would just learn on the job. Boy, was I sick of school work."

"Well, you do learn on the job, of course," Eileen explained, "but taking formal courses and other training is often necessary to be successful and move ahead."

"I wish I hadn't ignored the chance to attend the word processing courses," Pamela said. "What can I do now? I really need a job and like working here."

"I'm sorry I can't keep you in my department," Eileen said, "but I know that the research and development department has an opening for someone with your skills. I'm pretty sure I can get you that position if you'd like to try it."

"Yes, I certainly would!"

"Okay, but I know that they will also convert to word processing next year. That means you will not only have to learn a new job but also soon have to learn word processing as well, if you want to stay."

"I think I've already learned one lesson," Pamela said a bit ruefully. "I've got to be willing to keep learning not only to keep a job, but to get ahead. Well, I need to work, and I want to get ahead, so I guess it's back to school for me."

1. Describe the state of Pamela's motivation at the beginning of the interview. To what degree is she motivated? To what level of needs do you think she is responding?

2. How would you describe Eileen's motivation? Can you identify some of the needs she might be meeting? How does Pamela's motivation at the beginning compare with Eileen's?

3. Is there a change in Pamela's motivation by the end of the interview? Describe the change. To what level of needs is she responding now?

CASE 2

How Relative Importance of Needs Changes

Many writers... have speculated that the strength of the various needs in the population has been changing over the past 60 years. They argue that only recently has a significant proportion of the population been concerned with needs such as self-actualization and autonomy... The concept of man as a self-actualizing organism is essentially a development of the 1960s.

Two reasons are generally advanced for the emergence of higher-order needs. First, there is the rising level of education in our society... Second, the standard of living has constantly increased so that fewer and fewer people are concerned with satisfying their existence needs and, thus, can focus on satisfying their higher-order needs.

Unfortunately, there is very little evidence to either support or disprove the view that the strength of needs is changing... There are, however, some data that can be said to support the view that higher-order needs have become more important. [A higher standard of living suggests that higher-order needs probably are more important, and studies indicate younger managers place greater importance on self-actualization than older managers do.]

There is also some direct evidence that higher-educated people are more concerned with self-actualization. Finally, there is the fact that the idea of self-actualization has gained fairly wide attention in our society. It now seems "in" to talk about self-actualization.... In summary, although there [are] little direct data to support the view, it probably is true that, in general, people are somewhat more concerned with satisfying higher-order needs than they used to be.

- Think of yourself, your friends, and what you see and hear. Considering everything, discuss the quotation above. Decide whether you agree or disagree with the author that, in general, people are more concerned today than in the past with higher-order needs. Give reasons and evidence for your position. In your discussion, consider the popular nicknames different generations have had: Lost Generation, Beat Generation, Me Generation. What do these names suggest in regard to motivation and needs?

From Edward E. Lawler 3d, *Motivation in Work Organizations, Behavioral Science in Industry*, Series 11, Victor H. Vroom, ed. New Haven: Yale University Press: 39.

CASE 3

What Is Important to Us?

"Gail, I've thought about your offer to me of a position with our overseas operation in South America. I've decided to turn it down."

"I wish you would give it some more thought, Paul. We need

someone with your experience there. It would mean a promotion, a big raise—a great future."

Gail, vice president in charge of operations for a large electronics firm, was talking with Paul, one of her top line managers. The company was expanding its international operations. Gail had the responsibility for finding managers to operate the overseas offices. Paul was exceptionally qualified, and so his refusal to take the job was hard for her to accept.

"Paul, we'll pay all your expenses there and back. We will guarantee you a promotion at the end of the first year, if the operation does at all well—and with you there, I know that it will. You can have a month's home leave each year with all travel expenses paid for you and your family."

"Look, Gail, it sounds great. I'm flattered that you want me so much. But I just cannot do it," Paul said.

"Paul, if you don't take it," Gail said, trying another tactic, "you could get a reputation for not being willing to take tough assignments. It could hurt your career."

"I'll just have to take the chance you really mean that," Paul responded.

"You'll do well regardless, Paul. All I meant is that you would probably move ahead faster and enhance your reputation considerably if you would take this assignment. I just don't understand why you won't do it."

"I want to get ahead as fast and as much as anyone else," Paul said. "But I have other things I value also, such as my family. My son is doing well at school. My daughter just entered high school, and my wife is doing very well in her career. It's not a good time for me to ask them to move to another country. I value my family first, and I am not going to disrupt their lives just to advance my career."

"Well, Paul, I have to respect the fact that you know what is important to you," Gail told him. "A lot of other people would jump at this chance without a second thought. But you have weighed it against all the other things that are important in your life, and you have made your decision."

Paul smiled. "Life is full of difficult choices. I just have to know what has real value for me. And in this case I think that I do."

- List the six prominent values—achievement, altruism, autonomy, comfort, safety, and status—in their apparent order of importance to Paul. Give your reasons. Explain your answer.

THE WORK PERSONALITY: How We Express Ourselves as Working Persons

We are free when our actions emanate from our total personality, when they express it....
Henri Bergson

enri Bergson (1859–1941) was a philosopher best known for his ideas about "creative evolution" (he won the Nobel Prize for Literature in 1928). Although Bergson was not a psychologist, what he wrote in the quotation cited is not too far away from the theme of this chapter. Bergson would probably agree with psychologists that you are most "free" when you are able to express your potential to its fullest. There is a sense in which the driving force in life is for each living organism to realize its potential to the fullest extent possible under the circumstances. This is true for single-celled organisms, plants, birds, fishes, animals, and of course, humans. Personality is the term psychologists use to capture how all the various aspects of the potential of a person are organized and integrated. Expressing personality, then, is equivalent to realizing human potential.

▼ THE INCEPTION OF PERSONALITY

What is personality? The word comes from the Greek word for the masks that Greek actors used in ancient times to let the audience know what role they were playing. A single actor could put on a whole play, acting out all the roles with the help of different masks. The word's origin connotes:

- Something seen or manifested, as contrasted with, say, *character*, which is considered to be something deeper, hence not always detected until some crucial situation.

- A social phenomenon. If personality is to be seen, personality results from social consensus. There is no need for the concept of personality for a Robinson Crusoe or a hermit or anyone alone on a desert island where there is no one to see the personality.

personality
the characterization of a person as a unique individual

In what follows, the term **personality** is used in a more technical manner to mean the characterization of a person as a unique individual; specifically, the unique pattern of stable characteristics that identifies a person as a distinct individual.

Personality Reflects Differences

The perception of personality relies on how one person *differs* from others. Each character (characteristic, trait, attribute) by which an individual is described has to be something that differs among people. We may all be alike in some respects and some of us may be alike in many respects, but none of us are alike in all respects. If everyone were alike in every respect, such a concept as personality would not exist. The concept of personality, then, relies on the fact that people differ.

Personality Theories

Differ in what? The answer to that question is what personality theories are all about. One theory, for example, might state that the basic personality characteristic on which individuals differ is masculinity versus femininity. Another theory might say it is introversion (shyness) versus extroversion (outgoingness). Still other theories might say it is flexibility versus rigidity, or dominance versus submissiveness, or people orientation versus thing orientation, or initiating action versus responding to external control, or all of the above.

Some personality theories focus on traits or stable characteristics, others on "dynamic" or changing characteristics; some on single dimensions (characteristics), others on multiple dimensions.

Fig. 11-1

The word *personality* comes from the Greek word for the masks actors in ancient Greece wore to let the audience know what role they were playing. A single actor could act out all the roles in a play using the different masks.

▼ RESPONSE CAPABILITIES AND REQUIREMENTS

The personality theory used in this text encompasses many (if not most) of these other theories. Its starting point is the interaction of a person with the environment. Remember that the environment has several aspects, with social and physical aspects being among the most important.

When interacting with the environment, you show your **response capabilities**. These are your skills and abilities that you use when you are *active*, that is, you initiate events, or *reactive*, that is, you respond to events. The environment has its own response capabilities. You and the environment interact because you have **requirements** of each other. You need something from the environment, and the environment needs something from you.

A simple example of the interaction between you and the environment can be demonstrated in a family and child relationship. The family requires the child to behave in certain ways, such as to do some chores. The child may or may not be capable of doing these. The child also has its requirements, such as to be left alone (private time). The family may or may not be capable of providing for this (such as when the family is large and poor). The child may initiate events, such as staying in the bathroom for long periods. The family may react to this in permissive or punishing ways. The family may also initiate events, such as setting a schedule for the child. The child reacts to the family initiative either obediently or rebelliously. The child-family interaction goes on, and who it is that acts and who reacts may get blurred.

response capabilities
capabilities of person and environment for interacting with each other

requirements
the demands made on each other by person and environment

You begin interacting with the environment even before birth. Because of your genetic makeup, you have certain requirements for growth—nutrients, oxygen, relief from discomfort and stress. As you develop, your response capabilities also develop. Soon you can move your limbs; then you are sensitive to touch; then you can focus your eyes; next you can smile; next say a word; and so on. Development of response capability has many aspects—physical and motor, cognitive and emotional, social and moral—which were discussed in Chapter 8.

Requirements Increase

As you develop, your requirements of the environment increase. In the beginning, your requirements were mainly physiological—meeting your physical needs. After birth and during infancy you had other requirements: regularity of schedule (feeding, sleeping), contact with mother, sensory stimulation, and play activity.

In childhood you developed more requirements, adding social requirements to your physiological and emotional ones. Usually these requirements are needs, but as you learned in Chapter 10, they may also be values or interests. Because they "move" people to act, to behave, they are often called *motives.*

Motives can be viewed objectively, that is from an observer's point of view. When viewed objectively, motives are identified by the stimuli that elicit behavior. (If you see a person drinking water, you identify the need or motive as thirst.) Or motives can be viewed subjectively, from your own point of view. (Perhaps you were just getting a bad taste out of your mouth.)

When viewed subjectively, motives (or requirements) together with response capabilities are organized around the "self," the "I" that is differentiated from the rest of reality. This is the center of experienced reality. Some personality theories place great emphasis on "self" in their accounts. Others do not use the concept at all.

You might say that "self" is the view from within, while " personality" is the view from without. It is important to be aware of the view from within, but our account is essentially the view from without.

The two sets of characteristics with which we describe personality, *response capabilities* and *requirements*, together **predispose** people (make people likely) to behave in certain ways. To give some simple examples: If you had high verbal ability as one of your response capabilities, you would tend to be a talker; if you had high manual dexterity, you might tend to be a woodcarver. If you required social stimulation, you would tend to be gregarious and sociable, but if you required structure, you would tend to be regular and orderly.

predispose
to make likely to behave in a certain way

Note the use of *tend to* be rather than *are*. This is because personality is *predispositional*, and behavior depends not only on personality but on the situation as well. You might be a "talker," but you would be silent at a funeral service. You might be a "silent type," but you might talk a blue streak when you meet an old and dear friend whom you haven't seen for ages.

▼ PERSONALITY STRUCTURE

Structure is the term psychologists use to refer to the pattern that they find best describes the relationships among various characteristics of people. You have read of the radex pattern that describes the relationships among abilities, the six dimensions that describe the relationships among needs, and the hexagon pattern that describes the relationships among interest themes. These are all "structures," so that we speak of the structure of abilities, the structure of needs, and the structure of interests.

Personality structure, however, refers to more than just relationship patterns, although it includes them. Personality structure refers to the overall organization of personality characteristics. It is as if the personality characteristics were building blocks put together to form some kind of "structure." As you have read, different personality theories emphasize different personality characteristics, which also means that they come up with different personality structures.

In the theory we are using, the basic characteristics of personality are your response capabilities and your requirements. These tend to become stable when you reach physical and emotional maturity ("tend" because for a very few individuals, they may not become stable at all). Because they are stable, we can think of them as the building blocks with which to construct your personality structure.

Basic Dimensions

Response capabilities are best described as skills. The pattern of relationships among skills can be described by referring to a set of dimensions we call *ability dimensions*. In other words, skills can be described in terms of their ability dimension components. The ability dimensions, in turn, can be used to describe the relationships among skills. Thus, the ability dimensions make up part of your basic personality structure.

In a similar manner, requirements are best described as needs. The pattern of relationships among needs can be described by referring to another set of dimensions: *value dimensions*. Needs can be described in terms of their value dimension components and value dimensions can be used to describe the relationships among needs. Therefore, the value dimensions make up part of your basic personality structure.

So we can say that abilities and values constitute the basic dimensions, the "building blocks," of personality structure. Abilities and values do not always go together. Persons with the same abilities may have different values, and vice versa. As you have read, there are many possible combinations of abilities and values, or personality "types," each type being predisposed to a distinctive set of behaviors.

Higher-order Dimensions

If abilities and values are building blocks, what do they build? They build what researchers call *higher-order dimensions*. These dimensions are formed by combinations and interactions among abilities and values. One example of higher-order dimensions is *interests*. For example, if you had high verbal ability and preferred social reinforcers, you might develop interests in politics and other social-interaction activities; but if you preferred internal reinforcers, you might develop interests in writing and other literary activities. If you had high manual dexterity and preferred social reinforcers, your interests might be in service activities where you come in frequent contact with people. But if you preferred internal reinforcers, you might develop interests in artistic activities.

Another example of higher-order dimensions of personality structure are what we usually call *personality traits*. These are dimensions that have been popularized by the "personality test." The personality test is not a test in the same way that an ability test is a test. An ability test is designed to find out what your best performance is and you are told to "do your best" (hence, you are "tested"). A personality "test" is actually a questionnaire that asks about your "typical" behavior, either directly or indirectly. Direct questions ask you "Do you usually behave this way?" Indirect questions ask about your opinions, your attitudes, your beliefs, your interests—questions that try to get a picture of your habitual behavior.

One big difference between a personality questionnaire (or personality inventory—more correct than calling them "tests") and an ability test is that on an ability test, you cannot show yourself as having *more* ability than you have, although you can show yourself as having *less* ability than you actually have. Whereas on a personality questionnaire, you can show yourself as being *higher* or *lower* on a trait, for example, as being *more* extroverted or *less* extroverted than you really are. Psychometricians call this *bias error* (the other kind of error is chance error). In other words, bias error is only one way—downwards—for ability tests, but two ways—up or down—on personality questionnaires.

No doubt you are familiar with many personality "traits." A personality trait is a tendency to behave in a particular way, given a particular situation. At bottom, personality traits depend on whether you were able and willing to behave that way in the past and how frequently you behaved in that way. That is, personality traits at bottom depend on abilities and values.

Two psychologists once counted about 20,000 words in English that refer to personality traits. Using "traits" appears to be a popular way of describing people. Of course, many of these trait names are very similar in meaning. Psychologists have attempted to narrow their number to a manageable few that can represent the personality adequately and that can be measured reliably in personality questionnaires or inventories. Most constructors of personality-trait measures limit themselves to about a dozen, and no more than twenty, traits.

Five Basic Traits

Recent studies of these personality questionnaires have shown that the various traits they measure can be described along five higher-order dimensions. That is, five dimensions can form a "structure" that best organizes and integrates the different personality traits measured by the different questionnaires and inventories. These five higher-order dimensions are:

- **Extraversion:** The high end of the dimension describes individuals as outgoing, assertive, energetic, and talkative, and the low end, by contrast, as shy, passive, reserved and quiet.

- **Agreeableness:** High-end individuals are described as kind, trusting, cooperative, and warm, contrasted with low end individuals, who are hostile, distrusting, uncooperative, and selfish.

- **Conscientiousness:** High-end individuals are described as reliable, thorough, and organized, whereas low end individuals are described as unreliable, negligent, and careless.

- **Emotional Stability:** The high end of the dimension, emotional stability, is contrasted with the low end, which describes individuals as moody, temperamental, nervous, fearful, and anxious.

- **Openness:** High-end individuals are described as open-minded, curious, imaginative, and creative, contrasted with low end individuals who are described as close-minded, opinionated, imperceptive, and conventional.

Fig. 11-2

Chart of dimensions

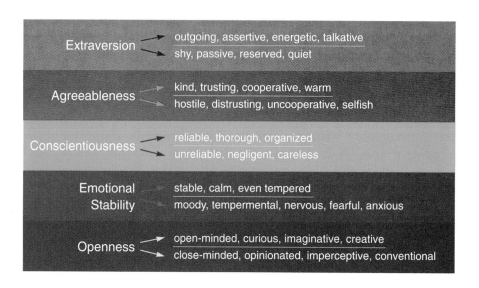

Some personality theorists preferred to construct personality structure around only one higher-order dimension. Most famous among these theorists is Carl Jung, who gave us the original *introversion-extraversion* dimension. For Jung, the most significant aspect of personality is whether your psychic life is directed inward and you are oriented toward your inner reality (introversion), or whether your psychic life is directed outward and you are oriented toward the outside reality (extraversion). More recently, Julian Rotter studied *internal* versus *external locus of control of reinforcement*, which has a bit different focus than introversion-extraversion. In Rotter's theory, your personality is oriented around your belief about who holds control of your reinforcement (and in effect, your life). Either you believe you control your reinforcement (internal) or you believe that others (or society or fate) control your reinforcement (external). Another example is Milton Rokeach, who studied the *closed mind* versus the *open mind*, similar in concept to the openness dimension described above. But the consensus among personality-trait theorists today is that personality structure is best described as multi-dimensional.

▼ PERSONALITY STYLE

In addition to its structure or content, personality can also be described in terms of its style. *Style* refers to the characteristics describing the person's typical interaction with the environment. Whereas *structure* can point to what kind (content category) of behavior to expect, *style* describes how that behavior would be manifested over time. In other words, style describes the dynamic aspects of the manifestation of personality structure in behavior.

There are four dimensions of personality style, which correspond to behavioral aspects studied in the laboratory. These style dimensions are:

- **Celerity:** How quickly or how slowly you initiate behavior

- **Pace:** How much energy or intensity or effort you invest in the behavior

- **Rhythm:** The pattern of the pace of the behavior, whether it is steady or cyclical or erratic

- **Endurance:** How long you maintain the behavior

If you are a bit familiar with laboratory experiments in psychology, you will notice that the four personality style dimensions correspond to the laboratory variables of *response latency* (for celerity), *response intensity* (for pace), *response pattern* (for rhythm), and *response duration* (for endurance). One difference between the laboratory variables and personality style dimensions is that the latter are developed over a relatively long period of time and eventually become tendencies or traits (recall that traits are behavioral tendencies). Your personality style, described in terms of the four style dimensions, is your tendency to behave in a characteristic style, for example, to initiate behavior quickly and intensely, but with up-and-down swings of energy and for short durations, or to initiate behavior slowly, with gathering but moderate intensity, and maintain it steadily for long periods. Personality style appears to be more related to abilities than to values, and to be influenced more by biological heredity than by environmental factors, but definitive research on these questions has still to be conducted. For the time being, it is best to consider personality style as a separate side of personality, separate from personality structure.

Studying personality alone will not enlighten you about how you can realize your potential. To do this, you have to study how your personality interacts with your environments and what happens from this interaction. In the remaining chapters, we will discuss in more detail how you interact with your social environment (Unit 4) and your work environment (Unit 5). Before we do that, however, we need to sketch a general picture of what the *work personality* is, how it interacts with the work environment, and the general consequences of this interaction.

▼ THE WORK PERSONALITY

work personality
those aspects of personality that
are appropriate to the work environment and are involved in the individual's interaction with the work
environment

As you have read, your **work personality** structure consists of the two sets of
characteristics: (1) response capabilities to meet the requirements of the
work environment, or work skills, and (2) reinforcer requirements that can
be met by the work environment, or work needs.

Work Skills

work skills
response capabilities that are
required by the work
environment

Work skills are the behaviors that you use to perform and complete your
work tasks. We define a "work skill" as the behavior required by a work
task. In other words, each work task defines a work skill. There are in
principle as many work skills as there are work tasks. In our modern world
of work, there are literally thousands of work skills.

For some jobs, the work skills can be learned on the job. The worker
can be taught the required work skills in a matter of hours or days. For
most jobs nowadays, however, workers need to be equipped with a
minimum set of work skills before they can be considered for hiring.
Workers learn these minimum sets of skills in formal training courses. Some
of these courses might be provided by the hiring companies themselves, but
most often training courses are provided by educational institutions, both
public and private.

Many work skills, for example word processing, are taught in high
school. Many more are taught in postsecondary institutions. A nation's
work skills are developed for the most part by its educational institutions.
School complements work in very important ways.

As workers go about their work tasks, they may learn better, more
efficient ways to do the job and revise their work skills accordingly. Often,
the skills that an experienced worker uses are not quite the same as the
skills that a beginning worker brings to work the first day on the job.
Because of your capability to learn, you are capable not only of improving
your work skills but even of changing them. Studies in Great Britain and in
this country show that experienced workers differ from inexperienced workers in their *work methods*. That is why things seem easy for an older worker.
That is also why it is such a senseless waste to retire older workers automatically when they reach a certain age.

Sometimes the same work task can be accomplished in a shorter
time without new technology by doing it in a different way—that is, by using
what in effect is a different work skill. Such possibilities were pioneered by
Frederick Taylor, the originator of time and motion study. By studying how
workers performed a certain task and revising the skill to take advantage of
the body's natural configurations, Taylor was able to improve work productivity to an astonishing degree.

Unfortunately, unscrupulous employers used Taylor's methods to improve productivity without fairly increasing wages for the worker. In effect, workers were required to produce much more for the same wages. This gave "Taylorism" a bad name, even if Taylor himself strongly advocated that workers should be compensated adequately for their gains in productivity. Today, collective bargaining agreements between managements and labor unions are designed to ensure that workers benefit from productivity gains that are the direct result of their work performance.

Work Needs

When you go to work for the first time, you have at least two basic reinforcer requirements, or **work needs**:

1. Pay at the level you expect (not necessarily at the level you want to be paid)

2. Work (that is, work tasks) that you can do under reasonable working conditions

You may have other needs, for example, for a considerate boss and for congenial coworkers. If these are important needs, you, of course, have more reinforcer requirements of the work environment and the work environment has to provide more reinforcers.

Typically, not all of your reinforcer requirements are met at the levels you would consider adequate. Some requirements are more than adequately met, in which case there is a surplus of reinforcement. But others are not met to your satisfaction. Also, as you develop as a worker, your minimum requirements may change: some going up, others going down. At any given time, you have to feel that overall, your reinforcer requirements are being met; otherwise, you begin to become dissatisfied with your job.

Some of your requirements for **work reinforcers** are learned after you begin to work. The most prominent of these is pay. True, you may learn about pay by receiving an allowance for doing chores around the house or by doing below-minimum-wage jobs, such as babysitting, mowing lawns, and shoveling sidewalks, or by working at part-time jobs during high school. It is different, however, from the feeling one gets upon receiving the first paycheck on a full-time job.

You may learn something new from that feeling. For example, you may learn to see the paycheck as the measure of your success and accomplishment, and pay can become a very powerful reinforcer. On the other hand, you may learn to see pay only as providing you with the necessities of life and look for the measure of your success in other things, such as in

work needs
reinforcer requirements that are met or can be met by the work environment

work reinforcers
those rewards and other motivators offered by the work environment to meet the worker's needs

correspondence
the state in which the individual meets the requirements of the work environment and vice versa

Fig. 11-3

Time and motion studies developed early in this century by Frederick Taylor helped make workers more productive. Unfortunately, Taylor's methods were abused by employers who did not compensate workers fairly for the workers' increased productivity, and the result has been to give Taylor's method a bad reputation.

family life or hobbies. In this case, pay will be less of a reinforcer requirement than it would be in the first instance.

However you develop your reinforcer requirements, fulfillment in work is probably important to you. Whether or not you go about it systematically, you do seek suitable work environments. If you fail to find the suitable work environment, you try to make the present one as suitable as possible.

▼ CORRESPONDENCE IN WORK

"Correspond" originally had the meaning of co-respond, that is, to respond mutually to one another. **Correspondence** in work, then, means that the individual and the work environment mutually respond to each other's requirements; they are "co-responsive." Correspondence refers to the state in which the individual meets the work environment's requirements and the work environment meets the individual's requirements. Behavior in work can therefore be said to be motivated by the desire to achieve and maintain correspondence. **Discorrespondence** is the term used to describe our failure to achieve correspondence.

discorrespondence
failure to achieve correspondence

Satisfactoriness and Satisfaction

When you meet the work environment's requirements, you are rated as a satisfactory worker. **Satisfactoriness** is the term for this condition. When the work environment meets your requirements, you are satisfied. **Satisfaction** is the term for this condition. Satisfactoriness and satisfaction, therefore, result from correspondence and are indicators of correspondence. You may be either satisfactory or unsatisfactory, satisfied or dissatisfied.

satisfactoriness
the condition produced when the worker meets the work environment's requirements

satisfaction
the condition produced when the work environment meets the worker's needs

There are four possible combinations of satisfactoriness and satisfaction:

1. You are both satisfactory and satisfied. In this case the work environment will want to retain you and you will want to remain in the work environment.

2. You are satisfactory, but dissatisfied. In this case you can become unhappy enough to leave the work environment.

3. You are unsatisfactory but satisfied. In this case the work environment can become unhappy enough to terminate your employment.

4. You are unsatisfactory and dissatisfied. In this case you are not suited for that work environment, and a mutual decision to part company may be made.

Satisfactoriness and Productivity

Satisfactoriness is a necessary condition for productivity. A worker without skills will not be productive. Without satisfactory workers, factories, offices, farms, mines, even schools cannot have productivity. But satisfactoriness alone is not sufficient to guarantee productivity.

That you work hard and can do the required tasks well does not automatically mean you are productive. That you do your job does not mean your company is productive. Productivity depends on several things in addition to satisfactory workers. Chief among these is technology. Equally hardworking workers with unequal technologies will not be equally productive.

TO THE POINT

Large businesses increasingly are taking steps to make sure that they hire people who will be suitable in the job and for whom the job will be suitable.

Toward this end, many businesses conduct training programs for managers who have hiring responsibilities, to help them evaluate and identify suitable candidates. A key player in the effort to match job and candidate is the industrial psychologist.

High grades and good references do not alone guarantee there will be correspondence (that is, a good match of an individual with the work environment) once a person starts on a job. The industrial psychologist helps managers identify and evaluate the skills and motivation of a job seeker. The industrial psychologist can also administer psychological tests to develop an individual profile that a manager can use to evaluate a potential worker's likelihood of fitting into the company's work environment.

There are critics of psychological testing of job applicants, and the process is open to abuse, not the least of which is the invasion of privacy. Used professionally and ethically, however, such prehiring screening by industrial psychologists can save both applicant and company from subsequent discomfort and unhappiness.

Productivity also depends on how work is organized. Mismanagement has often negated the hard work of rank and file. And then there is luck, or what lawyers call "acts of God"; these are unforeseeable and uncontrollable events that affect productivity, satisfactory work performance notwithstanding. Ask farmers about droughts, floods, or out-of-season freezes.

Satisfaction and Productivity

How about satisfaction—does it affect productivity? Yes and no. There is evidence that satisfied workers, if also satisfactory, are productive workers and that some dissatisfied workers are less productive. But not all dissatisfied workers are less productive. During the Depression, dissatisfied workers were as productive as satisfied workers—because they feared losing their jobs when there were no other jobs to be had! So there was a strange phenomenon: The more dissatisfied the workers, the more productive they were—up to a point.

Fig. 11-4

Productivity depends on several things in addition to satisfactory workers. Chief among these is technology. The American farmer and the farmer in a developing country may work equally hard and equally long, but the American farmer with superior technology will outproduce the developing country's farmer by a huge margin.

Satisfaction and Self-Fulfillment

When young people first start going to work, correspondence is not usually high, but because of a "honeymoon effect," they may express high satisfaction. In the "honeymoon period," the job's reinforcers appear more satisfying than they really are, and the job tasks appear more interesting and less demanding than they really are.

cognitive distortion
difference or discrepancy between
perceived reality and actual reality

This **cognitive distortion** (difference or discrepancy between perceived reality and actual reality) occurs because you want to think that you made the right decision—the right choice of career, the right choice of job—and you shape (or distort) your perceptions to fit in with that conclusion. This is an example of *cognitive dissonance reduction* as discussed in Chapter 5. Once you have made a decision, you are more likely to defend it and even make necessary adjustments in your goals to accommodate it. In this sense, your decisions become self-fulfilling.

Changes in Satisfaction

As you become more experienced at and habituated to the work setting and the work routine, you improve your correspondence to work, and your satisfaction has a more substantive basis. With time, workers undergo changes in their job satisfaction. There are two schools of thought about these changes, which can be called the V-shaped trend and the straight-line upward trend.

V-Shaped Trend

This school of thought holds that after an early period of high job satisfaction, disillusionment (or reality!) gradually sets in as the novelty of working wears off, so that by middle age, workers generally hit the low point of their job satisfaction cycle. They begin thinking that they are not moving ahead fast enough or that the job is not interesting enough. Then they either remain in their jobs and are promoted or otherwise rewarded or move to a new job that they find more satisfying. In any event, they eventually become more satisfied. See Figure 11-5.

Straight-Line Upward Trend

Another school of thought holds that satisfaction continues to improve as the years go by. According to this school, discounting the "honeymoon period" when perceptions are distorted, the youngest workers have the lowest job satisfaction. Some of them continue to be satisfied with their jobs (those whose work environments are truly correspondent), but many become dissatisfied and either change jobs or do something about their jobs to improve their job satisfaction.

There is a gradual "weeding out" process, with the satisfied workers remaining and the dissatisfied workers leaving. Therefore, what appears is a straight-line upward trend in satisfaction, with the younger workers being least satisfied, the older most satisfied, and those in the middle years also in the middle in job satisfaction.

Both Trends Exist

Because the above are group trends, both schools of thought are right for the simple reason that some individuals experience the V-shaped trend, whereas some experience the straight-line upward trend, and still others experience mixed trends. Do not expect one trend or the other to happen automatically for you.

The Most Satisfied

Who are the most satisfied workers? The evidence shows that those workers able to use their abilities fully are generally the most satisfied. In relation to this, studies indicate that the higher the skill level required and met, the more satisfied the worker. Thus professional workers are most satisfied, laborers are least satisfied; upper-level managers are more satisfied than lower-level managers; skilled workers are more satisfied than semiskilled workers.

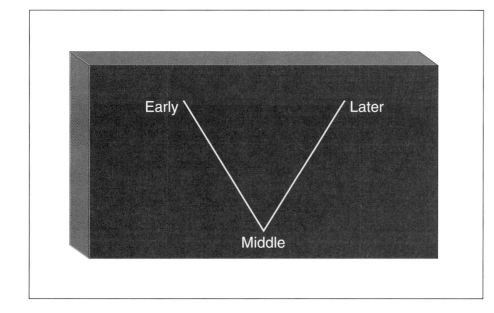

Fig. 11-5

This graph illustrates the "V-shaped phenomenon": workers experience high satisfaction in both the early years and the later years, and lower satisfaction in the middle years.

The higher the skill level, the more likely a person's abilities are used to the full, and the more satisfied the worker. *Dissatisfaction* occurs also, however, if the skill level required is higher than the worker's ability to achieve. When a worker's abilities and required skills do not match, in either way, discorrespondence results. Generally speaking, among unskilled workers, it is the *more* able who are dissatisfied, whereas among professional workers, it is the *less* able who are dissatisfied.

The above indicates that self-fulfillment—the realization of your potential, the highest use of your abilities—is closely linked with satisfaction. Satisfaction reflects self-fulfillment. But because satisfaction can also reflect the fulfillment of other needs, satisfaction alone is not the most accurate indicator of self-fulfillment. You have to know that you are satisfactory as well—that the use of your abilities has resulted in real accomplishment. In fact, it is when you *see* real accomplishment that you *feel* the sense of accomplishment, which in turn is sensed as a feeling of self-fulfillment.

Considerations of Style

Earlier, you read of an aspect of personality called style. Personality style includes whether you respond quickly or deliberately (celerity), how much energy you invest in responding (pace), what the pattern of your pace is (rhythm), and how long your energy lasts (endurance). Style considerations do enter into your correspondence with the work environment.

If the work environment requires rapid response and you are more deliberate, if it requires a higher pace—or a lower pace—than you are accustomed to, if you have to be steady when you are cyclical or vice versa, and if you lack the endurance required, you will be discorrespondent with your work environment even if you have the requisite abilities and the work environment has the requisite reinforcers.

Such style considerations show up eventually in your satisfactoriness and satisfaction. Some people are fortunate in that their work environments can accommodate a wide range of styles. But others are not that fortunate. For the latter, style considerations can make the difference between correspondence and discorrespondence, between satisfaction-satisfactoriness and dissatisfaction-unsatisfactoriness.

▼ ALIENATION

alienation
a kind of dissatisfaction common in industrial societies, characterized by a feeling of distance from, or lack of involvement with, other people or one's work

A certain kind of dissatisfaction is particularly characteristic of our industrial society: **alienation**. Two kinds of alienation have been identified:

1. Alienation from work
2. Alienation from fellow human beings

Alienation from Work

Alienation from work, a concept popularized by Karl Marx, is a product of modern assembly-line production processes. Assembly-line methods break work down into small, efficient tasks. But these tasks are meaningless and boring to the workers, who do not see the end result of their efforts. Not seeing the end result of their labors or not feeling part of the process causes workers to feel alienated from their work.

It is difficult for most workers to use their full potential when their work consists of tightening up 16 nuts on an assembly line, or slapping labels on bottles, or sewing cuff buttons on shirt after shirt hundreds of times a day. Workers cannot experience a sense of accomplishment when they feel like tiny, insignificant, replaceable cogs in a gigantic machine. More and more, "pride in work" has become a thing of the past. More and more, self-fulfillment is not being found in work but in after-work activities.

Fig. 11-6

Alienation from our work is one form of dissatisfaction that has resulted from modern assembly-line production methods. Workers can become alienated by the mindless, repetitive tasks required.

Alienation From Fellow Human Beings

The other kind of alienation, a concept popularized by Sigmund Freud, is also a by-product of industrialization: alienation from fellow human beings. Because most workers are interchangeable and expendable, a high rate of mobility exists. Because of competition in the marketplace, companies come and go and jobs come and go. The average worker changes jobs once every four years, and in any given year, a fourth of all workers change jobs. As a consequence of all this mobility, relationships with fellow workers, friends, neighbors, and even family are lessened and fleeting at best. Once the exception, the phenomenon of the individual who is afraid to develop emotional attachments to others because of fear of their being cut is fast becoming the rule. The current popularity of "support groups" reflects the extent to which alienation from fellow humans has infected society.

Alienation and Discontent

With the pervasiveness of alienation of both kinds, some observers detect an undercurrent of discontent. This undercurrent is thought to manifest itself in a variety of ways, such as in the:

- Counterculture movement
- Antiwork ethic

- Decline of productivity
- Sloppiness of both goods and services
- Erosion of standards
- Frightening epidemic of alcohol and drug abuse
- Burnout phenomenon
- Increasing incidence of suicides

These problems, of course, do not all result from a single cause. Each of these phenomena have multiple causes, and discontent could actually be only a minor cause. On the other hand, even a tiny straw could make the breaking of the camel's back that much more probable, and underlying discontent could be that straw.

Other, possibly more optimistic, observers, however, do not see any increase in underlying discontent. They see discontent as part of the human condition, changing in manifestation as human cultures and societies change. They believe that the discontentments of industrial society would have had their counterparts in preindustrial societies and will have them in postindustrial societies. Further, they believe that, on the whole, industrialization has improved the lot of humankind.

▼ NEED FULFILLMENT AND WORK MOTIVATION

In the chapter on motivation (Chapter 10), you read that you behave in order to meet or fulfill your requirements, and because your requirements never stay met or fulfilled, you continually behave to fill them. You also read that your requirements—which are called needs—are basically of three kinds, depending on the source of the reinforcers that meet them:

1. Physical or environmental
2. Social
3. Self or internal

Needs that have to do with physical reinforcers include physiological needs as well as safety and comfort needs. These are universal. Needs that require social reinforcers are of a different kind, because language, communication, and meaning are indispensable to the effectiveness of these reinforcers.

To illustrate, you would have a hard time being affected by social reinforcers if you found yourself in a country whose language you did not speak and whose people did not speak your language. However, in that country, food and shelter and other physical reinforcers would be just about as effective as in your own country.

Needs that require self or internal reinforcers are the most different of all, because each person builds a unique system of internal reinforcement (in his or her head) that is only partially discernible from the outside.

All three kinds of reinforcers—physical, social, and self—exist in the work environment. For some people, only work can provide all the reinforcers they require. For others, work can only provide some reinforcers and there are a few for whom work is no provider of reinforcers at all. In other words, work motivation depends in the first place on each individual's needs, or her or his requirements.

Some students of work motivation—Frederick Herzberg, an industrial psychologist, in particular—classify work motivators into two kinds:

1. **Extrinsic motivators:** Involve the context of the job and relate to physical and social reinforcers.

2. **Intrinsic motivators:** Involve the content of the job and relate to self or internal reinforcers.

Extrinsic/Intrinsic Motivators

Extrinsic motivators are those that are related to primary needs. Pay, fringe benefits, vacations, and job security are examples of extrinsic motivators. These motivators are not inherent in the job. People do the job to realize them, but they are *outside* the job, which is what *extrinsic* means.

Intrinsic motivators exist within the job itself, and a worker's needs are satisfied by actually doing the job. It is not necessary to wait for later rewards, such as pay, if the work itself is satisfying. An intrinsic motivator would be the aspect of a job that allows a worker to use his or her abilities to the fullest.

Herzberg believed that extrinsic motivators were more important for dissatisfaction, whereas intrinsic motivators were more important for satisfaction. In other words, he believed dissatisfaction and satisfaction are two separate phenomena. There is evidence to support Herzberg's contention. It is known that negative emotion (negative feelings, such as anger, fear, anxiety, or irritation) involves a different brain process from positive emotion (positive feelings, such as love, pleasure, or excitement).

Herzberg believed that extrinsic motivators (or the lack of them) could only dissatisfy and would not satisfy, whereas only intrinsic motivators could satisfy. The evidence on this assertion is mixed. Even if satisfaction and dissatisfaction are separate phenomena, extrinsic as well as intrinsic motivators (reinforcers) could lead to satisfaction as well as to dissatisfaction.

Herzberg assumed, as did Abraham Maslow (who formulated the hierarchy of needs theory you read about in Chapter 10), that needs or requirements are organized in the same way for all individuals. We know now that this is not the case.

KITA Motivation

Herzberg's other assertion is less controversial. He faulted employers for emphasizing the KITA ("Kick in the . . .") theory of motivation instead of accentuating the positive. Current work motivation, in Herzberg's view, concentrates on getting rid of dissatisfaction rather than on promoting satisfaction. KITA managers believe workers are motivated by a desire to escape punishment and will not work unless driven.

Theory X and Theory Y

An earlier student of work motivation, Douglas McGregor, had a similar view. He identified and criticized the usual methods of motivating workers, such as emphasizing punishment, putting the fear of God into the workers, distrusting workers, watching them all the time, making them do things only the way you would do it, and not giving the workers much responsibility. He named this approach to motivation **Theory X**.

Theory X
a style of work motivation described by Douglas McGregor in which extrinsic motivators, especially negative ones such as punishment, are emphasized over intrinsic motivators

McGregor, going against conventional wisdom, argued for emphasizing rewards, trusting workers, giving them more responsibility, letting them "do their own thing," and taking into account their opinions and suggestions when making decisions at work. He called this preferred approach to motivation **Theory Y**. Broadly speaking, the KITA approach and Theory X rely on extrinsic motivators, whereas Theory Y relies on intrinsic motivators.

Theory Y
a style of work motivation described by Douglas McGregor in which intrinsic motivators, such as trust, responsibility, and self-direction, are emphasized over extrinsic motivators

Theory Z

Theory Z
a style of work motivation drawn from Japanese culture and business that emphasizes worker participation even more strongly than Theory Y. Workers and supervisors work together to achieve consensus. Often quality circles are established

A third approach, called **Theory Z**, has gained acceptance more recently. Drawing on examples from Japanese culture and business, Theory Z emphasizes worker participation even more strongly than Theory Y. Workers and supervisors work together to achieve *consensus*, or common agreement, on work-related decisions. "Quality circles" are established in which workers directly involved in production are asked for input on how to make the product better, how to improve production techniques, and so on. This focus on worker input and involvement can improve worker morale and enhance production. Theory Z emphasizes improved human relations among workers and supervisors and tries to achieve long-term improvements in productivity, efficiency, and worker satisfaction.

Job Enrichment

Herzberg advocated an approach to work motivation, similar to Theory Y, that focuses on intrinsic motivators. Of course, the extrinsic motivators should not be neglected. Herzberg recommended enriching the content of the job so that intrinsic motivators, such as being able to use one's abilities or having a feeling of accomplishment, come into play.

Job enrichment is not accomplished by job rotation (moving workers from one boring job to another) or by job enlargement (simply adding more monotonous tasks). Rather, job enrichment requires a radical redesign of the job to make greater use of a person's abilities. Herzberg and his students have shown that jobs can be redesigned to become more satisfying to the workers.

There are, however, many jobs that need doing that cannot be redesigned to become intrinsically motivating. Also, feelings of monotony and boredom, like beauty, are in the eye of the beholder. A job that one person might find monotonous and boring, another person might find to be exactly what the doctor ordered.

Job redesign can be expensive and can sometimes have unforeseen negative consequences, such as creating problems about rates of compensation. Before resorting to job redesign, the more efficient strategy is to try to match the person's and the job's requirements. Which brings us back to an earlier theme—what matters is how suitable the job is for you and how suitable you are for the job.

As it is, the introduction of the computer and its offspring, the robot, is well on its way toward revolutionizing the design of work. More and more of the tedious, repetitive tasks are being taken over by the machine, leaving the human to operate at his or her creative best. But computers notwithstanding, remember that human motivation remains essentially the same in its basic contours and patterns. Only the specific details are changing.

In work motivation, you are still bound by your capabilities and requirements. You will still need work—even if you have to invent it—that matches and challenges your capabilities and provides the reinforcers appropriate to your requirements. Things may change, but these remain the same.

TO THE POINT

Whether a job is boring or stimulating more often than not depends upon the worker. If there is correspondence between the person's needs and the job's reinforcers, probably the person will not see the job as boring. Consider the following excerpt taken from an article on "Careers in Office Automation," by the Datapro Research Corp., Delran, N.J.

Manpower consultant Roy Walters, head of a New Jersey management firm, lists the following as the 10 most boring jobs:

1. Assembly-line worker
2. Elevator operator in pushbutton elevator
3. Typist in office typing pool
4. Bank guard
5. Copying machine operator
6. Keypunch operator
7. Highway toll collector
8. Traffic controller in tunnel
9. File clerk
10. Housewife

When interviewers from *U.S. News and World Report*[15] spoke to workers in seven of these occupations, not a single one found his or her job boring or monotonous. Factors that people consider important in their careers vary widely. It is important for a smoothly operating work environment that management select and hire individuals who not only have an aptitude for the jobs but also consider the work enjoyable and rewarding.

People often have misconceptions about certain jobs because of their own misunderstandings or the prejudicial opinions of others. Often those who actually work in the jobs have entirely different attitudes. The article cited as an example word processing, which is often described as dull and boring. Yet researchers found that 67 percent of people interviewed in these jobs said that what they liked best about what they were doing was the variety of work!

SUMMARY

1. Your personality develops from at least two sets of characteristics: response capabilities and reinforcer requirements.

2. Your response capabilities are organized in terms of skills, and your reinforcer requirements in terms of needs. In turn, your skills are described by referring to ability dimensions, and your needs by referring to value dimensions.

3. Your personality structure consists of your abilities and your values.

4. Abilities and values are the building blocks of personality structure, and combinations and interactions among them result in higher-order personality dimensions such as interests and personality traits.

5. Five basic higher-order personality traits have been identified: extraversion, agreeableness, conscientiousness, emotional stability, and openness.

6. In addition to structure, your personality has style, which describes your typical way of interacting with the environment. The four dimensions of personality style are: celerity, pace, rhythm, and endurance.

7. Your work personality consists of your work skills and your work needs.

8. Correspondence in work means that the person and the work environment mutually respond to each other's requirements: you meet the work environment's requirements (you are satisfactory) and the work environment meets your requirements (you are satisfied). Satisfactoriness and satisfaction are indicators of correspondence.

9. Satisfactoriness is a necessary condition for productivity, but does not guarantee it. Satisfaction can affect productivity, but many dissatisfied workers are productive workers.

10. Satisfaction changes with the work life. Some think satisfaction starts high in the early years, drops in the middle years, and rises again in the later years, in a V-shaped trend. Others believe satisfaction continues to increase with the years in a straight-line upward trend, as dissatisfied workers leave to find other jobs more correspondent with them.

11. Self-fulfillment—the realization of your potential, the highest use of your abilities—is closely linked to satisfaction. But satisfaction alone is not enough to indicate self-fulfillment; you also have to know that you are satisfactory as well.

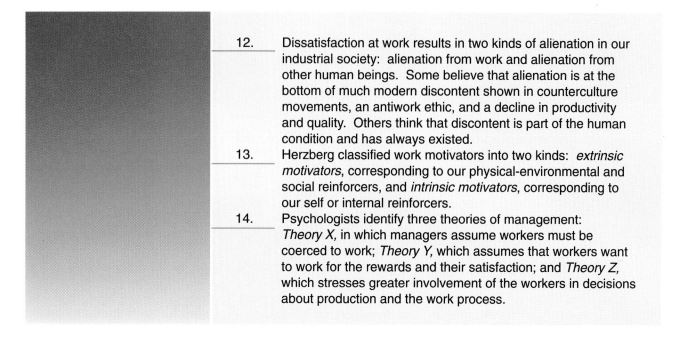

12. Dissatisfaction at work results in two kinds of alienation in our industrial society: alienation from work and alienation from other human beings. Some believe that alienation is at the bottom of much modern discontent shown in counterculture movements, an antiwork ethic, and a decline in productivity and quality. Others think that discontent is part of the human condition and has always existed.

13. Herzberg classified work motivators into two kinds: *extrinsic motivators*, corresponding to our physical-environmental and social reinforcers, and *intrinsic motivators*, corresponding to our self or internal reinforcers.

14. Psychologists identify three theories of management: *Theory X*, in which managers assume workers must be coerced to work; *Theory Y*, which assumes that workers want to work for the rewards and their satisfaction; and *Theory Z*, which stresses greater involvement of the workers in decisions about production and the work process.

KEY TERMS
Define the following:

Agreeableness
Alienation
Celerity
Cognitive distortion
Conscientiousness
Correspondence
Discorrespondence
Emotional stability
Endurance
Extraversion
Extrinsic motivators
Higher-order dimension
Interests
Intrinsic motivators
Needs
Openness
Pace
Personality structure
Personality traits
Predispose
Requirements
Response capabilities

QUESTIONS FOR REVIEW AND DISCUSSION

1. What is meant when we say that response capabilities and requirements predispose people to behave in certain ways?
2. Define personality structure and personality style. What are the components of each?
3. What are higher-order dimensions? Give examples.
4. What are the five basic personality traits? Give a brief description of each.
5. Draw the distinctions between "work task," "work skill," and "work method." Likewise, distinguish between "work need" and "work reinforcer."
6. What is correspondence? Describe when it occurs.
7. Explain and illustrate the difference between satisfactoriness and satisfaction in the work environment.
8. Explain what is meant by the V-shaped trend and the straightline upward trend in job satisfaction. Which really exists?
9. What does alienation stem from, and what two kinds have been identified? Give examples of each.
10. How do extrinsic and intrinsic motivators differ? Give examples.
11. Briefly explain *Theory X* and *Theory Y* as put forth by Douglas McGregor. How does *Theory Z* relate to them?
12. What is meant by job enrichment?

ACTIVITIES

1. List five occupations. Estimate your satisfactoriness for each occupation on a scale of 1 to 10 (1 = Very Unsatisfactory; 10 = Very Satisfactory). Similarly estimate your satisfaction, if you were to enter the occupation, on a scale of 1 to 10 (1 = Very Dissatisfied; 10 = Very Satisfied). How easy or difficult is it to make such estimates? These are called "global" ratings because you consider everything all at once.

2. Now, take one of the occupations. List as many work skills required by the occupation as you know (don't go overboard; list 10 or so most important ones). Also list the work reinforcers available in the occupation (to your best knowledge). Do the satisfactoriness and satisfaction estimates again on the same 1- to-10 scales, but this time do satisfactoriness ratings for each of the required work skills you have listed, and do satisfaction ratings for each of the work reinforcers. These are called "work aspect" ratings for obvious reasons. How does rating by aspect compare with rating globally?

3. Take the descriptions given for the five basic personality traits (extraversion, agreeableness, etc.) and construct a 1-to-10 rating scale for each trait, with 10 being high on the trait and 1 low. Rate yourself on the five basic traits. Put your ratings away and don't look at them for a week. Then rate yourself again on the five traits without looking at your first ratings. Compare the two sets of ratings. Did you rate any trait differently?

4. Do Activity 3 but this time on the four personality style dimensions. Use the following instead of high vs. low for your 1-to-10 scales:

    Celerity: deliberate vs. impulsive
    Pace: vigorous vs. laid-back
    Rhythm: steady vs. up-and-down
    Endurance: short (low) vs. long (high)

    You can put either description (word) at 1 on the scale and the other at 10. Rate yourself, put it away, then rerate yourself a week later. How does this compare with Activity 3? easier? harder?

5. From your own experience and feelings, discuss with your classmates which management style—Theory X, Theory Y, or Theory Z—you would prefer to work under. Give your reasons. Also discuss which style you feel would be the most effective in terms of encouraging productivity and why you think so.

CASE 1

What Is In a Job?

"Well, Chris, you graduate this spring. Have you been lining up job interviews?"

"Dad, I've been thinking a lot about what I want to do when I get out of college. But I really don't have any definite idea right now."

Chris was home on winter vacation. His father, like most parents, wanted to help his son start on the road to a meaningful, happy, and successful life.

"It can take a while," the father now said, "and going on job interviews is not a fun thing, I know. But you should get started right away. Check the classified ads. Go to employment agencies. See the school counselors."

"I'll do those things, Dad," Chris replied. "But I don't think it's that simple. I want to be sure I make the right choice."

"I guess I can understand that," his father said. "There are so many job opportunities, and it seems technology changes them every day. I know too many people who are not happy in their jobs to urge you to rush into anything until you have had a chance to check things out."

"Thanks, Dad. I appreciate your understanding. I want to make sure that I find a job that will satisfy my needs," Chris said.

"What kind of needs?" his father asked. "You mean making a lot of money, being recognized and successful, having an important position?"

"Sure, those things are important," Chris said. "But there are other things as well. It's important for me to have a job that will challenge me and help me develop my talents. If I could not use my abilities, I don't think I could be happy, even if it paid well and gave me a lot of power. Also, I think I'd like some independence. You know, not have someone looking over my shoulder all the time telling me what to do."

"I think I see," his father said. "Anything else?"

"Yes, there is," Chris replied. "I know that I could never be really happy in a job that was not making a contribution to society."

"I guess I understand," his father said. "But you haven't mentioned some things I thought most people wanted in a job. Things like security and the chance to get ahead."

"They are important, also," Chris agreed. "My problem is sorting out which things are the most important to me right now and for the future, and then finding the right job."

1. Discuss Chris's approach to finding a job in terms of what you have read in this chapter.

2. What work reinforcers do you think will be important to Chris, and what type of job will he be happy in?

3. Which management style would most motivate Chris? Which would least likely motivate him?

CASE 2

Suitability at Work

Louise Lisle was a very talented painter. She specialized in watercolors and painted extremely beautiful pictures of landscapes with lovely old buildings or of waterscapes with towering clouds and churning waters. She sold her paintings from time to time, but not frequently enough to enable her to live on the earnings. From time to time, she had to work in a commercial studio to earn enough money to live on.

When she worked in the commercial studio, she had to paint exactly what the clients wanted. She was not allowed to use much of her own ideas or creativity, except in carrying out a client's idea. Also, she had to meet deadlines. A specific painting had to be completed by a specific time. She preferred to follow her own sense of when to work on a painting. In her own work, she would sometimes keep working and reworking a painting for days or weeks before she decided it was done. At the studio, the painting had to be done by the deadline, period.

In addition to meeting deadlines, Louise had to paint during studio hours—9 to 5—in a large room surrounded by several other people. The art director was constantly looking over her work as she did it. Left to herself, she preferred working from sunrise to noon and then doing something else for the rest of the day. Also, she preferred to work by herself, identifying the problems and finding her own solutions.

Louise endured the days working at the commercial studio, sustained by the thought of the good money she was making. But she looked forward eagerly to the day when she could stop working in the studio for good. And while she worked there, she turned to her own paintings in the mornings for satisfaction before going to the studio.

1. Discuss Louise's situation at the studio in terms of what you have read in this chapter.

2. Aside from Louise's leaving the studio, were there other things that could be done to make Louise a more satisfied worker? Assume the studio believed she was such a satisfactory worker that they wanted to keep her.

Unit III

RESEARCH STUDY

Designing an Extra-Curriculum

You are the resident psychologist in a small (500-student) residential school for young (pick your gender: boys, girls, or both). The school spans Grade 7 to Grade 12 and all the students and teachers reside on campus. The school's trustees want the curriculum "updated," especially the school-provided and-supervised extra-curricular activities, to base them more on "current principles of psychological science." You have been asked to draft recommendations for the extra-curricular program. Your task (for this exercise) is to draw up a list of such recommendations, with a short rationale (reason behind it) for each recommendation.

1. Use the chapters of this unit as the basis for your recommendations. Take each chapter in turn, starting with Chapter 8, through Chapter 11, and for each chapter think up at least two recommendations. You may wish to divide your recommendations in two: one set for early adolescent students (Grades 7 through 9) and another for late adolescents (Grades 10 through 12).

2. The recommendations can be broad and general (such as principles or requirements, e.g., "All extra-curricular activities must be...or must have...etc.") as long as they are applicable to actual extra-curricular activities. Or, your recommendations can be narrower and more specific (such as recommending a particular activity). You must have a (short, 1-2 sentence) rationale for each recommendation that is based on the Unit III chapters.

3. One test you can apply to your recommendations is to ask if in your own experience it helped in your development, or if you observed that it helped the development of others. "Helping in development" means it contributes to your maturing physically, mentally, socially, and emotionally; that it contributes to your becoming more of an adult and less of a child.

4. Pay particular attention to the motivational side of things. Will your recommendations help meet the young people's needs, values, interests, and preferences? Will they be happier persons in addition to being more mature? Will the young people feel they are gaining more control of their lives?

Remember, each recommendation should have a short rationale based on the material in Unit III.

Social Relationships

Humans are social beings. For a long period after birth, you depend completely on other humans for survival. This bonds you to your parents and other humans. It also sets the stage for your ability to communicate, especially speech. Human speech is extremely complex, but human communication goes beyond speech and is even more complex. What humans have accomplished through speech and communication over the thousands of years since learning to communicate is truly awesome.

In this unit, you will learn how to communicate your thoughts, feelings, needs, and goals; how to relate to others; and how to "read" other people's thoughts, feelings, needs, and goals. Because you will always be in human groups of various kinds, it is helpful to learn how groups interact. Lastly, you can prepare yourself for leadership. Successful leadership depends on many factors, some beyond your control, but learning about leadership skills and leadership values is within your control.

▶ COMMUNICATING:
How We Convey Our
Thoughts, Feelings,
Needs, and Goals

*Speech is civilization itself. The word, even the most
contradictory word, preserves contact—it is silence that
isolates.*
Thomas Mann

Communication is something we need and desire. With it individuals, organizations, and society can accomplish much. When communication fails, so do aspects of our lives, the success of personal and organizational endeavors, and sometimes the efforts of society. Even sanity is partially defined by successful communication.

In this chapter, you will read of the need to communicate to survive and to function socially. Over the course of human development, many methods of communication have been devised, and this chapter examines the ways people communicate both with words and without words. You will follow the communication process from the formation of an idea to the response to the message. You will also consider communication in the workplace, how information travels, and the styles people use to communicate. And you will examine some of the impediments to successful communication.

▼ THE NEED TO COMMUNICATE

Human beings communicate to survive and to relate socially with one another. Being able to speak and read language are important skills that you begin to acquire, consciously and unconsciously, when you are young, and continue to develop through your adult life. In addition, you learn hand motions, facial expressions, and body movements that, added to language, form the mixture of words and gestures that constitute communication.

Former U.S. Senator S. I. Hayakawa said, "The meaning of words is not in the words, they are in us." It is, after all, the meaning and understanding behind words that are the essence of communication. Communication is a complex process, and you must use some effort to master it to succeed in daily life and in work organizations.

Communicating for Survival

"Help! Fire!" is one level of communicating for survival. You warn another of danger by shouting an alarm, by waving your arms to chase someone away from trouble. Children cry, and parents ask where it hurts. Traffic lights and warning sirens all communicate to us for our survival. None of these seem to be very subtle survival tools. But communication for survival can be very complex as well, humanly and technologically speaking.

We are all born helpless except for the ability to communicate with our parents by crying; and we soon learn that certain sets of sounds can produce the desired attention. Parents can almost always distinguish a child's cry of pain from one of frustration, hunger, or tiredness. Later in our development we learn the subtleties of tone and expression in our parents'

Fig.12-1

Imperfect communication results in disagreements and laws to deal with those disagreements—but laws can be misinterpreted too, which is why courts exist.

communication, sometimes so well that a certain glance from them can be enough to affect our behavior.

As adults, we extend this awareness in turn to our children, as well as to spouses and friends. A certain tone of voice or choice of words can be all that is needed for warning or reassurance.

Technologically, society has developed very sophisticated warning systems for everything from fire and break-ins to missile detection, on which people rely to provide them a measure of safety. Weather satellites now provide enough information to predict the track of storms, enabling people to prepare in advance for hurricanes, tornadoes, and blizzards. Hundreds of lives are saved because of this new communication survival tool.

Social Communication

You communicate also to recognize other human beings, to exchange information, and to solve day-to-day problems at work and at home. You also communicate purely for enjoyment. Social communication can vary tremendously in substance, from the "have a nice day" that completes many commercial transactions, to the complex negotiations between nations, businesses, and even individuals. To communicate for fun, people share sight gags, jokes, and puns and draw cartoons.

The purpose behind this social communication, however, is to create *understanding* among people. Understanding creates the interrelationships among humans that define society.

Although there is a certain level of casual communication in the business office, nearly all the work conducted there is communication for understanding. How well that communication is done, how well one understands what is done or said, determines the level of stress or ease of a person's work life. Misunderstandings can vary from minor ones easily solved between two people to major misinterpretations that may require resolution by a mediation board or court of law.

If social communication among human beings were always perfectly successful, there would be no need for contracts, regulations, policies, laws, or even the Supreme Court.

▼ METHODS OF COMMUNICATION

verbal
of, relating to, or consisting of words

nonverbal
communication that uses gestures or signs, either alone or simultaneously with verbal communication

Generally, communication is divided into verbal and nonverbal communication. **Verbal** means of, relating to, or consisting in words. Though common usage today often defines verbal as spoken words, *any* communication that uses language is verbal. **Nonverbal**, then, encompasses all the communication that uses gestures, signs, or symbols, either alone or simultaneously with verbal communication.

Effective communication uses a combination of verbal and nonverbal expression. These combinations are often what distinguishes individuals, family groups, organizations, and even whole cultures. Let's take a closer look at verbal and nonverbal communication.

Nonverbal Communication

You often use and respond to nonverbal communication unconsciously. Babies only one day old use the nonverbal communication of smiles, and they quickly learn the meaning of threatening gestures and gentle touches, long before they grasp language. But nonverbal communication is also developed consciously and is taught to members of society in such forms as good manners (offering a firm handshake when meeting someone) or the system of highway signs.

Nonverbal communication is both a process and a product, analogous to speaking and writing. Let's consider some forms that nonverbal communication can take.

Use of Symbols

symbol
something that stands for or suggests something else

The use of **symbols** for nonverbal communication is ancient. Sometimes the symbol is a pictorial representation of something real like an animal, a bird, or an artificial object that is identified with a particular meaning (for example, a lion often symbolizes courage, whereas a dove symbolizes peace).

Symbols can also be abstract, a visible sign of something invisible. Examples of this are the dollar sign ($) and the notations used in music. Certain businesses and professions like chemistry, medicine, or engineering have symbols that a person entering the field would need to learn and understand to communicate accurately.

Colors, like symbols, communicate nonverbally. In our culture, red is used to symbolize danger or warning. In Asia, red is the color of joy and celebration. Use of color, like any symbol, is a culturally learned thing and becomes part of your unconscious after a while. A businessperson traveling in the East might respond unconsciously with feelings of alarm upon seeing red used there in a celebratory way.

Body Language

Body language encompasses all those things you do with your hands, feet, posture, and facial expression when you are communicating with another. Like symbol and color, body language is sometimes used and responded to unconsciously, even though much of it is learned behavior and culturally influenced. But by understanding body language and using it consciously,

Because nuclear waste dumps are needed to hold the already existing stockpiles of dangerous radioactive waste materials, the problem of how to warn future generations of danger in these places has created an interesting problem for nonverbal communication

Much of this waste has a half-life of 24,000 years, so that the danger of it will probably outlive our language. A team of researchers has been seeking examples of symbols and structures used since earliest civilization to provide warning of danger or to frighten people away.

A selection of these will be used to designate radioactive dumps in the hope that future generations will understand the warnings and avoid contact with them.

TO THE POINT

you can gain a powerful tool for communication. Make sure you use it to work for you, not against you. The most commonly used elements of body language are:

- Eye contact
- Hand gestures
- Facial expressions
- Posture
- Tone of voice
- Personal appearance
- Face-to-face distance between speaker and listener

There is evidence that your credibility as a speaker rests primarily on *how* you speak rather than on *what* you say. Direct eye contact; hand gestures that "suit action to the word"; and a relaxed, confident tone of voice convey truthfulness and sincerity. Your sense of ethics, however, should prevent you from using these tools to tell lies convincingly.

In some circumstances, standing up to speak is appropriate, especially in front of an audience. At other times, it is preferable to sit down, because that expresses a receptive and attentive mode for listening and conversing. An erect, but not tense, posture shows interest and confidence. You can probably think of times when someone, slumping in a chair, possibly with feet up, and arms folded across the chest, sent you a nonverbal message that what you had to say was of little interest to that person.

Most body language behavior is an unconscious extension of your personality. How you dress, however, is one aspect of your personal appearance that you consciously manipulate daily. You probably have had the experience of wearing clothing that seemed to affect your behavior: perhaps it made you feel comfortable and confident, or relaxed and fun-loving.

Other people's responses to how you dress also affect your behavior. Businesspeople customarily find that suits, conservative shirts and blouses, and understated accessories increase their own professional self-image and reinforce that image for others as well.

Proximity

Attention has been paid in recent years to the significance of the distance people prefer to keep between themselves and those with whom they are communicating in a face-to-face encounter. Researchers have found that this, too, is a cultural trait, and that the distance preferred by North Americans, for example, is different from that regularly used by South Americans or Europeans.

In this culture, most people regard up to about four feet around them as personal space, and the only other people they feel comfortable having within that space are close friends or associates. From four to ten feet away is considered comfortable for most impersonal and business transactions, such as interviews or meetings. Beyond that is public space, the distance for any nonprivate communication, such as lectures or speeches.

You may find yourself uncomfortable talking with someone who does not use the same distance for communicating that you do. Or you might add a different meaning to what they say because of it. Consider, for example, how it might seem if a coworker standing right at your elbow asked you to go to lunch; then consider the same invitation delivered across your desk or in the company of a third person. People who do business internationally may need to understand spatial relationships in other cultures to communicate successfully with foreigners.

Sign Language

Some body language like pointing or beckoning is a form of sign language. Traffic officers communicate almost entirely by sign language. But sign language can also mean the language used by deaf people to communicate with one another and with people who can hear.

American Sign Language, or **Ameslan**, is a formalized system developed in the nineteenth century that assigns specific meanings to certain hand motions and combinations of gestures. Used with the finger alphabet, Ameslan's vocabulary is an animated system of communication that is really a form of verbal communication, because many of the signs stand for words. Much of it, however, is recognizable to hearing people because so many gestures have universally understood meanings, both symbolic and literal.

In Ameslan you point to yourself to say "I" and to the other person to say "you." This is a gesture anyone can understand, whether they "speak" Ameslan, English, or Swahili. The sign for "open" is made by holding your hands out, palms down, and then moving them apart and turning the palms upward simultaneously, like the lid of a box opening. The sign for "ape," tickling your ribs, also is universally understood—at least by anybody who has seen an ape scratch its sides.

Verbal Communication

As noted earlier, verbal communication means the use of *words* to communicate. Words either are spoken aloud in **oral communication**, or are written. Our world is full of words.

Ameslan
a formalized system developed in the nineteenth century that assigns specific meanings to certain hand motions and combinations of gestures

oral communication
spoken, as opposed to written, communication

Fig. 12-2

Ameslan helps deaf people communicate with one another and with people who can hear.

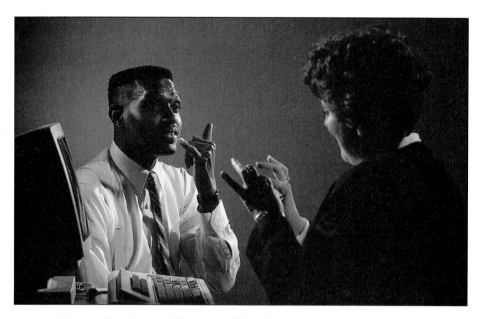

Each of us in our lifetime will probably see new words created and old words acquire new meanings, sometimes as a result of technology, sometimes because of social changes. Consider, for example, some of the new words developed as part of the computer industry: byte, software, microchip, and hard copy. Additional narrow meanings have been given to words like menu, prompt, enter, and save. In fact, scientists have developed computer "languages," such as C or PASCAL, that are used to write software programs.

Every trade or business has its own special language. When you go into a new job, you will have to learn its language, or jargon, to communicate successfully. Using jargon may interfere with communication, however, because usually only others in the business know the jargon, too, and using it can exclude others from participating in the conversation.

Most people expect to hear jargon; they might even feel uncomfortable if it wasn't used. For example, newscasters use a certain language and style that most people find comfortably familiar and that they associate with the evening news, weather, and sports.

Learning jargon can be fun and is a way of feeling like an insider. When you do business with people outside your profession, however, remember to be aware of the extent of your listener's or reader's knowledge of the subject. Define your terms as you speak or write, and double-check to be sure your listener understands what you have said. This is especially critical for those who are involved in marketing or communications. A customer's understanding may be directly proportional to how much she or he is willing to spend.

Speaking and listening (oral communication) and writing and reading (written communication) are entirely different experiences. Imagine the difference between hearing a political candidate's speech at a rally and reading an account of the same speech in the newspaper. Let's consider some of the elements of each of these two major communication methods.

Oral Communication

Think about hearing a political speech at a rally. The candidate is speaking, and you and others are listening. It is possible that the candidate's voice is amplified and that spotlights are trained on the podium. The hall may be decorated colorfully with banners and signs.

You probably are watching at the same time and taking in the candidate's whole appearance: dress, body language, and facial expressions. You are aware of changes in tone and inflection in the candidate's voice. At the same time, you may observe other people listening, watching, and responding to the speech. It may be that from time to time you and others will applaud or cheer what the candidate says.

Not all oral communication, of course, will be as dramatic as a political speech. But all oral communication is a sensory-rich experience. Oral communication, appealing to the whole person, can seem like a more complete experience than written communication. You can see and hear the speaker and often respond immediately. There is a much better chance for the communicators to sense one another's moods and feelings in oral communication.

Written Communication

Imagine now that you are reading an account of the same speech reported in the newspaper. You are probably seated and have the newspaper no more than two feet away from your face. You probably are not paying much attention to noises or people around you and are concentrating on the words in print. You might form a picture in your mind of the hall as it is described by the reporter—in fact, there might be a photo in the paper. As you read the candidate's words, you might stop and reread to get a clearer understanding or form a mental question. You will learn how the crowd responded through the reporter's interpretation of the event.

Of course, it might be that you are the reporter writing the description of the speech. Even then, you will probably be working alone, concentrating on the paper or word processor screen before you, and tuning out noise and conversation around you. You will have to select words to describe what you saw, and even if you are trying to be objective, chances are you will reveal your point of view by your writing.

cathy®

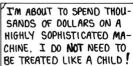

Fig. 12-3

Bad communication results when two people don't speak the same language.

Writing and reading, because they are not the sensory-rich experiences entailing immediate response that speaking and listening are, provide an opportunity for thorough review and analysis of communicated messages, especially complicated ones. Each experience has intrinsic biases, advantages, and disadvantages. In a later section, you will read of some of these advantages and disadvantages and consider strategies for working with them.

▼ THE COMMUNICATION PROCESS

Whether you are communicating with the spoken or the written word, the process of forming and expressing an idea is essentially the same. In this section, you will examine the parts of the process that you use no matter how you are communicating. In the next section, you will consider the special requirements of speaking and of writing.

The communication process is imprecise. To begin with, it is difficult to find the right words and ways to express exactly what you mean. Then, there is so much interference—both physically in the environment and mentally in your intended audience—that even well-prepared messages have difficulty getting through. Recall reading in Chapter 4 how people obtain data, how physical and mental filters prevent people from hearing or seeing accurately, and how these filters may make them misinterpret what they do hear or see. Because it is by nature imprecise, the communication process requires your careful attention.

In his book *Human Relations at Work: The Dynamics of Organizational Behavior*, Keith Davis gives six steps in the sequence of communication. These steps are:

1. Ideation
2. Encoding
3. Transmission
4. Reception, or transfer of initiative (to the receiver)
5. Decoding
6. Response (of the receiver)

Let's take a closer look at each of these steps.

Ideation

ideation
the process of creating an idea
or choosing a fact to
communicate

Ideation, according to Dr. Davis, is creating an idea or choosing a fact to communicate. This thinking process must be done clearly. Fortunately, having to express an idea or a fact often forces you to think more clearly. As the sender, you must have something meaningful to say to the receiver, especially in the workplace, where time is money and communication must be to the point.

Usually, ideation becomes encoding (see below) almost immediately. In conversation, it seems, you speak your thoughts almost instantly. On the other hand, when you are preparing a speech or a report, ideation is a longer, more involved process, in which several ideas must be presented, linked together in a logical, meaningful sequence.

Ideation requires sorting through all the possible ideas and combinations of ideas to select the ones that will accomplish your purpose. Whether you plan to write or speak, be sure that you have your main purpose in mind first and that subsequent ideas support it. Prepare an outline, and check it for clarity. Anticipate questions, and include answers and definitions.

Even though the processes of ideation and encoding are the same in speech and writing, there are important differences in the way they occur. When writing, you can move back and forth between the ideation phase and the encoding phase, making sure that the encoding has accurately expressed your idea. You revise until you get it right. There is also a lapse of time between writing the message and sending it, which gives you time to think about the best way to say what you need to say. In speech, on the other hand, there is almost no time between ideation and encoding. More importantly, you have no opportunity to revise your statements: once you have said something, it is final; the receiver has heard and processed the message.

Encoding

Encoding is the translation of the idea or thought to be communicated into symbols that the receiver can understand. In verbal communication, the symbols used are words, though as you learned earlier in this chapter, nonverbal symbols, such as hand gestures or signs, can also be used. In short, encoding means putting thought into words or action.

Encoding also involves the selection of the media that will attract the receiver's attention. **Media** (singular, "medium") in this instance are the methods or tools used to communicate, such as radio, newspapers, TV, magazines, billboards, telephones, computers, and so on. An idea, such as the promotion of pharmaceutical products, will be encoded in one way to reach doctors in a professional journal (print medium) and in a different way to reach the general public by television (electronic medium).

Because each person learns in a different way, choosing a successful medium is an important part of encoding. Some people learn best if they

encoding
the translation of an idea or thought to be communicated into symbols that the receiver can understand

media
the methods or tools used to communicate, such as print, spoken word, or television

read, others if they hear, and still others if they are shown. Most people require some combination of these methods. By choosing either to write or to speak, you limit to a certain extent your encoding capabilities. That is why books have illustrations and why speakers often use visuals such as slides or diagrams.

Transmission and Reception

transmission
the act of sending an encoded communication to the receiving individual

Because these two processes happen almost simultaneously, they will be considered together. **Transmission** refers to the act of sending the encoded communication from you to the person you are addressing—whether in a letter, in person, or on the telephone. You may be accustomed to thinking in terms of radio or television transmission from a transmitter to the receivers in your home, but any message is transmitted: voices through the air or over telephone wires or words on paper. (Remember what you read of sound waves and light waves in Chapter 4.) When you speak out loud, you use your vocal chords and the air around you to *transmit* your message to the listener.

reception
the point at which a message is received in the form transmitted

Reception or transfer of initiative means that the message is received in the same form in which it was sent. In other words, you as receiver can hear the sender's voice or read the words on the paper passed to you, and you are now expected to respond in some way, once you have decoded the message.

You may have had experiences with bad transmission. A favorite tune comes on the radio, someone in the house turns on an appliance, and all you can hear is buzzing; or you are talking on the phone, and all of a sudden a humming noise keeps you from hearing distinctly what the other person is saying. But bad transmission can occur in face-to-face conversation and in written communication as well.

Part of the responsibility you have in communicating, whether you are the sender or the receiver, is to reduce the *interference* in transmission and to make sure that the reception is clear. In the workplace it might mean shutting the office door and having someone else answer the phone so that you can have an uninterrupted conversation. At home, it might mean waiting until a family member is not deeply involved in a project to ask a question.

Decoding

decoding
the process of turning a received message into its meaning

Decoding is done by the receiver and is the process of turning the message into meaning. The closer the receiver's interpretation of the meaning is to the meaning intended by the sender, the more successful the communication is. Even a simple statement of fact can be subject to a variety of interpretations, because the person receiving the message considers the context and the sender's intent along with the substance of the message.

The responsibility for how accurately the message is decoded is shared by the sender and receiver. Some specific strategies for avoiding these problems will be discussed in a later section.

Response

Response in this sense refers to the action taken by the person or group receiving the message. This completes two-way communication and ideally should provide feedback to the sender so that the sender will know that the message has been received and understood. Very often a new sequence of ideation, encoding, transmission, reception, and response is set in motion,

response
the action taken by the person or group receiving a message

Effective spoken communication depends both on the transmission of the messege and on the response from the audience.

which can result in a continued dialogue. Communication stops when the sequence is interrupted or stopped.

Some communication, like conversation, for example, is designed to promote dialogue; other kinds of communication, by their natures, hinder dialogue. It is hard to imagine how to respond to a magazine article or television show, even though those are also communication. When you read or watch TV, you are acting only as receiver, and your response, if there is any, remains with you.

▼ LEVELS OF COMMUNICATION

One way to describe communication is to refer to its "direction." It can be downward, upward, or horizontal. When parents talk to children or when teachers talk to students, communication is described as flowing downward. When children talk to parents or teachers, communication flows upward. And when peers talk to each other, the communication is horizontal. Similarly, in most companies, people fill positions that are divided into supervisory and nonsupervisory levels. When supervisors talk to the workers reporting to them, communication flows downward. When workers respond to their supervisors, communication flows upward. Workers or supervisors talking to others on their supervisory level are communicating horizontally.

Linguists have found that the form of the communication changes, depending on whether it is up, down, or horizontal. A simple example might be how you would ask someone to hand you a pen. You might say, "Could you hand me that pen, please?" or you might just say, "Hand me that pen." One factor in your choice will be your relationship with the other person: Are you a supervisor? A peer? Do you report to that person? While we are all aware of these differences in how we speak in different situations (you can probably think of similar examples), they are subtle compared with the differences in some languages. Japanese, for example, has a very complex set of grammatical rules that deal *only* with this sort of distinction. By contrast, our forms of upward and downward communication are very simple and not all that different.

The pattern may be the same, but downward communication from parent to child is quite different from downward communication between supervisor and worker. If your employer spoke to you the way your parents did when you were a child, you probably would not like your employer at all. In the same way, upward communication does not mean being subservient or cringing; it simply means that the speaker and listener have different roles in that particular social structure (family, work, school, etc.).

Downward Communication

Downward communication certainly does not mean that supervisors or teachers speak condescendingly to workers or students. Supervisors must routinely talk with workers in lower-level positions if the company's business is to be accomplished. A good supervisor will know how to use downward communication without making the worker feel inferior.

An example of downward communication in the workplace is a manager giving instructions to employees. The manager makes job assignments, either orally or in writing, including who should do the job, what should be done, why it should be done, and when and where it should be done. Smart managers also provide information about their expectations of the quality of the product. Instructions may be spoken or written, depending on their complexity and number and on which medium the manager believes will be more effective in getting the message across to the particular employees involved.

A corresponding situation between teacher and student might be the assignment of a term paper or other work. A parent telling a son or daughter to clean up, take out the garbage, or do homework is in a similar position. In each case, although the specific relationships vary, the way the message is communicated is similar. The speaker tells the listener what to do and expects to be obeyed. Compare this with a child asking a parent for something, a worker or student asking a supervisor or teacher to do something. The tone is quite different.

Even though the supervisor or parent expects his or her instructions to be followed, it is important for the health of the relationship that that person not be too bossy. You should always phrase directions by asking for rather than ordering cooperation. Ordering is the opposite of being condescending, but it has the same negative impact. It may get the job done, but people work best when their pride of achievement, self-motivation, and dignity are preserved. Most people naturally resist being given orders and respond cooperatively to requests.

How well the supervisor or teacher communicates downward is directly proportional to the results produced by the workers or by the student's time in class. If employees do not understand their instructions or do not know how their work fits into the big picture, they may not work productively and the company will lose profits. Of course, if students cannot understand a lecture or do not realize the significance of an assignment, they will not learn what the teacher is trying to teach them.

For another example, the supervisor might talk to employees about things the employees want to know, such as work methods, shop rules, pay practices, employee benefits, appraisals, and advancement practices. Supervisors who keep their staffs informed about company news and direction will find that it fosters healthy two-way communication. Parents, too, are always answering questions. Working to do so openly, in a way the child can understand, will improve communication in both directions.

Upward Communication

Much communication flows upward from the employee to the supervisor, from the student to the teacher, or from child to parent. If this upward flow of information is not encouraged, severe problems may result. Employees will need to discuss their specific responsibilities, performance standards, quality of production, problems encountered, and solutions developed. Students will want assignments clarified and difficult subjects explained or interpreted, and they will need their performance periodically evaluated. Parents' relationships with their children are much less formal than either of these, but a similar give-and-take of evaluation, encouragement, and clarification definitely occurs. Information provided regularly and honestly prevents many problems of misunderstanding.

People will also want to discuss controversial matters such as complaints, criticisms, and disagreements. This kind of information may help a supervisor or parent solve problems before they multiply. You are probably familiar with examples from school. A teacher who is willing to listen to the students is more likely to generate trust and effective communication than one who is not. Finally, employees may also want to discuss how they feel about their work or about personal matters that have an effect on work performance. Supervisors and staff who communicate with each other openly and helpfully are likely to develop a healthy commitment to one another and to the workplace. Parents and children who communicate openly are also likely to develop strong commitments to each other and to the family as a whole.

Horizontal Communication

Good group relations, whether in business, at school, or at home, require horizontal communication as well as downward and upward communication. Coworkers use horizontal communication when seeking and giving advice on both business and interpersonal problems, when training replacements or new workers, or when meeting at small conferences or company social gatherings. Brothers and sisters communicate horizontally when doing chores together, giving advice, or helping with homework or social problems. Students do the same when helping each other with assignments, working on student council committees, playing on the same sports teams, dating, and so on.

Fig. 12-5

Employees use upward communications when they discuss work with a supervisor.

Besides the benefits of the feeling of belonging, good horizontal communication gives people incentive to try out ideas and share information informally, without the pressure of formal analysis by supervisors or teachers.

In their book *In Search of Excellence* Thomas Peters and Robert H. Waterman described a number of companies that actively encouraged horizontal communication by providing small, easily accessible meeting rooms with chalkboards where staff could gather to knock around ideas. Staff were encouraged to spend time out of their offices, talking with their peers. New products and better methods of doing business resulted from these informal exchanges, which added considerably to the companies' profitability.

▼ STYLES OF COMMUNICATION

Communication occurs formally and informally. You may have grown accustomed to certain kinds of information being presented in a certain way. In school, you are accustomed to factual information being presented formally through a lecture or textbook. At work, news of a promotion, mentioned to you only casually in a hallway by your supervisor, would not seem real, because the more formal setting of a planned meeting in the supervisor's office to discuss the new responsibilities is what you would expect. How a message comes to you may affect its meaning for you.

Whether you plan to communicate formally or informally, once you learn some rules of thumb for speaking and writing and become aware of

Fig. 12-6

Friends use horizontal communication when discussing personal issues, giving each other advice, or making each other laugh.

some of the pitfalls, experience and practice will improve your ability as long as you remain open to learning from your mistakes and successes. Good speaking and writing share some basic steps.

First, you decide what it is you want to say (ideation). Sometimes in the workplace you may be assigned the topic. For example, your supervisor might ask you to prepare a report. Second, you determine who will be hearing or reading what you prepare, answering such questions as, What will be the audience's level of knowledge about the topic? Third, you gather and process the information you intend to present, selecting the facts that will support your topic (encoding). Fourth, you choose and use a method of communication (transmission) by writing or speaking aloud.

Formal Communication

Most businesses formalize certain types of communication. When you first begin a job, you need to learn how the company expects you to communicate, just as you need to learn its jargon.

Written messages, such as sales orders, invoices, and letters to customers or suppliers, may have to be formatted in a certain way and sent on special forms or paper. In-house memos, reports, proposals, even phone messages may have to be prepared in a specific way.

Formal written messages are used outside of work as well. Letters asking for credit, information, or products or services; resumes; invitations; writings for publication (articles, letters to the editor, etc.); and college application essays are all examples of formal written communication. In each case, generally accepted rules govern the way the message is presented. Also, the language you use reflects the degree of formality of your message. Responding to an invitation with a simple "Thanks, I'd love to!" conveys a very different message from "Ms. Jane Doe gratefully accepts the invitation to attend the wedding of Barbara Smith and Joseph Allen."

Formal oral communication occurs at business meetings with prepared agendas. Job interviews, performance appraisals, presentations, and speeches are all characterized by formal communication. You may need to become aware of your company's etiquette in these formal situations. In a meeting, for example, you might need to know if it is customary to raise your hand and wait for recognition by the chair or just speak up when there is a pause.

Oral communication in a classroom may be formal or informal depending on the teacher's style and the school's approach. It can be formal in other areas as well, as at a formal dinner, a funeral, or a meeting of a community organization. When meeting someone for the first time in such a setting, you would probably use a phrase like "How do you do," or "I'm very pleased

to meet you," as opposed to a simple "Hi!" or "How's it going?" When you speak at a public meeting, you will choose words that reflect the fact that you are speaking formally and not just among friends.

Informal Communication

Informal communication takes place all the time in all areas of life. Employees and supervisors alike often discuss with each other or with their peers matters pertaining to work, without resorting to formal communication, such as calling a meeting or writing a memo. Of course, informal communication can be spoken or written. Letters to friends, conversations between classes or at a party, and casual encounters on a bus are all examples of informal communication. A conversation with a teacher after class often is informal, as opposed to the more formal exchange that takes place while class is in session.

Phone calls, face-to-face questions and answers, business lunches, even conversations over coffee during a break can accomplish work with informal oral communication. Notes penciled in the margins of a report, newspaper or magazine articles photocopied and highlighted, or notes left on a desk all constitute informal written communication. In the course of much informal communication, however, there are pitfalls—opportunities for rumor and gossip, which will be discussed in the next section.

Generally speaking, written communication is more formal than oral. Simply deciding to put something in writing can make it a formal message. There are a number of reasons for this. First, writing, as you read earlier in the chapter, distances the sender of the message from the receiver. This distancing effect is also a characteristic of formal communication. You are informal with your friends, those you are close to, and formal with people you are not so close to. Second, written communication tends to be more standardized, which is another characteristic of formal communication. When you speak with friends, you might drop your final gs, say "gonna" instead of "going to," and use other informal, nonstandard forms of speech. People expect you to follow the rules in writing, so to speak—spell correctly, use proper grammar, and avoid sloppy or shortened forms of speech like "gonna." This use of very correct language also helps to make written communication a more formal method of conveying a message than speech. Finally, because written communication is more or less permanent, it is a more reliable record than speech and represents you to people in general. This means that people tend to be more formal when writing words down than they are when speaking.

▼ COMMUNICATION ROADBLOCKS AND DANGERS

Good communication is a lot like good health: you never notice it until something goes wrong. Blocked communication or miscommunication, evidenced by insecurity, hostility, conflict, and, ultimately, nonproductiveness can create serious difficulties at home, in the workplace, and among friends. There are some identifiable causes of bad communication and strategies for working around them.

Physical Roadblocks to Communication

Patricia, in a hurry, stops by the reception desk, located next to the copier, where two people are running off some letters and discussing the mailing. The receptionist is on the phone, but without waiting for the receptionist to finish the call, Patricia, in a stage whisper, tries to leave a message about where she will be for the next hour. When the receptionist later gives the wrong information to an important caller, Patricia gets very annoyed.

Patricia tried to run four physical roadblocks to successful communication, and ultimately got stopped: time, space, complexity of the message, and the sender's and receiver's sensory limitations.

Time

Careful communication takes time and good timing. Delivering a message in a hurry means you have no chance to be sure your message was received as you intended; taking a message hurriedly prevents you from asking a question that might clarify meaning. Similarly, reading too quickly through a memo or a set of instructions can cause you to miss the fine print, and an error can result.

Space

Where a message is delivered is sometimes crucial to accuracy. A busy room, with background noise of phones ringing, machinery running, or

TO THE POINT

Public speaking becomes more important the higher up in an organization a person rises. Here are a few tips about speechmaking:

1. Decide on a central message. State the purpose of your talk in the first sentence, and keep your opening simple.
2. Limit the talk to 15 to 20 minutes. You can always elaborate later if there is time and if your audience asks you leading questions.
3. Use conversational language. Choose active voice over the passive; use vivid verbs and descriptions.
4. Make sure your remarks work for you. They should flow and support your main purpose.
5. Don't patronize your audience, but don't be unnecessarily modest.
6. Adjust your tone to your audience and message.
7. Use quotes, statistics, and jokes cautiously. Facts and figures may bog you down; quotes and jokes may seem trite.
8. Emphasize your concluding message. Repeat the essence of your message in a sentence or two.

people conversing, can scramble a message. It is hard to concentrate on what was written or what is being said when there is distracting noise. You may be accustomed to some level of noise where you work, but if a message is really important, it is worthwhile to minimize background noise.

Complexity of the Message

The more complex the message, of course, the more care has to be taken in communicating it. Patricia would have had better luck writing down her schedule for the next hour and giving it to the receptionist rather than trying to explain it aloud. Also, the more complex the message, the better it is to wait until the receiver has provided some response to help you judge his or her level of understanding.

Sensory Limitations

Sensory limitations can be caused by something as simple as a bad telephone connection and poor lighting or by some degree of deafness or poor eyesight or by a more complicated disability such as dyslexia, which you read about in Chapter 4. Being aware of physical limitations, yours or another person's, can help you overcome them by helping to prevent misunderstandings. Being aware of the limitations inherent in the environment can also help.

Mental Roadblocks to Communication

Mental roadblocks to communication are more complicated than physical ones but are not insurmountable. Because they hinge on psychological feelings and attitudes, they involve a person's emotions, values, and judgments, all of which may conflict with those of another person. It is hard to change such roadblocks in yourself and impossible to change them in another person. Sometimes differences between people can be resolved when both make an effort to understand, but sometimes it requires the help of a mediator.

Personal Interests

Although somewhat overused in recent years, the word *relevant* explains what is meant by personal interest. Information that relates directly to your own experience, life, or needs is much more likely to be received accurately and completely than something that seems to have no relevancy or meaning to you. You pay attention when your personal interest is addressed. If you hope to communicate with your audience, tell them right away why they need to hear what you have to say.

Cultural Conditioning

As you read earlier in the section on nonverbal communication, the many meanings behind body language, color, and symbols are culturally defined. Within the country as a whole, there are regions that can be identified as culturally distinct from one another. For example, a word can change meaning depending on where you are: a sandwich made in a long roll might be called a grinder, sub, hoagie, or Italian sandwich, depending on where you are. How you are raised and the attitudes you are raised with are all part of your cultural conditioning and will affect how you communicate and respond.

Awareness of your own and others' cultural biases and tendencies can improve understanding. Just knowing to expect a bias can help to prepare for it. When you travel abroad, you expect that occasionally there will be misunderstandings or lack of communication. But it can happen at home, too. If it does, stop for a moment to think about why the miscommunication is occurring. Then, if you can, spend some time with the person with whom you are miscommunicating to see if together you can discover the differences.

Abstraction

You read about abstractions in Chapter 5. You recall that an abstraction is a generalized concept of an existing object separate from a specific example. For example, house, cat, and dog are abstract categories as opposed to a specific house, cat, or dog. Concepts such as contentment, patriotism, or love are abstract ideas. They consist of feelings, reactions, or behaviors.

Because each of us has had a different upbringing and life experience, we are likely to identify abstractions differently from one another. Contentment, for example, will mean different things to different people. Depending on experience, even the idea of a house will vary: a child raised in a city will describe a house in a different way from a child raised in the suburbs.

The problem this can pose to communication lies in the different concepts each person has about abstractions. You cannot assume that someone else will form the same mental picture as yours when you speak about an abstraction. If you do assume so, it can lead to misunderstanding. If it seems that misunderstanding is occurring because of this, stop for a moment to ask what the other person means by the idea. It is all part of trying to speak the same language.

Stereotyping

stereotype
an oversimplified abstraction or attitude held by an individual or group about the members of another racial or national group, gender, or even profession

A **stereotype**, a form of abstraction, is sometimes a product of cultural conditioning, sometimes merely personal opinion. It is defined in *Webster's Dictionary* as "a standardized mental picture . . . representing an oversimplified opinion, affective attitude, or uncritical judgment." A stereotype is usually an attitude held in general by the members of a racial or national group, gender, or even profession about people of another such group.

Although there may be a core of truth to a stereotype, the danger to communication is that many people hear what they think they are going to hear. When your expectations of a group, or members of it, are predetermined, you are prevented from understanding individual differences. You may not even hear clearly what a member of that group really means when he or she speaks.

You can be tipped off to stereotyped attitudes in yourself or others when you hear the words *always, never*, or *all*. The truth is usually too complicated to fit neatly into such packages as, for example, "all women...," "men never...," or "salespeople always...."

Misinformation

Misinformation has two sides. Sometimes misinformation is unintentional; it is often derived from one of the communication problems already mentioned or from lack of knowledge or incomplete information. The mistakes resulting from unintentional misinformation can be at best irritating or at worst dangerous, but it usually does not have the adverse psychological impact that intentional misinformation has.

Intentional misinformation—deception, lying, or hiding of the truth—sabotages communication by undermining the trust that enables us to understand what someone means. As noted earlier, successful communication relies on an open and reliable exchange between people. Deliberate misinformation closes off the exchange and confuses communication.

Misinformation occurs sometimes when someone, afraid of the consequences of the truth, wants to avoid punishment or when someone seeks to manipulate a situation for personal advantage. Office politics is an example of that: A person may misinform to appear more knowledgeable or competent than he or she really is or even to make someone else seem incompetent.

The Grapevine

Any organization with a healthy level of informal communication is likely to have an active grapevine—an informal network for sharing news. The

Fig. 12-8

Office gossip is considered part of the grapevine. This gossip can be an effective method of informal communication or could be destructive if it is mostly rumor.

term goes back to the Civil War, when intelligence telegraph wires were strung from tree to tree. Some thought the wires resembled grapevines. The messages transmitted by these lines were often garbled and unclear, so a grapevine is often regarded as an unreliable source of information. There are good and bad sides to a grapevine.

Rumor is the bad side of the grapevine. Rumor is at best ambiguous, at worst untrue, information of great interest to a group of people, moving rapidly along a grapevine. It is subject to informal editing as it is filtered through each person's perceptions of the truth, in the process usually becoming less and less reliable.

Rumor occurs when there is inadequate formal communication. One of the best ways for managers to combat rumor is to open all channels— upward, downward, and horizontal—of formal communication.

A grapevine is not all bad. In fact, office gossip is a natural, normal, and indestructible method of informal communication. Smart managers learn its characteristics, listen to it, and try to influence it.

▼ COMMUNICATION VIA MACHINES

Communication via machines is a common feature of modern daily life. Most of us have telephones, many of us have telephone answering machines. At work, some of us may use computers or faxes in addition to telephones and intercoms. Depending on the machine you use, you may have to adjust the way you communicate slightly to accommodate the machine's capabilities or limitations.

Telephones

Telephoning, in a way, is a half step between oral communication and written communication. It gives you the oral communication advantages of being able to hear vocal inflections and to respond immediately to what is said. It has the written communication disadvantage of not allowing you to observe body language. But it does enable people to communicate over great distances, just as the mail does.

In addition, using a telephone means that you can demand attention without asking for it in advance. This is an advantage if you are doing the calling. But a disadvantage if you are the receiver. Perhaps you have done business with a person who is constantly interrupted by other customers calling. The telephone has thus gained a reputation of being a troublesome source of interruptions.

Keeping these things in mind, when you plan to make a phone call, think through what you want to say (just as you would for any other medium); try to organize well enough that you can do all your business in one call. When you reach the person you want to talk with, ask "Is this a good time to call?" or "Do you have a few moments now to talk?" Providing an opportunity for them to call you back later when they are less distracted will improve the chances that your message will be received clearly. Once you proceed, keep to the point and conclude your business promptly.

If you are taking a phone call when you are busy and your caller does not give you an opportunity to decline the call gracefully, ask if you can call back later, and explain that you are not able to talk right now. Terminating an unduly long phone call can be difficult because your caller cannot see you looking anxiously at a clock or shifting around in your chair. You have to provide a verbal message, such as "Well, thank you for calling, but I really must hang up now."

To minimize interruptions, many people use telephone answering machines. Because they are so common, it is a good idea to prepare a brief message (in addition to preparing for a longer conversation) to leave on a tape in case you should need to.

If you choose to use an answering machine to handle your calls, keep in mind that you are taking responsibility for responding to all calls that are left on your machine. If you truly want to ignore your phone, better not hook it up to an answering machine.

TO THE POINT

"In Praise of Office Gossip," an article by Walter Keichell III in the August 19, 1985, issue of *Fortune*, lists some of the benefits of grapevine communication:

1. Office gossip supplements official channels and can serve as an early warning system: Employees can think through their responses to news; the boss can hear bad news that staff are afraid to tell. Formal communication can then be opened with less stress.
2. Office gossip helps forge corporate culture as new staff informally pick up on company values.
3. Gossip can pull a company together, foster closeness among staff members, sharpen awareness, and refine understanding among staff.
4. Office gossip can provide an opportunity for venting grievances, so that by the time a problem has to be discussed formally, people have gotten some immediate reactions off their chests.
5. Managers who participate in office gossip have to be careful not to be shut off from the source of news by getting a reputation as a blabbermouth.
6. Everyone needs to weigh office gossip against real evidence in order to keep an accurate perspective.

Keichell reported that few managers he interviewed liked to admit they gossiped, but they all admitted that gossip consistently happens at work and in social situations.

Computers

Communicating via computers is verbal communication—writing electronically—but with immediate delivery. In some businesses the office computers are connected to one another through a mainframe; in other branches of the same company in different cities are also connected electronically. Information storage repositories, or data banks, are computerized, and it is possible to acquire access to them from anywhere in the country.

Person-to-Person (Interactive Computers)

The image of computers, despite industry efforts to make them "user friendly," is still that of high technology, cold, logical, and impersonal. One study showed that people who communicated via computers tended to use a more brusque and impersonal style of verbal communication than they would if they were communicating face to face. It is important to remember that there is always a person reading the screen and often waiting at a keyboard to respond to your message. Good computer messages are like any good written communication, with the added benefit of immediate feedback and response.

E (Electronic) Mail

One of the drawbacks, especially at work, of communicating with telephones is what is called "telephone tag." You place a call, but the person isn't in, so you leave a message for them to call back, which they do at a later time perhaps when you are not there to take their return call. Telephone tag can be very annoying and a time waster, especially if you are seeking information or a decision without which you cannot proceed.

Computers, however, enable you to leave messages for another person to which they can respond at their earliest convenience, whether or not you are there. People who use this feature eagerly return to their machines after being out of the office to "read their mail"—both new messages and replies to messages they sent earlier.

Communicating With Computers

Communicating with computers can teach you valuable lessons in communicating with people. A computer is a very exacting and logical communicator and will not "catch your drift" if you are imprecise. You need to speak the computer's language if you hope to use it as a tool. It requires certain commands and codes, which you must give very accurately for it to respond as you wish it to. The only time a computer makes a mistake is when it has been misinformed. A computer holds up its end of the operation as long as the operator is communicating responsibly.

Communicating with people is certainly more satisfying emotionally and psychologically. If people were as logical as computers, communicating could be very boring. Communication among people, however, would benefit from greater attention to precise language, clarity, and accurate and truthful information.

SUMMARY

1. Human beings communicate to survive and to relate socially with one another. Communication is a complex mixture of language and gesture that requires effort to master. People begin to learn communication skills as babies and continue to develop them as adults.

2. The purpose of social communication is to create understanding among people. Understanding creates the interrelationships among humans that define society.

3. Effective communication uses a combination of verbal and nonverbal expression. Verbal communication uses language, whereas nonverbal communication uses gestures, signs, or symbols, either alone or simultaneously with verbal communication.

4. Nonverbal communication is both a process and a product, analogous to speaking and writing, and can include the use of symbols, color, sign language, body language, facial expression, and even personal appearance.

5. Verbal communication means the use of words to communicate, either written or spoken (oral communication). New words are created all the time and old words acquire new meanings.

6. Oral and written communication are very different experiences, and each has intrinsic biases, advantages, and disadvantages. Oral communication is a sensory-rich experience during which communicators can observe one another's gestures and feelings and respond immediately to each other's messages. Writing and reading provide an opportunity for thorough review and analysis of communicated messages.

7. There are six steps in the sequence of communication: ideation (formulating an idea); encoding (putting thought into words or action); transmission (sending the message); reception, or transfer of initiative (the receiver's taking the message as it arrives); decoding (the receiver's turning the message into meaning); and response (the receiver's formulating a message in response).

8. Communication can be described as occurring downward, upward, or horizontally, depending on the relationship between the sender and the receiver. Downward communication occurs, for example, when supervisors talk to the workers under them, when teachers talk to students, or

when parents talk to children. When workers or students respond, communication flows upward. Peer-to-peer interaction is horizontal communication.

9. Communication can be formal or informal, whether written or spoken. Formal written communication can include memos, reports, proposals, sales orders, resumes, invitations, articles for publication, and college application essays. Formal oral communication includes business meetings with prepared agendas, job interviews, public meetings, presentations, and speeches. Phone calls, face-to-face questions and answers, business lunches, and conversations over coffee can accomplish work with informal communication.

10. Communication can fail because of physical roadblocks. Time, space, complexity of the message, and the sender's and receiver's sensory limitations are basic elements of physical communication. Providing enough time to communicate in a setting free of distractions will help a message be received accurately.

11. Mental roadblocks that create miscommunication hinge on psychological feelings and attitudes and involve a person's emotions, values, and judgments that may conflict with those of another person. Some broad categories of mental road blocks include personal interests, cultural conditioning, abstraction, and stereotyping.

12. Miscommunication also occurs because of intentional or unintentional misinformation. Unintentional misinformation usually results from lack of knowledge or incomplete information. Intentional misinformation is deception, lying, or hiding of the truth. The latter sabotages communication by undermining the trust that enables people to communicate.

13. The grapevine, or office gossip, is a natural, normal, and indestructible method of informal communication. It can be a benefit or a disadvantage, depending on the reliability of the messages traveling along it.

14. The use of machines to communicate is widespread in home and work life. Depending on the machine you use, you may have to adjust the way you communicate slightly to accommodate the machine's capabilities or limitations.

15. Communicating via computers is verbal communication—writing electronically—and, because it may seem impersonal, it is especially important to remember that there is always a person reading the screen or waiting at a keyboard to respond to messages. Good computer messages are like any good written communication.

QUESTIONS FOR REVIEW AND DISCUSSION

1. Human beings communicate to satisfy two basic needs. Name them and give an example of each from the text.
2. No matter what need you are meeting by communicating, what is the purpose of communication? How does that differ from an exchange of information?
3. Define verbal communication. Explain how it relates to oral communication.
4. List some of the methods used in nonverbal communication. Provide an example of each.
5. Explain the similarities and differences in written and spoken communication. Be sure to include the characteristics they share. Identify the advantages and disadvantages of each.
6. Provide an example of each of the following kinds of communication, written or spoken, that might be found in a business: formal horizontal, informal downward, informal upward, formal upward, informal horizontal, formal downward.
7. Describe the similarities of and differences between abstraction and stereotyping.
8. Compare and contrast interactive communication via the telephone and a computer. Identify the advantages and disadvantages of each as completely as you can.

KEY TERMS
Define the following:

Ameslan
Decoding
Encoding
Ideation
Media
Nonverbal
Oral communication
Reception
Response
Sign language
Stereotype
Symbols
Transmission
Verbal

ACTIVITIES

1. Open a newspaper to the sports pages, and select an article that is particularly jargon-filled. Rewrite the article in standard English, understandable to anyone, even if the reader is not a sports fan. You may have to ask friends or refer to a dictionary of colloquialisms to accomplish this task.
2. Using the steps in the communication process from ideation to response, prepare a short presentation to your class. Identify each step as you progress, and where appropriate list the decisions you have to make in order to accomplish the task.
3. Arrange to go to an event (a game, a lecture, or a film) with a friend. While you are there, each of you should take care to be as observant as possible and remember, without taking notes or comparing ideas, as much as you can about it. When it is over and you have gone home, each of you should write an account of the event, being as objective and accurate as possible. Share your accounts with one another. Consider how much the other person's account matches your recollection of the event. Try to identify each other's point of view; note choice of words and

selection of facts that each of you made. How did those choices affect the account, and how do they affect your perception of the event now?

4. Prepare a short message to anyone on any topic. Thinking through exactly what you would have to do and writing the process down as you do so, explain how you would deliver the message in each of the following ways: informally along the grapevine, formally in a letter, upward in an organization via a telephone call, downward via a written in-house memo, formally to one of your parents. Do you find the language changes? What gestures do you think you would use with one that you might not use with another? Would it make any difference what you were wearing in any of those situations?

CASE 1

Communication at Work

"Hey, George!" Val shouted, "come over here. I want to show you something."

George, the supervisor in the office, was talking with a typist two desks away from Val. The office, in which insurance policies were typed, was rather noisy with the word processors and printers all running. When George continued talking to the other typist, Val thought that maybe he did not hear her.

"Hey, George!" she shouted even louder. "I said come over here. I want to show you something. Hurry up!"

This time George looked up at Val. A shadow of annoyance passed over his face. "Is something wrong with your machine?" he asked her.

"No, not really. I want to show you something," Val called back.

"I'll be with you in a minute," George said, and turned back to continue talking to the other worker. He took his time getting over to Val's desk.

"Okay, Val, what's the problem?" George asked when he finally did get to her station. Even Val noticed that he did not seem very interested or particularly friendly.

"Don't sound so grumpy, Georgie," Val said. "I just wanted to show you that my machine has not blocked once and I'm right on quota for the day."

The supervisor's face turned a little red when Val called him "Georgie," but he did not say anything about it. But he did say, with a trace of annoyance, "You mean you were yelling at me when I was busy solving a problem with another worker just to tell me that you had no problem?"

"Don't be such a sourpuss," Val said. "I thought you would be pleased. Last week I kept having trouble, and we were under quota. Remember?"

"Yes, I remember, Val." George said. "Let's see if you can keep the machine running properly." With that he walked away.

A short time later during the coffee break, Val talked with her friend Peggy who worked next to her.

"Boy, did you hear that?" Val asked. "What a grouch that George is. Here I wanted to give him some good news, and he acts like he doesn't even want to talk to me."

"Gee, Val, maybe it's the way you communicate with him. You know, the way you talk to him," Peggy suggested.

"What do you mean, the way I talk to him?" Val asked. "I talk to him just like I do to everyone else."

"Well, maybe that's what's wrong," Peggy said. "I heard you call him 'Georgie.' He is our boss, you know."

"Oh, I use nicknames with everyone," Val said. "That's just the way I am. It doesn't mean anything."

"I can see doing it with our friends and even with George away from work if he is a friend," Peggy said. "I just feel it doesn't sound right in the work situation, and from the look on George's face I don't think he thinks it's right either."

"Well, he still didn't need to be so annoyed," Val said. "Only you and I heard it."

"But before that, Val, you were shouting at him. The whole room heard you call him over and tell him to hurry up. There was no emergency. But you shouted at him twice," Peggy said.

"I was excited because I saw I was going to make quota easily today," Val explained. "I thought he would be happy to know it."

"He probably would have been happy to know it," Peggy said, "if you hadn't tried to summon him over the way you did. He is the boss of all these people, and I don't think he appreciated being yelled at. Other workers will think he lets you get away with things or that anyone can treat him like that. Either way, it's not good for him."

"I just treated him like I treat everyone else," Val said, somewhat annoyed herself just now. "I'm not going to say 'Yes, sir' and 'mister' and play up to him just because he is the boss. That's not my style."

"Well, it's not my style to play up to the boss, either," Peggy insisted. "But I do think we have to talk to people who are our bosses at work at little differently from the way we talk to friends."

The break ended before Val could reply, but she began thinking about what Peggy said as she returned to her machine.

1. In what ways do you think that Peggy was correct in her assessment of Val's behavior?

2. Do you think that the other workers in the office would react as Peggy said they would? Why or why not?

3. If you could rewrite the script, what changes would you make in Val's communication with George that would make it possible for her to share her good news with him without jeopardizing their working relationship?

CASE 2

Imprecise Written Communication

"Hank, I'm really upset. Did you know that several dozen of our plants died?" Ethel, the owner of Pots-of-Flowers Plant Store, asked.

"Well, I'm sorry to hear that," Hank said, "but it's not my fault because I was away on my vacation. I guess my replacement must have made a mistake."

"You're right. You were on vacation, and yes, your replacement did make a mistake, but. . ." Ethel said.

"I don't understand that," Hank interrupted. "I left him written instructions, just like you asked me to. And I'm sure that I wrote down everything that he was supposed to do. I even typed them so there could be no misunderstanding. "

"Yes, Hank, you did type out the instructions," Ethel said. "But you weren't careful about how you wrote them. That, I'm afraid, is what caused the problem."

"But, Ethel, I don't know what you mean. I'm sure I put down everything the replacement needed to know. He must have misread the instructions."

"No, he didn't misread them," Ethel replied. "I checked them when I discovered so many of the plants were dying. I have them here. Look at what you wrote about watering and fertilizing:

'It's important that you water the plants and feed them fertilizer. Be sure you do not do this more than every other week because too much food will hurt the plants.'"

"So, what's wrong with that?" Hank asked. "I clearly told him that it was important to water the plants and warned him not to give them too much fertilizer."

"I think what went wrong," Ethel said, "is that your written note actually told him not to water the plants more than once every other week. In your first sentence you talked about the need to water and fertilize the plants. In your second sentence you wrote that he should not do 'this' more than once every two weeks. 'This' refers back to the whole first sentence, both watering and fertilizing, because you did not make it clear what 'this' referred to."

"Well, anyone should know that you have to water plants more often. You would assume he could have figured that out," Hank grumbled as Ethel walked away.

1. Ethel feels that Hank has let her down, and Hank feels he fulfilled his responsibility. Do you think Ethel is justified in her criticism?

2. Is there something she should have done, or ought to do in the future, to prevent this sort of misunderstanding from happening again?

3. How would you rewrite Hank's instructions so that they would not be ambiguous?

► HUMAN RELATIONS:
How We Relate to Others

*Treat people as adults. Treat them as partners; treat them with
dignity; treat them with respect. Treat them —not capital spending
and automation —as the primary source of productivity gains.
These are the fundamental lessons....*
Thomas J. Peters and Robert J. Waterman

CHAPTER 13

human relations
a course, study, or program designed to develop better interpersonal and intergroup adjustments

organizational behavior science
the study of how people behave in organizations

personnel and human resource management
a specialized field of human relations that focuses on employer-employee relations

Many companies changed the name of the personnel office to the "office of human resources," acknowledging the truth of the principle Peters and Waterman state in the chapter quote. Human beings are the most valuable resource a company has. Good human relations is the way to tap that resource.

The study of **human relations** is one of the behavioral sciences, specifically an applied aspect of **organizational behavior science** or the study of how people behave in organizations. Human relations combines practical information about working with people with an understanding of how they behave in organizations.

Organizational behavior science closely relates to anthropology, psychology, and sociology. It is a relatively new field of study developed during the 1960s. Many other fields and professions that deal with human behavior in the workplace have stemmed from it. The study by organizational behaviorists of such things as motivation, stress, and communication in organizations has done much to increase understanding of what creates a successful workplace.

The theories and research findings of organizational behavior and human relations can be used to develop specific techniques and tools for human resource offices and personnel specialists. A specialized field of human relations is called **personnel and human resource management**, whose practitioners focus on employer-employee relationships. These specialists apply their knowledge of human relations to developing employee training programs, attitude surveys, benefit programs, and many other similar applications to improve the work environment.

In addition to being more aware of the value of their employees, more companies are becoming aware of their need to be responsive to their customers. Henry Ford was famous for saying that Ford's customers could have their choice of any car color as long as it was black. Few companies today feel that they can afford to ignore the customer's demands.

Staying in touch with the public has become a hallmark of the really successful companies. At some of these companies, the chief executive officer will even take time to visit stores and talk with customers personally. Domestic and foreign competition has emphasized the financial advantages of good human relations with customers.

▼ WHY CONSIDER HUMAN RELATIONS?

Human relations are simply relations among people. Everyone, both in and out of the workplace, has to deal with people. How well you can deal with people on the job will be a factor in your success and your sense of fulfillment. How well you deal with people off the job will be a factor in how happy and pleased you will be with yourself and your life.

Your career can be adversely affected by poor human relations without your being aware of it. Although job ability counts, you must be able to get along with people on all kinds of jobs. One study of the reasons workers in one corporation were not promoted revealed that only 10 percent were passed over because of technical skill deficiencies. Almost 80 percent were denied promotions because of reasons having to do with human relations.

The need for good human relations is just as great in private and home life as well. Many of life's difficulties are caused by individuals who botch their human relations.

You learn human relations consciously and unconsciously. You consciously learn rules for behavior—from religious commandments to traffic regulations—that prescribe basically good human relations. As you grow up you acquire a sense of ethical behavior toward other humans by hearing the advice of your parents and other influential adults and observing their actions. You unconsciously learn other ways of relating to people as you imitate family members and your peers. Social learning and reinforcement that you read about earlier are at work here.

Human relations begin in the family. You may have had the experience of meeting a friend's family and being struck by how similarly to one another they behaved, even in tone of voice and gesture. Chances are very good that they will relate to others similarly as well. Good and bad habits in behavior can be passed along for generations.

In this chapter, you will examine the social needs that human relations fill, how those needs develop, and how people learn to relate to others socially. Then you will read of some of the specific skills that you can use for successful human relations.

▼ MEETING SOCIAL NEEDS

As you have already learned, humans are social animals. They form groups to raise their young, accomplish work, and have fun. Families, businesses, and organizations both fulfill and create human social needs. In Chapter 10, you learned about Maslow's hierarchy of needs. Developed to help explain how people are motivated in the workplace, Maslow's theory can be as useful in understanding how and why humans relate to one another.

You recall that Maslow identified levels of human needs, beginning with those satisfying requirements for survival and ending with the need for self-actualization. Further, some of the needs Maslow identified can be met largely through successful human relations. They are the need for affiliation

Fig. 13-1

People learn how to relate to others when quite young.

and the needs for esteem and self-esteem. Let's take a closer look at these two sets of needs.

Need for Affiliation

Nicole has just graduated from college. She wants to get a job, but the opportunity she really wants doesn't exist in her hometown. Except for her time at school, she has never lived away from home on her own, and even though she is looking forward to it, she is a little concerned about where to start looking for a new home and job. One possibility she is going to explore is moving to the city where her friend Margaret lives and works. She and Margaret got along well when they had a summer job together, and Nicole feels better starting her career where she has a friend.

Whether in a new situation, as Nicole is about to experience, or in familiar surroundings, people feel the need to be liked and to belong, or to be *affiliated*. For children these needs are satisfied by being part of a family, with parents and possibly siblings, grandparents, and other relatives who love them. Adults meet this need by becoming affiliated through groups of friends, businesses, organizations like churches or social clubs, or by creating a new family unit of their own.

When a family unit does not function normally—when a child is abandoned or abused or the family is dysfunctional in some way (perhaps by one parent being an alcoholic or one child having special needs that eclipse the needs of others)—a family member may develop psychological problems. Those problems may affect not only the person's affiliation needs but his or her esteem and self-esteem needs as well. An individual's ability to have healthy human relations may be impaired by early experiences.

To satisfy the need for affiliation, most people behave in a way that is acceptable to others. Much of this behavior is at the heart of good human relations: the need for affiliation creates cooperation, sharing, and friendliness. It also creates conformity and dependence that can work against good relations by creating exclusiveness. Too great a need to affiliate can make a person seem cliquish; too little a need may make a person appear to be aloof. Maintaining a healthy balance is the key to success.

Need for Esteem and Self-Esteem

Once secure in their sense of affiliation, people often find themselves needing recognition and the respect, or **esteem**, of others. At the same time, they may develop a need to respect themselves and take pride in their accomplishments, to feel **self-esteem**.

esteem
recognition and respect

self-esteem
self-respect, pride in oneself

You first experience esteem and self-esteem in your family settings. You earn your parents' respect by your accomplishments, even learning to walk and talk, later by your work in school or success at activities such as sports or playing a musical instrument. You may also learn from your parents that you can be accorded respect and esteem just for being.

In this culture one of the ways that people earn esteem and self-esteem is through work and careers. Think back to the last time you met someone new socially. Chances are you learned each other's name first. Then possibly one of you said, "Are you from around here?" As soon as you established where you lived and came from, one of you probably asked, "What do you do?" or "Where do you work?"

Having meaningful activity, whether it is remunerative or not, is a source of both self-esteem and the esteem of others. At first, it may be that someone will become involved in a project to satisfy a need to achieve (self-esteem). If others show supportive recognition (esteem), it may encourage the person to continue in the activity. The process might be reversed: someone may accomplish something to please others, discovering that it is actually very self-satisfying.

Under some circumstances, people will do things without expecting or needing recognition. This behavior is called **altruism**. Altruism is defined as "a regard for the interests of others," but it has also come to mean a selfless helpfulness. An altruist dives into icy water to save a drowning person without first hoping for a medal for bravery.

altruism
a regard for the interest of others; selfless helpfulness

As with affiliation, the need for esteem and self-esteem varies tremendously from person to person. People who are insecure about their abilities may need more recognition for their last accomplishments than

Fig. 13-2

Becoming involved in a project can satisfy the need for self-esteem and the esteem of others.

people who are confident. Too great a need can encourage people's competitiveness to the detriment of their relationships or make them susceptible to flattery.

How altruistic anyone can be depends a great deal on abilities as well as attitude. A person who can't swim will not attempt to rescue a drowning person by jumping into the river but might run to get help or throw out a life preserver.

Understanding the need for esteem and self-esteem can remind you that in your relations with others, you can easily meet their need for recognition, appreciation, and support. Chances are your efforts will be reciprocated.

▼ UNDERSTANDING HUMAN BEHAVIOR

Making assumptions and generalizations about people is risky. But because people strive to fill their needs in the order suggested by Maslow, there are discernible patterns to human behavior just as there are to the weather. If you have an idea of what signs to look for, you can make some reliable predictions about what to expect and can plan to act accordingly. In this section you will look at some assumptions you can reasonably make about people and at some patterns of human behavior you can look for in your human relations.

People Like to Feel They Matter

People like to sense their importance. They want to feel they matter, that they are "somebody." This is closely related to the need for affiliation and self-esteem, but a little different. If others, especially those who matter to you, act as if they consider you unimportant, you will probably become upset. For example, if a person you considered a friend held a birthday party and did not invite you, you would be angry and hurt.

This need to feel they matter can make people resistant to change, especially if they have not been consulted or asked about the change. This is particularly so for people who experience a sense of security and a feeling of importance with familiar routines and surroundings. New routines or other changes threaten this. As a result, some people become resistant to change without being aware of it.

As you will read in Chapter 16, the world of work is changing rapidly today, mostly as a result of new technologies, such as computers. Because change appears inevitable, you must be ready to deal with your sense of being threatened by it. If you are ever a manager who must make changes in a work routine, try to involve those who will be affected by the

Good human relations begin with yourself. You need to have a sense of self-esteem and a good mental image of yourself. It has been said often that in order to like others you must like yourself first. However, how well you like yourself may depend on how well others like you.

A study conducted at Adelphi University by Rebecca Curtis and Kim Miller shows that your human relations depend to some extent on your perceptions of how others feel about you. In the study, a group of subjects were paired off for 5-minute get-acquainted sessions. After the sessions, the experimenters arbitrarily told some subjects their partners liked them and others that their partners did not. None of this reflected actual feelings.

When meeting again with their partners, subjects believing themselves to be liked tended to act more at ease and confident. Those led to believe their partners disliked them tended to be more withdrawn, to make less eye contact, and to keep their distance.

Students who had not been told one way or another about their partner's feelings tended to follow the lead of those who were told, in other words those expecting to be liked acted more friendly, and those expecting to be disliked were more distant with their partners.

TO THE POINT

change in planning how to implement it. This is good human relations and will meet the need of people to feel they matter. People will be more ready to accept change if they feel they have been involved in bringing it about.

Each Individual Is Unique

There is one assumption about people that is perfectly safe to make: each individual is unique. Not only do you like to be viewed as unique, but in fact you are unique in many ways. You are made up of a complex of physical and personality traits that is never exactly duplicated anywhere on earth.

You may at any time behave in a predictable way or show traits typical of a culture or group, but chances are very good that you will put your own individual twist or interpretation on your activity. In human relations, it is essential that you look for those unique factors in each individual in order to relate to them appropriately.

The Whole-Person Concept

Monica returned to her career once her youngest child entered preschool. She and Frank wanted to save money for their children's education. Right now Monica is having second thoughts about working. It is hard to find a reliable babysitter for the time each day between the end of preschool and when she gets home. And to make things worse, Monica's mother is gravely ill.

As the only nearby family member, the responsibility for her mother falls on Monica. Doctors call her at work during business hours sometimes, and lately the news has not been encouraging. Monica tries hard not to let these worries affect her work, but she is sure the stress must be showing.

whole-person concept
the idea that, in any given situation, the individual is the embodiment of multiple roles. For example, one person may simultaneously be a parent, a child, and an employee, with each of those roles making certain demands on the person

Behind the **whole-person concept** is the idea that no matter where you are or what you are doing, you are the embodiment of multiple roles. As you can see in the illustration above, one person may simultaneously be a parent, a child, and an employee, with each of those roles making different demands.

You accumulate your roles through your lifetime, born to some, choosing others. You may be more active in one role at one point in your life than in another, but some roles you can never relinquish (for example, you will always be your parents' child even after you have become an adult). Even if you are not continually aware of all your roles, they all act upon you, subconsciously affecting your behavior and your relationships with others. Some roles continue to affect your behavior long after you have ceased to fill them actively.

Sometimes your roles coincide and conflict. It is hard to get through life without having personal and work roles vying for your attention from time to time. When they do conflict, they can adversely affect either home life or work, or sometimes both. In the workplace, sensitive coworkers and supervisors, if they understand the situation, can do much to be supportive and helpful.

Even within one role, for example, as an employee of a company, a person may have multiple roles. It might be that one person would be a subordinate under a boss, a supervisor over others, plus a leader of a project group. Each of these roles might require slight differences in attitude. They also might conflict.

More and more, people are integrating their life roles. People who wish to be active as parents seek jobs in companies that provide child-care facilities or offer flexible working hours so that parents can be with children after school. No longer willing to relocate—a customary prerequisite for promotion—some people prefer to stay in one community because of a spouse's job or children's schooling.

More progressive companies consider their employees as whole persons and accommodate these needs. From a human relations point of view, this is a smart way to do business. In the competition for employees, these companies are more attractive. Employees who are under less stress from conflicting life roles should be more productive. And these companies are more likely to retain employee loyalty and suffer less attrition.

The Concept of Human Dignity

Harry Truman once said, "We must build a new world, a far better world—one in which the eternal dignity of man is respected." Dignity—the quality of being esteemed, honored, respected by other humans—is a highly valued condition.

Most people can recognize human dignity and know that it goes beyond just the idea of formal and reserved behavior to encompass a person's whole quality of life. It cannot be taken for granted because it is not always respected by everyone in a society. In this culture, human dignity is a combination of human rights and responsibilities. Freedom from slavery, poverty, and discrimination are some elements of dignity. So are having responsibility for yourself, being considered trustworthy, and being allowed to participate in government. Society as a whole seeks to preserve these aspects of human dignity.

But human dignity is also a personal thing, preserved by good human relations. Freedom from personal humiliation, inappropriate physical contact, and manipulation are elements of human dignity that can be preserved at home or in the workplace. Your personal dignity is acknowledged when you are allowed to act independently, are relied upon, and are valued for yourself. Good human relations are all founded on recognizing these aspects of human dignity and acting upon them.

Human Potential Movement

Simply stated, the human potential movement has meant to most people an interest in discovering their potential as human beings and in developing it to the extent they are able. Maslow would identify it as achieving self-actualization. This movement had its greatest growth during the late 1960s and the '70s and has encouraged many to seek greater psychological well-being and growth.

The interest in human potential has reached institutional and business organizations as well. Churches sponsor marriage enrichment programs, peer drug counseling for young people, and support groups for people with special needs, such as single parents and the recently widowed. Business organizations offer workshops for their employees on stress management, career planning, and coping with job burnout.

Evidence of the human potential movement in the workplace can be seen in the widespread use of *transactional analysis* and *assertiveness training*. Both of these provide ways to think about patterns of human behavior and techniques for improving human relations. Let's take a closer look at each.

Transactional Analysis

transactional analysis
a theory of personality that identifies patterns of behavior based on the common experience of being a child and learning how to be an adult by observing parents

Developed by Eric Berne, **transactional analysis** provides another way of looking at patterns of human behavior, especially in communication. Understanding such a pattern and knowing what to expect when you encounter it can help you improve your human relations.

Transactional analysis, or TA, describes certain types of behavior as "adult," "parent," and "child" behavior. The terms are not used literally but in a descriptive sense to suggest a pattern of behavior. Everyone is a complex of all these behaviors. When you interact with others, you display one or another of these aspects, often in response to the aspect being displayed to you.

The "child" aspect of your personality is the emotional and creative side. When this side is in control you are likely to express yourself emotionally, be adventuresome, but also act or speak without thinking. Your "child" self also likes someone else to take control and lead, letting someone else make the decisions and take responsibility. The "child" aspect is often competitive and selfish.

The "parent" aspect of your personality likes to make and enforce rules, give orders, and be in control. The "parent" in us says "you should," "you ought" to do this or that. Your "parent" aspect can be judgmental, often reacting critically without thinking, and relying unquestioningly on beliefs learned when you were young. Your "parent" side can also be nurturing and caring. When your "parent" self sees someone hurt or needing help, it reacts sympathetically, providing comfort and help. This aspect likes to see growth and creativity and will encourage and praise it, though sometimes condescendingly.

The "adult" aspect of your personality is a questioning one and considers all the facts before acting. Your "adult" self is objective and rational. It does not lead automatically nor expect to be led. When this aspect of your personality is in control, you are likely to preface your remarks with "I think" or "my opinion is."

Transactional analysis theorists believe that interactions among people can be controlled to some extent by which aspect of the personality happens to dominate at the time of an interaction. Certain mixes of personality types result in better human relations than others. Personality types can interact successfully when they agree on the type of interaction they are involved in. For example, a "parent"-type personality can be bossy as long as it can find a "child" type who wishes to be bossed. The bossy "parent" aspect won't succeed with an "adult" type, who expects to be treated as an equal partner.

There may be times when another person's personality aspect will call forth an aspect of your personality as an unconscious reaction. The "child" aspect of a coworker who is evading responsibility may hook your "parent" aspect. Your impulse might be to take that person to task. From a human relations point of view, it would be better for you to react as an "adult" and weigh the pros and cons of getting involved.

No person is ever completely one type of personality. No one is ever just an "adult" or just a "child." All three aspects of personality are present in and can be exhibited by the same person. At different times, different aspects will dominate.

At times, one personality aspect is more suitable than another, but none is ever completely negative or positive. The "adult" personality is the more reasonable one, but a person who always takes time to think things through might end up being considered a cold individual, which would not be good for human relations. Also, in some situations it is important that a "parent" personality take command to make a quick decision or take fast action.

The "child" aspect of your personality also has its place. Sometimes a situation calls for spontaneity or creativity. There are times, too, when it is best to sit back and let someone else be the leader. For example, when you enter a new job, you will have better human relations if you let the "child" aspect of your personality take over, and at first have others lead and show you what to do.

Being able to recognize different aspects of your personality and knowing which you have to control and which are suitable for various situations can help you have good human relations.

Another concept of transactional analysis is that as a result of early influences everyone develops a "life script" that leads to a "life position." This life position influences how an individual behaves. Transactional analysis identifies four life positions:

1. "I'm okay, you're okay": the mature adult, accepting and getting on in life

2. "I'm okay, you're not okay": the "parent" ego state, wanting to be in command and dismissing others

3. "I'm not okay, you're okay": the constant "child" state, passive, feeling inadequate

4. "I'm not okay, you're not okay": pathological state, unable to cope

Assertiveness Training

Assertiveness training aims at teaching people three things:

1. To know how they feel
2. To say what they want
3. To get what they want

Assertiveness training attempts to train people to be assertive and to avoid both passiveness and aggression.

passive behavior

allowing things to happen without telling how you feel

Passive behavior is shown when people allow things to happen to them without expressing their feelings or volunteering their opinions.

aggressive behavior

getting what you want without much consideration for others

Aggressive behavior is shown by people who are frequently opinionated and offensive, getting what they want without much consideration for others.

assertive behavior

leaving no doubt what you want without being offensive

The middle ground between passive and aggressive is assertive. People showing **assertive behavior** deal with most situations directly, honestly, and clearly. They know how to state their needs without offending anyone but leave no doubt about what they expect.

Through assertiveness training, participants learn to recognize how they feel, state what they want, and get what they want. In order to do this, most people need to learn how to:

- Take criticism without defensiveness, withdrawal, or aggressiveness;

- Express an opinion or make a request clearly and confidently without resorting to manipulation, anger, and bossiness;

- Work with others maturely to solve problems in a way that meets the needs of most.

Some methods of psychotherapy are used in assertiveness training workshops. Role playing, role reversal, and modeling are effective ways to practice the skills listed above.

In **role playing**, the participants act out true-to-life situations while practicing appropriate assertive behavior. **Role reversal** is a form of role playing in which the participants take turns in the adversary role. These activities give each participant the experience needed for real situations in the future.

role playing
acting out true-to-life situations to practice assertiveness

role reversal
taking the role of another person to learn how one's own behavior appears from the other person's perspective

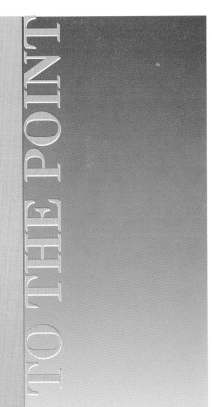

The first step toward developing assertiveness is to become aware of your own behavior. These questions can help you think about your own passive, aggressive, or assertive inclinations.

1. I say exactly what is on my mind.
2. I dread facing a confrontation with a coworker.
3. I believe that if I can't say something nice about someone, I don't say anything at all.
4. I feel comfortable declining invitations even if I don't have a prior engagement.
5. I let people smoke in my house even if I really wish they wouldn't.
6. I make sure I collect on all the benefits coming to me at work.
7. I can show affection to people I care about.
8. If someone is being disruptive in the movies, I make sure the manager does something about it.

If you answer "yes" to 4, 7, and 8, you are probably inclined to be assertive. A "yes" on 1 and 6 suggests aggressiveness; a "yes" on 2, 3, and 5 passiveness.

TO THE POINT

Fig. 13-3

Assertiveness training teaches people to avoid aggression or passivity.

modeling
imitating someone who knows how to behave assertively

Modeling is a method that relies on the participants' imitation of someone who knows how to behave assertively and does it well. Role playing and role reversal can then reinforce the new skills learned by modeling.

▼ HUMAN RELATIONS BLOCKS

Why any two or more people may not get along together is often very complicated and, as indicated, involves the whole range of factors, beginning with the individual, including the individual's background and culture. In this section you will read about three common human relations blocks and the behavioral consequences of them.

Poor Self-Esteem

You probably have heard someone say, "If you don't like yourself, you can't expect anyone else to like you either." People who don't like themselves— who don't have self-esteem or a positive *self-concept* may have difficulty getting along with other people.

A poor self-concept is characterized by a lack of self-confidence and feelings of inferiority. Persons with poor self-concepts may be hypersensitive to criticism and blame themselves for things that go wrong. Or perhaps such persons will "act out" in antisocial ways, alienating others, reinforcing their own opinion that no one likes them and that they are not good persons. Sometimes a poor self-concept is covered up by an attitude of superiority and vanity, and bossy or bullying behavior toward others.

Here are some steps you can take to develop assertive behavior.

1. Set your goal. Identify your situation and what you expect to achieve.

2. Identify what you have done in the past to avoid assertive behavior and what you will gain by not avoiding it now.

3. Identify what assertiveness will do to accomplish your goal.

4. Identify what may keep you from being assertive. (Consider old ideas such as your parents telling you that nice people didn't do that or not believing you have a right to assert yourself.)

5. Identify what you can do now to replace these ideas with new ones. (Consider reviewing your irrational responses and replacing them with a belief in your rights in a situation, identifying your real feelings, and deciding how to verbalize them.)

6. Decide what you can do to relieve any apprehension you may have about asserting yourself.

7. Prepare for asserting yourself by having a goal and by identifying your feelings and how to state them.

8. Be ready to listen to and understand the other person, to state clearly how you feel, and to state clearly what you want.

TO THE POINT

People with self-esteem usually can accept and adapt to change, can take suggestions and criticism well, and are more tolerant of others. In the workplace, they work well either in a team or in a leadership role, being neither manipulated nor manipulating.

Fortunately, a poor self-concept can be corrected even in adulthood. But it requires a great deal of self-awareness and sometimes a lot of work with a professional counselor. At some points in life, everyone, even a self-confident person, experiences moments of poor self-concept, when self-concept doesn't seem to match expectations. These moments often happen when a person is experiencing something new: going to a new school, or a different job, or becoming part of a new community. Remember what you read of people not liking change because it threatens their sense of being important.

As you adjust to the new situation, you stop feeling uncomfortable and find that you both change and are changed by new surroundings, until the match between your own and others' expectations is made. This transition can be helped along by other people extending themselves to help your self-esteem by recognizing your worth, and you can do that for others in such a situation.

Another time when this drop in your self-esteem can occur is when your expectations are not realized. You might, for example, expect a promotion, but not receive it. Disappointed, you may blame yourself for being inadequate, or feel anger toward the person who got the promotion.

It is natural to be disappointed. The difference between someone with a truly poor self-concept and someone with a healthy self-concept can be measured by how long it takes for them to adjust to the disappointment and go on to productive day-to-day activities. Pessimistic people tend to blame themselves and give up when disappointed. Optimists look for help and answers.

Dissonant Backgrounds

When two individuals or even groups have had substantially different life experiences, it can create a block to good relationships between them. It is possible to see this in the relations between generations, between people of different ethnic backgrounds, between foreigners and natives, and between different social classes.

Sometimes the characteristics of a society or group are so deeply ingrained that they are practically unconscious. If, for example, you lived in a society where eating meat was taboo, you would probably be horrified at seeing someone else do so. You might never overcome your sense of revulsion in order to feel comfortable with meat-eaters.

Other differences in background that might exist between people are more consciously adopted and even cherished. For example, graduates of traditionally rival universities may tend to favor fellow alumni over those from the other school. You are likely to feel most at ease with those similar to you in background and experience. Barring a shared experience, the next best way to establish good relations between people of different backgrounds is to provide information to each about the other society or group, expose them to one another and explore what they have in common.

Politically different countries seeking rapport with one another find it useful to have cultural exchanges, for example, exchanging ballet companies for performances in the other's country. Or each might encourage their citizens to travel to the other's country. An office Christmas party or a company picnic serves a similar purpose within a business organization. If no attempt is made to learn about people from another group and to establish good relations with them, stereotyping and prejudice can result.

Stereotyping and Prejudice

Encouraging travel among countries does much to increase international understanding.

A couple of engineers were eating lunch together in the company cafeteria. In a meeting that morning with some of the company's sales representatives, they learned that there were problems with one product line.

"I knew those people from sales were going to complain about that line. All they're interested in is how the product looks," said one.

"Yeah, I know. They never understand how things work and what goes into them," said the other. "I wish we didn't have to deal with them."

In the last chapter, stereotyping was defined as forming a standardized mental picture, usually oversimplified, and usually about a group of people. It is a form of abstraction, about which you read in Chapter 5. Stereotyping, as you can see from the exchange above, can be a block to communication. Not being able to communicate freely with someone certainly will be a block to good human relations.

Fig. 13-5

Stereotyping has resulted in certain jobs being considered male or female. Legislation and heightened social awareness are contributing to reducing these stereotypes.

A stereotype can, but does not always, result in a person making an insufficiently or incorrectly informed judgment about an individual member of a group based on ideas or expectations about the whole group. When that judgment is adverse and harmful, it is considered to be **prejudice**.

prejudice
an adverse or harmful judgment about an individual member of a group, based on insufficiently or incorrectly informed ideas or expectations of the whole group

Sometimes people have prejudices because of personal reasons or experiences, often out of fear. If you had purchased a certain make of car and had a lot of breakdowns and problems with it, you probably would not buy another car of the same make. Even if there was little evidence that all cars of that make had problems, your fear of a repeat of the experience could prejudice you against that make of car.

It is not necessary that someone have a bad experience with another person or group of people to develop prejudices. Fear of the unknown is sometimes sufficient for a prejudice to form and discrimination to result. That is why minority groups often suffer from prejudice: other people simply are not familiar enough with them not to be afraid of them.

Because prejudice often results in unfair treatment of certain groups of people, much legislation has been passed by the federal government to protect almost everyone from discrimination in the workplace, in housing, and in educational opportunities on account of race, color, sex, national origin, ancestry, age, religion, or physical handicap. Prejudice is a social problem in human relations and cannot be legislated away, but at least its worst effects can be reduced.

In addition to being unfair and possibly against the law, generalizing about an individual at work is bad from a human relations point of view because everyone likes to be treated individually, as well as equally. Each individual wants to be treated like "somebody." It is a good practice for you to stop to think every now and then about why you might hold the opinions and prejudices that you do, and always attempt to deal with people one-on-one, not just as a member of a group.

▼ HUMAN RELATIONS AIDS

Think for a moment about someone you feel gets along and works well with people and is liked by most. Mentally list the positive personal attributes you think this person has. Chances are you have just come up with a list of attributes that you might find helpful in developing the kinds of human relations skills to be covered in the last section.

credibility
the sense of being believable

Self-Confidence

As you read in the section on blocks to human relationships, a person with a poor self-concept (or low self-esteem) often lacks self-confidence. Self-confidence is a basic requirement in good interpersonal relationships.

There is no formula for self-confidence. In the ideal case people who are self-confident know their capabilities as well as their limits. They value their time and use it productively to accomplish their goals. They do not allow other people to control their behavior, and they do not seek to control others. They are able to make independent short- and long-range decisions about their lives and are not dependent on other people or institutions for direction, nor do they turn to drugs or alcohol to avoid reality. They understand their own motives and their behavior.

Honesty and Credibility

Honesty and credibility go hand-in-hand. **Credibility**, the sense of being believable, is derived from other things besides just truthfulness. In your everyday behavior, you have to be honest in more than just factual information. Individual facts are subject to different interpretations and can be disputed by different people. You have probably heard someone say that statistics can be used to prove anything. Giving facts alone does not add up to honesty.

Honesty also depends on what you and everyone else expects from an exchange. Generally, as long as you find your expectations met, you will feel that you have been dealt with honestly. Both you and the people with whom you are dealing have the potential for creating those expectations. Honesty provides solid ground for good human relations. You no doubt have heard "honesty is the best policy" and "truth in advertising" so often that the phrases seem trite now, but they are still cornerstones for good business practice and good human relations.

Personal credibility, especially in the workplace, is earned not only by knowledge of your field, your company, and your own capabilities, but also by the consistency and quality you demonstrate in your interpersonal relationships. The idea of sincerity, the phrase "paying lip service," and the old saying "actions speak louder than words" all underline the need for consistency between what others hear you say and what they observe you doing. A lack of consistency shakes confidence and damages credibility.

Tolerance and Flexibility

Dick and Douglas worked together in the mail room of a large plastics firm. They had to cooperate to get the mail out fast in the morning but could not agree on the best method.

"Sort the mail by floors," Dick said. "That's best."

"Sort the mail by people's names first," Douglas said, "That's the fastest way."

"Start at the top floor and work down," Dick declared.

"I always work from the bottom up," Douglas said.

"You should stamp the destination on the top envelope after you put a rubber band around the bundle," Dick said.

"Stamp each piece in case it gets separated from its bundle," Douglas insisted.

Neither one listened to the other. Each had learned different ways of doing things, and neither was going to change. Because they spent so much time arguing, they were always late in delivering the mail, and finally they were fired.

It is easy to see in this exchange how unproductive intolerance and inflexibility can be. Carried to its fullest extent, that kind of behavior almost always results in someone winning while someone else loses. If Dick and Douglas each had been willing or able to give up a little of their closely held ideas, they could have formed a successful team and could have held onto their jobs.

The basis of tolerance and flexibility is the principle of reciprocity, which is recognized in the golden rule, "You should behave to others as you would wish others to behave to you." If you show patience with or tolerance of others, you find them being tolerant of you. When others bend a little to accommodate your needs, you are likely to return the favor.

It has been said, "To understand everything makes one tolerant." It is a lot to expect to understand everything about yourself, another person, or a situation. But it certainly is true that the more you understand, the more tolerant you are likely to be. Let's look more closely at the concept of understanding.

Understanding

Like honesty, understanding works on more than one level. At the basic level of **understanding** is the ability to grasp information—procedures and the meaning of words, for example. Another level is the ability to find patterns and discern the significance of things, from environmental phenomena—like the weather—to communicated messages and human behavior.

Once you recognize patterns to things, you can predict what might happen and can act accordingly. That brings up a further meaning of understanding, which is a willingness to show a sympathetic or tolerant attitude. To develop good human relations, it is not enough to recognize another person's needs. It is necessary that you extend yourself to be sympathetic, tolerant, and helpful.

So far in this chapter you have explored a number of ways of understanding others and knowing what to expect in many different situations. Combining your understanding with a few specific human relations skills will help you interact successfully with others.

understanding
the ability to grasp information or find patterns; the willingness to be sympathetic, tolerant, and helpful

▼ HUMAN RELATIONS SKILLS

Most days when Ann, a division supervisor, comes into work she walks past Suzanne's desk without saying good morning. Sometimes when Suzanne, who is her administrative assistant, has a question, she goes into Ann's office, saying, "Excuse me a moment, I have a question about this." Ann does not always look up at Suzanne when she says, "What is it?"

Suzanne used to wait patiently until Ann looked up before she spoke, but most often Ann did not. One day Suzanne said to Ann, "It is important to me that you look up when you speak with me, Ann. That way I know I have your attention." Ann looks up more often now, but still isn't very consistent about it.

Most people think that human relations skills are just common sense and will somehow just happen automatically. The truth is that, as Will Rogers observed, "Common sense isn't very common." A situation like Ann and Suzanne's is more frequent than you might think.

Human relations is a combination of your actions and your communications with others. In Chapter 12, you read of effective communication, which is the primary way you relate to others. As you saw earlier in this chapter, it is important to be consistent in what you say and what you do. In the balance of this chapter, you will concentrate on the skills needed for successful human relations.

Be Self-Aware

Good human relations begin with you. You certainly can learn a great deal about dealing with people from others. In fact, you will probably learn a great deal about how others like to be treated from the way they treat you. But being aware of your own needs and how you might appear to others is essential.

What you appreciate in another's behavior toward you is a good first guideline for human relations. Do you like being greeted with a smile? Do you appreciate it when someone else offers to give you help with a project? If you do, chances are that people you live and work with will, too.

Once you are involved with people with whom you must relate successfully, self-awareness can help you analyze the interactions. How does someone seem to respond to what you say? Ask yourself "are they reacting to what I said or to how I said it?" You can experiment to see if you can get different results with different approaches.

Because it is so difficult to see yourself as others see you, some companies provide employees with a videocamera during training for public speaking or dealing with the public. It is sometimes startling to see yourself in this way, but it almost always does a great deal to improve self-awareness.

Anticipate Behavior

It is possible to look for and find patterns that might help you know what to expect from a person or situation, as you have read. Anticipating your own or another's behavior is one activity you can use in human relations, as long as you follow it up with an appropriate approach to dealing with someone.

You might ask yourself if, for example, you react badly when someone uses a parental tone when asking you to do something. Do you find your "child" personality aspect coming forth, making you feel rebellious? Understanding this pattern in yourself will help you anticipate your reaction and enable you to summon up your objective "adult" side in the transaction.

Once you have developed a successful approach, then you need to remember it. Remembering is practical for two reasons. One reason is you can save time by preparing for an exchange with someone so that it accomplishes your purposes the first time. The other reason is that knowing what to expect saves you the personal stress of surprise or disappointment. In the process of getting to know people, you will accumulate a mental catalog of successful ways of working with them individually and in different situations.

For example, you might learn that a coworker, one who is usually very self-confident and articulate working one-on-one with you, becomes nervous and disorganized in a group meeting. If you know how to anticipate this behavior, you can ease that person along in a meeting by being encouraging and prompting with helpful questions.

Develop Sympathy and Empathy

Sympathy and empathy are similar but not quite the same. Both require sensitivity to people. *Sympathy* means that two people are affected similarly by something; both feel or react in the same way. *Empathy* means that one can experience through imagination another person's feelings and can communicate that understanding to the other.

Sympathy is especially helpful for developing goodwill among people. It can help lay the foundation of trust, essential to good human relations. You might feel that if someone felt as you did about one thing, they might very well understand your feelings about something else.

Empathy helps you solve problems and make changes. It is one of the characteristics of a leader. Being able to imagine how another person is affected by something provides the kinds of insights needed to analyze a project, policy, or interpersonal circumstance to improve or change it. As you develop sympathy and empathy, you may find it increasingly possible to risk self-disclosure.

Disclose Your Feelings

Mutual trust and liking is the basis of good human relations between people. In order to trust and like another person, you need to know what that person thinks and feels and where he or she stands on various issues. You learn this when a person discloses himself or herself to you.

Self-disclosure is revealing your thoughts, feelings, fears, aspirations, likes, and dislikes to another person. It is a necessary step in establishing a relationship with another person. In doing so you show what psychologists call your *authenticity*, your real self. For most people this seems to be risky. After all, if someone knows you well enough to help you in need, they know how to hurt you as well.

self-disclosure
the process of revealing private thoughts, feelings, and personal history to others

When people do share feelings and thoughts, however, it encourages a reciprocal reaction. Perhaps you have experienced this when you shared your thoughts or feelings with a friend and found that friend in turn sharing his or hers with you. Disclosure encourages disclosure. This is known as the *dyadic effect*.

Self-disclosure can enrich your private life, but it has its place at work as well. In the workplace, you may find a colleague with whom you

The level of disclosure we are willing to reach with a friend indicates the intimacy of the relationship. Here are ten topics, each more revealing than the first, that you might discuss with friends. The more you can feel comfortable sharing with a friend, the closer you are to that friend.

1. Where I live and what I do for work
2. My political opinions
3. My feelings about loaning my possessions
4. My family life as a child
5. My religious opinions
6. My income level
7. My relationship with a spouse or loved one
8. What I fear most
9. How my feelings can be hurt
10. My sexual preferences

can share a great deal even if it may seem inappropriate to disclose yourself intimately to other people. But as you read in the section on assertiveness training, it is necessary to know and state your feelings clearly and honestly. In resolving conflicts, it is necessary to be willing to accept responsibility for how you feel, to identify and state your feelings. All this is a form of self-disclosure.

Express Acceptance

Acceptance is the next necessary step to creating trust and liking in a relationship. Acceptance does not mean that you like everything about another person. It does mean that you understand the person and are willing to accept the whole person while perhaps rejecting a certain aspect.

Generally, people communicate acceptance by showing caring, authenticity, and empathy. Caring is expressed both verbally (by stating feelings of interest, concern, and liking) and nonverbally (by listening attentively, and by keeping an open and friendly attitude).

Authenticity, as we saw in the discussion of self-disclosure, is revealing your real feelings and thoughts clearly and honestly. It is important that your feelings and thoughts be consistent with your nonverbal expressions. If you avoid eye contact, for example, while telling someone you care about how the person feels, he or she may doubt your authenticity.

It is not enough for you to feel empathy for another person; in order to show acceptance, you must communicate it, too. You each need to know that you understand one another, and you communicate this through listening and responding.

Help to Support and Change

Supportive helpfulness encompasses all the kinds of positive actions one can take to encourage others. Sometimes it is necessary to make changes, and helpful criticism can aid the process. In the section on esteem and self-esteem, you read how important recognition is to the development of a person's potential. Being able to provide both positive and critical recognition is essential for good human relations.

Recognition can take many forms. The simplest is appreciation; saying thank you makes another person feel worthwhile. The next step is learning from one another about what made a project successful. Providing specific information about what you liked will encourage someone to do more of the same. And you won't have to keep thinking of new ways to praise the job, which could verge on flattery.

Similarly, providing specific information about what you disliked is one of the most successful ways to criticize while preserving good relationships. In the workplace, criticizing the project, not the person, allows the person to maintain her or his self-esteem and still make changes.

Praise without flattery and criticism without blame are key ideas. Of course, someday you may have to reprimand someone for a clear infraction or personal offense. A confrontation, though it may not be pleasant or easy, can be handled well from a human relations point of view.

Patricia kept a small box containing aspirin, bandages, and miscellaneous supplies at her workstation. One day she returned from coffee break to find Judy looking through the box for some aspirin. Patricia thought to herself that she would have been happy to give Judy an aspirin if Judy had asked for it, but it bothered her that Judy would poke through her belongings to find it.

She approached Judy, and quietly and firmly said, "I am sorry you have a headache, but I feel that the things at my workstation are my private property. From now on, if you need something, please ask me for it first."

Patricia could have mishandled the situation by being angry with Judy, accusing her of being a thief, and demanding that from now on, she stay away from Patricia's workstation. Instead she chose to avoid an emotional, blaming tone of voice, stated her needs clearly, and, at the same time, left communication open between her and Judy.

Use Diplomacy and Humor

Diplomacy is the ability to perceive sensitively the nuances of a situation and act appropriately without creating uneasiness. Humor can help defuse tense situations and release anger constructively.

Diplomacy can be learned. It includes tact as well as being at ease in human relations. It can be as complicated as a skillful communication or as simple as knowing a few rules of etiquette. Knowing how to behave in many situations will give you the self-confidence to practice many of the other human relations skills you have been reading about.

Comfortable human relations, especially in the workplace, are acquired by observation and practice. You need to work at your human relations skills, but keep in mind that the more you are exposed to different people and situations, the more skill you can acquire.

Humor can be used very effectively in human relations, but it can also backfire if inappropriate. Use humor only when you are confident about your ability to use it appropriately. Do use it to help you personally keep matters in perspective. The ability to laugh at yourself is priceless, and others are much more likely to feel at ease around people who do not take themselves too seriously.

Avoid Problems

One excellent human relations skill is simply to avoid problems. This is possible to do if you can recognize the signs that some people will exhibit from time to time that tell you that no matter how hard you try, you will not be able to establish good human relations with these people.

Human relations problems arise in interaction with people exhibiting any of the following behavior patterns:

- Having a tendency to treat other people as objects rather than as human beings

- Being overly sensitive or overly eager to prove themselves, which indicates a sense of inferiority

- Depending unreasonably on others for material or emotional support

- Expecting too much from others

- Being unable to become emotionally involved with others

- Being continually hostile or suspicious

Fig. 13-6

The secretary could have handled this situation a little more diplomatically, but don't you wonder about her boss's human relations skills, too?

"Mr. Carmichael from Purchasing is here, sir. What was it you said you wanted done with him?"

Once you have identified one of these tendencies in a person and have discovered that nothing you do makes a difference, it is wise to stop thinking you can improve the situation.

Extend Yourself

Good human relations do not just happen. Anyone can create good or bad human relations. Knowing what it takes to create good human relations is not enough. This knowledge must be paired with a desire and will to work at successful interactions with people. Getting along with others may be the hardest work you ever experience, but the results are among the most satisfying.

SUMMARY

1. _____ Human relations are simply relations among people. How good those relations are affects people's happiness and productivity in their personal and work lives.

2. _____ Everyone has a need to affiliate, to belong and to be liked. Everyone also has a need for esteem, or recognition and respect from others, and a need for self-esteem, a self-respect and pride in accomplishment often provided by meaningful activity.

3. _____ You can understand human behavior better if you realize that each individual is unique and everyone, while having multiple roles, is a whole person. Good human relations preserve human dignity.

4. _____ The human potential movement has encouraged many people to achieve self-actualization and has given us tools, such as assertiveness training and transactional analysis, for improving human relations skills.

5. _____ Assertiveness training identifies passive, aggressive, and assertive behavior patterns and helps people learn to express their feelings and needs clearly and honestly.

6. _____ Transactional analysis is a theory that identifies three aspects of personality to describe behavior: "adult," "parent," and "child." These aspects exist in everyone and can both help and hinder human relations.

7. _____ Blocks to good human relations can include a poor self-concept, people's dissonant backgrounds, stereotyping, and prejudice. Stereotyping prevents good human relations when people make generalizations or judgments about a whole group. Prejudice is an adverse and harmful judgment based on lack of information or misinformation.

8. _____ Legislation now protects almost everyone from discrimination in the workplace, in housing, and in educational opportunities on account of race, color, sex, national origin, ancestry, age, religion, or physical handicap.

9. _____ You can develop a number of qualities that are helpful to human relations. They include self-confidence, honesty and credibility, tolerance and flexibility, and understanding. These should be combined with specific human relations skills, including self-awareness, anticipation of behavior, and sympathy and empathy.

10. _____ Encouraging others with appreciation and recognition is important for good human relations. Criticizing while

preserving good relationships can be done by providing specific information about what you dislike while avoiding a blaming or emotional tone.

11. Self-disclosure, revealing one's real feelings and thoughts, and acceptance, shown by caring, authenticity, and empathy, builds the basis of liking and trust necessary in relationships.

12. Diplomacy, tact, and good manners make it possible to act appropriately and easily in many situations with many kinds of people. Humor, when well used, eases tension and helps one maintain perspective.

QUESTIONS FOR REVIEW AND DISCUSSION

1. Why is it necessary to study human relations?
2. Which human needs in Maslow's hierarchy of needs are affected by human relations? How?
3. These needs sometimes have a side that does not contribute to good human relations. Identify some of those instances.
4. Explain what is meant by the whole-person concept. How can understanding it affect human relations?
5. Describe each of the three personality aspects presented in the theory of transactional analysis. Why is it helpful to understand this theory?
6. Show the connection between a healthy self-concept and good human relations.
7. How are stereotyping and prejudice linked in their effect on human relations?
8. The text identified three levels of understanding. Describe them. Which relate directly to human relations?

ACTIVITIES

1. Select a piece of your favorite fiction, and look until you find a section of dialogue. Keeping in mind what you learned about transactional analysis, read through the dialogue. Identify each exchange according to the personality aspect ("child," "adult," or "parent") the speaker shows. How do the aspects shown affect the relations between or among the speakers?
2. Take a trip to a store of any kind. While you are there, try to observe the ways that the store and its employees are trying to relate successfully to you, the customer. List them. Be sure to

KEY TERMS
Define the following:

Aggressive behavior
Altruism
Assertive behavior
Assertiveness Training
Credibility
Dyadic effect
Esteem
Human relations
Modeling
Organizational behavior science
Passive behavior
Personnel and human resource management
Prejudice
Reciprocity
Role playing
Role reversal
Self-disclosure
Self-esteem
Transactional analysis
Understanding
Whole-person concept

consider everything from signs to store layout to help from clerks. If you were the store owner, what would you do differently? List the changes you would make and tell why they would improve human relations in the store.

3. _____ Locate a videocamera. Organize a group of your classmates to have lunch together, and set the camera up to film your group eating and conversing together. You probably will all feel self-conscious at first, but try to keep it going long enough to overcome that. Later, either in a group or independently, review the tape; and as you watch, write down the behavior you see in yourself that you were not conscious of. Now that you are aware of your behavior, is there any aspect of it that you would want to change? Which might affect your relationships with others?

4. _____ Write your own name and the names of one family member, one friend, and one person you know from a work situation or school at the top of four pieces of paper. Keeping in mind what you learned about the whole-person concept, list as many life roles as you can think of or know about for each person. Then talk with the people to see if your lists encompass all the roles they feel they are filling. Are you surprised at how much or how little you know about these people and their roles? Go back over the list, and next to each role, note a specific example of how that person showed he or she was filling that particular role.

CASE 1

Human Relations Are Always Needed

"I'm going to be an accountant. A good one. Fortunately, I won't need to know how to get along with other people," Les said.

"Well, I'm going to be an accountant, too," said Wendy, "but I'm glad we'll be learning about human relations."

"What's to know?" Les asked. "You get along with people or you don't. People you don't like, you stay away from. The ones who don't like you leave you alone. It's that simple."

"I don't think it's that simple," said Wendy. "Sometimes you have to deal with people whether you like them or not. We have to go to class with 30 or more people every day. Some of them I don't like much."

"Oh, sure," Les agreed. "but you can just ignore the ones you don't like. That's what I do. Anyway, when we are out of school, we can pick the people we want to be with."

"Not on the job. Not really," Wendy corrected him. "When you go to work for a company, there may be a lot of other people around, and you may not get along with them all."

"Well, that's why I want to be an accountant, because accountants work alone," Les said. "I'll just do my job and not bother with anyone else. Human relations. Who needs it?"

"What if you work for a large company and there is a whole accounting department full of people?" Wendy asked.

"Who said I was going to work for a large company?" Les answered. "I plan to start my own business. It's going to be a small one. Just me."

"Well, if you are going to have your own business," Wendy said, "it seems to me that human relations are going to be even more important."

"Why? I just told you that it will be a one-person business," Les replied. "I'll be my own boss and my only worker."

"What about your customers?" Wendy asked. "Unless, of course, you plan to be your own customer, too."

"Don't be cute," Les said. "Of course, I'll have customers."

"Well then, you'll have to deal with them and convince them you are a good accountant. Knowing how to get along with people would help your business a lot."

"Yeah, I suppose you have something there," Les said. "I guess it won't hurt to think a little more about human relations—just in case."

1. Do you think Les has the right expectations of what his career is going to be like?

2. How do you think he deals with family and friends?

3. From what you learned about esteem and self-esteem, how would you describe Les's level of need for esteem? For self-esteem? How about Wendy's level of need for esteem and self-esteem?

4. Wendy showed her human relations skills as she dealt with Les. Identify some of the particular skills she used.

CASE 2

Job Skills Alone Are Not Enough

"I want to know why I didn't get the promotion to department manager," Linda said angrily, speaking to her boss, Tom.

"Well, Linda, you know that both you and Sarah were being considered for the job. We decided that Sarah was more suited for the position at this time," Tom explained.

"But that doesn't make sense," Linda said, "I know a lot more about this job than Sarah does."

"Just knowing about the job isn't enough for a promotion," Tom answered. "There are other considerations."

"Like what?" Linda asked. "It seems to me that the most important thing for a manager is knowing what the work is all about."

"Well, that is certainly necessary," Tom said, "but a manager has to get along with people in order to be effective. From observing you at work with others, it appears you need to work on your human relations."

"What do you mean?" Linda said.

"During your manager training period, you tended to be too bossy. You were always telling people what to do without asking their opinion or taking into consideration their abilities and knowledge," Larry explained.

"Well, for goodness' sake," Linda said, "that's what a boss is supposed to do, tell others what to do. They always got the job done."

"It's true that they got the job done, but you can't expect people to be loyal to the company if they don't feel that they are being treated with trust and aren't given responsibility," Tom commented.

"Well, I guess I wouldn't put up with that either," Linda conceded. "Do I get a second chance for a promotion?"

"I think so, Linda," Tom replied, "You seem to want to succeed. Are you willing to put a little effort into learning to work with people?"

"I guess I'd better," Linda said.

1. In Linda's interaction with her boss, which aspects of her personality could be characterized as "parent," "child," or "adult"? Which one predominates? What about Tom's personality?

2. Reread this, changing the whole conversation to an "adult" to "adult" exchange. Now does Linda sound like a good candidate for a promotion? Why or why not?

3. Imagine you are Tom; design a training program for Linda that will increase her self-awareness and improve her human skills.

14

▶ **GROUP DYNAMICS:**
How We Behave in
Groups

All for one, one for all.
Alexander Dumas Pere

In his nineteenth-century novel *The Three Musketeers*, Alexandre Dumas's central characters pledge loyalty to each other and to their group. "All for one, one for all" concisely sums up the perceived benefits of forming and joining groups. Groups form for the good and protection of the individual. And, conversely, the individual is expected to help maintain the group.

The study of people in groups emphasizes the fact that human beings are social animals from birth to death. Our inclination is to join with others, and throughout your life you are a member of many groups, by chance and by choice. By chance you are a member of a family, a clan or tribe, a neighborhood, a community, a state, a country. By choice you belong to the boy or girl scouts, a religion, a school, a sports team, a debating society, a work group.

You make a conscious decision to join a group for any one or a combination of several reasons. A major reason for joining a group is to achieve a goal or to do a task. Political parties and committees are examples of this. If you feel strongly that taxes should be reduced or used differently, you will join a political group to elect people to achieve this goal. If you are concerned about hunger in the world, you might form a group to obtain food for the starving.

You join a group sometimes because you like the activity for which the group was formed. You join football teams because you like to play football. You join swimming teams to enjoy swimming, bridge clubs to play bridge, chess clubs to play chess, gardening clubs to and to exchange information with others having the same interest. In addition to providing the environment for carrying out the activity, the group also provides you with important information and help about your abilities and interests.

You also join groups because you like the other members. Such social groups may be very loosely organized, such as a group of coworkers who get together for lunch and coffee breaks. These groups have no goal beyond the immediate pleasure that people derive from being in them, although other benefits can and do accrue to the members. Among such benefits is their ability to work together harmoniously. Another potential benefit is that if one member of this informal group moves by promotion to a position in which he or she can make promotions, group members may be favored.

You often join groups simply because you want to belong. As you have read, we all have a need for affiliation or belonging. This need represents an exceptionally powerful motivation for joining a group. This need strengthens such involuntary groups as the family and is what makes even those who consider themselves independent and self-sufficient want to be members of some group.

No other country has as many different groups living within its borders as does our country, the United States of America. We live in a pluralistic society. A pluralistic society is one in which many different ethnic, religious, racial, or cultural groups exist—reason enough to know about groups.

Your country has been and continues to be involved in the greatest social experiment ever carried on. Since its founding by immigrants, the United States has mostly had an open door policy so that people from different countries and backgrounds could come and live together here. The experiment has been to see if all these different groups living in freedom could coexist with each other. Mostly the experiment has been successful. No other country has so great a mix of people living together in one society. Although open, the door to immigration is not open fully to all people, and more people have tried to come here than could be legally admitted. As a result many people live here as illegal aliens. In the 1980s, a law was passed to allow many of these illegal aliens the opportunity to gain citizenship.

One theory about people coming to this country was that presently they would drop their different ways and we all would be similar, as in one big group. This was the "melting pot" theory. Interestingly, this has not completely happened. While changing in some ways, many groups have also kept a lot of their original heritage, including customs and, to some degree, language. The result has been that we have a richly varied society made up of many groups that, while incorporating many aspects of life from their new country, keep many of their own traditions alive.

TO THE POINT

▼ NATURE OF GROUPS

All groups, to remain in existence, develop structure and function. Without structure and function, a group will eventually cease to exist as a unit. Structure is the essential makeup or organization of the group. Function is what the group does.

Structure

Just as individuals differ, so do groups. As individuals have certain structures, so do groups. The first element of groups is membership. All groups must have members. Further, group members must be "tied" in a web of relationships that are determined by roles. Most groups have roles that members must fill. Groups have leaders and members named to do certain tasks. These roles may be official or unofficial, permanent or changing.

Roles may be changed on a regular pattern, such as at elections, or by chance. You will read more about roles later in this chapter.

In addition to members and their roles, the structure of a group requires that there be communication among members. If members fail to communicate, the group will cease to exist.

Finally, there must be rules and regulations. These do not have to be written down as they are in *Robert's Rules of Order,* but they need to exist and be mutually accepted, even if unspoken. The custom of serving refreshments at meetings may have developed informally and may have become a rule without much conscious thought. The host of a weekly poker party would definitely follow this rule or risk being excluded from the group. Rules and regulations give a group its sense of identity, the knowledge of what makes it different. Rules make it possible for the group to continue as a unit. Without them, there would be no regularity and, eventually, no group.

Functions

To succeed and survive, groups must carry out functions directed toward achieving two basic goals: task goals and maintenance goals. The extent to which these goals are important will be determined by the type of group, but they are important to a greater or lesser degree to all groups.

Task Goals

task goal
the basic purpose for the existence of a group, for example, to raise funds or elect a candidate

The **task goal** of a group is the basis for its existence, the reason that it formed in the first place. The task goal can be to raise funds, to get a candidate elected to public office, or to improve the public image of a particular group. The task goal can be a service, such as helping the handicapped or stopping litter. It can be simply social or an activity for its own sake, such as playing soccer. The task goal of a family is to provide a nurturing environment for its members.

Maintenance Goals

In addition to task goals, however, a group must achieve maintenance goals to maintain its existence. The purpose of these goals is to keep the group together, to maintain it. Sometimes a group will stay together after completing its task goal and thus has no primary reason to continue to exist. But the urge to maintain a group is very strong, and if the group has a strong sense of its maintenance goals, it may continue, at least for a while, to exist for its own sake. In such a situation, it is meeting its members' needs to belong, which, in a sense, becomes its task goal.

A maintenance goal that is very important is obtaining and keeping members. To do this, a group must continue to make itself attractive to new members and at the same time minimize conflicts among existing members, as well as between new and old members. A maintenance goal would include some standards for membership, whether they are actually stated or simply implied.

Other maintenance goals may require that there always be a strong leader or that members of the group behave in a certain way. The pressure to conform is a major factor in achieving the maintenance goal of any group. You will read later in this chapter of the effect this pressure has on individuals and what the good and bad consequences of it are.

▼ KINDS OF GROUPS

Groups exist everywhere, and large groups contain small groups. You, like everyone else, belong to many different groups. The work organization itself is a group. And within that work organization many other groups exist. Wherever large numbers of people get together—at work, at school, or at play (all groups themselves)—groups form naturally.

You can become a member of a group that is temporary, formed for a limited period of time. You can become a member of a group that is permanent. You may become a member of a group involuntarily, as in the case of your family. Involuntarily means it happened without conscious effort on your part. And you can become a member of a group voluntarily, that is consciously and with forethought, such as by deciding to join a service organization. You will read more about different kinds of groups below.

Temporary Versus Permanent Groups

From the point of view of social scientists, many groups are not worth studying. People waiting at a bus stop form a group with a common purpose, but it is a *temporary* rather than a *permanent* group. Other examples of temporary groups would be people gathered to watch a movie, listen to an opera, or cheer for their team in a football game.

Some of these groups can acquire permanence and thus acquire more meaning as a group. Fans of a particular football team may form a club and hold regular meetings and social events. Fans of a particular film personality may form a fan club. Consequently, these people become something more than just a temporary group of individuals watching a ball game or a film together.

temporary groups
groups that form and stay together for only a short period

permanent group
a group that stays together for a relatively long period

Another example of how a temporary group can change into a permanent one is that of a group of commuters who keep receiving poor service from the train or bus company. They may form a permanent committee to bring pressure to bear on the company to improve its service.

In a more restrictive definition, **temporary groups** do not have structure, whereas **permanent groups** do have structure. Permanent groups must have members who agree on a set of beliefs and values and have common interests, such as goals and objectives. For the group to be perma-

Fig. 14-1

A political convention is an example of a purposive group that is voluntarily formed. The convention itself is a temporary group, although it may be made up of permanent groups from different states.

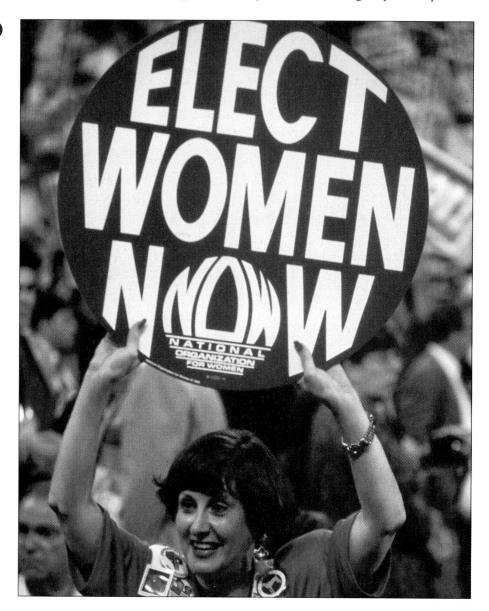

nent, members must think of themselves as members of the group, and others must think of them in this regard. People waiting for a bus do not think of themselves as members of a particular group beyond the sense of feeling they are in a crowd or the momentary sense of sharing annoyance at a late bus.

However, as noted, a group can change from being only temporary to being permanent because of changes in the environment or a continuing problem or interest.

Although you can decide which of many different permanent groups to join, you also belong to permanent groups involuntarily. You are, for example, a member of economic and social groups, depending on the status of your family and, subsequently, your own efforts.

Purposive Versus Spontaneous Groups

Groups can be characterized as being either **purposive** or **spontaneous**. Purposive groups are those formed to achieve a specific goal. Spontaneous groups are those that form merely by chance. Spontaneous groups include people waiting for a tardy bus, people shopping in the same supermarket, students assigned the same homeroom or taking the same course, patients in the same hospital, and soldiers assigned to the same squad or barracks.

purposive
formed to achieve a specific goal

spontaneous
formed merely as a matter of chance

Purposive groups form voluntarily. An example of a purposive group is one formed by the commuters who organized to get better transportation service. They changed their involuntary, temporary status into a purposive one. Like individuals, groups can change their nature.

In the work environment, there are many examples of purposive groups. The work organization itself is a purposive group. So are many groups or teams set up within it to do a particular task or job. Some jobs require the coordinated work of a group of three or more people. These groups are purposive. Constructing a house requires a group including carpenters, electricians, and plumbers. For the sake of completing the house, they form a purposive team. It is a temporary one if they disband when the house is completed, or a permanent one if they have formed a company to build many houses. Within the purposive group formed to construct a house, spontaneous groups exist: all the carpenters make up one group, the electricians another; or inexperienced workers one group, and skilled workers another.

Formal Versus Informal Groups

In any large work organization you will find both formal and informal groups. In a general way, purposive and formal groups are similar, and to a lesser degree so are informal and spontaneous groups. Formal groups within a work organization are purposive: they are formed deliberately to achieve company goals. But an informal group can also be purposive.

The overall work organization is a formal group. Depending on its size, it will be broken down into several smaller formal groups. An **organizational chart** is a written diagram of a work organization broken down into smaller formal groups—divisions and departments. The chart is also known as an organizational flowchart because it shows the flow of responsibility from one level to another.

Within the formal group structure of the work organization, two other formal groups exist, identified as to whether they are line or staff positions. Line personnel have direct responsibility and control. They are the ones who make the decisions and carry them out. Staff personnel provide research and other necessary services. Organizational charts usually show the relationship of staff groups in broken line. Both groups are formal, though.

organizational chart
a written diagram of a work organization broken down into smaller, formal groups—divisions and departments

Formal Groups

The departments and sections, which are formal groups, may be arranged according to the tasks that they must accomplish: assembly, shipping, filing. They may be arranged by the particular product they turn out. Book publishers, for example, often arrange divisions according to the type of book they produce: textbook, general reference book, fiction. A group identified by functions that it performs would be the payroll personnel.

However it is set up, the strength of the group feeling depends upon several factors. If members must communicate and work closely together to accomplish their tasks, there will be strong group feeling. If they do not need to work closely together or communicate, there will be only a weak group feeling. A group of assemblers might be doing the same tasks in the same room but not have a strong group feeling. The same would be true of people in a typing pool or a word processing pool, or messengers who get together only occasionally during the course of a workday.

A factor in their environment, of course, could change a weak group feeling into a strong group feeling. If the assemblers, for example, decided they were not receiving fair pay for their efforts, they might decide to act collectively for a raise (work closely together or communicate) and in doing so would develop strong group feeling with the structure and function of a group. But in terms of the work environment, it would be an informal group, as you will read below.

Task-oriented work groups are common formal groups in the work environment. Other kinds of formal groups are special committees formed to plan a particular project or study a given problem. Perhaps there has been a big advance in the technology that a company is using. The company

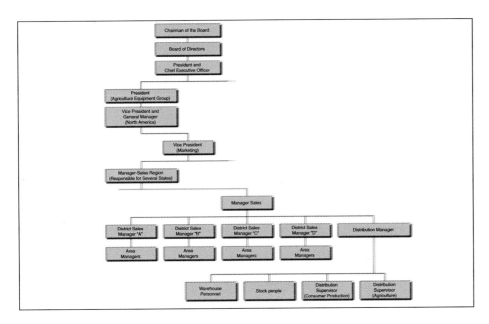

Fig. 14-2

The formal groups in a work organization are often indicated on an organizational chart that shows the various levels of responsibility as well as the different divisions and departments.

may, in response, set up committees to study the new technology to see how it will benefit the company. Large corporations usually have standing committees made up of representatives from the various divisions. The purpose of such groups is to give people from different divisions a chance to meet and exchange ideas and discuss common problems.

Informal Groups

Informal groups are usually more numerous than formal groups in large work organizations. Furthermore, they can often foster a greater sense of cohesiveness and mutual loyalty. The sense of belonging to an informal group can be so strong that members sometimes put more effort into maintaining such a relationship than they put into their work.

A formal group is one created deliberately by the company to achieve its purposes or goals. A production team formed to produce a specific part and a company-sponsored baseball team are both formal groups. The baseball team helps the company achieve its goal of high worker morale.

Informal groups form without the sanction or support of the company, and their goals may or may not be the same as those of the company. A group of workers may have been brought together to achieve a particular goal of the company. Perhaps they were put on a special committee to determine what new system should be introduced. This is a formal group. They may decide they do not want to disband when the company goal is achieved. Instead, they may continue to meet and function as an informal group, seeking to influence company policy.

Fig. 14-3

Factors in the environment help determine how quickly and strongly a group forms. If workers must communicate and work closely together, group feeling can become strong. If they do not need to work closely together or communicate, group feeling may be weak.

Workers whose tasks may not require them to communicate or function strongly as a group in the formal structure may still develop into an informal group, as in the case of the assemblers who band together to take joint action for better pay.

Informal groups can form around a natural leader or an individual with a lot of experience. Perhaps the formal leader—the person with the title of office manager or supervisor on the organizational chart—is not a good leader or is very new and inexperienced. If, at the same time, there is a natural leader in the group or a member with a great deal of experience, an informal group might form around such a person. The result could create problems for the formal leader and even for the organization.

Informal groups can form simply on the basis of friendships. Several people working in the same area or room with one another will eventually begin forming groups independently of the needs of the job. These groups based on friendship may stay job-related or may extend to outside activities as well.

Groups of workers with similar sports interests may join to attend games. They may form their own bowling or softball league. Many companies, recognizing that such groups will form, actively support them as a means of maintaining worker morale. How quickly groups based on friendship or outside interests form depends to some extent on the nature of the work. As noted earlier, if the nature of the work prevents much contact during the working hours, groups may not form very quickly.

A dramatic example of the potential importance of informal groups is labor organizations. In almost every case, these organizations began as informal groups when people doing the same tasks banded together to improve their working conditions. Over time these informal, loosely knit groups acquired the structure and functions of permanent groups. They may have started spontaneously, but today union organizations are purposive groups. And in many work organizations, unions are no longer informal groups but part of the formal working organization, helping to set working conditions and even in some cases overall company goals.

The 1990s have witnessed a decline in the strength and size of unions in the workplace. Probably several factors, both psychological and economic, played a part in this decline. One possible factor is that people are more individualistic, that is, less group-oriented.

Advantages of Informal Groups

Informal work groups superimposed on or intertwined with the formal groups can exert tremendous power for good or ill, both for the organization itself and for the workers. To some extent these groups and their influences can be controlled by the organization, and to some extent they cannot. In any event, managers and workers should be aware of their potential effects.

A definite positive advantage of informal groups is that they can help create pride among workers, both in themselves and in the work they are doing. An informal group formed by workers sharing a demanding job or performing exceptionally well may foster a sense of solidarity and spirit in its members that often a formal work organization may not.

Informal groups strengthen communication. Some of this communication may not be more than the spread of rumor or idle chitchat, but informal groups also help spread needed information quickly. The increased communication within an informal group can serve as a supplement to the formal communication of the work organization. It can even be used when the organization wishes to convey some information with less than the full power of an official, formal announcement.

The interaction of members in an informal group can be useful when a work problem arises or a crisis develops. At such times, the ability to communicate easily and quickly makes it possible for the members to work quickly and well. They can do this in part because they know one another and know what to expect. In a sense, by interacting in an informal group, they have developed additional skills beyond those of simply carrying out their appointed functions.

Disadvantages of Informal Groups

You read of one potential disadvantage of an informal group that forms around a natural leader when the formal leader is weak or inexperienced. Such an informal group could create problems for the formal leader and the organization, particularly if the organization were trying to make changes in the operations.

Even the most loosely structured informal group—such as a loose group of worker friends only lunching together—can under some circumstances create problems in a work environment. If strong bonds develop among the group members, management may find it difficult to discipline a particular member, no matter how justified, without having to deal with the whole group. If the group bond is strong enough, any discipline given out to one member will be resented by all.

Informal groups can create problems for the individual as well. The groups give the individual support and a sense of belonging. But as the motto "all for one, one for all" at the beginning of this chapter indicated, the group also makes demands. An individual in an informal group might face demands to act in a way not in her or his best interest. There could be pressure to slow down, not to try for a raise or promotion, and even to overlook improper conduct by other members.

Another problem of an informal group is the danger of its becoming a **clique**, which is a group that has drawn in on itself, is exclusive, does not admit new members readily, and looks with suspicion and even hostility on other groups. Although communication within the group might increase, communication decreases between the group and others. The members might become defensive and argumentative when faced with what they consider a threat to the solidarity of their group. Members might become preoccupied with their status in the group and maintain its exclusiveness to the extent of making it difficult for the company to maintain desired productivity.

One characteristic of all groups, but particularly of informal ones, is the pressure to conform. This is a two-edged sword, in that it can be a force for good or bad.

clique
an informal group that has drawn in on itself, is exclusive, does not admit new members readily, and looks with suspicion and even hostility on other groups

▼ PRESSURE TO CONFORM

All groups—even just a spontaneous gathering of people—exert pressure on individuals to conform to the expectations of the group. For example, consider an audience's reaction. At the end of a speech or play the audience applauds, because that is clearly the time. Unless the play or speech is particularly bad, almost everyone joins in, even those who might have slept through the performance or did not particularly enjoy it.

Often, applause breaks out during the speech or play. Frequently it is started by one or two individuals. Gradually others conform by following suit. Some people might boo at intervals or at the end. But such people must feel the urge to express this negative reaction very strongly before showing it, because the pressure is to conform by applauding. If, however, everyone was booing, an individual would find it difficult to applaud.

We All Conform

Studies indicate that we all tend to conform to some extent in a group situation. One of the most well known of such studies was conducted by Solomon Asch in the early 1950s. His experiment was quite simple. A subject was given two cards. One had one line on it; the other had three lines of different lengths. The subjects were asked to say which of the three lines was the same length as the single line on the other card.

In the experiment, the subject believed he or she was one of several people involved. In reality, all the other "subjects" were working with the experimenter and were told to give unanimously wrong answers. The test was organized so that the bona fide subject answered last, after hearing all the wrong answers. Under these circumstances, 36.8 percent of the subjects bowed to the group pressure and also gave a wrong answer, even though it was very clear which line on one card matched the single line on the other card.

Some people gave in to group pressure almost all the time. Not everyone gave in, however, and a few subjects, about one-fourth, stuck to their opinions throughout. Follow-up studies indicated that even those people who resisted pressure to conform under these circumstances did conform at times, depending on other circumstances.

Factors Affecting Urge to Conform

Circumstances can affect your likelihood of conforming. For example, if you are dealing with something familiar to you, you will be less likely to conform than if you are dealing with an unknown factor.

Studies also indicate a strong connection between certain personality traits—submissiveness or dependence—and conformity. Or, stated another way, "conformity" is part of the definition of submissiveness or dependence. People with lower levels of learning ability and mental development tend to conform more readily than those with high learning ability and mental development.

Another factor affecting our inclination to conform is the makeup of the group. A group composed of experts exerts strong pressure on

Fig. 14-4

We all feel the pressure to conform. If we are in an audience in which everyone is applauding, we will most likely applaud also even if we did not care much for the performance. We would need to feel very strongly to boo in such a situation.

individual members to conform if there is general agreement among members. A group that is especially important in a person's life exerts strong pressure; for example, it is very important to adolescents to belong to a social group, and consequently, peer pressure to conform is great.

In situations such as emergencies or unfamiliar circumstances, we conform more easily and readily. When you are in an unfamiliar situation, you look around to see what others are doing and copy or conform to that. A simple example of this is the person from a poor background suddenly thrust into the company of wealthy, socially active people. At the huge dining table, the newcomer, awed by the unfamiliar choice of silverware, will wait to see what others use and then conform.

Value of Conformity

If no one conformed, there would be no groups. Therefore, whatever value groups have for individuals depends on the individual's willingness to conform. To conform means to accept the rules or beliefs of the group—not necessarily all of the rules and beliefs and not necessarily all of the time, but at least enough of the rules enough of the time so that the group can cohere. Our society is made up of groups, and without our willingness to conform, society as we know it could not exist. Conforming is valuable and necessary, but it also can have negative results.

Danger of Conformity

An unappealing aspect of our tendency to conform has often been exhibited by mobs. A mob is a huge group of people brought together more or less spontaneously by some outside event: a police officer making an arrest, an accident, a fire, some crime. This loosely knit mob can often be turned into a cohesive group with a single, determined purpose, which is reinforced by the natural tendency of individuals to conform. Individuals acting in mobs have done things that they never would have done as individuals, such as lynchings and beatings.

Not only can unthinking conformity result in bad actions but it can prevent positive change from happening. If everyone always gave in to group pressure, many worthwhile changes would have been lost to society. Most great people tend to conform less. Indeed, many of their contributions to society grew out of their unwillingness to conform. If the founders of our country had conformed to the dictates of English trade, our democracy might never have been established.

An example of the benefits of refusing to conform can be found in the women's movement of the 1960s and '70s. For years women conformed to the social pressure that said they could not work at certain jobs, they

Fig. 14-5

Because of the unwillingness of our country's founders to conform to an English law, our country was born.

could not handle their own finances, and their place was in the kitchen. At first a few brave, nonconformist women began to refuse to conform entirely to the accepted notions. The result has been that society, in general, has benefitted by opening the way for women to make the many contributions they are capable of making instead of playing one role, which, although important, was limiting.

A danger of new movements, which themselves grow out of a refusal to conform, is that they often exert even greater pressure to conform to their new norm. A new movement may demand total conformity from its members. An extreme willingness to conform is marked by an individual's abandonment of his or her own critical judgment, a willingness to accept whatever the group demands, and a rejection of all those outside the group.

Politicians and mob leaders use the tendency of people to conform to achieve their own goals, regardless of whether these goals will really benefit the individuals in the group or society as a whole. When conformity causes us to follow such people, the results are often bad.

The pressure to conform becomes even greater when groups are under stress. The clearest example of this is when a country is at war. A country is made up of many different groups. Nonetheless, when the country is threatened by an outside aggressor, all the diverse groups join together and conform. Unfortunately, unscrupulous leaders use this conformity, or patriotism, brought out by war to maintain themselves in power.

If a group feels that it has all the answers, that it is invulnerable, it may exert such pressure to conform on its members that they will fear any hint of nonconformity. In such a situation, members tend to accept stereotyped views of outsiders, often seeing them as evil. Self-censorship is eliminated, and leaders protect the group from adverse information.

When a group gets into this mode, the members fall into what social observers have labeled **groupthink**. In this situation, members have abandoned all efforts to think for themselves or to question the wisdom of the group, and they see all outsiders as hostile. The result of groupthink can be disastrous for the group. The administration of President Richard M. Nixon, the only president to resign from office, fell prey to groupthink. The people in the administration began to believe that whatever they did was right because they alone knew what was good for the country. If anyone disagreed with them or criticized them, that person was regarded as an enemy. In fact, the Nixon administration actually kept lists of American citizens they considered "enemies." Caught in their groupthink mode, members of the administration even broke laws of the nation and then tried to cover up their actions.

A horrifying example of destructive groupthink occured in Waco, Texas in 1993. Rather than surrender to Federal authorities, a cult led by David Koresh apparently chose to commit mass suicide by fire. Clearly, groupthink, an extreme example of conformity, can cause an individual to lose sight of his or her own best interests and to act in an irrational manner.

groupthink
a situation in which members of a group have abandoned all efforts to think for themselves or to question the wisdom of the group, while seeing all outsiders as hostile

Groups and Conflicts

Groups can come into conflict with one another and prevent one another from achieving goals. Some competition between work groups in a work environment can be healthy, and friendly rivalry can lead to increased morale and productivity. Management must work to ensure that this rivalry does not escalate to the level of conflict. If the rivalry takes the form of fighting over company resources, such as office space or money in the budget to buy new equipment, the situation can become counterproductive to the achievement of company goals.

In such situations, a competing group will put group goals, such as obtaining a bigger share of company resources, ahead of everything else. The group then gets into a situation in which it cannot win because the company cannot accede to its wishes. When a group finds it cannot win, its morale suffers, loyalty to the organization declines, and in an extreme case, the group may resort to slowdowns, sabotage, and other antisocial methods of achieving its goals.

Management's biggest problem with regard to group conflict in the work environment is knowing whether to try to control the conflict, eliminate it, or let it continue because it can have healthy effects. Management has several courses of action when dealing with group conflict. These include using persuasion, providing more open communication with the groups, and encouraging greater interaction among groups. Management can also fall back on its authority and simply order groups to cease unwanted behavior. The latter solution, however, may do little more than achieve an apparent resolution while driving the conflict underground.

The threat of a common enemy can cause conflicting groups to forget their differences and unite. Groups within work organizations often overlook their intramural differences to unite in competition against other work organizations. A favorite theme of science fiction writers is having all the countries of the world forget their bickering and unite in the face of a common enemy from outer space.

Group conflict can sometimes be resolved by finding more responsible or competent leaders or by getting rid of troublemakers or outside agitators. Work organizations make a mistake, though, if they always attribute group conflict to outside agitators. This has been a ploy used by some managements to discourage or do away with union activity. In conflicts between two union groups, the charge of outside agitators is sometimes used by one combatant against the other.

More than one presidential administration has blundered because its members fell into the groupthink mode. Groupthink occurs when a group demands a high level of conformity from its members, deludes itself into thinking it is infallible, and feels it is invulnerable. In these circumstances, actions are often taken without being critically examined.

Groupthink often sets in after a president has won a large electoral victory and he and his team begin to think they can do no wrong. A psychologist, Irving Janis, examined an incident of groupthink in the administration of President John F. Kennedy that occurred in 1961 shortly after Kennedy took office.

The administration attempted to overthrow the government of Fidel Castro by supporting exiled Cubans in an invasion of Cuba. The Bay of Pigs invasion was a total failure, and all those taking part were captured in a few days. It was the administration's worst hour.

Janis suggested several techniques a group can follow to avoid the trap of groupthink. These include:

- Making sure members are aware of groupthink dangers
- Having the leader remain impartial
- Encouraging members to express objections and doubts
- Having members play devil's advocate
- Listening to outside experts (consider more than one point of view)

TO THE POINT

Developing overall goals that conflicting groups can accept is another method of reducing the conflict. Usually, such goals have to be suggested by a third party. Using a third party as mediator is a common device to resolve group conflicts, especially in the work environment.

None of these methods of resolving group conflict is foolproof. Often several must be used, sometimes in combination, to determine which works best. Because group conflict can be healthy and helpful, management must be careful not to attempt to eliminate it in every instance, forcing conformity on all.

▼ DIFFERENT ROLES

Just as you are a member of different groups at the same time and at different times throughout your life, you also fill different roles. You will fill different roles in different groups as well as within the same group. Sociologists describe **role** as a pattern of actions expected of a person in that person's interaction with others.

role
a pattern of actions expected of a person in that person's interaction with others

Your role is determined by the position you occupy in both the formal and informal social systems or groups. If you know what your role is, then you know what is expected of you. If you know what others' roles are, you know what to expect from them. This is true not only in groups such as the work organization but in all other areas of your life, such as at school, at home, and even at play. In each of these areas you fill different roles, and in each you probably fill several roles. Depending on where you are and what you are doing, one role will dominate at any given time.

In your family you may have the role of parent or child, sister or brother, aunt or uncle, niece or nephew. In a social context, you may have the role of member of an organization as well as secretary of the group. At work, you may be a data processor, office supervisor, and chairperson of the committee planning the annual company picnic.

When interacting with others, you should keep in mind that in addition to the role you see a person filling, that person also has other roles that could have an impact on his or her current actions. A parent with a sick child at home will probably find the parental role dominating in the work environment instead of the usual work role. The result could be different work behavior.

The same person can fill the role of parent and child, buyer and seller, adviser and seeker of advice. In the work organization many people are both supervisors and subordinates, managing people under them and reporting to people above them. And each of these roles requires a different type of behavior.

Roles are important for the orderly interaction and communication among people in a social environment or group. Your perceptions of particular roles guide your thinking as to how to behave and what to expect. Knowing a person's *role* is a quick way of knowing the person. Role is an abstraction of the real person, which, as you read in Chapter 5, represents all the characteristics of a group of similar individuals. Although useful, there is a danger that by using a person's role to identify the person at any given time, you end up misunderstanding the person. That is why it is a good idea to keep in mind that any given person fills many roles in addition to the dominant one that you are reacting to at any given moment.

Our ability to assume different roles represents the most complex set of responses of which we are capable. All the various activities and characteristics that make up a particular role are referred to as a **role set**. By using a few of these characteristics, we deduce one or more roles that a person fills and, as a result of that, reach conclusions or generate expectations about that person's behavior.

role set
all the various activities and characteristics that make up a particular role

For example, if you see a young person carrying books on a campus or sitting at a desk in a classroom answering or asking questions, you know from these characteristic activities that the person is filling the role of a student. Knowing the person is a student would cause you to expect the person to perform certain other activities, such as doing homework or research in the library. You would expect also to see other familiar characteristics in the way the person dresses, talks, or otherwise behaves.

These collective expectations make up the role set. If you see an older person in similar circumstances, you might decide the role the person is filling is that of a teacher. You could, of course, be wrong if the person is someone returning to school as a student after having worked for several years. You could also have been wrong about the younger person if she or he were a recently hired teacher just out of school. Role sets are useful ways of determining a person's role and place in a group, but they must be used with caution.

Role set in a work organization is determined by the nature of the job and by the organization's expectations. If there is a large difference between an organization's role expectation and an employee's role expectation, the result will be miscommunication, deteriorating motivation, and inefficiency. For example, if the managers see their roles as tough, hard drivers of workers, whereas the workers expect managers to be supportive leaders and problem solvers, conflict will result.

Perhaps some people want or need a dictatorial type of manager who lays down the law, does all the thinking, and expects unquestioning obedience. Workers with such expectations would not do well if they had managers who were only supportive. Conflicting expectations can create problems.

Fig. 14-6

We all fill many roles throughout life. At different times we are family members and workers, children and parents, and teachers and pupils, among other things.

Problems also develop when role expectations are not known or when roles are ambiguous or not adequately defined. When it is difficult to predict how a person or group will act, you cannot be sure what your response should be or how you should interact. It is important to communicate, and to do this you must have a full understanding of your own role, what others expect of you, and what action you should take.

1. Humans are social animals; our inclination is to join with others. Throughout your life you are a member of many groups, by chance and by choice.

2. We join or form groups for many reasons. A major reason is to achieve a goal or to do a task. You join sometimes because you like the activity the group has formed to carry out. You also join groups because you like the other members. And you often join groups simply because you want to belong.

3. To remain in existence, all groups develop structure and function. Structure is the essential makeup or organization of the group. Function is what the group does.

4. Structure consists of the members, communication among members, and the rules and regulations, spoken or unspoken, that govern the group's operations.

5. A group's functions are divided between two basic goals: task goals and maintenance goals. The *task goal* of a group is the reason for its existence, the reason that it formed in the first place. The maintenance goal is to keep the group together, to maintain it.

6. You may become a member of a group involuntarily as in the case of your family. (*Involuntarily* means it happens without conscious choice on your part.) And you can become a member of a group voluntarily, that is consciously and with forethought, such as when deciding to join a service organization.

7. There are temporary and permanent groups. People waiting for a bus are an example of a temporary group. Temporary groups can become permanent, such as when commuters form an organization to protest poor bus service. Until they develop structure, however, groups remain temporary.

8. Groups can be characterized as being either *purposive* or *spontaneous*. Purposive groups are those formed to achieve a specific goal. Spontaneous groups are those that form merely by chance.

9. In any large work organization you will find both formal and informal groups. Task-oriented work groups are common formal groups in the work environment. Informal groups are usually more numerous than formal groups in large work organizations. A formal group is one created deliberately by the company to achieve its purposes or goals. Informal groups

form without the sanction or support of the company, and their goals may or may not be the same as those of the company.

10. _____ Informal work groups can exert tremendous power for good or bad. A positive advantage is that informal groups can help create pride among workers, both in themselves and in the work they are doing. Another advantage is that informal groups can strengthen communication. If informal groups put their own goals ahead of company goals, however, problems can result.

11. _____ All groups exert pressure on individuals to conform to the expectations of the group, and studies indicate that we all tend to conform to some extent in group situations.

12. _____ Circumstances in the environment, your personality, and the makeup of the group can affect your likelihood of conforming.

13. _____ If no one conformed, groups could not exist. To conform means to accept the rules or beliefs of the group—not necessarily all of the rules and beliefs and not necessarily all of the time, but at least enough of the rules enough of the time so that the group can adhere.

14. _____ Unthinking conformity can be a bad thing. If everyone always gave in to group pressure, many worthwhile changes would have been lost to society. Most great people tend to conform less. Indeed, many of their contributions to society grew out of their unwillingness to conform. When members totally conform without thinking, the group enters a *groupthink* mode, which can be disastrous for the group.

15. _____ Groups can conflict and prevent one another from achieving goals, although some competition between work groups can be healthy.

16. _____ Just as you are a member of different groups at the same time and at different times throughout your life, you also fill different roles. Sociologists describe role as a pattern of actions expected of a person in that person's interaction with others.

17. _____ Your roles are determined by the positions you occupy in both the formal and informal social systems or groups. Our ability to assume different roles represents the most complex set of responses of which we are capable.

QUESTIONS FOR REVIEW AND DISCUSSION

1. Explain the statement that to remain in existence all groups develop structure and function. Give examples to support your explanation.
2. What are the distinguishing characteristics of purposive and spontaneous groups? Give an example of each.
3. Describe the part informal groups play within the work organization.
4. Discuss the ways in which conformity is both a necessity and a danger.
5. How do sociologists describe role?
6. Explain the importance of roles.
7. Explain the possible problems in using roles to understand and interact with others.

KEY TERMS
Define the following:

Clique
Groupthink
Involuntarily
Maintenance goals
Organizational chart
Permanent group
Pluralistic
Purposive
Role
Role set
Spontaneous
Task goal
Temporary groups
Voluntarily

ACTIVITIES

1. As you read, we all belong to many groups during our life, different ones at different times as well as different ones at the same time. Think back about your life and all the groups to which you have belonged. Make two lists: one showing groups you belonged to in the past and one showing groups you belong to today. Limit the temporary groups (attending a show, at the beach, and so on) you have been in to three examples.
2. Take the list you have made of your current groups and identify each group as a spontaneous or purposive group.
3. We all feel the pressure to conform. Often we conform. Sometimes we do not. Think of some examples in your life when you have felt the pressure to conform. Write a brief description of this experience. Try to think of times when you did not really want to conform, but did. Think of a time when you refused to conform. Describe your feelings in each situation. How did you feel? Was it difficult to refuse to conform? Discuss these experiences with your classmates.
4. In this chapter you read that through their refusal to conform, great people have made contributions to society. Give one example of this.
5. Complete conformity can be bad. From history or current events find an example of total conformity having bad results in mob action or groupthink.
6. Make a list of all the roles that you currently fill. Consider how you act in each and what is expected of you in each. Do you find you act differently in different roles?

CASE 1

Power of an Informal Group

The organizational chart at Lakeport Press, Inc., showed that Janice Dorcey was the supervisor of the mail room and that the mail clerks—Bill Yates, Mae White, Pedro Delgado, and Roberta Jones—reported to her. Jan had responsibility to make the work assignments, to answer questions, to solve problems for the group, and to get the work done on schedule.

Jan was new in her position. She had come to it after special training in the company's managerial training program. She had been chosen because she was young, intelligent, and eager to try new things that the company felt were necessary to keep its competitive position. Her supervisors had particularly told her to change the old procedures.

Bill Yates had been in the mail department for many years. He was a likable, outgoing man who, through years of experience, knew a lot. The other members of the department turned to him for advice as often as, if not more often than, they turned to Jan. Bill believed in the old ways of doing things. He told the other workers that the new ideas Jan was trying to introduce would not work.

"Yeah, Jan means well," Bill said to Mae White, who had asked him about a new procedure Jan suggested she try, "but she's got a lot to learn yet; better keep doing it the way you know."

Another time, when Jan was showing Pedro a different technique, he said he had better go check it out with Bill.

At coffee breaks and lunch time, Jan found that the workers would gather around Bill. When they had a problem with their job, Bill was the one they turned to.

Jan was finding it impossible to implement the many changes that the company expected to make the operation more efficient.

1. Describe what is happening here and why.
2. What do you think Jan can and should do?

CASE 2

A Closed Group

"George, I understand that Marcie Berkowitz is planning to leave. That's too bad. She is a good worker according to everything I hear. What's happening? You hired her less than a year ago."

"I really can't say, Juan," George said. "She certainly does have the production expertise and is a good worker. That's why I hired her. But she doesn't seem to be fitting in."

George and Juan were in Juan's office. George was the production manager and Juan the operations manager of a large manufacturing concern. George reported to Juan, and on this day they were having their weekly review of George's departmental activities.

"You have a good group, George. They seem to have spirit and work well together. But you also seem to be having trouble filling this position. Marcie is about the third person you have hired in the past two years, and now she is planning to quit."

"Well, the other workers don't seem to think she's just right for our department," George said.

"Yes, I notice they don't spend much time with her. She takes her coffee and lunch breaks alone," Juan said.

"I know," George said. "And the others don't help her as much as they help each other. Marcie dresses a little differently, you know, a little more formally. That might be part of it. The group just doesn't seem to want to accept her."

"Or any other new employee," Juan added. "You have a problem, George. What do you think it is?"

"I'm not entirely sure," George said. "I know the people I have are good workers. Morale is high. Production is good. They get along well with each other. But, you are right. We really need to increase the size of the group to handle increased business, yet whenever a new person has come in, she or he soon leaves."

"Well, we've got to solve this problem. Your department cannot handle all the increased work that will be coming along without additional personnel. You've got to find good people and get them to stay. Talk with Marcie some more to see what she says. What are her real reasons for leaving? Also, I think you have to talk to your people to find out what exactly is happening there."

1. Describe what is happening in George's department. What is good about it and what is bad?

2. What can George do to improve the situation?

15

▷ LEADERSHIP:
How We Develop Our
Potential to Lead

Good followers do not become good leaders.
Laurence J. Peter and Raymond Hull

In their book, Laurence Peter and Raymond Hull take exception to and contradict the old saying that "You have to be a good follower to become a good leader." They maintain that the qualities required of a leader differ so much from those required of a follower that the latter seldom make good leaders. So, which is right? As with most broad statements, each contains an element of truth despite their contradictory assertions.

The truth contained in the old saying "You have to be a good follower to become a good leader" is that you must understand the people you hope to lead. A good leader identifies with her or his followers, understands their needs, and knows what motivates them. To the extent that you learn these things by being a follower yourself and do not forget them when a leader, the old saying holds true.

It does not follow, however, that all good followers can become good leaders, and this is the insight of the quote from *The Peter Principle*. This book emphasizes that those qualities that make a good follower and those that make a good leader are different. A person who is very good at carrying out difficult and demanding orders may not enjoy giving them, or even have the ability to do so. Not everyone likes to have the responsibility that comes with leadership.

In this chapter you will read of some of the characteristics of leadership, particularly those required for success in the work environment. Whether you aspire to a managerial, or leadership, position will depend on the extent or intensity of the various needs that you have. Not everyone will seek leadership positions, and some will even refuse them. A skilled classroom teacher, for example, who enjoys and is fulfilled by the day-to-day encounter with students will not eagerly or wisely give this up to sit alone in the office as principal.

▼ NATURAL LEADERS

charismatic
the ability to inspire others to strive for common goals and to endure sacrifice and hard work

There are **charismatic** leaders, that is, people with the ability to inspire others to strive for common goals, endure sacrifice, and work hard. Such natural charismatic leaders are few. They can inspire for good or for evil, because it does not necessarily follow that a person with charismatic ability will use it in a good cause.

Adolph Hitler is an example of a charismatic leader with evil goals. It was Hitler, in fact, who noted that the main characteristic of a charismatic leader was the ability to move people with speech. He wrote in *Mein Kampf*, "I know that one is able to win people far more by the spoken than by the written word. And that every great movement on this globe owes its rise to the great speakers and not to the great writers." These statements are certainly open to argument, but it is true that charismatic leaders are effective speakers.

Many great religious leaders were charismatic for good goals. George Fox, the founder of the Society of Friends; Martin Luther, whose work led to Protestantism; and Ignatius Loyola, the founder of the Jesuits, are a few examples. Great charismatic leaders of recent times include Franklin Delano Roosevelt, who led this country out of a deep depression; Sir Winston Churchill, who led the United Kingdom to victory in World War II; and Martin Luther King, Jr., who awakened this country to the need for civil rights reform.

These men were all powerful speakers, able to sum up and articulate the feelings of many people. They could sway the emotions of others and get them to work together toward particular goals. Roosevelt summoned people out of the apathy of the great depression and into action with his words "The only thing we have to fear is fear itself." Churchill rallied the British people during their low point in World War II, vowing, "We shall never give up." And King fired the hearts of many when he said, "I have a dream."

▼ MADE LEADERS

Up until the first third of this century, the belief was generally held that leaders are born and not made and that they were born into a certain stratum of society. That is, an inherited talent for leadership was passed from generation to generation—mostly in a particular type of family. This belief was bolstered by the existing evidence, which was that leaders came mostly from a limited number of families, usually the well-to-do and influential.

The realization began to dawn, however, that the reason more leaders came from a limited number of families was that they had the *opportunity* and *motivation* to become leaders, whereas others with similar talents, coming from poorer, limited backgrounds, lacked both. Recall reading in Chapter 10 that for motivated behavior to be possible, three conditions must be met. The individual must have:

1. Ability (actual or potential skills)
2. Opportunity
3. Both internal and external motivation

So a person may be capable of being a leader but not have either the opportunity or encouragement. Or the person may have the ability but no great desire to lead. Leadership is a quality that can be developed, and

Fig. 15-1

Martin Luther King, Jr., was a modern charismatic leader whose ability to inspire others helped bring about civil rights reform in this country.

although heredity may play a part in determining whether one can or will want to become a leader, the other factors are just as important.

There are many recent examples of leaders rising from poor families and minority groups to illustrate the point that when opportunity, encouragement, and desire exist, leaders develop. Some evidence suggests that if the person has an opportunity to exercise leadership skills at an early age, she or he will become an adult leader. This is not surprising in the light of what we know of learning and reinforced behavior. Here are some examples.

Company President at Twenty-Nine

Charles Percy, who became president of the Bell & Howell Company at the age of 29, had the opportunity to begin practicing leadership skills at an early age. He started his career at age 5 by selling magazines. This was not for boyish fun. It was a necessity. By the time he was 8, he had other boys working for him, thus gaining practice in supervising others. Through most of his years in grade school, he captained his grade's baseball team, and this provided more practice in leading others. In high school he supervised the distribution of a newspaper in his suburb and ran a parking lot at night. He started college with savings of $50, yet he went through and even made money by using his experience in leadership to organize a purchasing agency for fraternity supplies.

In 1943, at age 23, Percy was elected to the board of directors of Bell & Howell, and 6 years later he became president of the company upon the death of Joseph McNabb. By the time he ran for the U.S. Senate in 1966, Percy had some 41 years of experience as a leader in business and civic affairs, more leadership experience than many executives twice his age.

TO THE POINT

Ability, opportunity, encouragement (external motivation), and desire (internal motivation) are the key ingredients for becoming a successful leader. Where you come from is not as important. The history of the three Rittereiser brothers underscores this point.

Wall Street is the financial center of the world. To reach top positions in the powerful Wall Street firms, one usually had to have the right connections, come from the old, blue-blooded families (which generally meant white, Anglo-Saxon, Protestant), go to the right prep schools, and in short be tied into the "old boy network." The Rittereiser brothers were none of these things. They came from a blue-collar family in the Yorkville section of Manhattan. They played their ball games on the city streets, not on the manicured playing fields of New England prep schools. Their father worked in a slaughterhouse and was a truck driver.

This background notwithstanding, in 1986, Fredric Rittereiser was vice chairman of First Jersey Securities, Robert Rittereiser was president of E. F. Hutton & Company, and Thomas Rittereiser was a first vice president of Fitzgerald Securities Corporation. At the time they held these powerful positions all three brothers were still in their forties. Their colleagues referred to them as "superb executives."

They clearly had the desire, and their parents helped to see that they had opportunities and encouragement. Their father encouraged them to take risks. Their mother ran their home but with the whole family, acting as a committee, giving their views. Later, a brother was quoted as saying "I think that's how all three of us manage today . . . we listen to what everyone has to say, then we make our decisions."

The brothers were encouraged to be curious and seek answers through reading and their own investigations. They learned to compete among themselves, which gave them the desire. They all began work early and turned down college scholarships to get steady paying jobs. In this way they quickly gained valuable experience. Because they had the opportunity and encouragement, the brothers were able to realize their potential as leaders in a demanding, competitive business where often having the "right connections" had been the deciding factor.

Based on "Hometown Boys Make Good" by Priscilla Ann Smith, *The New York Times*, June 1, 1986.

First Black Woman in Congress

Shirley Chisholm was the first black woman elected to the U.S. House of Representatives. She was born into a poor family, but she had a gift for leadership, and she was able to persuade people in the black community of Bedford-Stuyvesant in Brooklyn, her home, to do things to help themselves. From 1953 to 1959, she was director of the large Hamilton-Madison Child Care Center in lower Manhattan. By this time she had become an authority on childhood education and welfare. She took the initiative to learn Spanish so that she could work better with Spanish-speaking children and their parents. Her ability as a leader carried her forward and upward, and she became educational consultant in the Division of Day Care of the New York City Bureau of Child Welfare.

Chisholm began to be more and more involved in community and civic activities, and this eventually led to a career in politics. She is extremely careful and thoughtful in decision making, but once she has made up her mind to act, she works relentlessly toward her objective. Her persistence, honesty, and forthrightness reflect true leadership qualities.

Labor Leader

Another outstanding American leader was the late Cesar Chavez, who was called one of the heroic figures of our time by Robert Kennedy, a presidential candidate and esteemed leader himself before his assassination. Chavez dedicated himself to improving the lives of his fellow Mexican Americans, particularly those who were farm workers in California.

He defied conventional labor leaders by organizing the United Farm Workers. Chavez has been described as a very quiet, thoughtful man, who evoked love, loyalty, and a sense of dedication in his followers. He stressed nonviolence and shunned giving people direct orders. Chavez knew his supporters intimately because he was one of them and worked with them, sharing their needs, values, and goals.

▼ BUSINESS LEADERSHIP

Although charisma can help a manager, it is not essential for becoming a successful leader in the work environment. What the business leader must do is link the company objectives to the workers' needs and values. A leader's mission is to get people to function as a team to achieve a company goal. To do this the manager must show the workers that their work toward the achievement of the company's goal helps them achieve their own personal goals.

This requires an understanding of the workers and their needs, knowledge of the goals of the company, and a way to connect worker needs with company goals. An ability to communicate is essential, although it does not have to be at the level of a charismatic leader.

In business, a leader needs the support and confidence of his or her followers. A manager's ability to relate overall company goals to personal individual goals, such as meeting the needs for economic security and emotional satisfaction, will determine how well he or she wins and holds that support and confidence.

In the 1930s, some behavioral scientists attempted to compile lists of what they called *leadership traits*. They reasoned that the physical and emotional qualities essential for leadership could be recognized in potential leaders. However, no agreement could be reached on what qualities belonged on the list, the terminology was poorly defined, and the ordering of traits in terms of importance varied from list to list.

Now there is little confidence that leadership qualities can be identified, but there is general agreement that the successful leader will exhibit four basic characteristics:

1. Intelligence
2. Self-confidence
3. Communication skills
4. Sensitivity to group needs

▼ THE GROUP THEORY OF LEADERSHIP

That there are differences among lists of leadership traits suggests that there is no single set of characteristics common to all leaders beyond the basic ones listed above. Some modern theorists have therefore suggested that leadership does not arise solely from the personality of the leader but depends largely on the wants and needs of the followers. The **group theory of leadership** holds that the needs of the group of followers determine when a leader will emerge, as well as the type of leader.

group theory of leadership theory that holds that the needs of a group determine when a leader will emerge as well as the type of leader that emerges

The rise to power of Charles de Gaulle is a case in which the group's needs produced a particular leader. De Gaulle and other French citizens escaped from France when Germany defeated it in World War II. In England the Free French rallied around this autocratic man, who personified the unconquered spirit of the French nation. He and his people fought on the side of the Allies to retake France from the Germans. After the war, when the French people were depressed spiritually and economically, de Gaulle's strong leadership and sense of nation were exactly what France needed.

In the middle of the last century, our country was nearly divided into two nations. The majority of people who wanted to prevent the splitting up of our country turned to Abraham Lincoln, who believed strongly in preserving the union. The desire to preserve the nation was so strong, at least in the northern states, that Lincoln, a gentle man who deplored killing, led the country into its bloodiest conflict.

Leading Is Not Bossing

Leadership implies influencing people. That does not mean, however, just being bossy. As noted above, a good business manager shows the workers how helping to achieve the goals of the business organization helps them achieve their own goals and meet their own needs. In this way a manager motivates people to do what needs to be done. As you read in Chapter 10, using our skills and our knowledge involves motivation.

In a sense the good manager provides the second and third conditions required for motivated behavior: opportunity and encouragement. The work environment itself provides the final conditions for motivated behavior in requiring something of the worker (his or her skills) and in providing something the worker requires (satisfaction of needs).

In Chapter 10, you read that the industrial psychologist Frederick Herzberg identified two kinds of work motivators: *extrinsic* and *intrinsic*. Extrinsic motivators relate to our physical and social reinforcers and include such things as salary, vacations, and other fringe benefits. Intrinsic motiva-

Fig. 15-2

Being a leader is not just a matter of bossing. A good manager provides opportunity and encouragement, essential for motivated behavior.

tors relate to our self or internal reinforcers and include task satisfaction, personal recognition, and a sense of worth.

Rarely do jobs combine all the right extrinsic and intrinsic motivators. Hence the task of the leader is to keep workers making a conscious effort to support company goals at all times. Three methods are generally used by managers to induce workers to cooperate. These methods can be referred to broadly as using coercion, giving rewards, and arousing commitment. Each has advantages and disadvantages.

Coercion

Coercion means *controlling* people with threats. Leaders relying on coercion condition their followers to expect that something unpleasant will happen to them if they do not do what is wanted. In an extreme form, physical punishment, even death, is threatened. In the work organization the threat is loss of pay, bonuses, benefits, or even one's job. This method of leading people relies on fear, which is a strong motivator for action.

Although this method may be initially effective, there are several problems with it. First, it generates worker resentment along with the fear. You can imagine your own reaction to a manager relying on coercion to motivate you. You would not like it. Even the suggestion of coercion can cause resentment and negative worker reaction.

In one instance, for example, relatively unskilled workers in a factory were paid high wages, yet they were not satisfied and went on strike about every 18 months. It was eventually determined that a cause of their dissatisfaction was a large sign displayed on the wall. In huge type, the sign bluntly stated shop rules and the penalties for breaking them, such as days off without pay. This was a form of constant coercion, and it displeased the workers.

Another problem with the use of coercion is that it tends to harden the workers so that they become accustomed to rough handling. The coercive leader must bully workers to get them to work. As the workers become accustomed to the bullying, the leader must continually escalate it to get anything done. A vicious circle begins that cannot be easily broken.

You no doubt recognized that managers relying on coercion are using what Herzberg called the Kick in the...(KITA) approach to motivating workers. KITA managers believe that workers are motivated by a desire to escape punishment and that if they are not driven they will not work. Coercion also relates to what Douglas McGregor called the Theory X method of management, which is based on the assumption that workers

Some managers use rewards to motivate employees. This method can be ineffective because workers may come to expect them.

cannot be trusted, they must be watched all the time, and they will work only if faced with punishment for failing to do so. (See Chapter 10.)

The main reason that coercion is not the most effective way to lead people is because it does rely on punishment to motivate people, and as you read in Chapter 9, punishment is not an effective way to motivate people. Punishment may cause behavior but often not what is desired, and it may result in unwanted behavior.

This was shown by the well-paid workers in the factory who nonetheless went on strike because of coercive conditions. It is not unusual for workers to strike because of dislike for the leadership methods, even if this is not their stated reason. This was indicated by a survey of striking and nonstriking workers employed in similar conditions. Many more striking workers than nonstriking workers expressed dissatisfaction with the leadership where they worked.

Rewards

Instead of punishment, some managers use rewards to motivate workers. The use of rewards, such as raises, bonuses, time off, goods, or services, is more subtle than coercion, but like coercion involves extrinsic motivators. You have no doubt heard of the "carrot and stick" approach to leading. It comes from the image of motivating a mule to move either by hitting it on the rear with a stick or tying a stick to its body so that a carrot attached to the end dangles just in front, but out of reach, of the mule's mouth.

As noted, Herzberg referred to the use of the carrot or rewards as positive psychological KITA as opposed to negative psychological KITA, which relies on punishment. With positive psychological KITA, workers are motivated to behave as required so as to achieve a desired result: a raise, promotion, time off. Negative psychological KITA motivates workers to behave as required to avoid an undesired result.

The closeness of the two methods of managing can be illustrated easily. Consider that the result of behaving as desired, that is, doing the work satisfactorily, is keeping or losing a job. If the worker perceives the result of doing the work is the reward of keeping the job, you could say positive psychological KITA is employed. If the worker does the work because of fear of losing the job, then negative psychological KITA is at work.

Both rewards and coercion rely on extrinsic motivators, and both have similar weaknesses. As punishment must be continuously escalated to ensure productivity from workers who become hardened to harsh treatment, so also must rewards continually be enhanced, or workers will simply come to expect them as deserved and will not be strongly motivated by them.

Commitment

The ultimate form of leadership wins the commitment of the workers by closely relating their goals and the company's. One way of doing this is by involving the workers in the process of setting the goals and also by developing systems by which the workers can share in the profits of the company.

Whereas coercion and rewards rely on extrinsic motivators, commitment comes from intrinsic motivators. Essentially, workers do the job not for some future reward or for fear of future punishment but because they want to do the job for their own self-satisfaction. Creating conditions in the work organization that stimulate commitment is a major challenge for managers.

Referring again to what you read in Chapter 10, recall that McGregor identified not only Theory X, which involved negative psychological KITA, but also the Theory Y method of management. Managers using the Theory Y approach strive to generate commitment by trusting the workers, giving them more responsibility, and involving them in decisions about their work.

▼ FORMAL VERSUS INFORMAL LEADERSHIP

In the previous chapter you read that in all work organizations there are formal and informal groups. Sometimes informal groups unite around a natural leader who holds no official managerial position. This can happen when the formal manager is new, inexperienced, or not a natural leader. Such a situation can create problems for the work organization, especially if the informal leader and the official manager do not get along.

The fact that these two kinds of leadership exist has been recognized by those who study the functioning of work organizations. Amitai Etzioni noted that "the power of an organization to control its members usually rests in a specific position, person, or a combination of both." In other words, authority is carried by a specific job title, such as "president," "office manager," or "supervisor," and by the person with the title.

Etzioni goes on to say that such individuals "whose power is chiefly derived from [their] organization position [are] referred to as. . . official[s]. An individual whose ability to control others is chiefly personal is referred to as an informal leader. One who commands both positional and personal power is a formal leader." To achieve effective management, work organizations strive to make sure that all *officials* are also *informal leaders*, that is, according to Etzioni's definition, formal leaders. Essentially, his message is that being an official—having a title and authority—does not necessarily make a leader.

Fig. 15-4

Some managers use unique rewards to motivate workers.

▼ CONCERNS OF LEADERSHIP

Managers manage. But as you read above, managing is more complicated than simply telling someone to do something. Knowing how to motivate people is obviously an important skill of a manager. Another thing you should know about managing is that little if any actual hands-on work is involved. Managers think, plan, and organize. They work at an abstract level. Their work is to get the work done through other people.

In the automobile factory, managers do not rivet bolts or put parts of automobiles together. At the fast food stand, they usually do not sell the hamburgers and serve the customers. If you prefer doing the hands-on work yourself, you might not be comfortable being a manager. Hands-on workers have the satisfaction of seeing the results of their efforts, some tangible evidence of what they have been doing. At the end of the day or the week, a manager may not have any tangible evidence of the work she or he has done.

Managers do work, however. They work hard. And if they have little tangible evidence of their hard work, what they do, how they manage, can mean the difference between a successful work organization and a failed one. The effects of their leadership are felt in many important areas, some of which are discussed below.

Productivity

The Industrial Health Research Board of Great Britain conducted an experiment intended to determine the efficiency of several different makes of typewriters. Experienced typists used one model for a year, and then they used another model the next year. Toward the end of the second year, experimenters thought they had identified the most efficient machine, based on worker output.

Then the supervisors were switched. It was discovered that under one supervisor all the typists improved in speed, regardless of which model they were using. The other supervisor was a somewhat tense and nervous person who, in turn, made the typists tense by constantly checking their work and urging them to do better. Under the more relaxed managerial style of the first supervisor, the typists were able to perform more efficiently. The leadership style of the supervisors had more effect on output than the typewriting machines.

Personnel Turnover

Managerial style can affect personnel turnover. No one willingly stays in an unpleasant environment, which is why, ultimately, Theory X or coercive managers are not effective. They are faced with constant turnover, an expensive proposition for the work organization because it costs to train new workers. If workers are unable to find other work, they may stay, but they will be disgruntled and probably less productive.

The records of two small factories in the same town demonstrate how leadership affects labor turnover. These competing plants made the same product, paid the same wages, and were generally similar except for their general managers. The general manager in one factory inspired workers' commitment. Labor turnover averaged about 15 percent per year. The manager in the other plant was coercive, using fear and intimidation to motivate the workers. Turnover in this plant averaged 55 percent a year. Every two years, the plant had to train an entirely new workforce. That is expensive, and new, untrained workers do not produce as effectively as trained ones.

Fig.15-5

Leadership styles can affect a worker's productivity, even when the work involves a learned skill, such as working on a computer.

Absenteeism

As a manager's attitude can affect labor turnover, it also can affect absenteeism, and for the same reasons. If people cannot escape completely from an unpleasant environment, they will do their best to avoid it as much as they can. Short of risking their jobs, workers with an unpopular manager will use all sorts of excuses to be absent from work.

Sickness is an often-used excuse to stay away from work. Some of it is feigned, but it is likely that people in an unpleasant environment actually become ill more often than those in a pleasant environment. According to research conducted by the Industrial Health Research Board of Great Britain, 80 percent of the office workers in one department of a large company were absent one Friday afternoon during an epidemic of colds. The supervisor of this department was a continual nagger, and the employees were glad to have a chance to stay away from work. In other departments with more effective managers, the rate of absenteeism at the same time was much smaller.

Safety

It would seem that a manager's style and ability to lead would be remote from aspects of worker safety, but studies indicate otherwise. Researchers at the Industrial Relations Center of the University of Chicago studied accidents for a five-year period in a firm with some 5000 employees. It was found that the departments lead by autocratic (Theory X) supervisors had accident rates four or five times higher than those of similar departments led by democratic (Theory Y) supervisors. When the supervisors were

434 UNIT IV SOCIAL RELATIONSHIPS

switched, the low-accident departments had increased accident rates, and the high-accident departments had decreased accident rates.

So, managers may not be involved in hands-on work in the day-to-day operations of a work organization, but what they do and how they do it has a direct impact on the overall operations, even apart from their basic function of planning and organizing to ensure smooth operations. Successful managers are those who derive satisfaction from working through and motivating others to do what must be done and who know that even though there may be no direct link between their own daily efforts and final tangible results, what they do makes it all possible. They desire to get results, and getting the job done is their reinforcer.

▼ LEADER'S SOURCE OF POWER

As you read earlier in this chapter, no one set of traits essential to leadership has been identified. It follows from this that no one "best" personality for leadership has been identified. In fact, studies show that many different sorts of people who have different types of personalities can be good leaders.

Consider two men who together built a great steel empire. One, Andrew Carnegie, was physically small, quiet, a tactful diplomat, and reserved in his relations with others. The other, Charles Schwab, Carnegie's highly paid right-hand man, was a physical giant, boisterous, and outgoing. Both were competent leaders.

Circumstances can thrust a person not otherwise of apparent leadership quality into a leadership position. On a destroyer escort in World War II, this happened to a young seaman, who was not only the youngest person on the ship but a shy and retiring man. One night during convoy duty in the Pacific, an enemy submarine attacked. The destroyer escort went to battle stations and positioned itself between the troop ship and the submarine. Unfortunately, as it began its run on the submarine, several members of the antisubmarine gun crews facing their first battle panicked. The young seaman took charge and with another man loaded and fired four guns until other sailors rallied round him looking for orders. He organized and led them. When the action ended, he was embarrassed to find a score of men waiting for him to continue telling them what to do.

Different types of work may call for different leadership methods also. This was illustrated by a study of naval officer cadets who were given two different kinds of work to do: mechanical assembly and committee work. Both jobs required problem solving among the cadets, but the assembly work was with tangible objects, whereas the committee work was with ideas and attitudes. The same men were required to do both types of jobs and were observed doing them.

The person-to-person interaction of the men differed with each job. Little spontaneous leadership was shown in either task, but disagreeing and arguing accounted for nearly 10 percent of the interactions in the committee work, compared with only 2 percent in the assembling work. These observations indicate that a leader of a committee will have greater need of the ability to get people to work together than the leader of a group whose work involves tangible things.

So circumstances often determine whether a leader will arise and what kind of leader he or she will be (group theory of leadership), and persons with varying types of personalities can succeed as leaders. In all of these circumstances the different kinds of leaders essentially drew their power from three sources in addition to the group itself.

Power of Office

Their offices or job titles give managers authority. Such authority will not make a manager who lacks leadership skills a leader. Parents, teachers, police officers, supervisors, and low-level managers have power over others because of the authority carried by their offices or social positions. But official position alone never makes a leader. You read earlier that Etzioni identified formal leaders as those who had both the authority and the ability as informal or natural leaders.

Nevertheless, people often make the mistake of thinking that an official position will make them leaders. They confuse leadership with authority. What they fail to understand is that leadership involves a meaningful relationship between the leader and those led, whereas authority, by itself, is purely arbitrary. Compare two parents. One says to a child, "Be quiet and do what I tell you to do!" The other says, "Now, don't you think that this is the best way to do it because ...." Both have authority, but only one is a leader encouraging the child to follow by explaining why something should be done in a particular way.

Aggressive people often try to achieve power by getting authoritative positions. Such people often prove to be bad bosses because they understand only the power and authority. They do not realize that a little bossing may go a long way but more bossing goes a long way further—the wrong way. They cause dissatisfaction among workers, and that is counterproductive for the company.

Power of Knowledge

An old adage states that "knowledge is power." Put in terms of this chapter, this can be stated as "knowledge makes for a more effective leader." We tend to follow people who obviously know what should be done, whether such people are designated leaders or not. The examples you read earlier of how workers will turn to an experienced leader when an inexperienced person is the official leader illustrate this. There are many instances in which the person with the position title and authority does not have leadership because of lack of knowledge.

The boss who is weak in knowledge is often bypassed. If the executive is uninformed and the secretary or assistant is informed, workers learn to ignore the boss and go to the secretary or assistant in whom effective leadership resides. Some people in positions of power and authority actually fear having individuals around them who are as knowledgeable or more so. They see these people as a threat, which indeed they are to the boss lacking in knowledge.

Being knowledgeable, however, does not mean knowing everything there is to know. That is impossible for anyone. An effective leader must have the ability to understand and lead people, coupled with a basic knowledge of the business. Beyond that, the successful executive surrounds herself or himself with people who have skills and knowledge to contribute to the organization.

In this way both the executive and the organization benefit. As Andrew Carnegie said, "The able executive is the [one] who can train assistants more capable than himself [or herself]." Another industrialist, Lammot du Pont, put it this way, "There's a trick about management that I learned early. It is to surround yourself with [people] who know more than you do and listen to them." These successful leaders knew that capable assistants

Fig. 15-6

Some people in positions of authority are afraid to hire people who may be more able and knowledgeable than they are, although effective leaders try to hire people who will challenge them.

"SORRY, MR. HEINSOHN. I MAKE IT A PRACTICE NEVER TO HIRE ANYONE I'D BE AFRAID TO FIRE."

contribute to their achievement. Successful leaders have knowledge and surround themselves with more of it.

Power of Understanding Others

Much research in group dynamics and social psychology shows that the power of leadership comes from the group being led. In other words the real power of a leader is not imposed from above on the group being led. The power comes from the group. It is imposed by the group's willingness to accept the leader. Even before scientific observation confirmed it, this important truth was recognized by our founding fathers. They established a system of government based on the people's willingness to be governed.

Every group has certain expectations of what its leaders should be like and how they should lead. The groups follow most enthusiastically the leader who comes closest to the group's expectations. It follows that those leaders who best understand their groups and what they want succeed most. Such leaders have empathy. As you read in Chapter 13, empathy means that one can experience through imagination another person's feelings. Empathy is essential to successful leadership. By knowing their group's expectations, leaders can successfully coordinate their activities toward the goals in which they are interested on behalf of the work organization.

Workers' expectations of leaders are usually constructive and reasonable. Workers seldom expect the leader to work beside them at the same kind of work they are doing. They realize leaders do not do hands-on tasks. They expect the leader to perform leadership functions, such as providing an acceptable environment, taking care of complaints, helping solve work problems, and setting the goals and objectives.

Two supervisors, quite similar on the surface, may have quite different levels of success leading their work groups. The difference can be a result of one leader's fulfilling of the expectations of the group and the other's failure to do so. A study of 208 office workers in a Kentucky factory showed that the productivity of workers under a leader who they believed understood them was measurably higher than that of those workers who believed the boss did not understand or relate to them. Some of the things that these workers looked for in their leaders were:

- Being available when workers have a problem
- Being uncritical of workers for problems that could not be avoided
- Being prompt to respond to complaints
- Making good on promises to workers
- Showing an interest in workers' ideas and suggestions
- Giving good explanations of how to avoid errors

- Giving sincere, direct answers
- Discussing why work changes may be necessary

▼ LEVELS OF LEADERSHIP

Whatever their level, all business leaders have three basic responsibilities:

1. Produce (either goods or services) to generate income
2. Keep costs reasonable to ensure profits
3. Maintain group spirit to ensure productivity and stability

In practice, most business leaders tend to emphasize the first two areas and neglect the third. This probably is due, at least in part, to the close and apparent connection between desired results and the first two functions, in contrast to the less obvious connection between group spirit and desired results.

Business leaders can be divided roughly into two broad categories, or levels, according to the functions they perform: supervisory and executive. A third level, which bridges the two, also can be distinguished in many work organizations. Members of this third group are referred to as *middle managers*, indicating their role between the other two levels. The distinction among the three groups will vary from organization to organization. In a small work organization, one person might fill both supervisory and executive roles. In large organizations, all three groups exist and the lines between them are clearly drawn.

Near the beginning of this chapter, you read that successful leaders require intelligence, self-confidence, communication skills, and sensitivity to others. These can be related to competencies that business leaders must possess:

- Knowledge of technical details
- Understanding of people
- Planning and judgment

Leaders at the supervisory level require a good supply of the first two competencies because they work closely with people doing the day-to-day tasks. For leaders at the executive level, the last two competencies are more important than technical knowledge. Advancement to higher responsibility often comes because of improved business judgment and the ability to handle people, not because of increased technical knowledge.

Let's examine the three levels of business leaders. We use the terms *supervisors*, *middle managers*, and *executives* as a way of easily identifying the broad categories. One person's job, however, might put him or her in more than one category at the same time. Also, as mentioned earlier, the lines between the categories are blurred in small organizations and more definite in large ones. Job titles themselves can mean different things at different work organizations. A person with the job title of "office manager" might be a supervisor. A person with the executive-sounding title of "vice president" might be a middle manager. And a person with the title of "general manager" might be a top-level executive.

Supervisors

Supervisors are at the first rung of the leadership ladder. They have direct and immediate contact with the workers. A supervisor may oversee just one other worker or may oversee dozens. The number is limited only by practical considerations. Because a supervisor is responsible for the performance of individual workers, giving them more individuals than they can realistically supervise would be pointless. The complexity of the work being performed will determine to some extent how many workers one supervisor can oversee. If the workers are fruit pickers, one supervisor can oversee dozens. If the workers are computer programmers, one supervisor might oversee only two or three.

To the worker, the supervisor speaks for the company. The supervisor is the conduit through which company policies and goals are relayed to the workers and through which worker needs and complaints are relayed to the company executives. Supervisors do the immediate scheduling of workers, handle the day-to-day problems, praise the good workers, and reprimand the poor workers. When they must be absent because of illness, workers call in to the supervisor, who must find a way to get the work of the absent worker done, even sometimes doing it himself or herself.

The importance of these front-line leaders cannot be overemphasized. In a contest called "My Job and Why I Like It," 47 percent of the employees of a large company who participated gave "ability and consideration of my immediate boss" as a reason for liking their jobs. By contrast, only 2.5 percent named the pension plan provided by the company.

Supervisors carry out company policy, but usually do not originate it. In some companies, however, supervisors and the workers are given a say in developing policies. Companies that involve everyone in the policy-making process operate on the theory that policies created by everyone will be supported by everyone, which is considered a sound psychological concept. Regardless of how they might feel about a company policy, however, supervisors to succeed must implement it, explaining it to the people under them and seeing that it is followed. Knowing policy is as much a part of a supervisor's job as technical knowledge.

Fig.15-7

Supervisors have direct contact with workers and manage their daily tasks.

Because they must possess considerable knowledge about the detailed operations carried out by people under them, supervisors are most frequently promoted from within the ranks of those they eventually oversee. Some supervisors find it difficult, especially when first promoted, to keep from spending all their time continuing to do the hands-on work. This can create problems.

A study of the production records of 600 office workers found that in offices in which the supervisor spent most of the time doing hands-on work as opposed to supervising, the production record was low. The supervisors in the high-output offices were more likely to spend their time supervising, coordinating group activities, scheduling, and organizing.

Middle Managers

Middle manager positions exist between front-line supervisors and the executive level. They are found mostly in large organizations. In a sense they are super-supervisors in that they usually have a group of supervisors reporting to them and have overall responsibility for the functions of these supervisors. Where middle managers do not exist, their functions are fulfilled by the supervisors or executive-level officials. In the 1980s and 1990s, the trend in large work organizations, however, was to simplify levels of organization, and as a result many middle manager positions were eliminated.

Middle managers are separated from the workers by the level of supervisors, although they often have direct contact with the workers and must have a high degree of technical knowledge in the areas of their responsibility. Middle managers often head divisions or departments. In a particularly large office, the person who is office manager may have responsibility for several departments, each headed by a supervisor, such as word processing, data processing, and mail distribution.

Middle managers and supervisors both have a great influence on the climate in their departments. One way in which such managers can create a relaxed atmosphere is by serving as shock absorbers for the pressures that come down from the upper levels of management. Serving as a buffer and toning down the outbursts from above—and there usually are some, even in the best of places—are important functions of the middle manager. Good middle managers must be able to absorb tensions without passing them along. They require a high tolerance for frustration.

Middle managers and supervisors must convince workers of their sincerity. That their sincerity improves worker morale was demonstrated by a study involving dissatisfied telephone workers. Workers rated their satisfaction with meetings with their managers on a scale of 1 to 3. Those managers whom the workers considered insincere were least able to relieve dissatisfaction by calling conferences.

Executives

A wide range of positions is covered by the term *executive*, and some executives are paid ten times the salary of others. These executives have titles such as "chief executive officer," "president," "chief operating officer," or "chairman of the board." They are responsible for the overall operating policy of their work organization. They set the tone and direction.

Executives lead by remote control. Most of their person-to-person contacts are with other executives and middle managers or, possibly, supervisors. Although not in direct contact with the workers, executives make decisions that can affect all of them. They can decide to expand a plant or to close one down. They can decide to move a plant from one location to another or to modernize the equipment. All of these decisions obviously have a great impact on the workers.

Executives deal with long-range policy. In large work organizations they may be carrying out the wishes of a board of directors, who represent the stockholders, who may number in the thousands. Although technically the stockholders own the company and are the final bosses, it is the top executive officer, even more than the board of directors, who has the real day-to-day power and authority. Boards of directors can and do replace top executives, and at annual meetings stockholders can also do this. But as a practical matter, this does not happen often.

The differences between supervisory-level leaders and executive-level leaders are reflected in the kinds of decisions each type makes. The following two lists compare the decision-making environments of supervisors and executives.

Supervisory Level

Many daily decisions
Few workers affected
Decisions related to current problems
Decisions made on the spot
Decisions concern tangibles
Results evident immediately

Executive Level

Few daily decisions
Many workers affected
Decisions related to future problems
Decisions made after extensive analysis
Decisions concern intangible policies
Results not evident for months

line officers
executives under a chief executive who have direct responsibility for operations or production

A chief executive in a large corporation will have many other executives under him or her to help create and articulate policy. Many of these are **line officers**. Line officers have direct responsibility for operations or production. This line of responsibility extends from the chief executive down through the supervisors. Chief executives also have other executives and aides to assist them who have no line responsibilities. These aides are called staff officers. They carry out many day-to-day tasks for the top executive and often provide research and advice for the line officers. All of these positions would be shown on an organizational chart (see Chapter 14). The relationships of staff officers to others in the organization are indicated by broken lines.

▼ PROFILES OF LEADERS

Intelligence, self-confidence, communication skills, and a sensitivity to others constitute the essential ingredients of good leaders. But how do these ingredients relate to the day-to-day activities of leaders? In what ways do effective leaders put them together to perform their jobs satisfactorily?

You read earlier in this book that the amount of compensation one receives for a job is not a good indicator of the actual value to society of the job. But salary does indicate the perceived value of a job, and top executives of large corporations are among the most highly paid people in the world, making much more than heads of state. In 1994, these were the five highest-paid executives in the United States, according to *Business Week:*

Michael D. Eisner	Walt Disney	$203,011,000
Sanford I. Weill	Travelers	$52,810,000
Joseph R. Hyde, III	Autozone	$32,220,000
Charles H. Mathewson	Intl. Game Technology	$22,231,000
Alan C. Greenberg	Bear Stearns	$15,915,000

Observers have often studied and described effective leaders in action. Here are two such descriptions, giving slightly differing perspectives.

Day-to-Day Responses

In a talk at the Columbia University Graduate School of Business, Chris Agyris described ten ways in which he said executives exhibit their effectiveness as leaders:

1. **They have a high tolerance for frustration:** Strange though it might at first seem, successful executives must be able to handle failure. Actually, people who ultimately succeed do so because they did not let failures—which happen to everyone—stop them. Executives do not get angry or sulk when things do not go as hoped. They hold their feelings in check and work enthusiastically for a long-range goal, even if not 100 percent certain of success.

2. **They encourage participation by others:** In reaching decisions, successful executives welcome participation by others rather than

insisting on their own ideas. This requires the ability both to keep an open mind for ideas that they might not like at first and to accept criticism of their own ideas.

3. **They continually question themselves:** This does not mean that they lack self-confidence, but rather that they have the confidence to be critical of themselves. They try to be as objective as possible in evaluating their own actions.

4. **They are competitive:** They realize that other firms and executives are out to beat them. They welcome competition and enter into it without a feeling of hostility.

5. **They control their impulse to get even:** They can take hostility from others without trying to get even with the instigator or showing hatred. An executive must be able to handle stress well.

6. **They win without exulting:** Executives avoid gloating when achieving a goal or winning a victory. They are graceful winners.

7. **They lose without moping:** This relates to the first characteristic. Successful executives can take a loss, put it behind them, and get on with the job.

8. **They recognize legal restrictions:** They accept restrictions imposed by laws and agreements even though those restrictions may make it more difficult for them to reach their goals. They do not attribute these restrictions to a malevolent force trying to get them.

9. **They are conscious of group loyalties:** They are loyal to lodge, club, technical society, management group, church, and close personal friends. They are anchored to these groups, which give them comfort when they make decisions that are unpopular with other groups. They are also conscious of group loyalties possessed by their employees outside the work organization.

10. **They set realistic goals:** They have realistic goals that are challenging enough so that they have to strive to achieve them, but the goals are achievable.

Formula for Success

Another description of those most likely to succeed as top executives was given by Melvin Sorcher, author of *Predicting Executive Success*. He identified eight attributes that the best top executives possess:

1. Ability to make things happen

2. Ability to affect the opinions and actions of others—an influence so subtle it may go unnoticed

3. A record of living up to their commitments

4. Extensive knowledge of organizational history

5. Ability to recognize and acknowledge their mistakes

6. Ability to express their views and perspectives in a novel and arresting way

7. Possession of penetrating insight into the nature of their organization or industry

8. Ability to think up and act on concrete ideas for positive change and organizational improvements

SUMMARY

1. Whether you aspire to a managerial or leadership position will depend on the extent or intensity of various needs and abilities you have. Not everyone will seek leadership positions, and some will even refuse them.

2. Charismatic leaders have the ability to inspire others to strive for common goals, endure sacrifice, and work hard. Such natural charismatic leaders are few. They can inspire for good or for evil purposes.

3. Leadership is a quality that can be developed, and although biological inheritance plays a part, opportunity, encouragement, and need or desire are equally important.

4. Although charisma can help a manager, it is not an essential for becoming a successful leader in the work environment. What the business leader must do is tie the company objectives to the workers' needs. A leader's mission is to get people to function as a team to achieve a company goal.

5. There is little confidence that leadership traits can be identified, but there is general agreement that the successful leader will exhibit these four basic characteristics: intelligence, self-confidence, communication skills, and sensitivity to group needs.

6. Some modern theorists have suggested that leadership does not arise solely from the personality of the leader but depends largely on the wants and needs of the followers. This *group theory of leadership* holds that the needs of the group of followers determine when a leader will emerge, as well as what type of leader will emerge.

7. Being a leader does not mean being bossy. The good manager provides the second and third conditions required for motivated behavior: the opportunity and an environment that both requires something of the workers (their skills) and provides something the workers require (satisfaction of their needs).

8. Coercion means to control people with threats. Leaders relying on coercion condition their followers to expect that something unpleasant will happen to them if they do not do what is wanted. This method of leading people relies on fear. Even if initially effective, coercion creates problems and ultimately is an ineffective method of leading. It generates

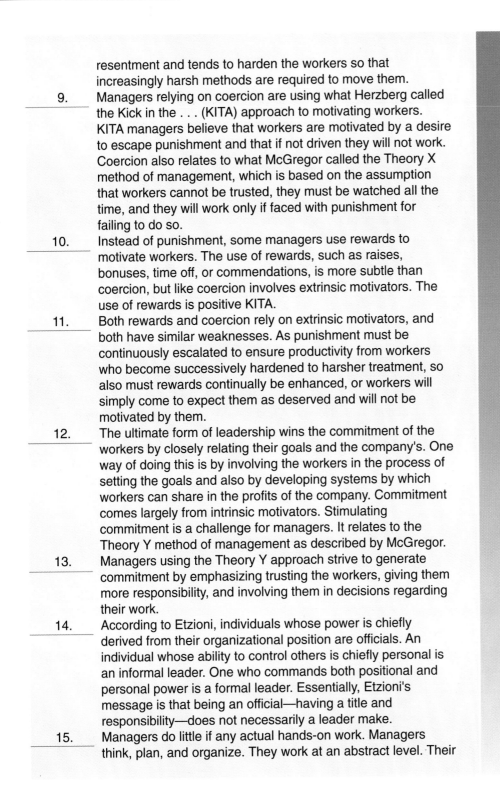

resentment and tends to harden the workers so that increasingly harsh methods are required to move them.

9. _____ Managers relying on coercion are using what Herzberg called the Kick in the . . . (KITA) approach to motivating workers. KITA managers believe that workers are motivated by a desire to escape punishment and that if not driven they will not work. Coercion also relates to what McGregor called the Theory X method of management, which is based on the assumption that workers cannot be trusted, they must be watched all the time, and they will work only if faced with punishment for failing to do so.

10. _____ Instead of punishment, some managers use rewards to motivate workers. The use of rewards, such as raises, bonuses, time off, or commendations, is more subtle than coercion, but like coercion involves extrinsic motivators. The use of rewards is positive KITA.

11. _____ Both rewards and coercion rely on extrinsic motivators, and both have similar weaknesses. As punishment must be continuously escalated to ensure productivity from workers who become successively hardened to harsher treatment, so also must rewards continually be enhanced, or workers will simply come to expect them as deserved and will not be motivated by them.

12. _____ The ultimate form of leadership wins the commitment of the workers by closely relating their goals and the company's. One way of doing this is by involving the workers in the process of setting the goals and also by developing systems by which workers can share in the profits of the company. Commitment comes largely from intrinsic motivators. Stimulating commitment is a challenge for managers. It relates to the Theory Y method of management as described by McGregor.

13. _____ Managers using the Theory Y approach strive to generate commitment by emphasizing trusting the workers, giving them more responsibility, and involving them in decisions regarding their work.

14. _____ According to Etzioni, individuals whose power is chiefly derived from their organizational position are officials. An individual whose ability to control others is chiefly personal is an informal leader. One who commands both positional and personal power is a formal leader. Essentially, Etzioni's message is that being an official—having a title and responsibility—does not necessarily a leader make.

15. _____ Managers do little if any actual hands-on work. Managers think, plan, and organize. They work at an abstract level. Their

work is to get the work done through other people. If you prefer doing the hands-on work yourself, you might not be comfortable being a manager.

16. What a manager does affects many important areas, such as productivity, personnel turnover, absenteeism, and safety.

17. Leaders draw their power to lead from three sources in addition to the group itself. These are their office, their knowledge, and their understanding of others.

18. In work organizations, leaders can be divided broadly into two groups: supervisors and executives. Supervisors directly manage the workers, interacting with them on a daily basis. They execute policy. Executives are remote from the workers and do the overall planning, organizing, and policy setting. In large organizations, a third level—middle managers—often exists between supervisors and executives.

KEY TERMS
Define the following:

Charismatic
Coercion
Formal leaders
Group theory of leadership
Line officers
Staff officers

QUESTIONS FOR REVIEW AND DISCUSSION

1. Discuss in what way the statements that "good followers do not become good leaders" and "you have to be a good follower to become a good leader" are both true.

2. What is a *charismatic* leader? Give some examples.

3. Leadership is a quality that can be developed, and although biological inheritance plays a part, the other factors are also important. Explain this sentence. What are the other factors?

4. Although charisma can help a manager, it is not essential to becoming a successful leader in the work environment. Explain what a business leader must do to succeed.

5. Although there is little confidence that leadership traits can be identified, there is general agreement that successful leaders have four basic characteristics. What are they?

6. What is meant by the *group theory of leadership*?

7. Discuss *coercion* as a method of leadership. What are its strengths and weaknesses?

8. In what way are coercion and rewards, as methods of managing, alike?

9. How does commitment help in leading people? How does it differ from coercion and rewards?

10. Describe what Amitai Etzioni meant by *formal leaders*.

11. Since managers do not do hands-on work in production or providing service, in what ways do they affect the operations of

the work organization?

12. Describe briefly the three levels of leadership found in a work organization.

ACTIVITIES

1. Read a biography or autobiography of a person who was reknowned as a leader. Try to find one on a business leader. For discussion note particularly the background from which the person came: his or her parents, social class, and upbringing. Make a list of the leadership characteristics the individual demonstrated. Note at what point in her or his life such characteristics started to become apparent. Were there opportunities and encouragement?

2. You have no doubt been in positions or groups in which others were leading you. Consider all the people you have known personally as leaders. Which ones did you think were the best? Which the worst? Without specifically identifying individuals, list the best and the worst along with those things you liked and did not like about the leader's methods.

3. While watching a favorite TV series or a movie, make an effort to identify which of the characters are officials, or hold authority in name only, and which are the real leaders. Remember Amitai Etzioni's definition of *official*, *informal leader*, and *formal leader*. Use these definitions to identify different characters as such.

4. Is leadership for you? Is it something you want? Review your life in terms of these questions:

- Do I have ability? Remember that leadership is not just a matter of personality. You may be shy or aggressive, neither of which will stop you from becoming, or guarantee you will become, a leader. Rather, ability refers to planning, organizing, and communicating.

- Would I enjoy working through others as opposed to doing the work myself?

- What opportunities to lead have I had? (Describe them.) If you have not had opportunities, consider ways you can get some: join a social, sports, or service club; do volunteer work; or get a part-time job.

- What encouragement have I received? (Describe it.)

- Make a plan for becoming a leader based on your history. Or give a convincing report on why leadership is not for you.

CASE 1

The Earmarks of a Leader

After World War II, young Bob Fildes helped support his family by selling milk and newspapers through the streets of the modest district of London where he lived.... Each Sunday, a sixpenny subway ride brought him a brief respite. He would while away the afternoon in the city's natural history museums sifting through drawers filled with insects impaled on stickpins, pondering a myriad of scientific puzzles.

He left home at 17 and held a variety of jobs with research groups while putting himself through the University of London, where he earned a Ph.D. in chemistry. One job he held required him to tackle and hold sheep so they could be vaccinated and marked with bright paint.

The ability to tackle daily chores with vigor yet still find time to dream has served Robert A. Fildes well. At 47, he is chief executive of Cetus Corp., a leading biotechnology company.

Prior to joining Cetus, Fildes held other positions. He was with Bristol Myers Co., where he was unsuccessful in getting money to start a biotechnology division. He left to become president of another company where his "take charge" approach clashed with the chairman. Fildes left to take over struggling Cetus.

He is considered a tough manager. "Acting angry is part of my management style." When displeased he demands to know who is responsible. His colleagues at Cetus gave him a spiked mace, which he displays in his office.

He conveys with obvious delight the sheer beauty of a science that may someday allow the pharmaceutical industry to defeat cancer and other deadly diseases.... But he is not about to leave the combat of business for the artistry of the laboratory.

1. Based on this report, what attributes and experiences contributed to Mr. Fildes's successful rise to a top executive position?

2. Were there any indications of what kind of manager Fildes is? Explain.

Report edited by Joan O'C. Hamilton and Lois Therrien, "How Bob Fildes is Engineering Growth at Cetus," *Business Week*, March 17, 1986: 80.

CASE 2

Who is the Leader?

Stan, Lynne, and Alice have just been named to head three new branch offices that their corporation was opening up. Delighted with their promotions, they are celebrating with a lunch and discussing their new responsibilities.

"I'm telling you," Stan emphasized, "you've got to take charge. People only understand one thing: authority. They want to be told what to do. You don't tell them, they won't work. I mean, that's what being manager is all about. You do the planning and ordering. They do the work."

"I'm not sure about that," Lynne replied. "Sure, the manager plans and has to give orders, but you should involve the workers. Ask them what they think. Let them have some input. You just don't say, 'Do this,' 'Do that.' People don't like that, and won't work as well."

"Yes," Alice said. "I'm going to be close to the workers in my branch, a pal to them. I'll let them know they can always come to me and that we are all partners in this."

"Well," Lynne said, "I don't know about being a pal to them. Sure, let them know they can always come to you with problems, but I think you must keep some distance between you and the people reporting to you."

"You're making more sense now, Lynne," Stan said. "You keep the workers in their place. If not they will take advantage of you. They just want their pay each week and don't care about anything else. And they want to get it with the least amount of effort. You have to make sure they know that if they don't do what you say, out they go. That way, you have no trouble."

"And no morale," Lynne said. "You don't need to be a pal, but you just can't drive them. You must involve them, let them know they are appreciated, and you can do that while at the same time making it clear you are the boss and not their buddy."

"Well," Alice said, "I think you both are going to be too tough and will alienate everyone. I don't like being ordered around. I'm not going to manage that way. My workers and I will be one big family."

1. Identify the leadership style or method each new manager will probably exhibit.

2. Based on their comments, which of the three new managers will most likely be the most effective leader? Explain your choice.

3. Who will probably be the least effective leader? Explain your answer.

Unit IV

R E S E A R C H   S T U D Y

All for None and One for One

The small (30-worker) company was having morale problems. Management was satisfied that all of the workers were qualified for their jobs, knew what their jobs were, and could do their jobs well. Yet the signs were there: cliques forming, minimal social interaction among groups, eating lunches separately and apart, petty complaints about one another, frequent verbal tussles–something had to be done!

You are hired to diagnose the problem or problems.

You resolve to approach this in a scientific manner, by forming hypotheses and testing them with data.

1. For each chapter in this unit, formulate at least two hypotheses about the company's problem. Be specific: One test of a good hypothesis is that you can collect data that can disconfirm the hypothesis (prove it wrong). In scientific logic, you can only disconfirm a hypothesis, you cannot confirm it. But if you (or others) can not disconfirm a hypothesis, you can have some confidence that your hypothesis is correct, and act accordingly.

2. For each hypothesis, specify the data that you need to collect in order to disconfirm the hypothesis.

3. Suppose you do not disconfirm a hypothesis–which gives you some reason to believe the hypothesis is correct–what course of action would you recommend to the company, based on the hypothesis, that will help them with their problem? Do this for each hypothesis.

This is called the "hypothesis-testing" approach to problem solving. With experience, you do not need to make a long list of hypotheses. You can quickly rule out many of them on the basis of immediately available information. You then concentrate on the few likely candidates. Then comes the "fun" (sometimes, very sensitive) part–looking for data to disconfirm as many hypotheses as you can–not unlike a detective trying to eliminate suspects.

Work Adjustment

The workplace has undergone major changes in the past few decades. Some of these changes occurred as a result of new technology; other changes stem from changing social and economic conditions. How you deal with these changes determines, to some extent, how successful you will be in the workforce. Other determinants are how you choose careers, your aptitude to learn job tasks, and how you deal with stress.

In this unit you will learn about the changing workplace and how people are adapting to it. You will find out that people often have several different reasons for entering into a specific job and several different ways to adjust. Finally you will learn how workers can turn stress into an advantage.

16

▷ THE WORLD OF WORK:
How Our Work and
World Are Changing

Do your own thing.
A sentiment that gained popularity in the Sixties

sociotechnological
both social and technological

Thanks for the most part to technology—the practical application of scientific discoveries—we in western countries are more free to "do our thing" than ever before in history. And "doing our thing" means not only doing the kind of work we prefer but also having more time to do whatever we want, that is, to play and pursue other hobbies or other dreams. In psychological terms, it means having more opportunity to fulfill more levels of our needs. At the same time, the **sociotechnological** (both social and technological) changes in our environment have required and continue to require psychological adjustments of us and present us with many choices to make, which can be both a boon and a problem.

The blessings of this greater freedom are real and obvious. The adverse effects are equally real if less obvious. For the most part, we no longer need to work constantly just to fulfill our basic physiological needs—for sufficient food and shelter, and a degree of security. Though this is welcome, a result has been that our higher-level needs—for belonging, the esteem of others, self-esteem and self-actualization—have become more important to us. There is nothing terribly wrong about this as far as it goes. Failure to fulfill a higher-level need usually will not result in death, as will the failure to fulfill a lower-level physiological need. But our higher level needs can be hard to meet. And although the result is not death, it is often dissatisfaction.

A modern person, faced with many choices and vague longings resulting from unfulfilled higher-level needs, may imagine there was an appealing directness in life lived at a basic level as it once was. At one time a person successfully hunted or gathered berries, ate and lived; or failed to do so and died. A modern person faces an ever-increasing number of choices, which can make it difficult to decide what to do, how best to spend one's life, even to decide "Who am I?" Such questions would not occur to a person struggling to meet basic needs.

As you read in Chapter 1, we face such typical, eternal questions constantly. The persons who can best answer them are the ones who are most self-aware—not self-centered or self-conscious, but aware of their talents, aptitudes, values, and interests. In Chapter 1 and in subsequent chapters, you read of ways to gain knowledge of yourself. Chapter 11 discussed the development of your work personality, and Chapters 6 and 10 identified personality aspects relevant to work. In this chapter, you will learn how the work environment has changed and is changing, what its effect is on you, and why knowledge of yourself and the work environment is important for making good career decisions.

▼ THE CHANGING NATURE OF WORK

At one time the connection between one's work and one's life was direct. One literally worked to survive. As humans increasingly organized themselves, socialized, and formed groups (see Chapter 14), the nature of work changed in many ways. Specialization began, and the link between survival and work became less direct. We must still earn a living, but most of us do not hunt or grow the food we eat or make the clothes we wear.

Working for Work's Sake

As the tie between survival and work became less direct, people eventually entertained the idea of work for work's sake. People still had to work to fill basic needs, but work was considered good to do for its own sake, almost apart from any other consideration. Essentially this view assumed workers could be *intrinsically* motivated.

People at one time held the strong belief that having idle time or leisure time away from work was somehow evil. A person should fill the days with productive labor or preparation for such labor, the belief went. On one day a week a person was not expected to work. This day of "rest," however, was to be spent in religious pursuits for the improvement of the spirit.

There was logic in maintaining a belief that work was in and of itself fulfilling because much hard, wearying work had to be endured to maintain society. By teaching that work contributed to spiritual betterment and would in itself bring dignity and emotional reward, society encouraged the people who performed the necessary drudgery. There was and is, of course, more than cynical logic and exploitation in the attitude that work can be rewarding for its own sake. Many people, especially today when they have choices, do find dignity and emotional rewards in their work. The fewer one's choices, however, the less the chance of emotional rewards and dignity.

The Concept of Leisure

Eventually the industrial revolution, with its increasingly sophisticated technology, brought about a fundamental change in our society, one that affected all our lives and influenced our perception of work and leisure. This shift in our economic system began in the latter part of the nineteenth century. It was to change the way we look at work and how we spend our lives.

Until the twentieth century, people had to work hard and long just to grow enough food or to make enough material things to sustain themselves and society. Then technology made it easier to produce food and other needed items. Soon one farmer could grow as much food as ten farmers could grow before. Highly productive factories replaced the less productive artisan and cottage industries. As a result, we moved from a society in which the major problem was how to produce enough to meet our needs into one in which the major problem is how to use everything we can produce.

The need to consume what people were able to produce coupled with excess time and money made leisure time acceptable for people other than the very rich. People no longer needed to spend all their time in productive work. This concept began taking root after the Civil War—hardly 100 years ago—and words such as vacation began to enter the vocabulary of the growing middle class. One interesting result was the appearance of a whole new industry offering employment—the leisure industry, a big industry today.

With work no longer taking up all available time, and with a bewildering variety of jobs from which to choose to earn a living, a person must think and plan a career and life carefully to achieve satisfaction. Making career decisions—good decisions—has become a new, demanding responsibility.

Working for Fulfillment

Although technology has made it possible for us to earn a living working fewer hours than our ancestors had to, we still must work for a living. But as earning a living has become relatively easy—compared with previous periods in history—we expect our work to bring us other rewards. Money, although always essential, is not by itself always sufficient. We want, as noted earlier, to satisfy some of our higher-level needs.

Fig. 16-1

It was only a little more than 100 years ago that our society accepted the idea of vacations for the working or middle classes. Before that, the prevailing belief was that leisure time was somehow wrong. Today, of course, vacations are considered right and essential, and a multibillion-dollar vacation industry thrives.

Put another way, after satisfying our needs for food, shelter, and security (wages and protection from arbitrary dismissals), we want to have work that is meaningful. Just how necessary meaningful activities are to our sense of satisfaction is only lately being realized. Recent studies have indicated that our sense of satisfaction is strongly affected by how much time we are able to spend doing things that are most meaningful for us, at which we are competent, and in which we take pleasure.

Some recent research has found that on average our opportunity to spend time on meaningful activities was a more powerful predictor of satisfaction with life than was health. In Chapter 11, you read that jobs that have no meaning for the worker—such as tightening bolts on an assembly line—can lead to dissatisfaction and alienation.

A major problem that technology has brought is the decline of meaningful work for young people. At one time every member of the family had a responsible job or task, even the very young. That has changed. Today, lacking meaningful work, the idle young present a problem for society. This situation has intensified the turmoil individuals experience at that stage in life when they undergo their greatest psychological and physiological change—the adolescent years. At a time when young people are struggling to develop a sense of identity and deal with role confusion (see Chapter 8), finding a place in society has become more difficult for them because society has few meaningful activities to offer at this stage, other than preparing for the future.

▼ THE CHANGING CHARACTER OF WORK

Apart from the farmer, upon whom we depend for our life-sustaining food, can you guess what single occupation has for the longest period been central to our civilization? The answer is blacksmithing. From the dawn of the Iron Age, which began about 1500 B.C., until this century, the blacksmith was essential to society. There were many blacksmiths in large cities, and no village existed without one. The blacksmith made and repaired iron plows, as well as pots and pans. Iron permeated life, and those who worked with it were among our first citizens.

If you had not guessed blacksmithing or even thought about such an occupation, that is understandable. Few blacksmiths remain today, and they are certainly not central to our society. The disappearance of the blacksmith not only symbolizes the change from an artisan society to an industrialized one but also dramatizes the speed at which change occurred. At the beginning of this century, blacksmiths still filled the important role they had held for more than 3000 years. Then within 50 years the trade virtually disappeared.

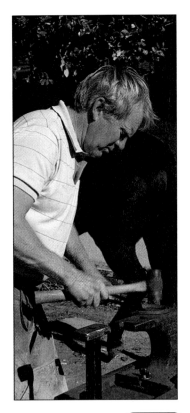

The blacksmith symbolizes the extent and rapidity of the changes technology has brought about. For more than 3000 years, until this century, blacksmiths played a central role in society. Then within the first 50 years of this century, the trade virtually disappeared.

In the second half of this century, another dramatic change is occurring in the workplace because of the computer. The computer is the most prominent of new tools that workers have to learn to use. It is a particularly significant new tool because it can change the nature of the work itself. Robots can replace workers on the assembly lines doing the mechanical and routine tasks, leaving workers free to perform more demanding jobs. In addition to affecting the production sector, computers are having a special impact on the service sector, which as you will read, is the fastest growing part of the workforce.

The business office controlling the flow of information is the center of just about all business activity, and the computer is influencing how office work is done by changing the way in which information is handled and processed. The computer not only speeds up the flow of information but also increases productivity by the way in which it can handle information. Essentially, you store information even as you create it. At one time, you would gather your information, work on it, type it, make copies, distribute it, and then file or store it. If you needed it again, you would have to go to the file for it. If you or someone wanted to change it, it would be necessary to begin again. With computers, the information is stored immediately, and it can be used, changed, and manipulated easily. Anyone who has access to a computer has access to tremendous amounts of information. Among other things, computers are one of the factors making it possible for more people to work outside the normal work environment. A secretary could work at home, for example, if connected via computer to the office.

From Blue-Collar to White-Collar

The rapid disappearance of the blacksmith anticipated the accelerated transformation of the United States from a predominantly production-based economy to a predominantly service-based economy in the second half of this century, and this is reflected in changes in the workforce. In 1950, only 17 percent of the nation's workforce held white-collar jobs (that is, they worked in offices and professions providing services) as opposed to blue-collar jobs (workers in factories producing goods). By 1992, white-collar workers made up 71 percent of the workforce and many new jobs being created are in the service industries. It is estimated that by the year 2000, nearly all new jobs will be in the service areas.

This means that fewer people work in factories producing things and more people work in offices processing information, in the professions, in stores or restaurants, or in recreation-related occupations. Because many service occupations require greater interaction with other people than did many manufacturing jobs, human relations skills assume greater importance.

Increasing Mobility

At one time having a successful career meant staying with one company or at least in one area. That is no longer true. As companies became larger, even if a worker stayed with one, the worker did not always stay in one area. Often advancement required moving from one community to another. Increasing transfers within one company from one part of the country to another were only one manifestation of the increasing mobility of the workforce. Rather than staying with one organization throughout one's working life—the traditional way to ensure security and advancement—workers began moving from company to company more often. A growing number even began to move from one career to another.

A third manifestation of the mobile workforce appeared in the 1980s when growing numbers of people joined the ranks of temporary workers. In fourteen years, from 1980 to 1994, the number of workers whose primary income was earned in temporary jobs rose from 471,800 to 1.4 million. If you consider all people doing temporary work—from one hour to full-time—their number in 1980 was 2.5 million. Now that number has tripled. People become temporary workers, moving from job to job, because temporary work gives them more freedom and autonomy. Not everyone has the temperament for this type of work, however, because, for one thing, it does not provide as much security, especially health care security.

As you learned in Chapter 10, research has found that values sometimes oppose each other and that satisfying the requirements of one seems to rule out being able to satisfy the other. The situation of the temporary

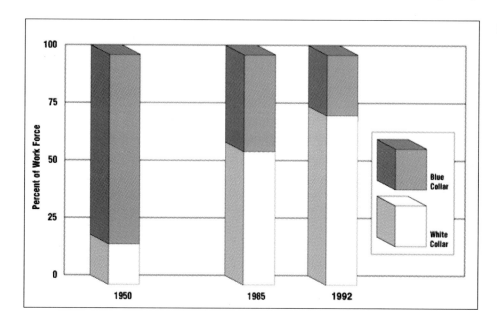

Fig. 16-3

White-collar workers make up 71 percent of the workforce.

workers illustrates this. A person might value the autonomy to set his or her own hours but also want (value, need) the safety a steady job affords. The temporary worker gives up the greater safety of a steady job.

In Chapter 11 you read of a negative consequence of mobility: that it can increase our alienation from fellow humans. We may fear forming relationships because we know they will not last. We sacrifice close relationships sometimes to meet our need for achievement.

▼ THE CHANGING WORKFORCE

As the nature and the character of work have been undergoing extensive changes, so has the workforce itself. Probably the single most significant change in this regard in the second half of the 1900s has been the increasing number of women outside the home. By 1992 almost 58 million women had entered the workforce. For an idea of the extent of this change, consider that as recently as 1970, only half of all women between the ages of 25 and 54 were in the workforce. By 1992, that number had risen to 75 percent. And these women were moving not only into the increasing number of service or office jobs but also into jobs customarily held by men. It is estimated that by the year 2000, 67 million women (80% of women between the ages of 25 and 54) will be in the workforce.

The movement of women from their traditional roles as homemakers or volunteers, or from limited low-paying jobs in the "pink-collar ghetto," continues to have major economic and psychological consequences. Because of the movement, our concepts of the family, rearing children, and the relative roles of men and women are changing. The line dividing these roles is no longer rigidly fixed. Other changes include the emergence of the dual-career family as common, a $1.6 billion child-care business to help working couples care for their children, and more discretionary income for young dual-career families.

As doors open, women enter the workforce to satisfy their need for self-fulfillment, recognition, more independence, and increased self-confidence, and to support their families. Their choices, though, are not always easy. Again they face conflicting needs and values, such as a need to have a family and a career at the same time. They are faced with the questions of when to have children, even whether to have them. Those having children then face the task of filling two, sometimes competing, roles—those of worker and mother. This creates stress for many. (You will read about dealing with stress in Chapter 18.)

Because society values the right and need of women to enter the workforce and also values family ties and women's roles as mothers, ways have been sought to help them fill both these desired roles. Laws require work organizations to grant women pregnancy leaves that enable them to have babies and enough time at home for their initial care. In 1993 Congress passed the *Family and Medical Leave Act*, which requires companies to allow parents (fathers as well as mothers) up to 18 weeks of unpaid leave to care for newly born or seriously ill children. The act reflects society's valuing of the family.

Minorities and People with Disabilities

Along with the increasing role of women in the workforce, the past three decades witnessed an increasing number of minorities and people with disabilities moving into occupations from which they had previously been excluded. This happened as a result of the growing realization in our society that these people had been systematically prevented from entering many types of jobs, just as women had.

This exclusion had, among other things, made it impossible for them to have the opportunity to develop their potential. As you read in Chapter 7, for many kinds of behavior your environment is crucial in your development. And in Chapter 10 you learned that for motivated behavior to be possible, three conditions must be met: you must be capable of the behavior, you must either require something from the environment or be required by the environment to carry out certain behavior, and *you must have opportunity*.

In the case of minorities, being kept out of many areas of the workforce prevented their learning and practice of particular behaviors, such as work skills. Even if many of these people—women, minorities, people with

Fig. 16-4

Women have more freedom today than they had in the past to develop satisfying careers in business and industry. To help them fulfill dual roles, society has enacted laws granting pregnant women leave of absence from work to have and care for their children.

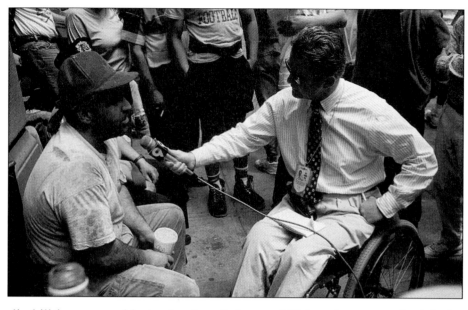

Fig. 16-5

Today many people with disabilities work in occupations from which they had previously been excluded.

affirmative action laws
laws enacted to correct the imbalance in employment opportunity for minorities and women

disabilities—were able to develop their capabilities, they were denied the opportunity to use them. In an effort to alter this situation and to provide equal opportunity to all, several laws were enacted.

As is often the case, it is sometimes easier to describe a problem than it is to correct it. Not everyone agrees with some of these laws or their interpretation. For example, statutes known as **affirmative action laws** have been strongly contested. These laws say that an organization in which there has been an obvious pattern of exclusion of women and minorities can and should take action to correct this pattern by hiring and promoting qualified women and minorities even if it means bypassing equally qualified or even more qualified white males. In 1987, the U.S. Supreme Court upheld affirmative action laws, saying employers may give preference to minorities and women as long as the purpose is to erase a "manifest imbalance in traditionally segregated job categories."

Affirmative action laws have been a source of debate because they embody conflicting values of our society. The laws' goal is to right a wrong by ensuring that people previously denied opportunity are now granted it even if it means passing over equally or more qualified white males. But doing this conflicts with the very value society is trying now to uphold, which is that people should be hired and promoted on the basis of their personal qualifications. The issues are subtle and troublesome and involve hard questions, such as whether denying jobs today to qualified white males to offset the results of past wrongs—for which they as individuals were not responsible—is not another form of discrimination itself. Societies, like individuals, must often contend with conflicting values.

The Broadening of Gender Roles

Women have not been the sole beneficiaries of the breaking down of the barriers that once limited their roles in the work environment. If it was found that women could perform work once considered the sole domain of men, the reverse was also true. Men could stay at home, for example, and raise children, to their own and their children's enrichment, without having to feel they were abandoning their "true" role. As noted earlier, companies may give unpaid leave to fathers as well as mothers to stay at home and care for their children.

In the working world, men have increasingly been moving into areas once dominated by women, as old stereotypes and perceptions have changed. Sometimes this movement by men into jobs once held exclusively by women was helped by such a simple thing as the changing of a job title: stewardess (female specific) became flight attendant (no gender indicated).

Men have moved into other fields dominated by women. For example, in the 22-year period between 1970 and 1992 the number of nurses who are men increased from 2.7 percent to 5.7 percent of the total.

The trend has also been seen in what is the country's second most overwhelmingly female occupation: that of secretary. (Dental hygiene is the most dominantly female occupation.) In the first half of the 1980s, the number of secretaries who are men doubled. Although they still make up only about 2 percent of the 4 million secretaries in the country, their numbers continue to grow. As with women, some men see the job of a secretary as a good entry-level position and a way to learn about a company in order to advance. Others see it as a career and a profession.

▼ THE MEANING OF WORK

The work environment is changing and complex. How do you fit in, not only in terms of a specific job but in terms of what work means to you? Because most of us must work for a living, the idea persists that work is something that we must do, as opposed to an activity that we want to do because it is enjoyable. Also, because our jobs and the wages received for them are closely intertwined, the idea is strongly entrenched that only work for which we receive money has value. Both these conceptions are faulty.

Even though we have been freed by technology from the unending toil previous generations had to endure simply to earn the necessities of life, we still must spend a great deal of time working. Because you spend the greater part of your adult waking hours working, you should strive to find a job that is satisfying and enjoyable. If you think that work is something you have to do without enjoyment, you will not make the effort to find that job you would enjoy.

Fig. 16-6

Men as well as women have benefitted from the breaking down of gender-specific barriers in the world of work. Men today find they can enter jobs once filled almost exclusively by women, such as that of secretary. Note that in the late 1800s, most secretaries were men. By the 1920s, most secretaries were women.

Although it is customary to define work in terms of money earned, this is not a completely valid definition. In 1972, a Special Task Force on Work in America defined work as "an activity that produces something of value for other people." The assumption may be that such work will be for pay, but the definition does not have payment as an integral part of it. This definition rests on the value of the work done, not the pay received for it. It is easy to think of work that people do without receiving a paycheck that produces something of value for others. The classic example, of course, is the homemaker who works, unpaid, to provide a nurturing, supportive environment for the family. Finding work of greater value to society than this would be difficult.

It is further misleading to use what people earn as a measure of their or their job's worth or value. In our society, a professional sports player can earn millions of dollars in a single year, whereas a master teacher in high school will earn about $40,000 in a year. The professional sports player gives us a few passing hours of excitement. The teacher influences our future as individuals as well as the collective future of our country. The pay each receives in no way reflects the relative value of their work to society.

As a measure of self-esteem, work is important to the extent that a person can take pride in it and feel successful in it. We want others to think highly of us, of course, but that alone is not enough. What others think is important, but other considerations may be more important. For example, a professional golfer who has won a round and is being congratulated may not feel satisfied. Her self-esteem could be low if she felt she played badly, no matter that she has won and that everyone else is saying how great she is. On the other hand, someone just learning to play the game may feel great about making a shot that any experienced player could have done with ease. Even though no one rushes up to tell the new player he played a great game, he still feels high self-esteem.

Work is also important because it helps define a person's role in society. It places people and determines their status. It is such a powerful influence in this regard that a whole family's status is often established by the type of work done by the head of the household. Often, however, status is mistakenly connected to money, which, as noted earlier, does not always reflect the true value of a particular occupation.

Thus, in addition to its fundamental purpose of supplying people with the means to earn a living, work is important because it gives people a sense of identity, provides a way for people to develop self-esteem, and helps establish a person's role or status in society.

▼ CAREERS, JOBS, FUNCTIONS, SKILLS

Careers, jobs, functions, skills: these are all related, but what do they mean? Just how are they related? What is their application to your actual working life? Let's define these concepts separately.

The Meaning of Career

As a rule when people speak of a **career** they mean employment for pay with a clear path for advancement or upward mobility. Some have applied the concept of a career very narrowly to the professions. Under this concept, you could have a career as a doctor, a lawyer, an educator, or an actor. Outside of professions such as these, according to this view, you did not have a career—you simply had a job.

career
how the individual makes a living; what you do with your life

Clearly, this concept of career leaves out the vast majority of people and the work they do throughout their lives. The implication is that most people only have jobs to earn a living, that is, to take care of their primary needs. But what about when those primary needs for food and shelter are satisfied? Everyone has higher-level needs, as you read, and once the lower-level needs are satisfied, a person will try to satisfy the higher ones. To satisfy your higher needs—esteem, self-respect, and self-actualization—you need a plan for life, for some meaningful activity. In short, a career.

This does not necessarily mean becoming a professional. It does mean planning your working life in such a way that you can satisfy higher- as well as lower-level needs. A job for pay may be central to your overall needs or it may be only a small part. Psychologists today see career as a process, a sequence of work-related experiences. What you decide to do to make your living and how you make your living is your career. It is what you do with your life. It may cover several kinds of jobs, or it may be only one. It is what brings you not only a living, but satisfaction.

The Job

Sometimes *job* and *career* are synonymous. An individual may make a career out of one job, such as being a secretary or an automobile mechanic. Sometimes *job* is only one part of a career, with a person moving through several jobs within a career. In the traditional Horatio Alger story, the individual begins as a gofer or clerk and moves through several jobs, finally becoming president of the company.

job
a group of positions with similar tasks

So, **job** refers to the specific work you are doing: chef, cashier, ballerina, computer programmer, or rock and roll singer. *Job* and *work* can mean the same thing, although narrowly speaking *job* refers to a group of positions with similar work, and *work* to what you actually do—your functions and tasks. As you will see, a job title is not always the best clue to what the job actually involves.

Functions, Tasks, and Skills

In an article in The New York Times[1] about a new staff member appointed in the White House, this sentence appeared: "Mr. Griscom's title is not assigned . . . but his function is already clearly defined. He has taken charge of the flow of paper, is assigning people to problems, and following through with options to the Oval Office." As the writer of this report was aware, the title by which a job is known does not necessarily reflect the functions to be performed.

Jobs with the same title could very well involve different functions, and jobs with different titles might involve similar functions. A job title is a convenient abstraction that makes it possible to think and talk about work in a generalized way without identifying all the functions and tasks involved. As you learned in Chapter 5, an abstraction is a general word or image that stands for the common characteristics of a group of similar individuals or images. Using abstractions can speed up our thought processes and communication. The danger is that in using abstractions, you might lose sight of the details that separate one thing from another. So it is with the use of job titles.

A prominent example of the fact that a job title does not always define the job is the title *secretary*. A person called a secretary might do some, all, or any combination of these activities:

- Typing
- Filing
- Taking dictation
- Transcribing dictation
- Scheduling meetings
- Greeting callers
- Screening visitors
- Making telephone calls
- Keeping an appointment calendar
- Making travel arrangements
- Doing simple bookkeeping
- Keeping expense accounts
- Preparing budgets
- Ordering supplies
- Opening and sorting mail
- Keeping the minutes of meetings
- Using a computer for word processing
- Data processing
- Creating graphics

Some job titles are more accurate indicators than others of what the work involves. Coal miner, fire fighter, and payroll clerk are examples of such descriptive titles. But even with such jobs, you will find that persons with these titles may do different things. A coal miner, for example, might work in an open pit as opposed to one underground. To understand fully what is involved in a particular job, you must look beyond the title to the functions and tasks involved.

Generally speaking, **function** defines the overall responsibilities of a specific job. It encompasses several tasks that require distinct skills to perform. For example, a secretary's function might be described as "preparing correspondence for mailing." This function would include the **tasks** of taking dictation, transcribing, typing or keyboarding, making corrections, addressing envelopes, mailing, and filing.

The tasks require skills of the secretary: shorthand or ability to use dictation equipment, typing or keyboarding, word processing. As you read in Chapter 6, skills are the basic units of response capability and are defined in terms of the tasks to be done. Skills are not only motor activities, such as typing, but also mental activities, such as remembering, reasoning, imagining, perceiving, sensing. For a secretary to file and retrieve a letter, memory and reasoning are clearly needed skills.

The functions, tasks, and skills required in a job are usually written down in summary form as a **job description**. Before you take a job or accept

function
the overall responsibilities of a specific job, encompassing several tasks

tasks
components of a job function that require distinct skills to perform

job description
a written summary of the functions, tasks, and skills required in a job

a job offer, it is a good idea to examine your job description carefully. The job description is part of the employment agreement between you and your employer. You should understand what functions you are expected to fulfill, what specific tasks you will be required to perform, what work skills you will need. For the employer's part, you should be held accountable only for those functions, tasks, and skills required as spelled out in the job description, and your performance appraisal should be based on it.

▼ WORK SUITABILITY

To be a satisfactory worker, you must find a work environment for which you have the necessary abilities to meet the job requirements. The work environment's requirements have ordinarily been described in terms of the functions or tasks to be performed. But the work environment's requirements can also be described in terms of other factors.

The tasks and functions, of course, are designed to meet the work organization's goals. Programming a computer to keep company records and using a word processor to type company letters are examples. A worker lacking technical or professional skills will not be suitable for a work environment requiring them and would not succeed in such an environment regardless of how appealing it might be.

Professional sports, for example, make up a work environment that appeals to many. It is an environment that meets several work needs: use of talent and abilities, opportunity for achievement and activity, high compensation, and much recognition. For most of us, however, there would be a big mismatch between a professional sports organization's goals and our ability to satisfy them. If you weigh 130 pounds, have poor physical coordination, and dislike physical contact, a career in professional football would not be suitable for you regardless of how satisfying the rewards might seem to you.

Lack of technical skills, however, is only one reason a person may not be suitable for a particular work environment. Lack of ability to adapt to the requirements of the work organization is another. For example, a person may have the technical skills to be a good construction worker, but if the person is afraid of heights, a construction company building skyscrapers may not be able to accommodate that person's desire to work close to the ground. Another example would be a work organization that requires employees to work overtime or to work on a flexible schedule or to work weekends. Other needs (family, social interests) may make it difficult or impossible for a worker to meet the company's need to use workers on a flexible schedule.

Some people have difficulty because their attitudes, morals, and other personal beliefs do not conform to the requirements of a particular

Fig. 16-7

A job title may not be an accurate indication of what the job involves. Even apparently obvious titles such as "coal miner" may involve different functions and tasks depending on whether the miner is working underground or in an open pit.

work environment. A person who believes that cigarette smoking is harmful will not fit into a job in an advertising agency whose main client is a tobacco company. A person concerned about nuclear waste would not be happy in a public utility running nuclear reactors.

▼ THE PERFECT CAREER

It may be impossible to find a career that fits you perfectly. Every job may have some aspects that do not suit you and lack some reinforcers that you would prefer to have. Also, you may not completely meet all the job requirements. The more you know of yourself and your prospective job, the better the chance of a "right choice."

Finding the right job is not an easy task. Herbert Greenberg, a clinical psychologist, estimates that as many as 80 percent of working Americans are in careers that are not satisfying to them. The symptoms of this failure are frustration, alienation from work, working for money only (reacting to extrinsic motivators alone), a dread of getting up in the morning, and an eagerness for breaks and quitting time. Considering that a person spends the greater part of life working, this is a sad situation.

Know Which Worker Traits Are Needed

What things in addition to the required skills are important to know about yourself and the job when selecting a career? One way to answer that question is to consider the general requirements—exclusive of specific skills—that jobs make on a worker. These requirements are many and they vary from job to job, but the U.S. Department of Labor, in its *Handbook for Analyzing Jobs* (1972), has organized them into six broad categories.

The handbook uses the phrase "Worker Traits" in discussing these attributes because the worker must possess them to meet the requirements of the job. Different jobs require different levels of different worker traits. Being aware of these general categories of requirements and the degree to which different jobs require them will allow you to analyze potential jobs to determine what their requirements are. You can then use your knowledge of yourself to judge whether you will be likely to achieve both satisfactoriness and satisfaction.

All jobs require certain worker traits. The handbook lists the following six categories of these traits:

TO THE POINT

Here are some examples of ordinary jobs defined in terms of functions and tasks.

TITLE: Chauffeur
Function: Provide private transportation
Tasks: Operate private car as required by owner or other passengers; assist passengers into and out of car; hold umbrellas in wet weather; keep car clean and polished; make minor repairs, fix flats, clean car, clean or change spark plugs, and adjust carburetor.

TITLE: Store detective
Function: Protect property and merchandise
Tasks: Protect property, merchandise, or money of store or similar establishment by detecting thieving, shoplifting, or other unlawful activities; gather information for use as evidence, know layout of building and area, be familiar with laws.

TITLE: Payroll clerk
Function: Prepare payrolls and maintain records
Tasks: Compute earnings from time sheets and work tickets using calculator or computer; operate computer or posting machine to post to payroll records deductions such as income tax withholding, social security payments, insurance, and credit union payments. Enter net wages on earnings record cards; prepare checks, check stubs, and payroll sheets.

Fig. 16-8

It's important to know which worker traits an employer wants.

"We're looking for somebody who's really special . . . somebody smart enough to do this job but dumb enough to take it . . .

1. Training
2. Aptitudes
3. Interests
4. Temperament
5. Physical requirements
6. Working conditions

Let us examine these six worker traits to achieve a practical understanding of job requirements. You can measure your suitability for specific jobs against these requirements and plan ways to acquire the necessary worker traits for a career of your choosing.

Each trait has subcategories that provide more detail. For example, the Training category is broken down into General Educational Development (GED) and Specific Vocational Preparation (SVP). GED refers to training or education that is applicable to a wide range of jobs. SVP refers to training for a particular job or group of jobs. Similarly, the other five traits each have their particular subcategories. Figure 16-7 lists the six worker traits and their subcategories, as well as the different levels that apply to some subcategories.

Training

Training, as you have read, refers to overall educational development as well as the specific vocational training a worker must possess to be qualified for a particular job.

Fig. 16-9

Six worker traits

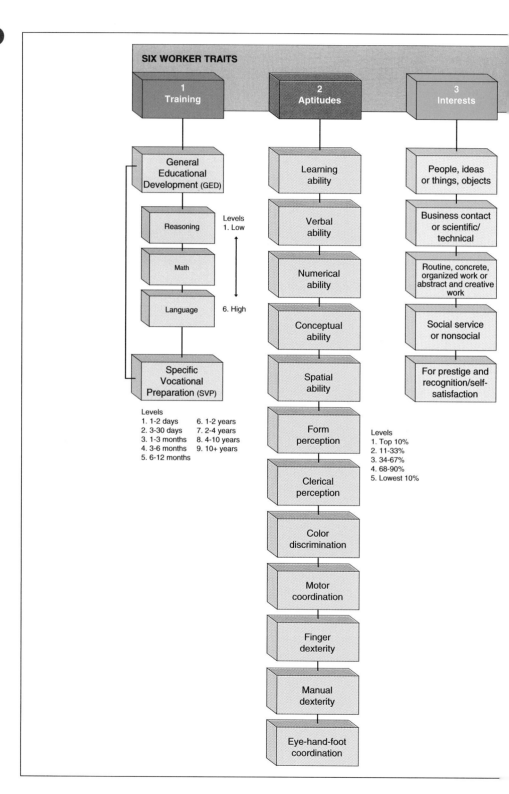

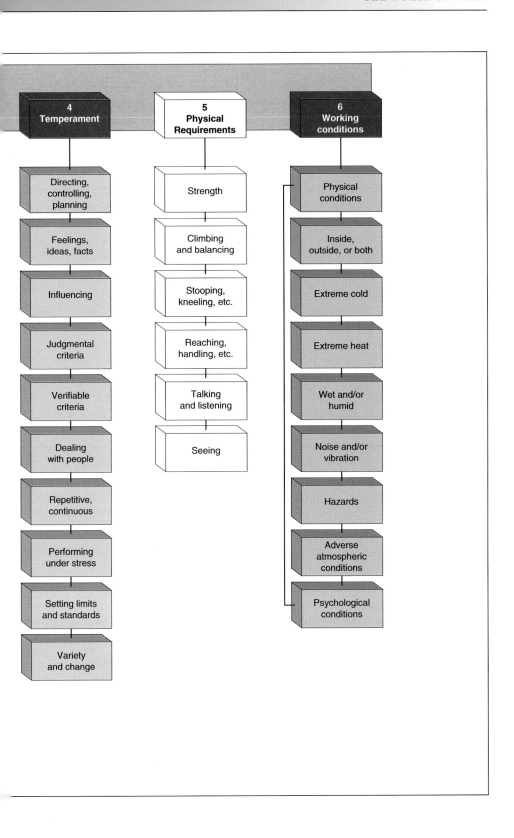

General Educational Development

General Educational Development (GED) refers to your formal and informal education and the extent to which you have developed your reasoning powers, your ability to use language, and your mathematical skills. These three broad areas of GED are listed in the U.S. Department of Labor handbook as Reasoning Development, Mathematical Development, and Language Development.

The handbook identifies six levels of development within each of these areas. Table 16-1 shows the levels, with examples of jobs corresponding to each level. These levels and samples are not precise but can be used as general guides. Also, most jobs would require a combination of the three, although not necessarily all at the same level.

Specific Vocational Preparation

The SVP scale quantifies the amount of time a worker would need to spend learning particular vocational skills to perform a job at a satisfactory level. The time involved, as defined by the handbook, is in addition to time spent in general educational development. Nine levels of vocational preparation are identified, ranging from those that require only a short demonstration to those requiring more than ten years of preparation. The levels with sample jobs are shown in Table 16-2.

Aptitude

aptitude
the special capabilities and natural talents that enable the individual to learn and perform selected jobs

As you read in Chapter 6, your **aptitude** is your potential to learn and perform a particular job. Aptitude is as important as training. If you lack the aptitude for a particular job, even extensive training is not likely to make you a master of it. Given strong aptitude for something and appropriate training, however, you can develop a successful career.

Nancy Kerrigan liked to ice skate when she was very young. Someone noticed her skill in skating, guessed that she had the aptitude for the sport, and arranged for her to have intensive coaching. This coaching enabled her to develop a natural aptitude into a career as a champion figure skater. Note that though you may not go far without aptitude, having aptitude will not alone guarantee success either. You must have coaching as Ms. Kerrigan did and, of course, the opportunity to use your talent.

Exceptional aptitude combined with lots of hard training and opportunity creates star performers in any field. You do not need to become a star, though, to have a successful career or simply to enjoy an activity. Few people have the aptitude to become star tennis players, but thousands have

TABLE 16-1

Areas and Levels of General Educational Development		
Area One: Reasoning		
Level	Description	Sample Tasks or Jobs
1	Use commonsense understanding to carry out simple one-or two-step instructions in routine situations with few or no changes.	Stencil identifying names or numbers on cartons; cover dry-cleaned clothing and household articles with plastic bags; sort articles for delivery; tend bandsaw; clean or pack eggs
2	Use commonsense understanding to carry out detailed but straight-forward written or oral instructions and deal with a few concrete variables.	Crossing guard, messenger, self-service laundry attendant
3	Use commonsense understanding to carry out instructions in written, oral, or diagrammatic form as well as deal with problems involving several concrete variables.	Answering service operator, shipping order clerk, molding machine operator, practical nurse
4	Use rational systems to perform work that requires solving practical problems and handling of a mixture of concrete variables for which there are only limited guidelines. Be able to understand a variety of instructions given in written, oral, diagram, or schedule form.	Electrician, internal combustion engine inspector, secretary, general duty nurse
5	Use principles of logical or scientific thinking to define problems, collect data, establish facts, and draw valid conclusions. Interpret large variety of technical instructions in mathe-matical or diagrammatic form. Work with several abstract as well as concrete variables.	Caseworker, claim agent
6	Use principles of logical or scientific thinking to handle a wide range of intellectual and practical problems. Work with nonverbal symbolism (formulas, scientific equations, graphs, musical notes, etc.). Deal with many abstract and concrete variables and understand obscure concepts.	Experimental psychologist, archae-ologist, judge, theoretical physicist

TABLE 16-1, continued

Area Two: Mathematical Development		
Level	Description	Sample Tasks or Jobs
1	Add and subtract two-digit numbers. Multiply and divide 10s and 100s by 2, 3, 4, and 5. Do necessary arithmetic to make change with a dollar. Understand units of measure for liquids, length, and weight (pint and quart; inch, foot, and yard; and ounce and pound).	Packing weigher, dipper (dips sheets of muslin in shellac), tender of some automatic machines
2	Add, subtract, multiply, and divide all units of measure and like or common decimal fractions. Calculate ratios, rates, and percentages; draw and read bar graphs; and handle all units of American money.	Sales route driver
3	Compute discount, interest, profit and loss, commissions, markups, and selling price using ratios, proportions, and percentages. Know algebra and geometry.	Payroll clerk, auto rental clerk, metals inspector
4	Have advanced knowledge of algebra (quadratic, rational, exponential, logarithmic, angle, and circular functions) and geometry (deductive axiomatic, plane and solid, and rectangular coordinates), and essentials of trigonometry. Able to apply in practical shop situations.	Quality-control technician, bookkeeper, surveyor
5	Know algebra, using exponents and logarithms, linear equations, quadratic equations, mathematical induction, and binomial theorem. Know calculus and statistics.	Civil engineer, industrial engineer
6	Know advanced calculus and know modern algebra. Work with mathematical statistics, mathematical probability, experimental design, statistical inference, and econometrics.	Physics professor, economics professor

TABLE 16-1, continued

Area Three: Language Development		
Level	Description	Sample Tasks or Jobs
1	Have 2,500 word vocabulary, read 95–120 words per minute; print and speak simple sentences using normal word order.	Deliveryperson (newspapers, telephone directories, following oral instructions or address list)
2	Have passive vocabulary of 5–6,000 words; read at rate of 190–215 words per minute; use dictionary for meaning, spelling, and pronunciation; follow simple written instructions, such as for assembling model airplanes.	Waiter, waitress
3	Read novels, magazines, atlases, encyclopedias; write reports and essays with proper format, punctuation, spelling, and grammar; speak before audiences, using correct English.	Typist, service station attendant (able to answer questions about repairs; give motorists directions)
4	Read novels, poems, newspapers, periodicals, journals, manuals, dictionaries, thesauruses, and encyclopedias; write business letters, expositions, reports following all rules of grammar and punctuation; speak in panel discussions, dramatizations, debates.	Employment interviewer, insurance sales agent
5	Read literature, reviews, scientific or technical journals, abstracts, financial reports, legal documents; write novels, plays, editorials, journals, speeches, poetry, songs, manuals; be effective and persuasive speaker.	Professional writer, newspaper reporter
6	Essentially same as Level 5, but even more advanced.	Corporation lawyer, college or university professor

TABLE 16-1, continued

Time Needed for Specific Vocational Preparation		
Level	Time	Sample Jobs
1	1-2 days	Packaging goods for shipment, stock clerk (put stock on shelves)
2	3-30 days	Library assistant, change-booth cashier, artist's model
3	1-3 months	Assistant in a greenhouse tending plants
4	3-6 months	Nursing aide, corrections officer, tractor-trailer truck driver
5	6-12 months	Secretary and stenographer, typewriter and office machine repairer
6	1-2 years	Bookkeeper, insurance sales agent
7	2-4 years	Kitchen supervisor, blaster
8	4-10 years	Industrial chemist, pastry chef
9	Over 10 years	Museum director, composer, managing editor

enough aptitude to become competent players, perhaps even neighborhood champions, and enjoy playing the game. In a career, success and satisfaction do not need to mean reaching the top so much as finding what you enjoy doing, finding the highest level at which you are good, reaching it, and doing it.

There are many different kinds of abilities by which aptitude can be assessed. The Handbook for Analyzing Jobs identifies 11 that are required to a greater or lesser degree for most occupations. Consider these work-related abilities when selecting a job. To achieve success and satisfaction, your abilities should match the job's requirements.

General Cognitive Ability

General cognitive ability refers to how well you can understand new information. If you can understand instructions and basic principles easily, can reason and make judgments, you have high learning ability. How well you do in school is an indication of this ability.

Verbal Ability

Verbal ability is the ability to understand and use words effectively. You need this ability to do well in school. Although closely related to intelligence, verbal ability is not the same. Because thinking is commonly expressed by speaking, verbal ability is often confused with intelligence. Do not underestimate intelligent people who are not glib speakers or overestimate the intelligence of those who are.

Fig. 16-10

Midori Ito, Kristy Yamaguchi, and Nancy Kerrigan all showed an aptitude for ice skating at young ages. They all had the opportunity to develop that aptitude through intensive training and then became Olympic medalists.

Numerical Ability

A person with numerical ability finds it easy to work with numbers—not only to add, subtract, multiply, and divide but also to reason with numbers. As with the two previous abilities, numerical ability is associated with academic success. Scores on tests of numerical ability can be used to predict grades in math, accounting, or other academic subjects involving numbers.

Spatial Ability

People with this ability are able to think visually about objects or forms of two or three dimensions and recognize the relationships of objects in space. Those who have high spatial ability may have the aptitude for careers as architects, industrial designers, drafters, or visual artists. Spatial ability is required, for example, to read or sketch blueprints or wiring diagrams.

Form Perception

Form perception is the ability to notice important details in objects or in pictorial or graphic material. It is the ability to make visual comparisons, to discriminate, and to see small differences in shapes and shadings of figures and the widths and lengths of lines. This ability is important for careers in the graphic arts (printing, engraving, typesetting), for example.

Detail Perception

Detail perception is the ability to perceive pertinent detail in verbal or tabular materials. Detail perception has the same relationship to words and numbers that form perception has to pictures and graphs. A high level of this ability is essential in business and office occupations. This ability has become increasingly important in this age of information as more and more workers are needed to work in offices processing data.

Color Discrimination

Color discrimination is the ability to recognize and compare different colors in terms of hue, saturation, and brilliance. Hue refers to the color itself, saturation to the purity of the color, and brilliance to the brightness of the color.

Note: All of the abilities discussed so far are *cognitive*, that is, they take place in your brain. The processes themselves cannot be seen, and as you read in Chapter 8, cognitive psychologists developed ingenious experiments to draw conclusions about what happens when you think. The remaining abilities pertain to motor skills, and although your brain is involved, of course, the actual motor processes are more easily seen.

The remaining four abilities, although the brain is involved, can be grouped together as motor abilities.

Motor Coordination

Motor coordination refers to the ability to coordinate your eyes and hands or fingers rapidly and accurately. Dentists or dental technicians using drills and other dental tools must possess this ability to a high degree.

Fig. 16-11

Motor abilities are very important in many occupations. You would probably not enjoy either the process or the result if a person with little or no finger dexterity styled or cut your hair.

Finger Dexterity

Finger dexterity is the ability to move your fingers accurately and rapidly to manipulate small objects. A concert pianist would have this ability to the highest degree, as would surgeons. Barbers and hair stylists, television and computer repairers also need to have this ability at a high level.

Manual Dexterity

Manual dexterity is moving the hands easily and skillfully. Juggling, for example, requires a high degree of manual dexterity. Meat cutters and butchers must possess this ability. Many manufacturing jobs require this ability, as do those of fire fighters and service station attendants.

Eye-Hand-Foot Coordination

Eye-hand-foot coordination refers to the ability to move your eyes, hands, and feet together in a coordinated way. This type of coordination is needed when shifting gears in a car with manual transmission. A gymnast, such as Mary Lou Retton, who in 1984 became the first American woman to win an Olympic gold medal for all-around performance, must be at the highest level of this ability.

Interests

Interests represent another category of worker traits identified as among those for which there should be a match between worker and job. Any career will require aptitude, but to have a satisfying career, you need more than the aptitude for it. You might be able to perform the job well, but not enjoy it especially.

Chapter 10 defined interests as your liking or disliking for activities. If you have an interest in a specific career, you will more likely persist in pursuing it in spite of difficulties. Donald Super and John Crites identified four types of interests in their book *Appraising Vocational Fitness*:

- **Expressed interests**: Specific interests made known by the interested person. You state your interest: "I like to work out doors. "

- **Manifest interests**: Interests expressed through participation in activities. By continuing to do something you like, you display—manifest—an interest in it.

- **Inventoried interests**: Estimates of your interests based on your responses to a large number of questions about your likes and dislikes.

- **Tested interests**: Interests manifested under controlled conditions, as opposed to those shown under actual situations.

One of the reasons for dissatisfaction among workers is their failure to consider their interests before exploring the world of work to find careers that suit them. Standardized measures for determining interests can help you discover interests that you might not realize you have. Your counselor can advise you in selecting an inventory that will help you choose a career.

Temperament

The dictionary defines **temperament** as a characteristic or habitual inclination or mode of emotional response. If you enter a job for which you are not temperamentally suited, you will not have the best chance of succeeding. When selecting a career, you should consider the kind of temperament that would most suit the job requirements.

temperament
a characteristic or habitual inclination or mode of emotional response

This can be difficult because it is easy to be misled about what a job requires in the way of temperament. For example, many shy people have found great success in the performing arts, even though on the surface it might appear that the performing arts should be the last career a shy person considers. A person with a retiring temperament might seem an unlikely candidate to succeed as a journalist, yet I. F. Stone, too retiring to ask questions at press conferences, was one of the most successful journalists of his day.

The success of people despite an apparent mismatch of temperament and job might be explained in two ways:

1. Their interest and aptitude were so great as to overcome the difficulties resulting from the apparent mismatch.

2. The job did not really require the temperament it appeared to.

In any event, the more you know about your own temperament and what a prospective career requires, the better able you will be to find a suitable career.

The *Handbook for Analyzing Jobs* defines ten broad categories of temperaments required for particular kinds of work environments. In reading the descriptions of temperaments below, think about yourself and which categories best describe you.

Directing, Controlling, Planning

This temperament accepts responsibility for planning, directing, and controlling the activities of others—will oversee entire projects or programs, plan for future. People with this temperament are found in the ranks of professionals, such as architects, teachers, business and project managers, accountants, and lawyers.

Feelings, Ideas, Facts

People with this temperament adapt to situations requiring the interpretation of feelings, ideas, or facts in terms of their personal viewpoint. Original and creative people—artists, photographers, choreographers, conductors, writers, and high-level computer programmers—have this temperament.

Influencing

The temperament to influence others is right for jobs that require motivating, convincing, or negotiating with others. Good salespersons, lobbyists, and group leaders have this temperament.

Sensory or Judgmental Criteria

This temperament generalizes, evaluates, or makes decisions on the basis of data received through the physical senses or on the basis of prior experience. Lawyers, interior decorators, and test pilots have this temperament.

Fig. 16-12

People whose temperaments make them good at influencing others can succeed at jobs that require them to function as counselors or group leaders.

Measurable or Verifiable Criteria

This temperament prefers to make judgments or decisions based on measurable, verifiable data. People with this temperament have become ship's captains, doctors, physical scientists.

Dealing With People

Persons with this temperament like to work with people to a greater extent than in simply giving or receiving instructions. They are suitable for jobs such as managers, salespersons, appointment secretaries, employment claims aides.

Repetitive, Continuous

People with this temperament adapt to performing repetitive work or doing the same thing continuously, following set procedures or processes. Persons with this temperament would be suitable on an assembly line, running automated machines, entering data into a computer, or typing addresses.

Performing Under Stress

People with this temperament are able to work under stress, handle emergencies, and handle critical, unusual, or dangerous situations. They are suitable for jobs in which speed and accuracy are essential elements. These people are found in such careers as deep sea or scuba divers, emergency medical technicians, fire fighters, animal trainers, racing car drivers, and police officers.

Setting Limits, Tolerances, Standards

People with this temperament like precise, exacting, meticulous work. Jobs for people with this temperament include that of pharmacist, operator of precision machinery such as diamond cutters, and secretary.

Variety and Change

This temperament is common in people who have the ability to move from one task to another task without loss of efficiency or composure. Good secretaries have this temperament. People with this temperament are suitable to be flight attendants, elementary school teachers, service station attendants, or organizers of recreational, physical education, or cultural programs.

Physical Requirements

All jobs make some physical requirements of workers, even the most sedentary—those that can be done sitting at a desk. In selecting a career, you must consider the extent to which you can meet the physical requirements.

Often the physical requirements of a job are apparent, so that matching them with your physical traits is easy. But that is not always the case. As with temperament, it is sometimes not easy to judge accurately the degree of physical requirements for a particular job, or, conversely, to determine a worker's physical suitability.

For example, people used to believe automatically that some jobs were not suitable for women because of the physical requirements. As more facts have been gathered, such perceptions have changed. Today women perform many jobs that it was once believed only men could do, such as those of fire fighter. Also, workers with disabilities today fill jobs that were once believed to be beyond their physical capacity.

The U.S. Department of Labor *Handbook for Analyzing Jobs* identifies six categories of physical demands jobs make on workers:

1. Strength, including what is required for standing, walking, sitting, lifting, carrying, pushing, or pulling

2. Climbing and balancing

3. Stooping, kneeling, crouching, and crawling

4. Reaching, handling, fingering, and feeling

5. Talking and listening

6. Seeing

As you can see, the physical requirements are defined largely in terms of functions that you must perform to carry out job-related tasks. Consider your own physical characteristics in terms of the functions on this list.

Working Conditions

Working conditions are an important aspect of the work environment that you should consider when looking for a suitable career. Working conditions can be either physical or psychological. Your temperament, interests, and aptitudes help determine your reaction to different working conditions.

Physical Conditions

The U.S. Department of Labor handbook identifies seven physical conditions workers encounter on different jobs:

1. Inside, outside, or both (carpenters, for example)

2. Extreme cold, with or without temperature changes (ice cream storage workers, for example, or scientists working in the Antarctic)

3. Extreme heat, with or without temperature changes (foundry workers, boiler tenders)

4. Wet and/or humid (garment pressers, fish cleaners, car wash attendants)

5. Noise and/or vibration (jackhammer operators, spinning machine operators, riveters)

6. Hazards (fire fighters, police officers, blasters)

7. Adverse atmospheric conditions (workers exposed to fumes, odors and toxic particles, such as in coal mines, cotton mills, chemical factories)

     Many jobs involve unpleasant physical conditions that workers must endure if they are committed to a career. Federal and state laws have been enacted to protect the safety of workers. These laws establish basic conditions that a company must meet to protect workers. For example, in factories where the noise level is high, the company is required to supply earplugs or take other steps to reduce the noise. When a job is dangerous, workers are required to take safety precautions. In jobs that expose workers to harmful fumes, laws require that air filters be issued and adequate ventilation be provided.

Psychological Conditions

Psychological conditions refer to what can be called the **work climate** or the style of the company. Is it easygoing and relaxed? Is it tense and regimented? Is it fast- or slow-paced?

    The work climate includes the leadership system. Is it harsh and dictatorial or open and free? Is the organization power-oriented? If so, you would like it if you valued power. If you valued achievement for its own sake, you may be unhappy in a power-oriented company.

Fig. 16-13

You cannot always tell who might succeed in a job on the basis of physical requirements. A woman may not appear to have the physical qualifications to be an electrical line repair worker, yet some women are.

work climate
the psychological conditions in a work environment

The size of a company is another aspect of working conditions to consider. The size of a company straddles physical and psychological conditions. Some people like working in large organizations. Some prefer smaller, more personal working conditions. The conditions can vary between large and small organizations. Knowing which you prefer can help you select the career in which you will most likely be satisfied.

Finding a Satisfying Work Environment

What makes a satisfying work environment differs, of course, for each person. Some studies, however, have indicated general vocational needs that most people rate highly. A study of high school students, for example, found that they rated these as the four most important work needs:

1. Use of abilities
2. Achievement (feeling of accomplishment)
3. Security
4. Advancement

These students listed the following work needs as the least important to them:

- Authority
- Independence (working alone)
- Social status
- Activity (being busy)

If these students found themselves in a work environment that only gave them authority and independence they might not achieve satisfaction. Of course, what the students rate as important before employment can change when they enter an actual work environment. Also, what a person feels is important can change over the years. Further, high school students in different eras may very well identify different needs as important or unimportant.

It is worth noting that this study found that although the vocational needs of all students were similar, there were differences between what young men and young women identified as most important needs. More young women than young men felt that they would be most satisfied in a job that made them feel they were performing a social service.

You probably recognized the work needs rated by the high school study as taken from the Minnesota Importance Questionnaire (MIQ), which you read about in Chapter 10 in a discussion of psychological needs and motivation. These work needs were referred to again in Chapter 11 in regard to work reinforcers. These work needs are also related to the hierarchy of needs identified by Maslow: basic physiological needs (food, sleep, and shelter), safety (security), affection, esteem, and self-actualization.

Although we tend to satisfy the needs on Maslow's hierarchy in order, different needs are important to different people and they may also change for the same person over time. To find a satisfying work environment, you should know what is important to you—what your needs are in terms of what you value. You must also, of course, know which jobs will provide the reinforcers that for you are important.

To make a satisfying career choice in a changing work environment that offers thousands of different possibilities, you should have a clear idea of what your needs, values, and interests are, because they are what motivate you. You will change and adapt your needs, values, and interests through the years but will always retain a basic cast that will inform your life.

The better you are able to clarify and understand your needs, values, and interests, the better you will be able to pick a satisfying occupation or career. If you really do not like working with people, you would probably not be happy in a job such as flight attendant no matter how much you like flying and traveling. Of course, liking a particular career does not necessarily mean you will succeed in it. You must possess the aptitude necessary to acquire the required skills and the temperament and interest to perform the work.

▼ DECISION MAKING IN A CHANGING WORLD

Because so many options exist and technology continues to transform the world of work, you will constantly face the need to make decisions. Your values, needs, and interests will shape the decisions you make, especially those affecting your overall life goals. Just as with any other mental process, you can follow an organized system of decision making to improve your chances of making the best one.

You make decisions constantly. You decide when to get up in the morning, what to wear, how to get to work or school, what to eat for breakfast. Most of these decisions you make automatically. They do not require much conscious thought. Sometimes the decision you must make is not so simple. Sometimes there is a conflict. Because of their increased opportunities, people today often face a conflict when deciding on whether or when to start a family or deciding between a career that will consume most of their time and one that will allow them more time with their families. To make the right decision in such situations—and there is no one decision that will be "right" for everyone—each individual must use her or his decision-making skills to select the best possible course.

When a decision, such as what career you will enter, will have far-reaching effects, you should spend additional time and effort to make a thoughtful and reasoned choice. In making a decision about your career, you must assess as many factors as possible. It is impossible to make a career decision with 100 percent certainty that it is the one and only choice. But it is possible to make a decision with a greater probability of success if you follow a logical decision-making process.

A decision, however, is never final. You can always change it, even a career decision. That does not mean you should be casual about making such decisions, but it does mean that you should not be afraid to make them. Some people become so fearful that one career decision made now will be the only chance they will have that they find it impossible to decide. Your initial career choices are major choices, but that is not the last time you will have to make a decision about your career, especially in the changing work environment.

All decisions entail some risk because they deal with the future and no one can foretell the future with certainty. The more you know about yourself and the present, though, the less risk you face in the future.

To ensure you make the best choice possible for yourself, follow the simple process given below when facing a major decision. Note how the steps parallel the problem-solving process you read of in Chapter 5.

- Recognize that a choice exists.
- Generate alternatives.
- Evaluate each alternative.
- Decide on one alternative.
- Act on your decision.
- Review.

Recognize That a Choice Exists

Because of technological and social changes, you have more options than ever before from which to choose. But if you are not aware of this, you won't be in position to make a good career choice. You might be inclined to take the first job that comes along. Whether jobs are plentiful or scarce, taking whatever happens to crop up when you look is not the best way to start a meaningful career.

People often make wrong decisions by failing to realize options do in fact exist. This is true in many situations, not only in deciding on a career. People who make the serious mistake of experimenting with drugs fail to recognize that they have other choices. Before taking any serious step, always remind yourself that choices exist, and look for them. In terms of careers, for instance, school, the experience of others, newspapers, books, and particularly reference books about careers are all ways to learn that choices exist and what these might be.

Generate Alternatives

This second step in the decision-making process is related to the first, but it involves making a more detailed examination of the choices that do exist and selecting the most promising ones for further evaluation. The important thing at this step is to think of as many realistic alternatives as possible. The more, the better for an eventually sound decision. Many people skimp at this point and do not generate enough possible alternatives. At times few choices may exist. Often, however, people do not take the time to gather information about all the alternatives that do in fact exist.

Few people are really adept at seeking information. This is a skill that must be learned. In making your career decisions, you must identify as many sources of educational and career information as possible, using career counselors, employment agencies, and want ads.

All the information you gather should enable you to list several possible alternatives in terms of your needs, values, interests, abilities, and aptitudes. Without enough information, people will sometimes make the mistake of excluding potential alternatives. For example, if a person liked working with people, particularly teaching, and also liked working outdoors, with only limited information she might decide she had to give up one of her interests because no jobs could satisfy both. To teach or work with people usually requires indoor work. However, a careful search would reveal possible jobs that do cover both interests, such as a ranger in the National Park Service, a naturalist, and a camp counselor.

Evaluate Each Alternative

Once you have generated as many alternatives as possible, you should then examine each one thoroughly and try to determine the consequences of taking each one. This is a weeding-out process. As far as you can, decide to what extent you will be satisfactory and satisfied in each of the various possible occupations. To do this, you must take into consideration what you require of the job and what the job will require from you.

It will probably not be possible to find the perfect job that will indeed satisfy all your needs. You must decide which needs and values are most important in terms of bringing you satisfaction. Most careers will probably combine elements that you want and need with ones you do not want and dislike. You must learn enough about the occupation to determine whether the part you like will be a strong enough reinforcer to counter the part you do not care for. For example, you might like working with people but dislike paperwork. Yet many jobs that allow you to work with people, such as a social worker or personnel official, require doing a lot of paperwork.

This step in the decision-making process requires you to look closely at the relationship between what you do and what effect the action will have. You might think about leaving college. You must try to imagine what effect that will have on future career choices and even on the reactions of others: If you decide to leave school, your parents will be disappointed, so you need to ask yourself if you can live with that. If you leave school, a particular career you wanted may be out of reach. Another example is a career choice that requires you to move to another part of the country or to live in a city. If you are interested in a career in television, you will almost certainly have to live in or near a city. If you do not enjoy urban living, you will have to be sure your career satisfies you enough in other respects to offset this.

objective data
statistics and other factual information

Objective data are necessary in evaluating the consequences of each alternative. But you must also consider the emotional effects of a decision. Personal values and feelings about oneself are especially important when making decisions about education and careers. You cannot eliminate the emotional and subjective part of decision making. You must be aware of its influence.

For example, Anne had strong mathematical ability and training, and job opportunities in computer programming were available to her. These objective facts all suggested that she consider a career in computing. Her subjective reaction, however, was unfavorable. She was not interested in working with computers. She was interested in playing the piano. Objective information showed that she also had an aptitude for this career. But the objective information also showed that there were fewer job opportunities for a pianist. Nonetheless, she decided that the emotional satisfaction a career in music would bring her was worth it. If she finds she cannot make enough money as a pianist to support herself, she may subsequently need to make another career decision. If she has generated enough alternatives, she may find one that combines both interests, perhaps programming a computer synthesizer to create music.

It is a good idea at this stage to rank your alternative careers in order of their importance to you. One way of doing this is to list them on a piece of paper along with your goals—make a lot of money, help people, retire early, whatever. You can write goals in one column, all the alternative careers in a second column, and the most likely ranking of the alternative careers in terms of meeting your goals in the third column. You are looking for the one "best" decision for you, but ranking your alternatives allows you to have a practical backup plan if for some unforeseen reason you cannot follow up on your first decision.

For example, Joel, a young high school graduate, faced the problem of what to do next and decided he wanted to enter a college premedical program to start training to be a doctor. A second choice was to train to be a paramedic. As it happened, Joel was not accepted into any premedical program, and so he turned to his next best alternative and trained as a paramedic. With this training, he became better qualified for more advanced study in medicine, which he could use to help him in a future attempt to enter a premedical training program. It is good to rank several alternatives to provide a backup course of action if necessary.

A useful tool to help you organize and evaluate your alternatives and relevant data is a **decision-making matrix**. This is simply a grid with your short- and long-term goals listed down the side and your alternative careers across the top. Using the information you have gathered about each alternative, you can check the appropriate box opposite each goal that may be fulfilled by that alternative. The alternative with the most check marks would be your top choice. You can refine this process by rating the alternatives on a simple scale of 1 to 3 according to how effectively they help you achieve each goal. The alternative with the highest numeric value would be the logical career choice.

decision-making matrix
a tool to help organize data and evaluate alternatives consisting of a grid with short- and long-term goals listed down the side and alternatives across the top

Fig. 16-14

Career decisions chart.

Career Decision Chart

Summer Jobs

		Bank teller	Construction worker	Invest in own hotdog stand
Short-term goals	Money for college	1	3	2
	Experience in accounting	3	1	3
Long-term goals	Degree in accounting	3	2	2
	CPA's license	3	1	1
	Own business	2	1	3
	Totals	12	8	11

Imagine, for example, that your problem is deciding what to do during summer vacation. Assume you have generated three possible summer jobs in your search for alternatives: working as a bank teller, doing outside construction work, or investing some money in equipment and supplies and having your own hot dog vending cart. Also imagine that your short-term goals are earning money for college and gaining experience for your future career. Your long-term goals are earning a degree in accounting, obtaining a certified public accountant's license, and, eventually, owning your own business. You arbitrarily rank your alternatives on a scale of 1 (lowest) to 3 (highest) in terms of how much they contribute to each goal. The matrix is shown in Figure 16-14.

Decide on an Alternative

This is the crucial step. By itself it takes only the few seconds for you to think, "That's it! I'll do it." These few seconds, though, should reflect the hours of work and thought that went into the previous steps. To help you reach this step, it might help to give yourself a deadline for making the decision. Deadlines are often forced on you, but if they are not, give yourself one that allows you ample time to examine the alternatives.

Act on Your Decision

The best decision means nothing until you act on it. Once you have identified your best alternative, act. This can mean seeking appropriate training, either on the job or through more formal training. Unlike the decision step, which can be done in an instant (after all the preliminary steps), acting on your career decision is a continuing project that will continue over the years.

Review Your Decision

No decision is forever. And no decision, no matter how carefully prepared, is so perfect that you will never need to review it. In the first place, it is impossible to tell what the future will really be, and all decisions must contend with the future. Conditions change. You change. New opportunities arise. Interests and aptitudes you were unaware of emerge through experience.

For example, a man who spent most of his adult life as a welder, working with things and not people, was once asked to explain the career of a welder in general terms to students at a local high school. The welder did and enjoyed the experience so much that he became interested in teaching.

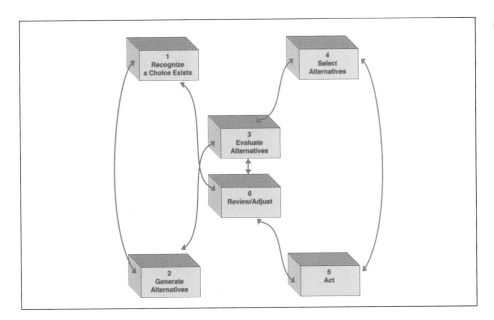

Fig. 16-15

The decision-making process can be thought of as a "lazy" figure eight. The steps in the process occur along this continuously flowing line without stopping the process.

When a position opened up for an instructor in welding at the night adult education course, he applied and was hired for the job. Eventually, he gave up welding for a living and became a full-time teacher. He was very satisfied with his new career.

The important thing in this changing world is to have a plan based on your knowledge of yourself and of available careers, keeping alert to the changing environment as well as changes in yourself. This will not guarantee satisfaction, but it will make it a lot more likely.

Many decisions are important, but few are forever. For a satisfying life, be ready to review major decisions and adjust to changes in yourself and in your environment. You can think of the decision-making process as represented by a continuously flowing self-contained line that takes the shape of a "lazy" figure eight, as shown in Figure 16-15. The steps in the decision-making process occur along this line, and although each step has consequences that interact with the other steps, none permanently stops the process, which can begin again at any point in reaction to new stimuli.

SUMMARY

1. Because of technological changes, we no longer need to work constantly just to fulfill our basic physiological needs. Although this is welcome, a result has been that our higher-level needs—for belonging, the esteem of others, self-esteem, and self-actualization—have become more important to us. Our higher-level needs can be difficult to meet. And even though failure to meet these needs does not usually result in death, the result is often suffering and dissatisfaction.

2. As a result of technology, we have moved from a society in which the major problem was how to produce enough to meet our needs into one in which the major problem is how to use everything we can produce. Also, as more people had more time and money, the concept grew that leisure time was acceptable and one did not need to spend all of one's time in productive work.

3. There has been a change in the United States from a predominantly production economy to a predominantly service economy, which is reflected in the workforce. Fewer people (blue-collar workers) work in factories and farms and more (white-collar workers) work in offices and the profession.

4. The workforce has become increasingly mobile through transfer within companies, through people moving from company to company for advancement, and through increasing numbers of people becoming temporary workers.

5. Probably the single most significant change in the workforce itself in the second half of the 1900s has been caused by the increasing number of women working outside the home.

6. The movement of women into the workforce has changed our concepts of the family, child rearing, and the relative roles of men and women. The line dividing these roles is no longer rigidly fixed.

7. Having more options has increased the potential for conflict between values and interests. Women particularly face the need to reconcile interests in having children while having a career. Society has attempted to help solve such conflicts with laws such as the Family and Medical Leave Act, requiring companies to grant unpaid leave for pregnancies and time off for parents (fathers as well as mothers) to care for ill or newborn children.

8. As with individuals, societies often must contend with conflicting values. An example is the effort being made

through affirmative action laws to right past wrongs by ensuring that minorities and women obtain jobs and promotions previously denied them. Doing so, however, sometimes conflicts with the very value of hiring and promotion on personal merit that the laws are intended to foster, and also may cause innocent people to pay for a situation for which they are not responsible.

9. _____ As a result of the liberalizing effect of women entering the workforce and the breaking down of old rigid lines separating jobs that men and women do, more men are taking jobs previously held mostly by women, working, for example, as secretaries, teachers, and nurses.

10. _____ Although it is customary to define work in terms of money earned, this is not a completely valid definition. In 1972, a Special Task Force on Work in America defined it as "an activity that produces something of value for other people." The definition does not have payment as an integral part of it. It is misleading to use what people earn as a measure of their or their job's worth.

11. _____ In addition to supplying people with the means to earn a living, work is important because it gives a person a sense of identity, provides a way to develop self-esteem, and helps establish a person's role or status in society.

12. _____ Psychologists today see the idea of career as a process or sequence of work-related experiences. What you decide to do to make your living and how you make your living is your career. It is what you do with your life. It may cover several kinds of jobs, or it may be only one. It is what brings you not only a living but satisfaction.

13. _____ Job refers to the specific work you are doing: chef, cashier, ballerina. A job's title is not always the best clue to what the job involves.

14. _____ Function defines the overall responsibilities of a specific job. It encompasses several tasks that require distinct skills.

15. _____ To be a satisfactory worker, you must find a work environment for which you have the necessary qualifications to meet the job requirements.

16. _____ Lack of skills, however, is only one reason a person may not be suitable for a particular work environment. Inability to adapt to the requirements of the work organization is another.

17. _____ It may not be possible to find a career that fits you perfectly. Every job will have some aspects that do not suit you altogether and lack some reinforcers that you would prefer to have.

18. _____ Six categories of worker traits have been identified by the U.S. Department of Labor as important requirements of jobs: training, aptitudes, interests, temperament, physical capabilities, and preferred working conditions.

19. _____ All jobs require some degree of general educational development in reasoning, mathematical, and language abilities, as well as specific vocational preparation.

20. _____ Your aptitude is your potential to learn and perform a particular job. Aptitudes are as important as training. If you lack aptitude for a particular job, even extensive training is not likely to make you a master of it. Given a strong aptitude for something and appropriate training, however, you can develop a successful career.

21. _____ Abilities related to aptitude for jobs are general cognitive ability, verbal, numerical, spatial, form perception, detail perception, color discrimination, and motor abilities.

22. _____ If you have an interest in a specific career, you will more likely be satisfied in it than if you had only aptitude.

23. _____ If you enter a job for which you are not temperamentally suited, your chances of succeeding will be lessened. It can be difficult to match job and temperament because it is easy to be misled about what a job requires in the way of temperament.

24. _____ Six physical demands workers will encounter are strength; climbing and balancing; stooping, kneeling, crouching, and crawling; reaching, handling, fingering, and feeling; talking and listening; seeing.

25. _____ Workers must be aware of and be able to adapt to working conditions. These include physical conditions, such as heat and cold, outside or inside, and psychological conditions, such as whether the work environment is open and easygoing or closed and strict.

26. _____ To find a satisfying work environment, you should know what is important to you—what your needs and interests are in terms of what you value. You must also know which jobs will provide the reinforcers that for you are important.

27. _____ A simple six-step process can help you make the best decision when the issue is a serious one, such as selecting a career:
1. recognize that a choice exists,
2. generate alternatives,
3. evaluate each alternative,
4. decide on an alternative,
5. act on your decision, and
6. review.

QUESTIONS FOR REVIEW AND DISCUSSION

1. What fundamental change did technology bring about in our society as we moved from the nineteenth into the twentieth century?
2. In what way has the character of our workforce been transformed in this century?
3. What is probably the single most significant change in the work force itself in the second half of the 1900s? Give statistics to support your answer.
4. Describe affirmative action laws, and give examples of the troublesome issues they arouse.
5. Meaningful work can be defined only in terms of the pay received. True or false? Support your answer.
6. Based on what you have read in this chapter, write a definition of career.
7. Explain why the title of a job does not necessarily indicate the true nature of a job. Give an example.
8. Explain what is meant by "general educational development." Name three broad areas of GED.
9. What are aptitudes, and why are they important in planning a career?
10. Name the four types of interest identified by Super and Crites.
11. Discuss why temperament is important when selecting a job.
12. Unlike with temperament, it is always easy to match the physical requirements of a job with a worker's physical traits. Is this a true or false statement? Give your reasons for your answer.
13. What are the two kinds of working conditions you will encounter? Give an example of each.
14. Identify the six steps to take when making a major decision.

KEY TERMS
Define the following:

Affirmative action laws
Aptitude
Career
Decision-making matrix
Expressed interests
Function
Inventoried interests
Job
Job description
Manifest interests
Objective data
Sociotechnological
Tasks
Temperament
Tested interests
Work climate

ACTIVITIES

1. Look in your school or local library for books describing occupations that existed in the nineteenth century. See how many you can find that do not exist or are of only marginal importance today (such as, blacksmith, maker of buggy whips, candle maker, iceman, and so on). Make a list of at least ten of them.
2. Check the *Dictionary of Occupational Titles* or the *Occupational Outlook Handbook*, and make a brief list of occupations that did not exist before this century. Identify some occupations that women now enter that they once did not.
3. Look in the classified ad sections under Help Wanted or Employment. Check more than one day's edition, and if possible,

in more than one major newspaper. (Most libraries subscribe to major daily newspapers.) Make two lists of the jobs advertised: one for service jobs and one for production jobs. Determine in which area most openings appear.

4. Based on any work experiences you may have had as well as experiences at home or in organizations to which you belong, make a preliminary list of what you see as your worker traits as defined in this chapter—training, aptitudes, interests, temperament, physical capabilities, and preferred working conditions.

5. Go to your school or local library, and look for the *Dictionary of Occupational Titles* (DOT) or the *Occupational Outlook Handbook* (OOH). Both are published by the U.S. Department of Labor. The DOT lists hundreds of job titles and brief descriptions. The OOH forecasts future demand for workers in hundreds of jobs. Skim the publications for an idea of the great variety of occupations that exist. From either publication select four occupations that appeal to you.

6. Pretend you must make a career decision right now. Follow the six-step decision-making process up to step 5. Be as realistic as possible. Consider what you know about yourself and your abilities, interests, needs, and values. Develop a list of potential occupations. For the sixth step— review—try to imagine what changes might occur and other factors you would consider after making a decision and acting on it.

CASE 1

What Makes a Career?

Cecilia entered the office of the career counselor and sat down in the offered chair with a cheerless air. "I'm confused," she blurted out.

"What's the problem?" the counselor asked.

"Well, I get my degree this spring, and I've had a couple of good job offers. "

"I wouldn't have guessed it by your expression," the counselor said with a smile. "Is the problem deciding between them?"

"I wish," Cecilia said, and then fell silent.

"Okay, what's the problem?" the counselor prodded. "I know your academic record is outstanding. If you don't like either of these two offers, I'm sure you would have no trouble getting others."

"You know what?" Cecilia asked. "I feel a lot of pressure to go out and get a job. To start a career. Get on the fast track. Make money. Make a name for myself. You know?"

"Well?" the counselor prompted.

"Well, I'm not sure that's what I want to do with my life. At least not right away."

"What do you want?"

Cecilia was quiet for a long time. "I'm almost embarrassed to say. A lot of my friends kid me about it."

"What?"

Cecilia began slowly. "I'm engaged, you know. I am getting married in the fall. What I really want to do is take care of a home, have children while I'm young enough, and stay home and raise them. There! That's what I want!"

"So? What's wrong with that?"

"What's wrong with it?" Cecilia repeated. "All my friends say I'm crazy. That it is a waste of my talents. That I should be getting out there and earning money! Staying home and being a housewife and mother isn't a career!"

- Pretend that you are the counselor. Based on your readings in this chapter, what advice can you give to Cecilia?

CASE 2

Issues of Work

At one time, the single most important issue in labor disputes and contracts was wages. But changing conditions changed that. Here is a report of an actual strike and settlement in 1987. From the start of the strike, the main issues have been over job security rather than wages. In fact, the wage increases in the new three-year contract are described by both sides as moderate ones. Some of the major areas of dispute were:

- Dismissal of employees for incompetence—employees whose work is considered unsatisfactory must be given a written explanation and reasonable time to improve or respond.

- Use of temporary employees—company has expanded rights to hire temporaries, particularly to replace employees promoted or transferred, but not to replace employees who have been laid off. Company must first offer laid-off, qualified workers temporary positions.

- Layoffs of permanent employees—the company wanted to eliminate need to lay off people according to seniority and base staff reductions solely on qualification. The contract allows the company to use qualification as a base for 25 percent of any layoffs, but the other 75 percent of layoffs must be according to seniority.

- Job crossover—the company wanted to eliminate the restrictions that prevented supervisors or others from doing different jobs. The new contract allows more supervisors to perform other jobs as well as more interchange of jobs.

1. Discuss how the issues in this strike and settlement reflect the changing world of work.

2. Identify what needs the workers were trying to protect and meet.

Report based on Lisa Belkin, "Writers at CBS Ratify Pact: Union Still On Strike at ABC," *The New York Times* (April 17, 1987).

17

▶ ## ADJUSTMENT: How We Cope in the World of Work

In our society there is no single situation which is potentially so capable of giving some satisfaction at all levels of basic needs as is the occupation.
Anne Roe

CHAPTER

Work means different things to different people. For most of us, work means a paycheck, which then translates into our means of living—food, clothing, shelter, and recreation—or our lifestyle—the kind of car, coffee, TV set, or vacation we can afford. For many, work is a responsibility freely (if sometimes grudgingly) accepted as a matter of duty or pride or conscience or religious belief. For some in our society (and for many in the "third world"), work is hard labor, exhausting, unending, demeaning. And for a fortunate and relative few, work is achievement, creativity, self-fulfillment, a vocation or calling. As Anne Roe, the pioneering work psychologist, wrote, work is the one situation in our life that is able to fulfill many, if not most, of our needs at least part, if not most, of the time.

In Chapter 10, you read about the needs you have: physiological needs that have to do with your survival and psychological needs that have to do with your well-being. To fill these needs, you require things from your environment, for example, air and food for your physiological needs and friendly people and situations where you can excel for your psychological needs. If you are like most people, you go to work in order to get the means to meet these requirements.

You also read how the environment, in turn, has its requirements or needs. In Chapter 16 you read about the different—and changing—requirements of the work environment. (You recall we use the term work environment as a general term to mean either your actual work place or the company or organization for which you work.) When you go to work, you are given job tasks to do; these are the main requirements of the work environment. There are other requirements as well, such as coming to work regularly and on time, and following rules (such as not using parking spaces or restrooms reserved for top management). What is called your work behavior is intended to meet these different requirements of the work environment.

When you are able to meet the requirements of the work environment, you are termed a "satisfactory" worker, which is to say, the work environment is satisfied with you and your work behavior. When, in turn, the work environment is able to meet your requirements, you are a "satisfied" worker; you are satisfied with the work environment.

▼ CORRESPONDENCE

correspondence
as used here, the state when the individual meets the work environment's requirements and the work environment meets the individual's work needs

When you are both satisfactory and satisfied, you and your work environment are presumed to be in a state that University of Minnesota researchers call **correspondence**. *Correspondence* is a term that was chosen to mean that the person successfully "responds" to the environment's requirements, and the environment successfully "responds" to the person's requirements; in other words, person and environment are mutually responsive (or "co-responsive," hence "correspondence") to each other's requirements.

Fig. 17-1

If a person successfully responds to the work and vice versa, correspondence has occurred.

Like many things in life, correspondence often does not last for long. People and environments change, which means their requirements and their ability to meet each other's requirements also change. When either party fails to meet the requirements of the other party, then we have a state the Minnesota researchers call **discorrespondence**, that is, at least one party fails to respond adequately to the needs of the other party.

Discorrespondence takes many forms. A change in any one of the following may produce discorrespondence, even if the rest do not change: (a) the person's requirements, (b) the environment's requirements, (c) the person's capability to respond to the environment's requirements, and (d) the environment's capability to respond to the person's requirements. Of course, two, three, or all four can change and produce discorrespondence.

Correspondence and discorrespondence are objective states, which means that different observers should be able to agree whether the state exists or does not. Satisfaction and dissatisfaction, on the other hand, are subjective states that only the person concerned can observe directly. And because the "environment" is made up of persons, its "satisfaction/dissatisfaction" is also subjective because it depends on the satisfaction/dissatisfaction of the persons who make up the environment. To illustrate from the world of sports: objectively, you either win or lose (this translates to correspondence or discorrespondence). Most winners are happy (satisfied), yet a particular winner may not be too happy (be dissatisfied) because the competition was weak. On the other hand, although most losers are dissatisfied, a particular loser might be very satisfied because she never expected to make the championship game or he expected to lose big but

discorrespondence
failure to achieve correspondence

indicator
a sign, symptom or index
of something

adjustment
the process of achieving and
maintaining correspondence with
the environment

lost by a very close margin. The same objective fact can be associated with different subjective experiences. As the research people put it, satisfaction and dissatisfaction are **indicators** of correspondence and discorrespondence, respectively, but they are not the same thing.

▼ ADJUSTMENT

The concept of **adjustment** can be illustrated by your home's heating system. We start with your thermostat, which you set to your desired room temperature. The thermostat acts like a thermometer that registers the actual room temperature. When room temperature goes above the setting (your desired temperature), the thermostat shuts off the furnace (for our purposes, we don't need to describe the mechanism for doing this). When room temperature drops below the setting, the thermostat starts the furnace, which in turn

Winning or losing a football game demonstrates correspondence or discorrespondence; it does not however demonstrate satisfaction and/or dissatisfaction. What is the difference?

provides heat to the room, until room temperature rises to the setting, at which point the thermostat shuts off the furnace, and we start all over again. (A cooling system works in a similar manner except in the other direction, and instead of a furnace you have an air conditioner.)

With the help of a thermostat and heating system (or cooling system), we can say that your room temperature is continuously being "adjusted" to the desired temperature. "Adjustment" therefore is the process of maintaining a desired room temperature setting by a series of shutting off and turning on of the furnace (or air conditioner).

Psychologists have adopted the term *adjustment* to refer to the process in which a person attempts to *achieve and maintain correspondence with an environment*. Correspondence is like the desired room temperature setting. When the person-environment relationship drops below the desired "setting" (that is, when discorrespondence sets in), the person behaves in some fashion to reduce the discorrespondence and regain correspondence. Later, you will read about the different ways people use to reduce discorrespondence. (We have focused on the person's adjustment, but in a parallel way, we can also describe the environment's adjustment, which is happening simultaneously.)

Adjustment Style

Like they do in other aspects of life, people differ in the way they adjust. We can describe these differences in terms of dimensions that collectively are called **adjustment style.**

Most people are able to tolerate a fair amount of discorrespondence before they feel they have to do something about the situation, but some people are able to tolerate greater amounts and others only smaller amounts. Differences in how much discorrespondence people can tolerate before they feel they have to do something can be described on a dimension called **flexibility**. You are more flexible if you can tolerate more discorrespondence and less flexible if you tolerate less discorrespondence. (The old term *frustration tolerance* is a lot like flexibility when by "frustration" you mean something blocks the fulfillment of your needs.)

When you can't tolerate the discorrespondence any longer, you "adjust," that is, you attempt to reduce the discorrespondence. Your behavior here is called *adjustment behavior* (as contrasted with *maintenance behavior*, which is behavior when you are not adjusting). Adjustment behavior occurs in two modes: it can be directed at changing the environment, in which case the adjustment mode is called **activeness**; or it can be directed at changing self (the person), the adjustment mode that is called **reactiveness**. Activeness and reactiveness are not opposite modes; rather,

adjustment style
the dimensions that differentiate how people adjust

flexibility
tolerance for discorrespondence

activeness
adjustment behavior that is directed at changing the environment

reactiveness
adjustment behavior that is directed at changing the self

they occur independently. This means that you can adjust both actively and reactively, actively but not reactively, reactively but not actively, or neither actively nor reactively, that is, passively. (Actually, you behave in degrees of activeness or reactiveness, such as high active and moderate reactive, or somewhat low active and somewhat high reactive.)

What is changed when you adjust actively or reactively? In the active adjustment mode, you attempt to change the environment's requirements or its ability to meet your requirements. If you, as low person on the totem pole, were expected to make the coffee but hated doing so, and therefore always found something more important to do when coffee-making time came, so that soon someone else got the job of making the coffee, you had adjusted in an active mode by changing the environment's requirements. If you went and persuaded the boss to move you from an inner location to one by a window, you had adjusted in an active mode by changing the environment's ability to meet your needs.

In the reactive mode of adjustment, you try to change your requirements of the environment or your ability to meet the environment's requirements. When you downgrade your requirements, or substitute one that can be fulfilled for one that cannot be fulfilled, you have adjusted in the reactive mode by changing what you require of the environment. When you learn new skills or improve old skills, you are adjusting in the reactive mode by changing your ability to meet the environment's requirements. As you can see, you should not think of reactive adjustment as always being negative. Likewise, you should not think that active adjustment is always positive; it can sometimes be negative—for example, note the difference between assertion (positive activeness) and aggression (negative activeness).

The last adjustment style dimension is about how long you continue your efforts at adjusting, at attempting to reduce discorrespondence, be it by the active mode or the reactive mode or both. This dimension is called **perseverance**. People who persevere in adjusting may eventually succeed in restoring correspondence. True, persevering is no guarantee of success, but not persevering is a guarantee of failure.

perseverance
continuing at efforts to adjust

People who fail to persevere in adjustment may either remain in the discorrespondent environment (and suffer the consequences) or leave the environment. Remaining in a discorrespondent environment may lead to the phenomenon of *learned helplessness*. In effect, the person learns that adjusting in any mode is "useless" and lapses into the behavior of doing nothing about the situation. In extreme instances, remaining in a discorrespondent environment may lead to *victimization* (as, for example, in the case of abused children or spouses, or oppressed workers).

Leaving the environment can take place either physically or psychologically. Physically, you leave the job and take another job. Psychologically, you remain on the job but lose your commitment to your work or the organization, perhaps doing your tasks perfunctorily, minimally and with no enthusiasm, or perhaps doing a lot of daydreaming or fantasizing, sometimes even losing touch with reality.

Your perseverance is also defined by how much discorrespondence you can tolerate before you feel you have to leave the environment. Viewed from this perspective, perseverance is similar to flexibility in that your flexibility is defined by how much discorrespondence you can tolerate before you feel you have to do something about it.

People differ in how much it takes to set them off; this is called a **threshold**. You have two *adjustment thresholds*: your *flexibility threshold* and your *perseverance threshold*. When discorrespondence rises above your flexibility threshold, this starts up your adjustment behavior, and when discorrespondence rises beyond your perseverance threshold, you stop your adjustment behavior. If your flexibility threshold is low, it does not take much discorrespondence to get you adjusting. If your flexibility threshold is high, it will take quite a bit of discorrespondence before you start adjusting. Likewise, if your perseverance threshold is low, you quit adjusting very quickly, but if your perseverance threshold is high, you keep on adjusting for a long time. Figure 17-3 shows how these adjustment thresholds operate.

What you have just read about is a general model of the adjustment process that you can use to understand how you adjust to work. We presented it at a general level in order not to get bogged down in details. But

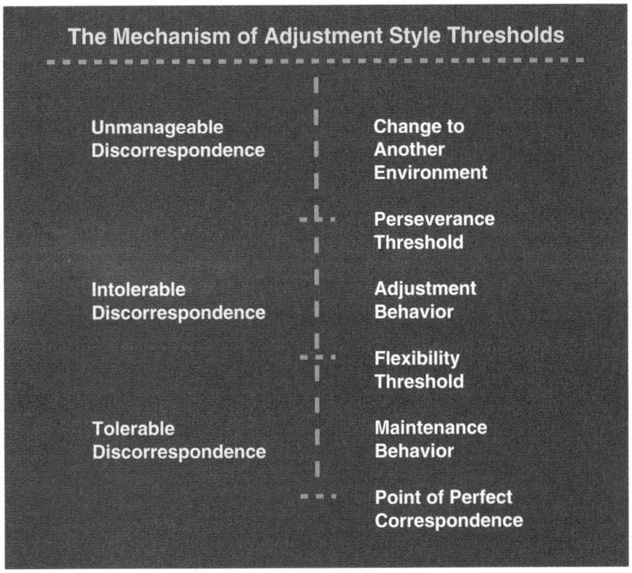

threshold
the point at which a physiological or psychological effect begins to be produced

Fig. 17-3

Adjustment style thresholds and adjustment behavior.

Adapted from: Dawis, R. V., & Lofquist, L. H. "Personality Style and the Process of Work Adjustment." *Journal of Counseling Psychology* 23 (1976): 55–59 (Figure 1, page 57).

adjusting to work requires getting down to details and down to earth. In the next sections, you will read about specific techniques and "tricks of the trade" that you can use to help you adjust better to your work.

▼ JOB DESCRIPTIONS

Many people feel anxious when they enter a workplace for the first time. As a new employee, you will ask yourself questions, such as, How will I do? Will they like me? Suppose I can't do the job? Questions like these indicate a basic human fear, the fear of a new experience. It is natural to be uncomfortable when faced with any new situation: you have to meet new people and remember their names, you have to learn new rules, and you have to face new problems. Knowing exactly what is expected of you in your job will do much to allay your natural fears and answer your questions.

The most important information you need at this time is a clear description of your job. A job description is a summary of the functions, tasks, and skills required in a job. Most large companies have formal, written job descriptions. If there are no written descriptions, your immediate supervisor has the responsibility of informing you of the job requirements. You might write them down yourself, when you have time, to be sure that you know what functions you must carry out and what tasks to perform.

A job description essentially answers the questions raised in the U.S. Department of Labor's *Handbook for Analyzing Jobs*. From your point of view as a new worker, these questions can be phrased as:

- What do I do in relation to data, people, and things (your functions)?

- What methods and techniques do I need to know (your skills)?

- What machines, tools, equipment, or other work aids will I need to use?

- What materials, products, subject matter, or service will result from my work?

- What worker traits are required of me (training, aptitude, interest, temperament)?

Obtaining the answers to these questions, either through a study of your written job description or through discussions with your immediate supervisor, will ensure that you can learn and adjust to your job.

Fig. 17-4

Newspaper job advertisements give prospective employees an idea as to what is expected in a particular job. However, they do not usually give a clear and complete description of that job.

▼ TRAINING

There is always a training period on a new job, during which your employer will expect you to make mistakes and ask questions. During this period, referred to as the "honeymoon period," both sides are more than usually tolerant and accepting of each other. During this period, despite initial anxieties, you will often probably feel greater satisfaction than in subsequent middle periods.

The training period may be formal or informal, depending on how complicated the work and how large the company is. Large companies often have half-day to full-day **orientation programs** for new employees during which they are shown around the company, introduced to key people, and informed about company policies. In smaller companies, the training may consist of nothing more than a veteran employee working with you and explaining the procedures as you work.

orientation programs
in large companies, half-day to one-day programs for new employees during which they are shown around the company, introduced to key people, and informed about company policies

Learning How to "Learn a Job"

Remember that, as you have read, although people do not like new experiences, people do have the ability to adapt. Here are some general guidelines to follow to ease your path and reduce the strain of the first few days on a new job:

- Be friendly, but not aggressively so.

TO THE POINT

Attending school has given you some idea of what going to work will be like. For both school and work you must leave home at a certain time, join others in common activities, and perform specific tasks. Thus your schooling provides you with experiences helpful for when you begin work. There are, however, many differences between a school environment and a regular work environment. Here are some of the differences to which you will have to adjust:

At School

> With friends
> Associates your age
> Groups based on friendship
> Intermittent work
> Short hours
> Frequent, long vacations
> Frequent feedback (tests and grades)
> Promotions each term
> Usually much homework
> Set time spent in one grade
> Little independence
> No earnings

At Work

> With strangers at first
> Associates of different ages
> Groups based on duties
> Steady work
> Longer hours
> Few, shorter vacations
> Infrequent feedback
> Promotions infrequent
> Little or no homework
> No set time in one job
> Feeling of independence
> Earnings

- Get acquainted with a few people a day, but avoid cliques.

- Ask older workers for advice, but do not try to show them up.

- Be a good sport if someone plays a practical joke on you.

- Be patient; expect it to be a slow process to come to know your coworkers and be accepted by them.

- Avoid trying to "prove" yourself in your first days.

- Spend more time listening than talking—you'll learn more.

Learning From an Expert

One of the best ways to learn about a job is from an expert who is doing it now. If you know what job you are going into and can find someone to tell you about it before you start, you will have done much to help yourself over the first-day hurdles. Often companies will assign an expert worker to help you. Even if that does not happen, try to identify such a person to turn to for advice. People are generally pleased if someone asks them for help and advice.

Even if experts might be willing to advise and teach, they are often not good at explaining in such a way that someone unfamiliar with the process can understand easily. Experts may know their work so well that they sometimes take too much for granted and assume learners know or understand more than they do.

Take the following steps to get the most out of any training:

- Learn the "why" before starting.
- Watch closely to see how.
- Try it to get the "feel-how."
- Keep trying for accuracy. Speed will come later.
- Want to improve.
- Believe you can improve.

If possible, stick to one instructor until you have gained some skill. Experts often use different techniques, and shifting from one to another may bring you more confusion than understanding.

Learning From Peers

You can also learn from your peers, that is your coworkers, simply by observing them, listening to them, and asking them questions. All the different ways of learning—classical conditioning, operant conditioning, and

TO THE POINT

An expert who is a good teacher will usually follow certain procedures when helping a newcomer. By knowing them, you can help the expert help you by asking appropriate questions. Here are sample procedures for instructing a new worker as adapted from Honeywell, Inc. by County College of Morris, N.J.:

Skill in Instructing

How to Get Ready

I. Have Training Timetable

Determine your training needs: Note the jobs. Decide who should be trained or retrained to do the jobs. Decide when they should be trained.

II. Break Down the Job

Note the important steps. (An important step is a logical segment of the operation when something happens to advance the work.) Pick out the key points of each step. (A key point is anything in a step that will make the job—not break it, prevent accidents, or make the work easier to do.)

III. Have Everything Ready

The job, including right equipment and material.

IV. Have the Workplace Properly Arranged

As the worker will be expected to keep it.

How to Instruct

Step I. Prepare the Worker

Put the worker at ease. Start with what the worker knows. Get the worker interested in the job. Place in the correct position.

Step II. Present the Job

Tell, show and illustrate carefully and patiently. Stress the key points—explain reasons. Instruct clearly and completely—one point at a time, no more than the worker can master. Repeat as necessary. Encourage questions.

Step III. Try Out Performance

Have the worker do the job—walk through—correct errors. Have the worker do the job again, explaining key points. Ask "W" type questions: Who? What? When? Why? Continue to have the worker do job until you know he or she knows.

Step IV. Follow Up

Put the worker on his or her own. Designate to whom the worker should go for help. Check frequently. Watch key points. Encourage questions. Taper off the extra coaching and close follow-up.

cognitive learning—you read of in Chapter 9 will be taking place as you learn your new job. Of these ways, cognitive learning, particularly observational learning, will probably dominate. Remember that observational learning involves four steps:

1. Paying attention and seeing the relevant behavior
2. Remembering the behavior in words, in mental images, or both
3. Converting the memory into action
4. Adopting the behavior

▼ REVIEW AND EVALUATION

Your immediate supervisor will probably be meeting with you frequently, especially at first, to assess your progress and give you feedback about how you are doing. Take advantage of these meetings to clarify any aspects of your job description you are not sure of and to make sure you have understood what the priorities are if your job requires you to perform different functions. Often, a written job description will indicate how much time a worker should spend on different duties.

At the beginning, your meetings with your supervisor will be aimed at teaching you your job. Subsequently, in the natural course of your work, you will be continually evaluated. Many companies have formal reviews in which a supervisor sits down with an employee at set intervals (semiannually, annually) and reviews the worker's performance. These reviews often relate the worker's performance to the job description and sometimes as well to additional written goals based on the job description and prepared by the worker and supervisor.

The purpose of periodic reviews is twofold: One, of course, is simply to see that you are doing the work you were hired to do and that the company is benefiting from it. The second reason is to see that you are rewarded for your good performance and given additional training if necessary to improve performance not considered adequate.

That your performance will be evaluated in terms of the job description is another reason for you to be thoroughly familiar with it. The job description and the performance evaluation provide the basis for an objective review of you as a worker. In this sense, they protect you from arbitrary or personally biased judgments about your worth as a worker. Although seniority is a major basis upon which pay raises and promotions are given, performance evaluation often also plays a part in determining the amount of a raise, for example, or the timing of a promotion.

TO THE POINT

In this sample job description of an information processing specialist, the percentage of time the worker is expected to spend on each specific task is given. The percentages are intended as guides to help the worker set priorities. Exact compliance with them would not be required, and on any given day a worker might spend 35 percent of the time on a task for which 5 percent is allocated. Overall, however, the time allocated for the tasks should reflect those on the job description.

TITLE: Information Processing Specialist

<u>Major Function</u>: Responsible for operating the integrated information system and providing support to system users. Primary emphasis is on coordinating the system to improve communication and information access through the use of software applications (such as word processing, spreadsheet, database, and communications software). Responsibilities also include the provision of necessary training and the administration of standards. The position reports to management and in some cases to the information processing manager as well.

<u>Specific Tasks</u>:

1. Performs site-specific coordination of the information processing system. Analyzes and monitors information needs. Designs information management system.(2%)
2. Establishes procedures for information processing, including information needs and sources, document formats, electronic file management, document distribution and controls, and use and operation of equipment. Monitors system and revises as needed. Monitors systemwide libraries.(5%)
3. Researches new capabilities of the system to improve information and communication access for both local and remote networks. Maintains a thorough working knowledge of the system. Uses new capabilities of the system and works with end users to define the needs for new applications.(3%)
4. Conducts applications training for system users, including training in word processing software, writing tools (spelling checkers, grammatical scanning tools, outlining tools), spread sheet software, database software, charting and graphics software, and integrated software. Provides network and computer literacy training to secretaries and office staff in file system, data storage, telecommunications, and data conversion software.   (5%)
5. Maintains the equipment inventory system and prepares reports based on database analyses. Defines and establishes

categories of database system. Updates database system regularly. Analyzes data and prepares reports based on analyses.(5%)

6. Gathers information on order requests. Verifies prices using databases and print sources. Processes order request documents: Enters, edits, files, and distributes documents electronically and in print (as appropriate). Forwards order request documents to purchasing department or directly to vendor. Follows up order requests and communicates status of order to originator of requests.(5%)

7. Processes documents for invoice billing. Coordinates and updates electronic invoicing system, including client information, project rates, and billing schedules. Retrieves billing and invoice information for the billing schedule, generates the invoice, files monthly invoice information, distributes information to billing clerk, and follows up invoice sent (reissues as appropriate).(5%)

8. Processes payroll records. Creates and implements electronic time record system; updates as necessary. Calculates totals, stores records, and directs information to accountant.(5%)

9. Processes business correspondence, including reports, letters, and memos. Gathers information from electronic and print sources. Formats, enters, proofs, and edits documents; stores documents; and distributes as appropriate. Integrates spreadsheet, database, and graphics data when necessary. Uses a variety of input devices (such as keyboard, digitizer, and voice). Uses advanced word processing features in document preparation.(35%)

10. Builds budget spreadsheets, processes financial information, and maintains spreadsheet files, utilizing all aspects of spreadsheet software. Submits departmental budget reports to the manager.(15%)

11. Prepares visuals for management presentations. Gathers information for graphics or visuals needed, uses applicable software to prepare them, integrates visuals in word processing documents, and produces computer-generated visuals in a variety of forms (for example, overhead transparencies, slides, and print). (2%)

12. Coordinates office communications. Establishes incoming/ outgoing mail system, establishes electronic phone and phone message system, and uses electronic mail systems for interoffice communications.(8%)

13. Coordinates staff schedules by arranging meetings, updating calendars, and taking minutes of staff meetings. Orchestrates interdepartmental meetings as necessary, using teleconferencing and/or videoconferencing.(5%)

▼ COMFORT AND CONFIDENCE

It takes the average person about six weeks to begin to feel at home after moving into a new house. It takes that long for people to change their previous notions of what a home should be like and to adjust to whatever changes they find in the new house. Just as in adjusting to a new home, the average person needs at least six weeks to begin to feel at home on a new job. The process will probably take a little longer for a person going to work for the first time or for a person who has worked a long time at another company.

In addition to your job description, you must learn what is considered acceptable social behavior. For example, people in some organizations use first names readily. In other organizations, last names are used with the appropriate social title. Keep your eyes and ears open, and do as others do in such matters. These customs may seem minor, but if you overlook them, others will say, "He does not seem to fit into our organization" or "She is a good enough worker but does not seem to be our type." It takes more than job skills to fit into an organization.

Practically all companies have factions or cliques. Some companies are riddled with factions scheming against each other. In studies of mental health in industry, Robert Kahn, an industrial psychologist,

TO THE POINT

Some kinds of behavior are particularly unsuitable in a work environment and should be avoided. Here is a list of behaviors that studies have indicated are most objectionable in the work environment:

Gossiping	Using baby talk
Cheating in games	Petty lying
Coughing on others	Bragging
Cracking gum	Sniffling
Being bossy	Spitting
Looking glum	Losing temper
Trying to be funny	Dominating conversations
Talking too loudly	Hurrying others
Continually criticizing	Coaxing
Putting on airs	Using high-pressure selling
Backslapping	Pushing to the front of lines
Using sexy talk	Being nosy
Having body odor or bad breath	Disrespecting the elderly
Gushing	Using endearing names
Giving unasked-for-advice	Seeking attention
	Overusing slang

Fig. 17-5

The sooner you learn and remember the details of a new job, the sooner you will feel at home. It takes the average person about six weeks to begin to feel at home in a new house. It takes at least that long to become fully comfortable and confident at work. Don't push it; let it happen.

conducted a nationwide survey of personal stress arising from such internal conflicts. About half of the employees and executives interviewed experienced stress because of contending factions within their work environment. You will read more about stress in Chapter 18.

On many jobs you will have to learn a new vocabulary. Practically every occupation or work organization has its own vocabulary, or at least a number of words that have special meaning for it. To fit in, you must learn this vocabulary. Each profession or trade has its own particular jargon that you learn as you learn the trade.

Jargon can vary from office to office, however. For example, most offices use computers today for word processing. But even if you know word processing from training or previous experience, you might still need to learn different terms, according to the word processing system being used. What one system calls "strikeover" another calls "replace" and a third calls "overtype." What is referred to as "boilerplate" in one office is called "glossary" in another and a "macro" in still another; "highlighting" in one office is "blocking" in another.

Staying Effective on the Job

A major difference between the work and the school environment is that at school your hour-to-hour activities were determined for you, whereas at work you more often than not have to determine your own hourly activities. This is more true on some jobs than on others, but it is true to a degree on nearly all jobs. Of course, you have a job title, and there is often a job description that describes the functions and tasks you are expected to perform. But, nonetheless, you must often determine exactly how and in what order you will carry out these activities to be successful and effective.

For example, suppose you are waiting tables and serving food. This seems a rather straightforward job with clear functions: see the customers enter, seat them, ask for their orders, and give the food to them. But you must also clear tables, wait on more than one group at a time, remember orders, get drinks, make up the bill, collect the money, all at a reasonable speed so people feel neither neglected nor rushed, and all the time you must be pleasant.

If you do not plan and think about how you will perform your function of waiting on tables (or any job in which you interact with others), you might end up annoying the customers by forgetting orders or, worse, giving the impression of ignoring customers. If you concentrate on clearing one empty table while diners wait unattended at another, you are certainly carrying out one of your tasks, but you have failed to plan and set realistic priorities. As a consequence, customers become annoyed and you are not performing your basic function.

Organizing Your Work

The essence of organizing your work effectively is to replace the less important activity with the more important activity. A waiter who concentrates on clearing an empty table while customers wait to give their orders has not replaced the less important activity with the more important one. Another example of a disorganized worker is one who puts off the big, important tasks until "there is enough time." There never is enough time for a disorganized worker who fills all available time with the small, less important tasks.

So develop the habit of tackling your important tasks without delay. But how do you determine what's important? Suppose you have several things to do? To identify important tasks, you must set goals for yourself and give your job some forethought, which is to say: plan. A person waiting tables who has thought about the job will realize that an important goal is keeping the customers happy and will plan his or her activities accordingly. Other jobs might require more thought and planning to identify what is important, but it can be done.

When starting a new job you must learn many details, several of which may not be directly related to the performance of the job itself, but knowledge of these details can help you be a more satisfactory and satisfied worker. Here is a checklist of questions you can use to seek such information. Many companies, especially large ones, automatically answer these questions in formal orientation programs or with printed brochures. Smaller companies may not. Do not expect to have all the answers after the first day, but be alert to find them in anticipation of needs.

- What is the company policy that you must follow when you are unable to report to work?
- Whom should you notify when you change your address?
- How do you request new equipment or repairs?
- Where should you report in case of an accident?
- What is company policy on using telephones for personal calls?
- Is medical advice available?
- Where do you report lost or found articles?
- Who explains company benefits and paycheck deductions?
- Where do you report a lost paycheck?
- Is there a policy for recommending a friend for a job?
- Does the company have such things as a tuition refund program so you can take formal training?
- What are the policies about raises and promotions?
- What holidays and vacations are given?
- What is the policy about personal days off?
- Can you cash a payroll check in the building?
- Can you borrow money from the company?
- Is there a discount policy for company goods?
- Is there a company library, and if so what policies govern its use?
- Is there a company newspaper, and if so how do you get news into it?

TO THE POINT

Sometimes organizing a job requires identifying all the tasks you do and how much time you spend doing them. If you do have a multitask job, logging your activities for a two-week period can be a useful exercise. It allows you to see exactly how you are spending your time. You might find that you are spending more time than you should on less important activities.

Planning Guides

planning guide
a breakdown of the day into blocks of time

A simple **planning guide** can be a useful tool if you have a multitask job. A planning guide is nothing more than a breakdown of the day into blocks of time. These blocks can be as small as an hour, but mostly they might be longer, perhaps even half a day. You assign activities to specific blocks of times. A planning guide should be broad based and not specific like a "to do" list, which you will read about next. Also a planning guide is infrequently changed, whereas the "to do" list is made up daily.

Keeping a log for two or three weeks can help you develop a planning guide. The point of a general planning guide is to organize your work to do similar things at the same time each day. Experts have discovered that when we do similar tasks, especially mentally demanding ones, at the same time, we seem to do them better because our brain is primed for them.

Studies have shown that we all operate on cycles. Some of us are morning people: We are full of energy and action in the morning or early in the day. Some of us are night people: We are sluggish early in the day, but as the day goes on we come alive. When you create your planning guide,

Fig. 17-6

A planning guide is a useful tool for organizing your work. The guide represents a typical working day. You block out major activity areas on it by drawing horizontal lines in the appropriate places and identifying the activity in the hours represented by the block. Time blocks can represent any length of time, but should usually be more than an hour. The planning guide is a broad-based guide, not a "to do" list.

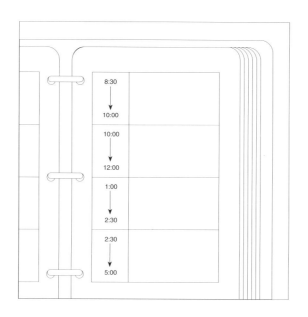

How effective are you as an organizer of your work day? Try this self-analysis quiz. Answer each question as honestly as you can. Do you:

	Never	Sometimes	Often
Keep a daily "to do" list?			
Weight or prioritize your lists?			
Have a special time for planning?			
Keep a "quiet" period?			
Deal effectively with interruptions?			
Do important work in your peak hours?			
Arrive at work and meetings on time?			
Finish projects on deadline?			
Keep your desk or bench uncluttered?			
Have a place for everything?			
Find things easily in your files?			

If you can answer "often" to six or more of these items and have fewer than five "nevers," you are rather well organized. Six or more "nevers" and fewer than five "oftens" suggests you could improve your organizational skills.

TO THE POINT

schedule important jobs and the time for your most demanding work to coincide with your peak energy hours. If you are a morning person, it is foolish to waste that energy doing routine work.

"To Do" Lists

Written daily "to do" lists are very helpful, especially when used in combination with an overall planning guide. Effective "to do" lists share these three characteristics:

1. Prepared daily
2. Written
3. Prioritized (activities identified and listed according to their importance)

A word of warning about "to do" lists. For some people they become an end in themselves rather than a tool for effectively organizing work. Spending time to plan and make lists is important. Spending a lot of time planning and making lists is wasteful.

The most effective way to keep a written, daily "to do" list is to start with a blank sheet of paper and a pen. Try to take a few minutes each

TO THE POINT

Here is an example of a ranked "to do" list. You can use any simple system to identify the priorities of items—numbers or letters—or you can use a combination if you wish more sensitive levels of priorities. You may have several "A" tasks and have broken them down in order of their importance, such as "A-1," "A-2," "A-3."

"To Do" List (Date)

Learn daily specials and prices.	A-2
Get new uniform from cleaners.	B-1
Check next week's schedule.	C
Clean out table.	A-3
Fold napkins.	B-3
Review tipping policy.	B-2
Wait on customers.	A-1
Call Marcia to work for me	C

morning to write your list for the day. Even better, try to do it last thing the day before, and then just make adjustments as necessary in the morning. The "to do" list is an extension of your planning guide, both of which should reflect your long- and short-term work goals.

Do not develop the habit of keeping your "to do" lists on any piece of scrap paper. Use a spiral-bound notebook, small enough to fit in your pocket. You want to be able to keep your list with you. The ideal "to do" list should be made up of a mix of your top priority and lesser priority items for each day. You will read about setting priorities in a later section.

If you have prepared a realistic "to do" list, you often will not complete it in one day. If you find that you are completing your list every day, you either are superhuman or are not creating your list as carefully as you could. The test is whether the activities you are completing are moving you toward your goal. If so, fine. If not, better rethink your lists and ways of setting priorities. The idea is not to complete a lot of tasks during each day, but to work on the right ones.

Your "to do" list should be a firm guide to action, but not an inflexible one. You will have to and should add to it those unexpected tasks that come up and must be done. Do actually write down the additional tasks so you have the satisfaction of seeing a complete list of what you accomplished during the day. Also, one day's "to do" list with its incomplete activities is the base for the next day's list.

Working Smarter, Not Just Harder

Nothing will substitute for hard work. To remain fresh and effective on your job and to advance, you must work hard. The American poet Henry Wadsworth Longfellow made the point more than a hundred years ago when he wrote that successful people did not suddenly become successful, "but they, while their companions slept, were toiling upward in the night." To be good at anything—a popular singer, a great actor, a doctor, accountant, nurse, or waiter—requires effort.

But simply working harder will not by itself ensure success. You must plan and develop planning guides and "to do" lists. A person may be working very hard—like the waiter scurrying around clearing empty tables while customers wait—but without effect. Some of the least productive and most unhappy workers are hard workers in terms of taking a lot of actions. But because their actions are not directed, they never seem to get ahead or achieve anything. In addition to developing planning guides and "to do" lists based on work requirements and goals, there are some other ways you can increase your productivity and job enjoyment.

The 80/20 Rule

The 80/20 rule was put forth by the Italian economist Vilfredo Pareto in the last century. Basically, what he said was that in any grouping, the significant items amount to only 20 percent of the total. Commonly cited examples are:

- Twenty percent of the customers provide eighty percent of the business.

- Twenty percent of the people control eighty percent of the wealth.

- Twenty percent of the workers do eighty percent of the work.

- Twenty percent of your effort will produce eighty percent of your results.

The final item in the list is the important one for your purposes. Of all the things you must do, some are more important than others. Also, of all your activities, some that you do will have a greater bearing on your productivity than others. As you work and keep track of what you do, you can learn which of your activities are among those 20 percent that produce 80 percent of your results. Use this knowledge to rank your activities according to their importance.

Setting Priorities

The 80/20 rule is a way to help you rank activities on your daily "to do" list according to what is most important. Another guide for ranking your activities is to relate them to your overall function or goals. Those that move you toward your goal have high priority; those that do not get a low priority. The waiter ignoring customers while cleaning off a table did not rank his activities very well because he failed to relate them to his overall function: serving customers.

Sometimes you must include as top priority activities not related to your overall functions. If the restaurant manager tells the waiter to clear the tables regardless of waiting customers, that rightfully becomes the number one task.

In setting priorities, ask yourself these two questions:

1. How *urgent* is this activity?
2. How *high* is its value?

Whatever helps you carry out your function or reach a goal has a high value. Some things, however, must be done even though they do not relate closely to your overall objectives. These are urgent tasks. If a task is urgent and also has high value, then that is a top priority task. But urgency alone does not necessarily make a task a top priority. Beware of letting urgent tasks shoulder out high-value tasks. Sometimes, the urgency is more apparent than real. To use the waiter example again, the pile of dirty dishes had to be cleared, and it was an urgent activity for the waiter (especially if not doing it now would mean staying late to do it). But the activity with high value was taking care of customers.

Once you have established your priorities, stick with them. Often, an A-number-one (A-1) task is a demanding, time-consuming one. Your desire to feel you have accomplished a lot often sidetracks you from tackling that tough, time-consuming activity. Then you spend a lot of time doing the easy but less important tasks. At the end of such a day, you can tell yourself you accomplished a lot. If you did not do the A-number-one task, however, your accomplishments do not amount to much. When tempted to put off a top priority but difficult task and do a lot of easy tasks, stop to consider the consequences of not doing your number-one task. What usually happens when you procrastinate (put off) doing the important but difficult task is:

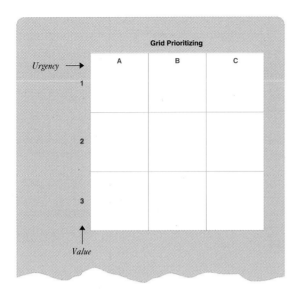

Grid Prioritizing

Urgency →

A   B   C

1

2

3

Value

Fig. 17-7

A priority grid helps in setting priorities. The letter and number values are as follows: high (A and 1), medium (B and 2), and low (C and 3). You place each activity in the box you believe best reflects its overall urgency and value. An activity in the upper left corner box has top priority: A-1. An activity in the lower right can be done last.

- The hard task becomes harder.
- More tasks intrude.
- You have less time.

The Importance of Subgoals

Most job functions or overall goals can be broken down into subgoals. Creating subgoals serves three useful purposes: (1) breaking a job up into smaller goals helps keep you fresh and alert, (2) developing subgoals helps you determine what is immediately important, which leads to setting priorities, and (3) identifying subgoals helps clarify ways to achieve main goals or the steps and activities required to carry out your assigned functions.

Subgoals not only help you develop your daily activities but also serve as progress markers and guideposts on how effectively you are organizing your work to accomplish your functions. Having a series of subgoals gives you the opportunity to experience the satisfaction of achieving a series of goals during the day. Lacking such satisfaction, you could become bored and uninterested.

Work Like a Computer

Computers impress us all by their ability to carry out complex tasks very quickly. Essentially what a computer does is break every big computing job it is given into little bits of positively and negatively charged electrical impulses and handle each bit as it comes along. You cannot really operate like a computer, but you can copy a computer's approach to a big job. When you find yourself procrastinating over a big A-number-one activity, take a good look at it and break it down into bits that you can handle.

You don't have enough time right now to do the big job? Perhaps not. But you certainly have time to do a bit of it. You might even start now—just to get going. Here are some ways of breaking that big job into smaller jobs you can handle:

- Look for the easy-entry bits—find a part of the big task that is easy for you and start with that.

- Look for bits that can be done quickly.

- Identify bits that match how you feel at the moment—if you must prepare a paper and just do not feel like writing, do the research and checking.

- Break your large task into bites that lead naturally into each other; make them steps toward completion of the big job.

- Vary your bites on a big task when you become tired or bored by taking a different bite of it and doing something a little different, but stay with it.

- Set meaningful deadlines for yourself.

Lifelong Learning

As you can see, learning takes place in areas other than school. You must learn a lot when starting a new job, no matter how well trained you have been. And even after learning your job, you must continue learning if you want to advance and avoid boredom. How well you learn while continuing through life and what you learn depend on many factors, such as determination, interest, curiosity, experience, and opportunity. You read in Chapter 9 that learning continues throughout life. You learn from new experiences daily. But it is the conscious, directed learning that is important to your continued growth.

As you were growing up, your learning was more or less directed for you. After high school, your learning is mostly self-directed. You decide whether you will learn, what you will learn, and the pace at which you will learn. Continued learning throughout life is important to having a successful and fulfilling life, that is, to achieving the higher goals on your hierarchy of needs. If you change jobs, you must learn the routine of the new job. Even if you do not change jobs, learning is often necessary to improve your skills and chances for advancement.

Fig. 17-8

The speed with which a computer tackles large, complex computational tasks is awesome. But the secret of its power is that it breaks every big job down into small bits. When faced with big tasks, do as the computer does and break them down into small bits that you can get started on easily.

Given the pace at which technology changes things, continued learning is probably more important than it ever was. In the last 20 to 30 years, technology has opened up thousands of new jobs requiring new skills and at the same time has made many jobs and their skills obsolete. The way this book you are reading is manufactured is but one example of this change: As recently as the 1960s, skilled workers, known as linotype operators, would have been the ones to set the words you are reading into type. All books, newspapers, and magazines required linotype operators to set their words into type. There were thousands of such skilled operators. Within 30 years, they virtually disappeared. Not one linotype operator worked on this book. Technology, mostly in the form of computers, eliminated the linotype operator's job. The skilled linotype operator had to learn other skills to have a job.

Curiosity and Learning

Your curiosity is what causes you to continue to learn. It gives you the desire. At different times, you will seek to gain knowledge and skill because it will be useful or valuable. Sometimes you want to know something or be able to do something just for its own sake. You might decide to make pottery, do crossword puzzles, or upholster a chair. You do these things as hobbies because you enjoy them.

You may have practical reasons for learning something that does not have to do with getting and holding a job or having a hobby. For example, you may take the trouble to learn what food is going to be on sale this weekend or where to go to buy a new suit for the lowest price. Learning can also be directed at changing your behavior. You might learn how to control a quick temper or how to break a bad habit, such as smoking.

Your efforts to learn may be brief or long-term. Some efforts to learn are primarily intellectual, others are emotional or attitudinal, and still others are designed to develop physical skills. Experts say that about 70 percent of all learning is planned by the learner (as opposed to spontaneous) and that everyone undertakes at least one or two learning projects a year. Some people engage in as many as 15 or 20 per year. Also, it is common for people to spend about 700 hours a year at learning projects. Some may spend less than 100 hours and others as much as 2000 hours a year in intentional learning.

Refer back to Chapter 9 for a discussion of the various kinds of learning and of ways to improve your memory, which is a key element in learning. You can learn with an instructor or alone, by imitation and by absorption or habituation. But for cognitive learning particularly—and that is the type of learning important for a fully successful life—the will or intent to learn must be strong. The extent of your curiosity and desire to learn and retain knowledge or to acquire a new skill has an influence on the extent to which you succeed.

Getting Started

Deliberate or intentional learning—planned as opposed to spontaneous—requires you to make decisions about what and how to learn. Nearly any kind of learning has some use to the extent that it exercises your mind, but undirected learning will not necessarily lead to fulfillment or success. There is so much to learn, and to do so in our society, you must choose and decide. Some people are prone to jump from one thing to another: "I'm going to learn programming;" "I'm going to learn to play the guitar." "I'm going to learn accounting." "I'm going to learn...." Such a person will learn a little bit of a lot of things and nothing well—not a good situation. As the poet Alexander Pope said, "A little learning is a dangerous thing." Dangerous, in that we may think we know more than we do, and useless as well.

Thus the first step in deliberate learning is to identify what you wish to learn. Then you should set realistic goals and stick with them. After that you must identify the resources that can help you attain the desired learning. These resources could be attending a formal program of education, receiving one-on-one tutoring from an expert, reading books and seeing films, and having the opportunity to practice.

Carrying Through

Evidence indicates that when we as adults act on our own initiative to learn, we learn more deeply and retain more of what we learn longer than when we are told to learn. Nonetheless, it requires dedication to continue and carry through on a learning project once you have made the decision to learn.

A way to ensure a successful carry-through of a learning project is to set yourself deadlines and intermediate goals. An overall goal may be to become an entry-level systems analyst, which could take a year or two of study, depending on how much time you have to devote to studying. Working for a year or two toward a goal can be difficult, hence intermediate goals help you achieve a sense of accomplishment during the period, and this sense reinforces your desire to continue learning.

Intermediate goals in this example could include learning the concepts of systems analysis, learning how to create flowcharts, and learning to analyze a simple system. Deadlines for reaching the subsidiary and main goals give you targets to shoot for. Deadlines should be realistic, taking into account how much available time you have; they should be tough enough to push you somewhat but not so tough that you can never realize them.

▼ CHANGING CAREERS

Career planning is a continuing process, but there are three particular times when you tend to face the need to make a career decision. These are early

Fig. 17-9

Formal learning can continue after retirement. Many people who no longer must work for a living return to school to learn new skills that they can use in interesting hobbies or just for the sake of learning itself.

career, when you are first starting out; middle career; and late career. You are at the early stage now, making your first major career decisions. The next important stage will come after you have been in a career a number of years. We call this the midcareer stage, but it could be nearer the beginning or the end. In Chapter 16 you read of the need to review all decisions after making them and of the example of the welder who decided late in his career to become a teacher.

Midcareer Change

It is becoming rather common for people to decide to change careers in midlife. At that time, many have to face up to feelings of restlessness and insecurity. At this point, people reexamine their values and lives. They ask themselves if they are doing what they really want to. The question has urgency if half or more of a person's working life has gone by.

Other factors require people to rethink their careers. Technological change brings new occupations and eliminates existing ones. When that happens, workers must be prepared to make a career change. Being able to adjust and make new career decisions, even after you are well into a career, and even if you did not particularly want to change, is important.

Third Stage—Retirement

The third crucial career change occurs when workers face retirement. Most workers today retire between the ages of 60 and 70. Retirement not only means a sharp reduction in income for most people but also the loss of that which has given them a major purpose in life. Remember that work's importance to us stems from the fact that it helps us establish our identity.

Retirement can be a shock for someone who is not prepared. Although it seems like a long time off when you are just starting out, it is not too early to give a little thought to it. In fact, one aspect of a career you should check out when selecting a job is whether you will be eligible for a pension when you retire. You are entitled to social security, of course, but a company pension can make retirement a lot easier. You should not make a pension the prime reason for taking or rejecting a job, but it is a consideration. If you take a job that does not provide for a pension, you should know this so that you can establish your own savings plan. Information about pensions will also have a bearing on choices you make when faced with midcareer changes.

Maintaining meaningful activity after retirement is also important. Remember that a career is not simply a job for pay. In planning a career, consider all aspects of the life you want to live. You may want to select a career that will allow you to develop hobbies and interests outside of your remunerated employment. Developing such interests not only will give you something to continue with after retirement but also will enrich all of your working life.

When the time comes to retire, you are stepping down from a job that has dominated most of your waking life until now. It will sometimes take courage to walk away from what has given your life so much meaning. Thus it is good to prepare before retirement for this step.

SUMMARY

1. After you obtain a job, your learning is just beginning. Despite prior training, you must still learn the specifics of your new job, which include learning not only the skills related to your assigned tasks but also the general policies that govern the operation of the work organization and interpersonal relations, both formal and informal.

2. When you are new on a job, the most important information you need is a clear description of your job. Most large companies have formal, written job descriptions. If there are no written descriptions, your immediate supervisor has the responsibility of informing you of the job requirements. Write them down yourself.

3. A job description answers these questions for you: What do I do in relation to data, people, and things (your functions)? What methods and techniques do I need to know (your skills)? What machines, tools, equipment, or other work aids will I need to use? What materials, products, subject matter, or service will result from my work? What worker traits are required of me?

4. Some general guidelines to follow during your first days on the job include the following: be friendly, but not aggressive; try to meet a few more people daily, but keep out of cliques; ask older workers for advice, but do not try to show them up; watch out for practical jokes, but laugh along if caught; be patient; avoid trying to prove yourself; do more listening than talking.

5. All the different ways of learning—classical conditioning, operant conditioning, and cognitive learning—will be taking place as you learn your new job. Of them, cognitive learning, particularly observational learning, will probably dominate.

6. Your immediate supervisor will probably meet with you frequently, especially at first, to assess your progress and give you feedback. Subsequently, you will be continually evaluated. These reviews often relate the worker's performance to the job description and sometimes as well to additional written goals prepared by the worker and supervisor. The evaluations often are the basis for determining promotions, raises, or further training.

7. Written job descriptions that include many duties or tasks often indicate in percentages the amount of time a worker should spend on each, as a guide for setting priorities.

8.   The essence of organizing your work effectively is to replace the less important activity with the more important activity.

9.   A planning guide can be a useful tool if you have a multitask job. A planning guide is a breakdown of the day into blocks of time, which can be as small as an hour, but mostly are longer, perhaps even half a day. You assign specific activities to specific times. A planning guide should be broad based and not specific like a "to do" list. A planning guide helps you organize your work to do similar things at the same time each day. Experts say that when we do similar tasks, especially mentally demanding ones, at the same time, we seem to do them better.

10.   Written daily "to do" lists are very helpful, especially when used in combination with an overall planning guide. Effective "to do" lists share these three characteristics: (1) they are prepared daily, (2) they are written, and (3) they set priorities.

11.   Working smarter, not just harder, leads to success. Ways to work smarter include using the 80/20 rule, setting priorities, having subgoals, and breaking your work down into manageable bits.

12.   Continued learning throughout life is important to having a successful and fulfilling life, that is, to achieving the higher goals on your hierarchy of needs.

13.   Deliberate or intentional learning—planned as opposed to spontaneous—requires you to make decisions about what and how to learn. When we act on our own initiative to learn, we learn more deeply and retain more of what we learn longer than when we are told to learn.

14.   A way to ensure a successful carry-through of a learning project is to set yourself deadlines and intermediate goals.

15.   Career planning is a continuing process, but there are three particular times when you tend to face the need to make a career decision: early career when you are first starting out, middle career, and late career.

KEY TERMS
Define the following:

Activeness
Adjustment
Adjustment style
Correspondence
Discorrespondence
80/20 rule
Flexibility
Indicators
Orientation programs
Perseverance
Planning guide
Procrastinate
Reactiveness
Threshold
"To do" list

QUESTIONS FOR REVIEW AND DISCUSSION

1. Being new on a job creates tension and anxiety. Describe some general guidelines you can follow to reduce the strain of being new on a job.

2. What is one of the chief difficulties you will face in a new job? Explain your answer. Give at least four examples of objectionable behaviors.

3. Describe planning guides and "to do" lists, how they differ, and what they are useful for.

4. Explain the 80/20 rule.

5. In a simple 1-2-3 ranking with 1 being high and 3 low, assign ranks to three tasks that are described as Urgent and Low Value; Urgent and High Value; and Not Urgent and High Value. Explain your ranking.

6. Describe the three major points at which people face the need to consider important career choices.

ACTIVITIES

1. An ideal way to learn about a new job is to learn it from a person who is experienced in it. Consider an occupation that interests you. Identify a work organization in which that occupation can be found or an individual you know who is in it. Write to the organization (address your letter to Public Relations or Personnel Department or President) or individual. Explain your interest and ask them if they would help you prepare for such a job by describing briefly the most important skills and worker traits required.

2. During the week, your days are controlled by your need to attend school and follow the routine there. On weekends you are free to plan more of your time. Prepare a planning guide for a typical weekend. Planning even for such free time can pay dividends. Without a plan, you might just fritter away the time without enjoyment or profit of any kind. Include housework you are required to do, homework, part-time jobs, recreational activities, and social and religious obligations. Remember that the planning guide should include just broad categories, not specific tasks.

3. Prepare a "to do" list for a typical day. Make a detailed list of your activities. Include as many as you can think of but not routine matters, such as dressing, eating, or sleeping. After making the list, go back over it and rank the activities.

4. Let's look way into the future. Think about retirement—your retirement. What would you like to do when you no longer need to

work every day for a living? Where would you like to live? What steps can you take now to prepare? Draft a brief plan for your retirement years. Consider what steps you should be taking now. Be as realistic as possible.

CASE 1

Setting Priorities

Mildred was very pleased to be promoted to office manager. After five years working in the office, she felt she knew everything necessary to do the job well. She knew she was popular with the other office workers and looked forward to helping improve morale. Under the previous manager, who was something of a dictator, morale had not been as good as it should. In fact, when the general manager promoted Mildred, he told her that her popularity was a factor in his decision to make her manager and that he hoped she could help improve morale.

"The main thing, of course, is our desire to reorganize the office and computerize more of the operations. You will be the key person acting as the liaison with the outside consultants. Your report and recommendations will be crucial because you have held all the different jobs in the office and have been training on computers."

Mildred said she was excited about the prospects, and the general manager continued, "Well, that's our top goal for the next year. Of course, you've got to keep the office running smoothly and efficiently. Your predecessor had things rather well organized, if a little too tense. So, finally, we want you to try to make the atmosphere a little less tense and more friendly. I think it's a matter of personality, really. It is possible to maintain control and keep things running smoothly without making everyone tense. Well, good luck."

Mildred said she would do her best and thanked her boss. As she was leaving, he reminded her that he would like to have her interim report on the reorganization and computerization in two months.

Mildred went happily to work. She spent a little time thinking about the reorganization report, but two months seemed a long time away and improving worker morale was more urgent. She got into the habit of spending a lot of time with the workers, helping them, answering questions, reassuring them about the reorganization, and generally working to relieve the tension that had existed.

At the end of a month, she began to worry about the report because she had not done much on it. It was such a big project that she never seemed to have enough time to get started on it, so she would often turn to some other task, such as catching up on the mail, checking the time cards, and spending a lot of time on worker problems. She kept telling herself she would get started on the report in a day or two when she had enough time.

She was also having difficulty keeping the work flowing smoothly. One problem, she knew, was that she spent so much time talking with and helping the workers on small problems that she did not have time to prepare the weekly work schedules. She drifted into the habit of handing things out as they came up and frequently changing assignments when workers complained about the workload.

Like the reorganization report, preparing the weekly work schedules took a lot of time, and she never seemed to have a good block of time to work on either one. Every morning when she arrived at work, she was full of energy and eager to get one of these big jobs done. But first, she always directed her energies to clearing away all the little things that had cropped up. She reasoned that once she got all those little tasks out of the way, she'd be able to concentrate on the big ones. The only trouble was that often by the time she had finished all the small tasks, she felt too drained to get started on a big one.

As the two-month period drew to its end, worker morale was indeed up, but the work flow was noticeably less efficient, and Mildred had hardly even started to prepare her report on the reorganization.

1. Discuss Mildred's problem as manager. What was she doing wrong? What should she have done?

2. Prepare a priority-setting "to do" list for Mildred based on her goals. Make up activities that would be necessary to achieve goals.

CASE 2

New on the Job

Phil felt a little nervous going to his first day on the job as a computer programmer, but he was determined not to show it. He knew he was well trained. His grades had been high in school. The company manager had been particularly pleased to hire him because Phil had been trained to program using the most recent computer language and the most up-to-date equipment. In fact the company had just upgraded its computers, so Phil would probably know as much about them as the senior workers.

Phil fixed these thoughts firmly in his mind to quiet his sense of anxiety upon entering his new work environment. He told himself that he would let the others know right away that although he might be young and just out of school, he really knew his stuff. To make this point and not appear ignorant, he decided not to ask any questions. When the shop supervisor showed him his work station and started to explain some things about it and the keyboard, Phil quickly interrupted her to say he knew what to do. She gave him a look, shrugged slightly, said, "Okay, good luck," and walked away.

A few minutes later, Phil was embarrassed because he found he could not turn on his computer. The regular switches did not work. He felt his face getting red as he sat there staring at a blank screen after pushing the switch back and forth several times. Eventually, he got up and went over to the supervisor to tell her his computer was broken and would not run.

"That's funny," she said, "it was working fine last night. Let's see." They went back to Phil's machine, and Phil demonstrated that it would not start when he turned on the switches.

"Well, that was one of the things I was going to tell you," the supervisor said. "To make sure the monitor, the computer, and the printer are all turned off, we use this switch and keep the ones on the equipment in the 'on' position all the time." Saying this, she showed Phil a master switch on the side of his desk. "I thought the manager had told you since you said you knew everything. Maybe I better show you..."

"No, no. I know how to run these things," Phil said quickly. He was more determined than ever to show what he could do without a lot of help like other new people might need. "I did a lot of programming on this system in school." The supervisor said, "Okay," and returned to her work station.

With the system on, Phil soon had it running and was busy working on his first assignment. It was a simple program, and he quickly wrote it into the system. But when he tried to test it by running it, he kept getting gibberish on the screen. He could not figure out what was happening. He kept trying the program, changing little things, but it would not run as it was supposed to. He became very frustrated and annoyed. Finally, he had to get up again and go to the supervisor. He knew other workers were watching him, and his face was red.

The supervisor came back to his station and looked at his screen. After a quick glance she called out, "Okay, who's the wise guy?" The other programmers were grinning and laughing. One of them got up and came over to Phil's work station. He sat down and input a few commands. "Just a little joke, man," he said to Phil with a big grin. "We sort of test the new programmers. "

Phil was not amused by the little joke. He felt everyone was trying to make him look bad. The supervisor explained that the older programmers sometimes changed the key definitions on new programmers' keyboards as an initiation joke. She said she warns newcomers, and they can sometimes figure out what was done and correct it when it happens. Anyway, it was a quick way for older workers to get to know new ones, she explained. She advised him to laugh along and forget it.

Phil did not feel like laughing or forgetting it. He was more determined than ever to show them. During the lunch break other workers said they hoped he did not mind the little joke and offered him any help any time. He said thanks, but to show he did not need help he talked about how much he knew about the system they were now working with.

After a few days on the job he realized the programmers would often help each other with problems, but he never asked for help. One day, though, as he was returning from a break he noticed that Joan, an experienced programmer near his work station, had a complicated program on the screen. He happened to have worked on a similar problem in school and knew a better way to do it.

"Hey," he said to Joan, "You got that all wrong. Or you could do it a lot neater. Look, I'll show you." He pushed in and began changing her program. "There, isn't that a lot better. You were doing it in a very clumsy, inefficient way. The way I did it is best. I guess you old programmers don't know some of these new ways like I do."

Although he did know programming and the system, Phil continued to make mistakes because he was slow learning company policy and the special ways the company had of doing things. Also, he was not getting to know the other workers, and even after several weeks he still felt like an outsider or newcomer.

1. Discuss Phil's approach to his new job. What did he do wrong?

2. What should he have done?

▷ STRESS:
How We Turn It To Our
Advantage

The diseases of stress have more than replaced the
dangers of working with heavy equipment or toxic chem-
icals
Earl Shorris

18

CHAPTER

In his book *The Oppressed Middle*,[18] Earl Shorris, noting our change from a production to a service society, makes the point that although more people now work in service jobs that are physically safer, they face increased risks from job-related stress.

In this chapter you will read not only of job-related stress but of stress that you will experience in other environments, examine the nature of stress, and learn some ways of coping with it. We all experience stress and have done so throughout our lives. You should be aware, however, that stress is not always harmful, nor is it always a negative factor in your life. Although too much stress is harmful, some stress is actually necessary. A life without stress results in boredom, indifference, and inaction.

▼ WHAT STRESS IS

stressors
specific conditions or events in the environment that challenge or threaten a person

Just what is meant by stress? As with so many other human experiences, stress is defined differently by different experts, depending on how they view it. Some describe it in physiological terms: your bodily responses to a situation in the environment will tell us if it is stressful or not. Others define stress through a person's psychological reaction: if you perceive a situation in the environment as stressful, it is a stress. According to Richard Lazarus, from the University of California at Berkeley, stress is an external load or demand on a biological, social, or psychological system. The stress process includes: (1) a causal situation (the **stressor**), (2) an evaluation that distinguishes what is threatening or unpleasant from what is not, (3) a coping process used by the mind (or body) to deal with the stressful demand, and (4) a pattern of effects on the mind and body, referred to as the **stress reaction**. A stressful situation may lead to a stress reaction in one person and not in another because people differ in their evaluation and coping processes.

stress reaction
a physical and/or psychological reaction to a difficult, demanding, or dangerous environment or situation, normally experienced as anxiety, fear, or extreme discomfort

A stress reaction is individually determined and has both psychological and physiological effects. It is perceived as emotional and physical arousal. Emotional arousal may be felt in many ways, such as anxiety, guilt, or anger. When encountering stress, your body prepares to respond in one of two ways: to fight or to flee. Your glands become active, increasing the supply of natural chemical substances in your body that increase your energy so you can react—by fight or flight—to the stressor.

Stress comes to you in two ways:

1. It is thrust upon you—having an accident, experiencing a death or illness in the family, losing of a job, taking a test, being blocked from satisfying a need, or being in a continually demanding or threatening environment.

2. You actively seek it by trying something new and challenging—applying for college, interviewing for a job, trying a new sport, starting a new career, or asking for a date.

As these examples indicate, change often presents you with stress, whether you seek it or it is thrust upon you. Lazarus draws a distinction among three kinds of stress: harm refers to psychological damage that has already been done, threat is the anticipation of harm that has not yet taken place but may be imminent, and challenge results from difficult demands we feel we can meet by using our abilities, skills, and coping resources. Change is upsetting and always requires adjustment on your part, so it is not surprising that change and stress are associated.

▼ NECESSARY STRESS

Some stress, or challenge, is necessary for people to perform well. Without challenge, according to some theories, people would not be energized to perform as well as they can. Some psychologists refer to the "optimal level of arousal," by which they mean an individual is aroused or stimulated to perform well. Without challenge, there would be no arousal. People need a "medium" or "moderate" level of challenge and arousal to perform at their peak. Too little challenge or too much challenge can become a bore or a threat and lead to poorer performance.

The optimum level of arousal depends in part on *task complexity*. Performance in simple tasks (unskilled physical labor such as loading or unloading) is higher when arousal is high. Performance in complex tasks demanding concentration (writing involved reports, negotiating difficult agreements) requires a moderate level of arousal for best performance.

You experience stress as the result of inevitable changes, either good or bad, in your lifetime: new schools, new jobs, getting married, having children, deaths in the family. Psychologists call stress associated with such expected experiences **normative stress**. At times, unexpected changes occur, such as being robbed or suffering a bad accident or a tornado. Psychologists call the stress accompanying these unexpected events **nonnormative stress** or **traumatic stress**.

Unpredictable or nonnormative events are usually more stressful than those that are anticipated. A worker whose day is filled with random, frequent interruptions faces a high degree of stress because of this. Reducing the unpredictability of the stressors (the events, actions, or conditions that cause stress) in the environment is an important way of diminishing stress.

normative stress
stress associated with unavoidable or normal life experiences (a death in the family, a new job or school, or marriage)

nonnormative stress
stress associated with unexpected or atypical experiences (being robbed, war, or a car accident)

▼ STRESS IN A CHANGING SOCIETY

Life was never easy, at any time or in any place. As you read earlier, life once was a struggle for existence. People hunted, farmed, fished, and traded to get the necessities of life. Failure led immediately to deprivation, starvation, and ultimately to death. Today, the struggle is not so directly tied to survival, but the greater number of choices available to us is increasingly a source of stress. Even as our physiological needs are satisfied more easily, the urge to satisfy higher psychological needs intensifies. And because satisfying these needs can be difficult and not at all assured, our susceptibility to stress reactions increases.

Society is complex and filled with contradictions. We often face trying to satisfy conflicting values, such as with the affirmative action laws, as you read in Chapter 16. We have the conflict between the need to stop pollution to clean up our environment and the need to have industries producing necessary goods while providing essential jobs.

The increased complexity of work, a result largely of technology, contributes to stress. Ancient farmers faced a bitter life-and-death struggle with nature in their effort to feed their families, but in this struggle they did

TO THE POINT

Experimenting with rats in the 1930s, Hans Selye, a scientist, identified a three-phase physiological reaction to stress, which, he concluded, was similar to what happened to humans in stressful situations. More recent research has challenged Selye's conclusions, particularly on the grounds that to some extent different types of stress trigger different responses. Nonetheless, Selye's concept appears to describe what happens to our body in many stressful situations. Selye named the physiological reactions he observed general adaptation syndrome, or GAS for short. The reactions consisted of three major stages:

1. Alarm Reaction. This stage is divided into two phases: shock and countershock. In shock, your initial response, your temperature and blood pressure drop, your heart quickens, and your muscles go slack. In countershock your body bounces back to concentrate on defending itself.

2. Resistance. In this stage you take action to eliminate or defend yourself against the source of stress.

3. Exhaustion. This stage occurs as the stressful situation and stress response continue. If the stress is great and continues long enough, exhaustion can result in collapse, even death.

not need to interact with many other individuals or perform in an environment in which the demands, rewards, and punishments are not always clearly defined or assured.

Today, the average worker earns a living in a large corporation in which one must cooperate and somehow get along with many coworkers, subordinates, and superiors (and often clients and customers). Often, the longer a person is employed in a modern corporation and the higher the person advances, the greater the stress. The irony is that one would think that increased experience and power would lessen stress, whereas the opposite is true.

A worker on an assembly line might begin to perceive the repetition as stressful and the new worker, perceiving the job as insecure, is exposed to the stress of insecurity. But the top officials often face greater stress both because their decisions can affect so many others and because the demands on them are so great. In short, success can generate stress just as failure can. The successful athlete feels pressure to continue as number one, the successful writer feels pressure to repeat the bestseller, and the successful executive feels pressure to continue increasing corporate profits. There are constructive and destructive ways of coping with these demands, as you will read.

Those living and working in cities—where most workers live or work—experience stressful situations before they even get to work. Their day begins and ends with struggles through clogged streets and freeways and on jammed trains and buses.

The changed nature of our jobs may present us with stress. Many jobs have been broken down into their simplest elements to produce assembly-line tasks that are boring, dull, and repetitious. At the same time, the technology with which every worker must cope is becoming more complex. A dull, boring job can be perceived as stressful, especially when the worker cannot see or understand how it fits into the overall production plan. And in the midst of this frustrating boredom, the assembly-line worker experiences the stressful threat of being replaced by a machine.

At one time, workers were able to see the meaning in what they did. There was a clear and obvious relationship between the tasks they performed and the end product. That relationship has disappeared from many jobs today. If the nature of the job has changed, so have the workers' attitudes toward it. Once workers felt that simply having a job was sufficient. Now, workers are constantly bombarded with the notion that they must keep moving onward and upward—go, go, go. A worker may be very happy as a secretary, but television, newspapers, and magazines will all scold the worker for not going farther. Tension results as the secretary struggles to win a management position—which may be less satisfying and thus generate still more unhappiness.

Fig. 18-1

In our crowded cities, just getting to and from the job can be a stress-producing struggle.

The idea of upward movement is a stressor for managers of work organizations as well as for the workers. The idea that a company must show a bigger profit every year, and often every quarter, is accepted wisdom today. Grow or die is the watchword, and the result is tremendous tension for the managers of such a company.

As an example of this tension-producing pressure to grow every year, executives at a huge corporation experienced a year of panic when sales did not increase by 10 percent over the previous year. The fact that the previous year had been a record year in sales was ignored. Also ignored was the fact that in the current year, sales were slightly over those of the previous year. In other words, the company was actually having another record year of earnings, but management kept the pressure on and generated tension because an expected rate of 10 percent growth was not met. Their concept of growth was so unrealistic that their anxiety grew extremely high when the growth rate fell below their expectations. In this way, they generated their own stressor, that of unrealistic expectations.

▼ WORK-RELATED STRESS

In a 1984 survey of 160 work organizations, Kenneth Pelletier, a professor of psychiatry at the University of California at San Francisco, found that training on handling stress was the most desired employee-assistance service. Some occupations, of course, involve more stress than others. As you read, unpredictable events are the most stressful, and those occupations in which workers must contend with the unexpected face the most stress.

Health care technicians and receptionists who must be able to respond to the unexpected visitors, callers, and complainers are among stress-exposed workers.

Air traffic controllers are another group of workers who must face tremendous stress on the job. These people are responsible for the lives of thousands of airline passengers daily, and they frequently face the unexpected. Reporters on daily newspapers face a special kind of tension as they must race to get all the facts of a story, get them right, and get them in time to meet deadlines. On each story, they face new conditions and situations that cannot be anticipated. Then their work is put into print for everyone to read—and criticize. Underwater workers, such as scuba divers, and construction workers on tall buildings face high levels of stress associated with their jobs partly due to the dangerous conditions and partly due to the need to deal with the unexpected.

Even jobs that do not have such obviously stressful environments can create stress reactions. The secretary whose word-processing computer malfunctions during a rush to complete an important report under deadline faces stress. If the computer malfunctions often, the secretary's level of stress reaction will probably increase. This is another example of the random, unpredictable event being stressful.

Work-related stress is now a subject of concern to public and private health officials. They have found that stress reactions can contribute to or make worse health problems such as heart disease, hypertension (high blood pressure), alcoholism, drug abuse, ulcers, and anxiety. Some consider stress reactions to be the number-one health problem today. In addition to adverse effects on health, stress reactions have two other negative effects:

1. They can result in poor performance at work. A person constantly exposed to stress cannot function as efficiently as when working under less stress. No one lives a stress-free life, and a degree of stress is normal and even necessary. In fact, many people in demanding jobs realize that experiencing a degree of tension helps them perform better. If they do not feel this tension, their work and effectiveness loses an edge. But continuing exposure to stress can exceed an individual's ability to cope, and the result is reduced capability.

2. A worker's personal life can become increasingly unhappy as a result of continuous exposure to stress at work. Continued stress tends to make us edgy and easily upset. Workers under such stress often carry their problems home and are often angry or anxious. As a result their family life suffers. The family might even disintegrate. The reverse can also happen. As you will read later in this chapter, work is not the only source of stress. Stress can occur at home and

in social settings. A worker enduring excessive stress at home can carry the results of it into the work environment, and performance can suffer.

Psychological Expectations

Besides the obvious stressors at work, such as the pressure to perform well, potential physical danger, difficult coworkers or bosses, continuous interruptions, the need to meet deadlines, and malfunctioning equipment, there are other factors that contribute to the stress a worker perceives. The degree of stress perceived on the job has been found to be related to one's psychological expectations of the job.

Our psychological expectations are met by what were referred to as *work reinforcers* in Chapter 7. Known familiarly as "rewards," they are called *reinforcers* because they maintain or strengthen work behavior. All workers have two sets of expectations for the job: those reflected by formal reinforcers, such as pay, vacation, and fringe benefits, and informal or unstated ones, such as reinforcers that help fill higher psychological needs for esteem, recognition, and full use of talents.

We all have certain expectations when we start a job. If our expectations prove wrong—that is, if the work does not provide the expected reinforcers—we will begin to perceive our job as stressful. For example, Mildred was unhappy in her job in the mail room. She worked alone mostly, except for handing out packages to the messengers when they came by two or three times a day. She liked people and thought she would prefer being a receptionist because receptionists see a lot of people and seem to have important positions. When an opening for a receptionist came along, she applied for the position and was selected for it.

At first she was happy, but she soon found that she was having too much contact with people and not in the way she had anticipated. The phone kept ringing, and people kept hurrying up to her with questions. Often she could not answer the questions, and the people became annoyed. Everyone expected to be dealt with right away. If they had to wait, they became rude and scolded her. With all the people bothering her, she found that she could not keep up with the filing work she was required to do.

Eventually she asked to leave the job because her psychological expectations were not realized and she was feeling too much tension because of the unexpected and unpredictable events that made it difficult for her to do her work. She was not really interacting with other people as she had hoped, and the job did not seem all that much better to her.

To avoid future stress, you must know as much as possible about a potential job and whether it will meet your psychological needs by providing the desired reinforcers. This means studying yourself to identify your needs, and studying the job to identify its potential reinforcers. Ideally, you should see how the job fits into the work organization, what interaction there will be with other workers, what recognition it provides, and how well what you find out matches what you want from the job in terms of meeting not only your financial needs but also your psychological needs.

Job Status

Work involves stress because it plays such an important part in our lives. As you have read, our work often provides us with our identity. A person is introduced as a "lawyer," "sales representative," or "computer programmer." When people meet, either at a party or as new neighbors, one of the first questions asked is, "What do you do?" What you do is important in terms of your perceived status—sometimes undeservedly so. Some occupations are perceived as having high status, and some have low status.

This perception may or may not reflect the job's actual value, but it does reflect the perceived value society places on it. The importance society places on a job's status is reflected in the way we change titles of jobs to increase their perceived dignity or value. "Custodian" suggests more value or dignity than "janitor." "Sanitation worker" or "sanitation engineer" suggests greater status than "garbage collector." Changing titles reflects a normal desire for status. What happens, of course, is that although at first a loftier title might influence the perception of a job's status, eventually the perceived status of the job influences the title.

Generally speaking, a job's status reflects the degree of skills required to perform it or the amount of training and education required. The greater the required skill and training, the greater the status. In terms of actual value to society, however, these criteria for determining status do not always make sense. A major problem facing society today is getting rid of its accumulating trash. Thus the lowly regarded garbage collector performs an increasingly essential service. A person concerned about status, however, might perceive a great deal of stress working in a job that has low status, regardless of how important it is, how easy it might be to do, or even how well paid and enjoyable it is.

Women and Job Stress

Whatever their occupation, women face particular stressors as they attempt to juggle roles: that of worker and that of wife-mother-homemaker. The personality traits necessary for a woman's success at work often are not suitable for success at home. At work she is required to be forceful,

Fig. 18-2

Job status can be a source of stress. A person in a job with low status who craves higher status will experience stress. To relieve this stress we sometimes try to change how a job is perceived by changing its title. In this cartoon, a man who is already a chief executive officer feels the need for more status, so he has put four general's stars on his shoulders.

assertive, competitive. At home she must often be supportive, nurturing, self-effacing. Children and husband may feel threatened by the wife and mother's job, especially if they believe that it means more to her or that they must compete with it for her time.

Women also face the additional stress of having to make their way in what was once considered the domain of men. The plight of the modern woman seeking to have a career was neatly summed up by a wry cartoon in a national magazine. A woman responds to a question from a man at a party by saying, "Why yes, you could call me 'a little homemaker.' I am the president of a construction company that builds single-family houses."

In today's climate, even if they elect to stay at home and make their career having and raising children, women still face stress. This partly reflects the stress we all face as a result of simply having more choices. But for women it also reflects their need for status. Although a fallacy, as you read in Chapter 16, it is customary to define work in terms of money earned. Because homemakers do not receive a salary, the job has little conventional status. In reacting negatively to the simplistic notion that a woman's place is in the home, we have tended inadvertently to downgrade the career of homemaker and mother, which means more stress for the woman who chooses the career of homemaker and mother but who may also long for status.

Work Organizations

In addition to psychological expectations and job status, another potential source of stress is the work organization itself and the demands it makes on a worker. To achieve success at work, all workers must give things up at times. For the executive driven to reach the top, the cost often can be less time with the family. This can produce feelings of guilt and anxiety. Sometimes to get a desired job, the worker must give up living in a preferred area or must work hours that interfere with one's personal life.

Increasing awareness of worldwide problems, such as air and water pollution, conflict among nations and peoples, and economic downturns, is another source of stress for people today. Many people ask themselves whether they should work for organizations that contribute to these problems. Many workers, in order to have a job, find themselves doing things they really do not believe in. Often this results in *discorrespondence* as you read in Chapter 17. When people have trouble making their attitudes, morals, and other personal beliefs conform to the requirements of a particular work environment, the result is discorrespondence and stress reaction.

The nature or style of a work organization can contribute to job stress. If the organizational style is **autocratic**—that is, the bosses make the rules, give the orders, and expect unquestioned compliance—stress increases if workers feel the need to have a say in the operation and want a more democratic style. Work organizations unresponsive to worker needs are stressful for everyone.

autocratic
as used here, a work organization style in which the bosses make the rules, give the orders, and expect unquestioned compliance

Burnout

Burnout is an emotional state that a worker might experience after exposure to continuing stress. Workers experiencing burnout suffer from emotional exhaustion. They seem to lose a sense of themselves as effective individuals. They might believe that their work is useless, that there is nothing they can do, that they have nothing left to give to the job or to others. They can become uncaring, depersonalized, and unproductive, saying to themselves, What difference does it make?

People in service occupations devoted to helping others, such as social workers, nurses, doctors, counselors, and clinical psychologists, are susceptible to burnout. Many people enter such careers with a strong desire to help and with a naive sense of how much they can accomplish. Soon they become overwhelmed by the extent of the problems and the number of people seeking help. They work as hard as they can to make a difference, but come to realize that regardless of how hard they work, problems will continue. They then experience burnout, feeling frustrated, apathetic, and useless.

burnout
an emotional state that a worker experiences after enduring continuing stress, characterized by emotional exhaustion, loss of a sense of effectiveness, and a corresponding sense of futility

People who succeed in careers likely to cause burnout develop ways to cope. They remove themselves from their work occasionally and they cut down on their working hours and take frequent breaks. At the end of the day they follow routines to wipe away the problems of work, such as jogging, taking a hot bath, listening to music, or just simply sitting and meditating. In a sense they learn how to withdraw from contact with others at times to reduce the tension they feel. Some, of course, try to cope by turning to drugs or alcohol to escape, and they fail. You will read about effective and self-destructive coping patterns in later sections.

▼ NON-WORK-RELATED STRESS

All of your environments can present you with stress. You no doubt are well aware that the school environment can be stressful, especially around the time of midterms or finals. Stress occurs when you feel outside pressure to perform, particularly to perform well. This pressure creates anxiety and causes you to question your ability to do what is expected or what you want to do, and you begin to doubt yourself.

If you decide to play a game of baseball or tennis, you create a stressful situation to the extent that you wish to perform well and win. If people watch, the situation becomes more stressful. A degree of stress reaction causes your body to release natural chemicals, so you have greater energy. If the stress is too great and you cannot control it, however, you will probably play poorly and thus enter a frustrating cycle of increasing stress and deteriorating performance.

Change—major or minor, expected or unexpected, desirable or undesirable—can be stressful. Whether the stress experienced at any given time will have harmful aftereffects—and studies have indicated a connection between severe or continued exposure to stress and illness—depends to a certain degree on the individual.

In your everyday life away from work, you face a multitude of changes that are potentially stressful. Poor health, loss of job, death of a loved one, aging parents, and financial problems are among the more common stressors. If the change is sudden, the stressfulness is greater. For example, the death of someone you love is always very stressful. But if the death comes as expected after a long life or illness, the bereaved's stress response is less than if the death is unexpected, the result of sudden illness, suicide, murder, or an accident. See the following To The Point box for a list of stressful changes social scientists have identified, along with values indicating their relative severity.

▼ FACTORS AFFECTING STRESS REACTIONS

Fig. 18-3

Although the Holmes and Rahe list on the following page looks as if we all tend to rank the severity of stressful events in the same order, different people react differently to different events. To an extent, you learn to appraise many potentially stressful situations through classical or operant conditioning that you read about in Chapter 9. Studies have also indicated that your personality often determines the events you consider stressful as well as how you react. Some people resist the negative effects of stress better than others; they are said to be more resilient. They typically think positively about situations, reflecting a personality trait of *optimism*. Of course, optimism can be learned, as you will read later. Furthermore, factors in the environment influence your stress reactions. An event that may be particu-

The relative strengths of various stressors help determine how stressful a job is. Jobs such as air traffic controller, where a mistake can cost many lives, can be very stressful.

larly stressful under some conditions can be less stressful under others. Let's review some of these factors, as well as learning and personality factors, as they influence our stress reactions.

Kinds of Needs Blocked

Stress reactions result when you fail to fulfill your needs, and the degree of stress reaction you feel will be determined by the needs not filled. Your level of stress reaction will be greater if you are stopped in trying to satisfy your

TO THE POINT

In the 1960s, Thomas Holmes and Richard Rahe, behavioral scientists, asked several hundred subjects to rank the severity of 43 potentially stressful events. They used marriage as a standard and asked the subjects to rate the other events by whether each would require a greater or lesser degree of adjustment. Here are some of the events and their ratings (100 indicating the most stressful event) as established by Holmes and Rahe:

Death of a spouse	100
Divorce	73
Death of close family member	63
Personal injury or illness	53
Marriage	50
Loss of job	47
Retirement	45
Change in health of family member	44
Pregnancy	40
Sex difficulties	39
Change in financial state	38
Death of close friend	37
Changing jobs	36
Mortgage or major loan	31
Change in responsibility at work	29
Beginning or ending of school	26
Changing personal habits	24
Trouble with boss	23
Change in work hours or conditions	20
Change in residence	20
Change in schools	20
Vacation	13
Minor violations of law	11

most important need. If you are really hungry or thirsty, you will react strongly to things that prevent you from satisfying these needs. Generally speaking, the more important the blocked need is, the greater your frustration and stress reaction.

Number of Needs Blocked

If circumstances prevent you from satisfying several needs, you experience a greater stress reaction than you would if your ability to satisfy only one need was blocked. If you were in a job that did not meet your need for recognition, you might feel some dissatisfaction but be willing to accept it because the job paid well and also met your need to be creative and independent. If none of these needs were met, you would experience a higher level of stress reaction.

Your Expectations

The greater your expectations, the greater your degree of stress reaction when you fail or are prevented from realizing them. If all you expect from your job is a modest paycheck and the chance to work 7-1/2 hours a day, 5 days a week, you will not perceive your job as very stressful if that is all you get. Usually, though, you will expect something more in terms of recognition, praise, eventual promotion, and fringe benefits. If your expectations for these things are not met, your job will seem more stressful.

Total Versus Partial Block

If you are completely blocked from achieving a goal, your job will appear more stressful than if you are only partially blocked. Say you have been expecting a promotion and a pay increase at work, but then you receive only a merit pay increase with a bonus but no promotion. You will experience frustration, but not as great as what you would feel if you received no part of your expectation.

Repeated Failure

Continually failing to achieve a goal, whatever the reason for your failure, is increasingly stressful, up to a point. But after multiple failures, most people experience a reduced frustration response. They may even experience the phenomenon you read about in Chapter 17, *learned helplessness*, appearing apathetic in the face of failure. They may appear burned out in that they continue to "go through the motions" without obtaining success and do not react "normally" to this frustrating outcome.

Availability of Options

Your stress reaction will be less if you have more than one way to fill a need than it will be if you have only one way and that way is blocked. If your need is to achieve recognition and you have a job that does not provide you with much opportunity for recognition, such as that of a factory worker in a large plant, you may find an alternative way to meet your need through outside activities. For example, you could work for a politician or run for public office yourself. If you are able to find other ways to receive the recognition you want, your stress reaction will be less if your remunerated work fails to provide the recognition you need.

Length of Time

The longer you are in a stressful situation, the greater your stress reaction. At work you will perceive stress when first faced with an impossibly difficult deadline or task. But if you take care of it and are not challenged with another immediately, your stress reaction will subside and soon passes. You think to yourself, this can happen now and then but I can handle it. If, however, you face difficult tasks daily, the stressors mount and the demands on you become increasingly unacceptable. You begin to think you can not keep this up. Your stress reaction increases the longer difficult tasks continue to stream in.

Acceptable Explanation

Your acceptance of the reason for failing to reach a goal can lessen its stressfulness. A person eager to be promoted to branch manager may be able to accept delay if she knows that the delay is the result of a general downturn in business. Because business slowed, no new branches opened; thus the need for new managers dropped. She will reason that when conditions change, the promotion will come, and thus her stress reaction will be less. If, however, new branches are being opened and she was not promoted to manager for whatever reason—less-than-satisfactory performance, a supervisor's personal dislike—her stress reaction will increase. If she determines it is indeed as a result of a personal dislike and not because of dissatisfaction with her performance that she is not likely to be promoted, her stress reaction will be even greater.

Status of Cause

The relative strength of the stressor will determine to some extent the level of your stress reaction. For example, if you recognize the cause as relatively unimportant or a thing that you can easily remove or do something about, it is less stressful than if the cause is powerful and outside your ability to control it.

Appraisal, Learning, and Self-Efficacy

As noted earlier, appraisal is that part of the stress process in which you distinguish what is threatening or unpleasant from what is not. Most of your appraisals are learned, such as your appraisal of a particular neighborhood as safe. A few appraisals have biological roots, such as the common appraisal of snakes as threatening. All appraisals may be modified through learning. You may reappraise a neighborhood as unsafe after the occurrence of a crime there. Snakes may be reappraised as nonthreatening after you undergo behavior therapy aimed at reducing fear of snakes.

Your learning often determines not only what you appraise as threatening but how you react. A simple illustration of this would be an executive who makes two or three seriously bad decisions after several years of successful management. Until the bad decisions, having to make difficult decisions was not threatening, but challenging to the executive. After the bad decisions and their consequences, being called on to make a tough decision is now a stressful situation. The executive has learned a stress reaction through a conditioning experience.

The executive may have also learned through observation (imitation or vicarious learning, as you read in Chapter 9) that the best way to handle the increased threat is to accept the possibility of error and go right on making decisions. Otherwise, if the executive begins to postpone making decisions, the threat will build up, possibly causing harm to the company and the executive.

An emerging notion in social and counseling psychology is that of **self-efficacy**, which refers to confidence in your ability to accomplish a task successfully. Self-efficacy, which is related to self-esteem, is largely learned. Essentially, early success experiences in childhood or in the early stages of a new job generate a belief within a person, a confidence in one's ability to do the job. People vary in their sense of self-efficacy for a given task, and those with higher levels are more likely to undertake new tasks. Remember you read in Chapter 17 about *perseverance*, how long you persist in actively or reactively adjusting to your environment. All other things being equal, those with greater perseverance cope more successfully with demands of the environment, which may lead to an increased sense of self-efficacy.

self-efficacy
confidence in your ability to accomplish a task successfully

Individual Predisposition

Individuals have different levels of tolerance for stress, which may be inherited. Some seem to thrive in situations in which others feel uncomfortably stressed. Also, some individuals appear to be more emotional and hence more sensitive to stressful situations. Other individuals actually seem to seek out stressful situations.

Studies in the mid-1980s revealed that some people live lives of deep emotional intensity. These people react more strongly to events around them, often interpreting the events in personal terms even when the events have no real connection to them. They tend to feel more strongly about things than others do. When an emotionally intense person has conflicting goals—a frequent occurrence because they tend to seek variety in their lives—they feel the conflict deeply. As a consequence they experience a greater stress reaction.

Another type of person likely to experience more stress has been identified as a **Type A personality**. Meyer Friedman and Ray Rosenman in their book, *Type A Behavior and Your Heart*, (New York: Knopf, 1974) identified such behavior as a "chronic, incessant struggle to achieve more and

Type A personality
a personality type believed to experience more stress, characterized by an incessant struggle to achieve more and more in less and less time, free-floating hostility, and behavior that appears to deliberately invite stress

---

TO THE POINT

Who you are is a factor in what you may find stressful and how stressed you feel. Judith Pliner and Duane Brown surveyed 229 students (123 females and 106 males) from four ethnic groups (white, African American, Hispanic, and Asian American) who were asked to estimate how stressful they would expect to find events in four different domains: academic, financial, family, and personal.[19]

Responses to the survey indicated that an individual's ethnic background is associated with what that person appraises as stressful. For example, according to their responses, older African Americans and Hispanics perceived more stress than older Asian Americans in dealing with events in the academic domain, and older Hispanics perceived significantly more stress than older whites.

African American men perceived greater stress in the personal domain than did African American women. Younger white women perceived more stress in this domain than did older white women.

In the financial domain, both African American and Hispanic subjects felt more stressed in meeting events than did either white or Asian American subjects.

Studies such as this indicate that although some events are inherently stressful for everyone—being in a burning building, for example—many other events are appraised as stressful or not according to an individual's background, gender, and conditioning.

more in less and less time" accompanied by a "free-floating hostility." Type A people appear deliberately to invite stress reactions. In their book, Friedman and Rosenman linked such behavior with increased rates of heart disease.

Although intensely emotional people and those with Type A behavior patterns may be subject to more stress, recent studies are indicating that, at least within limits, being emotional or a Type A personality is not all bad, nor does it guarantee illness. There is some evidence that on average such people live richer lives, experiencing challenge in stressors that others find threatening, are less likely to be harmed by many stressors, and if they become ill, are able to bounce back more quickly. Also, recent studies indicate that not all Type A personalities experience constant, undirected hostility.

Being unemotional or a Type B personality is not a guarantee of avoiding stress reactions. There is a general theory that too high or too low a level of emotional experience can result in either anxiety or boredom. In any event, what you are has a bearing on how you might react to stress and even what kind or degree of stress reaction you experience.

▼ COPING WITH STRESS

Stress that is challenging is beneficial, even necessary. But constant or sudden extensive stress that is threatening can be harmful, both mentally and physically. Therefore, scientists talk of our *coping* with stress. By coping they mean the process of reducing or avoiding a stress reaction by changing the unfavorable circumstance or altering the appraisal of it.

In general our coping strategies for changing the environment can be considered *behavioral coping strategies*; those for changing our own appraisals and therefore our stress reaction can be regarded as *psychological coping strategies*. All of these coping strategies can be effective for dealing with stress at any particular time. Many, however, become counterproductive when carried to extremes.

Changing the Environment

In general, behavioral coping strategies manifest themselves in physical action, as opposed to those for changing our appraisal of potentially stressful conditions, which are predominantly cognitive. But this distinction is not perfect. Any action requires mental activity. Let's examine some of the behavioral responses.

Aggression

aggression
a hostile reaction to threat

Aggression is a common reaction to threat. You attack. Sometimes this is best. But aggression can be self-defeating and counterproductive by generating even more threat from the original source. Social scientists have identified two kinds of aggression: *reactive aggression* and *instrumental aggression.*

Reactive Aggression

reactive aggression
an immediate or spontaneous, often not thought out, reaction to threat

Reactive aggression, as its name implies, refers to immediate or spontaneous reaction to threat. You may hardly think at all before acting. The advantages are that you have taken action quickly to reduce the threat you perceive. The obvious disadvantage is that by reacting quickly, with little thought and in the heat of the moment, you may make a bad situation worse. Reactive aggression does not mean you react instantly at the first perception of threat, but that at a given occasion in a stressful situation you react directly and quickly.

For example, suppose at work your boss has been treating you in a way you consider unfair. She has been giving you more than your share of work and criticizes you openly in front of your coworkers. As the days go by this causes you increasing frustration, and one morning when she gives you an assignment you know is unreasonable, you tell her off. That is reactive aggression. It might relieve your sense of frustration, but not produce any desired results.

Fig. 18-4

Many people react to stress with aggression. Psychologists identify two kinds of aggression: reactive and instrumental. Reactive aggression is immediate; instrumental aggression is planned. The executive in this cartoon is reacting to stress with instrumental aggression as he plans a series of "get even" meetings.

"At ten-thirty, you have an appointment to get even with Ward Ingram. At twelve, you're going to get even with Holus Wentworth at lunch. At three, you're getting even with the Pro-Tech Company at their annual meeting. And at five you're going to get even with Fred Benton over drinks."

Instrumental Aggression

Instrumental aggression lacks the immediacy or spontaneity of reactive aggression. It is the conscious use of aggression. It may be planned aggression. Given the stressful situation of having an unreasonable boss, rather than reacting openly and immediately, you might begin to work slower, try to undercut your boss with the other workers, or attempt to make your boss look bad in front of her superiors.

All of these manifestations of aggression might work for you, at least in giving you a way to vent your feelings if not to solve the basic problem. To solve the basic problem, you might plan a course of action that would include an unemotional discussion with your boss in which you laid out your objections and reasons, using your job description (see Chapter 17) and company policies to support your case. You could also take this approach in a formal way to the next in command, and, perhaps, seek a transfer. All of these approaches constitute an attack on the problem, which is instrumental aggression.

Fixation

Sometimes you might become fixed on a response to a particular stressor. There is nothing wrong with that if it helps you reduce or avoid stress reactions. If, however, the fixed response fails, yet you continue with it, then you are exhibiting fixation. **Fixation** is the process of persistent nonproductive responding to particular stressors. Perhaps the response did work at one time, but changing conditions have made it unsuitable. Despite the changing conditions, the person with fixation sticks with the old, unsuccessful response.

An example of fixation is the student who tries to write down everything the lecturer says, even though it is impossible and the effort causes him often to lose track of the main points being made. Furthermore, the notes, which may not even include some essential points, are so long it is difficult to review them for exams. The result is poor performance and increased frustration. The student should change and train himself to listen for and make notes only of the major points. Thus he can concentrate on listening and not on note taking. In this case, the notes he does take will jog his memory better, and he has already pinpointed what is important, which is helpful at exam time. But a fear of not writing down every word leads this student to exhibit fixation and to continue his unproductive actions.

Regression

When people experiencing a stressful situation throw a temper tantrum, they are reacting by **regression**. That means they are reverting to earlier forms of

instrumental aggression
the conscious, sometimes planned, use of aggression as a means to an end

fixation
repeating the same response to a particular problem or situation, even after experience has shown that the response will not bring about the desired results

regression
a reaction to stress characterized by reverting to earlier forms of reaction that were used in childhood, such as yelling, throwing tantrums, sulking, and so on

reaction that were learned in childhood. Such people yell, swear, or sulk, and in some cases exhibit aggression in their reaction, although often the extent of their aggressive behavior is to make a lot of noise or pound a table. If aggression takes the form of inflicting physical harm on others, it is also a form of regression.

Children often exhibit regression when frustrated. They may return to an earlier age by sucking their thumb again, for example. Regression represents a way of coping with stress by returning to an earlier age when we felt more effective in coping with stress. Crying may be a form of regression, but it also represents a functional response when it helps us relieve our pent-up feelings.

Withdrawal

withdrawal
a coping strategy that is not an attack on the problem but a decision not to act, to pull back from a goal, often producing depression and apathy

In a sense all of the coping strategies you have just read about are some form of attack on the stressor. The attack may or may not be suitable, but you are doing something. Although a response, **withdrawal** is not an attack on the problem. Withdrawal means just that: to decide not to act, to pull back from attacking the problem.

Withdrawal may be the most harmful and least effective response to stress, but at times it might be the most sensible response. If you are turned down for a raise on the first request, you would probably be better advised to withdraw by giving up your goal of an immediate raise rather than to quit. If at the same time you quietly begin looking for another job that pays what you desire, you are using problem solving as a coping strategy. But withdrawal without alternative action can result in apathy.

Avoidance

avoidance
a coping strategy characterized by attempts not to deal with a problem at all, for example by not thinking about it or acting on it

A somewhat different reaction from withdrawal, **avoidance** is an attempt not to deal with the stressor at all. One example of avoidance is to postpone thinking or acting. One of the most harmful avoidance tactics is a resort to the use of mood-altering substances—drugs. Excessive use of drugs, including alcohol and prescription and nonprescription drugs, alters a person's mood temporarily and makes stressful situations "go away." The situations do not really go away, of course, and the person is ultimately worse off.

Defense Mechanisms and Reappraisal

These coping strategies differ somewhat from those already described, with which you change your stressful environment by making a decision and acting or, as in the case of withdrawal, deciding not to act. Defense mechanisms provide ways to distance yourself from stressors, often allowing you to change yourself through changing your appraisal of potentially stressful events. Generally, defense mechanisms alone are not the most effective ways of coping with stress. When they permit the reappraisal of a threat as nonthreatening, they can make sense for an individual.

Freud identified **defense mechanisms** as strategies that we employ unconsciously; they are aimed at blocking our awareness of a problem. Because they are unconscious reactions, they are difficult to identify scientifically. But several types of defense mechanisms have been observed. **Denial** itself is one. Denying reality or refusing to acknowledge it can reduce stress temporarily, but it obviously is not a good long-term solution.

Other defense mechanisms we employ unconsciously include **repression**, which means that without conscious thought we banish stress-arousing ideas, conflicts, memories. **Fantasizing** is another defense mechanism. We all resort to it by dreaming about what might have been or what might be rather than reacting more appropriately to a stressful event. We abort or escape a practical reaction to stressful events by jumping to fantasy. It becomes harmful only if we fantasize to excess and our fantasies become our reality. Distancing yourself psychologically from the stressor without blocking it from your awareness can be achieved through the use of *humor, support from others,* and other methods suggested later. Such *distancing* has the advantage of temporarily reducing or avoiding stress reactions while allowing us "space" to select other coping strategies and change our appraisals.

▼ DESTRUCTIVE COPING BEHAVIOR

Prolonged stress reactions that we feel incapable of dealing with can lead to severe depression and, sometimes, even to suicide. People experiencing stress reactions beyond a point they feel that they can deal with should seek help from family, friends, and counselors. Help is usually there for someone seeking it. One response to stress, however, should be avoided: drug abuse.

Earlier in this chapter, you read that mood alteration through drug use was one example of *avoidance* that people used to minimize stress reactions. Because it is so destructive, and, unfortunately, has been resorted to by alarming numbers of people, drug abuse deserves special emphasis as a particularly destructive response to stress. Drug abuse, whatever the drug— alcohol, nonprescription (over-the-counter) drugs, and even an overreliance on prescription drugs—not only does not solve the problem but greatly impairs the user's ability to cope. The use of drugs itself is, in the long run, stressful on the mind and body. Furthermore, because they often produce a physiological dependency on their effects, the drugs themselves become the problem.

defense mechanisms
strategies employed subconsciously, aimed at defending the ego or self-concept as a means of coping with stress

denial
a defense mechanism consisting of simply denying or refusing to acknowledge reality

repression
a defense mechanism that involves banishing from consciousness ideas, inner conflicts, or memories that cause stress

fantasizing
a defense mechanism in which one dreams about what might have been or might be

In the 1980s the public became aware of the shocking use of drugs among professional athletes—a phenomenon probably symptomatic of a more widespread problem in the general public. The case of the athletes, however, commanded special attention because the young men involved were gifted, seemed to have everything in life, and, unfortunately, were role models for younger people. In a tragic case, one young basketball star died from drug abuse just after being named as a first round draft pick by a top professional team. The use of drugs among these athletes in part reflects the stresses they perceive to perform well and, ironically, the stresses of success. As the tragedy of drug abuse and addiction among athletes has made clear, no one is immune from the perception of stress, and coping with stress reactions by abusing drugs is destructive.

▼ REDUCING STRESS REACTIONS

You can use different techniques to reduce or your lessen stress reactions, either at work or in any other environment, such as the social environment or the home. You cannot eliminate stress completely, however, and you should not try to do so. A certain degree of stress (or challenge) is inevitable and even necessary and helpful, as pointed out earlier. The more responsibility you have, the greater the challenge you will experience. Some people, to perform at their best, even seem to need stress that most people would perceive as threatening. The right amount of stress often brings out the best in people.

Stress is a continuing part of business. The teams that put books such as this one together often face stressful situations that induce frustration. The designers do not have enough money to make the book as beautiful as they would like. Neither they nor the editors have enough time before the deadline to make the book meet their high standards for perfection. The production staff struggles with time and financial limitations. Out of all this stress, a creative tension arises that results in the best book for the reader at the lowest possible cost. Stress is not all bad; it can make people think and try harder to reach a goal.

To achieve more invariably requires you to face stress. But you can learn to cope with stressors and your stress reactions so that you can handle and channel them into creative actions rather than into self-destructive actions. Here are some techniques that you can consciously practice to reduce anxiety and frustration. Some will reflect coping strategies you have read of in this chapter. The situation you are in and the type of stress you face often determine what is the best coping technique.

▼ PROBLEM SOLVING

If you are facing stress because you cannot reach a goal for whatever reason, a good coping technique is to look for alternative ways to achieve that goal. Do not give up the goal; instead change the way you are trying to reach it. Other ways to achieve your goals almost always exist. If you do not get a raise when you first expect it, perhaps there is something you can do to bring it about in the near future. Ask your supervisor the reasons you did not receive a raise now and what exactly you must do to earn one in the near future. In short, approach the stressful situation as a problem to be solved by generating alternatives and picking the best one.

Again, keep in mind that although facing extreme and continued stress can be physically and mentally harmful, some stress is useful. If stress challenges you to do some problem solving and to come up with new ways to achieve goals, to react to your environment, or to change yourself or the environment, the results can be positive.

Avoid Stressful Situations

Although facing some stress is inevitable, often you can legitimately avoid certain stressors with a little forethought and care. This does not mean to run away from or deny the stress that is an integral part of your life and plans. But it does mean to avoid unnecessary stress to conserve your strength for coping with the inescapable stress. In short, choose your "battles" intelligently and carefully.

You may have an annoying neighbor or classmate who is stressful. Avoiding that person is a logical and effective way of coping. If heights are stressful, do not climb cliffs; if you become anxious trying to sell people things, do not try to become a salesperson. Not infrequently, however, you may have to face something you perceive as stressful in order to achieve certain goals.

Confront It

This is the opposite of avoiding stressors, but in some situations it is the best approach. Often it turns out that when confronted, the situation is not as stressful as anticipated. But more important, the more you confront the situation, the better able you are to cope with any stress reaction that it produces. For example, if you are like many people, you probably perceive public speaking to be very stressful. Yet many careers require you to be able to speak to large groups. Consequently, avoiding the situation can prevent you from realizing your career goals. Better to face your fear and learn how to speak in public. Each time you do it, you will probably find that you can

Fig. 18-5

Knowing what strategy to use is important when trying to reduce stress reactions. Often, avoiding the situation is not possible or good, but sometimes avoiding a potential stressor is the best reaction. The man being spoken to in the cartoon can and should avoid a potentially stressful event.

"No, I would not welcome a contrasting point of view."

cope a little better with your stress reactions. The reactions you feel when called upon to give a public talk will probably never completely disappear. This is good. Without that slight edge you experience as the adrenalin flows into your body when you face a stressful situation, you would probably be a less effective speaker. Women and men who have been acclaimed for their acting ability often confess that no matter how many years they have been doing it, they invariably experience stage fright, particularly on opening night. Their ability to confront this stress contributes to the quality of their performance.

Increase Physical Activity

In the last decade, the fitness fad has flourished. Tennis courts are crowded, health clubs booked solid, and swimmers, joggers, and runners fill their respective elements. For many people seriously concerned about both their physical and mental health, fitness is more than a fad; it is a way of life. We think of physical activity primarily as a way to tone up our muscles and keep our body in shape. Research has shown, however, that it is a great reliever of stress reactions.

endorphin
a class of brain chemicals similar in structure and effect to opiate drugs such as morphine

When you exercise, the neurotransmitter **endorphin** (see Chapter 3) is released in your brain. This natural chemical produced by your body enables you to endure more pain and discomfort and promotes a feeling of well-being. In addition to enhancing physical fitness and helping you cope with stress reactions, physical exercise may also have other benefits. In a

1985 Gallup poll of more than 1000 men and women, those who exercised regularly described themselves as more confident and creative than did those who did not exercise.

After a stress-filled day, jogging, riding a bike, or playing tennis are good ways to release your tensions. You do not need to wait until the end of the day. Many people jog during their lunch hour. Some business executives have said that the 20 or 30 minutes they spend jogging are the only times when they can be free of tension. You can even exercise by doing some calisthenics in the middle of many stressful situations and thus ease your anxiety.

Find Relaxing Alternatives

If you have chosen a career that has daily built-in stressors for you, you should make a point of finding some relaxing alternatives to turn to at the end of the day and on your weekends and holidays. Exercise, of course, is one example that has its own benefits in addition to getting you away from work-related or other kinds of stress. Hobbies can also be helpful if they really relax you and let you forget the cares of the day.

Many people who do well in jobs that involve a lot of stress have developed ways to put the stress reactions of the day aside when they get home. Soaking in a hot tub is one way to help yourself shift gears and get rid of the tensions of the day. Reading, spending some quiet minutes alone, listening to a favorite piece of music, or taking a long walk are among the gambits people use to get away from the tensions of the day. These are all valid ways of removing yourself from daily stress and helping your mind and body recover so it can effectively meet the next day's demands and stresses. It can also be a time to plan new coping strategies and alter appraisals of stressors you face.

There is a widely applicable generalization that applies to stress reduction: Change your situation or change your view of the situation. This is the basis of cognitive behavior therapy, and it is reflected in the serenity prayer: "God grant me the courage to change the things I can change, the strength to bear the things I cannot change, and the wisdom to know the difference." Getting counseling or simply talking with a supportive close friend can help one make these changes.

SUMMARY

1. We all face stress and have done so throughout our lives. Stress is not always harmful, nor is it always a negative factor in your life. Although too much stress is harmful, some stress may actually be necessary.

2. Stress is defined differently by different experts, depending on how they view it. Some describe it in physiological terms: your bodily response to a stressful situation in the environment. Others define it in psychological terms: your perception of a situation in the environment. A situation that causes a stress reaction in one person may have no such effect on another. In general, stress reaction is both physiological and psychological.

3. When encountering a stressful situation, your body prepares to respond in one of two ways: to fight or to flee.

4. Stress comes to us in two ways: It is thrust upon us as in an accident or unexpected change, or we actively seek it by trying something new and challenging.

5. Health researchers have found that stress reactions can contribute to many health problems, such as heart disease, hypertension (high blood pressure), alcoholism, drug abuse, ulcers, and anxiety. Some consider stress reactions to be the number-one health problem today.

6. Whatever their occupation, women face particular stress as they attempt to juggle the roles of worker and wife-mother-homemaker.

7. Burnout is an emotional state that a worker experiences after enduring continuing stress. Workers experiencing burnout suffer from emotional exhaustion. They seem to lose a sense of themselves as effective individuals. They might believe that their work is useless, that there is nothing they can do, that they have nothing left to give to the job or others. They can become uncaring, depersonalized, and unproductive.

8. Stress reactions occur when we feel outside pressure to perform, particularly to perform well. This pressure creates anxiety and causes us to question our ability to do what is expected or what we want to do, and we begin to doubt ourselves.

9. We tend to rank the severity of common stressful events in the same order. However, different people react differently to stressors. To an extent, we learn our reaction to many

stressful situations, quite often through classical or operant conditioning. Our personalities often determine the events we consider stressful, as well as how we react. Some thrive in situations that others perceive as very stressful.

10. _____ By coping, scientists mean making an effort to escape from or reduce the anxiety induced by stress either by changing what ever in the environment is causing our stress or by changing our own reaction to it.

11. _____ We have behavioral coping strategies aimed at changing the environment and psychological coping strategies aimed at changing our perception of a stressful event, even to the extent of denying its existence.

12. _____ Behavioral coping strategies include aggression, fixation, regression, withdrawal, and avoidance. Psychological coping strategies include denial, repression, and fantasizing.

13. _____ Drug abuse is a destructive response to stress that an alarming number of people have resorted to. Drug abuse not only does not solve the problem, it greatly impairs the user's ability to cope.

14. _____ Strategies for reducing stress reactions include cultivating problem solving, avoiding stressful situations, confronting the problem, increasing physical activity, and finding relaxing alternatives.

QUESTIONS FOR REVIEW AND DISCUSSION

1. _____ What are the two ways experts define stress?

2. _____ In what two ways does stress come to us? Give examples of each.

3. _____ What do psychologists mean when they speak of normative and nonnormative stress?

4. _____ Identify and describe at least two factors that can affect the severity of stress an event can generate in us.

5. _____ In general, our coping strategies for changing the environment can be considered behavioral coping strategies. Those for changing our own perception can be regarded as psychological defense mechanisms. Explain and give examples of each.

6. _____ Describe two strategies for coping with or reducing stress.

KEY TERMS
Define the following:

Aggression
Appraisal
Autocratic
Avoidance
Behavioral coping strategies
Burnout
Coping
Defense mechanisms
Denial
Endorphin
Fantasizing
Fixation
Instrumental aggression
Nonnormative stress
Normative stress
*Psychological coping
    strategies*

Reactive aggression
Regression
Repression
Self-efficacy
Stress
Stress reaction
Stressor
Traumatic stress
Type A personality
Withdrawal

ACTIVITIES

1. Try to remember some recent stressful events—a school exam, a first date, a fight with a friend, or a job interview. What were your feelings (fearful, anxious, angry)? How did your body react (dry mouth, tight throat, sweaty palms, tension headache)? Did you react differently to different stressful events? Write a one- or two-page description of the events and your stress reactions.

2. Anticipate a future event that you expect will be a stressful one for you, such as taking an exam, starting a new job, confronting a friend or neighbor, or making a presentation at school or work or in a social setting. Write down a plan for reducing your stress reaction, using some of the strategies for coping you read about in this chapter.

3. Although if used excessively defense mechanisms will not help us cope with stress, we all do use them from time to time, and they do help us reduce stress reactions, at least temporarily. Three kinds of defense mechanisms were identified in the text: denial, repression, and fantasizing. Try to think of times when you (or a friend or relative) have used these defense mechanisms. Were they helpful? Were there times when you think they might have been helpful? Describe how effective you felt the use of the defense mechanisms was.

4. Critically view one of your favorite TV programs or a movie. As a rule, the characters face several stressful events per episode. As you watch, take notes on a character's behavior in reacting to stress-causing events. Later, try to characterize the coping behavior you noted in terms of what you have read. A character might show more than one kind of behavior or different kinds at different times, such as aggression one time, avoidance another. Support your characterizations. Also decide whether the behavior was appropriate and effective or inappropriate and counterproductive. Prepare a brief report to discuss in class.

CASE 1

Work-Related Stress

"I'm quitting," Juan announced. "I can't take it any more. This company is asking too much."

"Now wait a minute," Susan said. "All I asked was that you be a little more careful when you check the originals to make sure the tapes are all right. Several promotional letters went out last month with typos in them. Marketing says that errors hurt sales."

"Those so-called errors could have been caused by the computer," Juan said. "Did anyone think of that?"

"Of course," Susan answered, "but there is no way to prove that. And you know that when anything goes wrong, marketing jumps on me because I'm the head of the office staff."

"Yeah, and then you jump on us supervisors," Juan said. "All the heat comes down on us. I'm sick of it, and I'm quitting."

"Now, don't do anything hasty," Susan cautioned. "You worked a number of years on keyboarding and looked forward to being promoted to supervisor. You have been doing it only a short time, and you have been doing well. Don't let a thing like this stop you. It is part of the job. It goes with the territory."

"Sure, it goes with the territory," Juan said. "But I do a good job under tough conditions. We have to meet a quota in turning out the letters. If I turn too many back, the keyboarders don't make the quota. Then everyone gets mad at me. If I slip up once in a while and let a small error go through, then you and the marketing department get on my back. It's a no-win situation for me."

"You're paid well for what you do," Susan reminded him.

"I know I make a lot more than I did as a keyboarder. But then I didn't take the job home with me. Now it's on my mind all the time. Last night I began worrying about the batch of letters I approved yesterday, and I couldn't sleep. I came to work early this morning to recheck them. They're okay, but that didn't give me back the lost sleep."

"I appreciate your being so conscientious." Susan said, "and you are one of my best supervisors. But you have to learn how to handle the stress better. Quitting is not the answer. You are going to find some stress on every job."

"How do you handle it?" Juan wanted to know.

"In different ways," Susan answered. "First, in my job I have learned to accept the fact that there will be some stress. Then I try to take a realistic look at what I do. I figure out just how much I can reasonably be expected to do, set my goals accordingly, and then try to reach them."

"Well, I can work on that, I guess," Juan said. "But what about the situation I'm in right now, with you telling me one of the batches I passed had errors in it? That makes me pretty tense."

"No one is perfect, Juan. You must recognize that you will make a mistake now and then and learn not to resent it when someone points the error out to you. You will actually make fewer mistakes if you realize you cannot be perfect and stop trying to be."

"But my job is to be perfect. I'm the supervisor, I have to set an example for the other workers."

"Your job is to do the best that you can. There is pressure enough without trying to be perfect. Try to relax and enjoy your work—you're very good at it."

1. Analyze Juan's reaction to stress. How would you characterize his reaction? How appropriate was it?

2. What factors affected the severity of the stress Juan was experiencing? Give evidence to support your answer.

3. What advice would you give Juan?

CASE 2

Avoiding or Confronting Stress

"Nancy, we are pleased to tell you we are promoting you to head our new training program for computer operators. You learned the system faster than anyone else. You have an excellent grasp of it, and you seem to have a knack of explaining it to your coworkers."

Nancy was naturally pleased and flattered to hear about her promotion. It was completely unexpected. She knew the company was planning to set up a training department, but had no idea she would be asked to head it. And she was very pleased with the large pay raise the general manager told her went with it.

"Now, you are part of management, Nancy," the general manager said, smiling at her. "You will attend the biweekly managers' meetings. I will introduce you and announce your new position at this week's meeting. At the next one in two weeks, I'd like you to make a small report about the new department and your general plans."

When she heard this, Nancy's initial glow began to fade. "Uh, you want me to make a report to all the other managers?"

"Oh, just a general outline, Nancy. I realize there will not be time for a detailed report. That can come later. Just plan to speak for

15 or 20 minutes. You can talk about what you have learned yourself as well as what you will be teaching others."

Nancy felt a cold knot gathering in her stomach. She dreaded giving talks before groups of people. All through school she had avoided speech classes and giving recitations in class. Because she was naturally smart, she was able to get good grades anyway, but she had never conquered her fear of public speaking. Even as she was thinking these thoughts, the general manager was continuing.

"Of course, you will be doing some traveling to carry out the training in our branches. I want you to visit all our branch offices to set up training programs. I think the best approach will be for you and me to visit them all first. We'll get all the employees together, even those who may not be working the computers, so everyone will know what is happening. I find that best and there are only 40 or 50 in each branch. I'll introduce you, and then you can talk about your training program. Plan a 30-minute talk. No more. You can give the same one at each branch, of course, so it will be easy."

By now Nancy was thoroughly dismayed. Although she was good, as she knew, in one-on-one situations and could explain and teach well, she could not possibly make these speeches the general manager was telling her she would have to do. She decided to reject the promotion and say that her family commitments made it impossible for her to do any traveling that kept her away from home overnight.

The general manager was very sorry to hear that and urged her to try to find a way. He pointed out that the promotion was a big one and opened up a whole new avenue of career advancement for her. Nancy regretfully declined. Just the thought of making speeches caused her stress and anxiety. Another person was given the promotion.

1. Analyze Nancy's reactions to stress. What behaviors did she exhibit? How would you classify her coping strategy?

2. Devise an alternate coping strategy for Nancy.

3. Do you think that Nancy's decision was right? Defend your answer.

Unit V

RESEARCH STUDY

A Case of Work Adjustment

An employee, considered unsatisfactory by the company, is sent to you for evaluation to see if the employee should be dismissed. You read the employee's personnel file and are surprised to find that the employee had very good credentials and very high recommendations. You also find that the employee's performance ratings were borderline at the start and declining ever since. You interview the employee, who reveals to you a deep dissatisfaction with the job and the work situation.

1. Making use of the three chapters of Unit V, draw up a list of realistic possibilities of what might be the underlying problem. (The more possibilities the better, but at least two per chapter. Be sure the possibilities overlap as little as possible. Choose the gender you prefer for the employee.)

2. Sort the possibilities into those that are open to change and those that are not. For those open to change, what can be done by the company? by the employee? Give details.

3. Sort the possibilities into those that are grounds for dismissal and those that are not. How would you decide how much of the fault can be assigned to the employee? (This is often what juries have to do in employee lawsuits challenging dismissals.) For how many of the possibilities you have drawn up is it the case that all of the fault lies with the employee?

1. Flanagan, JC: Project TALENT: A National Inventory of Aptitudes and Abilities. Pittsburgh, 1960, University of Pittsburgh.
2. Barron, F, Jarvik, ME, and Burnell, S, Jr: The Hallucinogenic Drugs. Scientific American, 210, no. 4, 1964: 33-35.
3. Nichols, RG and Stevens, LA: Listening to People. Harvard Business Review, September– October 1957: 85-89.
4. Ibid.
5. Cousins, N: Anatomy of an Illness. New York, 1979, Norton.
6. Posner, MI: Cognition: An Introduction. Glenview, Ill., 1973, Scott, Foresman.
7. Decision Making: A Demonstration of the Post-Decision Dissonance Effect, Journal of Social Psychology, 126, no. 5, October 1986: 663-665.
8. Adams, JL: Conceptual Blockbusting: A Guide to Better Ideas, ed. 2, New York, 1980, Norton.
9. Keith, A: Of On the Origin of Species by Charles Darwin, Introduction to the Everyman's Library edition as quoted in A Treasury of Science. New York, 1985, Harper.
10. Daniels, D and Plomin, R: Origins of Individual Difference in Infant Shyness, Developmental Psychology, 21, no. 1, 1985: 118-121.
11. Dennis, W: Causes of Retardation Among Institutional Children: Iran, Journal of Genetic Psychology, 1960: 47-49, 96.
12. Lofquist, LH and Dawis, RV: Adjustment to Work A Psychological View of Man's Problems in a Work-Oriented Society. New York, 1969, Appleton Century Crofts.
13. Kristof, ND: Disobedience Training of the 80's Is Done by Pet Psychologists. The New York Times, Aug. 31, 1986.
14. Murray, HA and collaborators: Explorations in Personality. New York, 1938, Oxford University Press.
15. Those Boring Jobs Not All That Dull. U.S. News and World Report, December 1, 1975: 64-65.
16. Berlo, DK: The Process of Communication: An Introduction to Theory and Practice. New York, 1960, Holt, Rinehart, and Winston.
17. Etzioni, A: Modern Organization. Englewood Cliffs, N.J., 1964, Prentice-Hall.
18. Shorris, E: The Oppressed Middle: The Politics of Middle Management, Scenes from Corporate Life. New York, 1981, Anchor Press/Doubleday.
19. Helpers among Students from Four Ethnic Groups. Journal of College Student Personnel, 26, no. 2, March 1985: 147-157.

NOTES

PHOTO CREDITS

Page 1: Elle Schuster. Pages 2 and 3: Lori Adamski Peek / Tony Stone. Page 5: Skjold / PhotoEdit. Page 8: Kaz Mori / Image Bank. Page 9: Phototeque. Page 12: Reprinted by permission of United Feature Syndicate Inc. Page 16: Curzon / Bettmann Archive. Page 19: M. Richards / PhotoEdit. Page 20: Barros & Barros / PhotoEdit. Page 21: Kay Chernush / Image Bank. Page 27: Gary Gay / Image Bank. Page 30: Susan VanEtten (top), Jeff Greenberg (bottom) / PhotoEdit. Page 46: Bettmann Archive. Page 50: Bettmann Archive. Page 56: Elle Schuster. Page 57: Elle Schuster. Pages 58 and 59: Chuck Savage / Stock Market. Page 61: G&V Chapman / Image Bank. Page 62: Chris Allan Winton / Image Bank. Page 65: John Allison / Peter Arnold. Page 79: EMC Publishing (Top), Anna Zuckerman / PhotoEdit (Middle), Ann Marie Weber / Stock Market (Bottom). Page 85: Tony Freeman / Image Bank. Page 92: Bettmann Archive. Page 94: Baron Wolman / Woodfin Camp & Associates. Page 100: Archive Photos. Page 105: Jules Allen. Page 106: Renzo Mancini / Image Bank. Page 117: Stuart Dee / Image Bank. Page 118: Alan Oddie / PhotoEdit. Page 119: Hans Wendler / Image Bank. Page 122: David Young-Wolff / Image Bank. Page 138: David Young-Wolff / PhotoEdit. Page 140: David Young-Wolff. Page 142: Jeff Greenberg (left), Mark Richards (right) / PhotoEdit. Page 151: Diane Pody / FPG International. Page 154: Tony Freeman / PhotoEdit. Page 157: Susan Van Etten / PhotoEdit. Page 175: Chris Allan Winton / Image Bank. Page 176: Tony Freeman / PhotoEdit. Page 177: Culver. Page 183: Steve Allen / Image Bank. Page 185: Alan Oddie / PhotEdit. Page 186: Lori Adamski Peek / Tony Stone Images. Page 188: Richard Hutchings / PhotoEdit. Page 192: Unicorn. Page 198: Elle Schuster. Page 199: Elle Schuster. Pages 200 and 201: Ronnie Kaufman / Stock Market. Page 203: Steven Simpson / FPG International. Page 204: Robert Brenner / PhotEdit. Page 205: Mug Shots / Stock Market. Page 207: Dennis MacDonald / PhotoEdit. Page 209: Tony Freeman / PhotoEdit. Page 210: Bill Anderson / Monkmeyer Press. Page 213: Mimi Forsyth / Monkmeyer Press. Page 215: UPI / Bettmann Archive. Page 219: Alvis Upins / Image Bank. Page 221: ATC Productions / Stock Market. Page 223: Alan Oddie / PhotoEdit. Page 231: Jeff Smith / Image Bank. Page 232: Gary Conner / PhotoEdit. Page 233: David Young-Wolff / PhotoEdit. Page 235: Alan Oddie / PhotoEdit. Page 238: Will Rapport / Photo Researchers. Page 239: Jeff Leedy / Image Bank. Page 243: Jeff Greenberg / Image Bank. Page 246: Mimi Forsyth / Monkmeyer Press. Page 251: Frank Wing / Image Bank. Page 252: Marc Romanelli / Image Bank. Page 255: David Young-Wolff / PhotoEdit. Page 263: Heinz Fischer / Image Bank. Page 266: Mug Shots / Stock Market. Page 271: John Neubauer / PhotoEdit. Page 279: Jeff Greenberg / PhotoEdit. Page 283: Bettmann Archive. Page 293: Gabe Palmer / Stock Market. Page 295: Bettmann Archive. Page 304: David Pollack / Stock Market. Page 307: Dennis MacDonald (Top), Paul Conklin (Bottom) / PhotoEdit. Page 311: William Taufic / Stock Market. Page 322: Elle Schuster. Page 323: Elle Schuster. Page 327: EMC Publishing. Page 329: Michael Heron / Stock Market. Page 334: Michael Melford / Image Bank. Page 335: Cathy Copyright 1985 Universal Press Syndicate. Page 339: HMS Images / Image Bank. Page 342: Paul Conklin / PhotoEdit. Page 343: Jon Feingersh / Stock Market. Page 345: Jose L. Pelaez / Stock Market. Page 347: Jon Feingersh / Stock Market. Page 351: Mug Shots / Stock Market. Page 363: Comstock. Page 364: Romilly Lockyer / Image Bank. Page 366: David Young-Wolff / PhotoEdit. Page 368: Tony Freeman / PhotoEdit. Page 376: Robert Brenner / PhotoEdit. Page 379: PhotoEdit. Page 380: Michael Neuman (Left), Tom McCarthy (Right) / PhotoEdit. Page 389: Drawing by Donald Reilly, copyright 1986 / The New Yorker Magazine, Inc. Page 395: Alan Oddie / PhotoEdit. Page 400: Paul Conklin / PhotoEdit. Page 404: Jon Feingersh / Stock Market. Page 407: David Young-Wolff / PhotoEdit. Page 409: Bettmann Archive. Page 414: Elyse Lewin / Image Bank. Page 421: Bettmann Archive. Page 422: Bettmann Archive. Page 424: Bettmann Archive. Page 428: Paul Conklin / PhotoEdit. Page 430: Jon Feingersh / Stock Market. Page 431: Reprinted by permission of United Feature Syndicate, Inc. Page 433: Gabe Palmer / Stock Market. Page 434: Reprinted with permission from the Saturday Evening Post, copyright 1986. Page 452: Elle Schuster. Page 453: Elle Schuster. Pages 454 and 455: Comstock. Page 457: Robert Brenner / PhotoEdit. Page 458: David Pollack / Stock Market. Page 460: Elan Sun Star / Tony Stone Images. Page 462: Leslye Borden / PhotoEdit. Page 465: Amy C. Etra / PhotoEdit. Page 466: Robert Brenner / PhotoEdit. Page 468: Jon Feingersh / Stock Market. Page 473: Alan Oddie / PhotoEdit (Left), P&G Bowater / Image Bank (Right). Page 475: Reprinted with permission from the Saturday Evening Post. Page 483: Paul Hanna / Bettmann Archive. Page 485: David Young-Wolff / PhotoEdit. Page 488: Mary Kate Denny / PhotoEdit. Page 491: Elena Rooraid / PhotoEdit. Page 507: L.D. Gordon / Image Bank. Page 509: Tony Freeman / PhotoEdit. Page 510: Tony Freeman / PhotoEdit. Page 515: Elena Rooraid / PhotoEdit. Page 523: Gabe Palmer / Stock Market. Page 533: Michael Newman / PhotoEdit. Page 535: Elena Rooraid / PhotoEdit. Page 545: Elena Rooraid / PhotoEdit. Page 550: Michael Tamborrino / Stock Market. Page 554: Drawing by Joseph Farris, copyright 1985 / The New Yorker Magazine, Inc. Page 557: Peter Yandai / Stock Market. Page 564: Drawing by Dana Fradon, copyright 1985 / The New Yorker Magazine, Inc. Page 570: Drawing by Bernard Schoenbaum, copyright 1985 / The New Yorker Magazine, Inc. Page 578: Elle Schuster.

80/20 rule A rule, formulated by Vilfredo Pareto, that in any grouping, the significant items amount to only 20 percent of the total.

Ability test An instrument and a set of standard procedures designed to measure a particular ability.

Absolute threshold The smallest amount of a physical stimulus that the brain will notice 50 percent of the time.

Abstraction General words or images that stand for all the common characteristics of a group of similar objects or images.

Accessibility The idea that all scientific study should be available to the public.

Accommodation (sensory) Changes in the shape of the lens of the eye that serve to focus objects at varying distances.

Accommodation In Piaget's theory, the modification of existing mental patterns to fit new demands (that is, mental schemes are changed to accommodate new information or experiences).

Acetylcholine A neurotransmitter involved in perception, learning, language, and memory.

Achievement value Importance of accomplishment through use of abilities

Active memory Memory used in tasks currently being performed, consisting of short-term memory and operational memory.

Activeness Adjustment behavior that is directed at changing the environment.

Adaptation The tendency to adjust ourselves to the environment, as, for example, when we stop responding to a stimulus when we have been constantly exposed to the stimulus.

Adjustment The state or process of achieving and maintaining correspondence with the environment.

Adjustment style The dimensions that differentiate how people adjust.

Adrenal glands Endocrine glands whose hormones arouse the body, regulate salt balance, adjust the body to stress, and affect sexual functioning.

Affective behavior Emotional behavior based primarily on the functioning of the inner brain and hypothalamus. (Compare cognitive behavior.)

Affiliation need The need to be associated with others.

Affirmative action laws Laws enacted to correct the imbalance in employment opportunity for minorities and women, requiring organizations with an obvious pattern of discrimination to hire and promote women and minorities over equally qualified or even slightly more qualified whites or males.

Aggression A hostile reaction to threat.

Aggressive behavior Getting what you want without much consideration for others.

Alienation A kind of dissatisfaction common in industrial societies, characterized by a feeling of distance from, or lack of involvement with, other people or one's work.

Alphabet writing A system of writing in which each symbol (letter) stands for a distinct sound or phoneme. (Compare syllable writing and word writing.)

Alternate-forms method A common method for evaluating test reliability where a test is given to a group along with another test designed to be equivalent to the first test.

Altruism value Importance of service to and harmony with others.

Ameslan A formalized system developed in the nineteenth century that assigns specific meanings to certain hand motions and combinations of gestures.

Amplitude The measurement of the height of a wave.

GLOSSARY

Amygdala Almond-shaped brain structure in the limbic system involved in aggresion and fear.

Analytic method The method of breaking the object of study into component parts in order to see how the whole functions as a result of the functioning of the parts.

Anterior chamber Part of the eye filled with watery fluid.

Applied science Scientific study of the use of science to address and solve human problems. (See technology.)

Appraisal The evaluation of worth, significance, or status.

Aptitude The special capabilities and natural talents that enable the individual to learn and perform selected jobs.

Assertive behavior Leaving no doubt what you want without being offensive.

Assertiveness training Behavior modification that teaches people to avoid aggression or passivity.

Assimilation In Piaget's theory, the application of existing mental patterns to new situations (that is, the new situation is assimilated to existing mental schemes).

Association A theory, developed by Aristotle, that our thought tends to run from one idea to another related idea.

Association cortex All areas of the neocortex that are not specifically sensory or motor in function.

Associative learning Learning that results from things going together.

Astigmatism The condition in which the eye's lenses are defective, not spherical or symmetrical, and as a result distort the image.

Attitudes Learned tendencies to respond to people, objects, or institutions in a positive or negative way.

Auditory canal The opening through which sound waves pass from the outer ear to the middle ear.

Auditory cortex Sites on the temporal lobes where auditory information registers.

Auditory nerve Cranial nerves connecting the inner ear with the brain and concerned with hearing and balance.

Auditory perception A broad ability measured by combinations of tests that measure both perception of speech and perception of music.

Autocratic A work organization style in which the bosses make the rules, give the orders, and expect unquestioned compliance.

Autonomy value Importance of independence and self-sufficiency.

Aversive stimulus A life-threatening or distressing stimulus.

Avoidance A coping strategy characterized by attempts not to deal with a problem at all, for example by not thinking about it or acting on it.

Axon A long fiber that conducts information away from the cell body of a neuron.

Basilar membrane A membrane in the cochlea supporting the organ of Corti.

Behavioral coping strategies Coping strategies for changing the environment.

Biofeedback The process involved in monitoring and mentally controlling functions previously considered involuntary, such as heartbeat, blood pressure, skin temperature, and so on.

Biological Referring to physical characteristics inherited from ancestors.

Blood-brain barrier A barrier that makes it hard for substances in the blood to enter the brain.

Brain stem The lower portions of the brain, including the cerebellum, medulla, and reticular formation.

Broad ability A common factor measured by ability tests.

Burnout An emotional state that a worker experiences after enduring continuing stress, characterized by emotional exhaustion, loss of a sense of effectiveness, and a corresponding sense of futility.

Career What an individual decides to do to make a living and how the individual makes a living; what you do with your life.

Causal Referring to a cause-and-effect relationship.

Cell Basic unit of the body.

Cell body The central part of the cell.

Central nervous system The brain and spinal cord as a combined system.

Central processes What goes on in the brain.

Cerebral hemisphere The right or left half of the cerebrum.

Cerebrum The enlarged upper part of the brain that is the seat of conscious mental processes.

Charismatic The ability to inspire others to strive for common goals and to endure sacrifice and hard work.

Chromosome A part of a human cell that transmits physical characteristics.

Classical conditioning The process whereby a neutral stimulus becomes an effective stimulus in causing a response as a result of association with an effective stimulus.

Clinical psychologists Psychologists with specialized training in the treatment of emotional and behavioral problems.

Clique An informal group that has drawn in on itself, is exclusive, does not admit new members readily, and looks with suspicion and even hostility on other groups.

Closure rule Perceptual tendency to complete figures by "closing" or ignoring small gaps.

Cochlea The inner ear.

Coercion The use of threats or force to control people.

Cognition The act of thinking.

Cognitive behavior Behavior based primarily on the functioning of the cortex.

Cognitive development Development of the ability to think, remember, learn, and use language.

Cognitive dissonance reduction An attempt to reduce the mental inconsistency resulting from the awareness of incompatible beliefs held simultaneously.

Cognitive distortion Difference or discrepancy between perceived reality and actual reality.

Cognitive learning Higher-level learning involving thinking, knowing, understanding, and anticipation.

Color blindness A total inability to perceive colors.

Comfort value Importance of the absence of stress and the presence of pleasant feelings.

Comparative method The method of comparing and contrasting observations, attempting to identify similarities and differences.

Compensate To substitute satisfaction of one important need for another.

Compensation The ability to understand that when a quantity of matter changes shape, its dimensions (height, length, and width) change accordingly. (An aspect of conservation.)

Concepts General ideas on a very high level of abstraction, which, together with images, are the primary form that thoughts take.

Conditioned stimulus A previously neutral stimulus that, through conditioning, is made to elicit a particular response.

Consciousness The state of having knowledge, being aware of one's own existence.

Conservation The ability to understand that equal quantities of matter remain equal regardless of their shape. An ability acquired during the concrete operational phase of cognitive development identified by Piaget.

Constancy (perception) The brain's ability to recognize that an object retains its size, shape, and color under varying conditions of perspective and lighting.

Constant (statistics) A factor that always has the same value in an experiment. The speed of light is a constant, or unchanging. (Compare variable.)

Construct validity When a test's pattern of correlations with other tests and other variables is consistent with theory.

Content validity When the content of a test appears to measure what it is supposed to measure.

Contiguity The state of being close together.

Continuity rule Tendency to extend perception of part to perception of whole.

Continuous reinforcement Reinforcement that occurs each time the operant behavior occurs.

Convergent thinking Designates "conventional" thinking (as opposed to "creative" thinking), characterized by the use of established thought paths to arrive at one "correct" solution. (Compare divergent thinking.)

Convergent validity When a test correlates with other tests that measure the same thing.

Coping Attempting to escape from or reduce the anxiety induced by stress either by changing whatever in the environment is causing the stress or by changing one's reaction to it.

Cornea A transparent tissue covering the front of the eyeball.

Corpus callosum The large bundle of fibers connecting the right and left cerebral hemispheres.

Correlated Ranking people (or observations) in a similiar manner.

Correlation coefficient A number that indicates the degree of correlation between two variables.

Correlational method A major method in psychology based on the study of correlations between variables.

Correspondence When the individual meets the work environment's requirements and the work environment meets the individual's work needs.

Counseling psychologists Psychologists who help individuals understand themselves, make choices and decisions, and solve personal problems.

Counterconditioning Conditioning to replace a conditioned response with a different response.

Credibility The sense of being believable.

Criteria Standards on which a judgment or decision may be based.

Criterion-related validity The validity of tests for particular uses.

Crystallized intelligence A broad ability that depends on experience, learning, and culture.

Cultural environment The system of ways of behaving expected within a community of people.

GLOSSARY

Cultural values The values attached to various objects and activities by the majority of people in a given culture.

Customs Accepted, habitual ways of behaving observed by all members of a community.

Cycle The passage of a single wave from peak to trough to peak.

Decibels Units of measurement of the loudness of a sound.

Decision-making matrix A tool to help organize data and evaluate alternatives consisting of a grid with short- and long-term goals listed down the side and alternatives listed across the top.

Decoding The process of turning a received message into its meaning. (Compare encoding.)

Deductive logic A form of logic that arrives at specific conclusions from general principles. (Compare inductive logic.)

Deductive method The method of studying current theory to deduce (arrive at) a suggested explanation of an existing condition, then devising experiments to disprove the explanation or find evidence for it.

Defense mechanisms Strategies employed subconsciously, aimed at defending the ego or self-concept as a means of coping with stress.

Dendrite Short fiber that conducts information from other neurons to the cell body.

Denial A defense mechanism consisting of simply denying or refusing to acknowledge reality.

Dependent variable The condition or activity which the experiment is designed to measure.

Determinism The doctrine that behavior is determined, completely produced by, and resulting from stimuli or unconscious motives.

Developmental psychologists Psychologists who study how behavior develops from (and even before) birth to death.

Difference threshold The smallest amount of change in a physical stimulus that will be noticed 50 percent of the time.

Discorrespondence Failure to achieve correspondence.

Discriminant validity When a test does not correlate with other tests that measure different things.

Displacement Redirection of the libido to objects or activities that are acceptable to the superego.

Divergent thinking A term to designate "creative" thinking (as opposed to "conventional" thinking), characterized by the use of new thought paths to arrive at unconventional solutions. (Compare convergent thinking.)

Dominant (Genetics) Mendelian characteristic that is always showing.

Dopamine A neurotransmitter involved in our experience of reward and pleasure.

Dyadic effect Reciprocating self-disclosure.

Dyslexia A reading impairment whereby the individual perceives words or numbers reversed from their proper order or form, and might, for example, read the word "may" as "yam."

Eardrum A thin tissue in the middle ear that vibrates when struck by sound waves, activating the anvil, hammer, and stirrup, which in turn activates the inner ear.

Ecological theory A theory that attempts to explain constancy in terms of the perceived relationships of objects to one another. (Compare unconscious inference theory.)

Educational psychologists Psychologists who study factors that influence learning.

Effortful retrieval Recall of information occurring in an unfamiliar context; recall with effort.

GLOSSARY

Effortless retrieval Recall of information occurring in a familiar context; recall without effort.

Ego A term used in the psychoanalytic model to refer to an area of the mind thought to be the seat of free will and perceiving, thinking, and remembering. The ego, or self, acts as mediator between the drives of the id and the demands of the superego.

Egocentric Believing that one is the center and cause of all that happens.

Emotional development Development of emotional traits; feelings.

Encoding The translation of an idea or thought to be communicated into symbols that the receiver can understand. (Compare decoding.)

Endorphins Neurotransmitters that behave like opiate drugs such as morphine.

Environmental Pertaining to the surroundings; factors outside the individual that affect the individual's development and behavior.

Enzymes Proteins produced by genes involved in the development of the body's organ systems.

Esteem Recognition and respect.

Etiquette The conduct or procedure required by good breeding or prescribed by authority to be observed in social or official life.

Eustachian tube A passage that runs between the middle ear and the throat area. One of its functions is to help balance the air pressure on the inner ear.

Excitatory Exhibiting or produced by excitement or excitation.

Experimental method A major method of psychology based on the use of experiment to study cause and effect.

Experimental psychologists Psychologists who use the experimental method in attempting to understand and explain basic behavioral processes, such as sensation and perception, learning and memory, cognition, motor skills, motivation, and emotion.

Expressed interests Specific interests made known by the interested person.

Extrinsic motivators Work motivators that relate to external physical and social reinforcers. (Compare intrinsic motivators.)

Factor What a test measures in common with other tests with which it is correlated.

Factor analysis A statistical technique to find out the parts (factors) that tests measure in common.

Fantasizing A defense mechanism in which one dreams of what might have been or might be.

Fixation Repeating the same response to a particular problem or situation, even after experience has shown that the response will not bring about the desired results.

Flexibility Tolerance for discorrespondence.

Fluid intelligence A broad ability that depends on biological inheritance and development.

Forebrain The front part of the brain, including the cerebrum, hypothalamus, thalamus, and corpus callosum.

Formal leaders As defined by Amitai Etzioni, people who combine their status as officials with their capacities as informal or natural leaders.

Fornix An anatomical arch or fold.

Frequency distribution A graph that shows how many people have the same score.

Frontal lobe The top front of the cerebrum that includes sites associated with the control of movement, the processing of smell, and higher mental functions.

Function The overall responsibilities of a specific job, encompassing several tasks.

Functional model A school of psychology that emphasized the functions of consciousness rather than its structure and the importance of psychology for practical purposes. (Compare structuralism.)

GABA A neurotransmitter that serves as an inhibitor in the nervous system. It is also involved in sleep.

General ability A common factor measured by all ability tests.

General Aptitude Test Battery Tests that measure job proficiency of workers in each of about 500 different occupations.

Genes The mechanism whereby characteristics are passed from parents to offspring. Specifically, parts of a chromosome that determine specific characteristics, such as eye or hair color.

Genetic code The chemical structure of genes.

Genetics The study of how traits are passed on through the genes from one generation to another.

Gestalt A school of psychology asserting that perception and cognition could not be broken into constituent parts: "The whole is greater than the sum of its parts." Also stresses the context of the individual in his or her environment in understanding the individual. (In German, Gestalt means "form" or "shape.")

Glia Cells that surround the neurons.

Glutamate A neurotransmitter that speeds up transmission across synapses.

Gonads The primary sex glands: the testes in males and ovaries in females.

Group theory of leadership Holds that the needs of a group determine when a leader will emerge as well as the type of leader that emerges.

Grouping method The method of categorizing or classifying observations in order to identify underlying rules or principles about the things observed.

Groupthink A situation in which members of a group have abandoned all efforts to think for themselves or to question the wisdom of the group, while seeing all outsiders as hostile.

Gustatory sense The scientific term for the sense of taste.

Habituation learning Learning by becoming used to something.

Hallucinogens Drugs that cause the user to have vivid sensory experiences that do not correspond to reality (hallucinations).

Hearing The act of sensing sound; specifically: the special sense by which noises and tones are received as stimuli.

Heritability index A measurement of the relative influence of heredity on a plant or animal characteristic.

Hertz A measure of frequency equal to one cycle per second.

Hindbrain The back part of the brain including the cerebellum, pons, and medulla oblongata.

Hippocampus Brain structure in the limbic system involved in memory.

Hormones Body chemicals carried by body fluids that have an effect on bodily functions and behavior.

Human behavior Human acts or activities, both mental and physical.

Human relations A course, study, or program designed to develop better interpersonal and intergroup adjustments.

GLOSSARY

GLOSSARY

Humanistic model A school of psychology that emphasizes free will, action as opposed to reaction, creativity, and the "whole person" in the Gestalt sense.

Hybrid intelligence A broad ability that is a mix of fluid and crystallized intelligence.

Hyperopia Farsightedness; difficulty seeing nearby objects.

Hypothalamus The small section of the brain that controls body temperature and influences hunger, thirst, and sexual behavior.

Hypothesis An explanation deduced (arrived at) from theories about an object, event, or condition.

Id Term used in the psychoanalytic model to refer to unconscious, unlearned, inborn instincts.

Ideation The process of creating an idea or choosing a fact to communicate.

Identity As used here, the ability to understand that a single quantity of matter formed into two different shapes remains the same amount of matter. (An aspect of conservation.)

If-Then Relationship in an experiment that states how the dependent variable changes as a result of changes in the independent variable.

Imagery Mental representation of things experienced.

Imitation theory A theory of language learning that holds that individuals imitate what they hear and continue to do so until they get it right. (Compare reinforcement theory.)

Incubation period A period of inactive or unconscious thought following intense concentration on a problem, often followed by the sudden appearance of a solution.

Independent variable In a scientific experiment, the factor or condition controlled by the experimenter.

Indicator A sign, symptom, or index of something.

Individuation The lifelong process of acquiring and clarifying values, as defined by Jung.

Inductive logic A form of logic that arrives at general conclusions from specific observations. (Compare deductive logic.)

Industrial/organizational psychologists Psychologists who study how people behave in their workplace environment.

Inhibitory One result of synaptic integration when the receiving neuron does not fire.

Innate ability theory A theory of language learning that holds that humans are born with an ability to learn the "rules" that govern language.

Instrumental aggression The conscious, sometimes planned, use of aggression as a means to an end.

Interests Preferences for activities; likes or dislikes as opposed to needs or values.

Interference As used here, the occurrence of new information that drives out or makes recovery of old information more difficult.

Intermittent reinforcement Reinforcement that occurs only sometimes when the operant behavior occurs.

Internal environment The environment within the individual's body, including the biochemical environment and the cognitive environment.

Internal sensors Proprioceptive sense receptors that receive data from internal organs such as the heart.

Internalize To make an idea, value, or attitude a part of one's way of thinking.

Interneuron A nerve cell that links other nerve cells.

Interval schedule In conditioning, a situation in which reinforcement depends on the passage of time, regardless of how many times the behavior is repeated. (Compare ratio schedule.)

Intrinsic motivators Work motivators that relate to self or internal reinforcers. (Compare extrinsic motivators.)

Introspective method The examination of one's own thoughts in order to understand cognitive processes.

Inventoried interests Estimates of interests based on responses to a large number of questions about likes and dislikes.

Involuntarily Without the individual's conscious control.

Involuntary Outside or beyond the individual's conscious control. (Compare voluntary.)

Iris The colored part of the eye that controls the opening of the pupil.

Job A group of positions with similar tasks. (Compare function and tasks.)

Job description A written summary of the functions, tasks, and skills required in a job.

Kinesthetic sensors Proprioceptive sense receptors, located throughout the body in blood vessel walls just under the skin, that allow the individual to sense the movement of parts of the body in relation to each other.

Laws of science Theories that are so universally accepted and unchallenged as to be taken for granted (such as, "the law of gravity").

Learning Changing behavior more or less permanently by acquiring knowledge, understanding, or skill through experience.

Libido Psychic or mental energy that originates in the id.

Limbic system A system of interconnected structures in the forebrain that are closely associated with emotional response.

Line officers Executives under a chief executive who have direct responsibility for operations or production. (Compare staff officers.)

Listening The act of perceiving sound.

Long-term memory All remembered material (associations) that is not in active memory.

Maintenance goals Goals that must be achieved in order for a group to maintain its existence, as distinct from task goals.

Manifest interests Interests expressed through participation in activities.

Maturation Behavioral development or change resulting from biologically predetermined patterns.

Maximum performance The limits of human performance.

Mean Occupying a position about midway between extremes.

Media The methods or tools used to communicate, such as print, spoken word, or television.

Medulla The enlarged stalk at the base of the brain that connects to the spinal cord and controls vital life functions.

Memory The mental capacity of storing, organizing, and recovering information.

Memory codes The different forms in which items are stored in the memory system.

Memory retrieval A broad ability to readily recall concepts, ideas, names, etc. from long-term memory.

Memory systems Cognitive mechanisms for storing information.

GLOSSARY

Mendelian traits Characteristics that depend on only one gene.

Method of limits A variant of the comparative method. The study of the extremes, or limits, of a phenomenon.

Midbrain The middle part of the brain consisting of structures linking the forebrain and the brain-stem.

Modeling Imitating someone who is a model.

Moral anxiety Defined in the psychoanalytic model as a disorder of the mind or emotions for which there is no apparent physical cause, arising out of a failure to satisfy the demands of the superego; guilt.

Moral development The development of the concepts of right and wrong.

Moral realism A tendency exhibited by younger children to judge an action solely by results and not by intent.

Morphemes The smallest units of sound that have meaning in a language, such as "by" or "-ly." (Compare phonemes.)

Motivation Internal or external condition or conditions that cause one to act.

Motor behavior Starting from the brain and ending in the environment.

Motor cortex Area of the neocortex associated with control of voluntary movements.

Motor development Development of the ability to use muscles purposefully, to make them do what is wanted.

Myelin sheath A layer of myelin surrounding some nerve fibers; called also medullary sheath.

Myopia Nearsightedness; difficulty seeing distant objects.

Nanometers A unit of measure for light wavelengths, consisting of 1 one-billionth of a meter. (From Greek, nano, meaning "dwarf," plus meter.)

Narrow ability A common factor measured by ability tests.

Need-satisfier Object or event that satisfies a need.

Needs The individual's requirements of the environment.

Neocortex The cerebrum's surface covering of neuron cell bodies.

Nerve A bundle of neuron fibers supported by connective tissue located outside the brain.

Nerve tract A bundle of neuron fibers located inside the brain.

Nervous system Body system that is made up of the brain and spinal cord, nerves, ganglia, and parts of the sensory organs.

Neural impulse An electrical signal transmitted from receptor cells or from neurons to other neurons, muscles, or glands.

Neural network Interconnected groups of neurons.

Neuron Individual nerve cell that forms the basic structure of the nervous system.

Neurotic anxiety Defined in the psychoanalytic model as a functional disorder of the mind or emotions for which there is no apparent physical cause, arising out of a failure to satisfy the demands of the id.

Neurotransmitters Chemical "messengers" that convey neural impulses between neurons.

Neutral stimulus A stimulus that does not produce any particular response.

Nonnormative stress Stress associated with unexpected or atypical experiences such as being robbed, war, or a car accident.

Nonverbal Communication without words; communication that uses gestures or signs, either alone or simultaneously with verbal communication.

Norepinephrine A neurotransmitter involved in arousal, learning, sleep, wakefulness, and mood.

Normal curve A bell-shaped curve characterized by a large number of scores in a middle area, tapering to very few extremely high and low scores.

Normative stress Stress associated with unavoidable or normal life experiences (a death in the family, a new job or school, or marriage).

Object permanence The ability to understand that objects continue to exist even when out of sight (an aspect of the first phase of Piaget's theory of cognitive development).

Objective Actually observable as opposed to being a mental idea or feeling; verifiable. (Compare subjective.)

Objective data Statistics and other factual information.

Observational learning Learning by observation of others; imitation, vicarious learning, or modeling.

Occipital lobe The back of the cerebrum that includes areas where vision registers in the brain.

Olfactory cortex Site on the frontal lobes where information on smell registers.

Olfactory sense The scientific term for the sense of smell.

Operant conditioning The process whereby behavior is influenced by its consequences (stimuli that occur after the behavior).

Operational memory Material stored in long-term memory that has been activated for use in active memory.

Oral communication Spoken, as opposed to written, communication.

Organ of Corti Minute hair cells in the cochlea that rest on the inside surface of the basilar membrane.

Organization The tendency to organize experience in coherent systems (Piaget).

Organizational behavior science The study of how people behave in organizations.

Organizational chart A written diagram of a work organization broken down into smaller, formal group divisions and departments.

Orientation programs In large companies, half-day to one-day programs for new employees during which they are shown around the company, introduced to key people, and informed about company policies.

Oval window The oval fenestra (opening) of the inner ear.

Pace The energy or intensity an individual invests in a behavior. (A dimension of personality style.)

Pancreas A large compound racemose gland of vertebrates that secretes digestive enzymes and the hormone insulin.

Parasympathetic division A branch of the autonomic system responsible for quieting the body and conserving energy.

Parathyroids Any of usually four small endocrine glands that are adjacent to or embedded in the thyroid gland and produce a hormone concerned with calcium metabolism.

Parietal lobe The top of the cerebrum that includes sites where bodily sensations register in the brain.

Passive behavior Allowing things to happen without telling how you feel.

Perceiving The act of interpreting and organizing the data received through the senses.

Perceptual set The tendency of an individual to perceive what she or he expects to perceive.

Peripheral nervous system All portions of the nervous system lying outside the brain and spinal cord.

Permanent group A group that stays together for a relatively long period. (Compare temporary group.)

Perseverance Continuing at efforts to adjust.

Personnel and human resource management A specialized field of human relations that focuses on employer-employee relations.

Philosophy The study of first principles or ultimate questions.

Phonemes The smallest sounds in a language that can be distinctly recognized, such as "b" or "ch." (Compare morphemes.)

Physical Perceptible through the senses and subject to the laws of nature; of or relating to the body.

Physical development Development of the body; physical growth.

Physical environment Natural settings, such as forests or beaches, as well as environments built by humans, such as buildings, ships, cities.

Physiological needs Needs that must be satisfied for survival.

Pineal body A small usually conical appendage of the brain of all craniate vertebrates that in a few reptiles has the essential structure of an eye, that functions in some birds as part of a time-measuring system, and that is variously postulated to be a vestigial third eye, an endocrine organ, or the seat of the soul.

Pitch Highness or lowness of a sound, determined by frequency of cycles.

Pituitary gland The "master gland" at the base of the brain whose hormones influence the output of other endocrine glands.

Placement The assignment of a person to a suitable place (as a job or a class in school).

Planning guide A breakdown of the day into blocks of time.

Pluralistic Containing many different ethnic, religious, racial, or cultural groups.

Polygenetic traits Characteristics that depend on many genes.

Pons Mass of nerve fibers that connect the cerebellum and medulla.

Potential An inherent range of capacity for growth.

Predispose To make likely to behave in a certain way.

Prejudice An adverse or harmful judgment about an individual member of a group, based on insufficiently or incorrectly informed ideas or expectations of the whole group.

Prepotent Referring to needs that have to be satisfied ahead of other needs.

Primary needs Needs that must be satisfied for the individual to survive. (Also known as biological or physiological needs.)

Primary reinforcers Reinforcers that meet biological needs.

Procrastinate To put something off, to wait to do something.

Proprioceptive senses Internal senses that react to stimuli from within the body instead of stimuli from the environment outside of the body.

Proteins Chemical compounds that are essential to the growth and development of the body; the "stuff of life."

Proximity rule Tendency to group items on the basis of closeness.

Psychiatrists Individuals with degrees in medicine and specialized training in the treatment of mental disorders.

Psychoanalysts Psychiatrists who study and practice Sigmund Freud's personality theories and treatment methods and have undergone psychoanalysis.

Psychoanalytic model School of psychology originated by Sigmund Freud, stressing unconscious motivations and defining the mind as made up of three regions: id, ego, and superego.

Psycholinguists Scientists who study language and its relation to behavior.

Psychological coping strategies Strategies for changing our own appraisals and therefore our stress reactions.

Psychological needs Needs having to do with the psychological or mental well-being of the individual. These higher level needs are also called secondary needs.

Psychology The scientific study of human physical and mental behavior. (From Greek, psyche, meaning "soul," and logos, meaning "to study.")

Psychometric psychologists Psychologists who design and use tests to measure a variety of characteristics, such as intelligence, aptitude, and personality.

Psychomotor Of or relating to motor action directly proceeding from mental activity.

Psychopharmacology The study of the effect of drugs on the mind and behavior.

Purposive Formed to achieve a specific goal. (Compare spontaneous.)

Radex A diagram that surveys the variety of human abilities.

Ratio schedule In conditioning, a situation in which reinforcement depends on repeating operant behavior a certain number of times. (Compare interval schedule.)

Reactive aggression An immediate or spontaneous, often not thought out, reaction to threat.

Reactiveness Adjustment behavior that is directed at changing the self.

Reception Transfer of initiative in communication; the point at which a message is received in the form transmitted.

Receptor sites Areas on the surface of neurons at which neurotransmitters "dock."

Recessive (Genetics) Mendelian characteristic that is not shown if paired with a dominant one.

Reciprocity When behavior toward others is based on how we would wish others to behave toward us.

Reflex arc The pathway that leads from a stimulus to the spinal cord to an automatic response, such as a knee jerk.

Reflex behavior Actions monitored by the spinal cord.

Reflexes Automatic physical responses to stimuli.

Regression A reaction to stress characterized by reverting to earlier forms of reaction that were used in childhood, such as yelling, throwing tantrums, sulking, and so on.

Reinforcement Consequences of an action that serve to maintain behavior or make it more likely.

Reinforcement theory Theory of language learning that holds that children learn or are conditioned to use language correctly by being reinforced for correct usage and punished when they make errors. (Compare imitation theory.)

GLOSSARY

Reinforcers Stimuli or stimulus requirements that figure in the consequences of behavior and thereby play an important role in strengthening or weakening behavior.

Reliability coefficient Index of the ability of a test to yield the same score each time it is given to the same person.

Replicability The ability to be repeated. A necessary condition for an experiment to be considered valid.

Repression A defense mechanism that involves banishing from consciousness ideas, inner conflicts, or memories that cause stress.

Requirements The demands made by person and environment on each other.

Response capabilities Capabilities of person and environment for interacting with each other; for a person, consisting of skills and abilities.

Response (communications) The action taken by the person or group receiving a message. This completes two-way communication and ideally should provide feedback to the sender so that the sender will know that the message has been received and understood.

Response (psychology) Originally, a term that referred to a reaction to a stimulus. Later expanded to mean behavior generally, especially learned behavior.

Retest method A method for evaluating test reliablity where a test is given to a large group of people and then given again to the same people after a period of time.

Reticular Activating System (RAS) A part of the reticular formation that connects with higher brain areas and that serves especially to activate or alert the cerebral cortex.

Reticular formation Network of neurons within the medulla associated with attention, alertness, and activation of higher brain areas.

Retina The photosensitive part of the eye onto which light is focused through the lens.

Reversibility The ability to understand that a quantity of matter converted to a different shape can be reversed to its original shape. (An aspect of conservation.)

Role A pattern of actions expected of a person in that person's interaction with others.

Role playing Acting out true-to-life situations (as in practicing assertiveness).

Role reversal Taking the role of another person to learn how one's own behavior appears from the other person's perspective.

Role set All the various activities and characteristics that make up a particular role.

Safety value Importance of order, predictability, and freedom from harm.

Satisfaction The condition produced when the work environment meets the worker's needs. (Compare satisfactoriness.)

Satisfactoriness The condition produced when the worker meets the work environment's requirements. (Compare satisfaction.)

Saturation That quality of colors related to their being very pure, from a narrow area of the spectrum, or free from mixture with other colors.

Schemata Mental structures, summaries, or outlines that are based on many different bits of information, used to handle all the sensory data to which an individual is exposed.

School psychologists Psychologists who study people in relation to educational environments. (Compare educational psychologists and counseling psychologists.)

Secondary needs Another term for psychological needs.

Secondary reinforcers Learned reinforcers that derive their effectiveness from their association with primary reinforcers.

Selection A process that results in the choice of some individuals but not of others.

Self-aware Sensibly aware of one's worth and potential.

Self-centered Excessively preoccupied with oneself.

Self-concept An individual's view of himself or herself.

Self-disclosure The process of revealing private thoughts, feelings, and personal history to others.

Self-efficacy Confidence in your ability to accomplish a task successfully.

Self-esteem Self-respect, pride in oneself.

Sensing The act of receiving data through sense organs or receptors.

Sensory Of or relating to sensation or to the senses; conveying nerve impulses from the sense organs to the nerve centers; afferent.

Sensory and perceptual behavior Starting from the environment and ending in the brain.

Sensory cortex Area of the neocortex that receives sensory or motor information.

Serotonin A neurotransmitter involved in mood, sleep, and appetite.

Short-term memory Material that enters active memory directly from the environment and is unlikely to be retained unless reinforced.

Sign language The gesture language used by deaf people to communicate with each other and with people who can hear.

Similarity rule Tendency to group items on the basis of similarity.

Skill Capability to perform a given task or tasks; the basic units of response capability.

Social development The process of learning that one is not the center of the universe and that it is necessary to interact with others and the environment.

Social psychology The study of how people interact.

Social roles Community expectations about social position and function, which define the power relationships in the community.

Sociotechnological Both social and technological.

Somatic sensory cortex The part of the parietal lobes that serves as a receiving area for bodily sensations.

Specific factor Part of an ability test that measures something no other test measures.

Speediness A broad ability that is measured by speed tests and speed of test performance.

Split-half method A common method for evaluating test reliability where a test is given to a group but the tests are divided in half and scored for each half of the group separately.

Spontaneous Occurring without plan or forethought. As used here, referring to groups that form merely as a matter of chance. (Compare purposive.)

Staff officers Aides under a chief executive, holding no line responsibilities, but who carry out day-to-day tasks for the chief executive and often provide research and advice for line officers. (Compare line officers.)

Standard deviation A measure of the dispersion of a frequency distribution.

Status value Importance of recognition and dominance.

Stereotype An oversimplified abstraction or attitude held by an individual or group about the members of another racial or national group, gender, or even profession.

Stimulus A condition that elicits a response. See also aversive stimulus, conditioned stimulus, and neutral stimulus.

Stress reaction A physical and/or psychological reaction to a difficult, demanding, or dangerous environment or situation, normally experienced as anxiety, fear, or extreme discomfort.

Stressors Specific conditions or events in the environment that challenge or threaten a person.

Structuralism The first school of thought in scientific psychology, which emphasizes the structure of consciousness and its elements: sensations, images, and emotions.

Subjective Based on a mental idea or feeling; not observable; not verifiable. (Compare objective.)

Subliminal Referring to sensory data that affects the individual below the conscious level.

Superego Used in the psychoanalytic model to refer to a portion of the mind in which are stored cultural and traditional morals, ideals, and values, learned primarily from parents.

Syllable writing A system of writing in which symbols represent sounds and stand for parts of words, or syllables. (Compare word writing and alphabet writing.)

Syllogism A form of deductive logic consisting of a major premise, a minor premise, and a conclusion.

Symbol As used here, nonverbal, visual representation of some concept or emotion.

Synapse The space between two neurons over which neurotransmitters travel.

Synaptic integration The accumulation of neural impulses.

Taboos Powerful customs that forbid specific kinds of behavior, such as murder or incest.

Talent Potential for learning to perform activities important in a culture.

Task goal The basic purpose for the existence of a group, for example, to raise funds or elect a candidate. (Compare maintenance goal.)

Tasks Components of a job function that require distinct skills to perform.

Technology The use of scientific theory and knowledge to address and solve human problems. (See applied science.)

Temperament A characteristic or habitual inclination or mode of emotional response.

Temporal lobe The side of the cerebrum that includes the sites where hearing registers in the brain.

Temporary groups Groups that form and stay together for only a short period. (Compare permanent group.)

Test battery A group of tests given to the same individual.

Test items Problems that measure particular abilities.

Test profile A graph that shows a person's relative standing on different abilities.

Tested interests Interests manifested under controlled conditions as opposed to those shown in real-life situations.

Theories Attempts to describe and explain reality.

Theory X A style of work motivation described by Douglas McGregor in which extrinsic motivators, especially negative ones such as punishment, are emphasized over intrinsic motivators.

Theory Y A style of work motivation described by Douglas McGregor in which intrinsic motivators, such as trust, responsibility, and self-direction, are emphasized over extrinsic motivators.

Theory Z A style of work motivation drawn from Japanese culture and business that emphasizes worker participation even more strongly than Theory Y. Workers and supervisors work together to achieve consensus. Often quality circles are established.

Threshold The point at which a physiological or psychological effect begins to be produced.

Thymus A glandular structure of largely lymphoid tissue that functions especially in the development of the body's immune system, is present in the young of most vertebrates, and tends to disappear or become rudimentary in the adult.

Thyroid gland Endocrine gland whose hormones help regulate metabolism (the production and expenditure of energy within the body).

"To do" list A daily written and prioritized list of tasks that organizes the tasks in the order in which they can be completed most efficiently.

Transactional analysis A theory of personality that identifies patterns of behavior based on the common experience of being a child and learning how to be an adult by observing parents. Describes various behaviors as "adult," "parent," or "child" and describes the individual as a complex of all three types of behavior.

Transmission The act of sending an encoded communication to the receiving individual.

Traumatic stress Stress associated with unexpected or atypical experiences.

Type A personality A personality type believed to experience more stress, characterized by an incessant struggle to achieve more and more in less and less time, free-floating hostility, and behavior that appears to deliberately invite stress.

Unconscious inference theory A theory that explains constancy as the result of unconscious "inferences" or explanations of the difference between the perceived object and what it is known from prior experience to be. (Compare ecological theory.)

Uncorrelated Having no consistent, systematic relationship.

Understanding The ability to grasp information or find patterns; the willingness to be sympathetic, tolerant, and helpful.

Valid When a test measures what it is supposed to measure.

Validate To test for effectiveness for a particular use.

Values Standards for evaluating things and events; a sense of what is important.

Variable A factor that can take on different values in an experiment. Height, weight, and age are variables. (Compare constant.)

Verbal Of, relating to, or consisting of words.

Vestibular sensors Proprioceptive sense receptors, located in the inner ear, involved in the sense of balance and in determining when the body is moving and in what direction.

Visual cortex An area of the cerebral cortex that receives afferent nerve fibers from lower sensory or motor areas.

Visual perception A broad ability that is measured by a combination of tests of visualization, spatial relations, and perceptual speed.

Voluntarily Resulting from one's own choices.

GLOSSARY

Voluntary Resulting from one's own choices. (Compare involuntary.)

Wavelength The measurement of the distance between the peaks of two consecutive waves.

Whole-person concept The idea that, in any given situation, the individual is the embodiment of multiple roles. For example, one person may simultaneously be a parent, a child, and an employee, with each of those roles making certain demands on the person.

Withdrawal A coping strategy that is not an attack on the problem but a decision not to act, to pull back from a goal, often producing depression and apathy.

Word writing A system of writing in which symbols stand for entire words or concepts. (Compare syllable writing and alphabet writing.)

Work climate The psychological conditions in a work environment; the "style" of the work organization.

Work environment The physical and social environment within which one works.

Work needs Reinforcer requirements that are met or can be met by the work environment.

Work personality Those aspects of personality that are appropriate to the work environment and are involved in the individual's interaction with the work environment.

Work reinforcers Those rewards and other motivators offered by the work environment to meet the worker's needs. (A form of secondary reinforcer.)

Work skills Response capabilities that are required by the work environment.

GLOSSARY

INDEX

INDEX

INDEX

INDEX

INDEX

INDEX

INDEX

INDEX

INDEX

INDEX

INDEX

INDEX

INDEX